A Cindy Book

c. 1964—1975

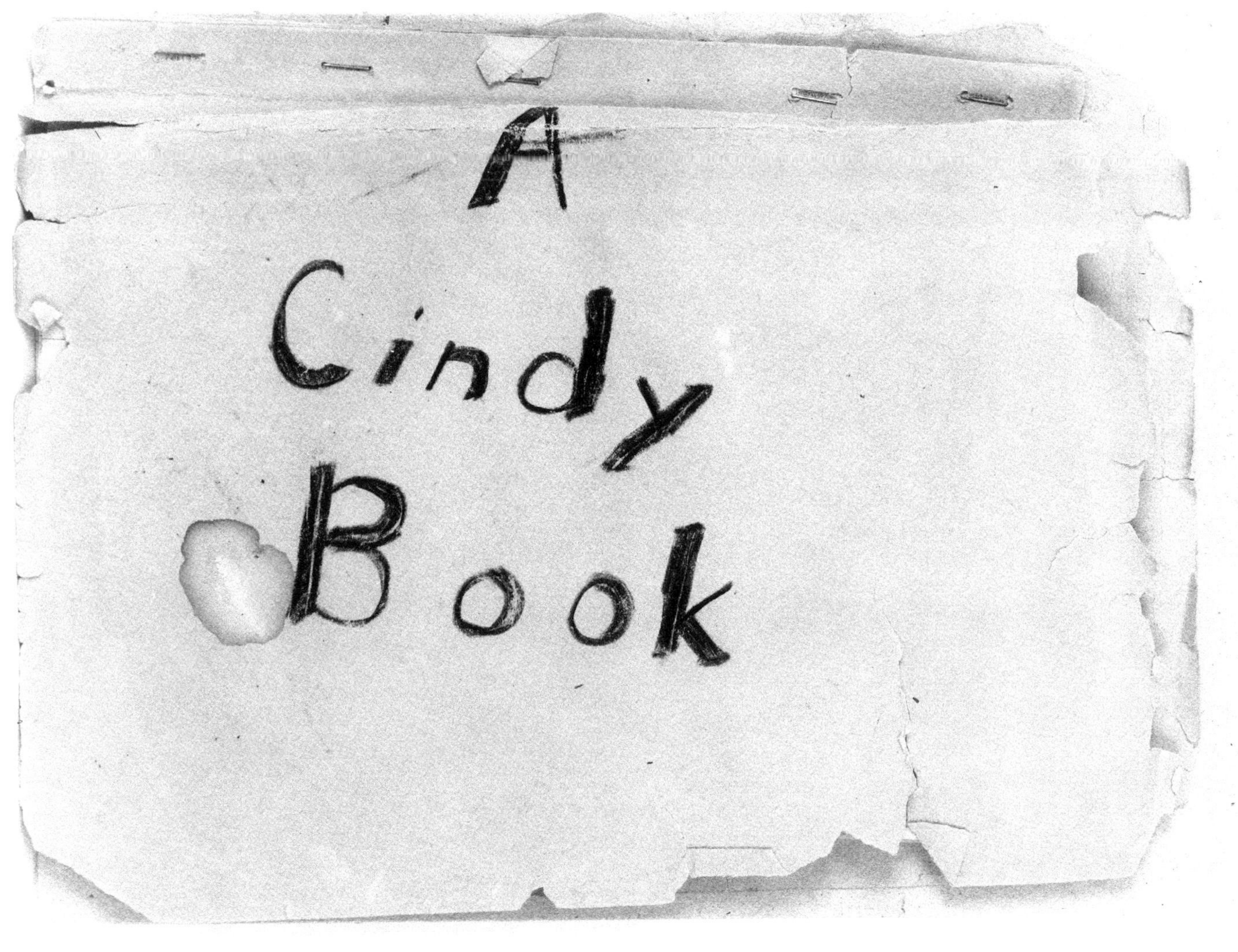

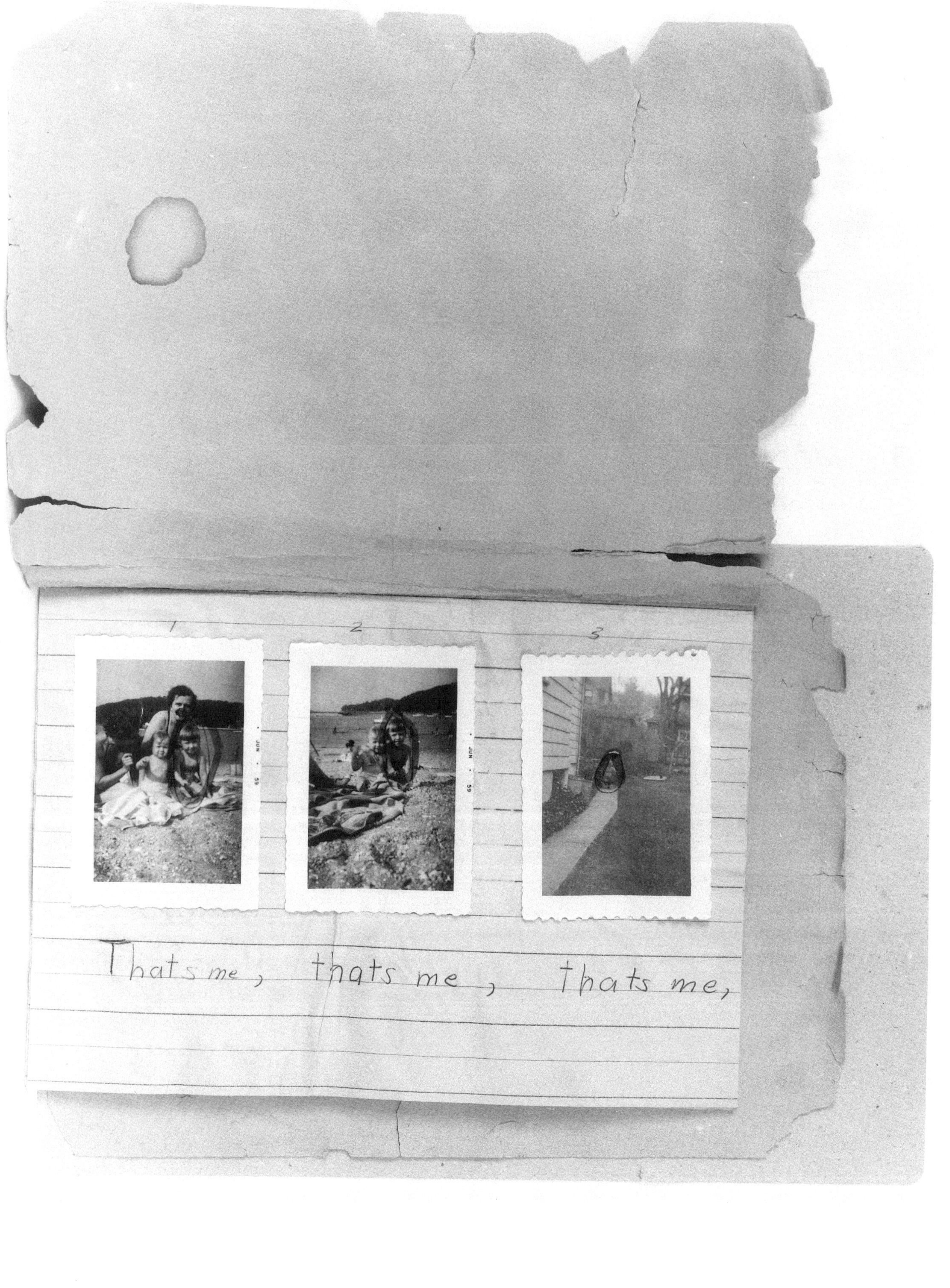
1
2
3
Thats me, thats me, thats me,

4

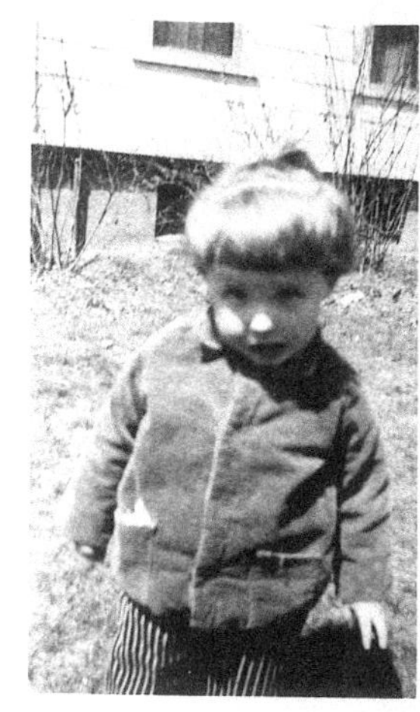

5

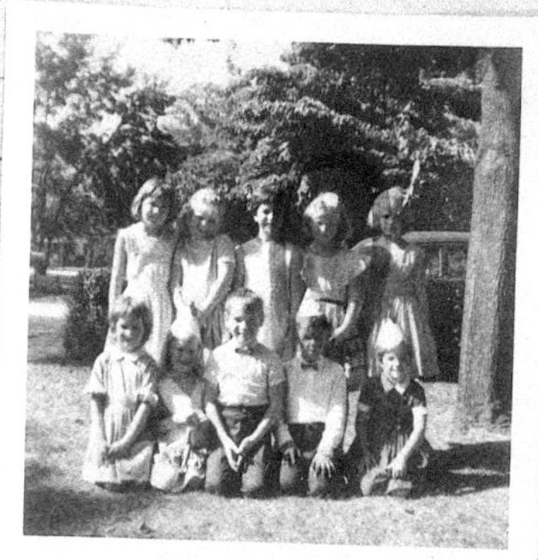

Thats me,

Thats me,

6

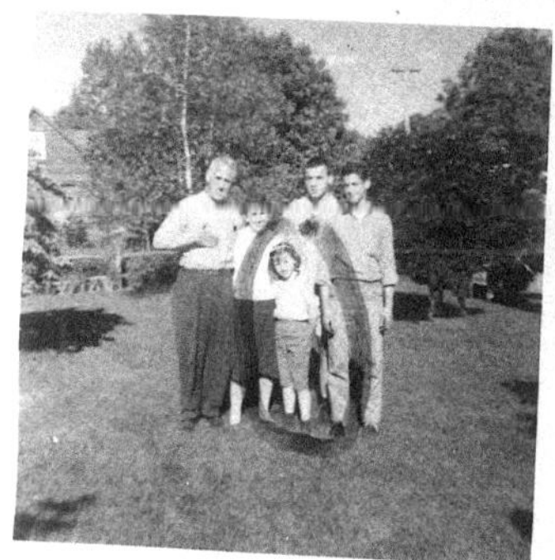

7

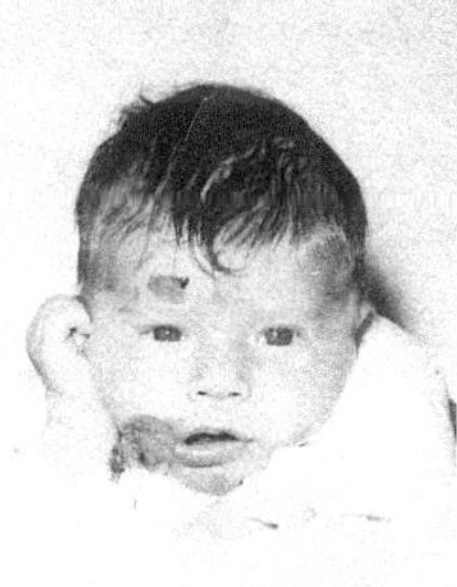

Thats me,

Thats me,

8

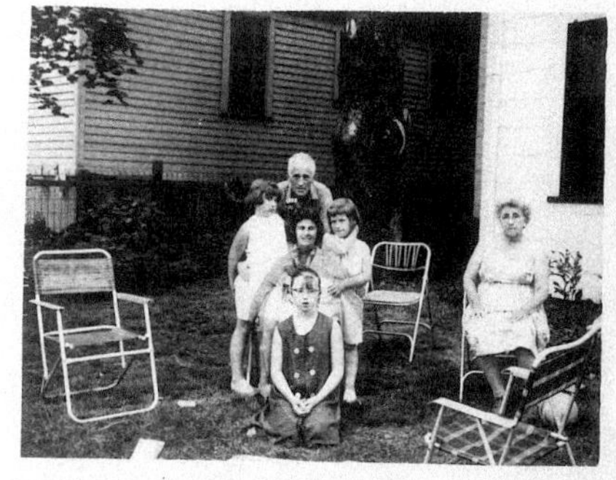

9

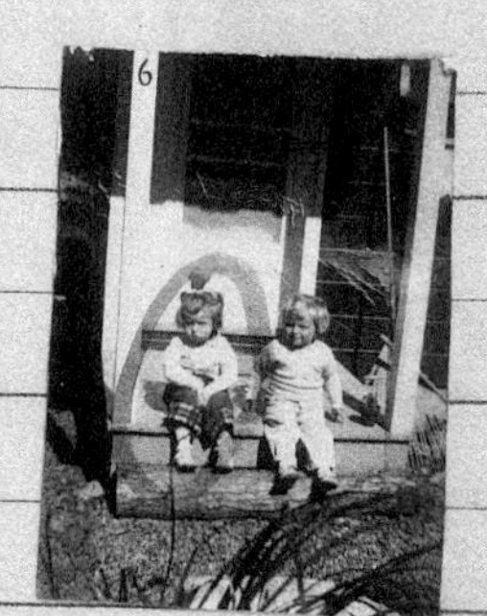

Thats me,

Thats me,

10

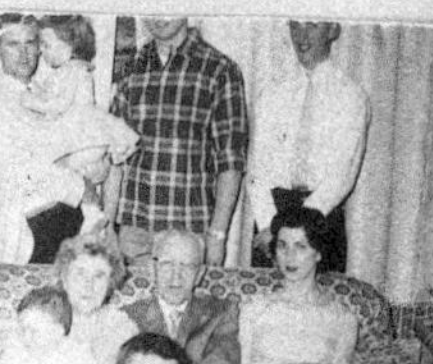

11

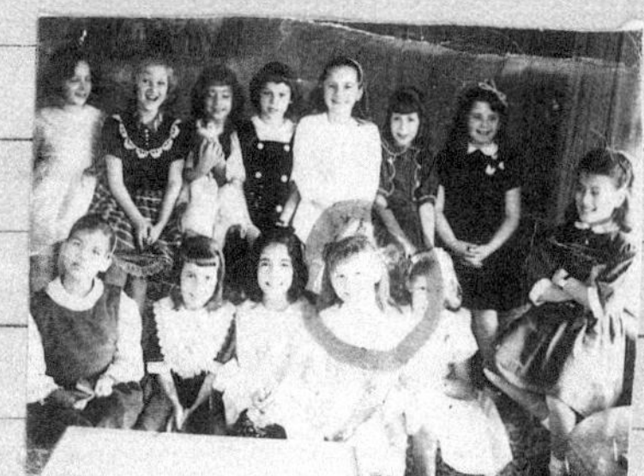

Thats me,

Thats me,

12

13

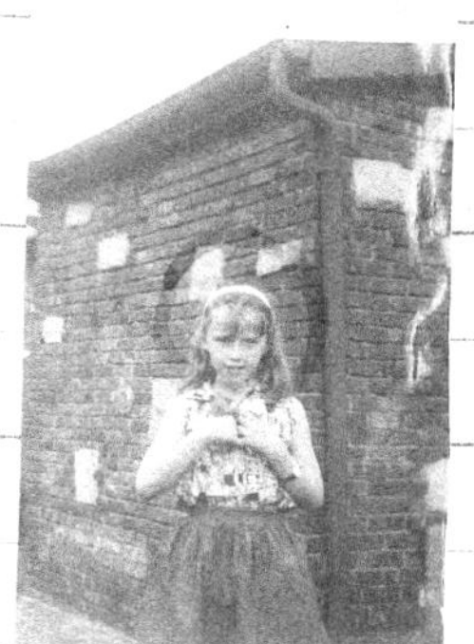

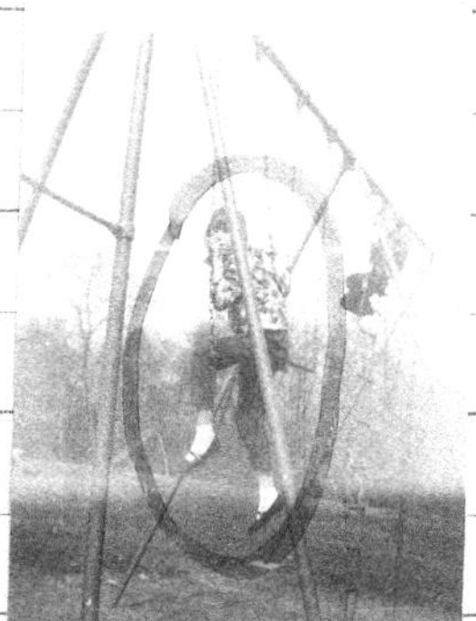

Thats me,

Thats me,

14

15

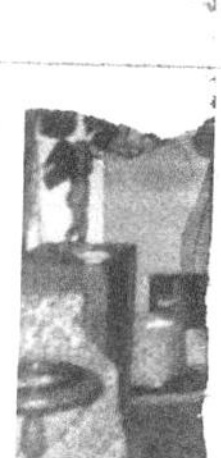

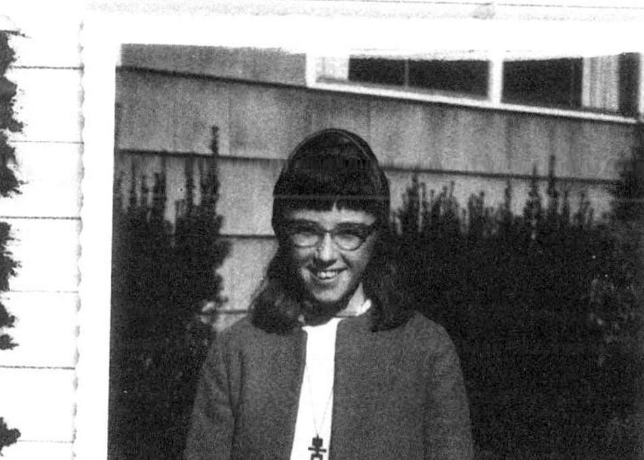

me,

That's me,

Thats me,

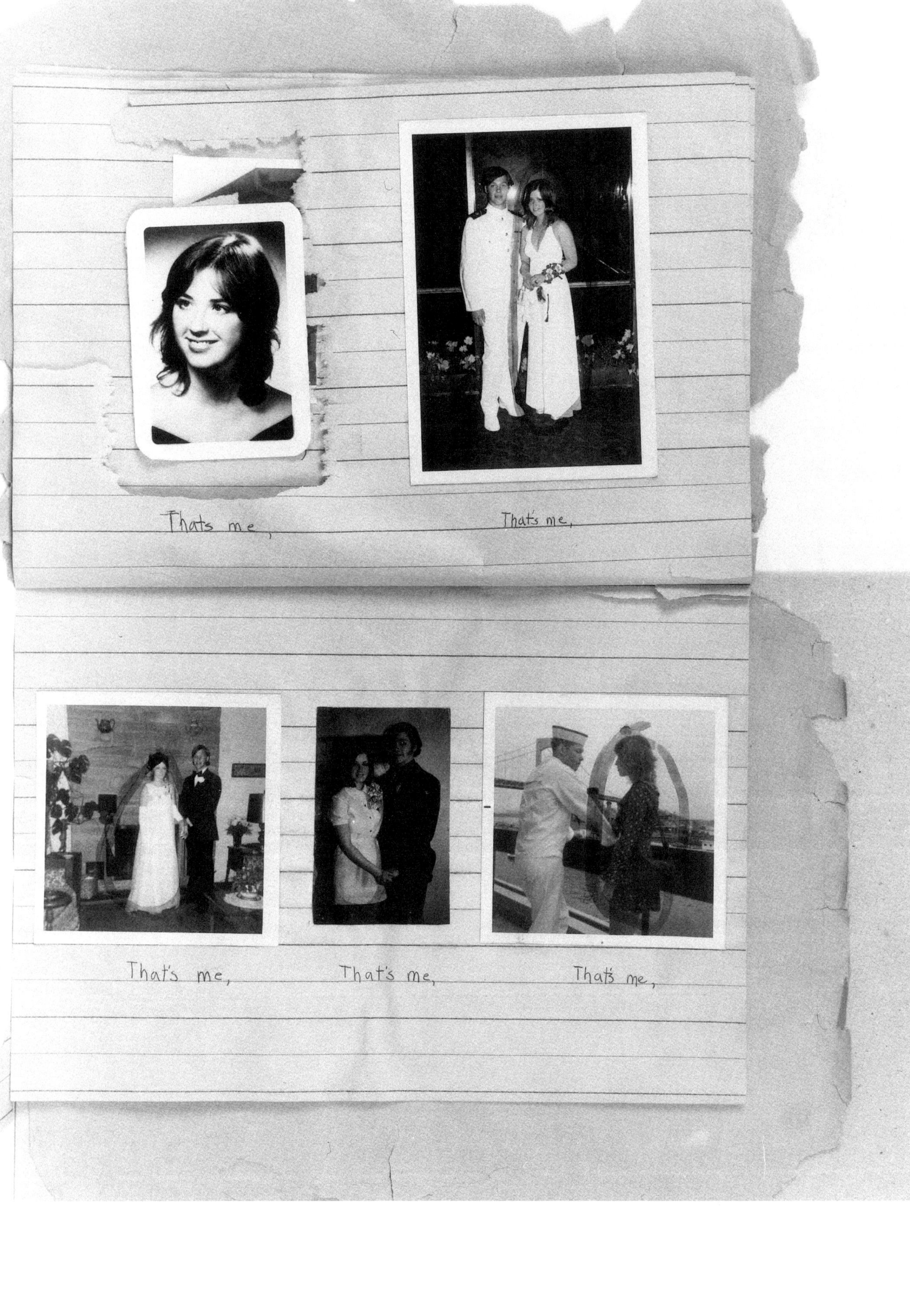
Thats me,
That's me,
That's me,
That's me,
That's me,

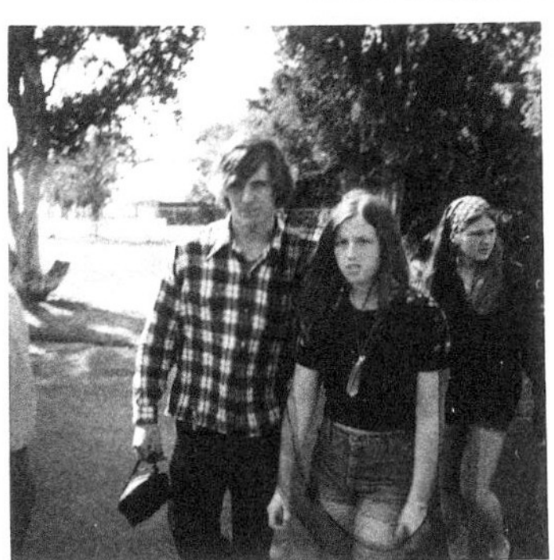

That's me

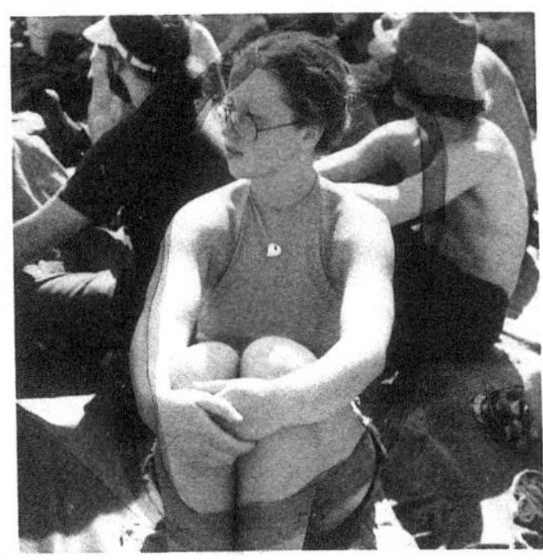

That's me,

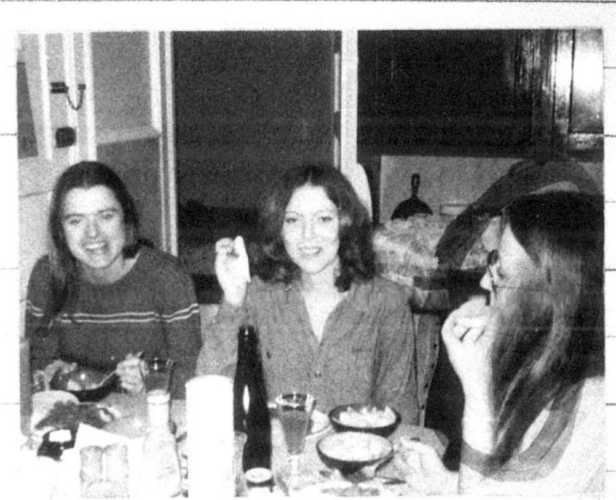

That's me,

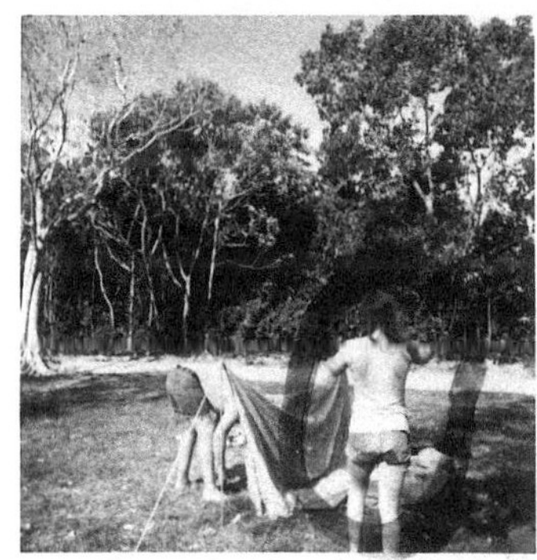

That's me,

That's me,
That's me,

Untitled A
Untitled D
Untitled B
Untitled C
Untitled E

1975

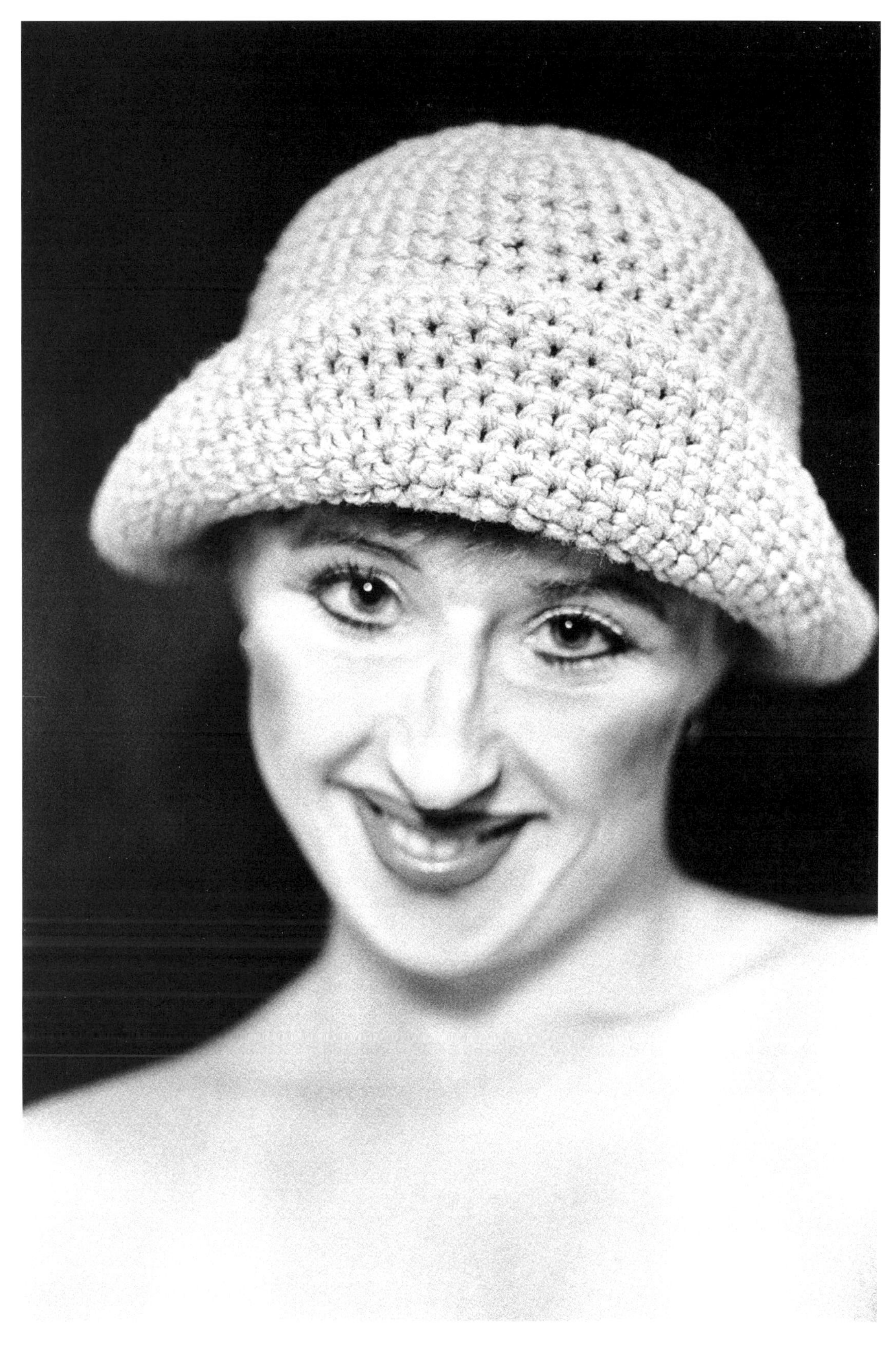

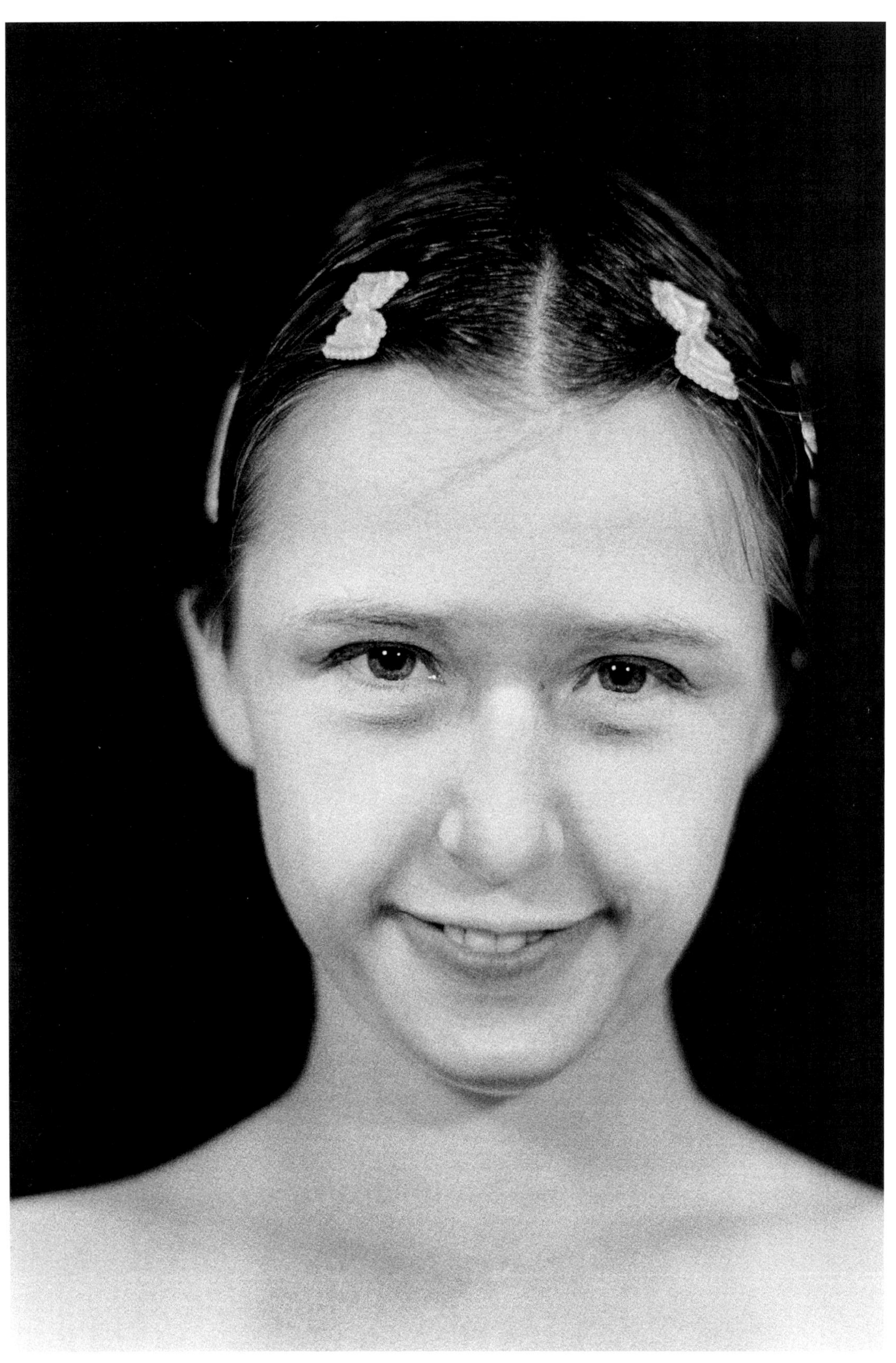

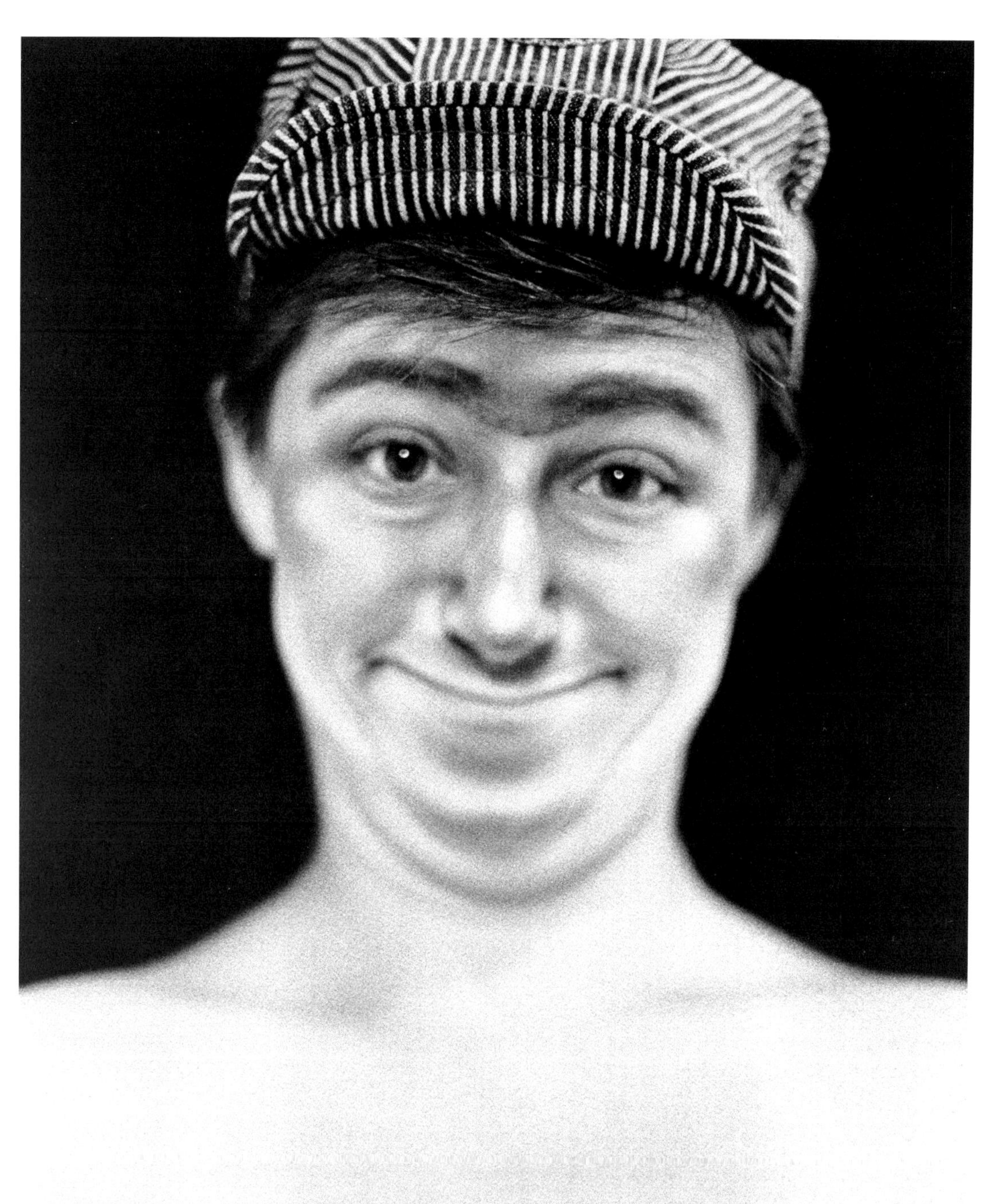

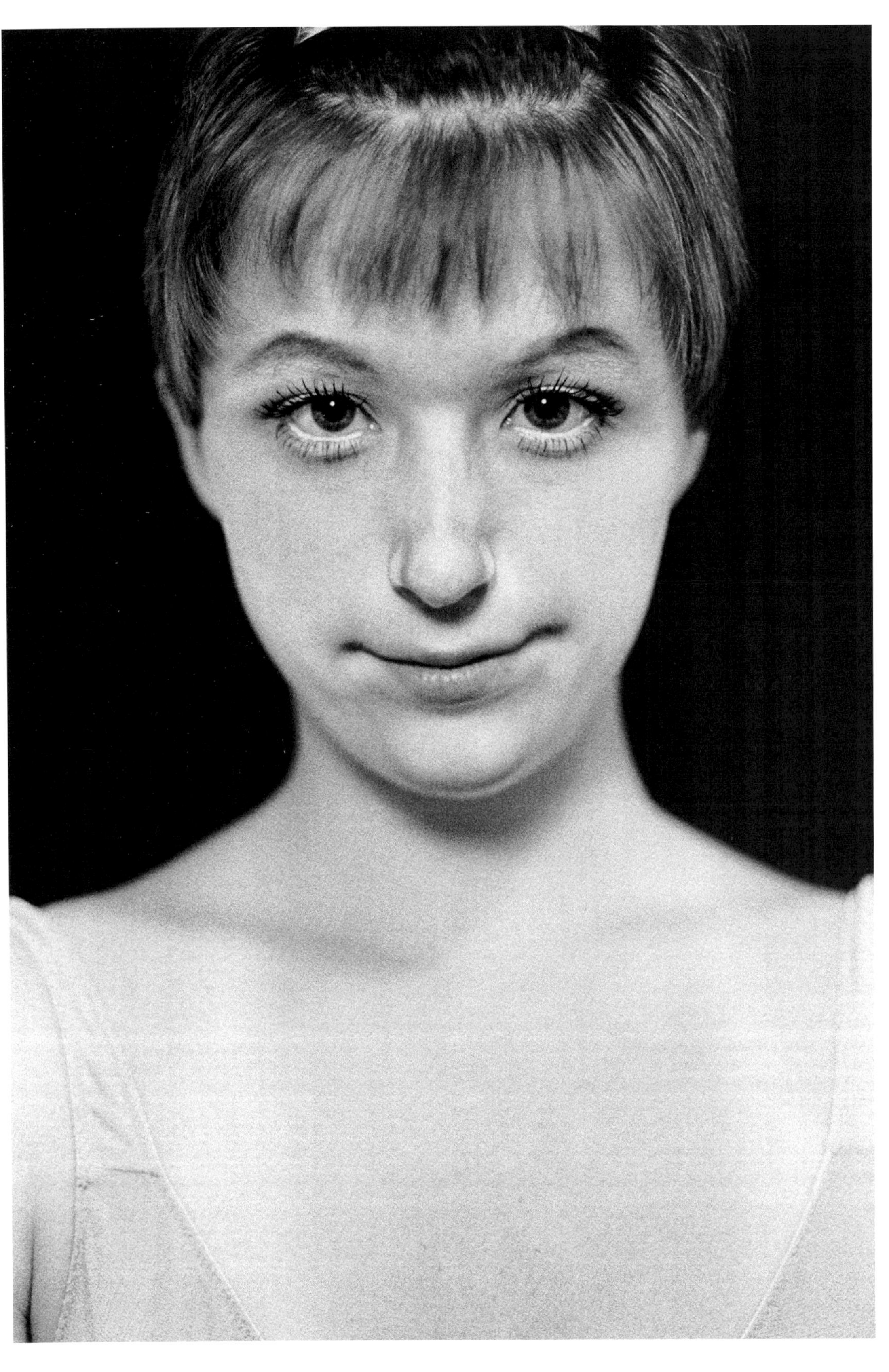

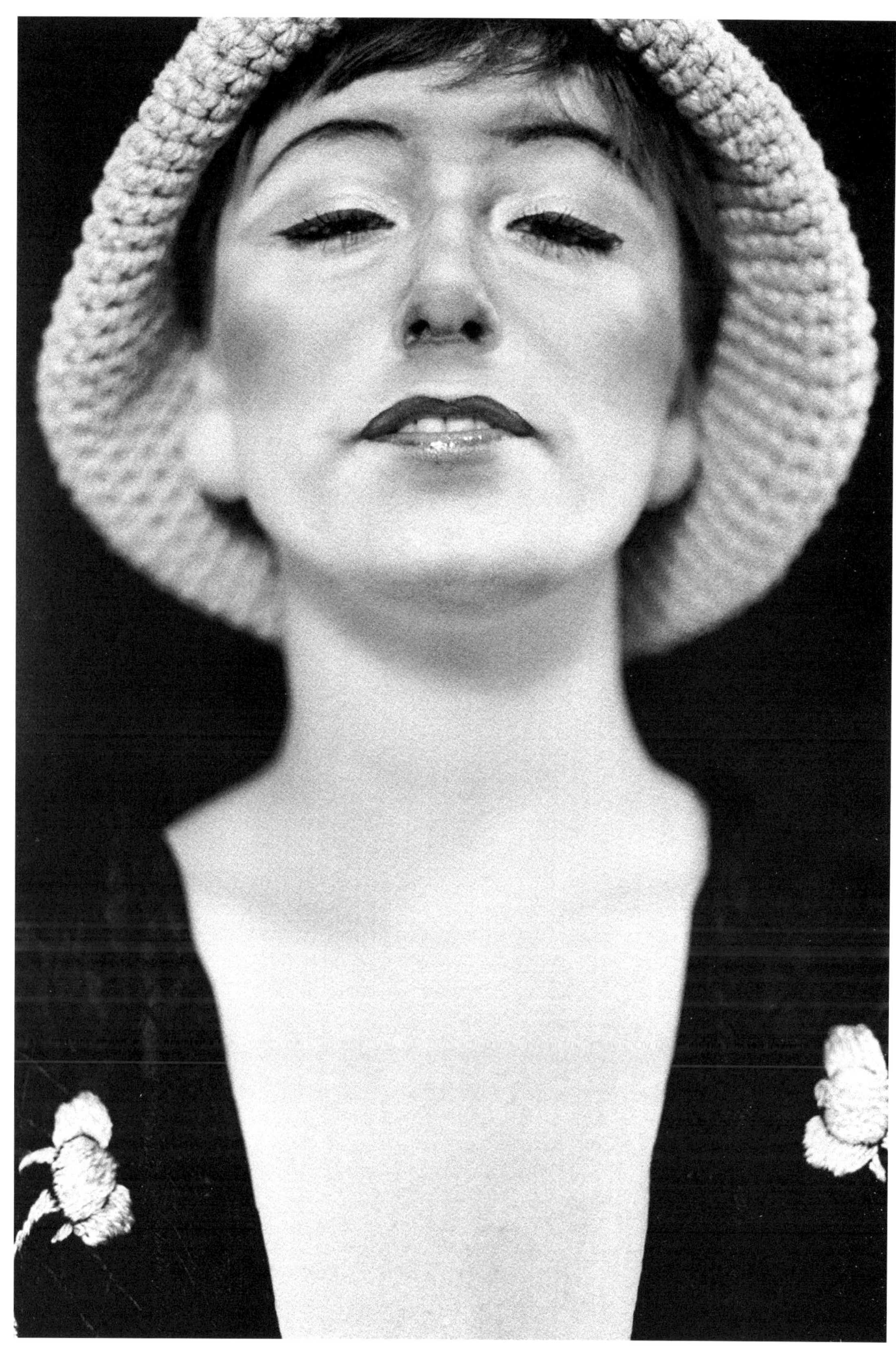

Untitled #363
Untitled #364
Untitled #365
Untitled #366
Untitled #367
Untitled #431
Untitled #369
Untitled #370
Untitled #371
Untitled #376
Untitled #433
Untitled #374
Untitled #375
Untitled #434
Untitled #377
Untitled #430
Untitled #368
Untitled #373
Untitled #372
Untitled #439

from Bus Riders

1976 — 2005

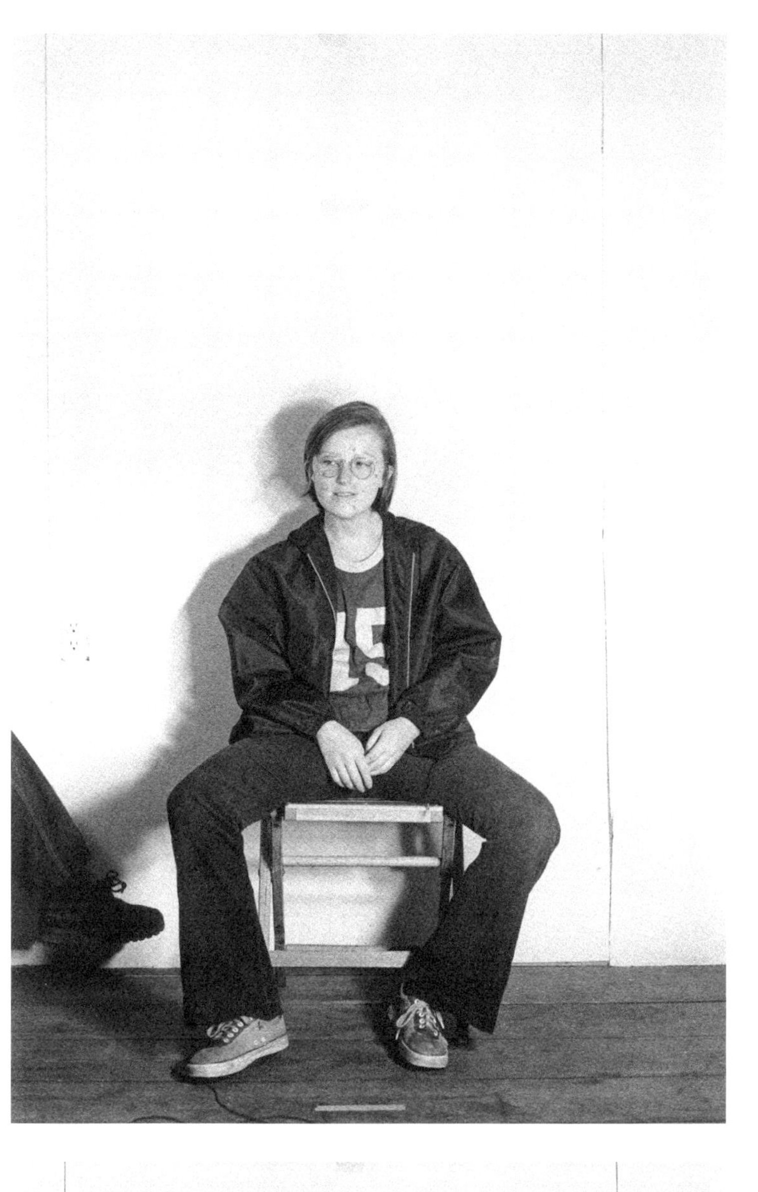
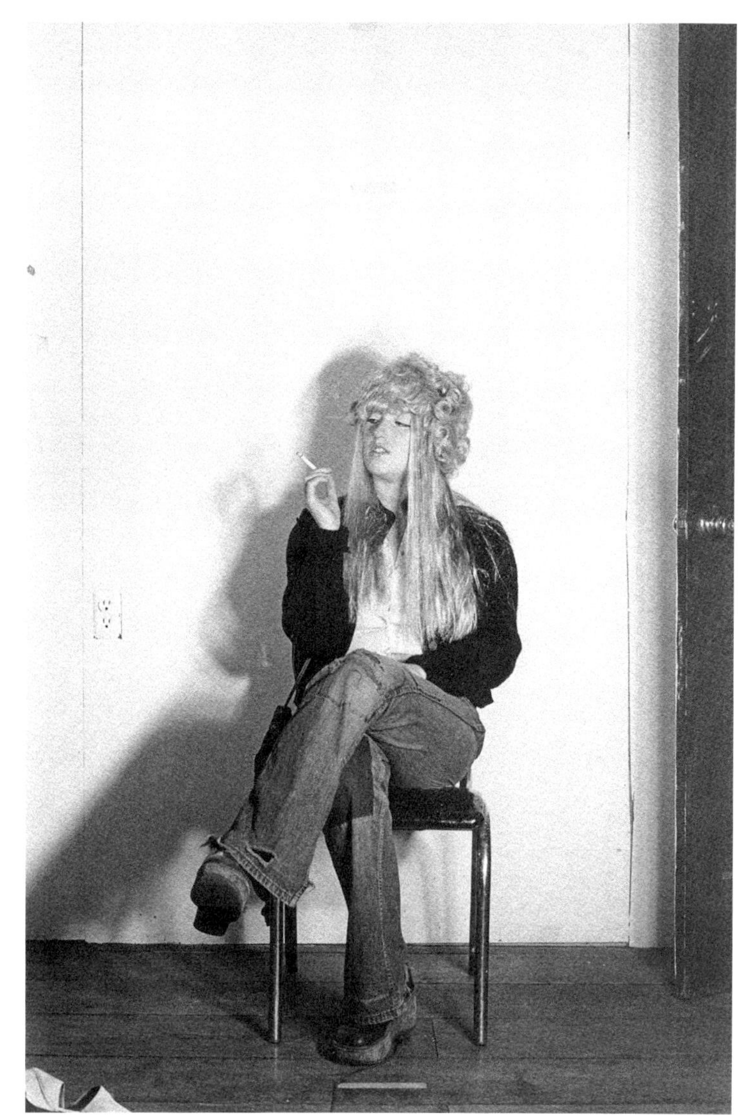
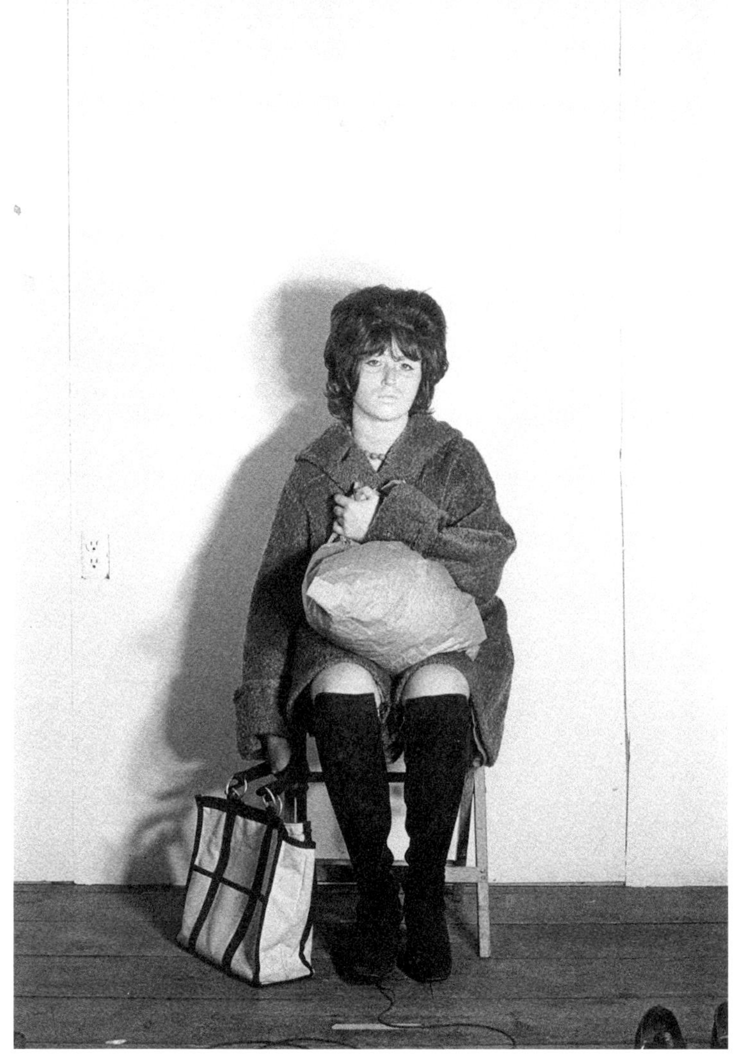
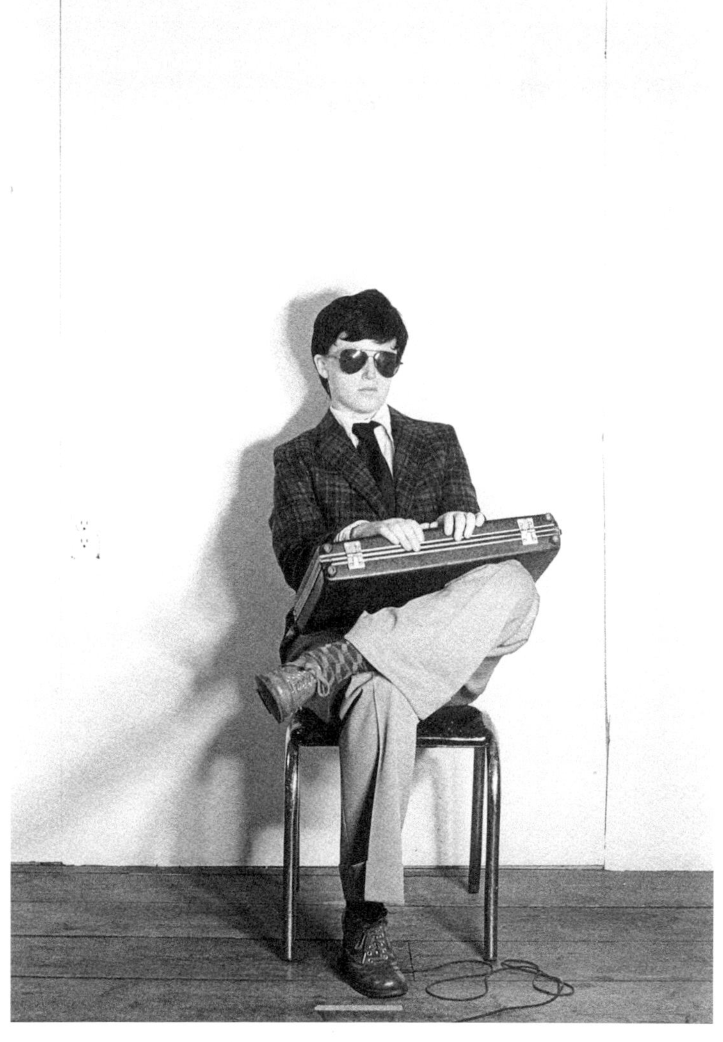

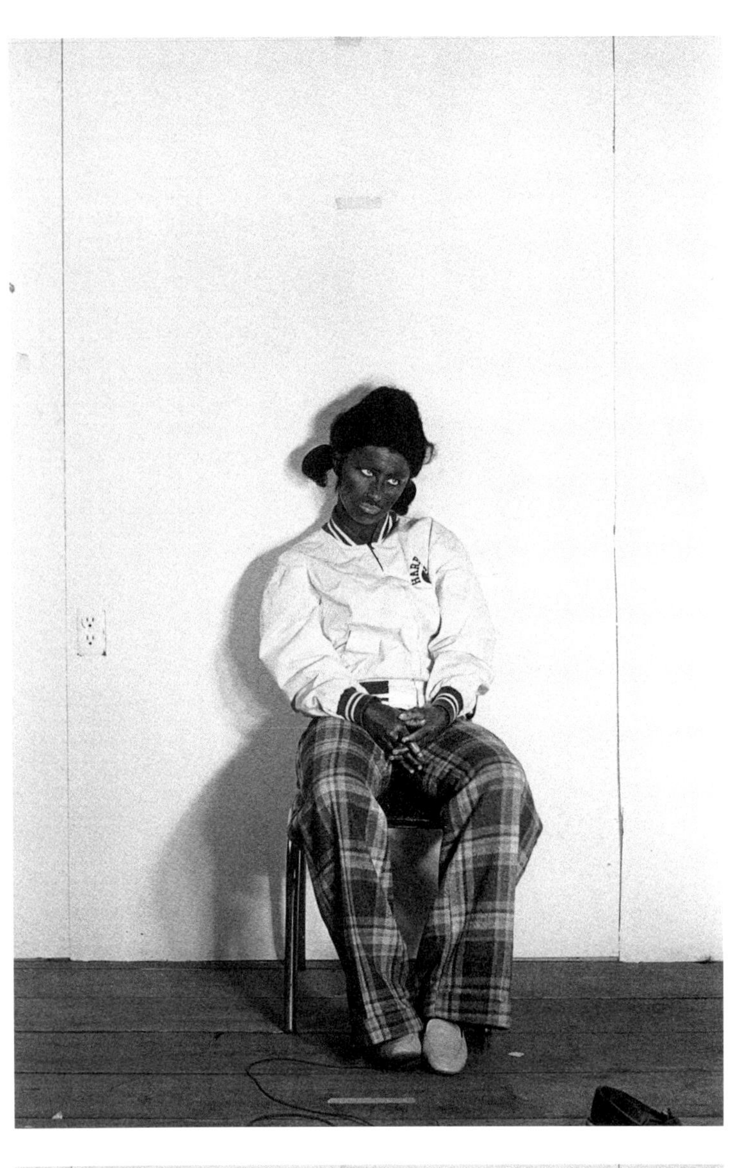

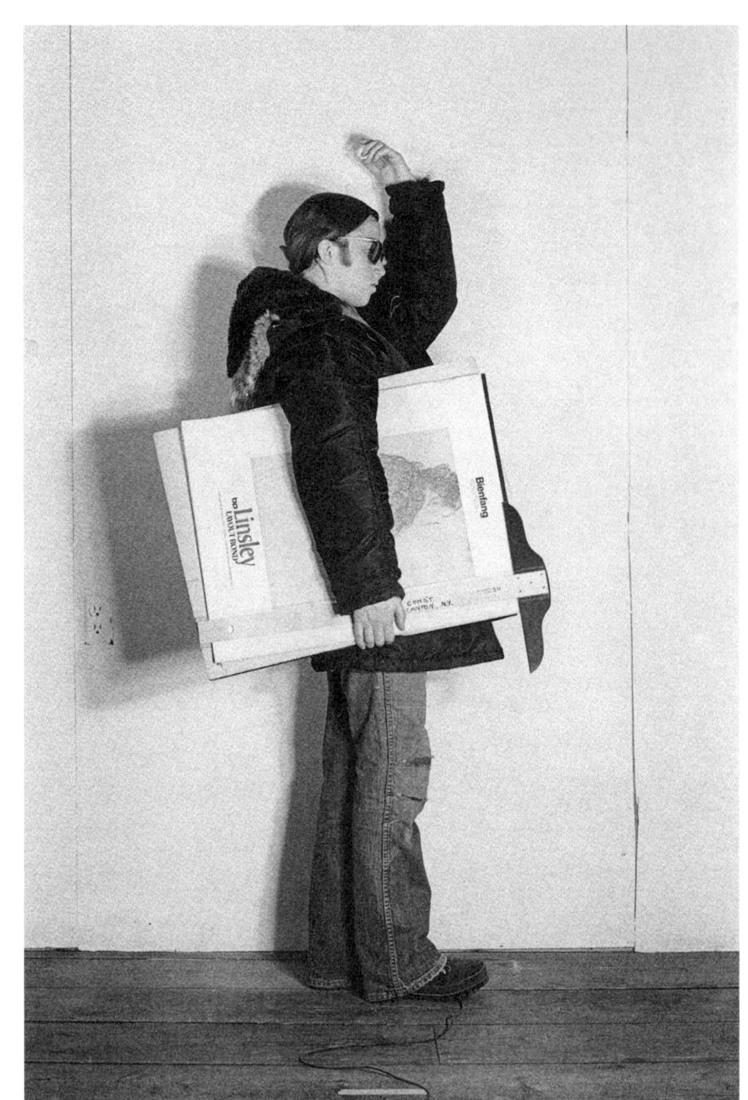
Linsley
Bienfang

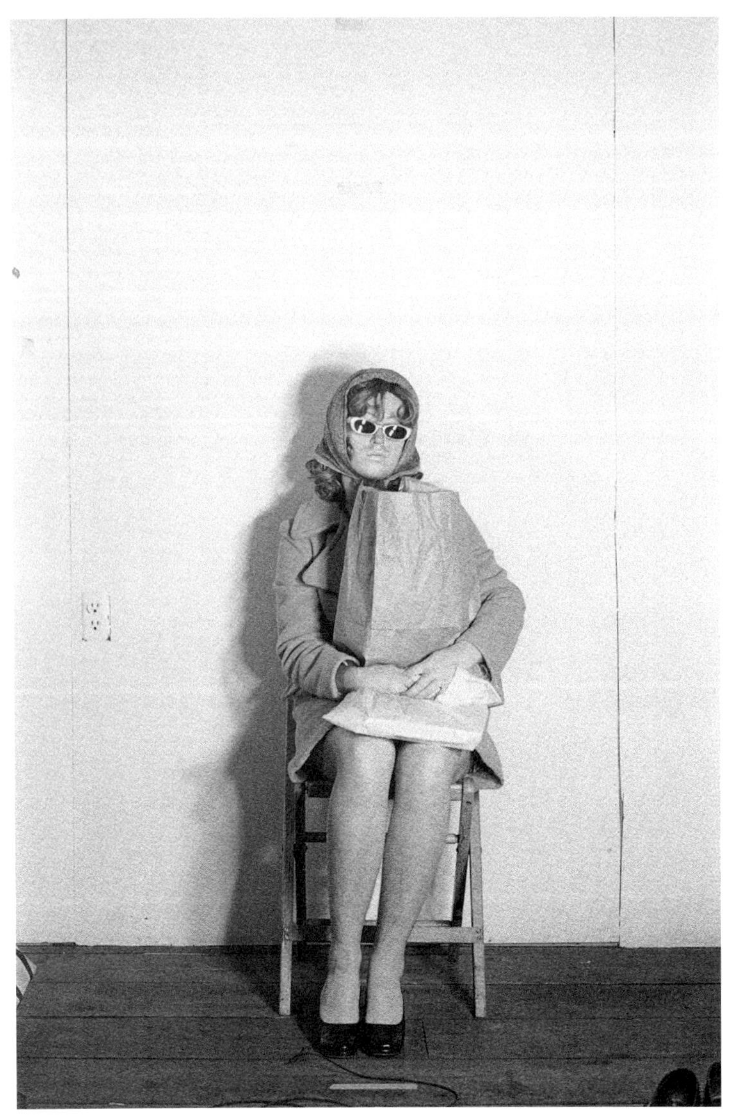

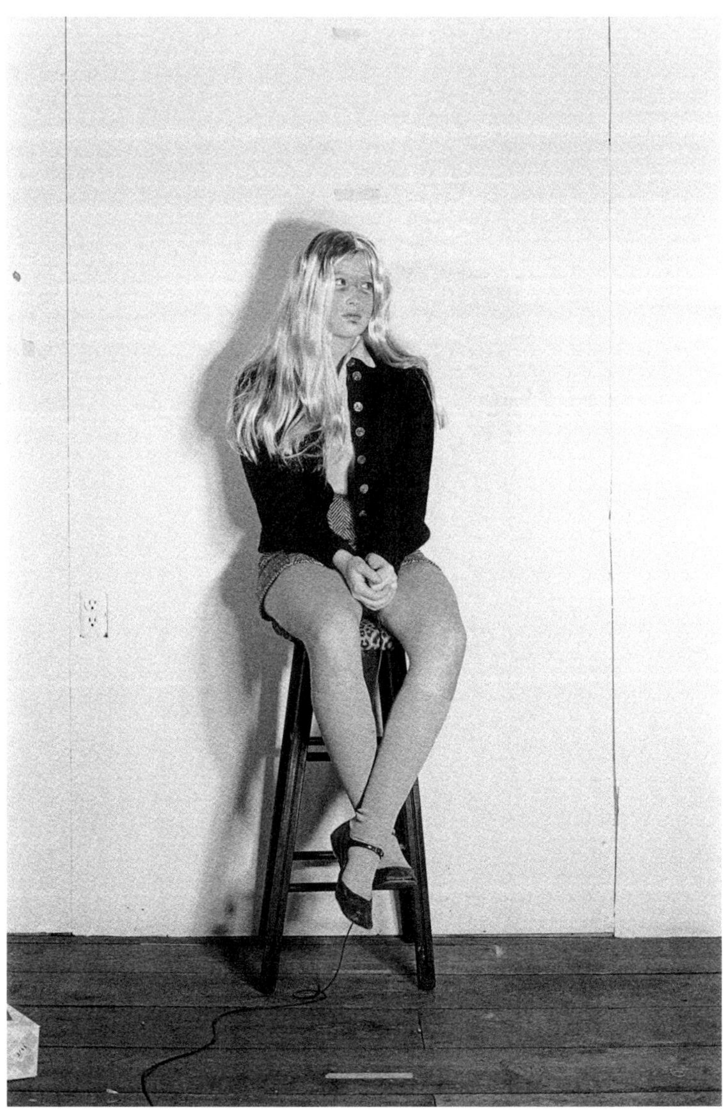

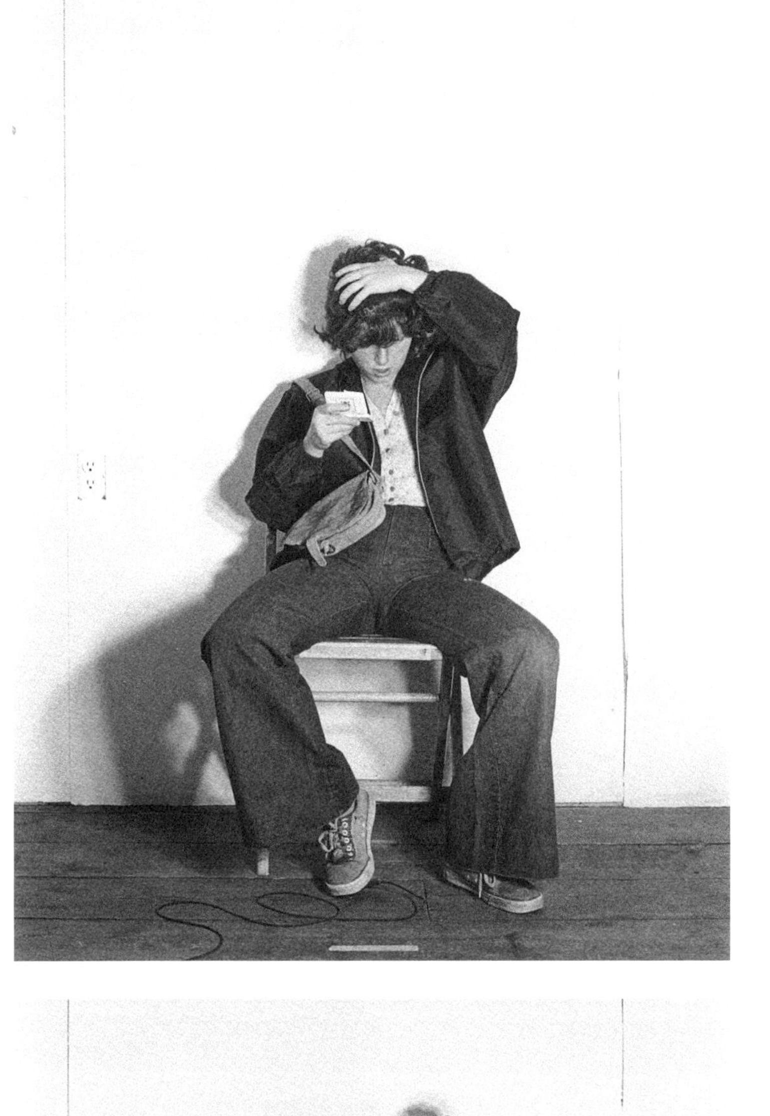
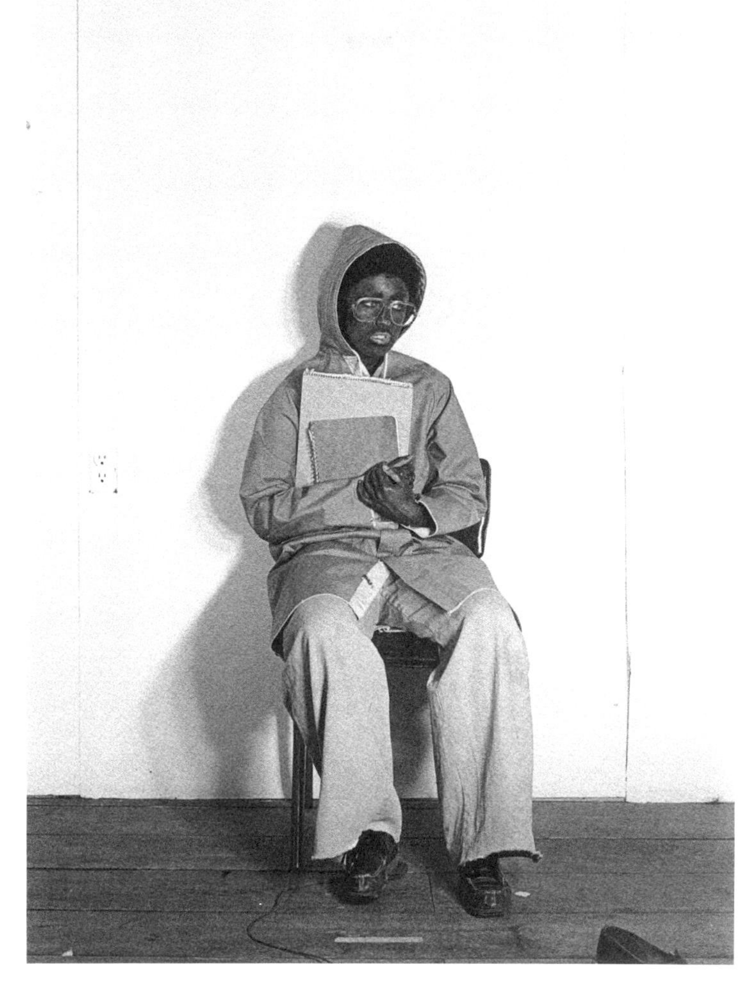
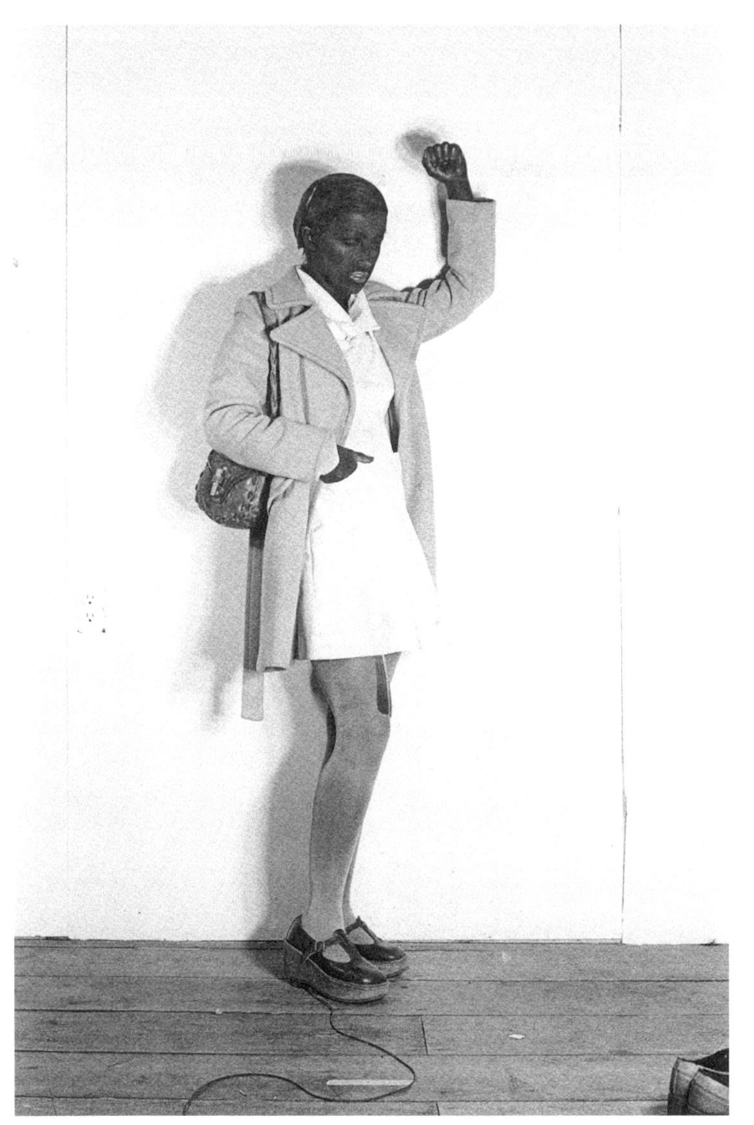
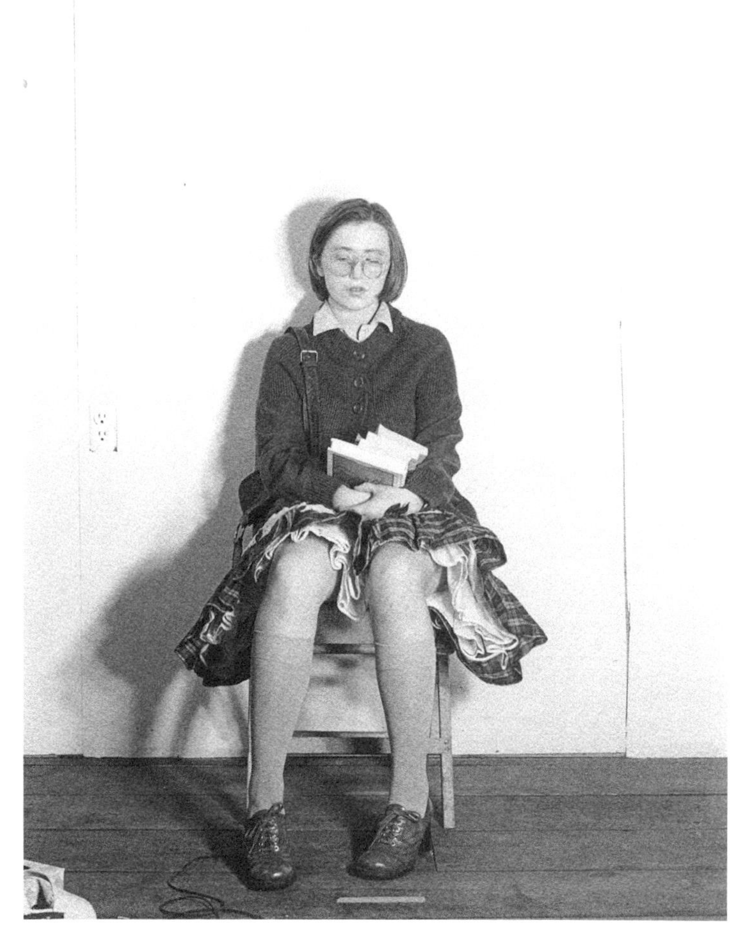

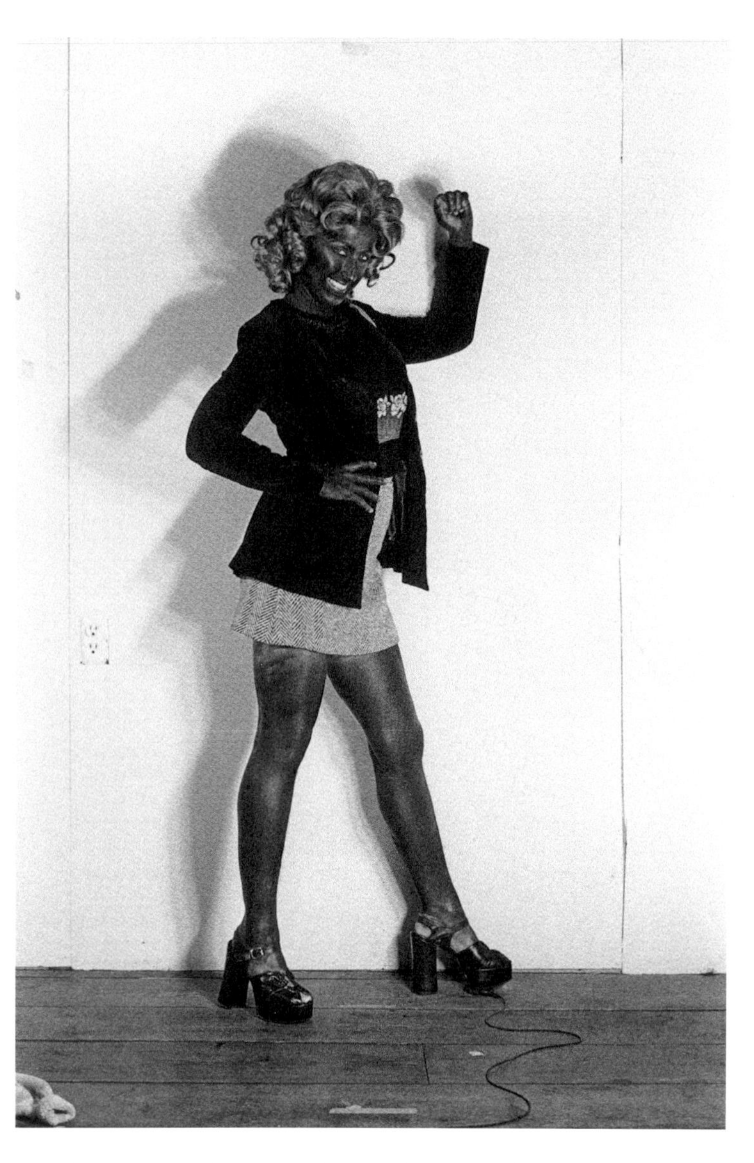

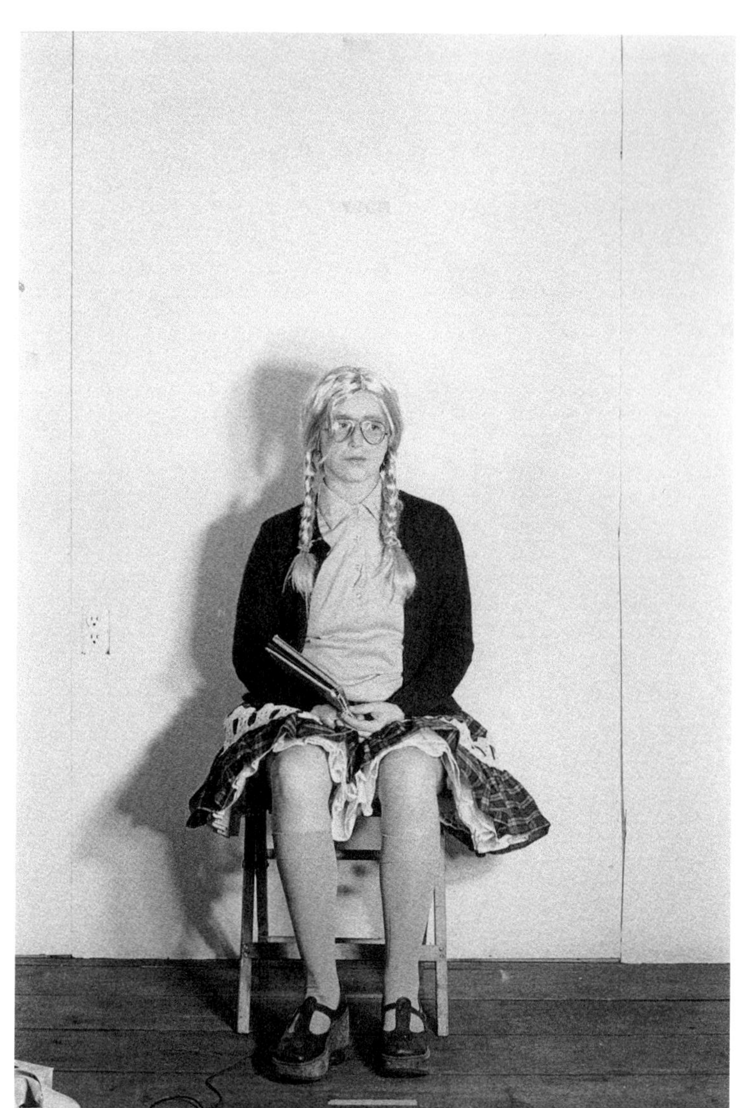

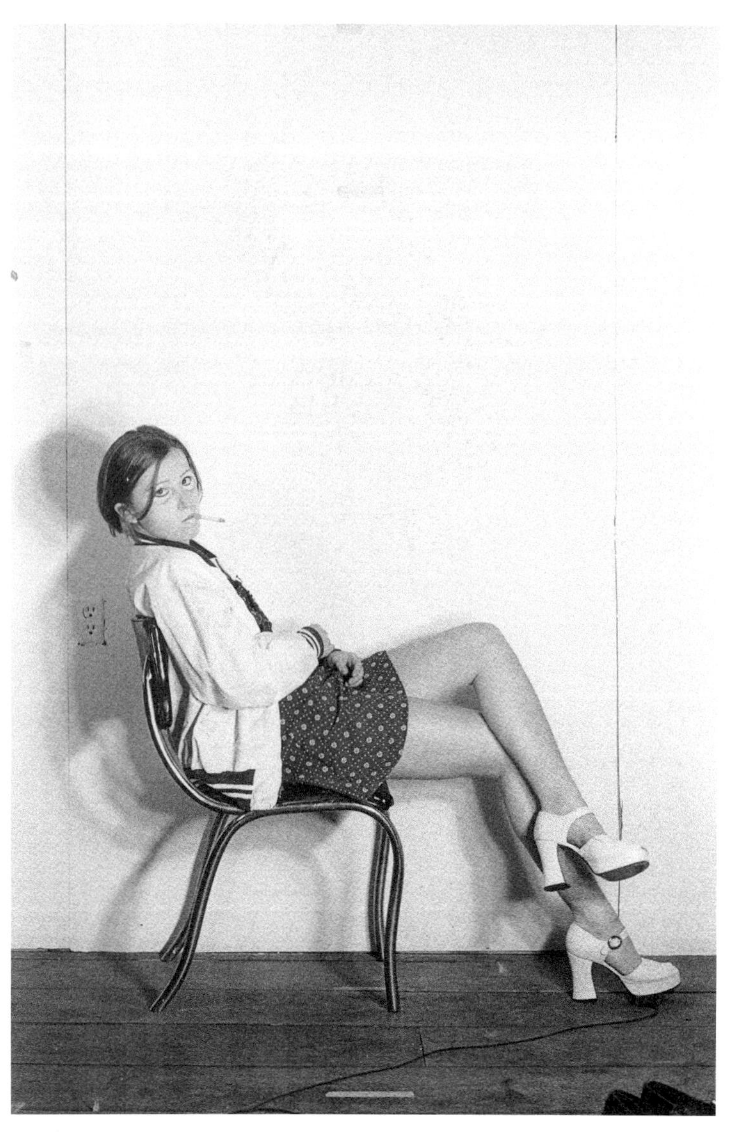

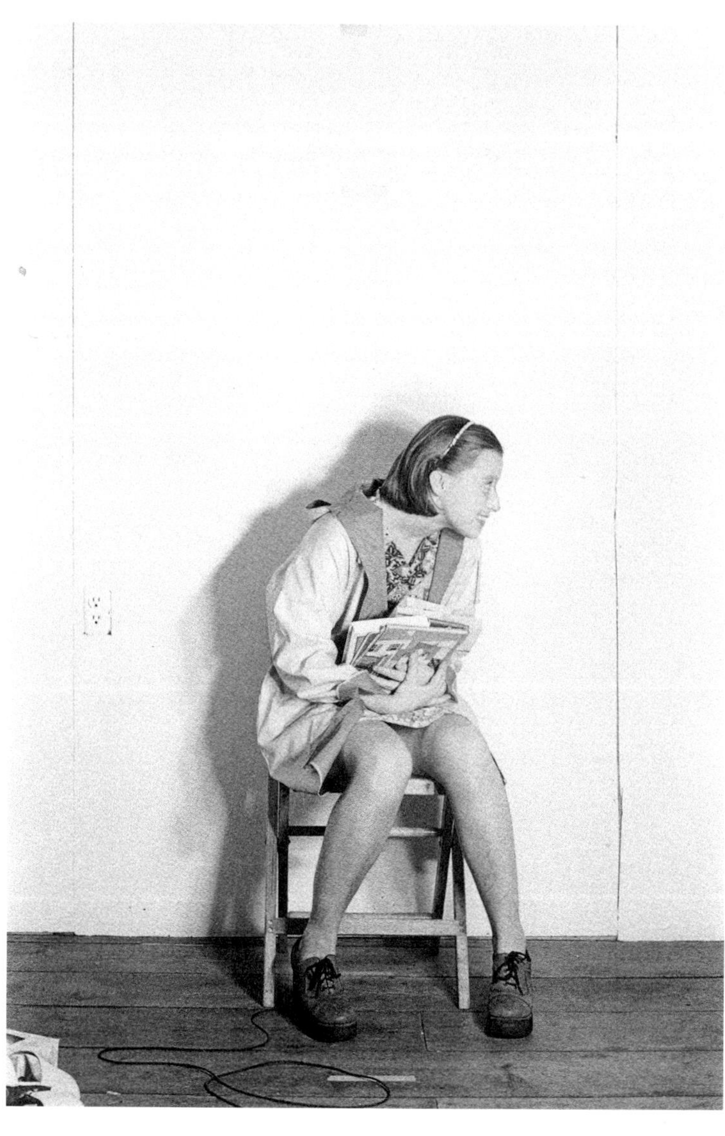

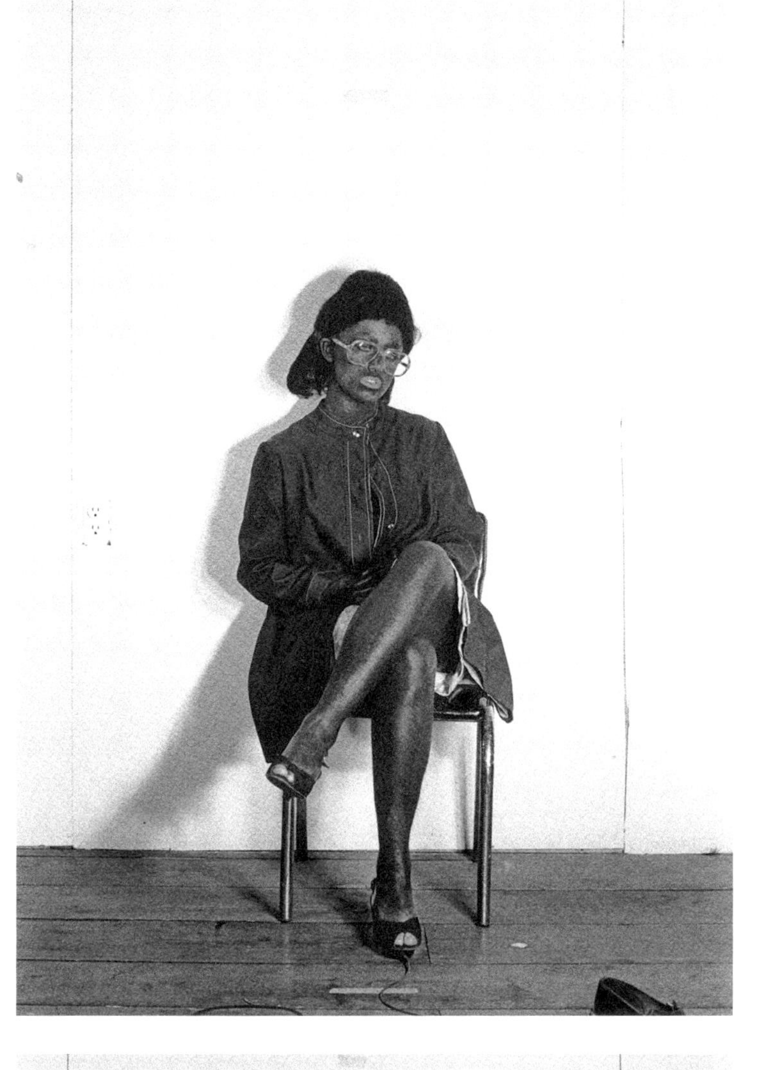
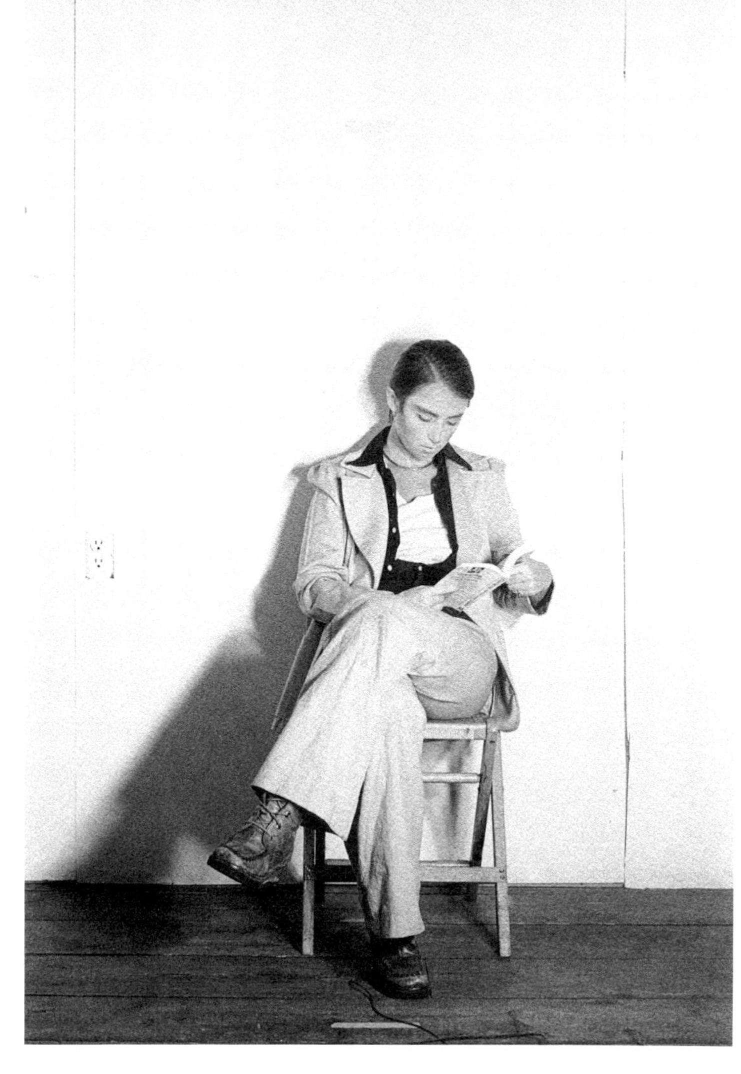
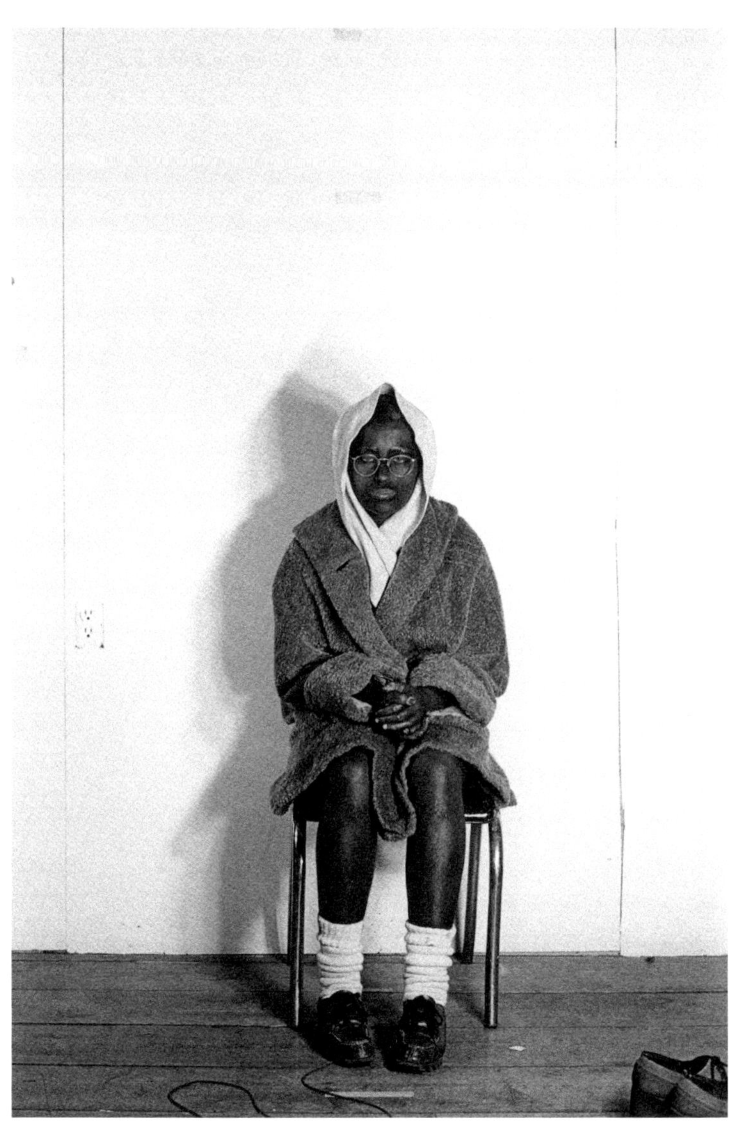
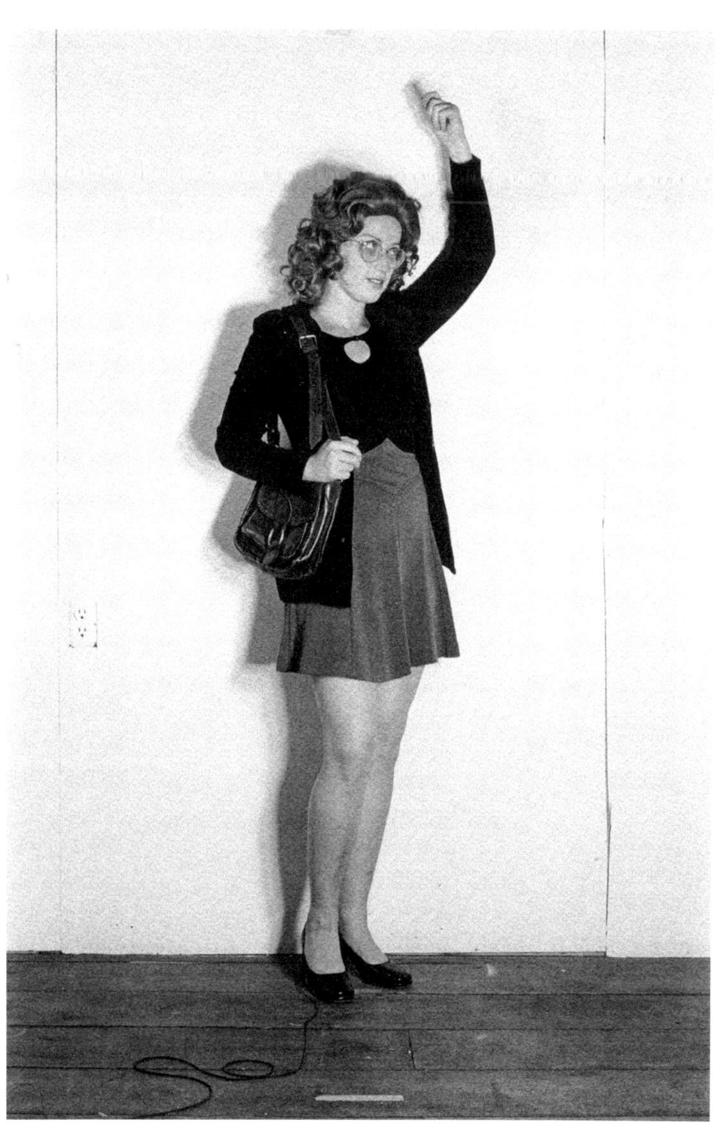

Untitled #379
Untitled #380
Untitled #381
Untitled #382
Untitled #383
Untitled #392
Untitled #385
Untitled #391
Untitled #393
Untitled #386
Untitled #390
Untitled #389
Untitled #388
Untitled #384
Untitled #387
Untitled #394
Untitled #378

from Murder Mystery

1976 — 2000

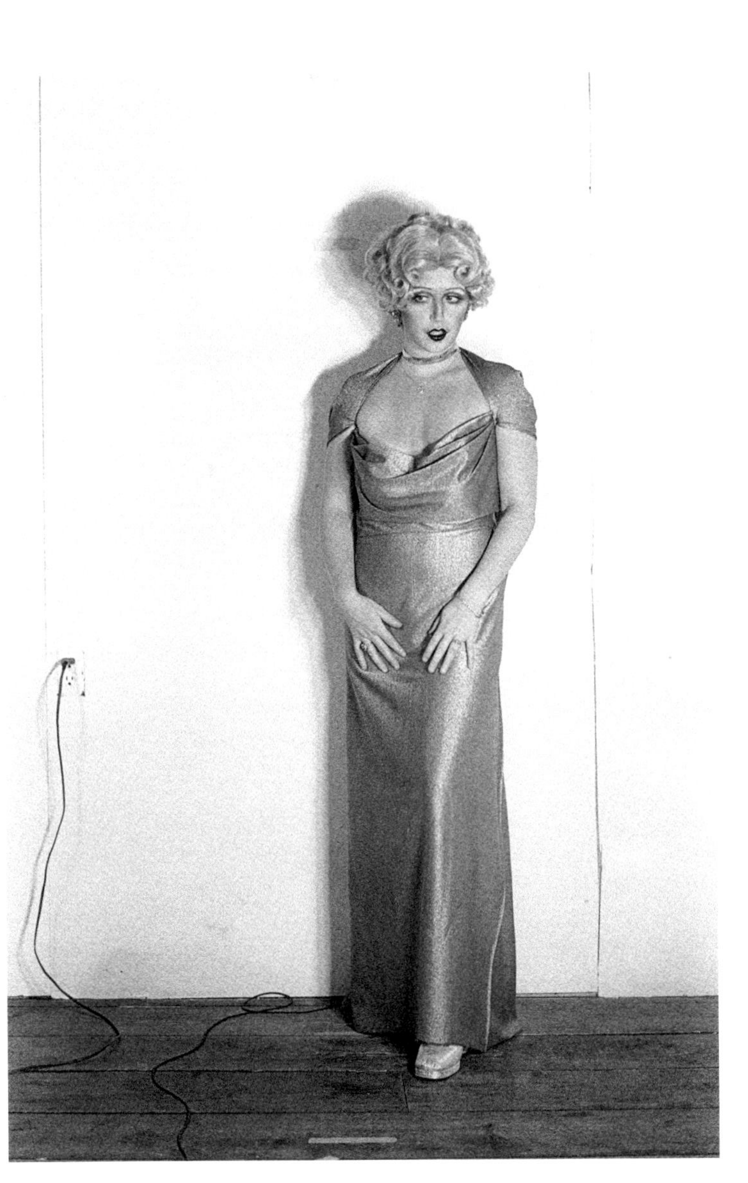

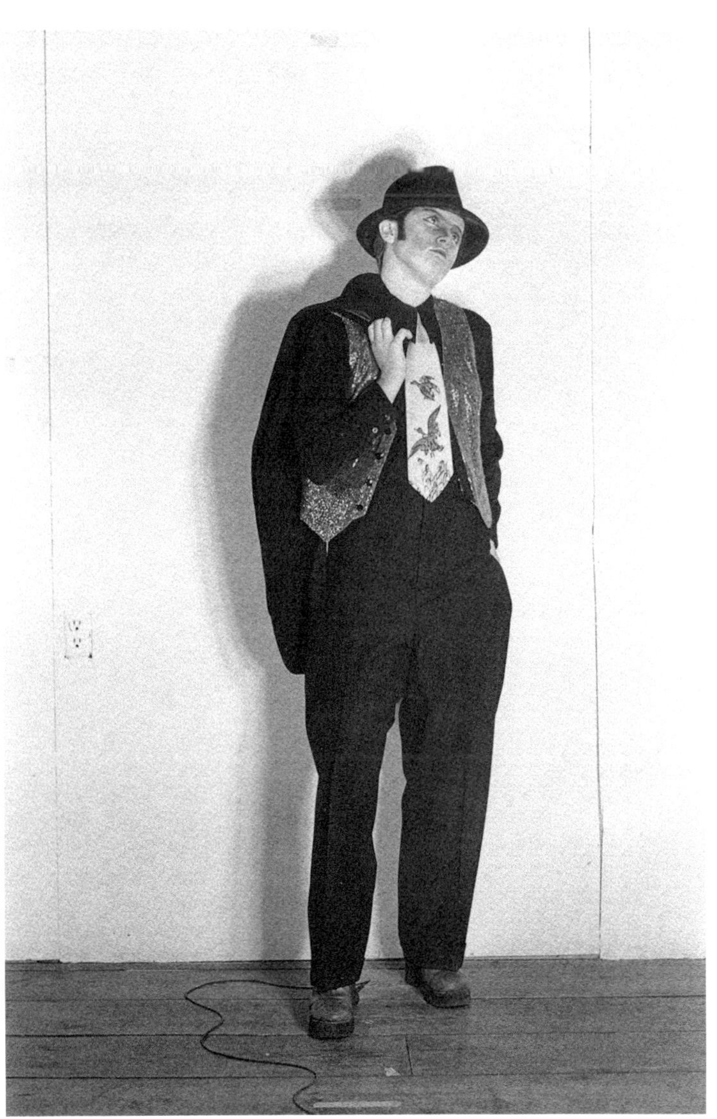

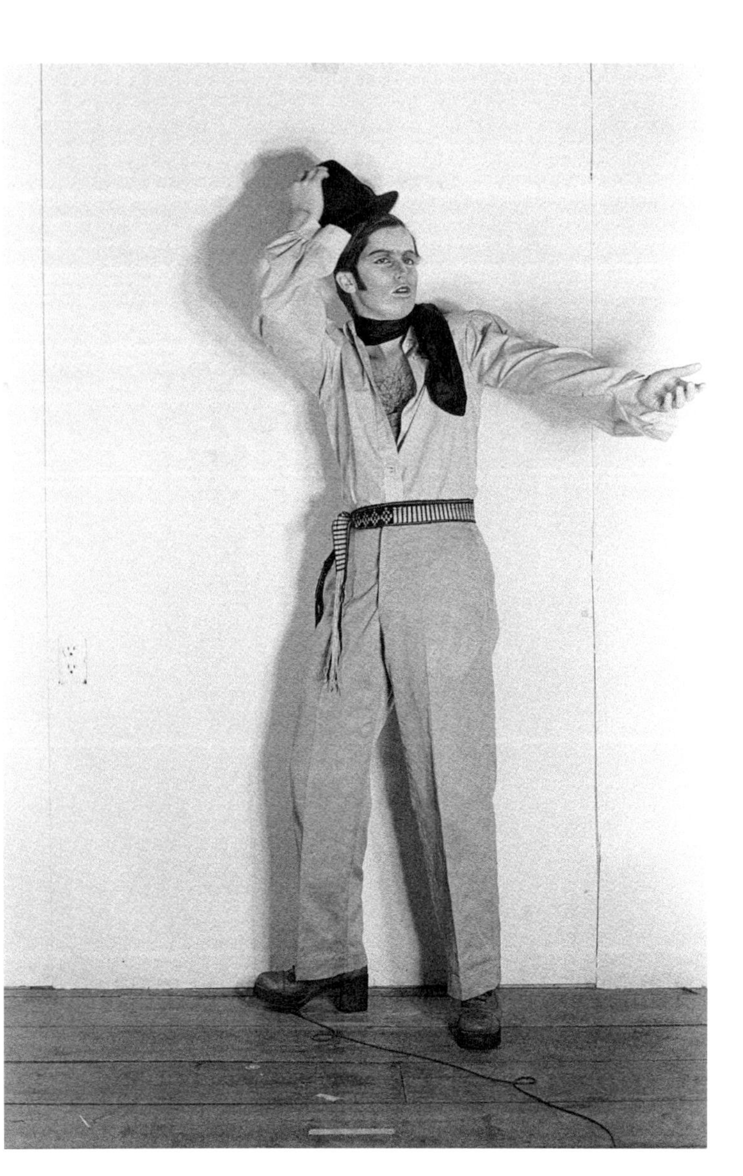

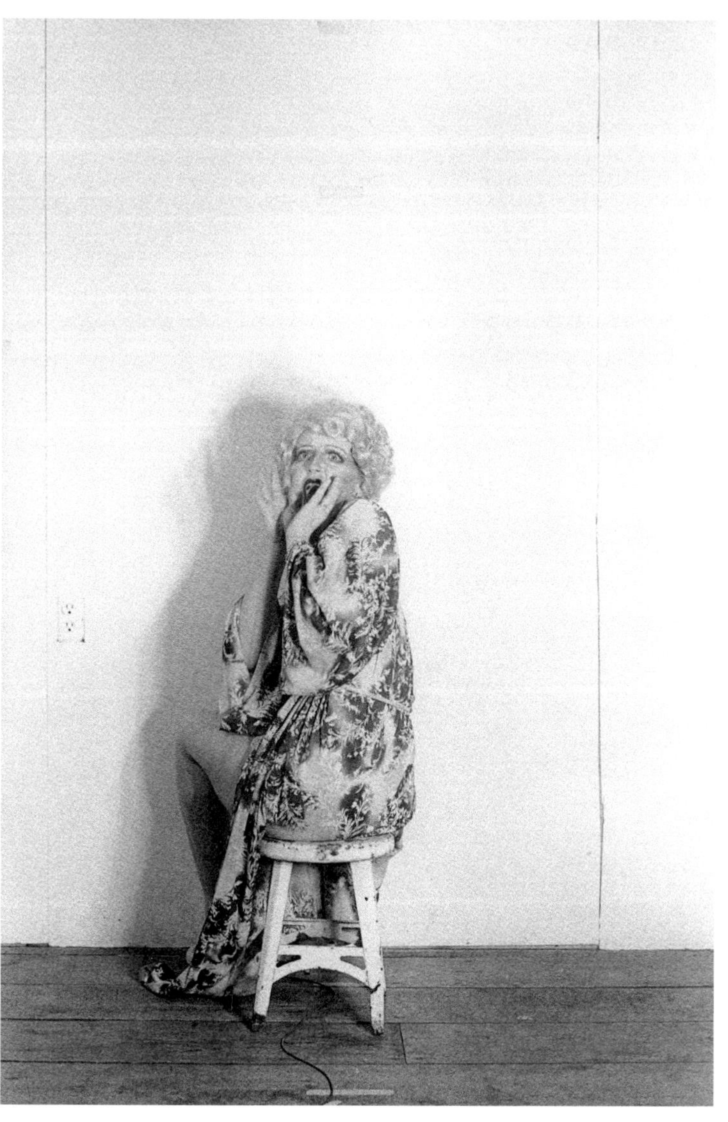

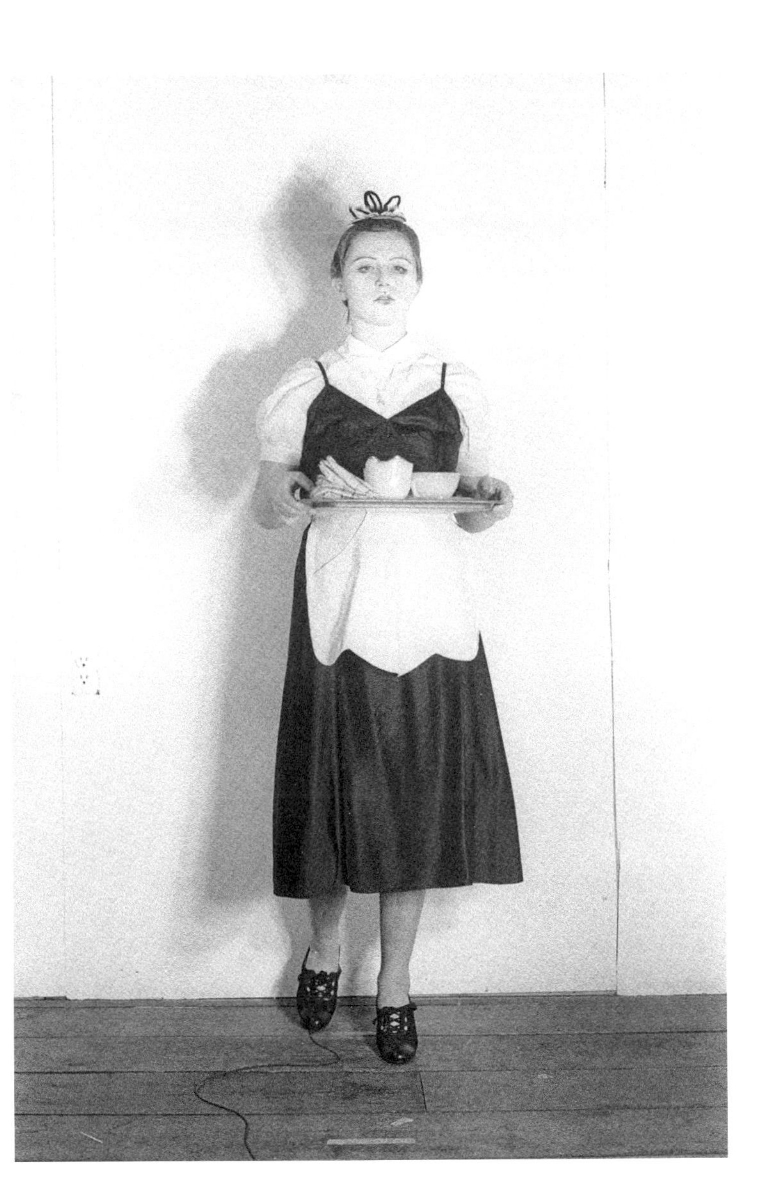

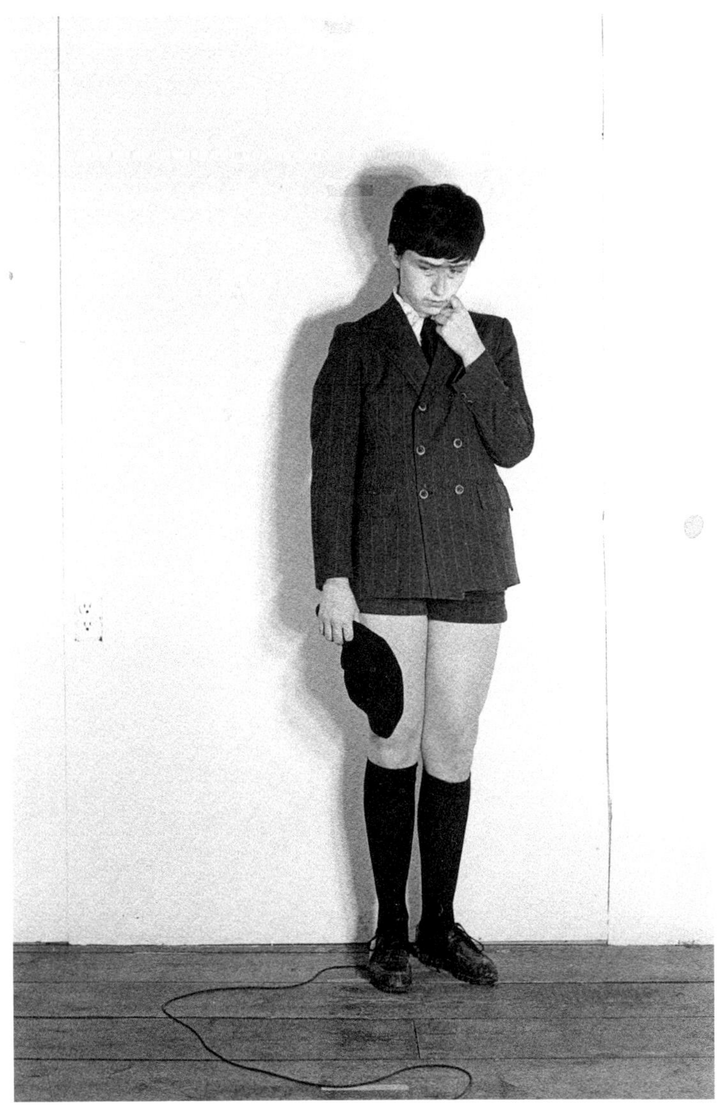

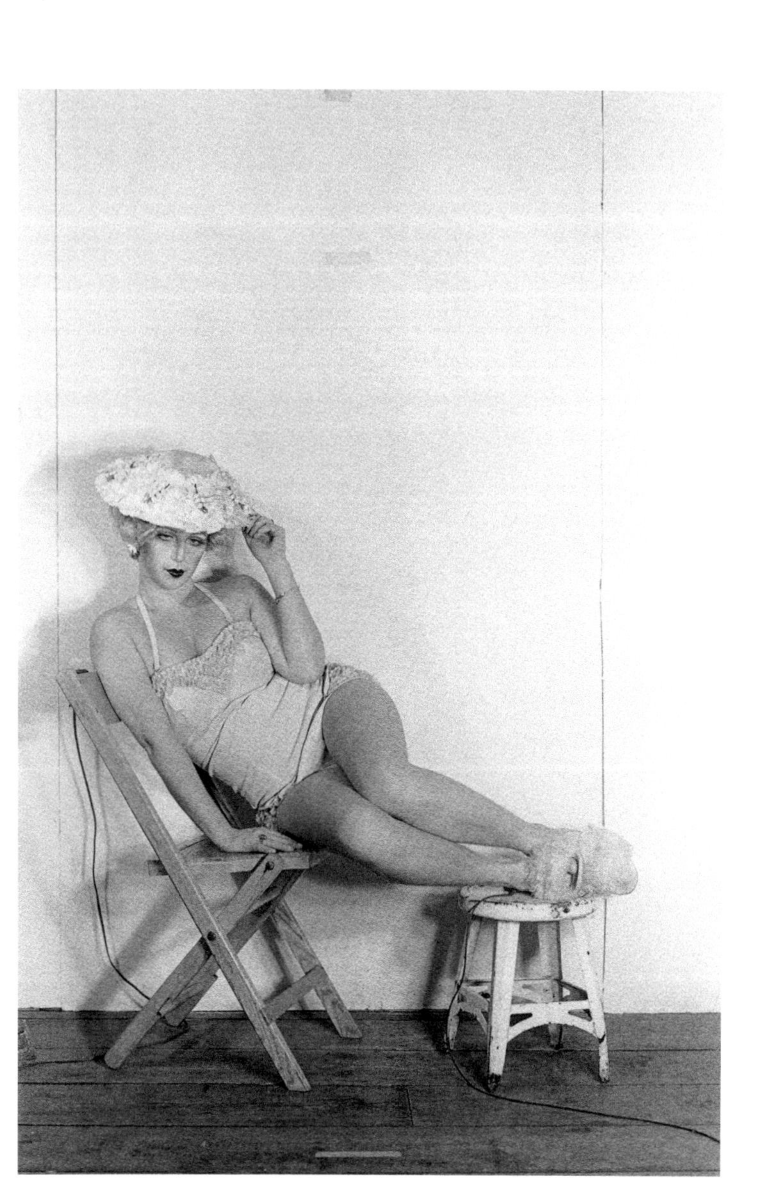

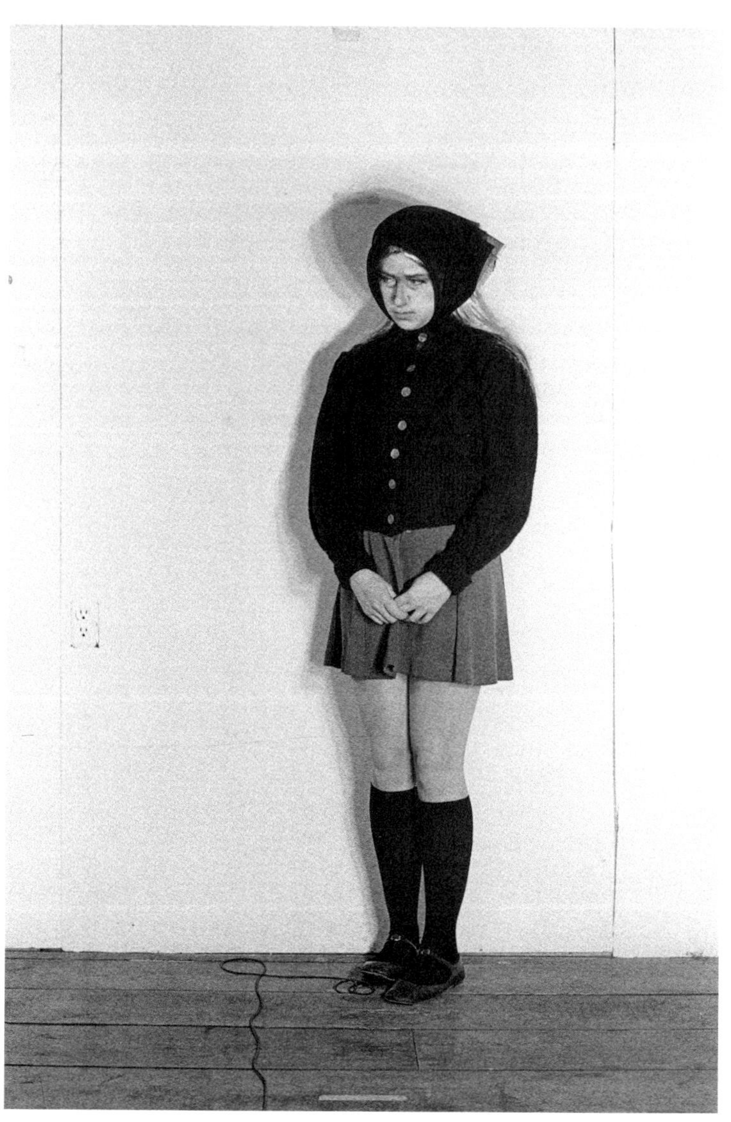

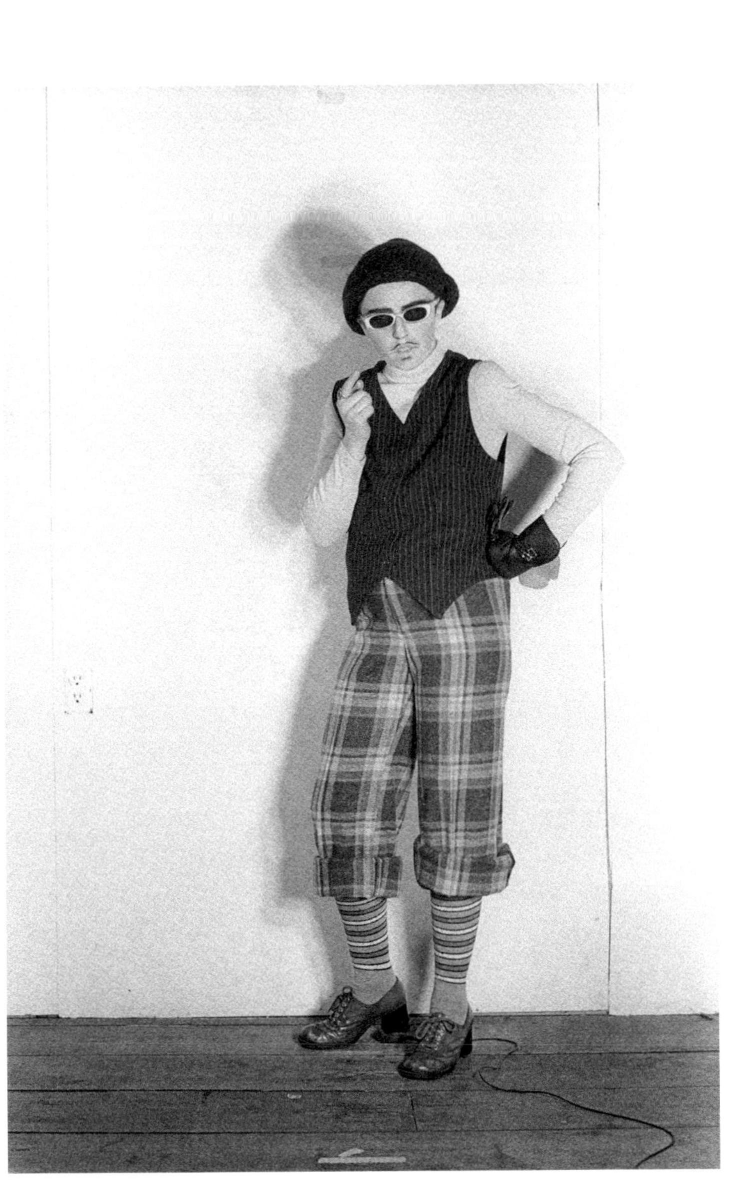

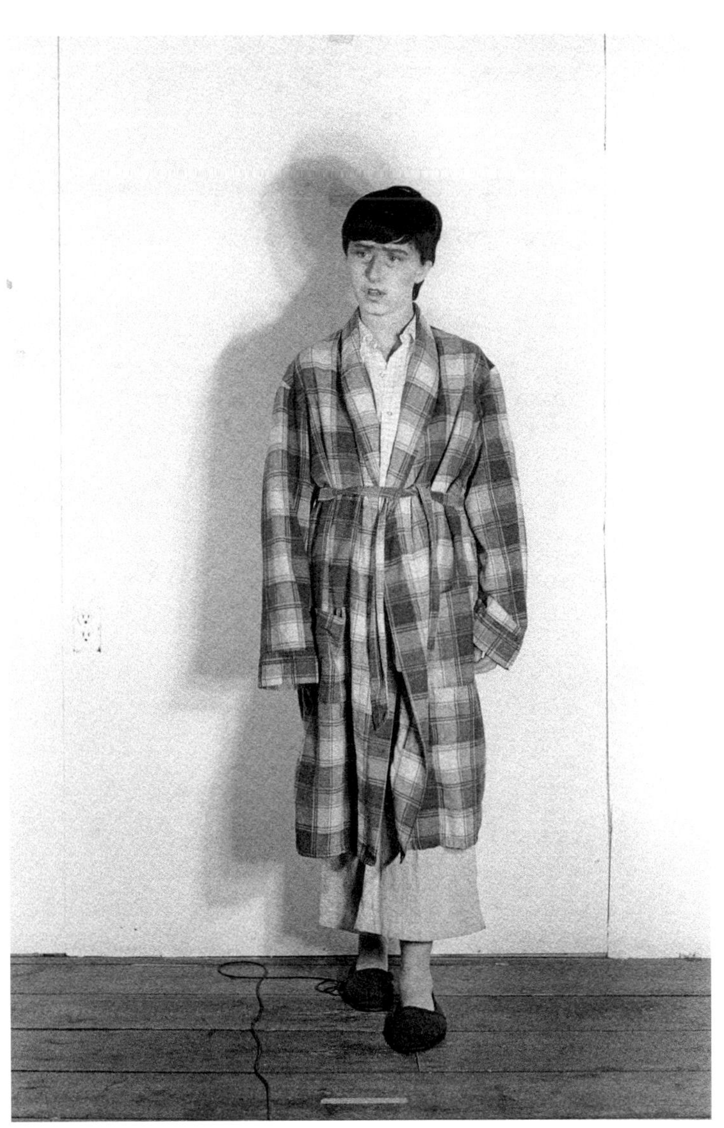

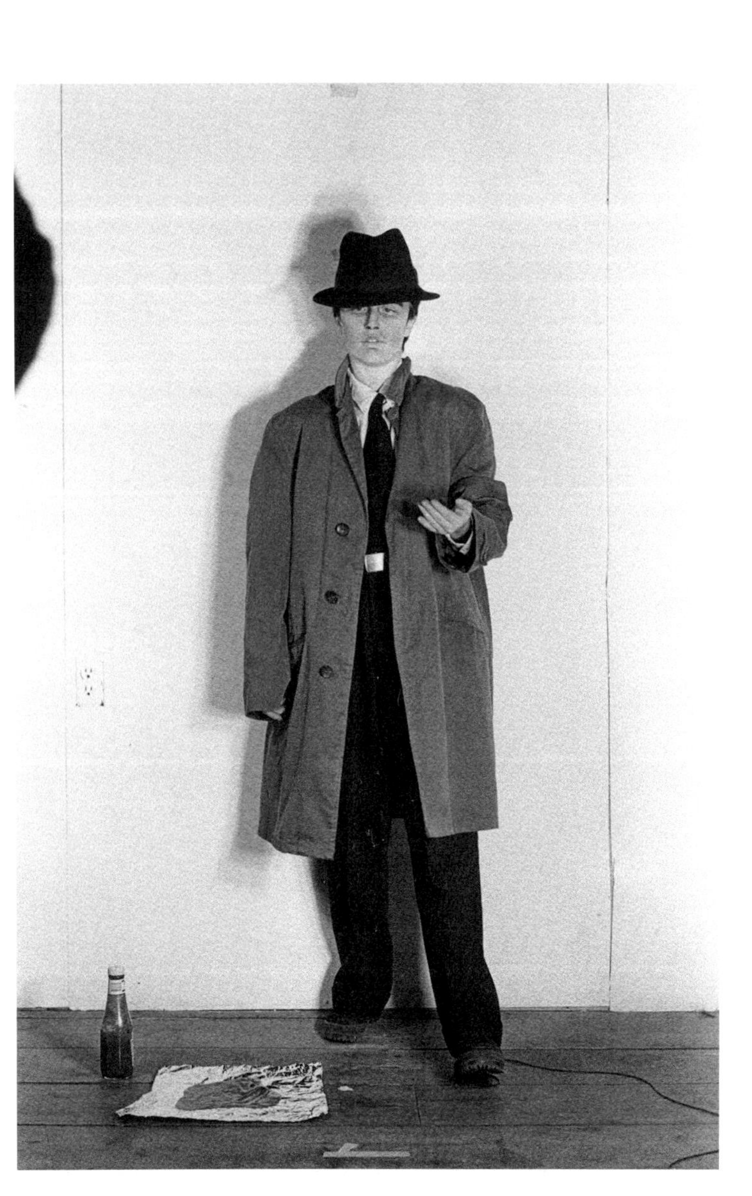

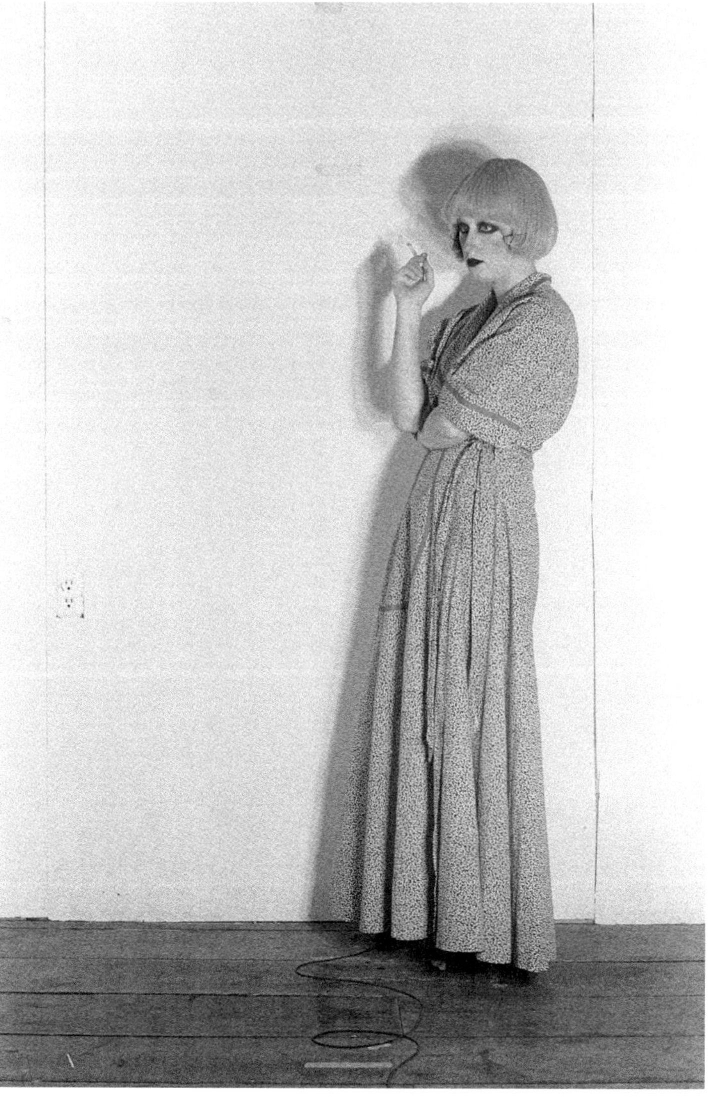

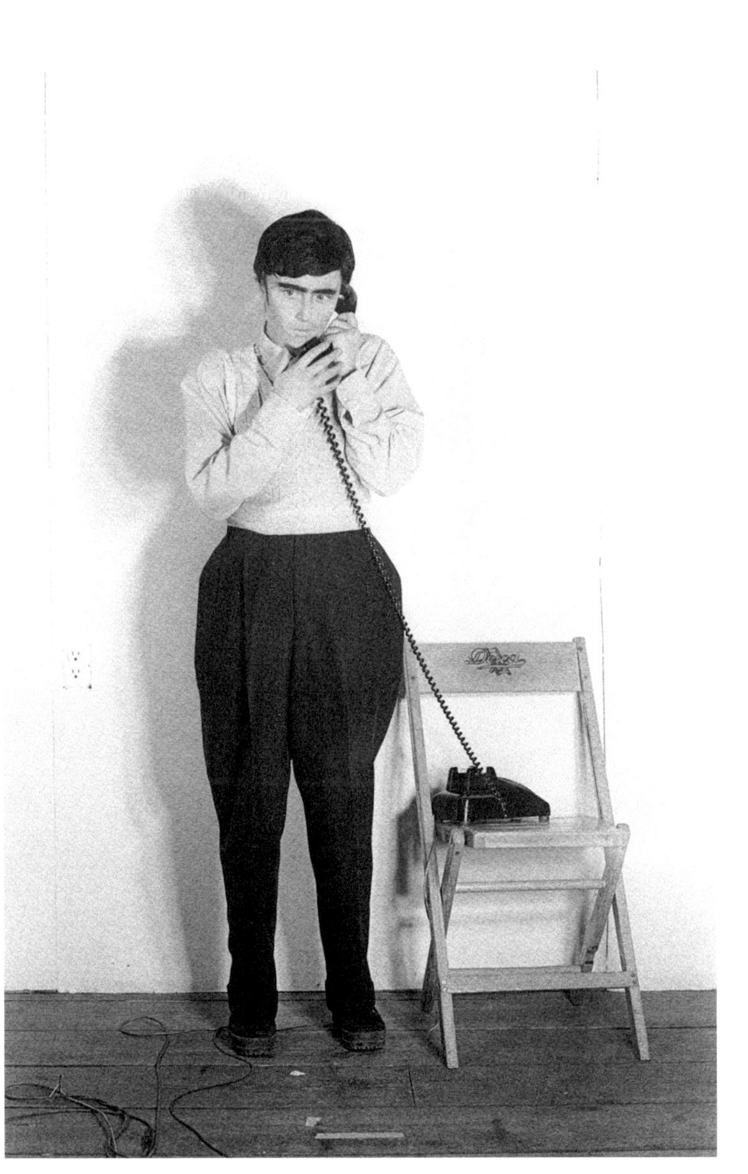

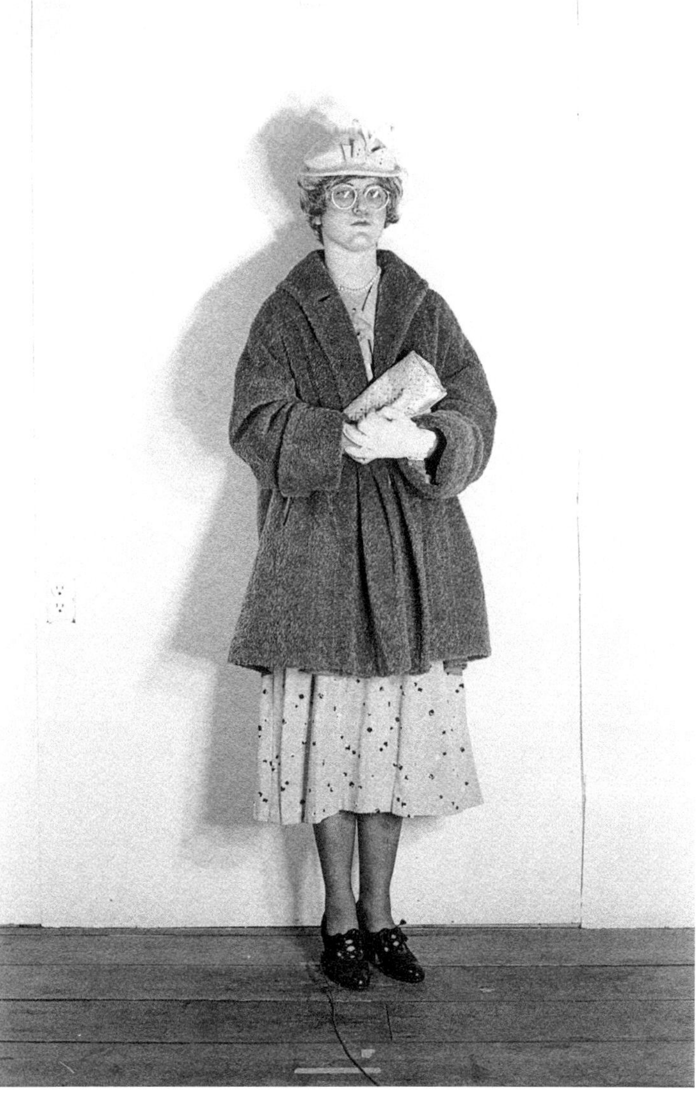

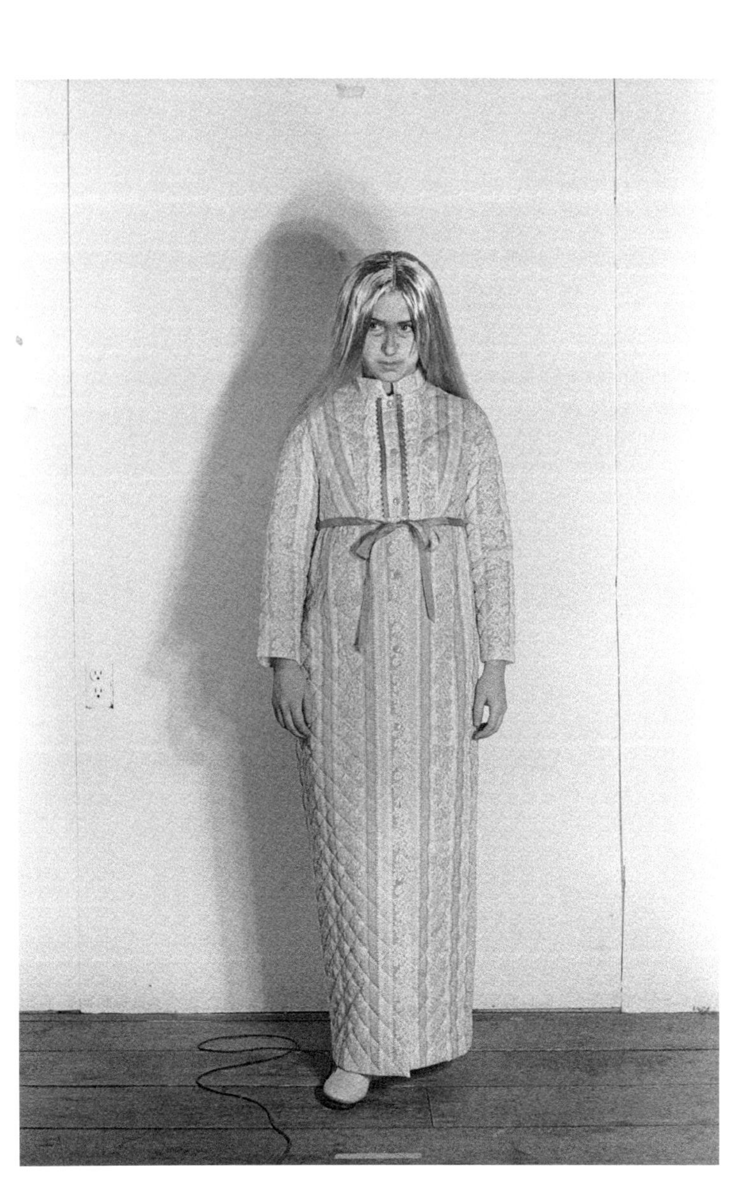

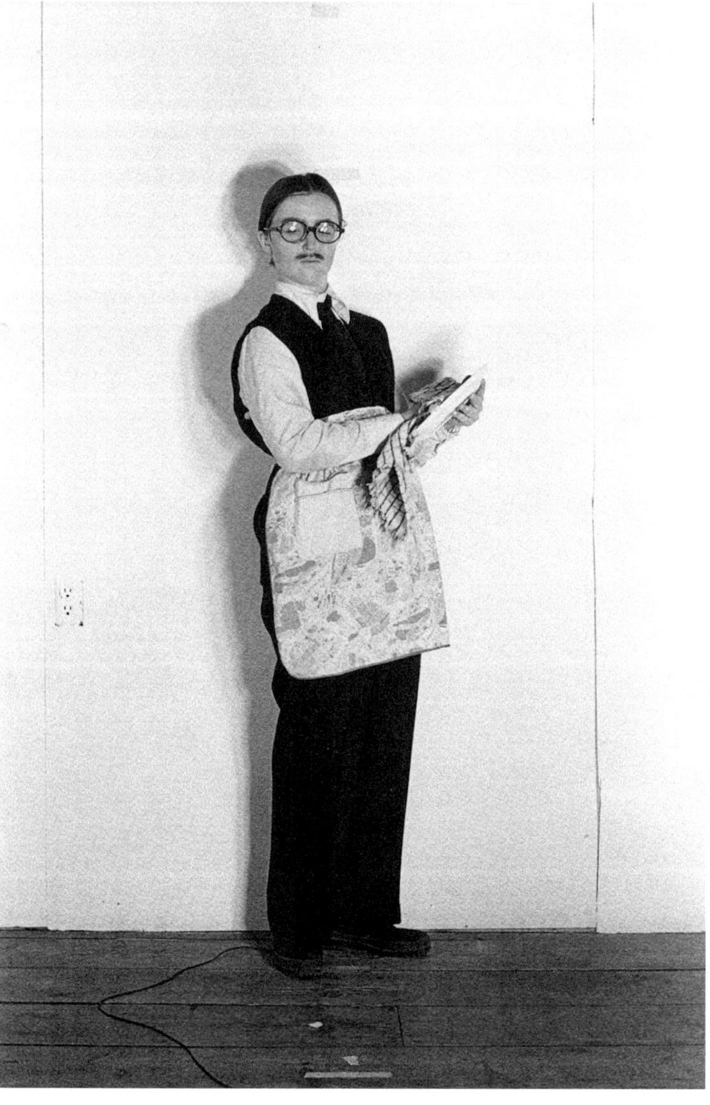

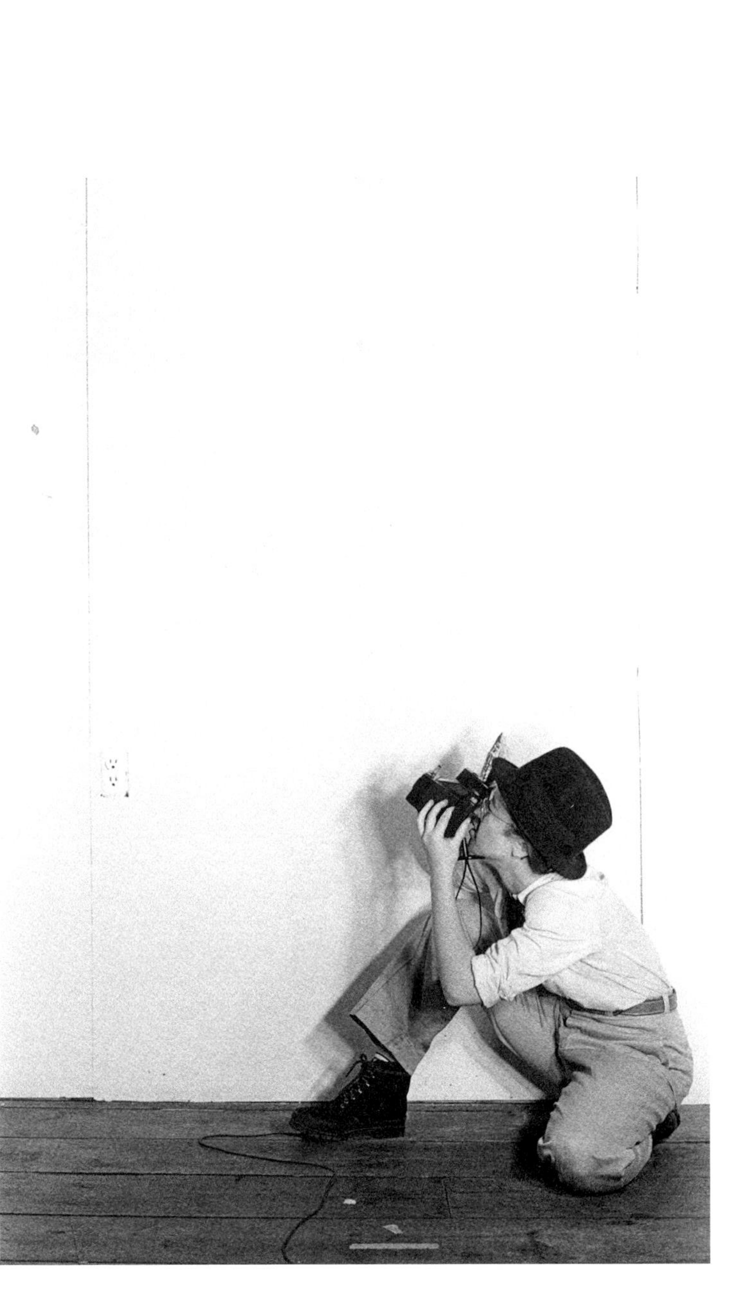

Untitled Film Still #1

Untitled Film Still #2
Untitled Film Still #3
Untitled Film Still #4
Untitled Film Still #5
Untitled Film Still #6

Untitled Film Still #8
Untitled Film Still #7
Untitled Film Still #9
Untitled Film Still #84
Untitled Film Still #10

Untitled Film Still #12
Untitled Film Still #13
Untitled Film Still #60
Untitled Film Still #11

Untitled Film Still #17
Untitled Film Still #18
Untitled Film Still #19
Untitled Film Still #20

Untitled Film Still #23
Untitled Film Still #21
Untitled Film Still #22
Untitled Film Still #25
Untitled Film Still #24

Untitled Film Still #15
Untitled Film Still #35
Untitled Film Still #26
Untitled Film Still #29
Untitled Film Still #28
Untitled Film Still #27b

Untitled Film Still #45
Untitled Film Still #46
Untitled Film Still #33
Untitled Film Still #34
Untitled Film Still #32

Untitled Film Still #31
Untitled Film Still #30
Untitled Film Still #14
Untitled Film Still #16
Untitled Film Still #51
Untitled Film Still #50

Untitled Film Still #43
Untitled Film Still #40
Untitled Film Still #38
Untitled Film Still #42
Untitled Film Still #44

Untitled Film Still #41
Untitled Film Still #39
Untitled Film Still #82
Untitled Film Still #81
Untitled Film Still #61

Untitled Film Still #36
Untitled Film Still #62
Untitled Film Still #53
Untitled Film Still #56

Untitled Film Still #47
Untitled Film Still #27
Untitled Film Still #49
Untitled Film Still #52
Untitled Film Still #37
Untitled Film Still #57

Untitled Film Still #54
Untitled Film Still #55
Untitled Film Still #48

Untitled Film Still #58
Untitled Film Still #59
Untitled Film Still #65
Untitled Film Still #83
Untitled Film Still #64

Untitled Film Still #63

1977—1980

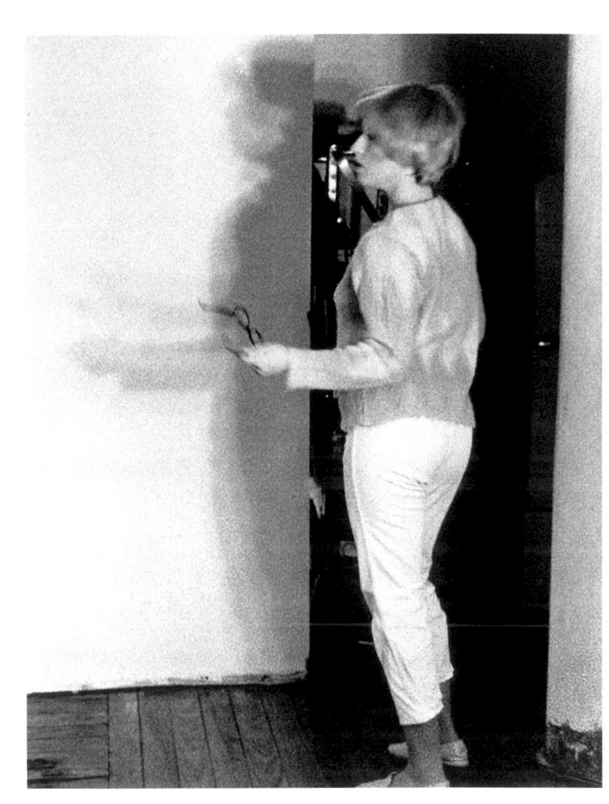

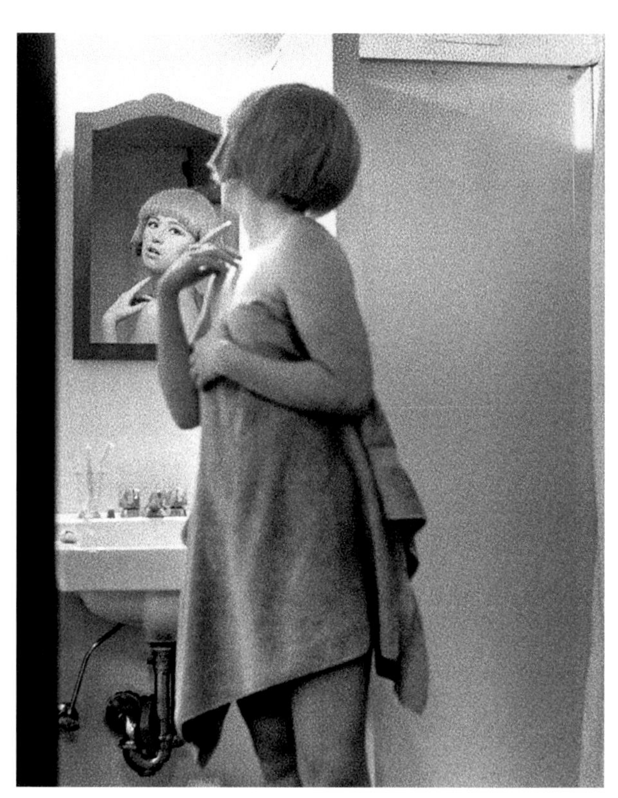

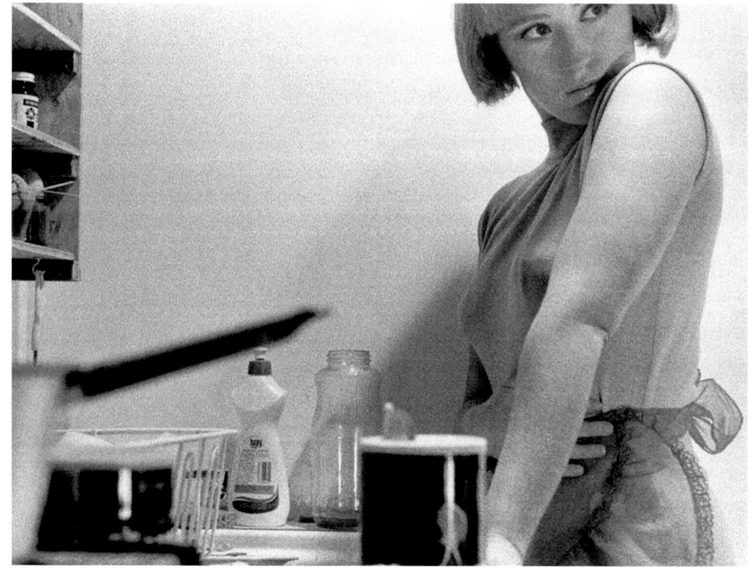

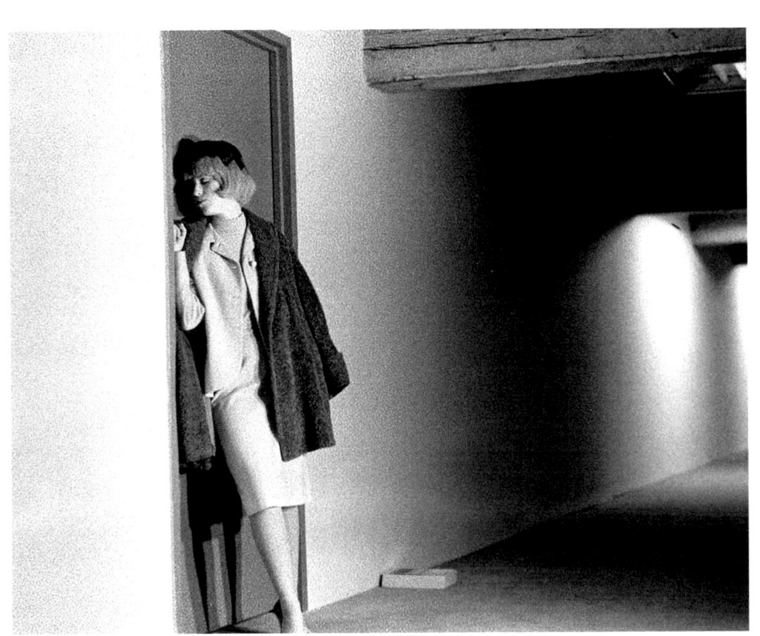

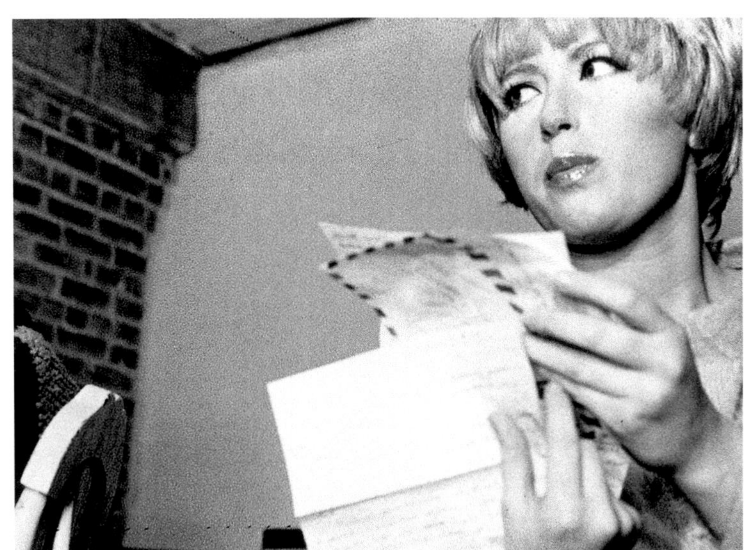

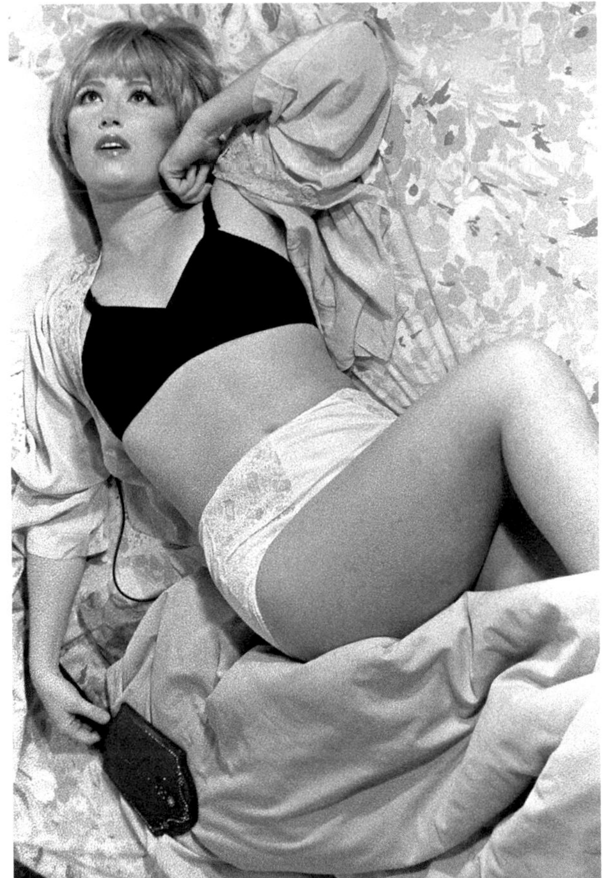

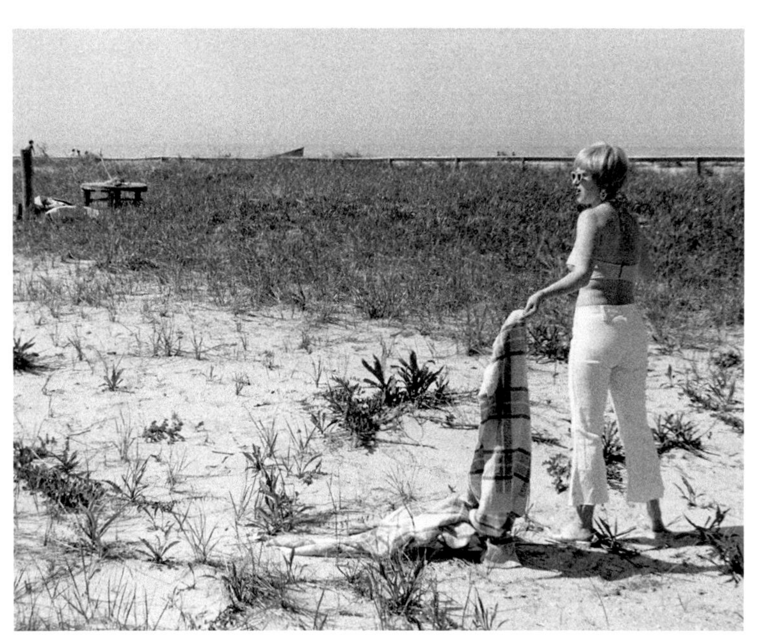

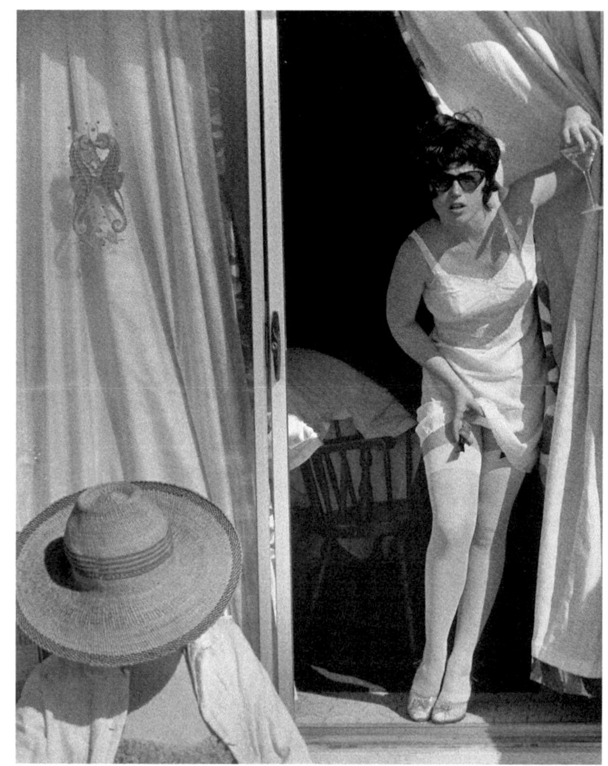

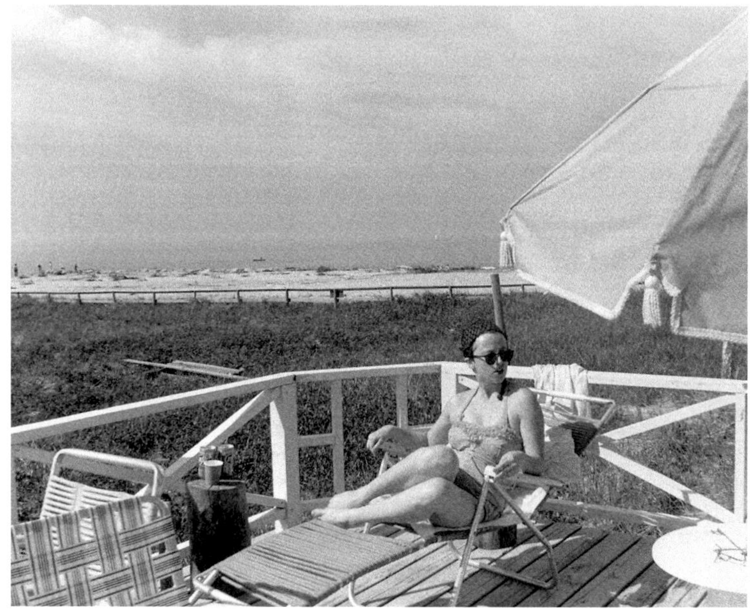

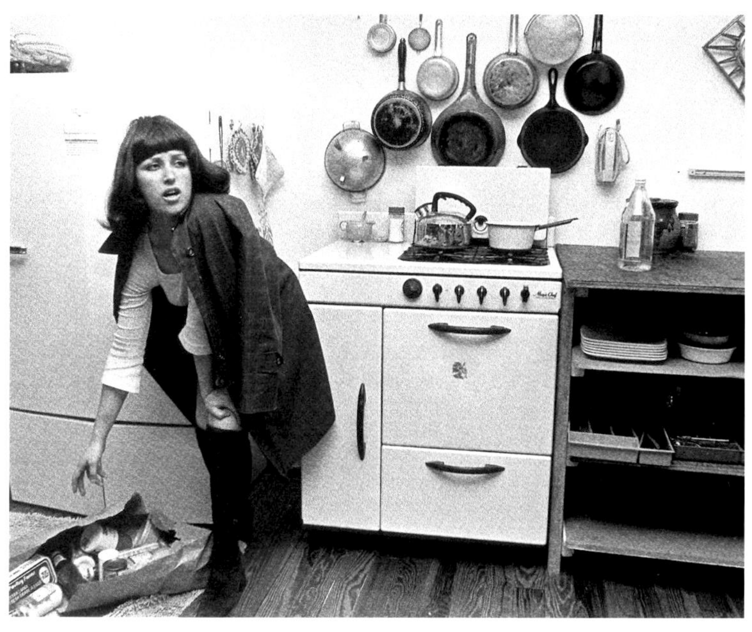

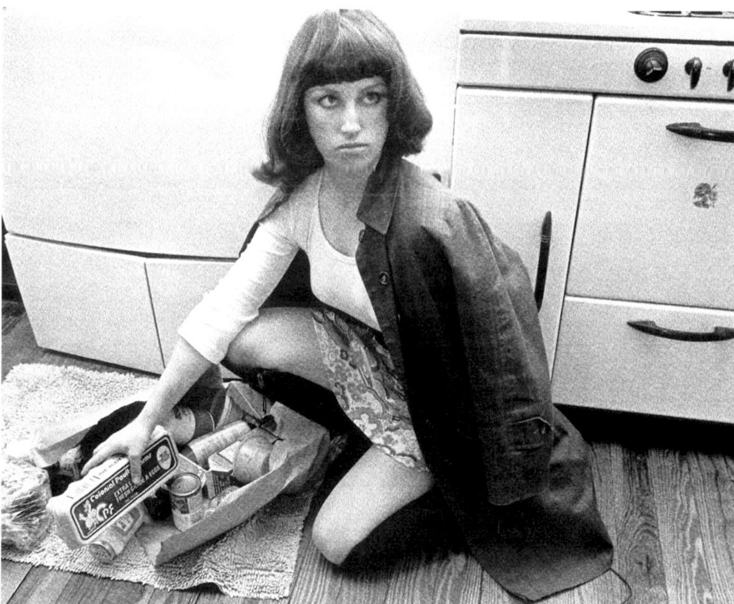

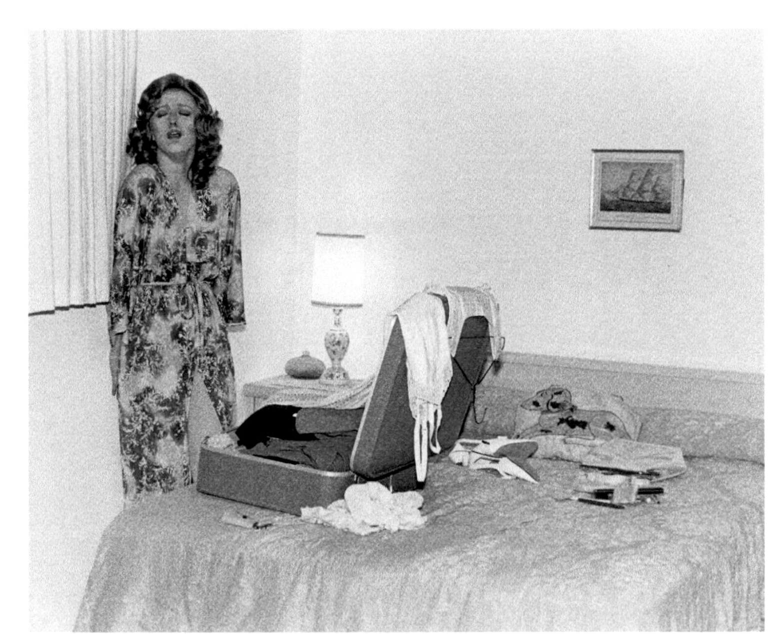

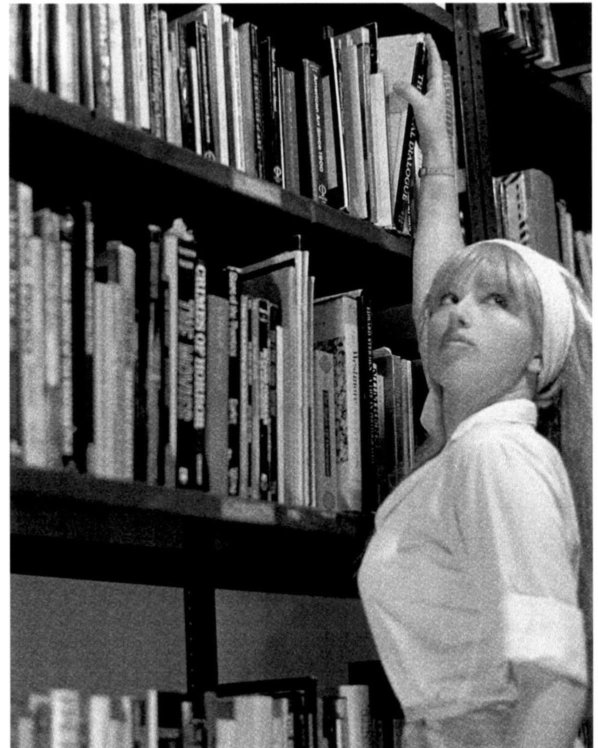

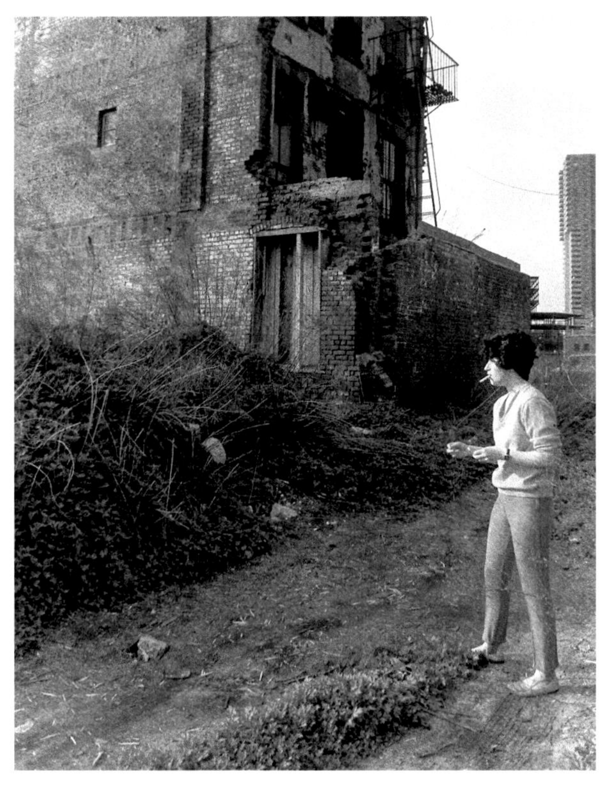

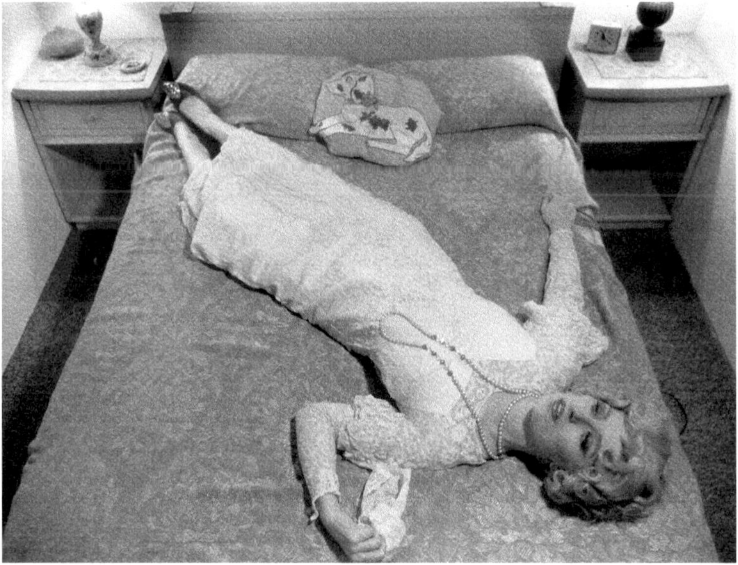

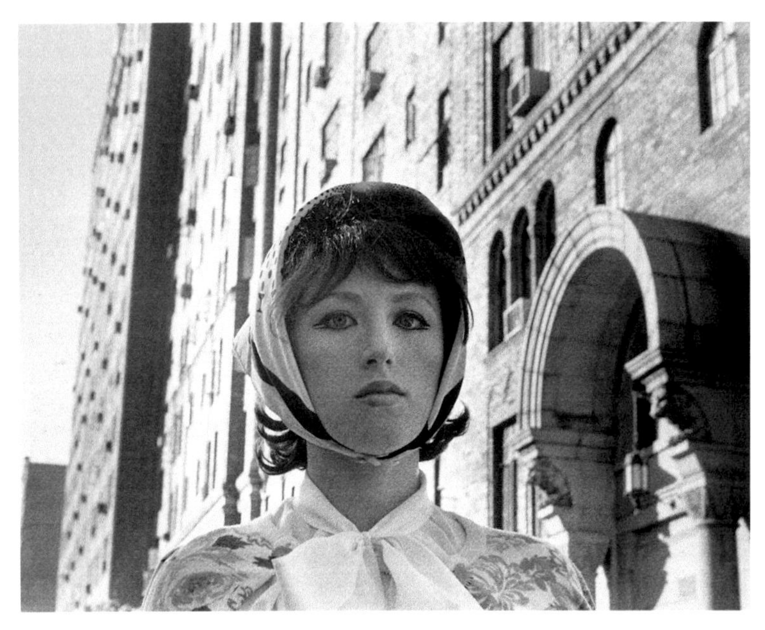

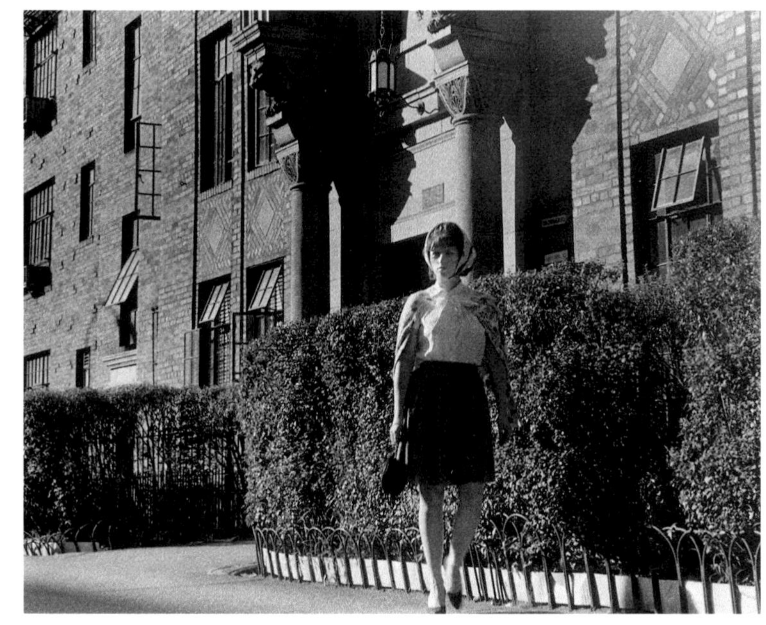

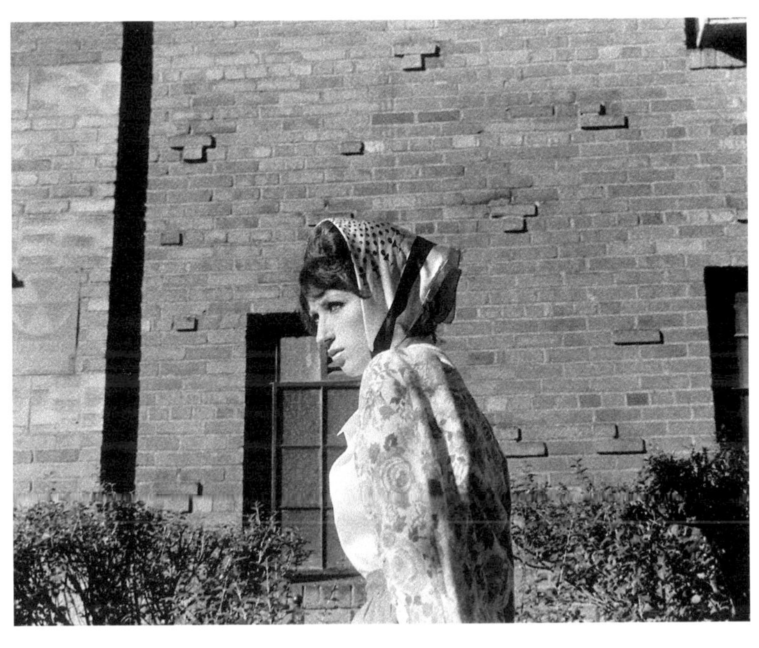

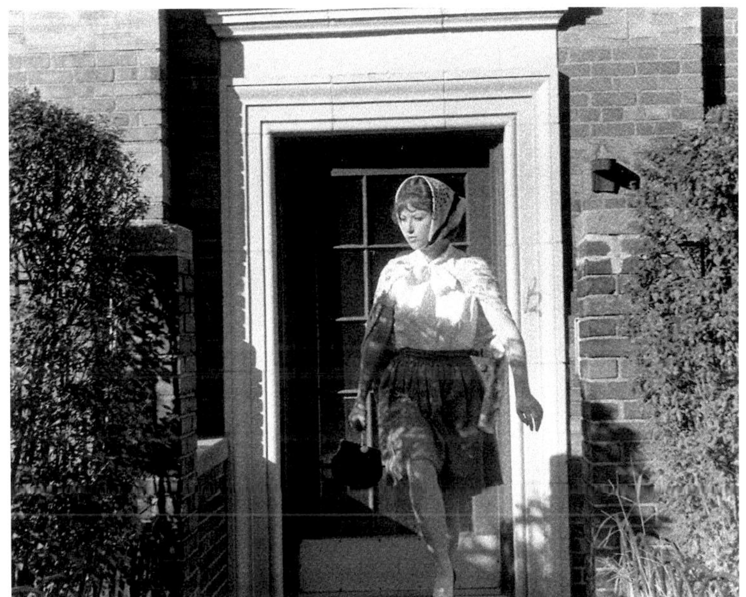

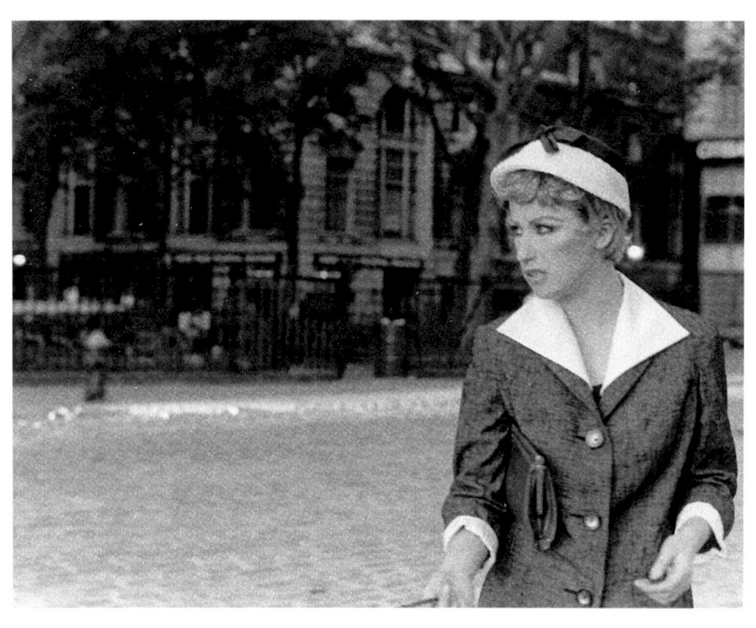

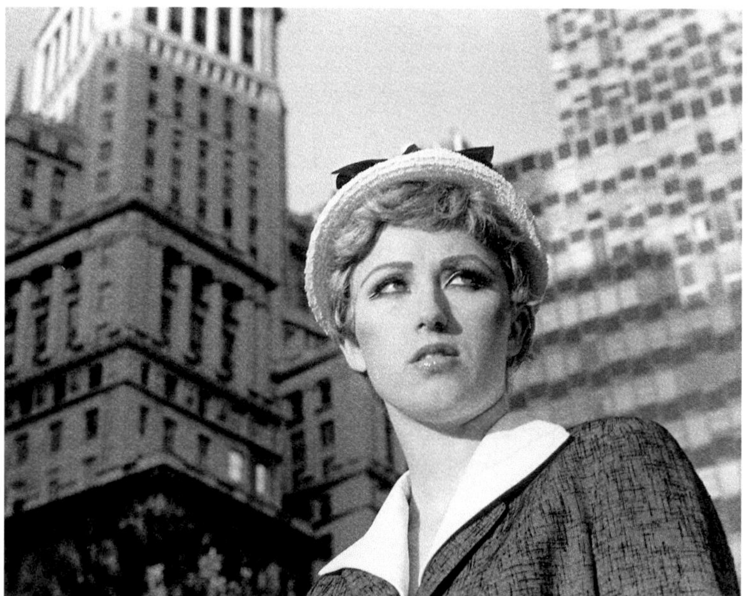

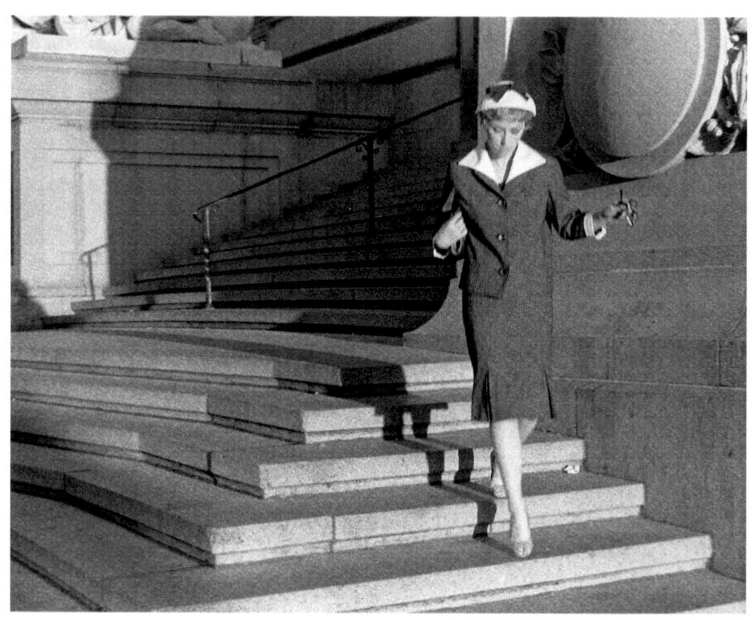

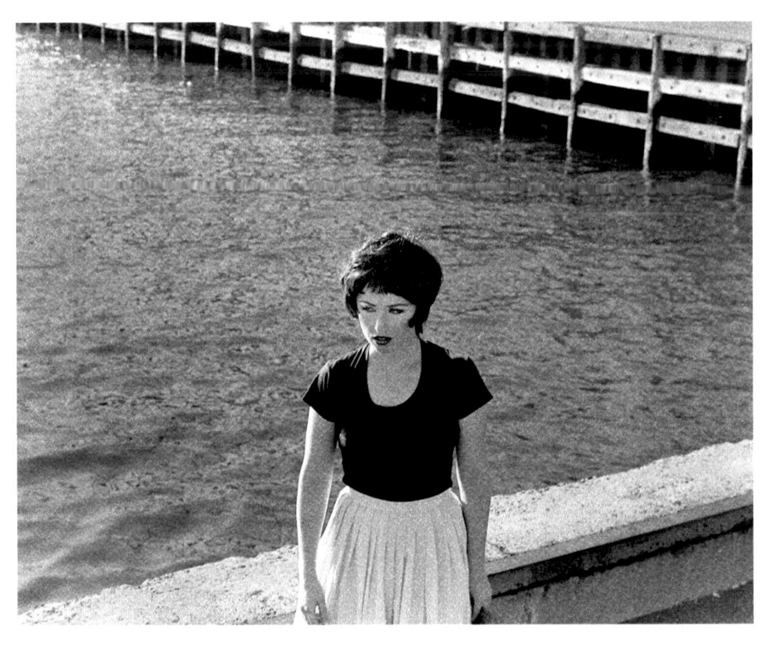

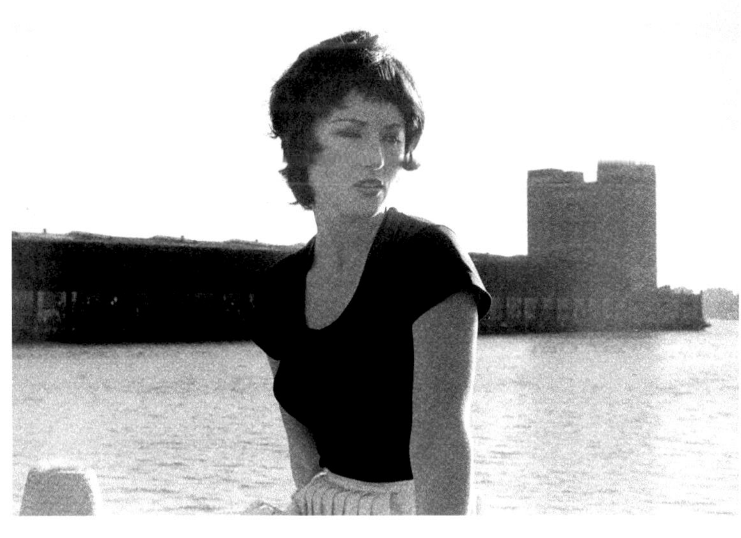

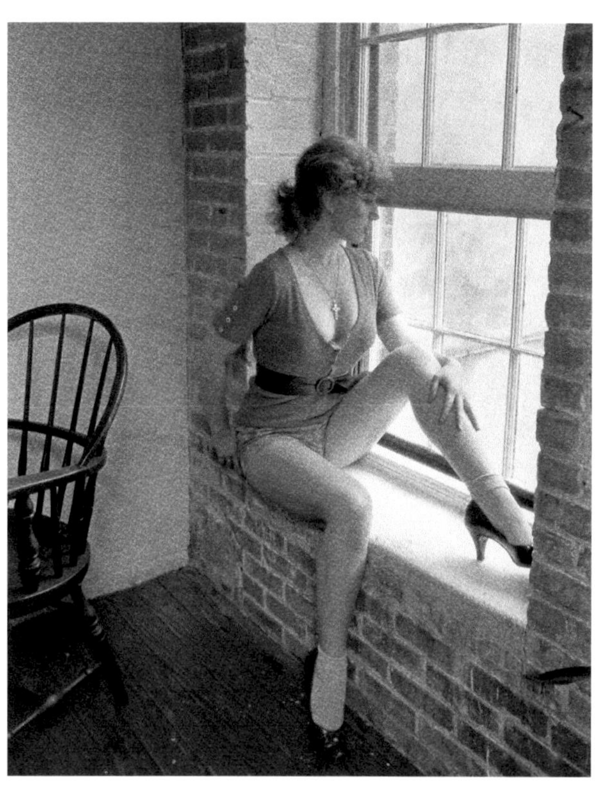
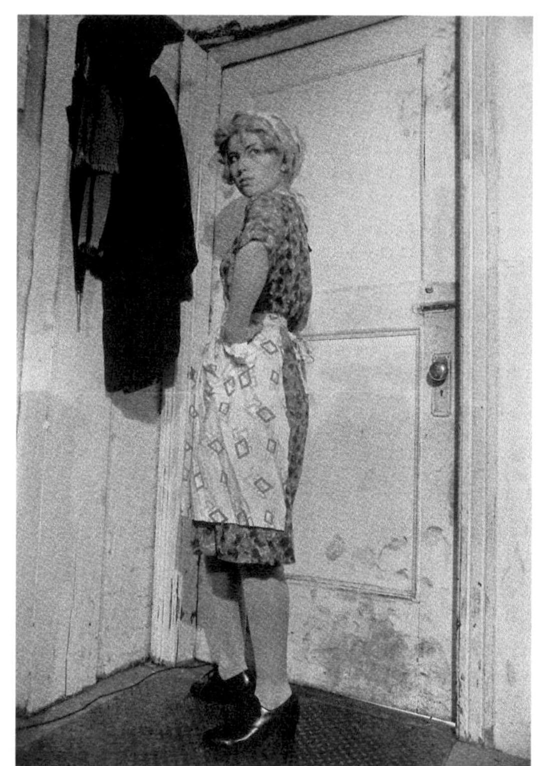
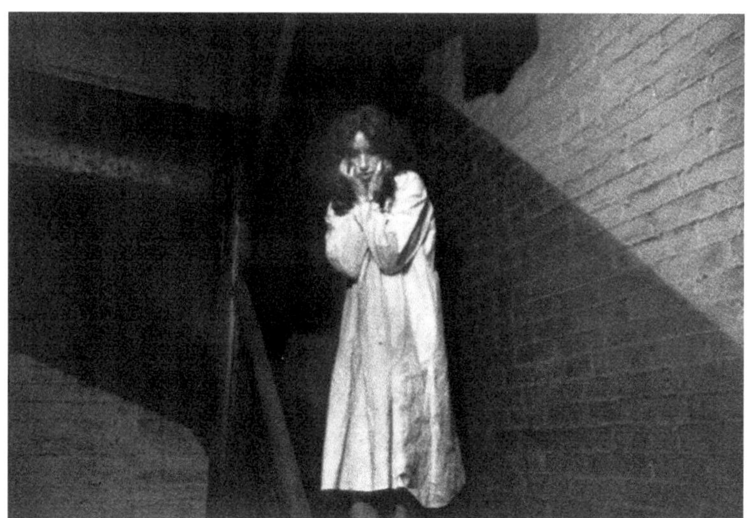

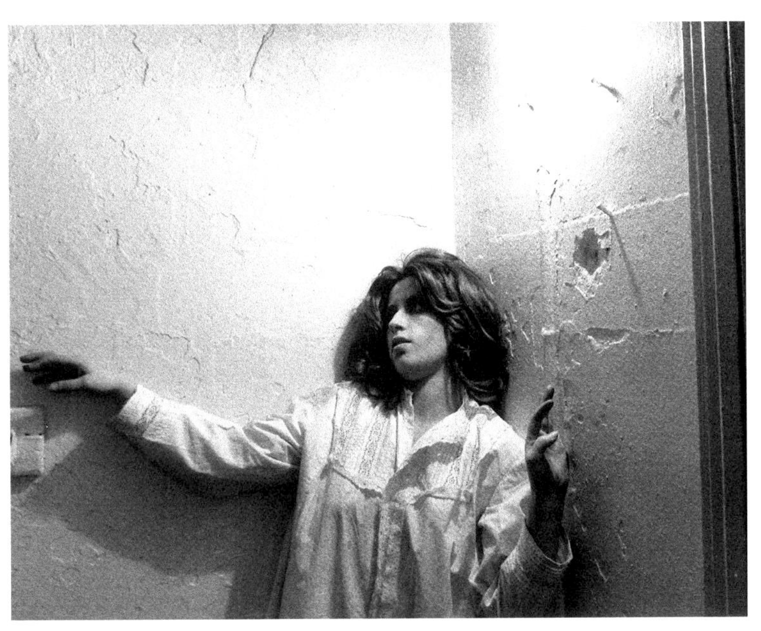

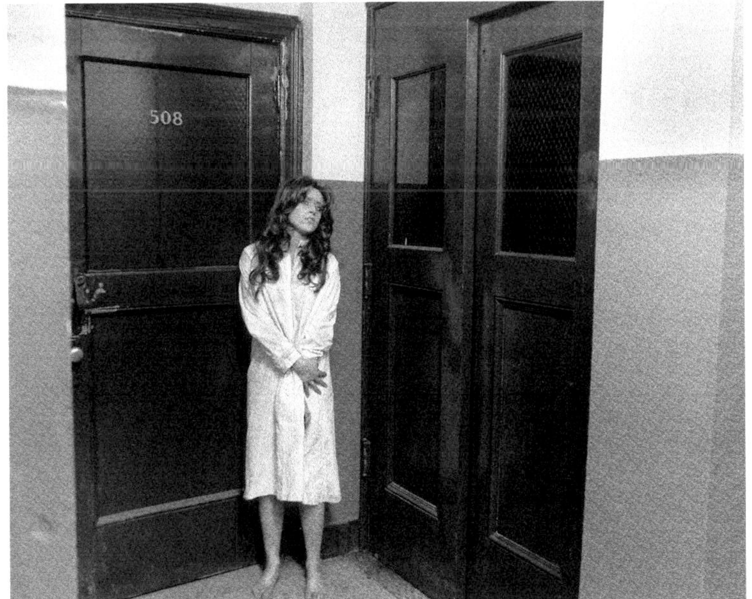
508

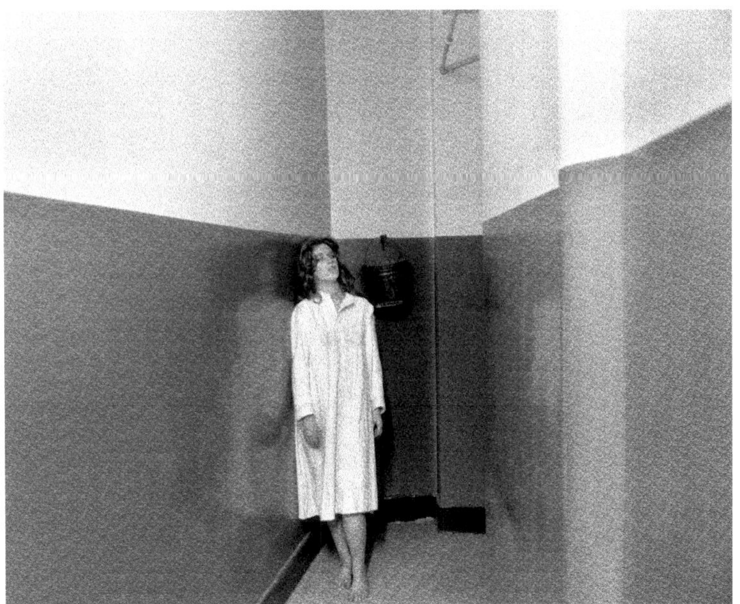

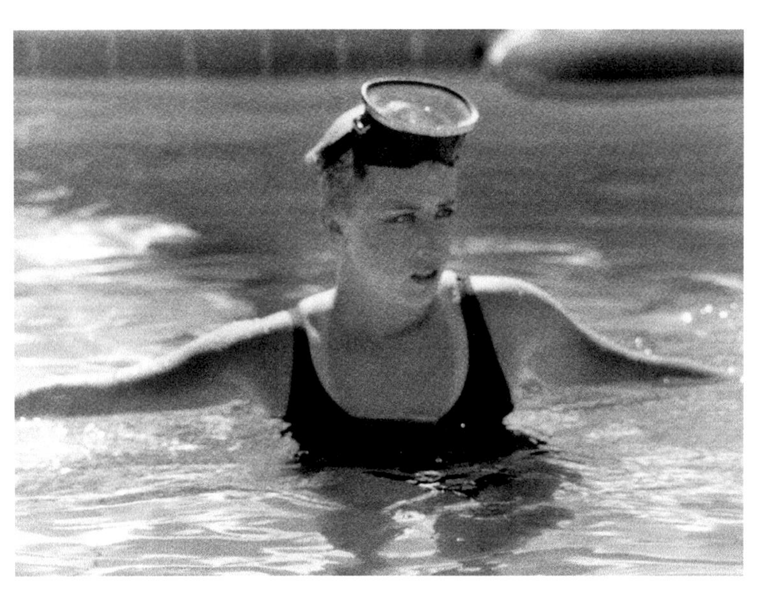

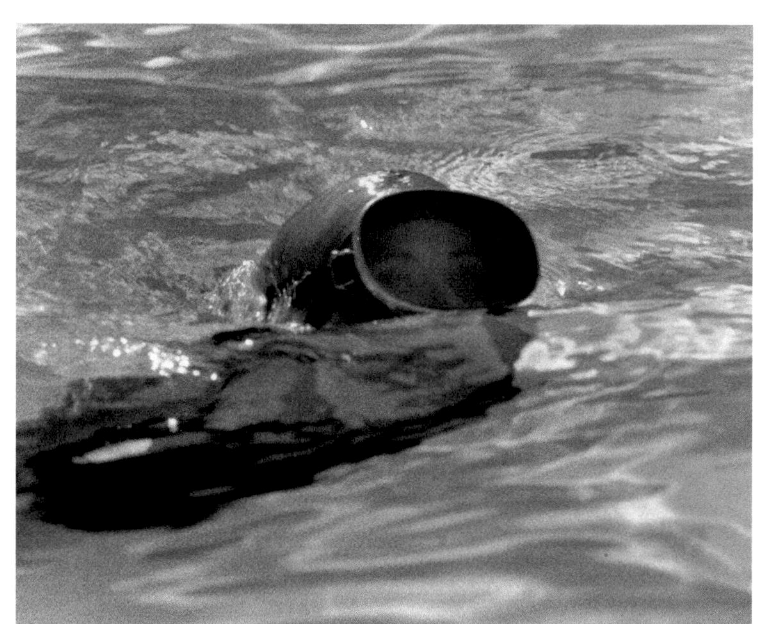

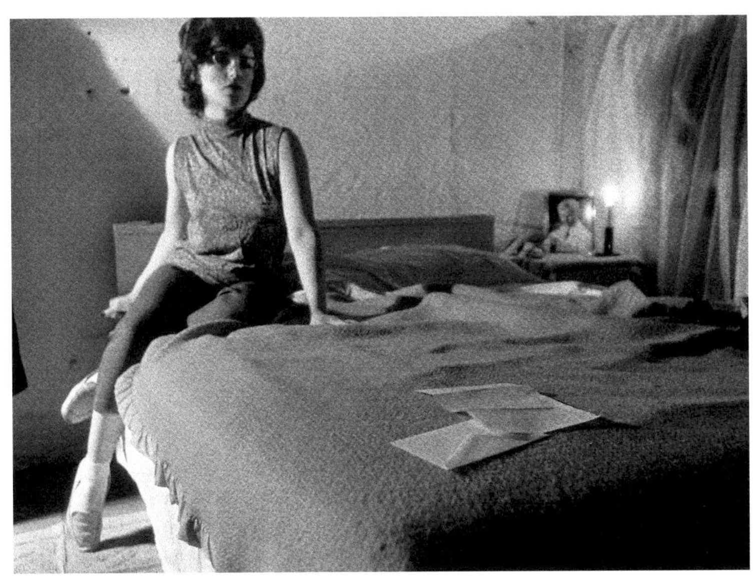

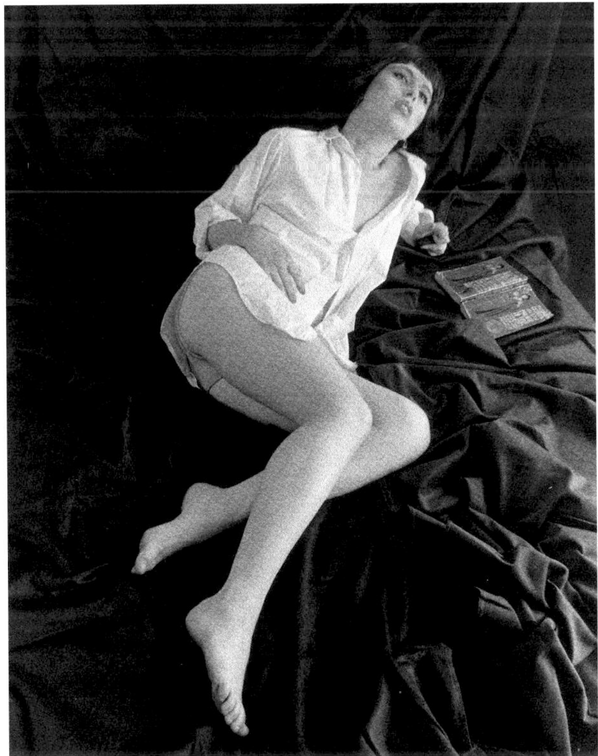

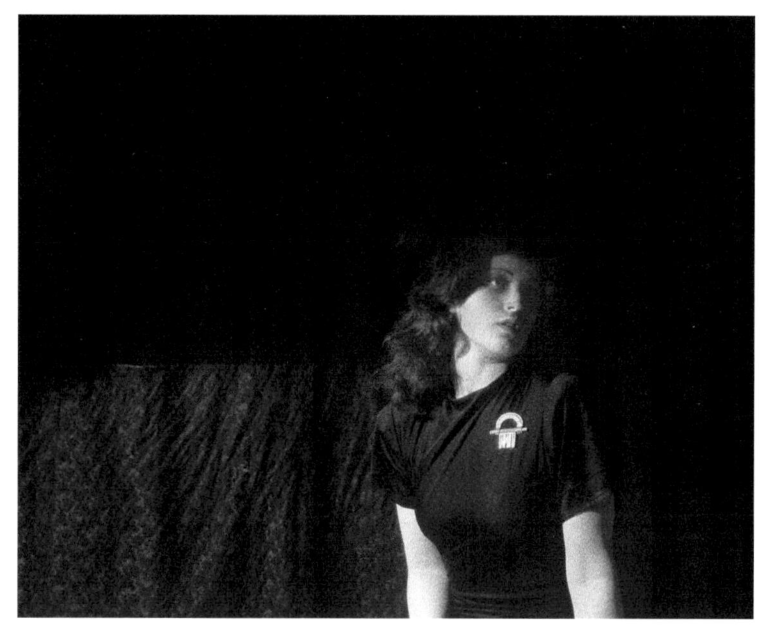

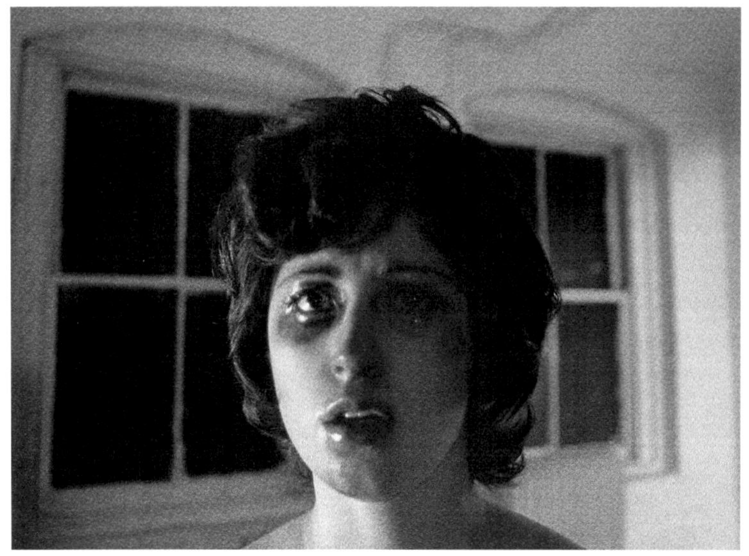

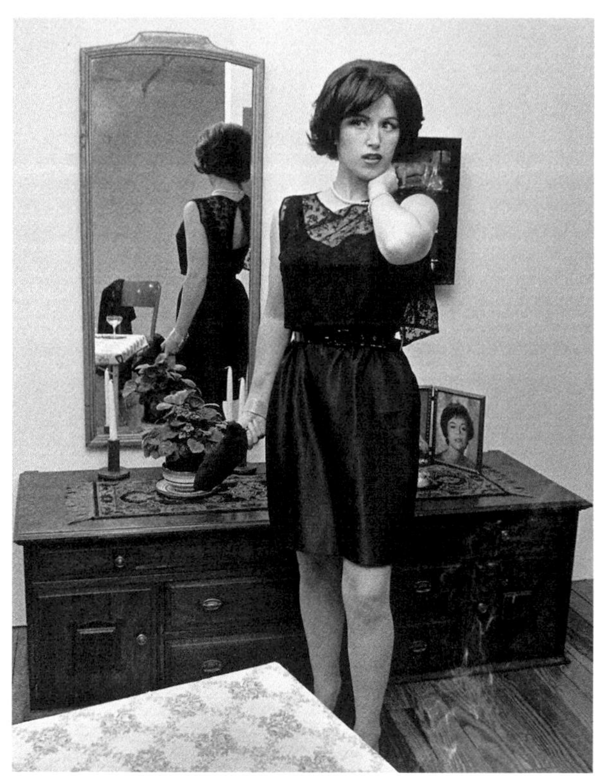

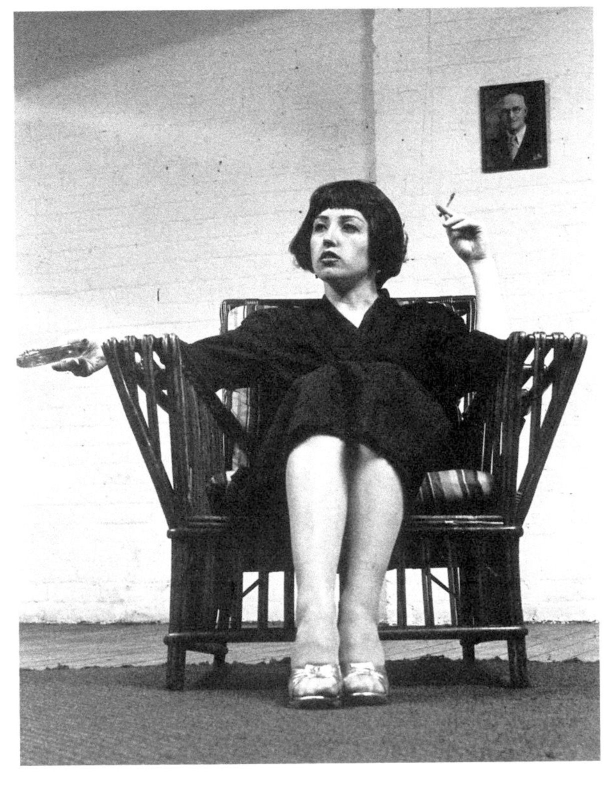

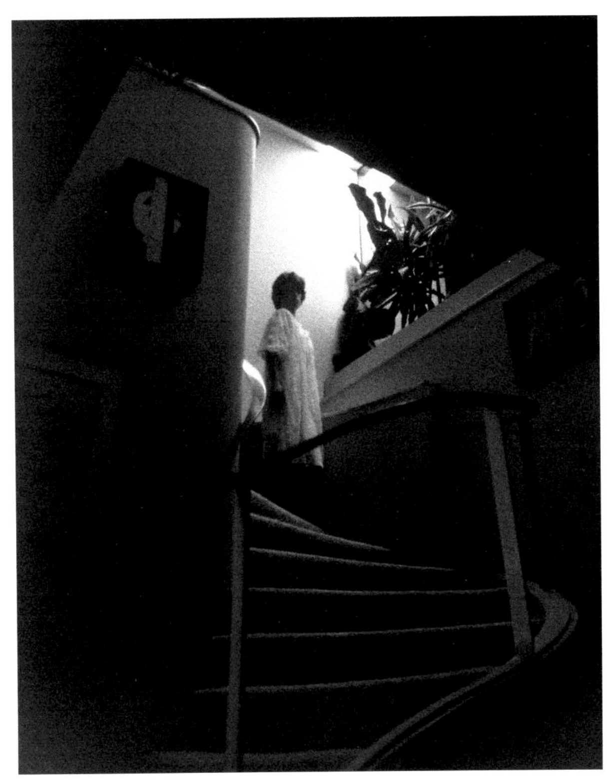

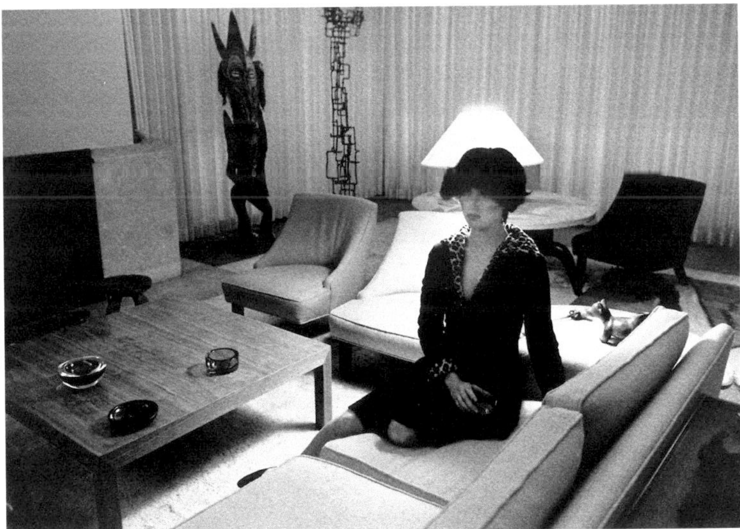

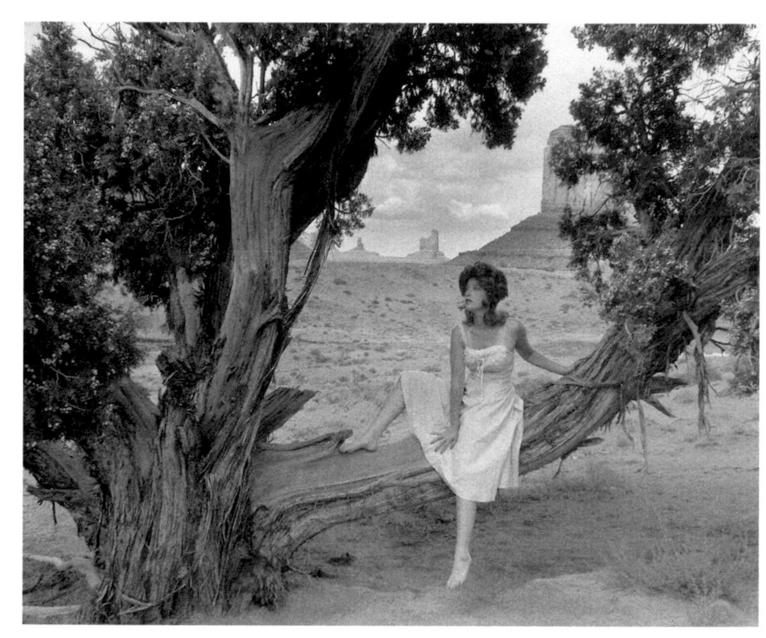

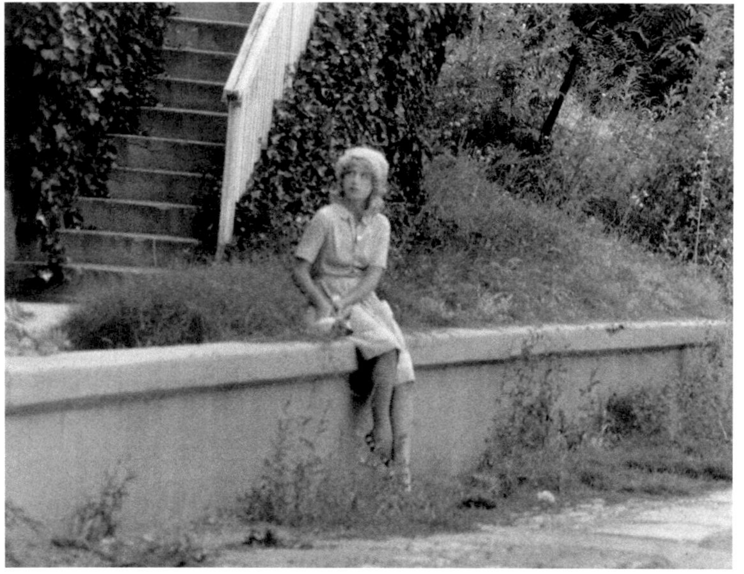

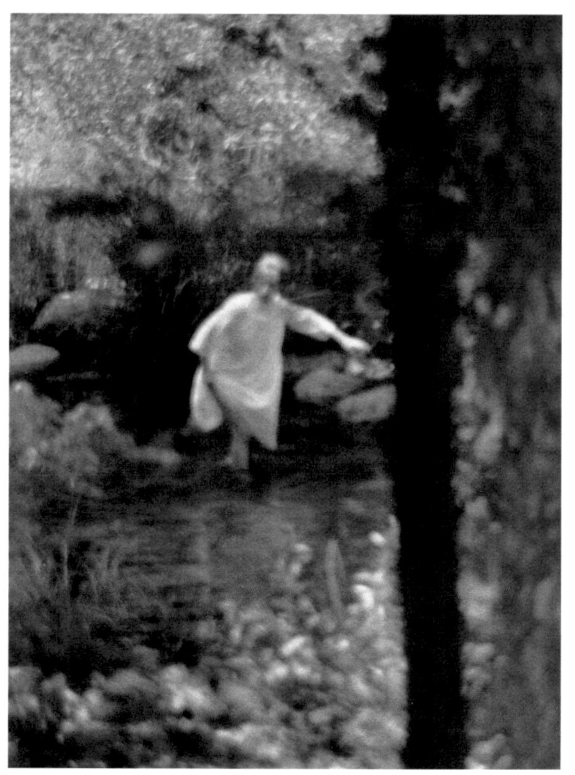

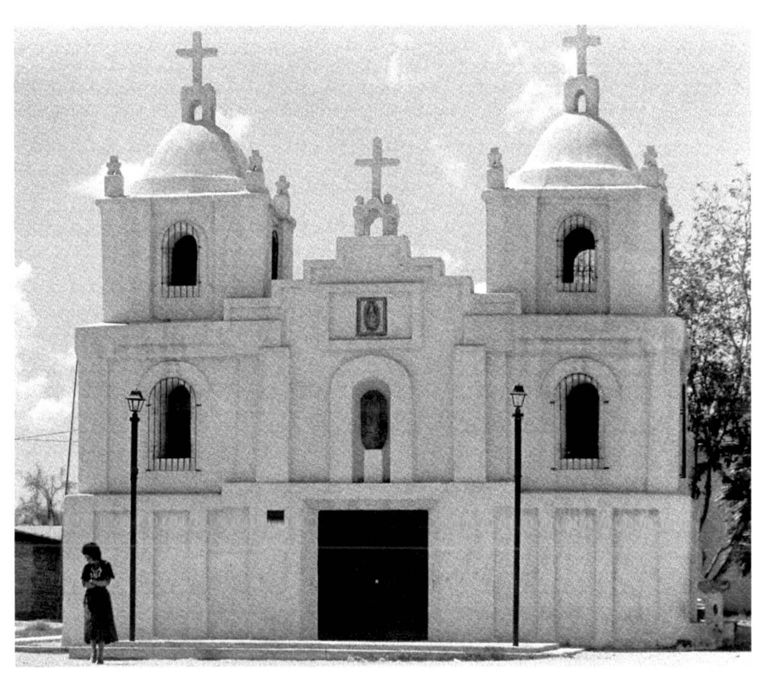

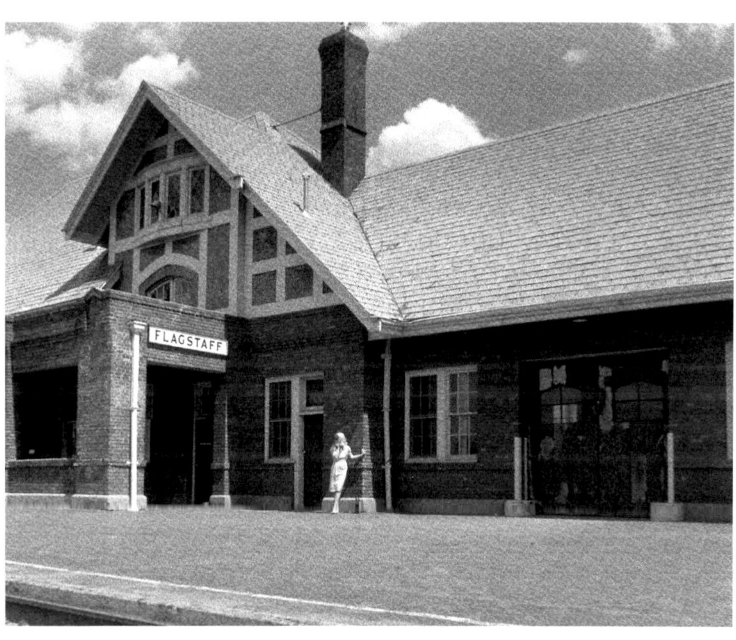
FLAGSTAFF

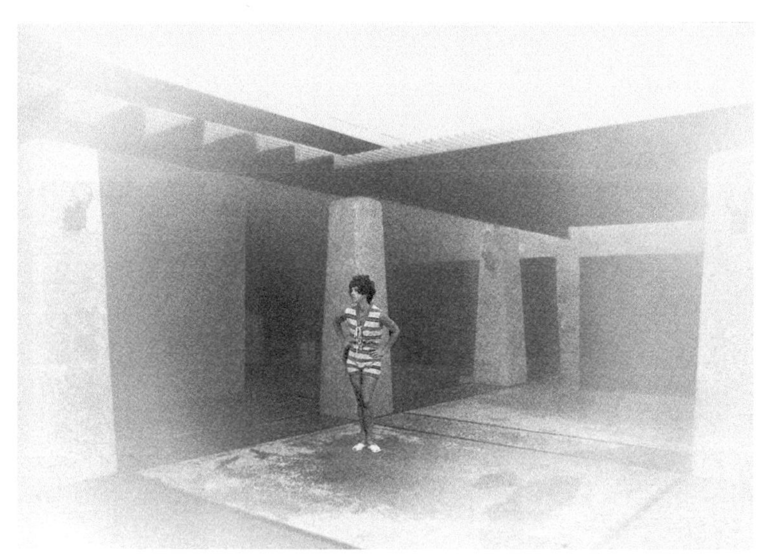

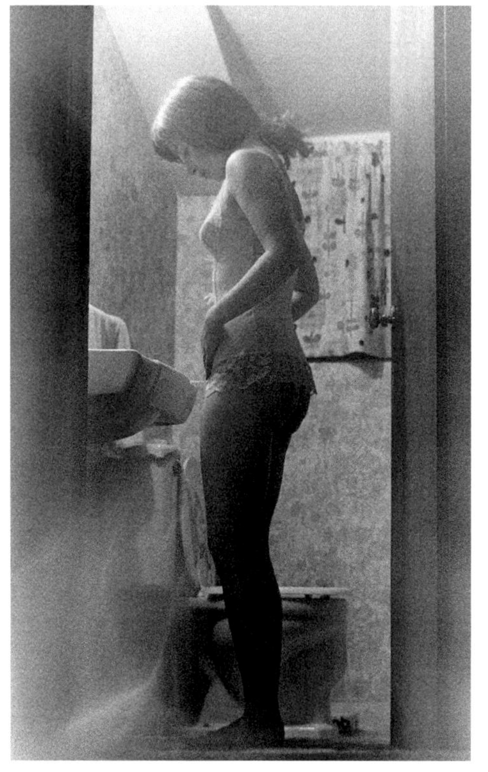

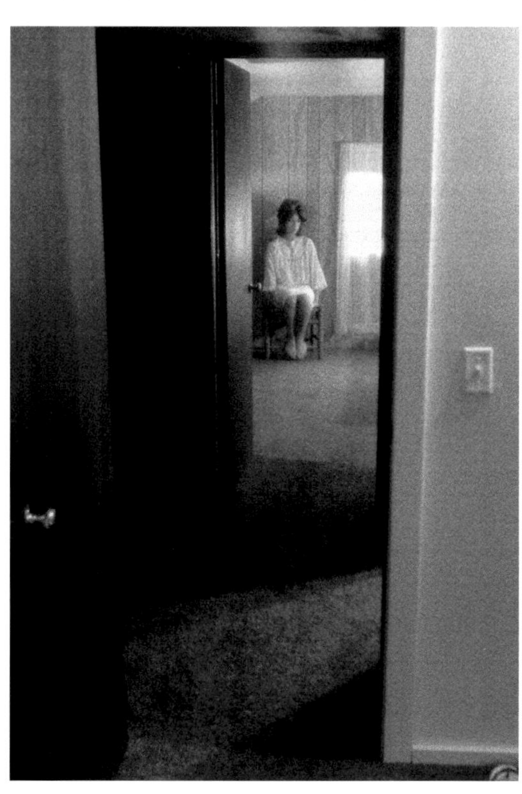

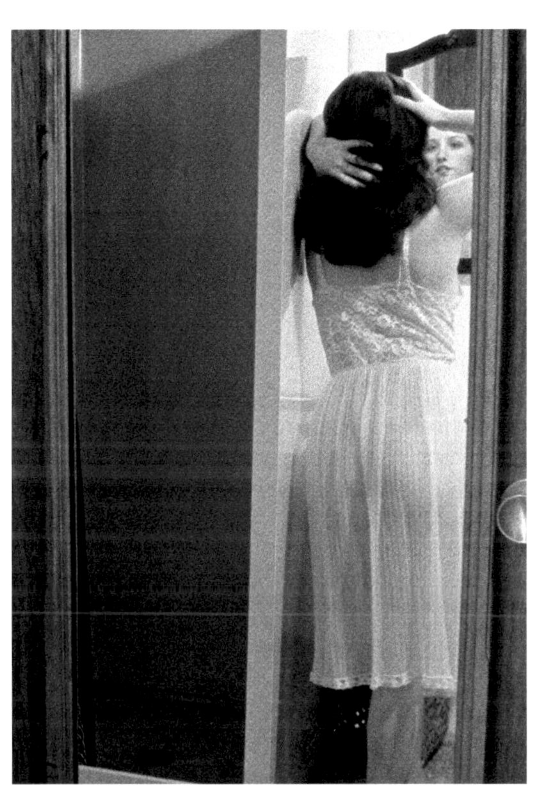
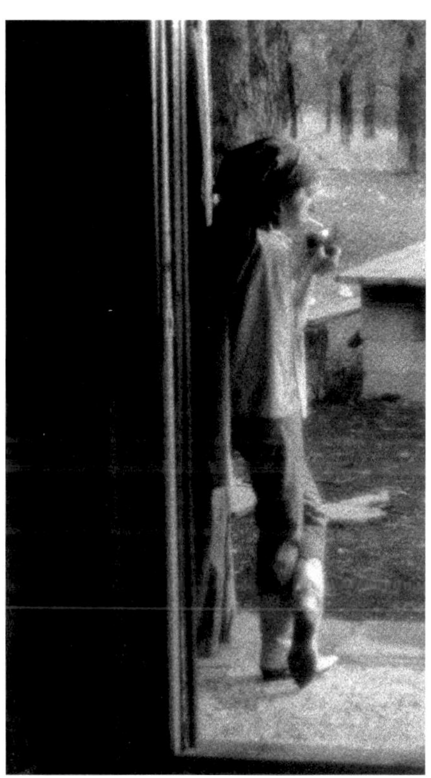

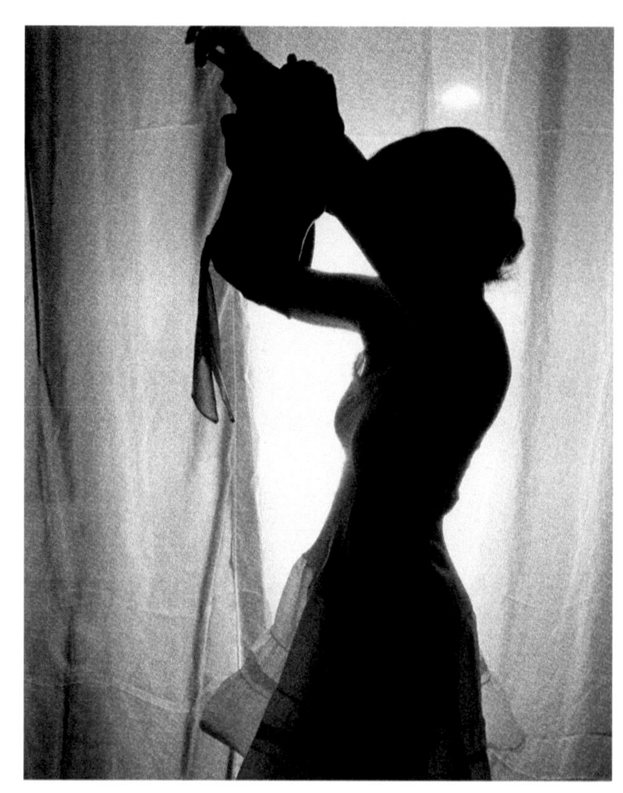

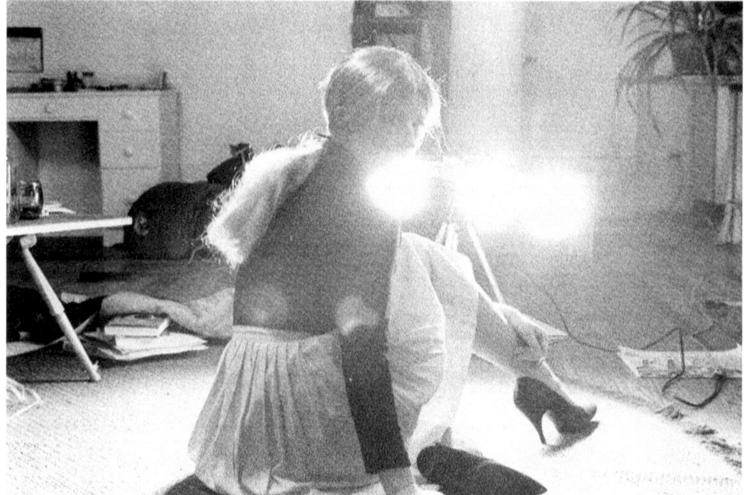

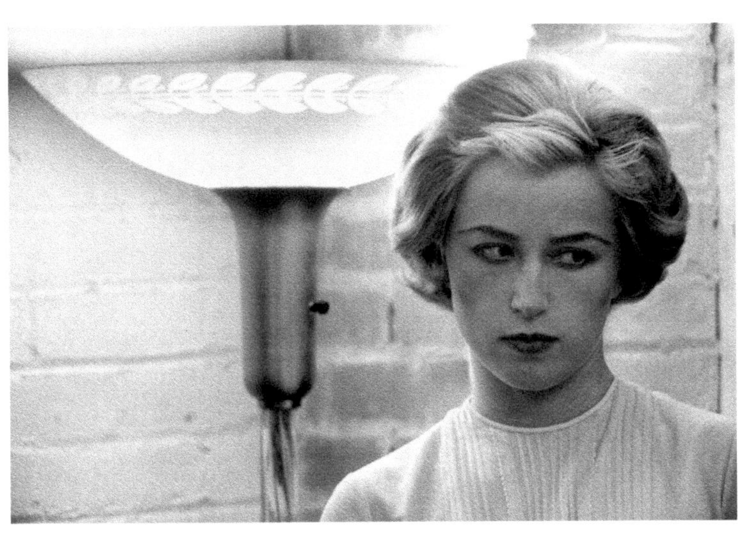

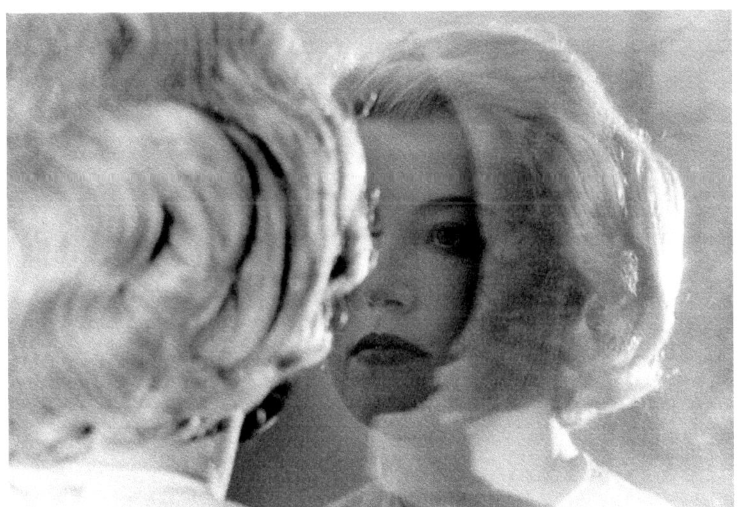

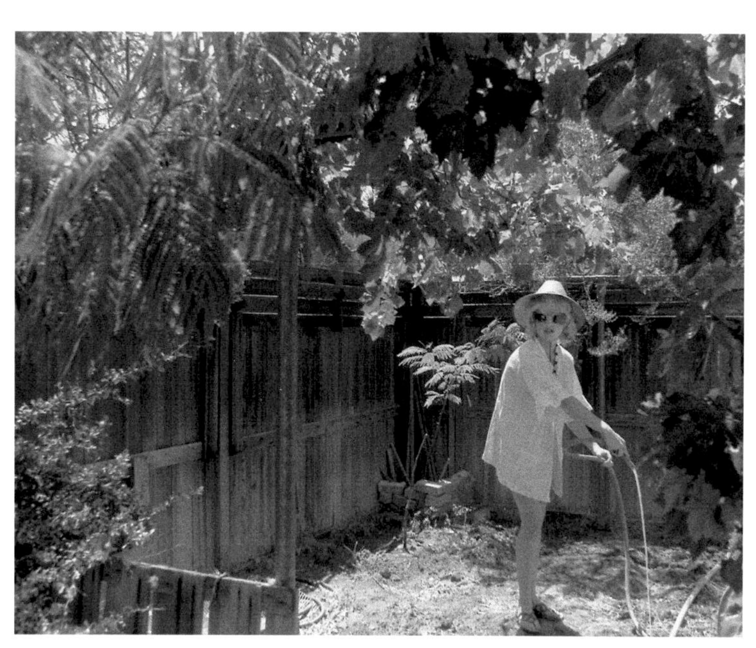

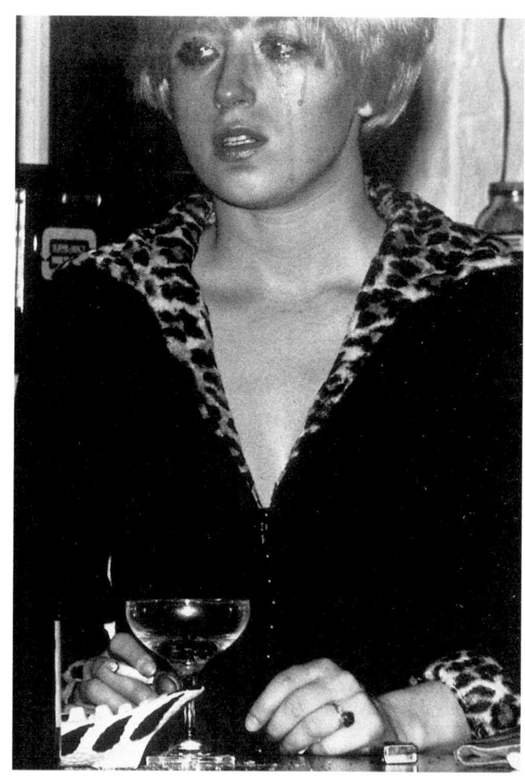

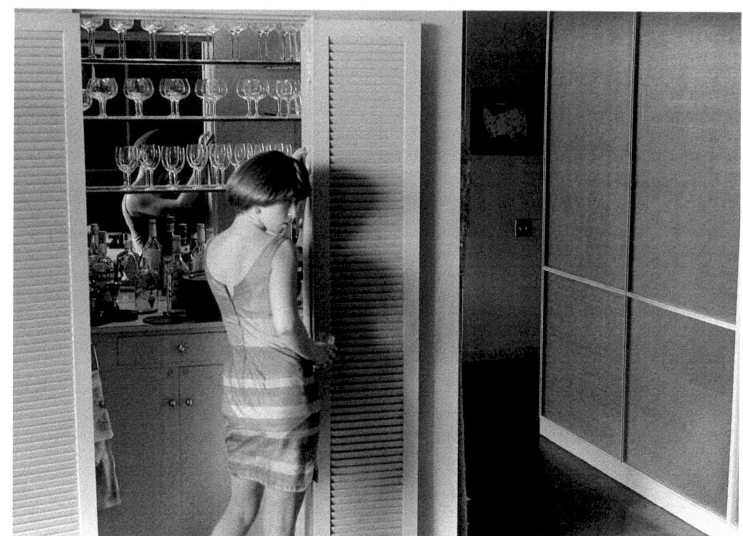

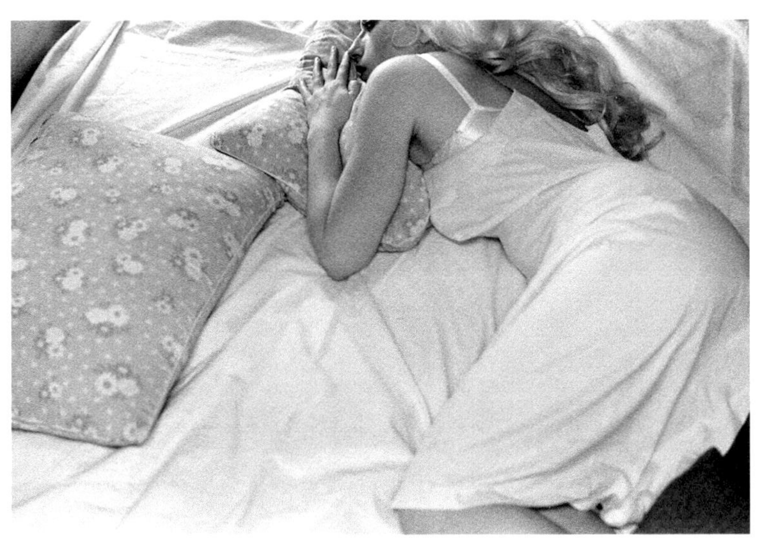

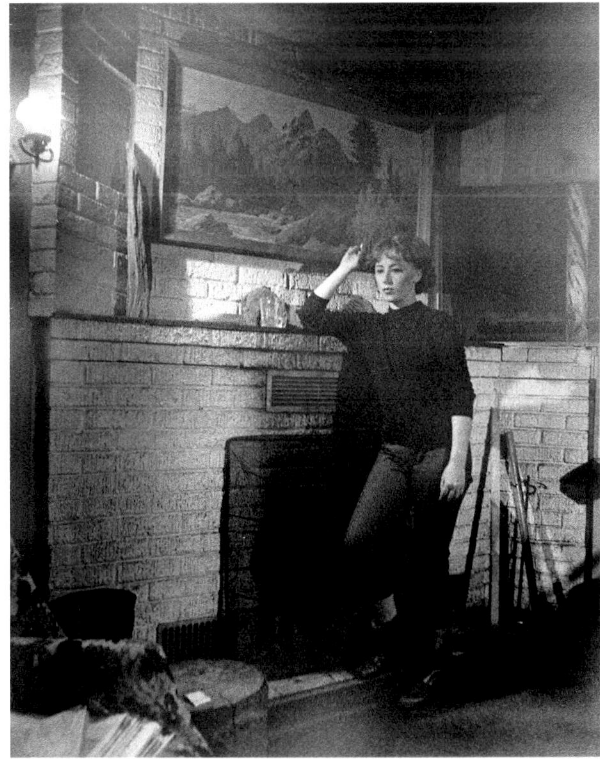

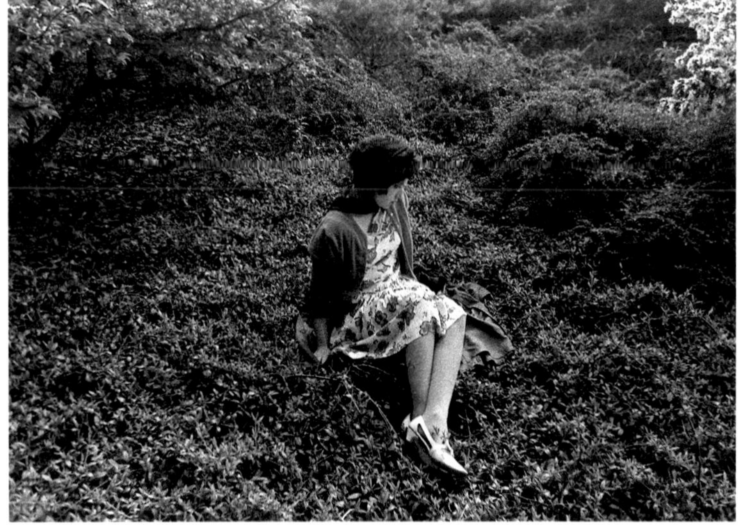

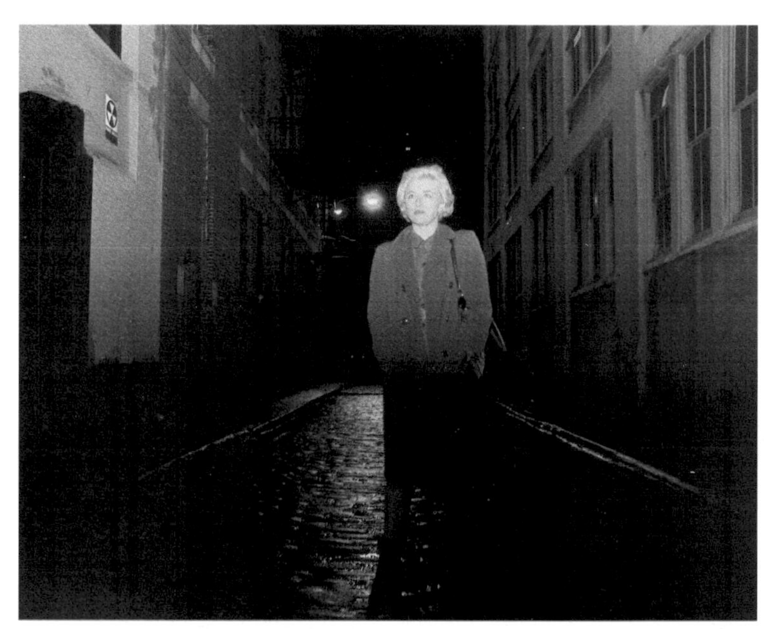

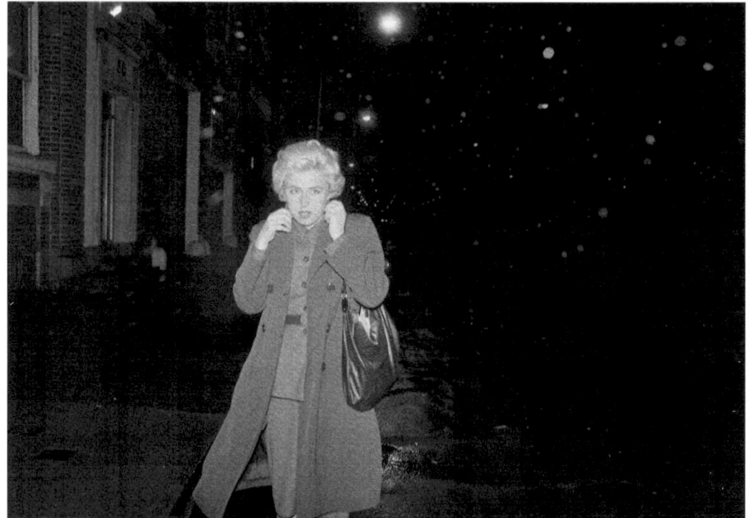

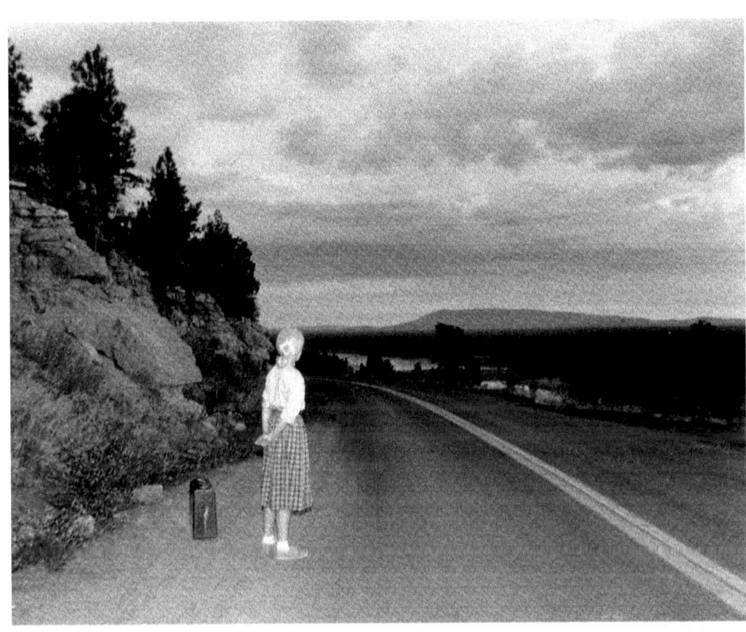

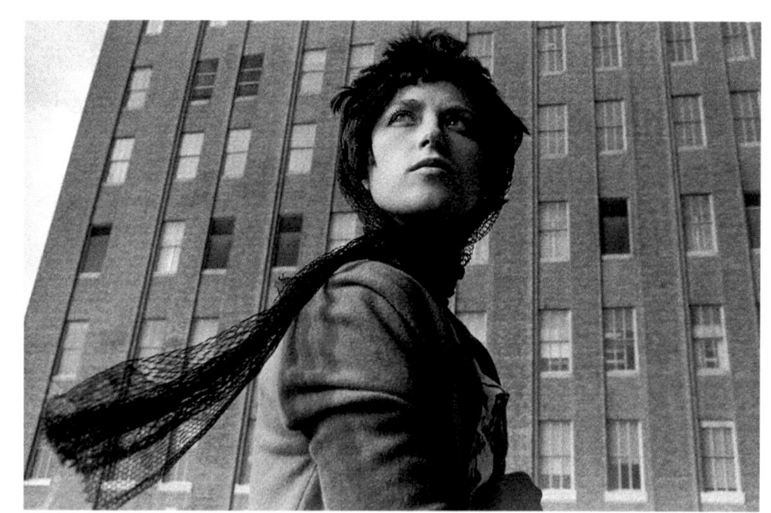

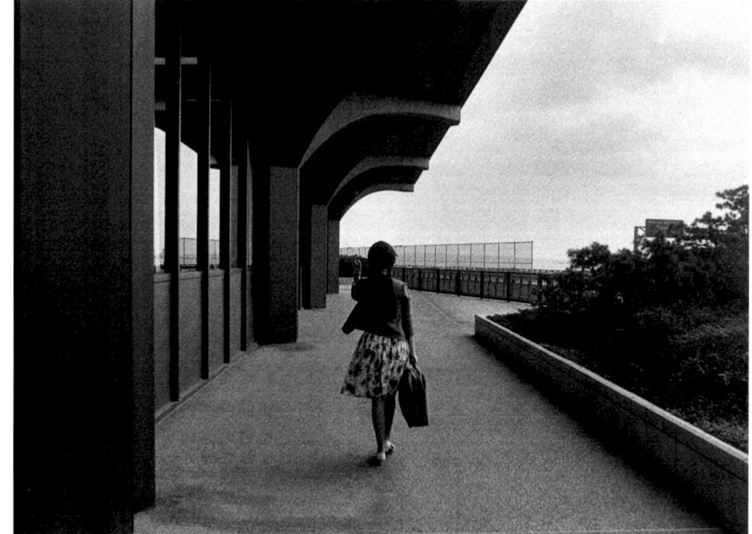

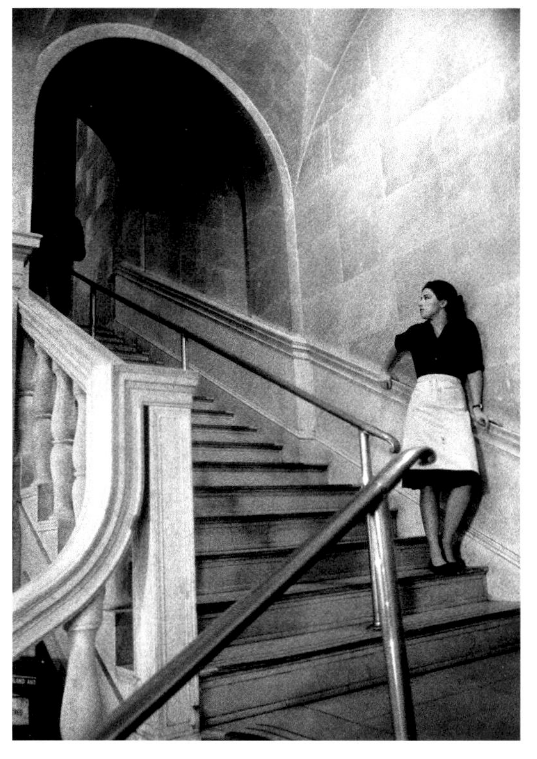

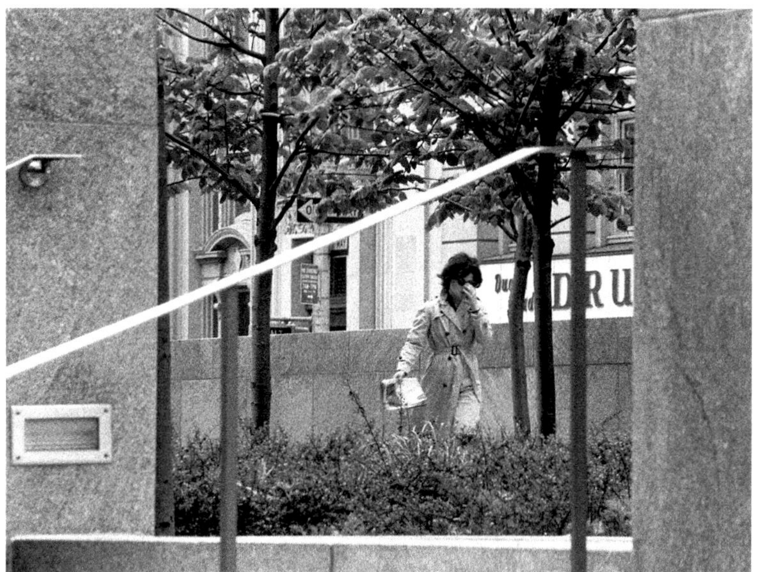

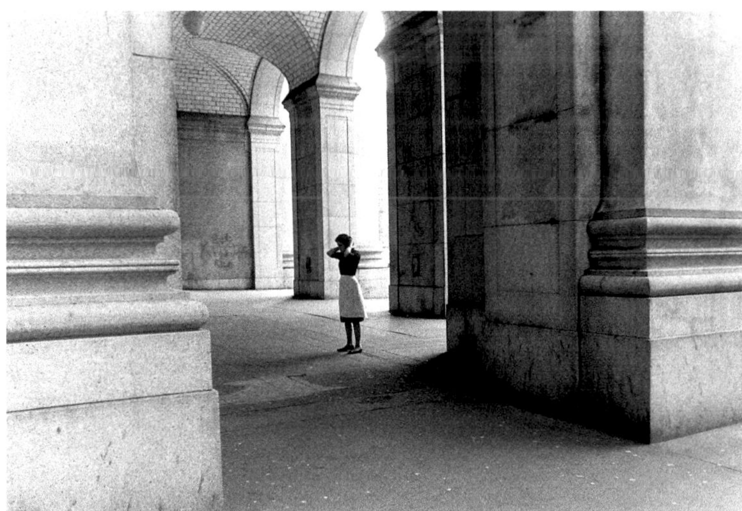

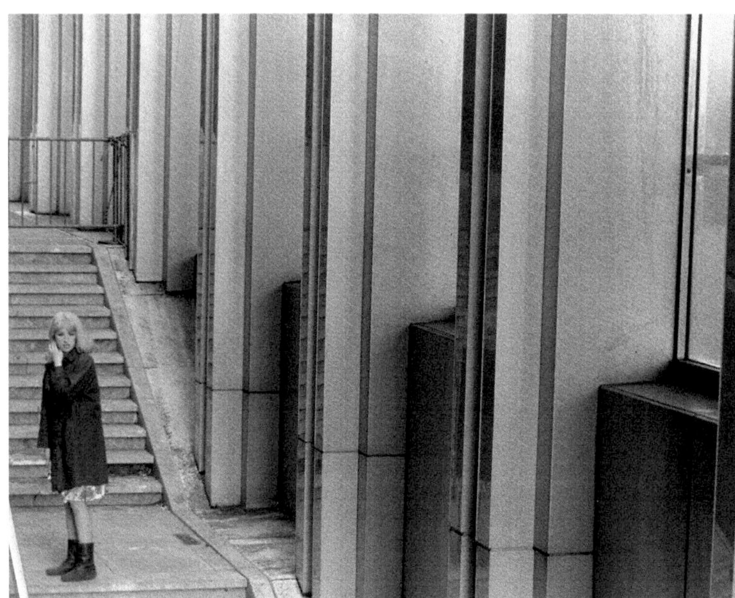

Untitled #66
Untitled #67
Untitled #75
Untitled #76
Untitled #71
Untitled #72
Untitled #78
Untitled #77
Untitled #74
Untitled #70
Untitled #79
Untitled #69
1980

[Rear Screen Projections]

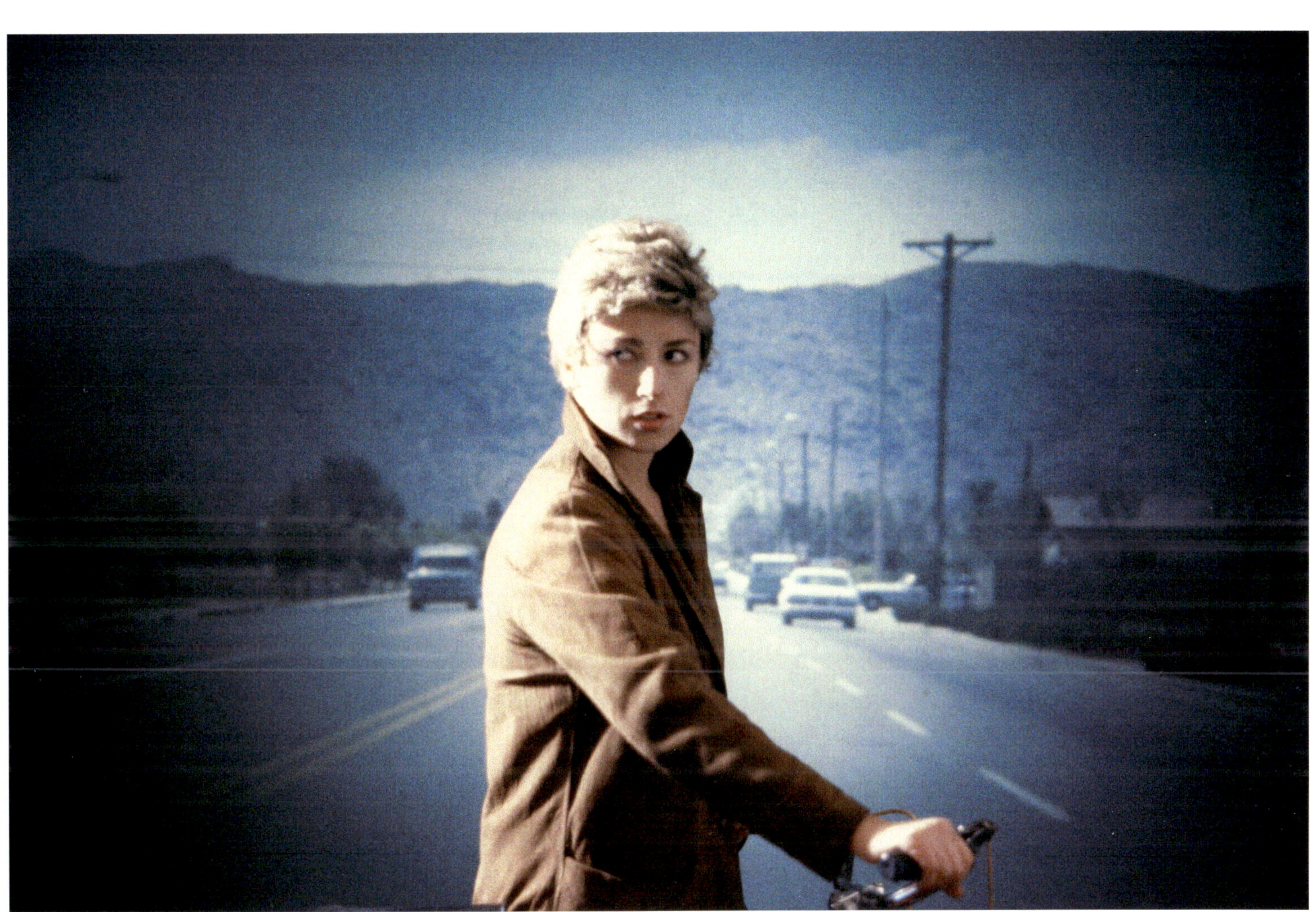

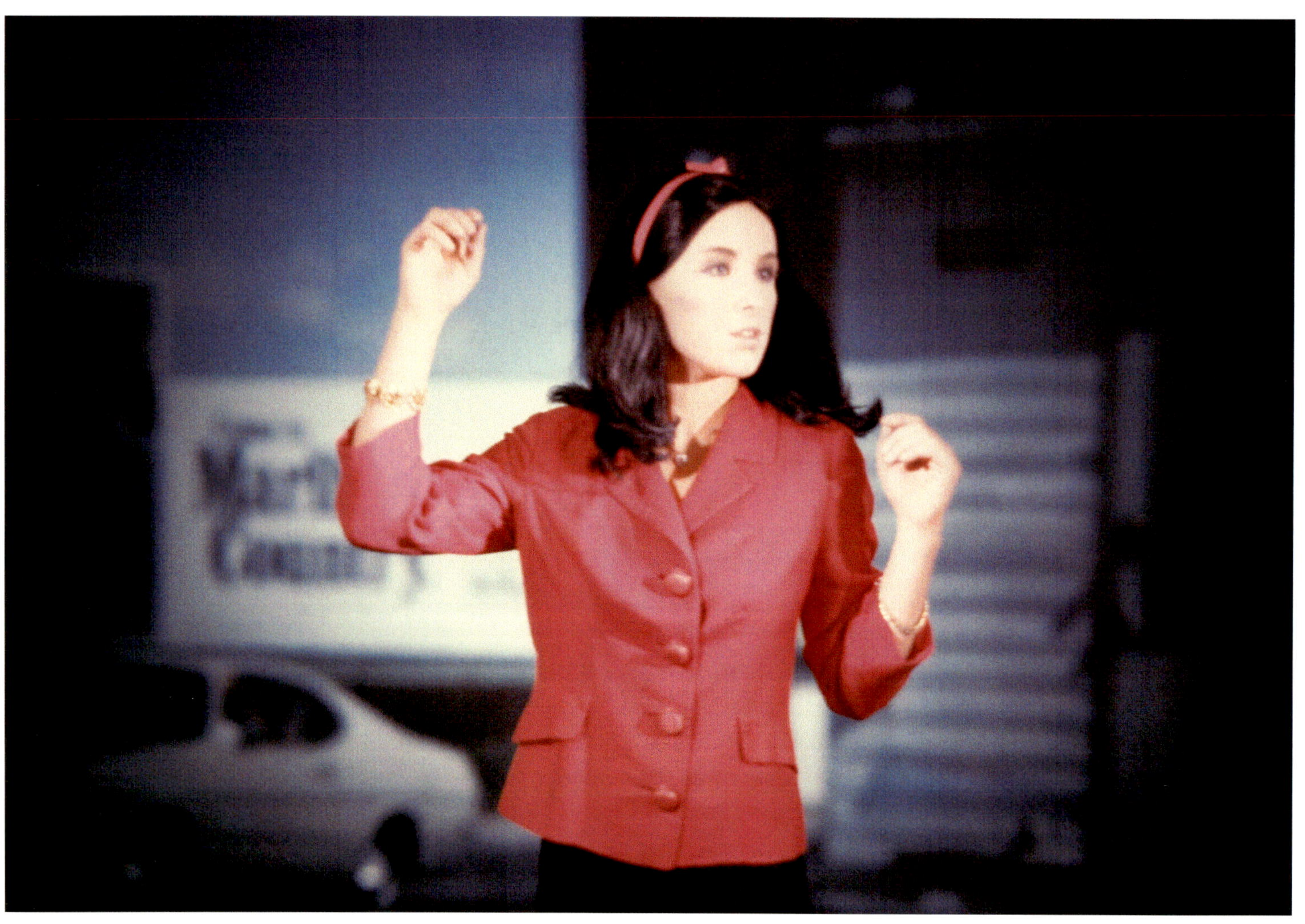

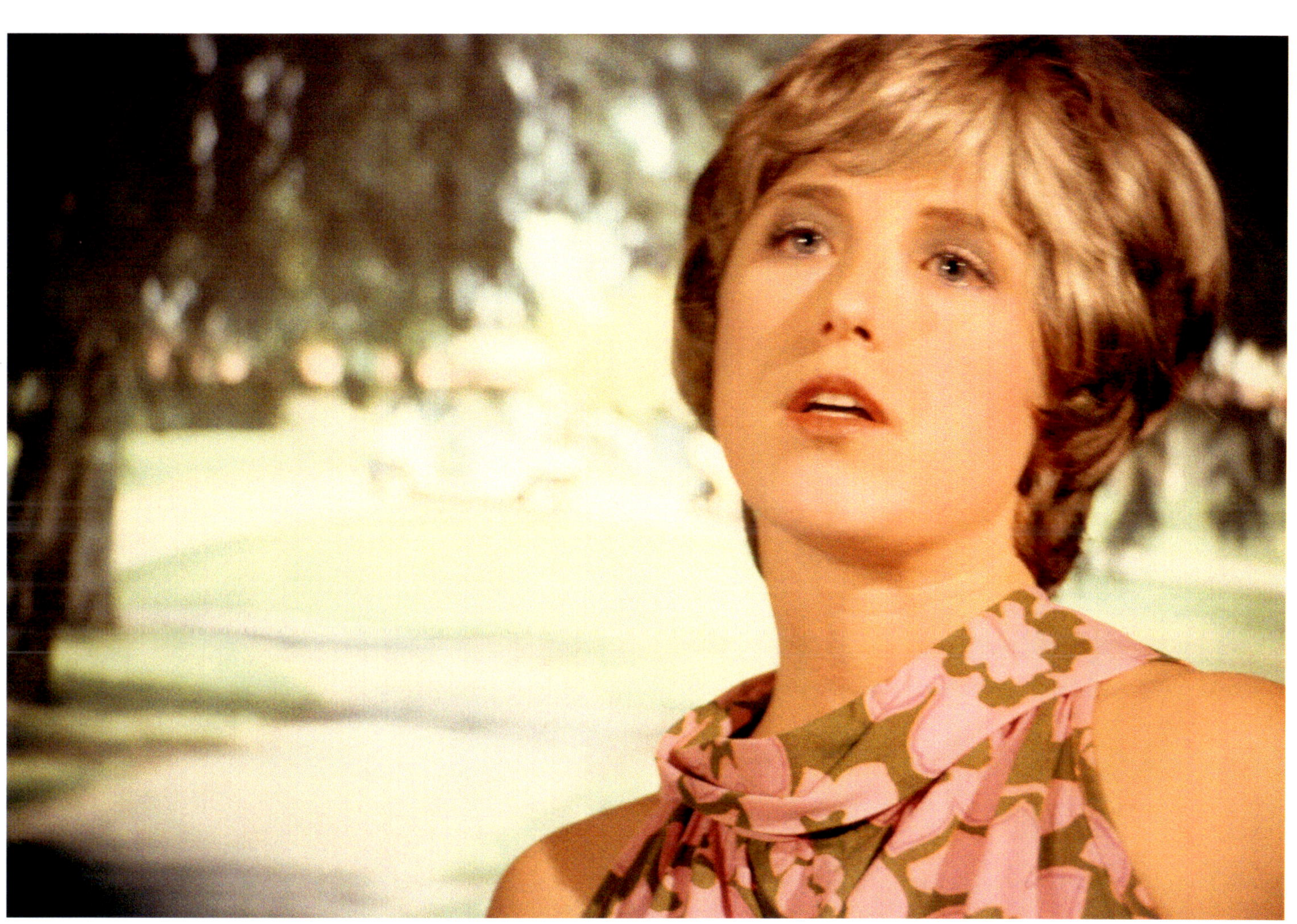

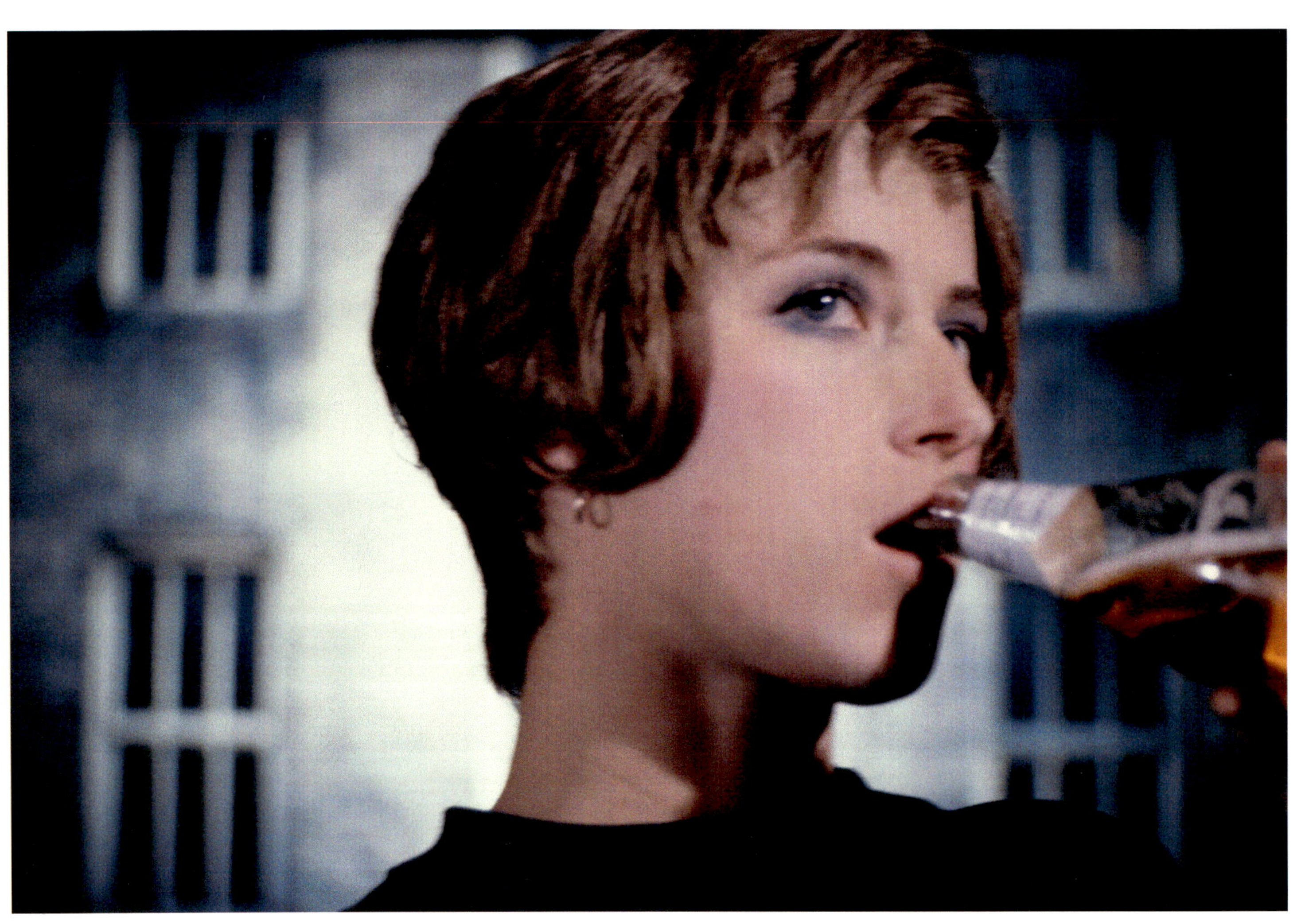

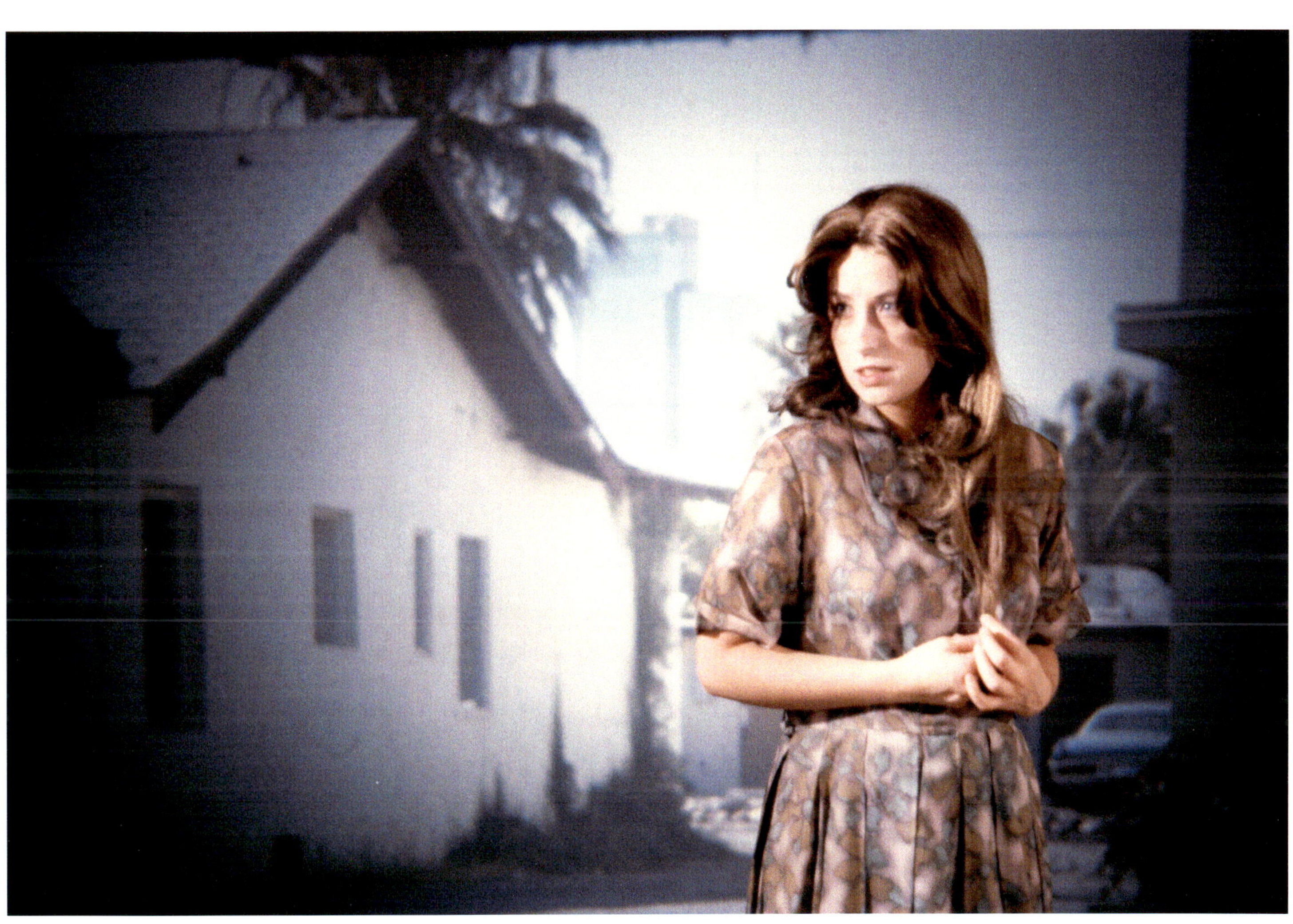

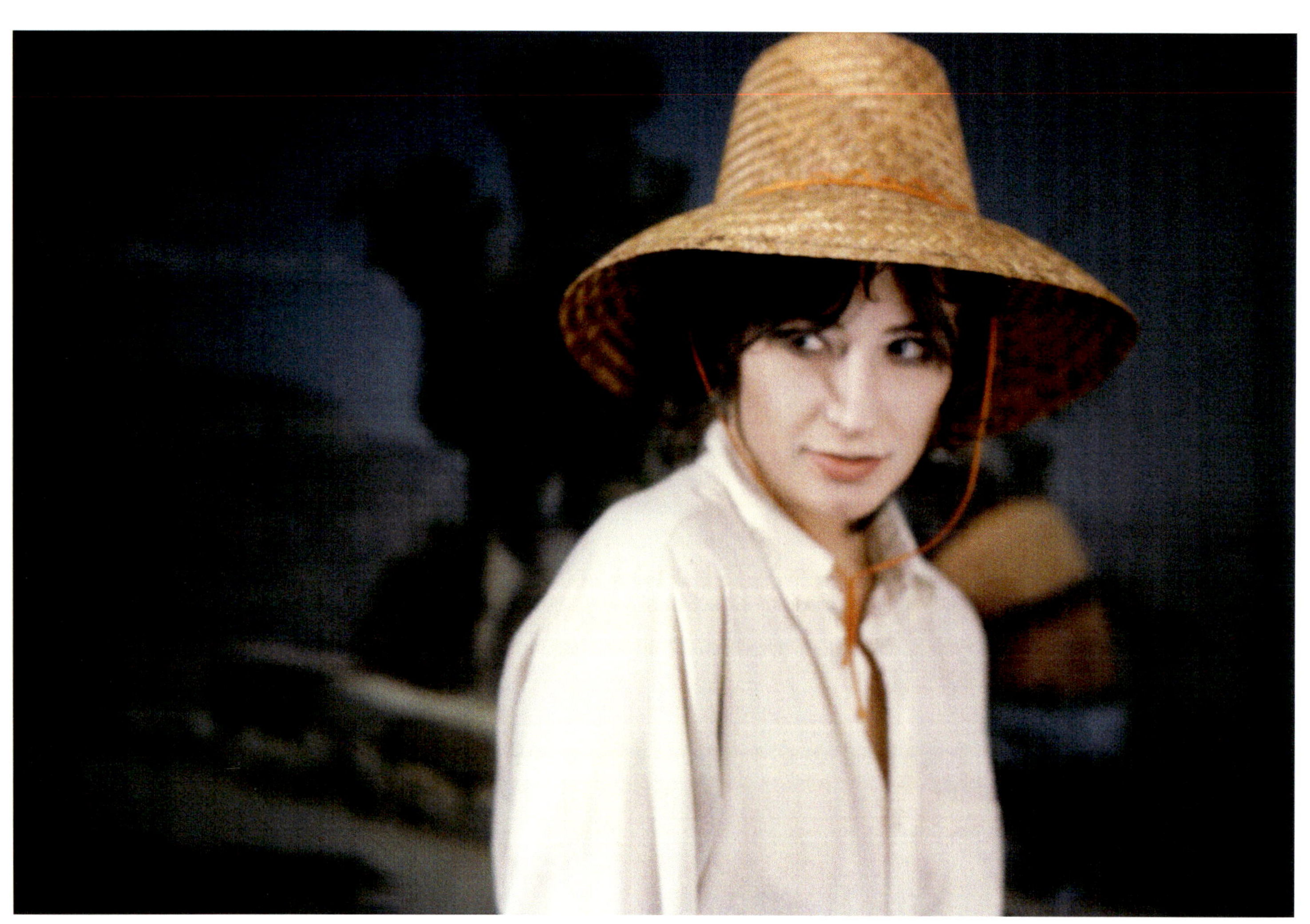

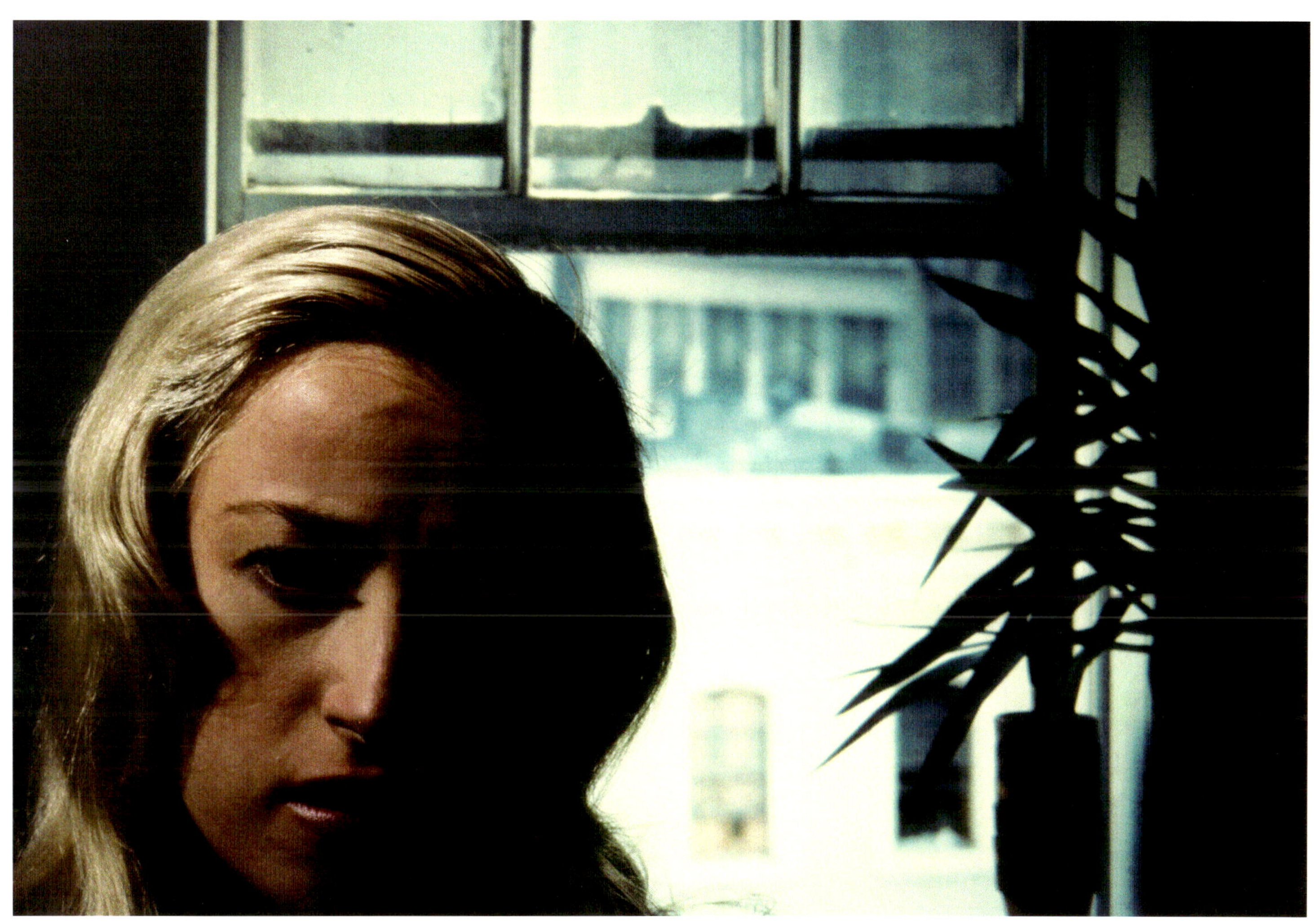

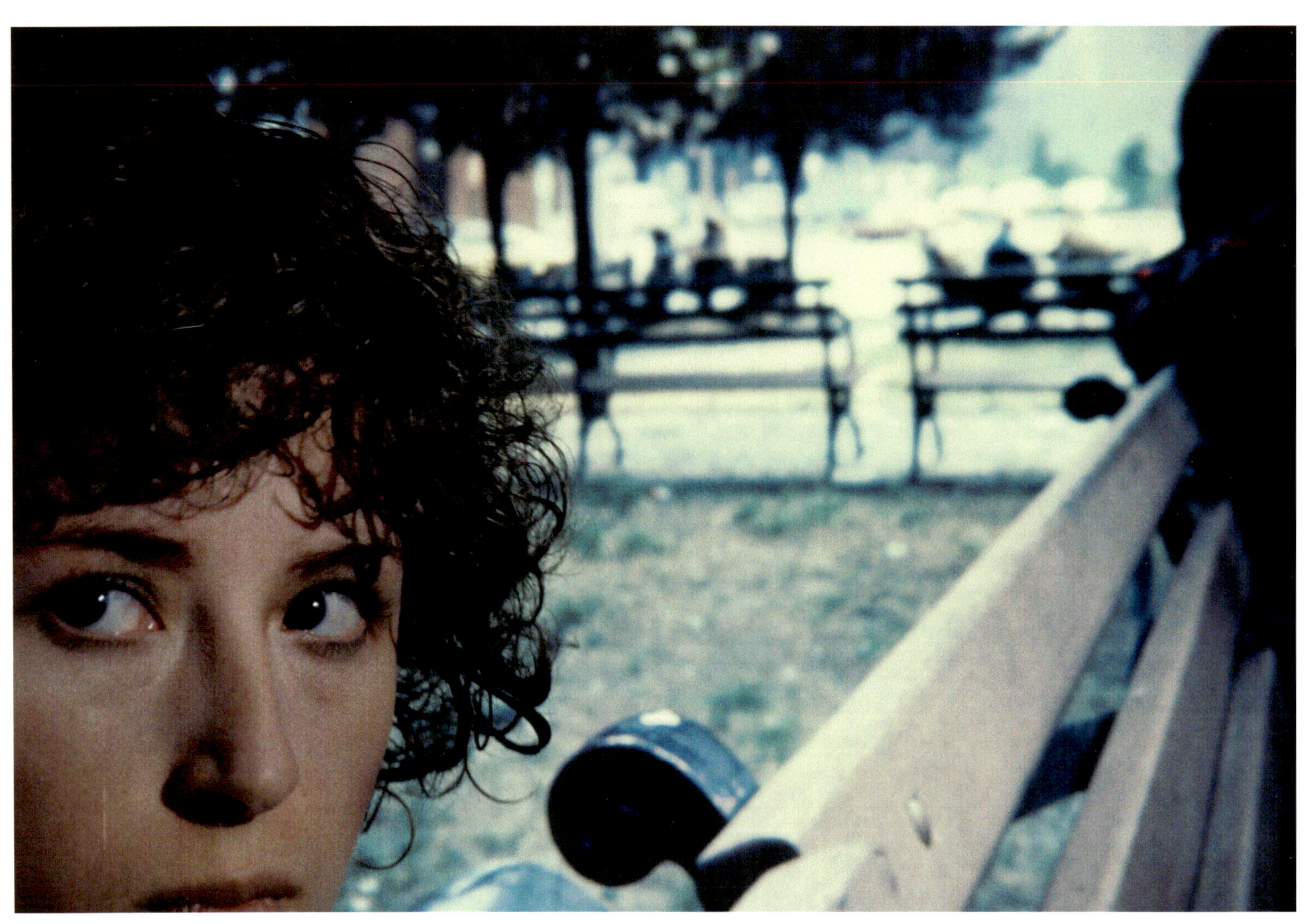

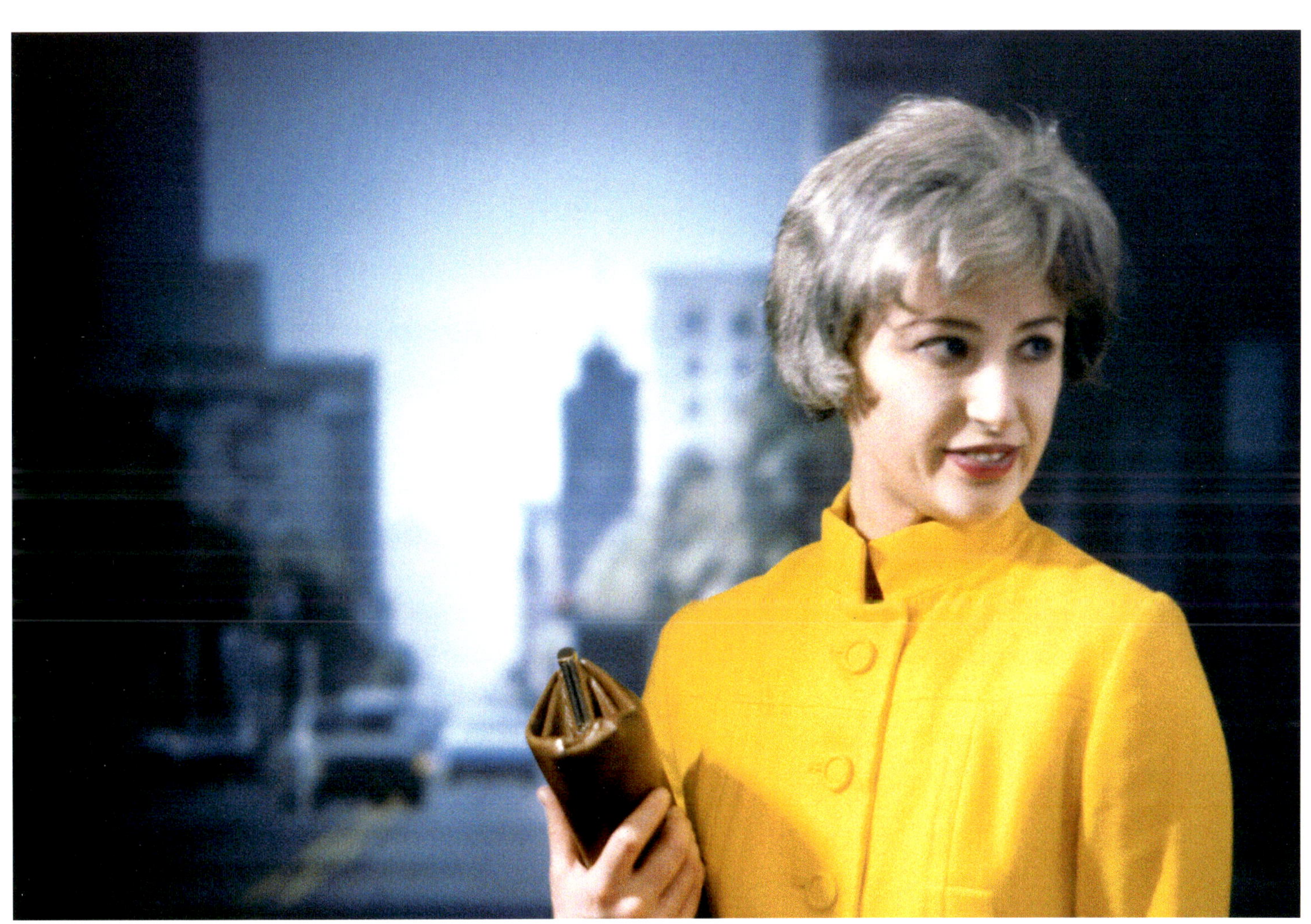

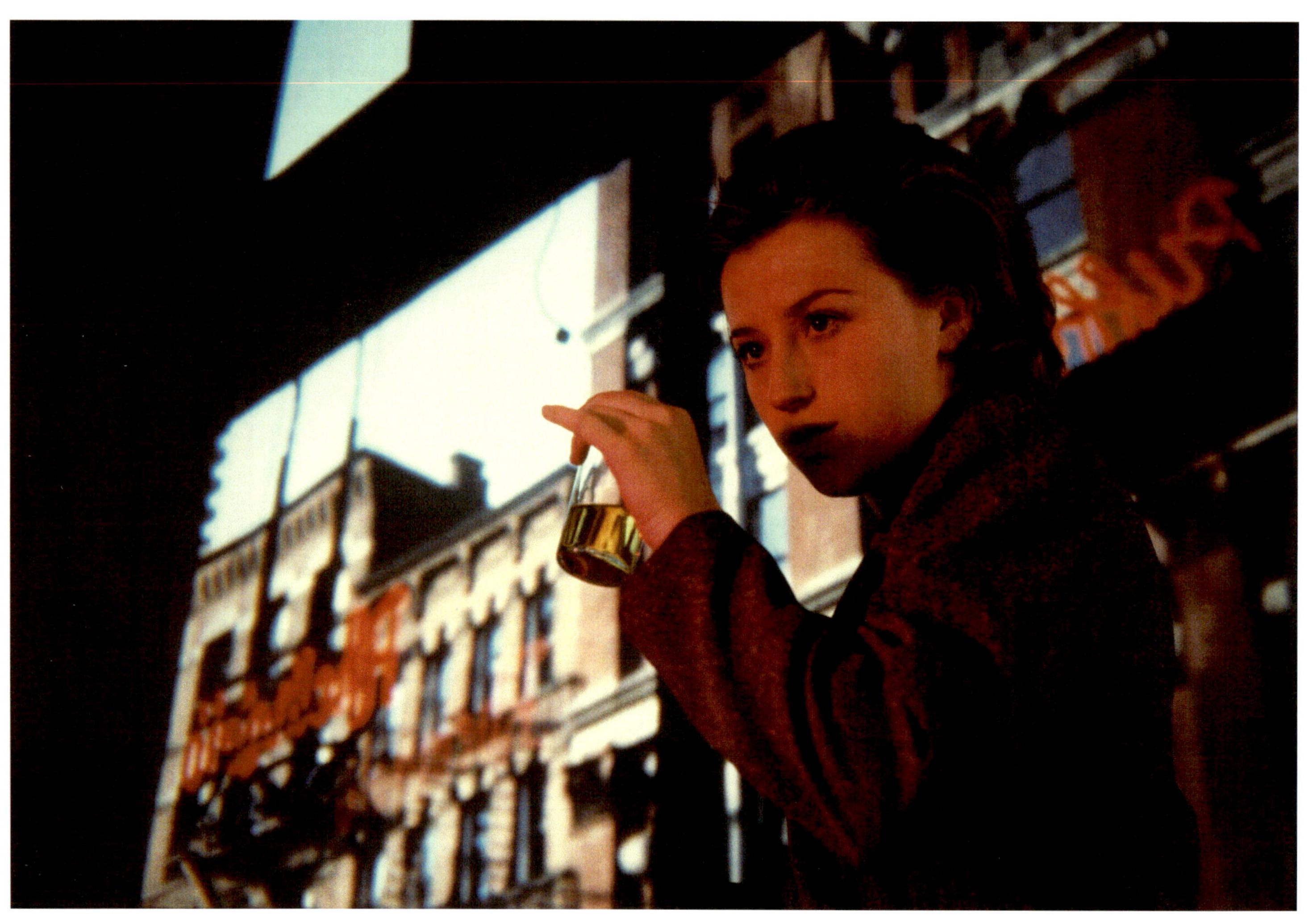

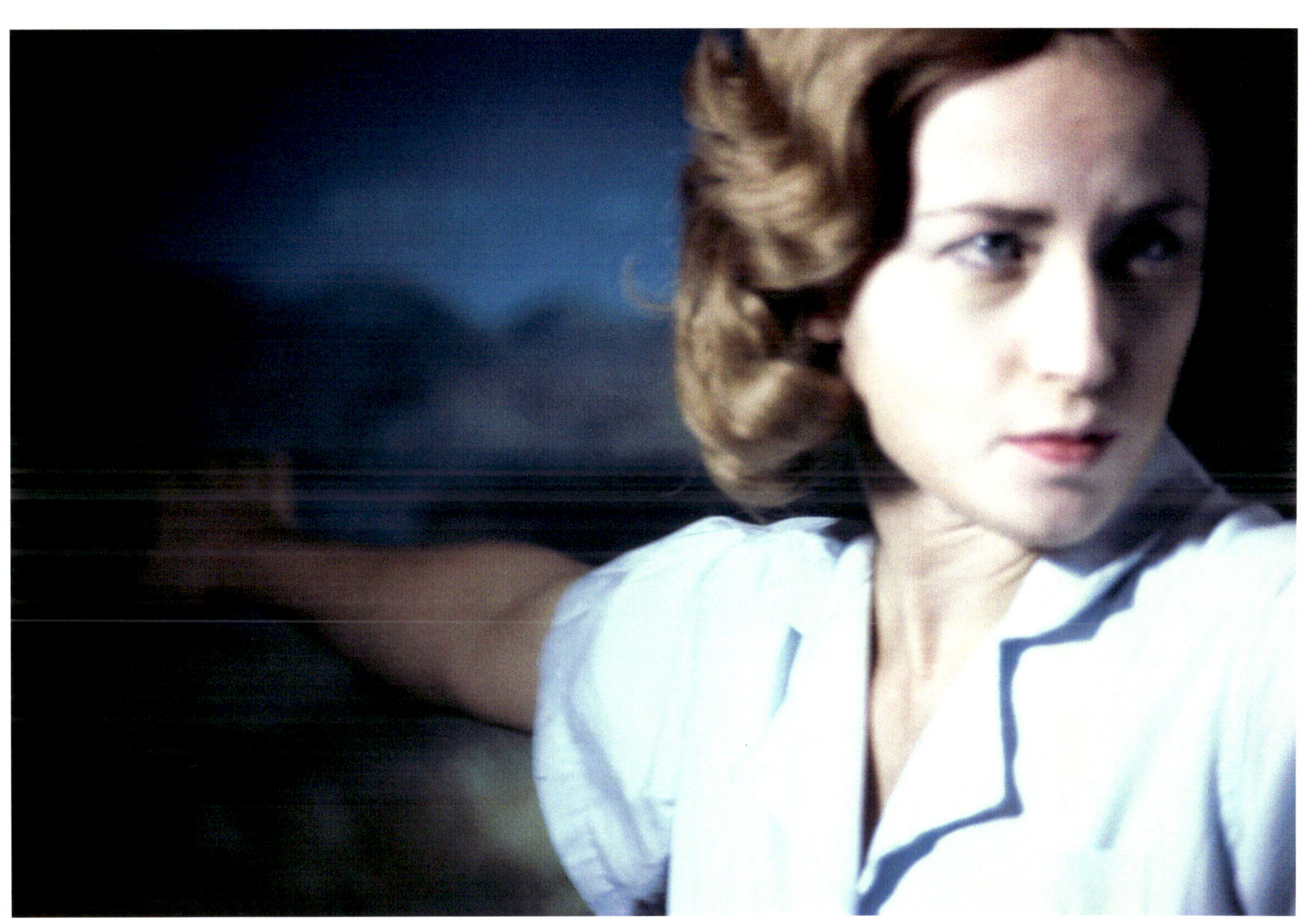

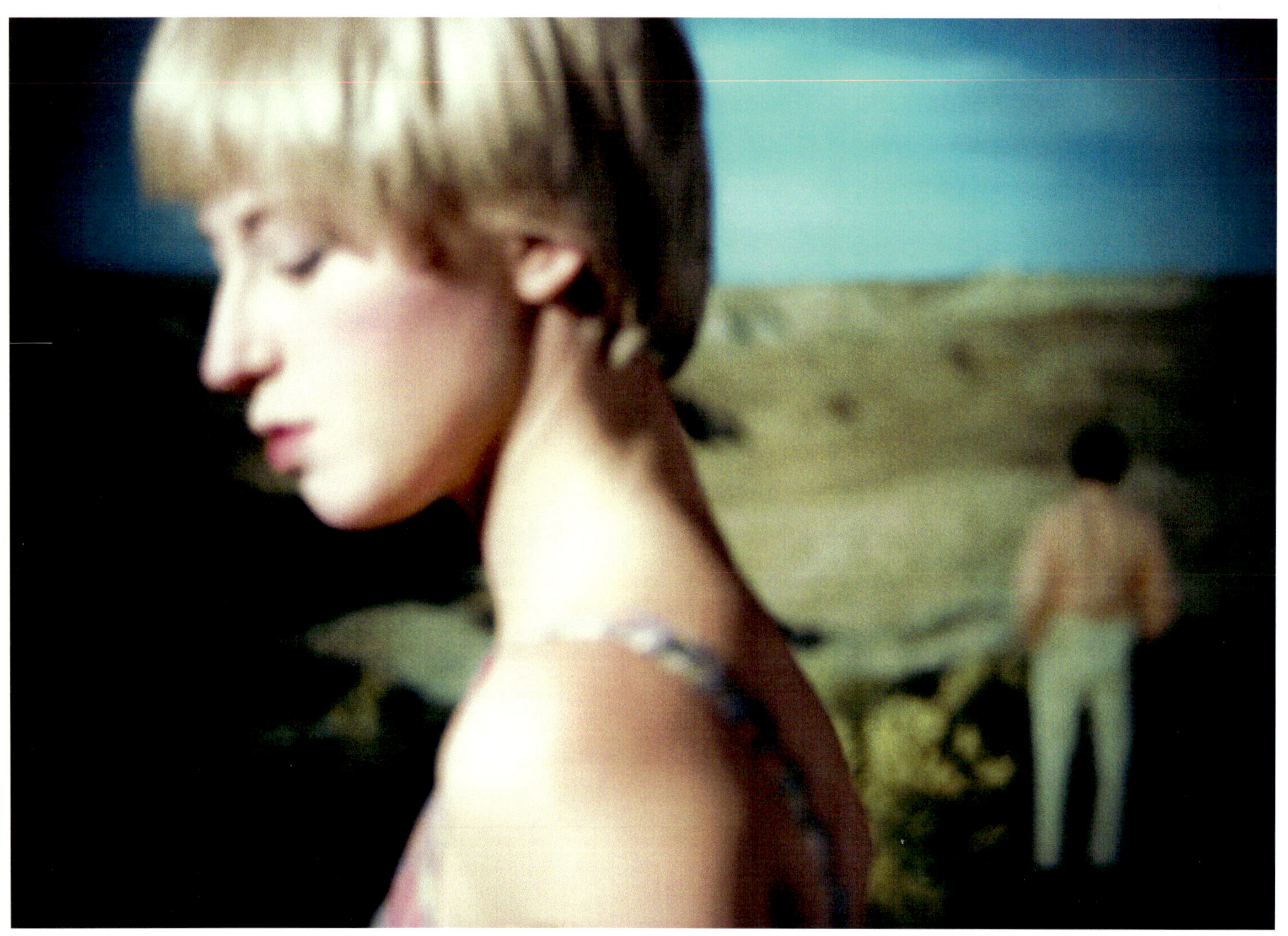

Untitled #92
Untitled #86
Untitled #88
Untitled #87
Untitled #89
Untitled #90
Untitled #91
Untitled #85
Untitled #93
Untitled #94
Untitled #96
Untitled #95
1982

[Centerfolds / Horizontals]

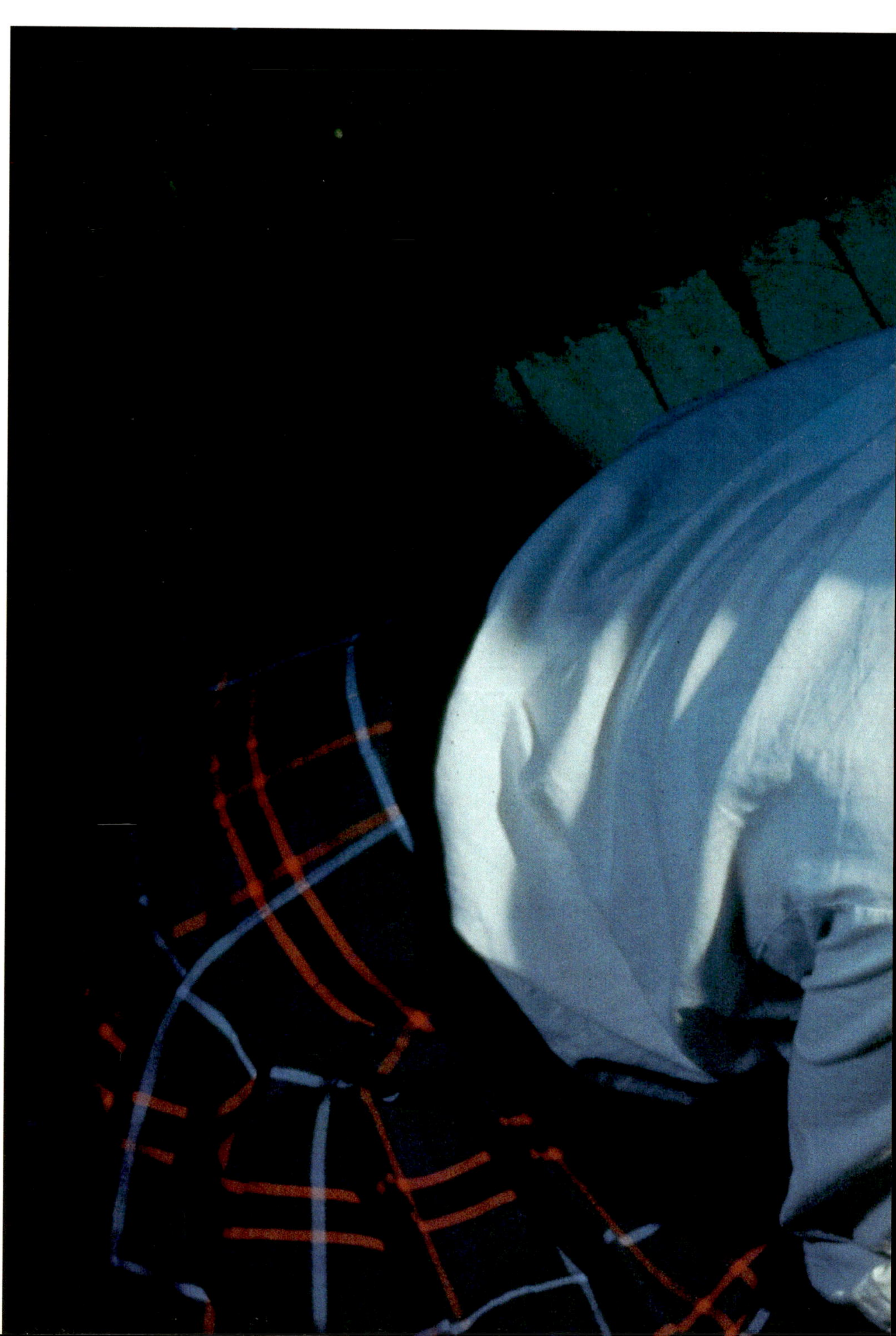

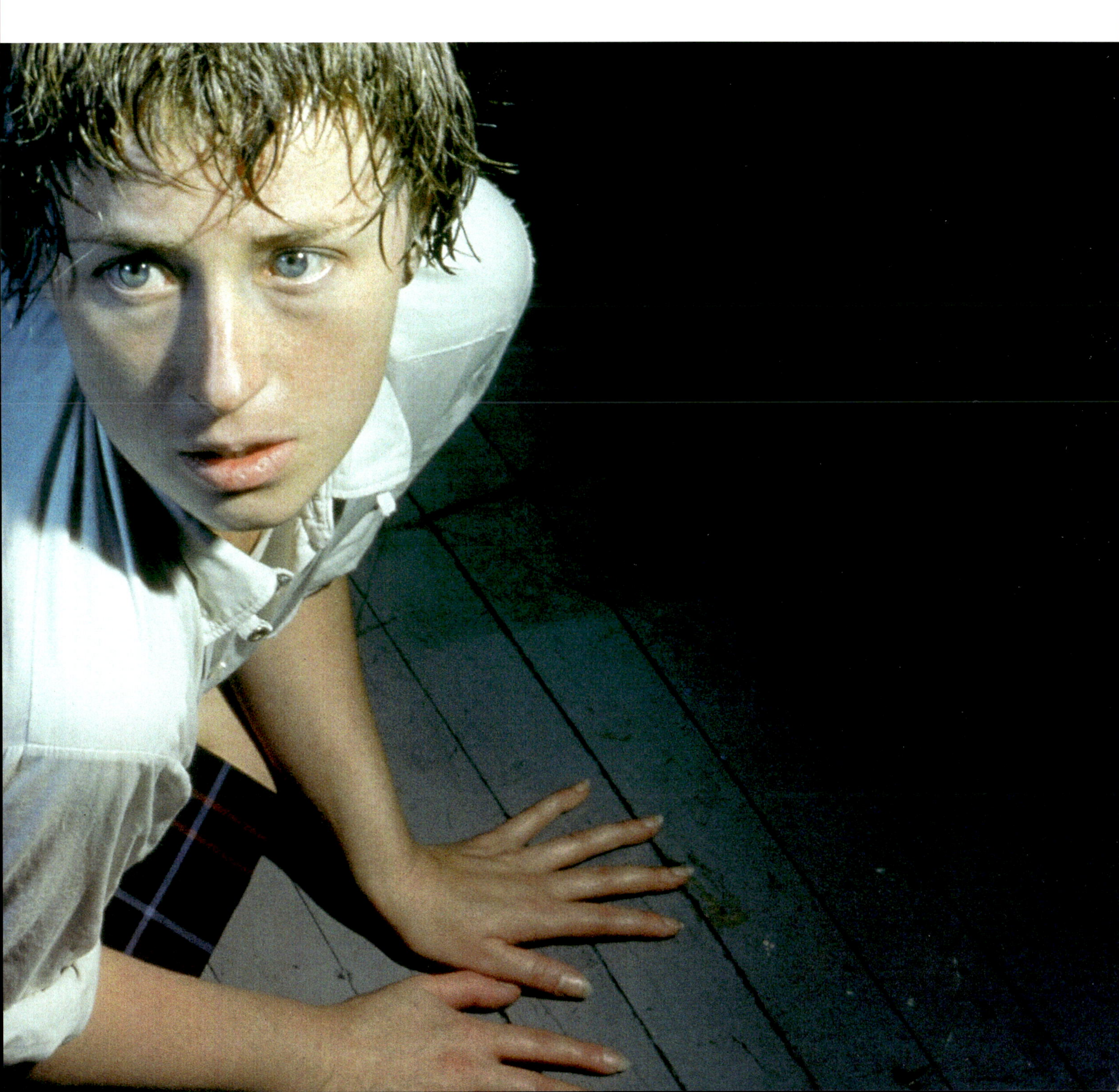

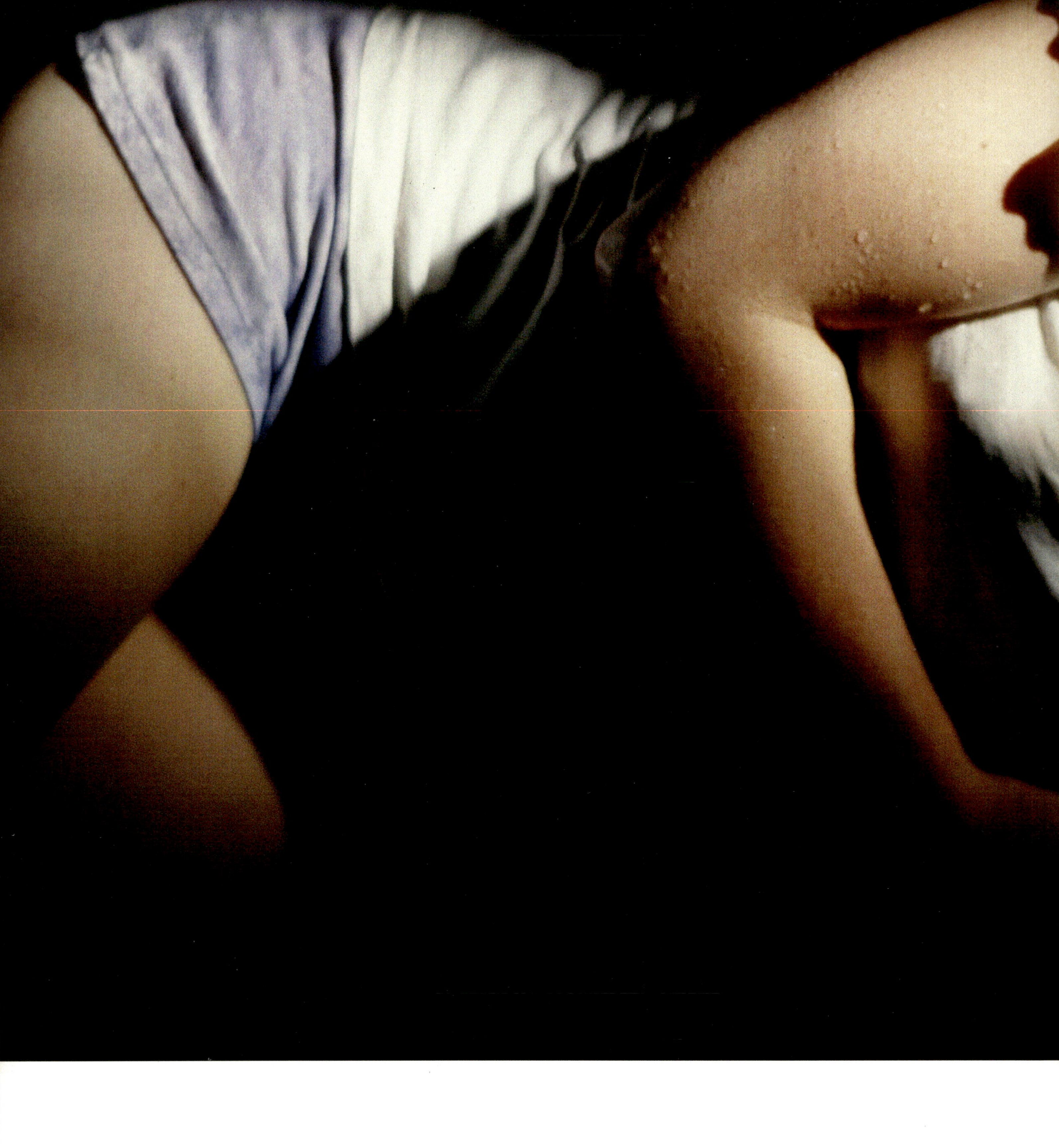

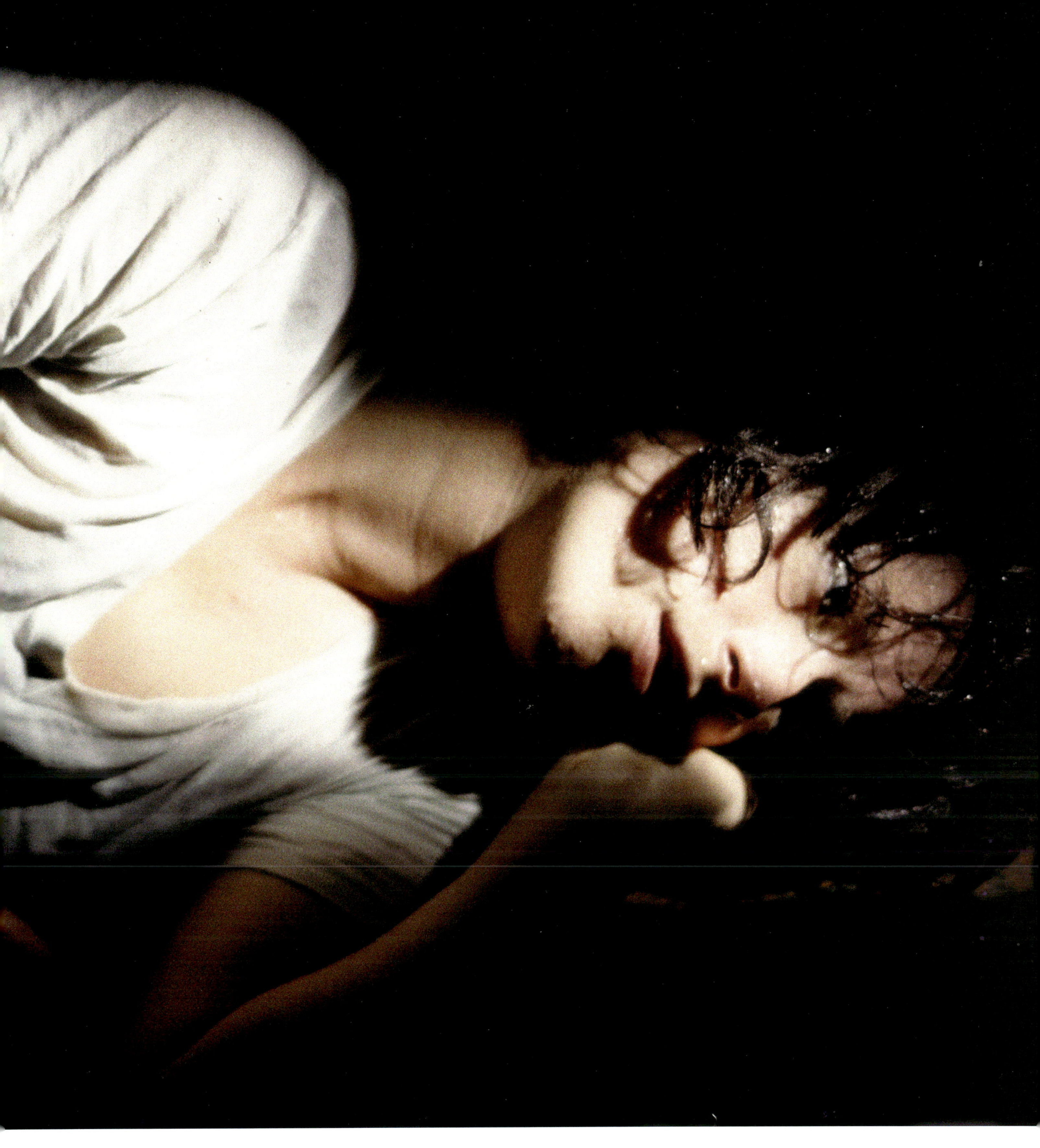

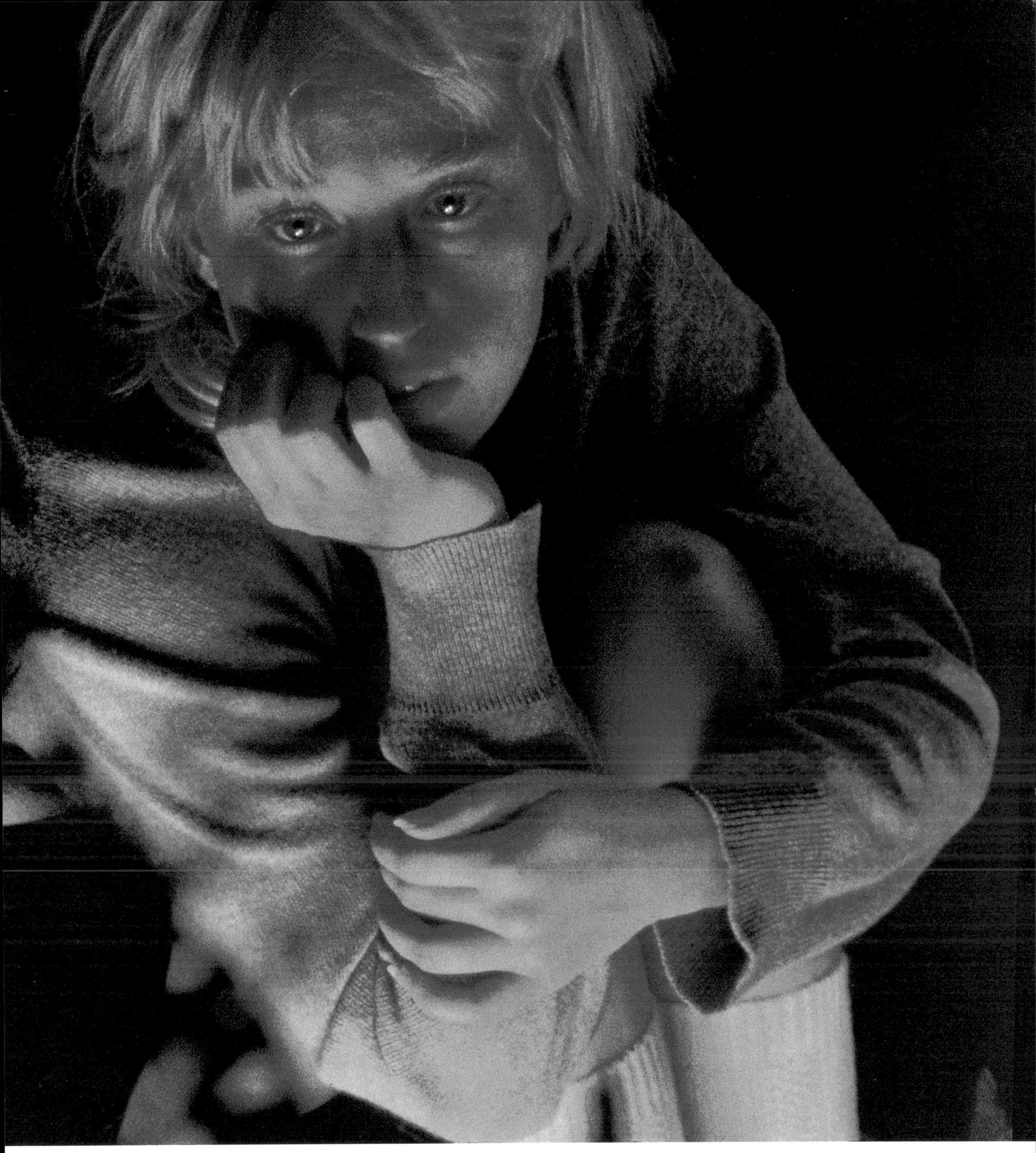

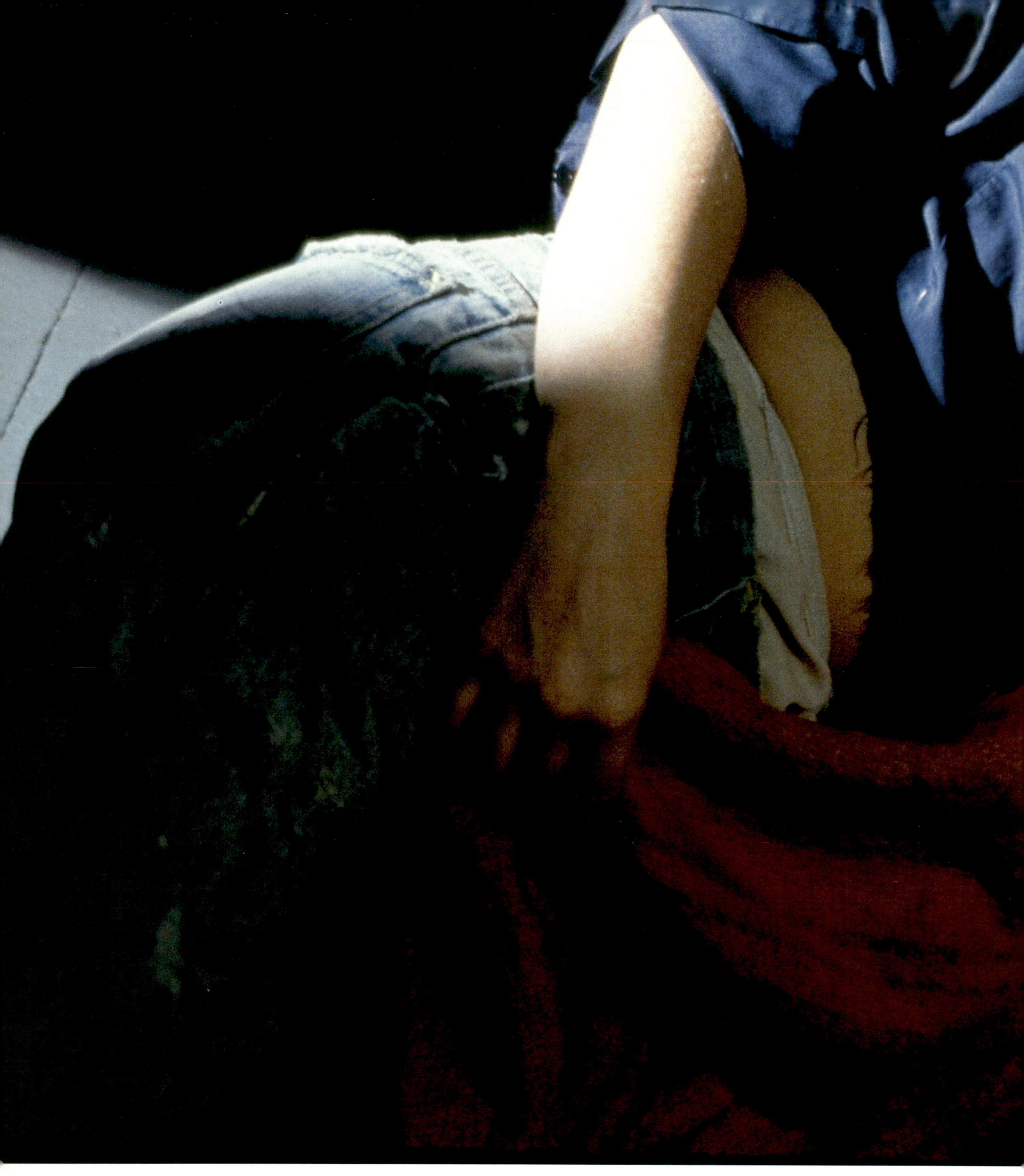

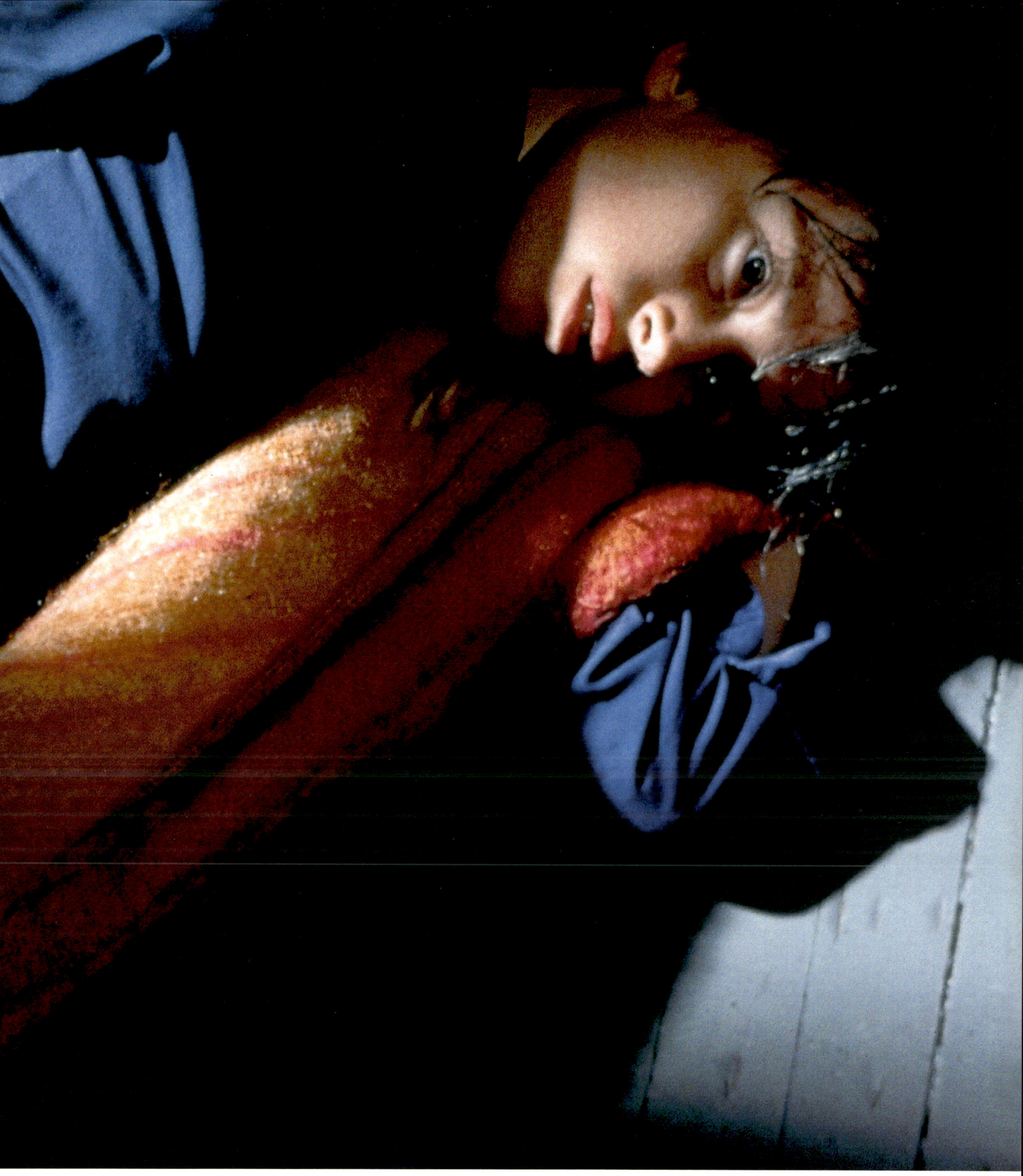

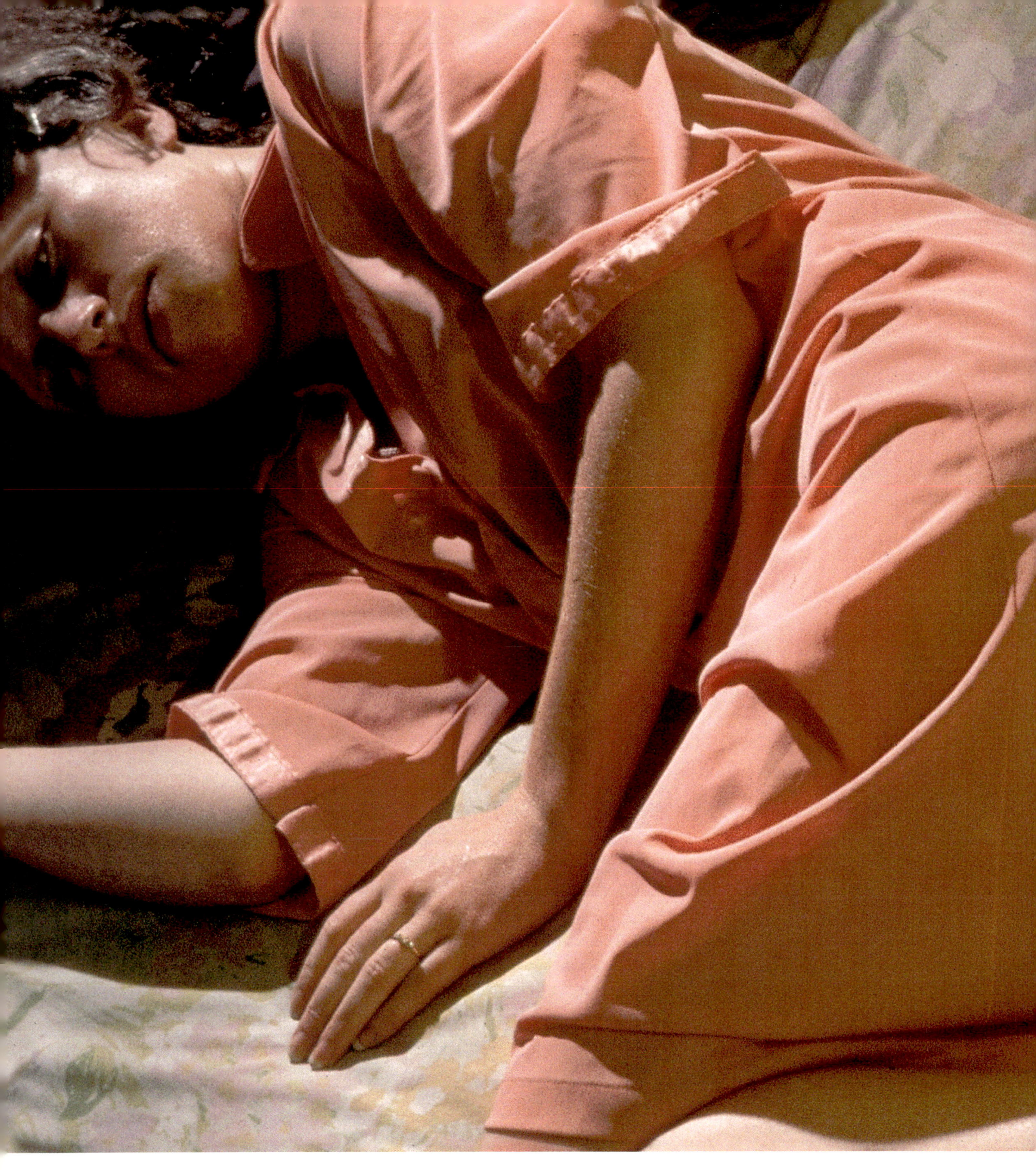

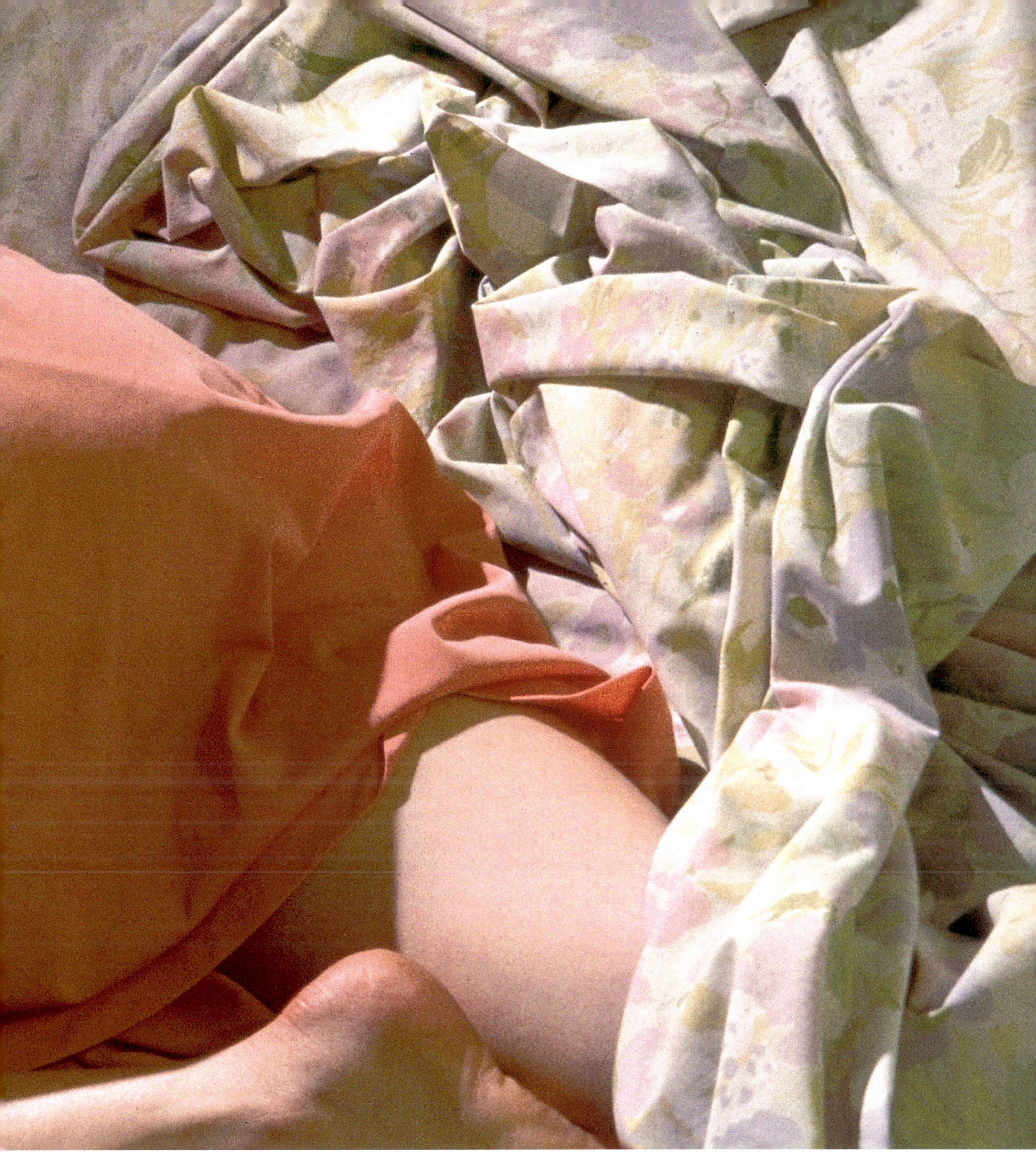

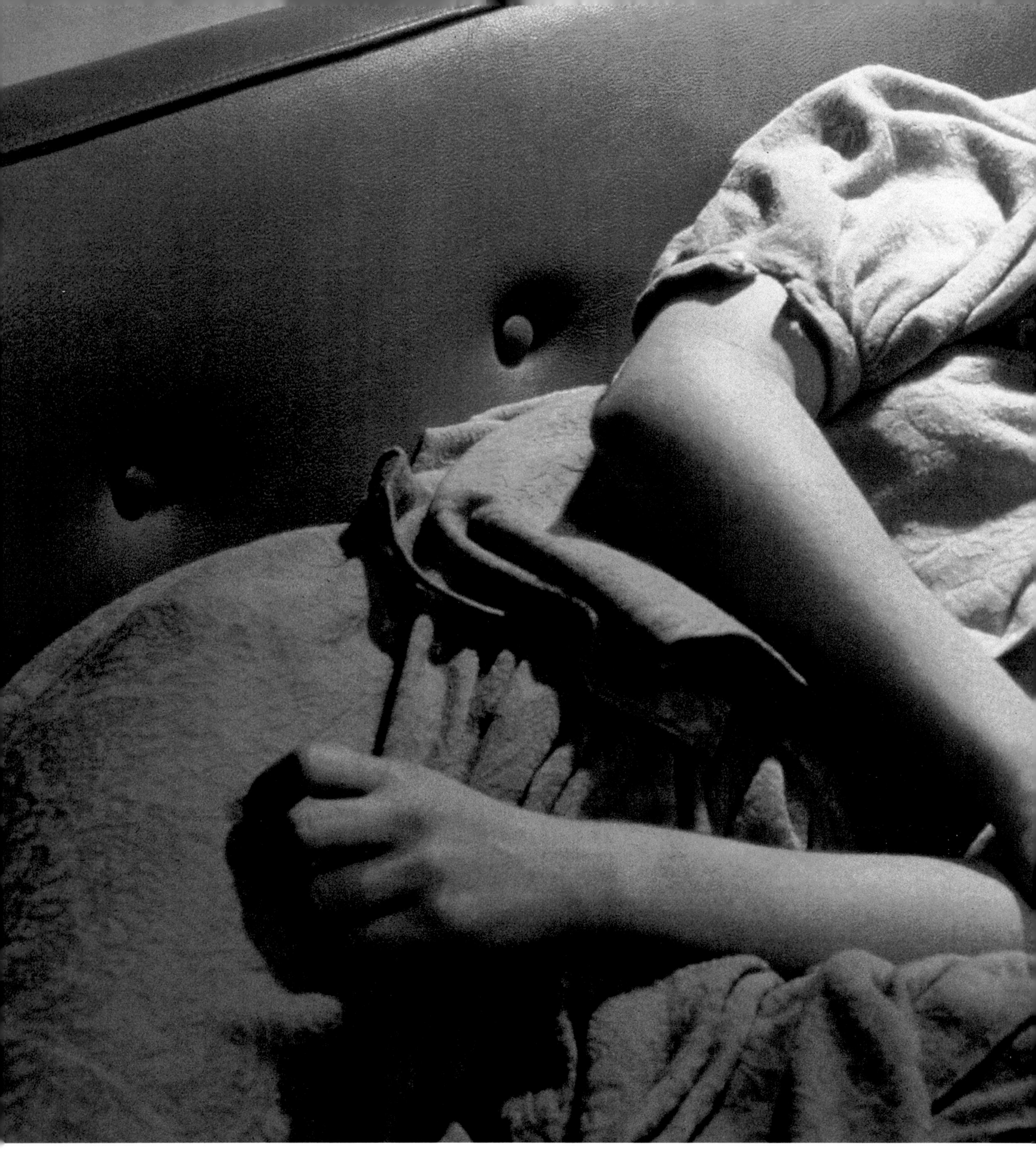

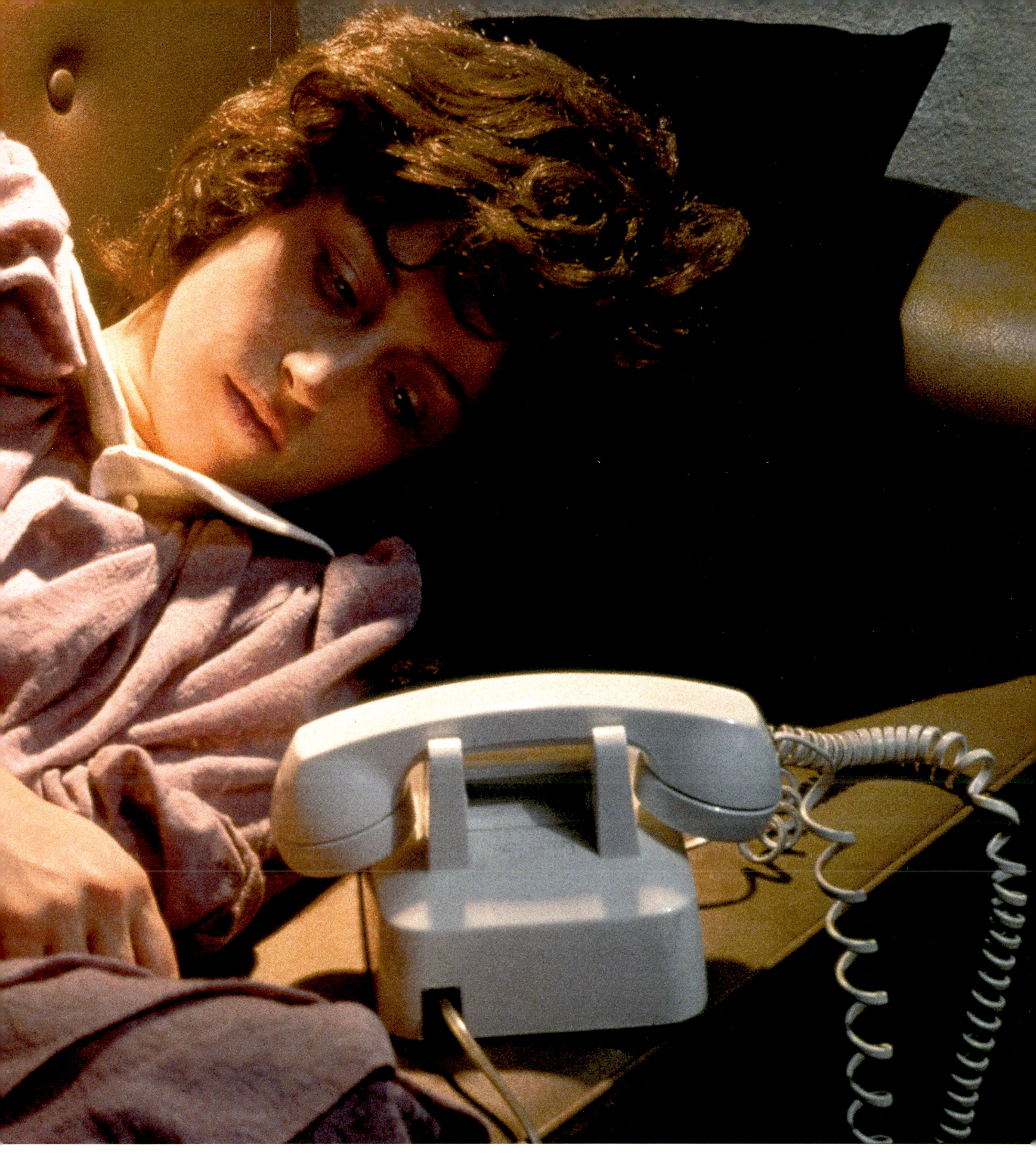

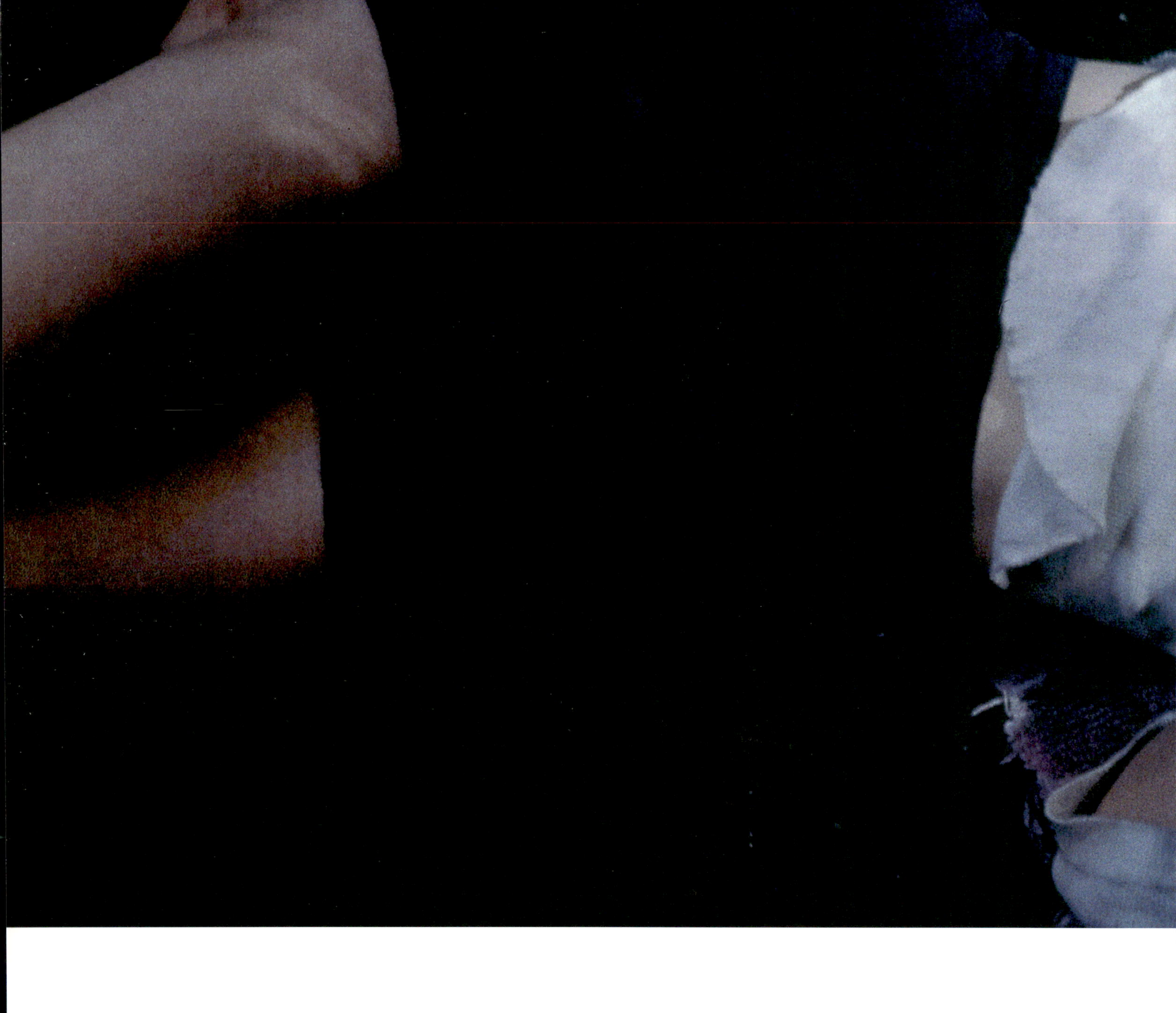

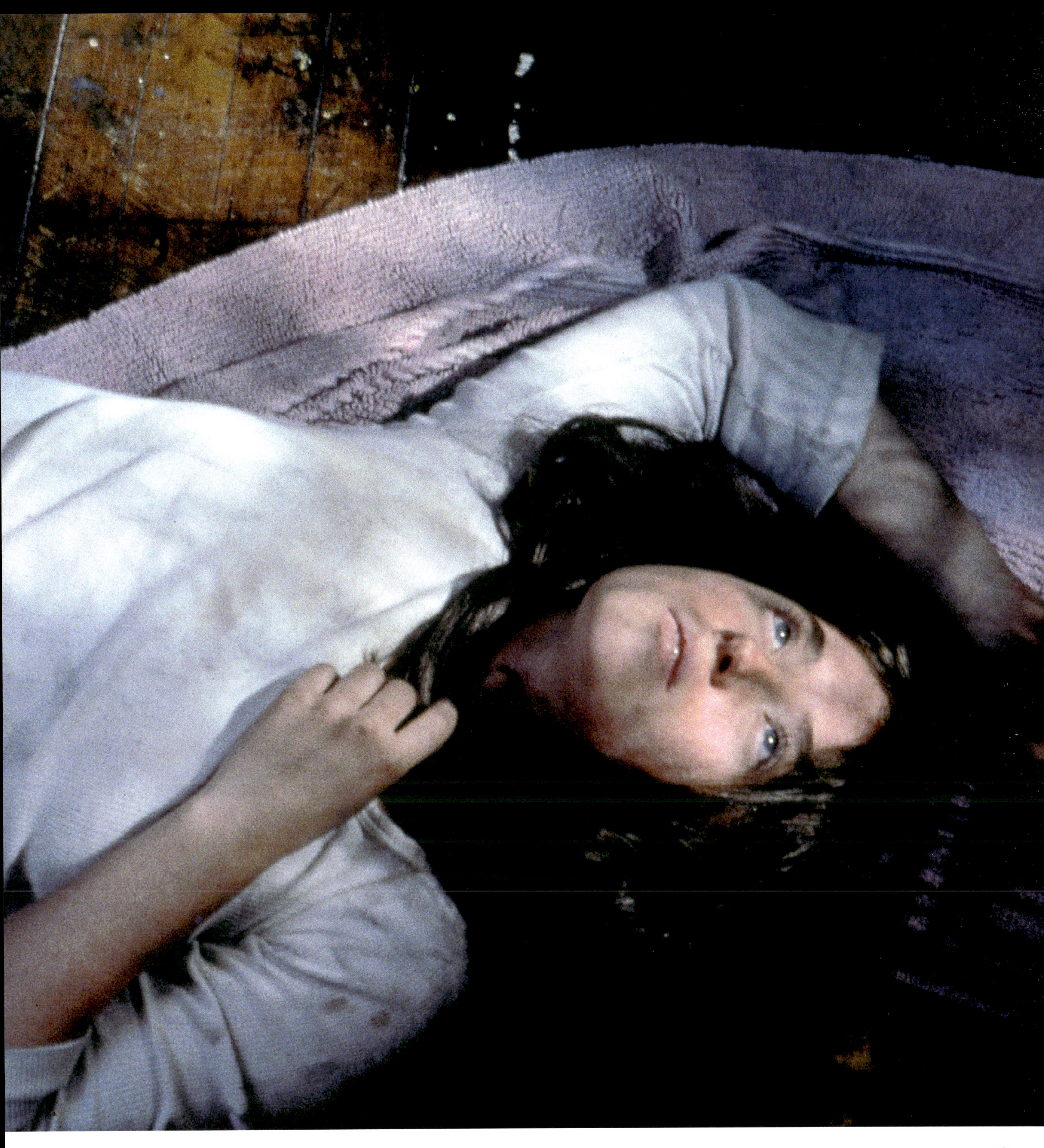

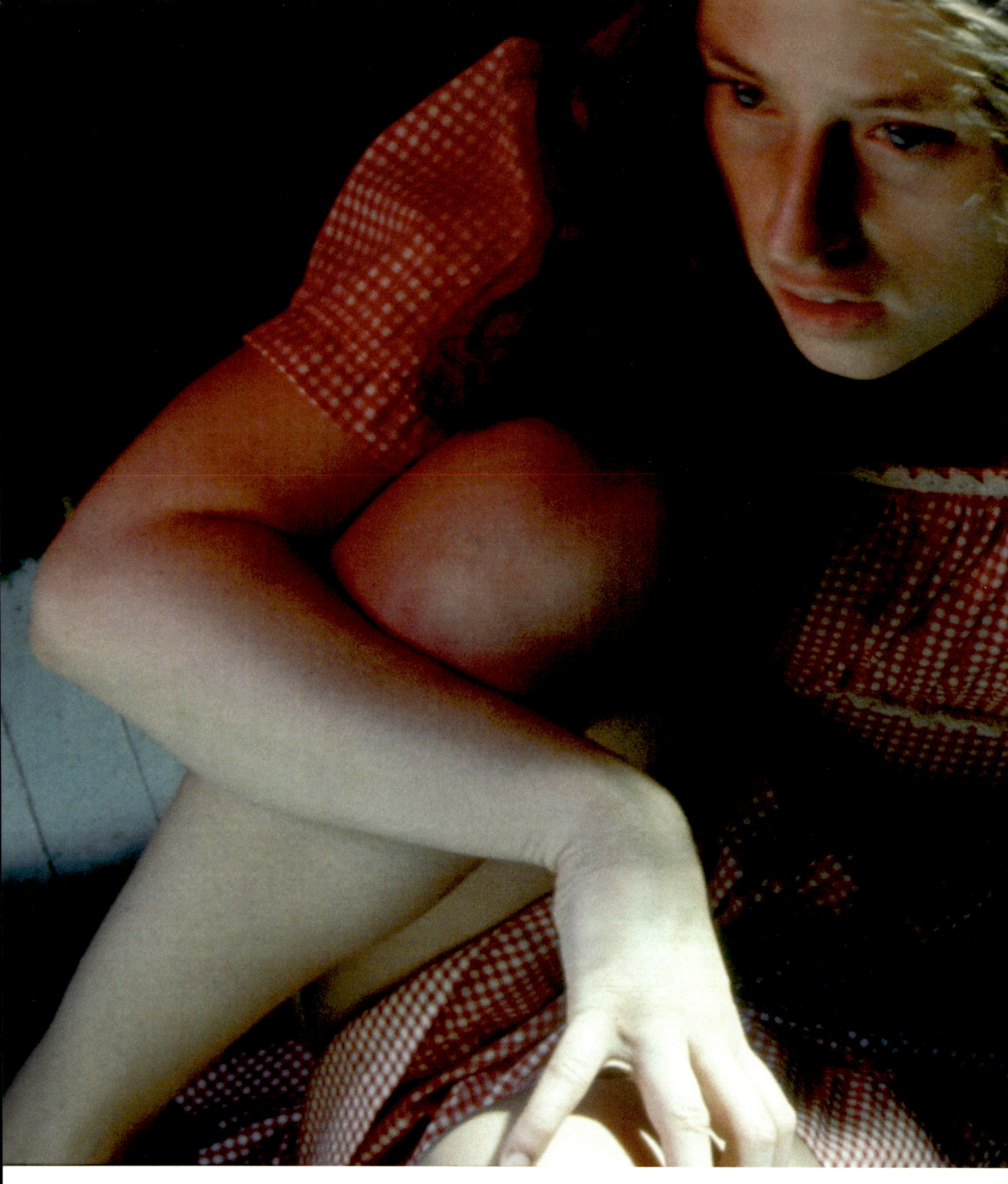

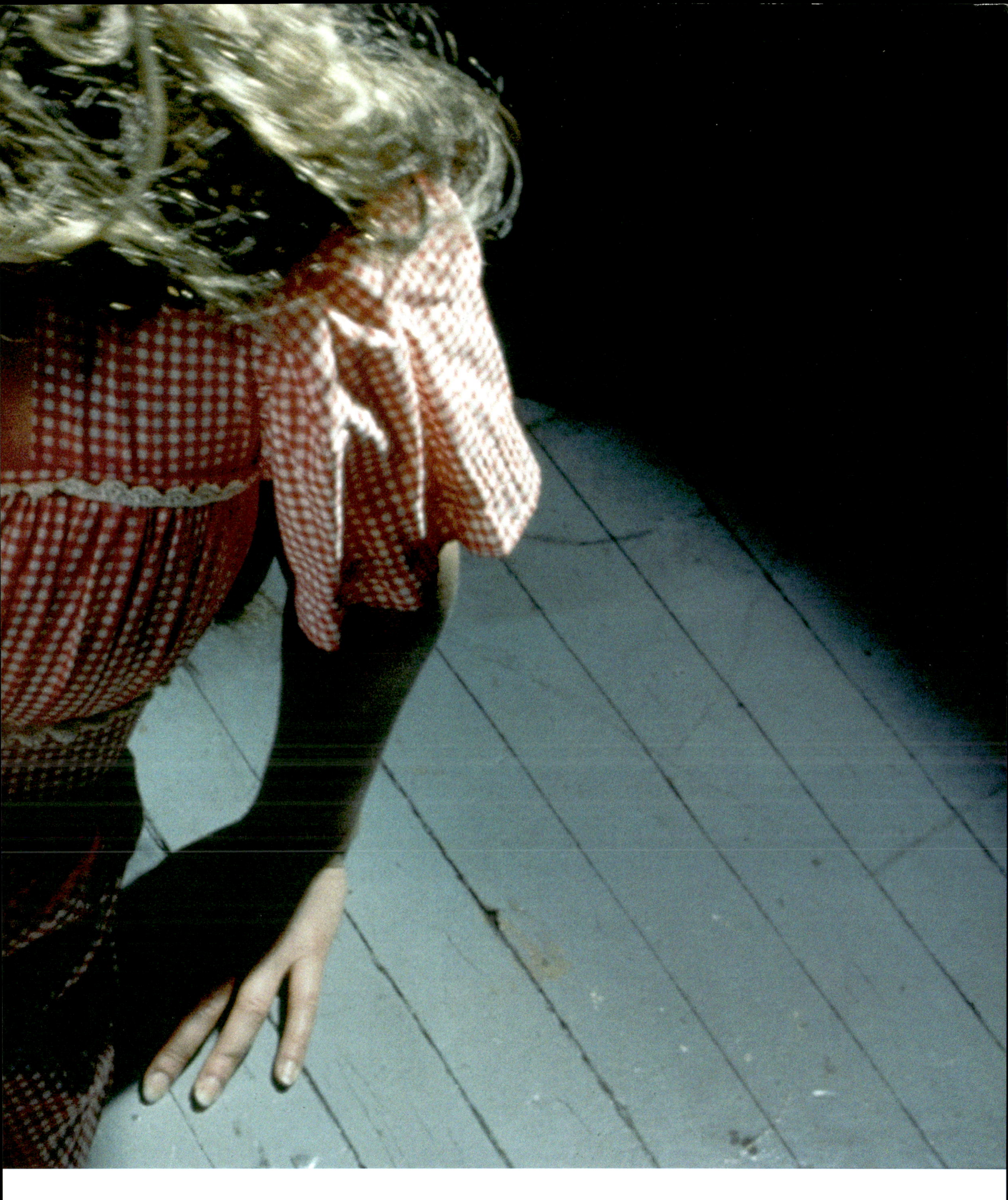

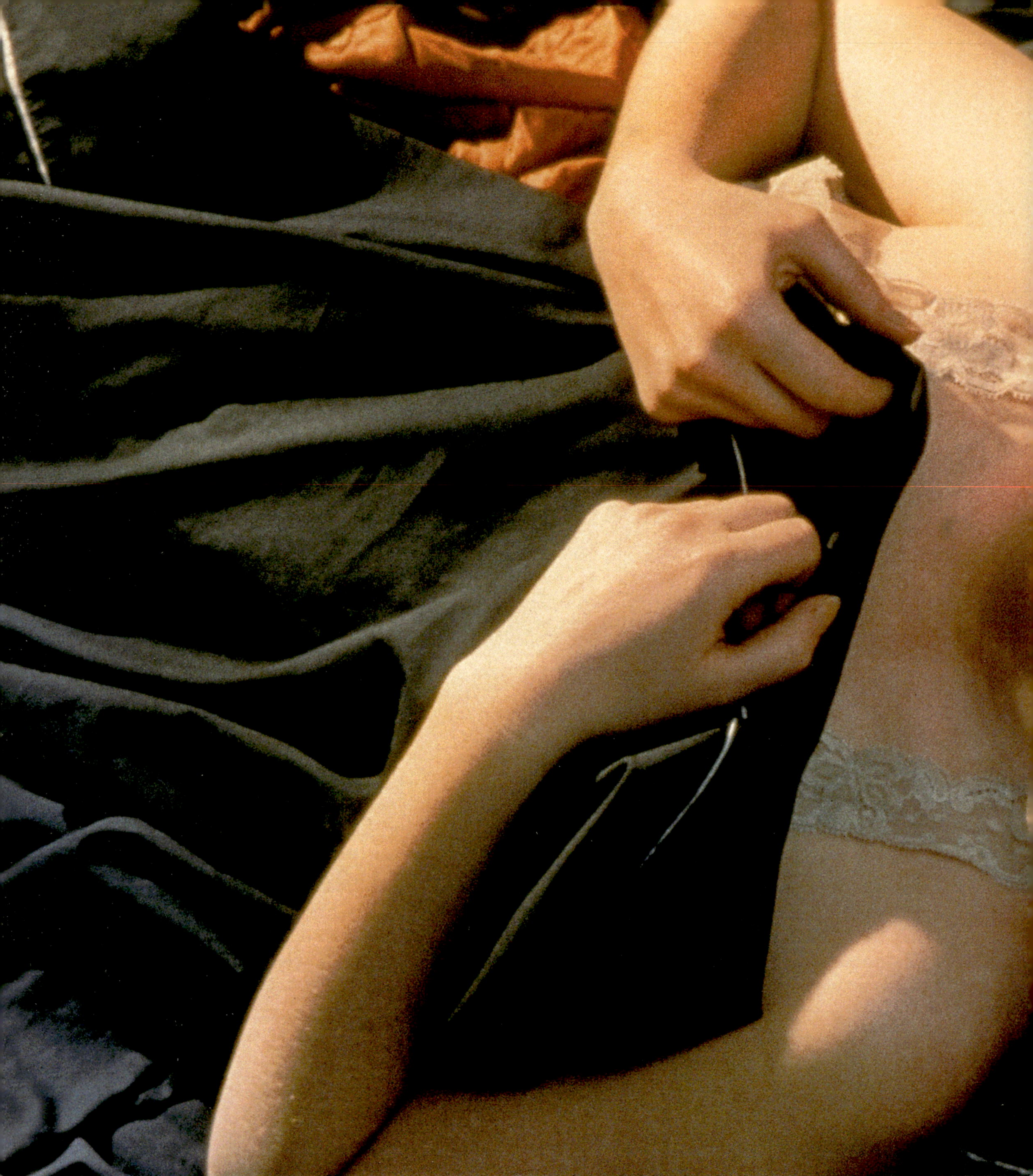

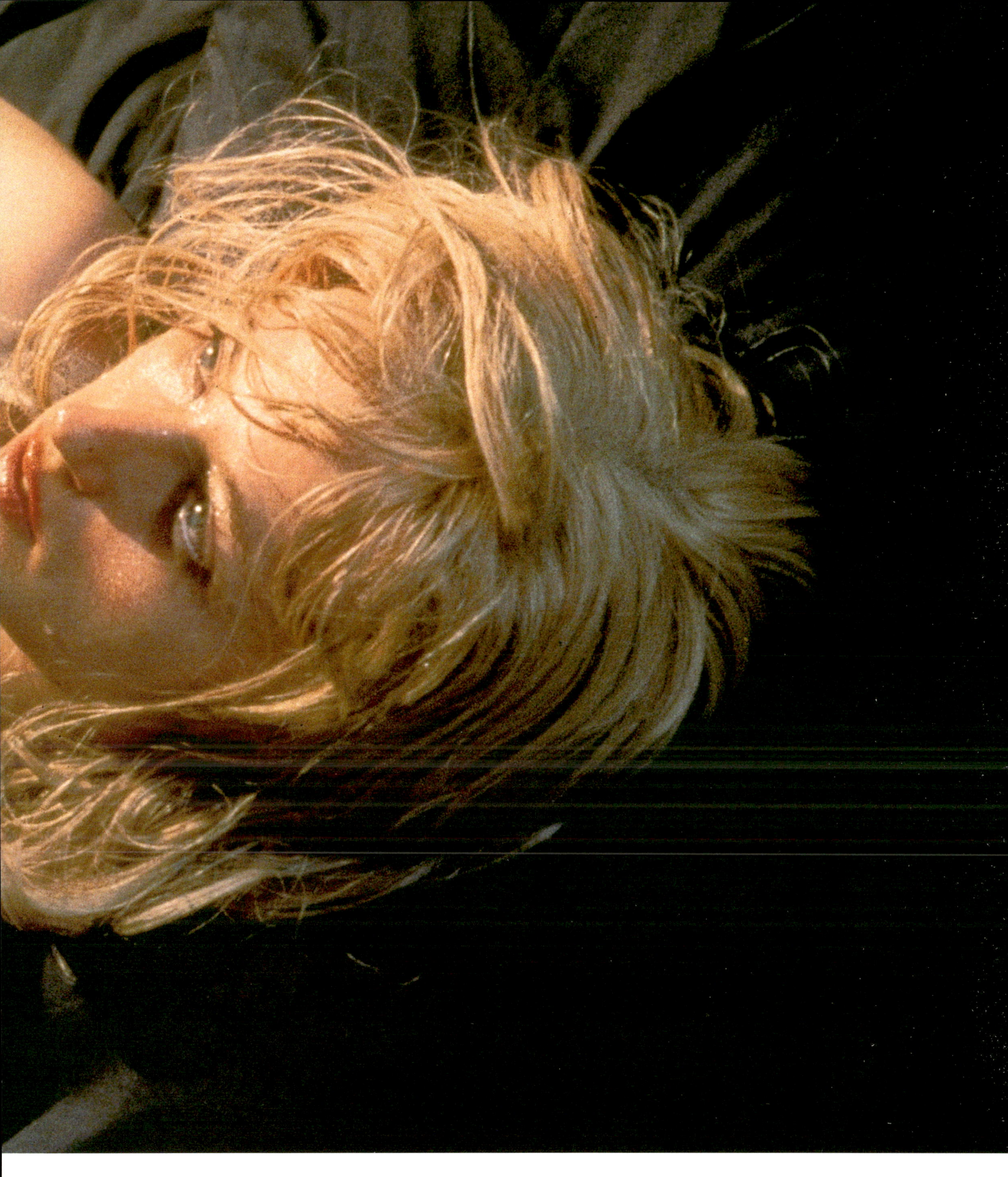

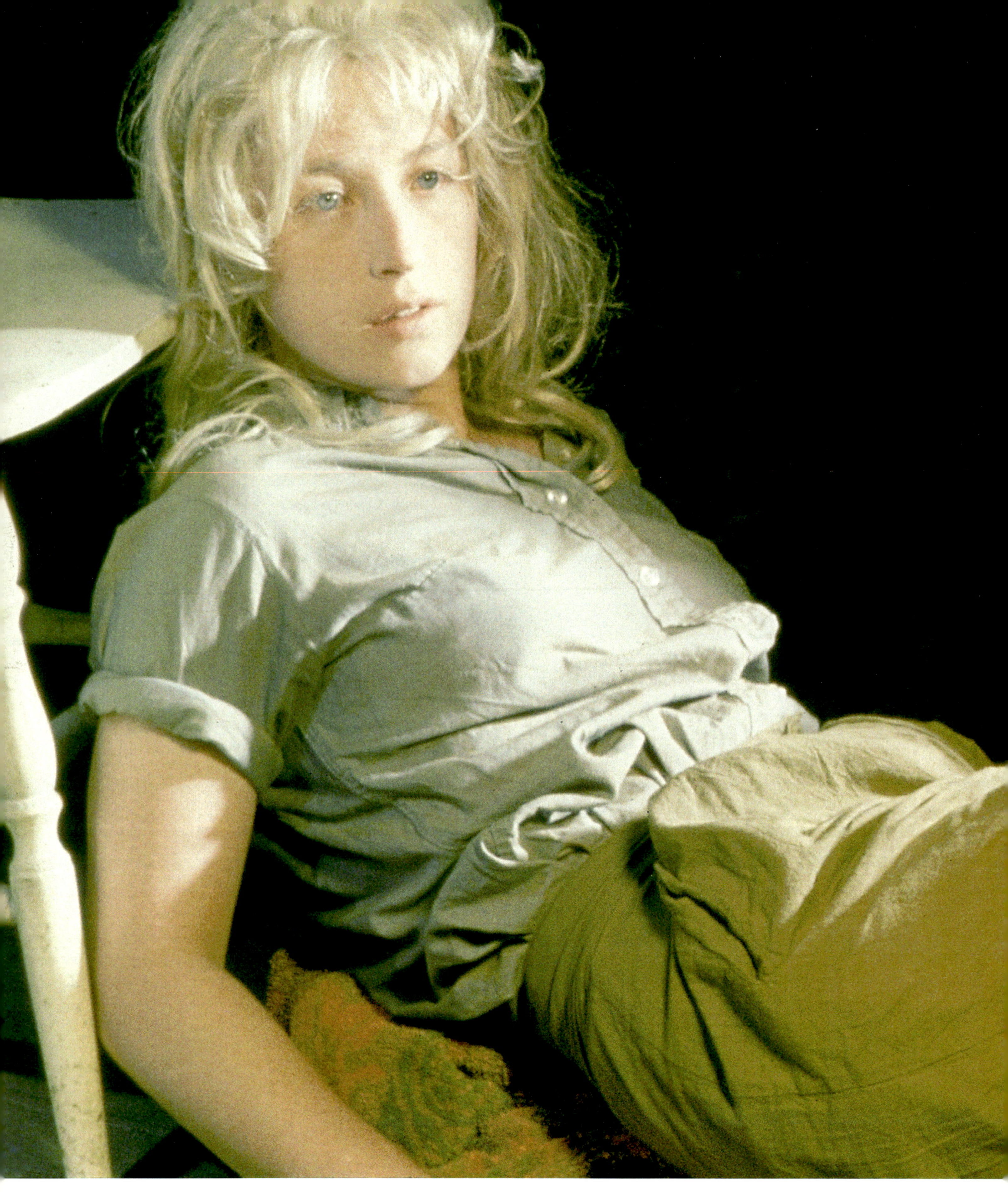

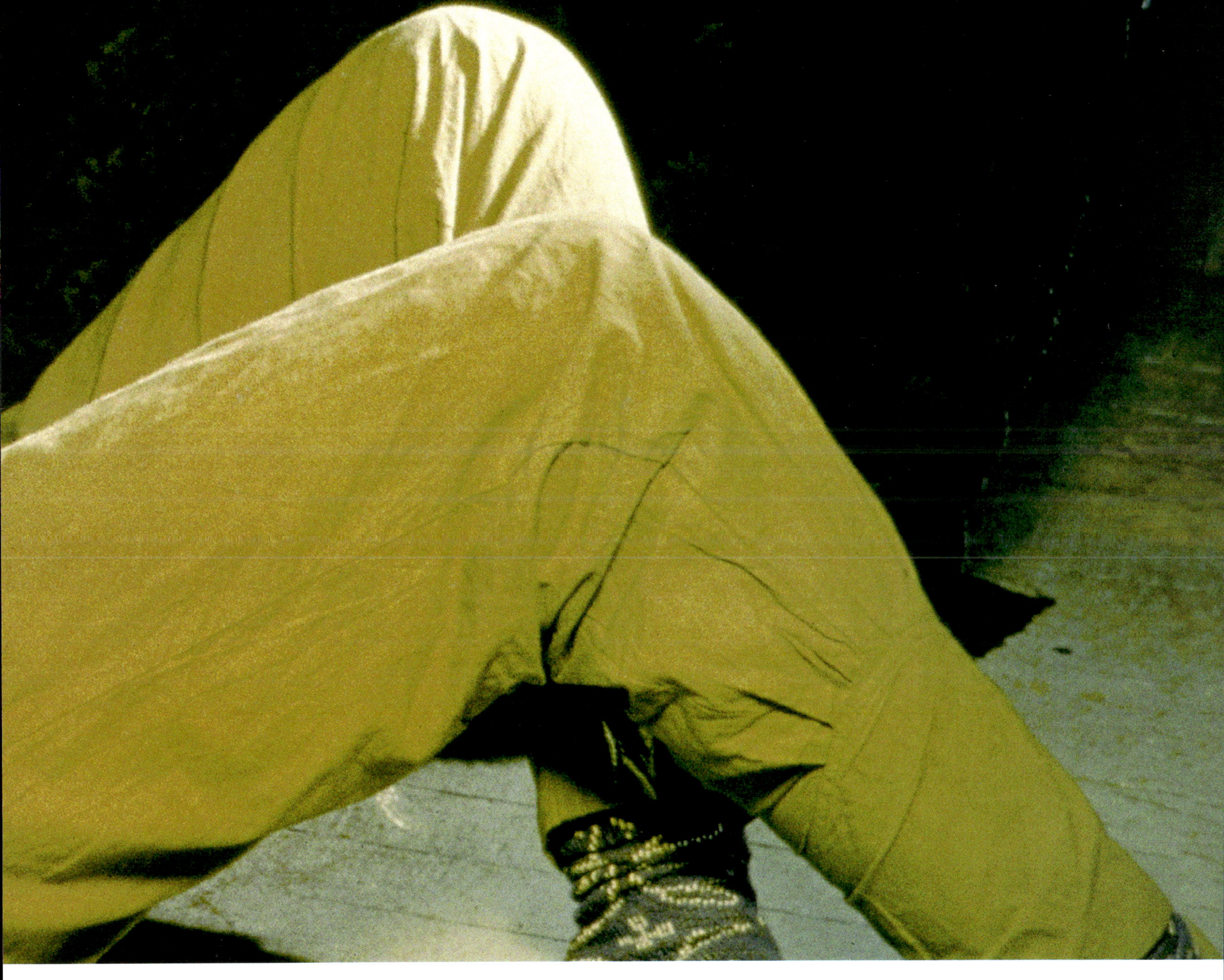

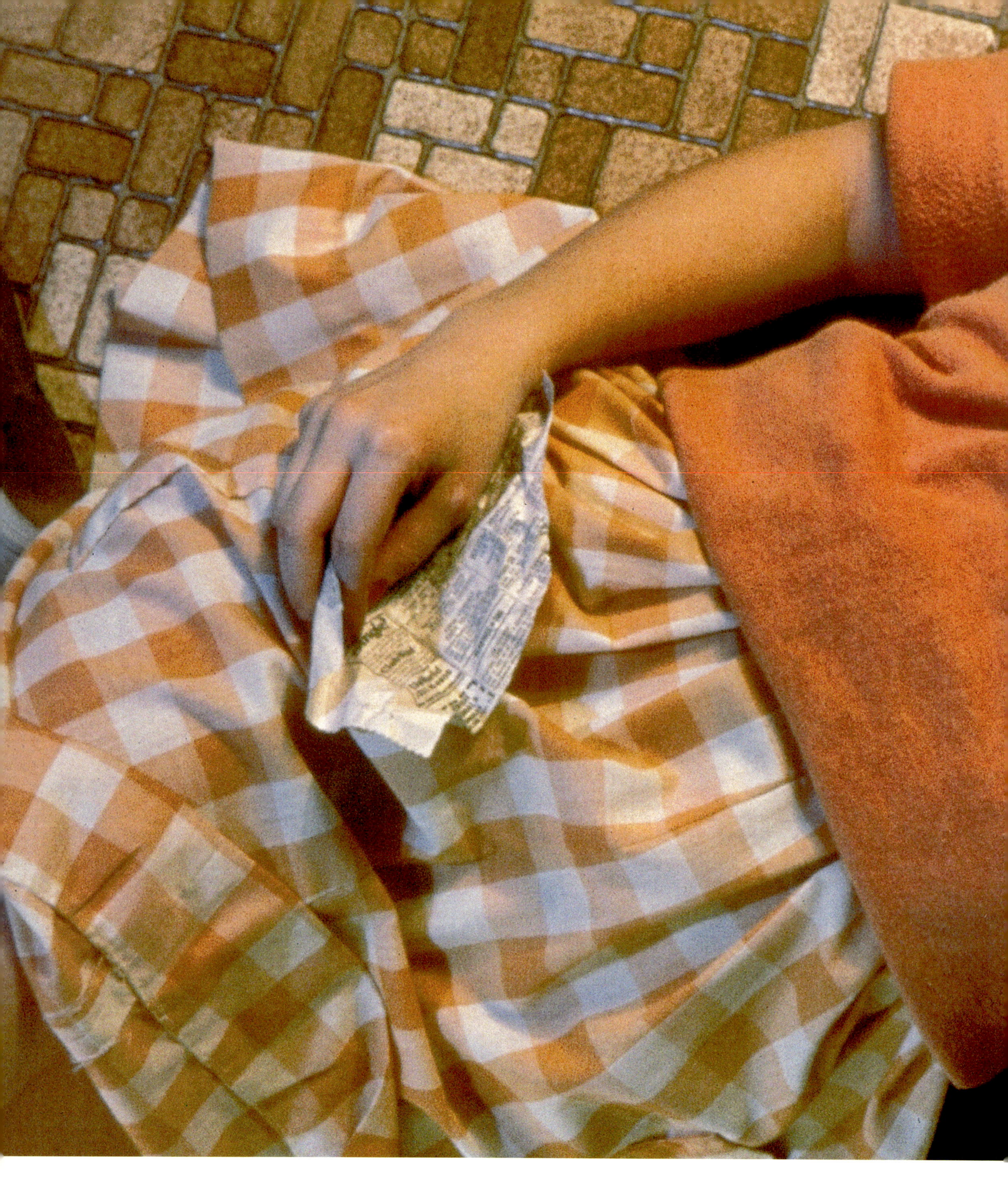

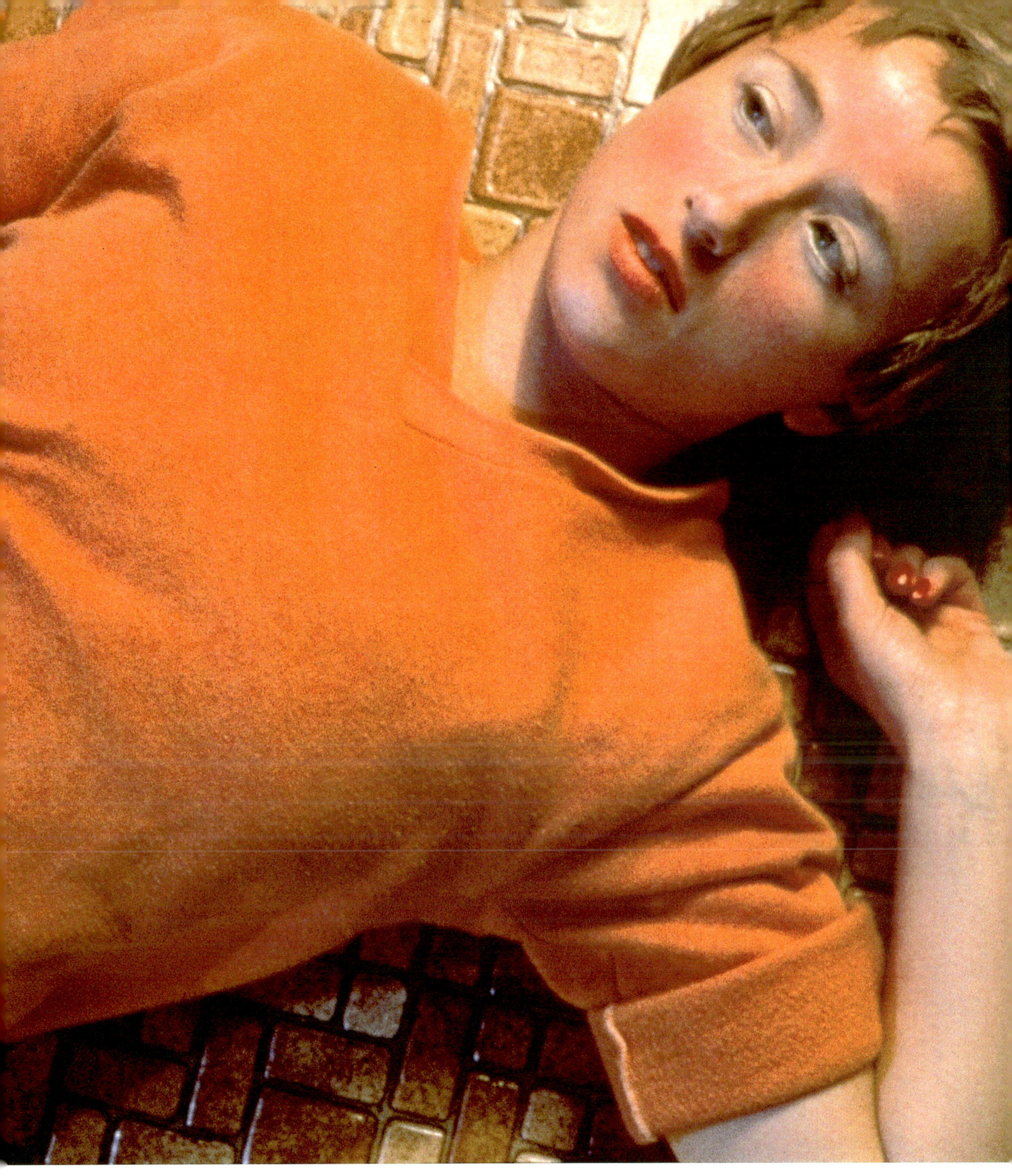

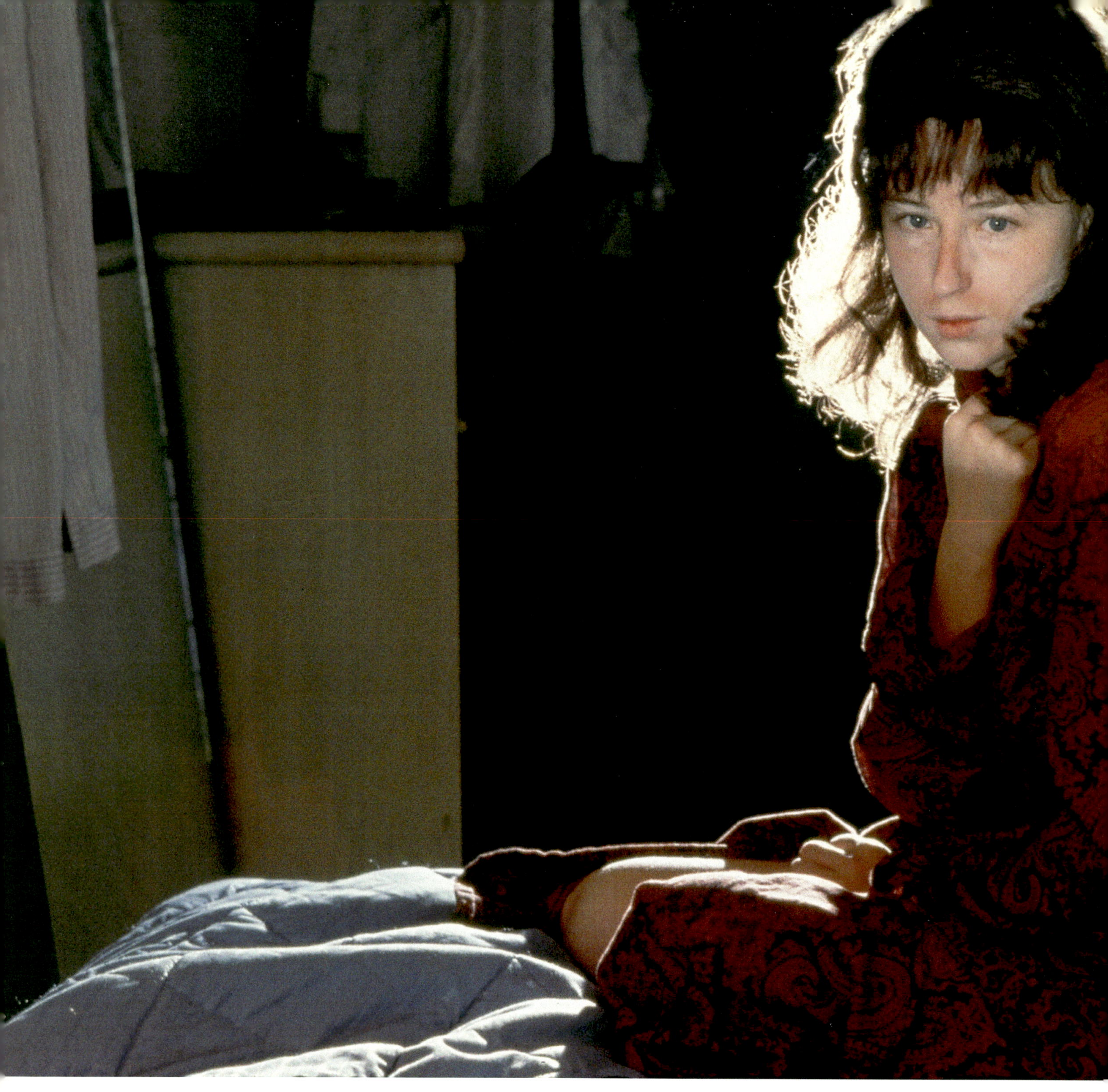

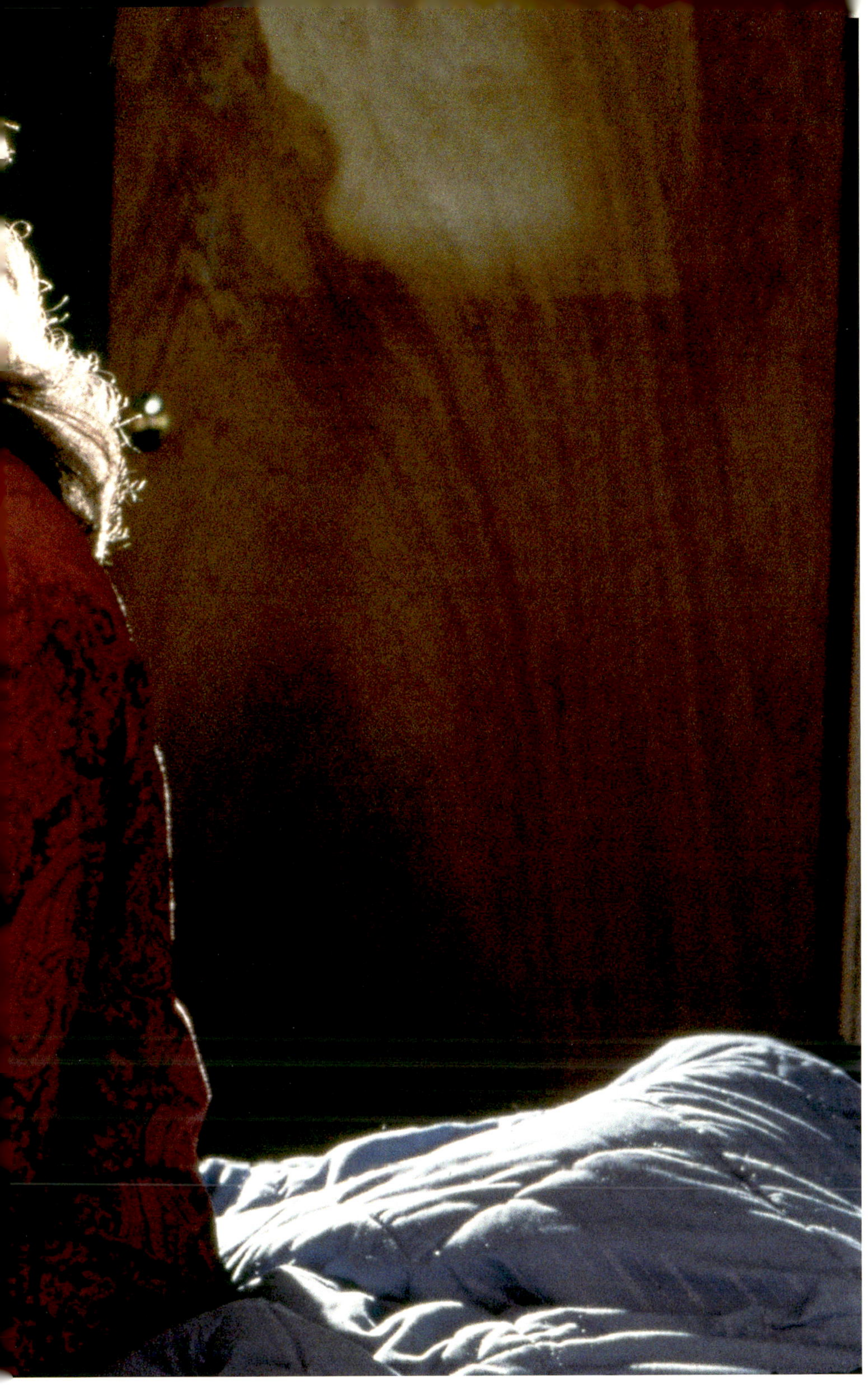

Untitled #97
Untitled #98
Untitled #99

1982

[Pink Robes]

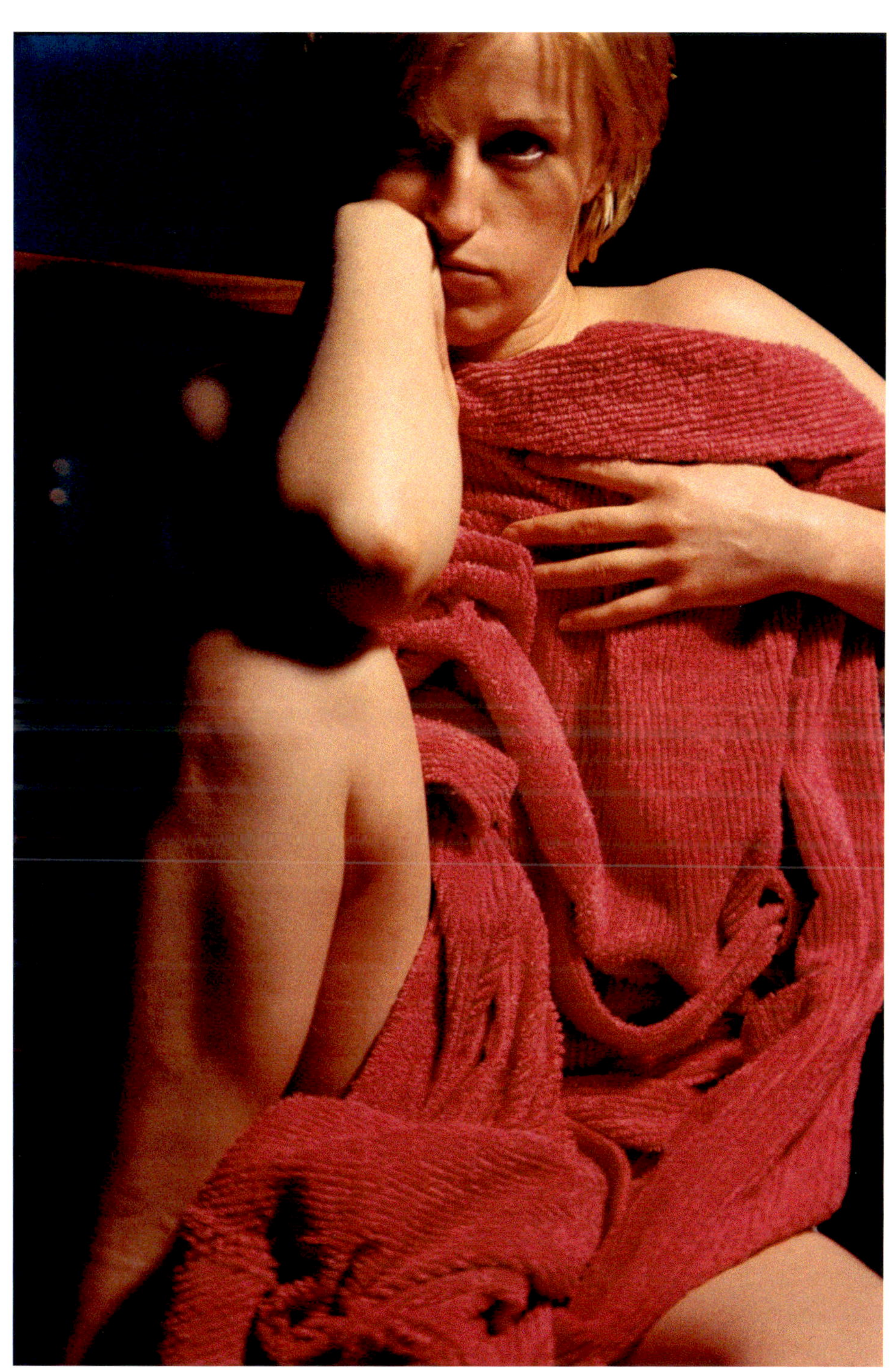

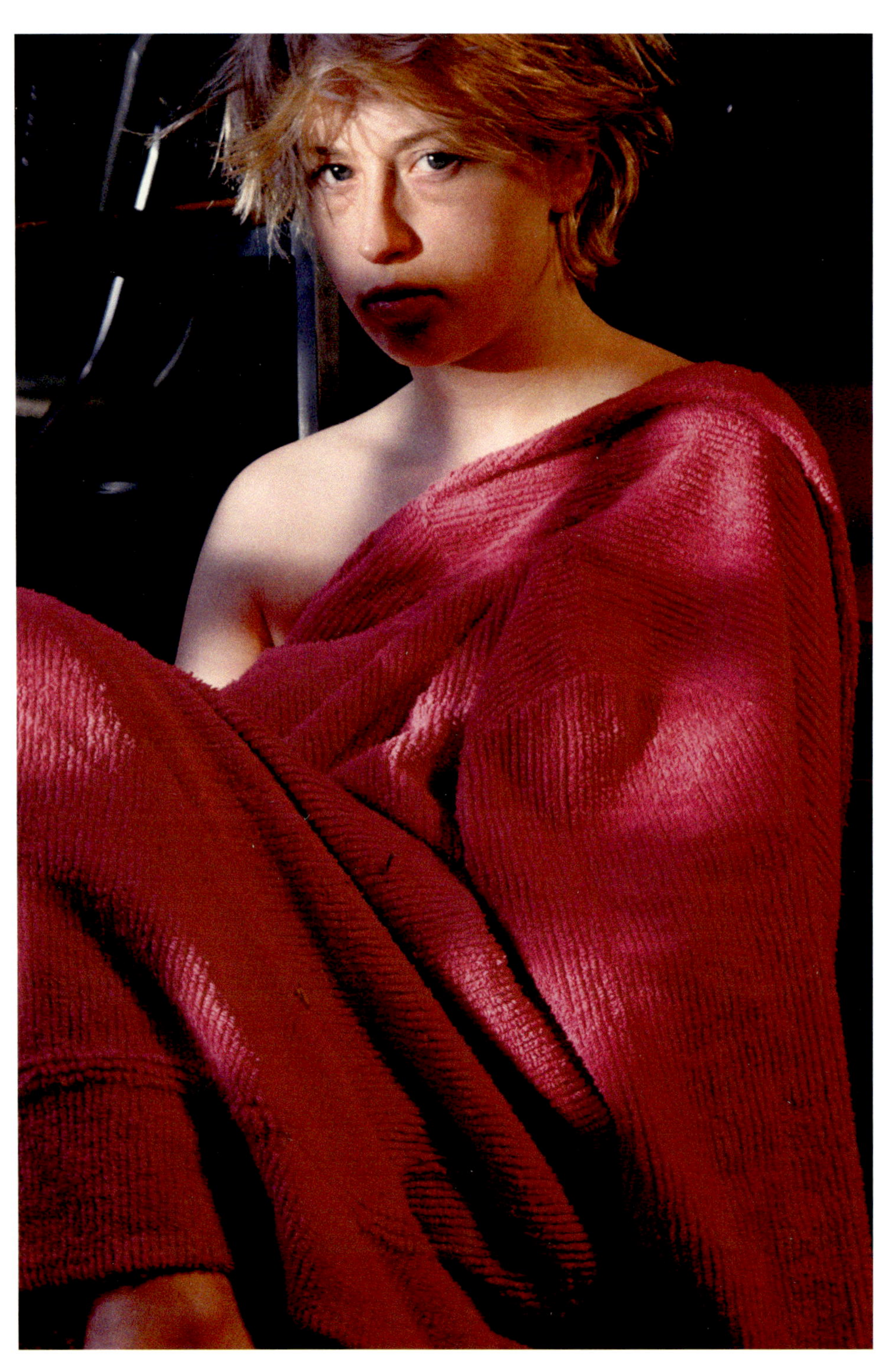

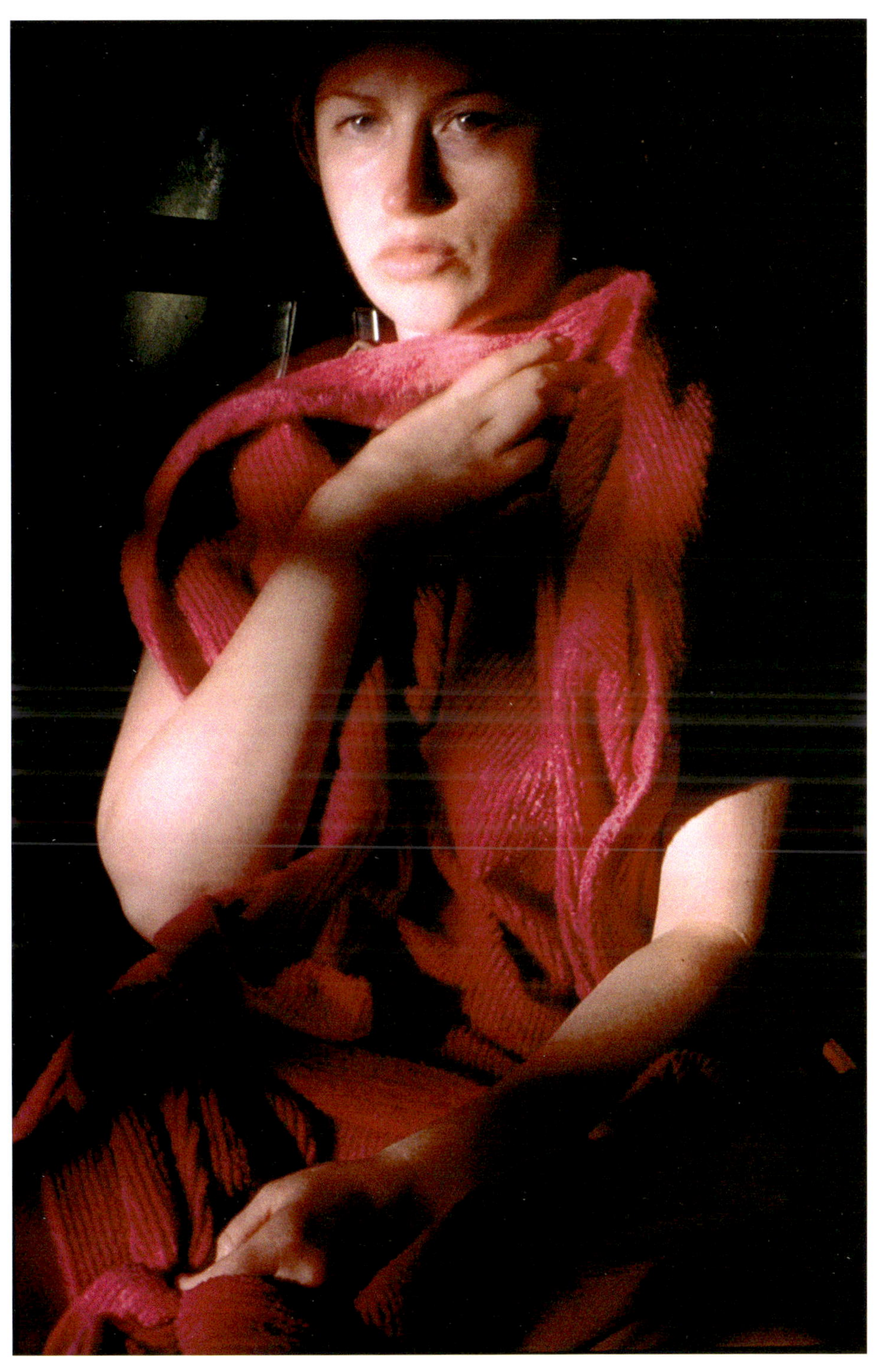

Untitled #103
Untitled #113
Untitled #114
Untitled #116

1982

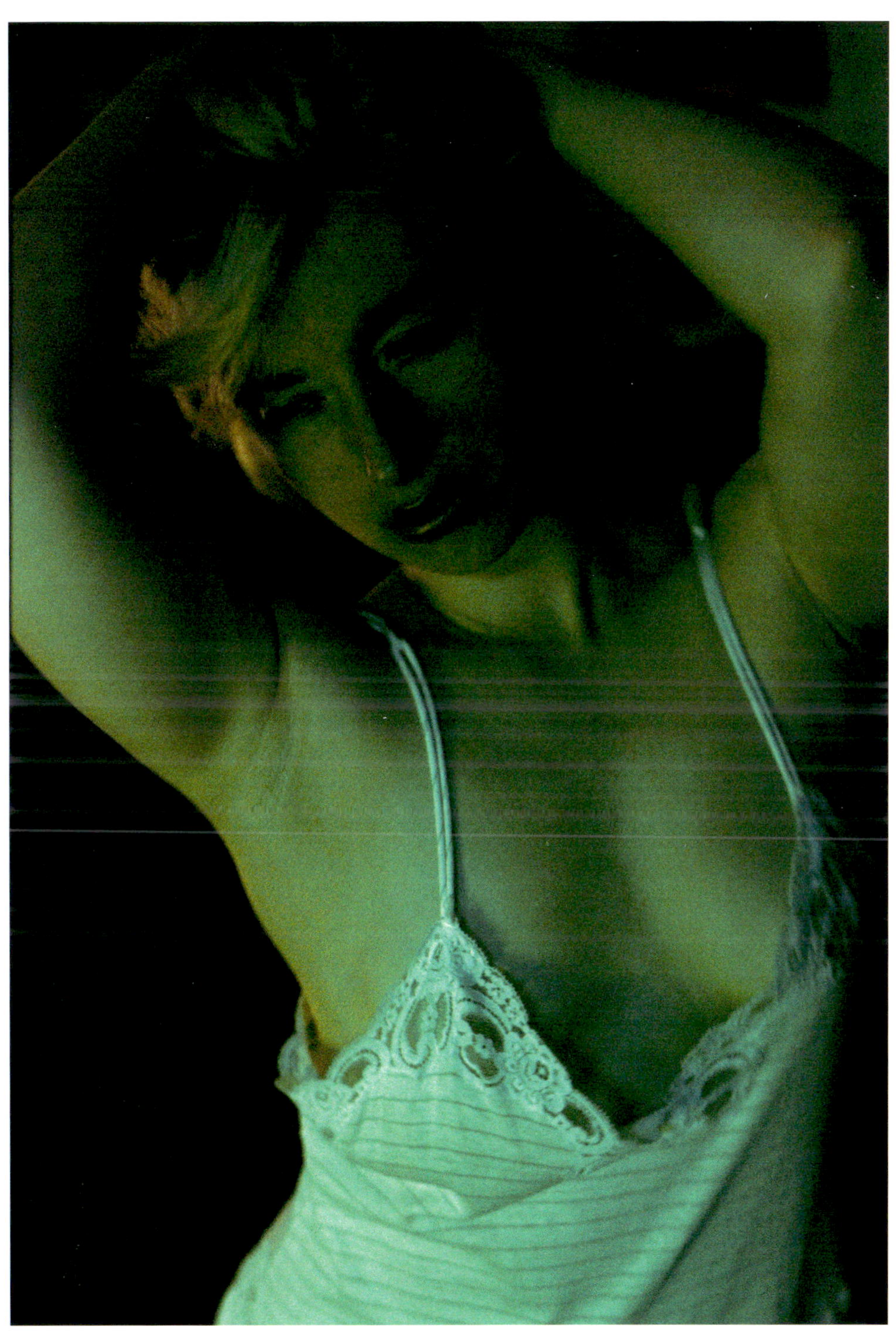

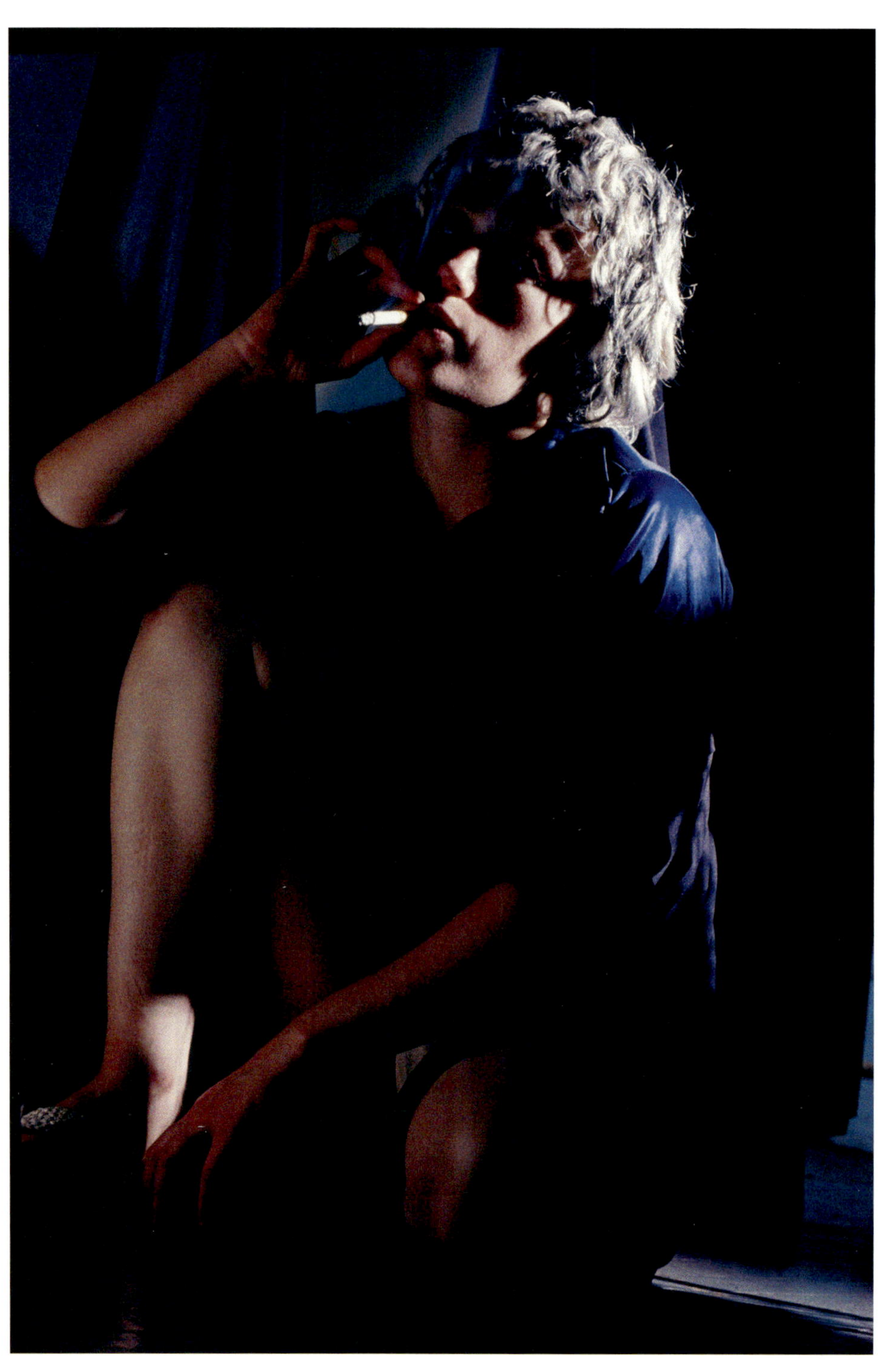

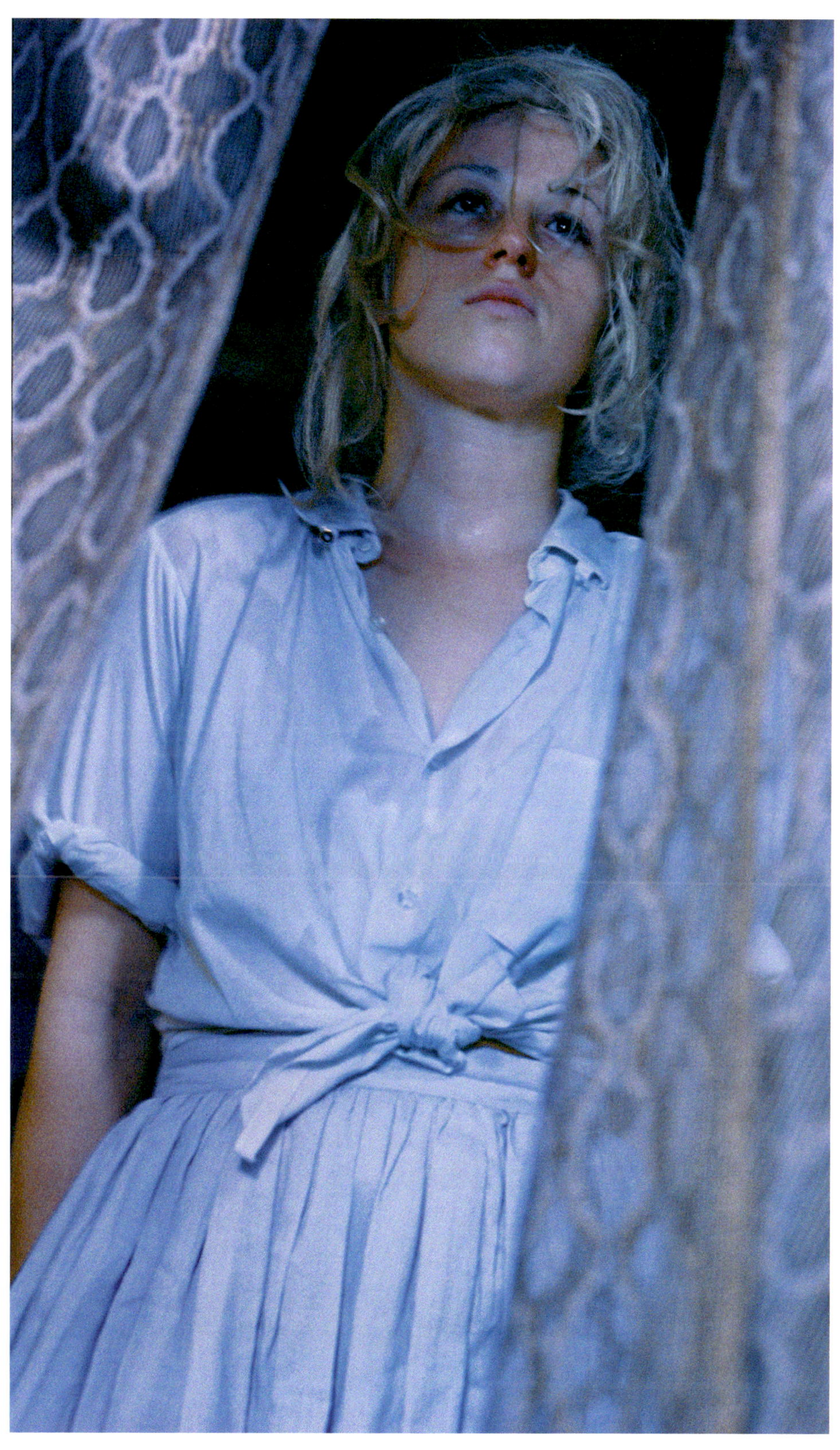

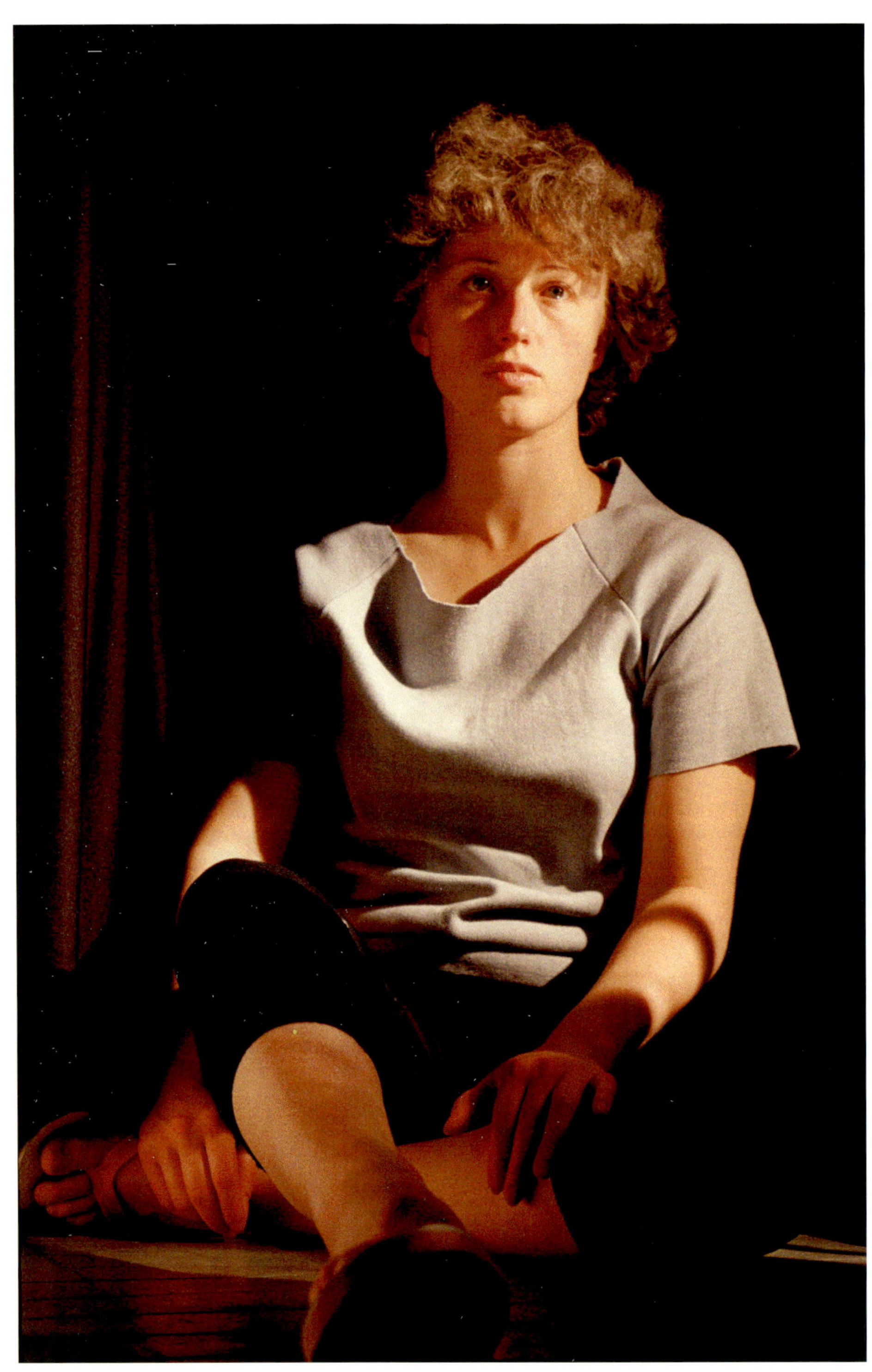

Untitled #122
Untitled #137
Untitled #131
Untitled #127
Untitled #133
Untitled #138
Untitled #126

1983-1984

[Fashion]

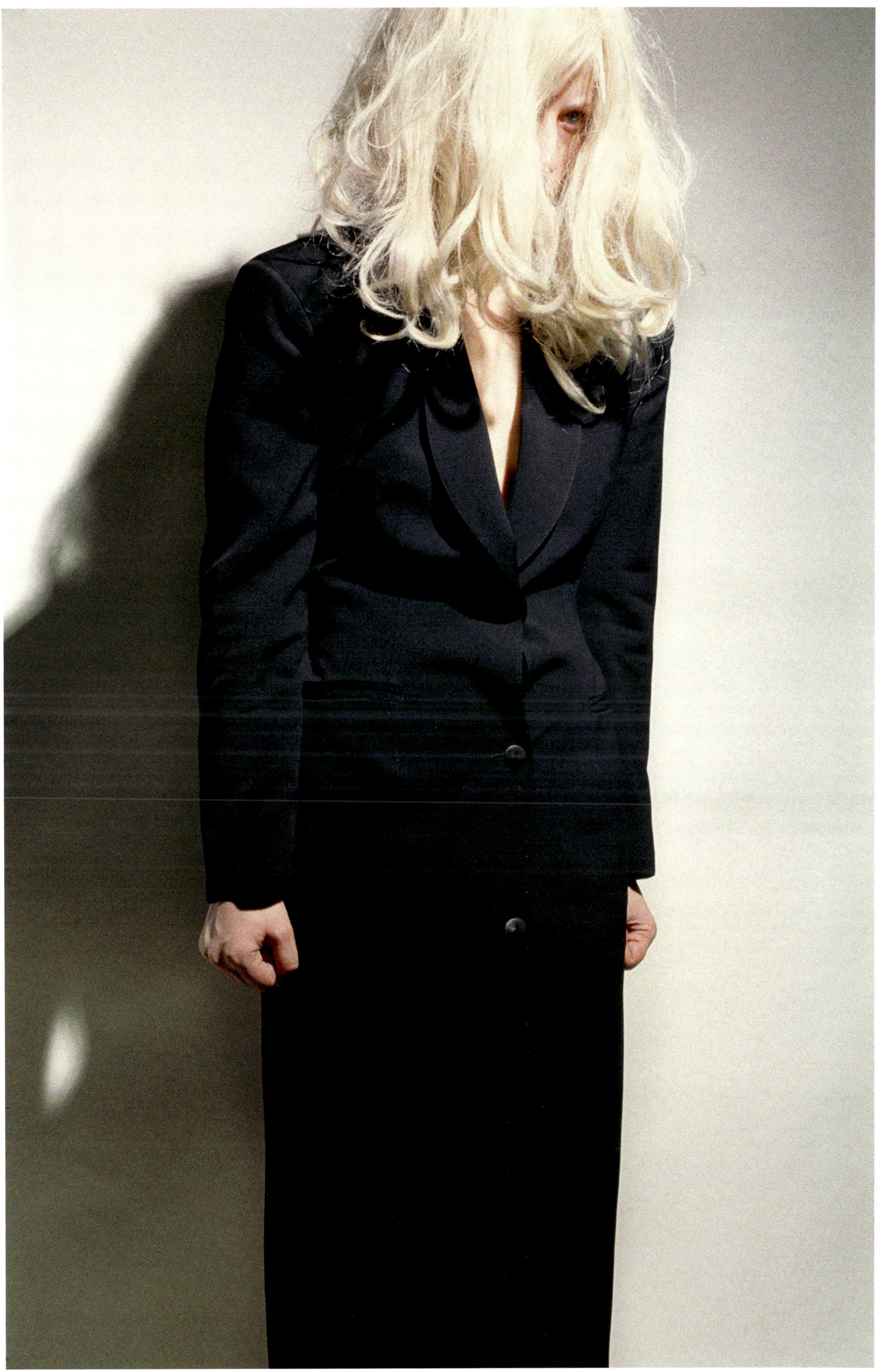

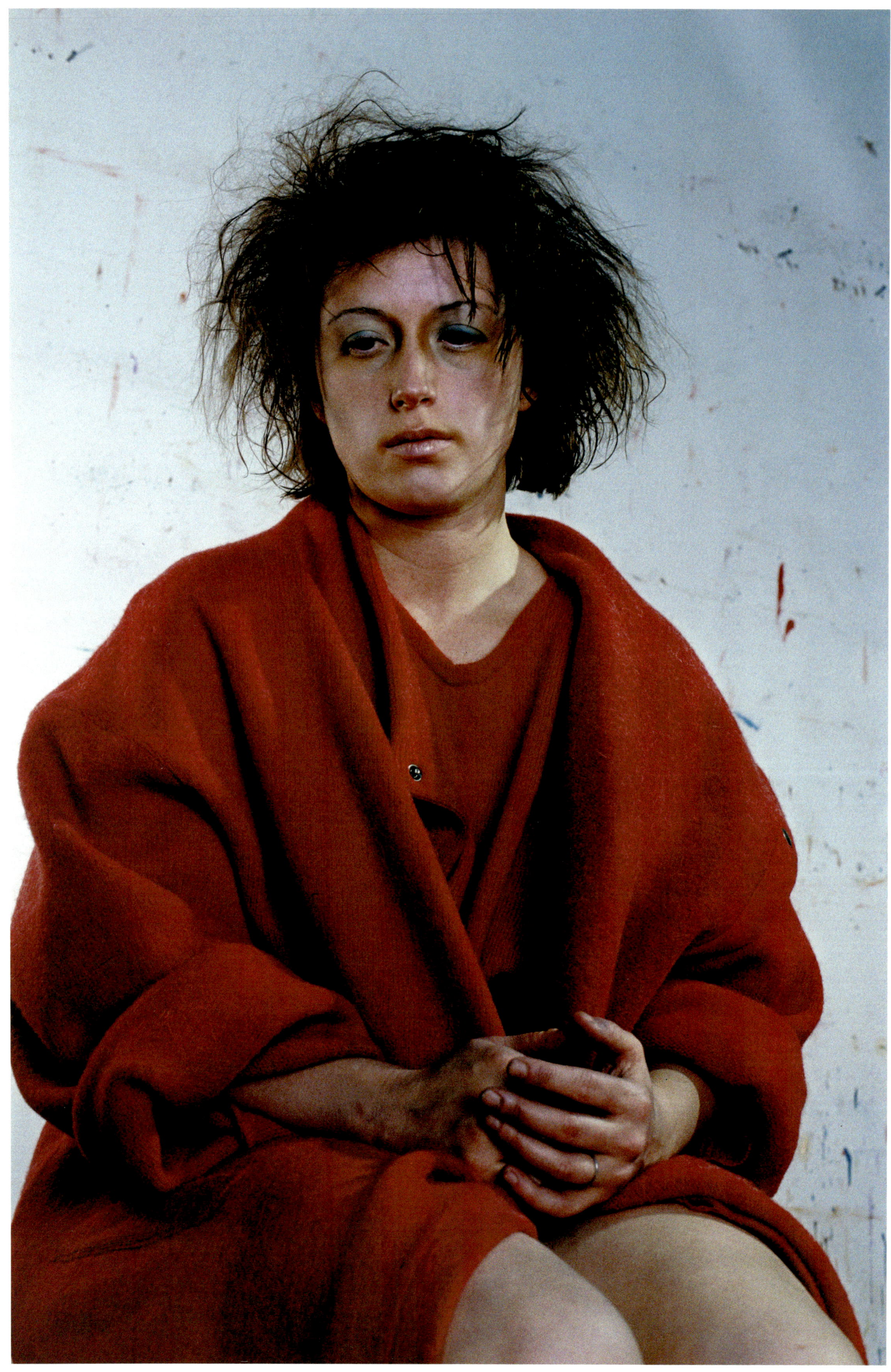

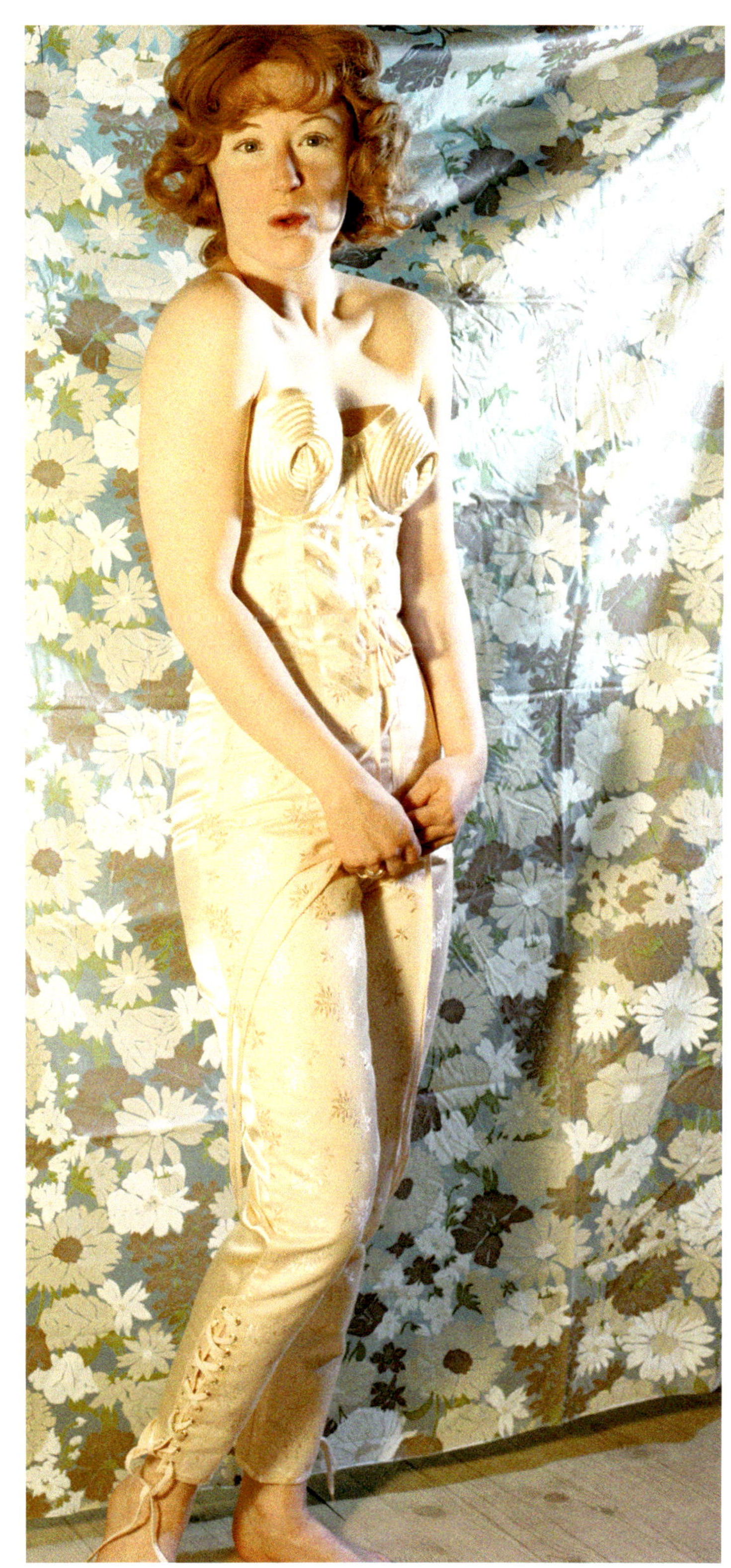

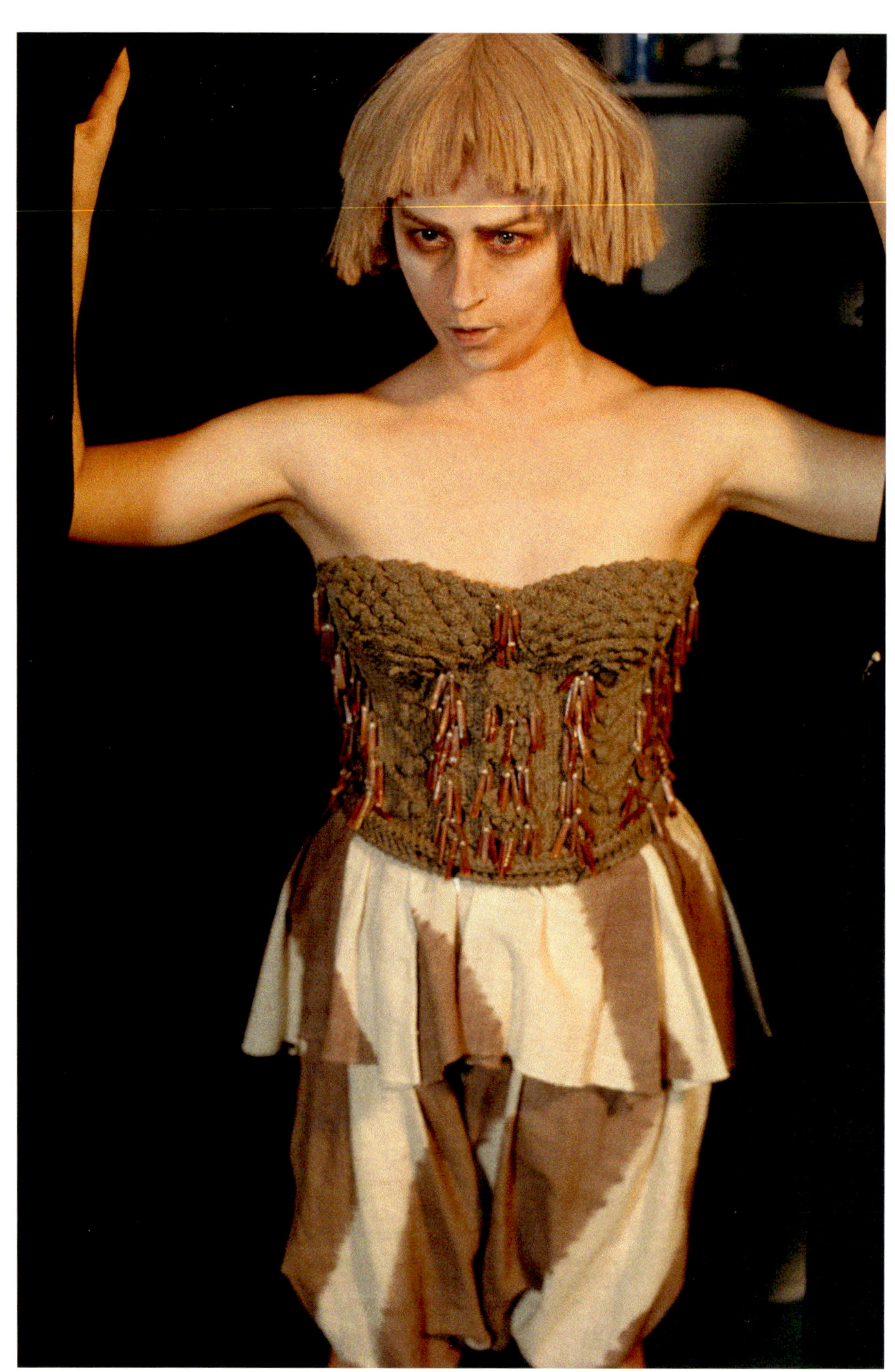

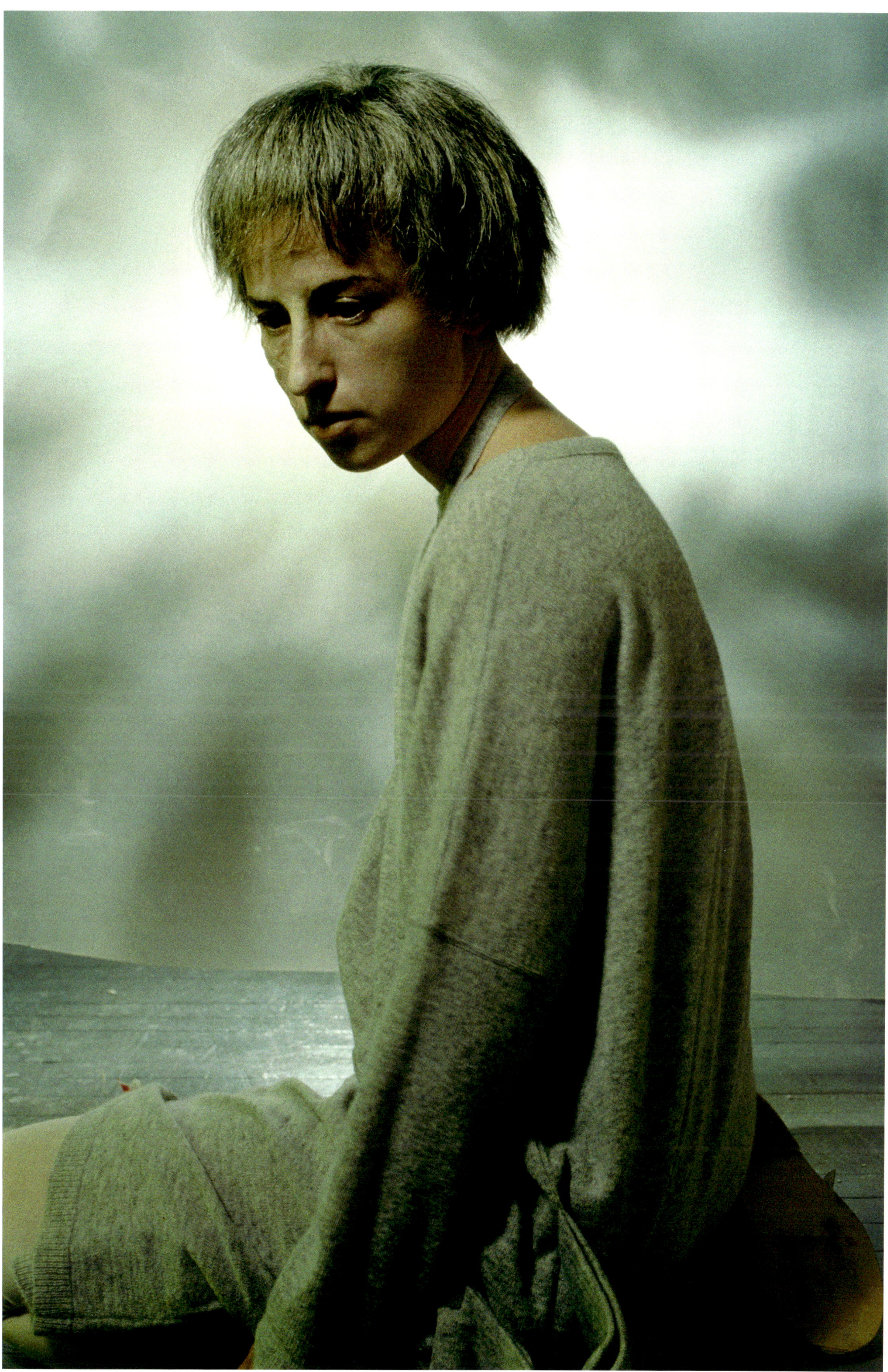

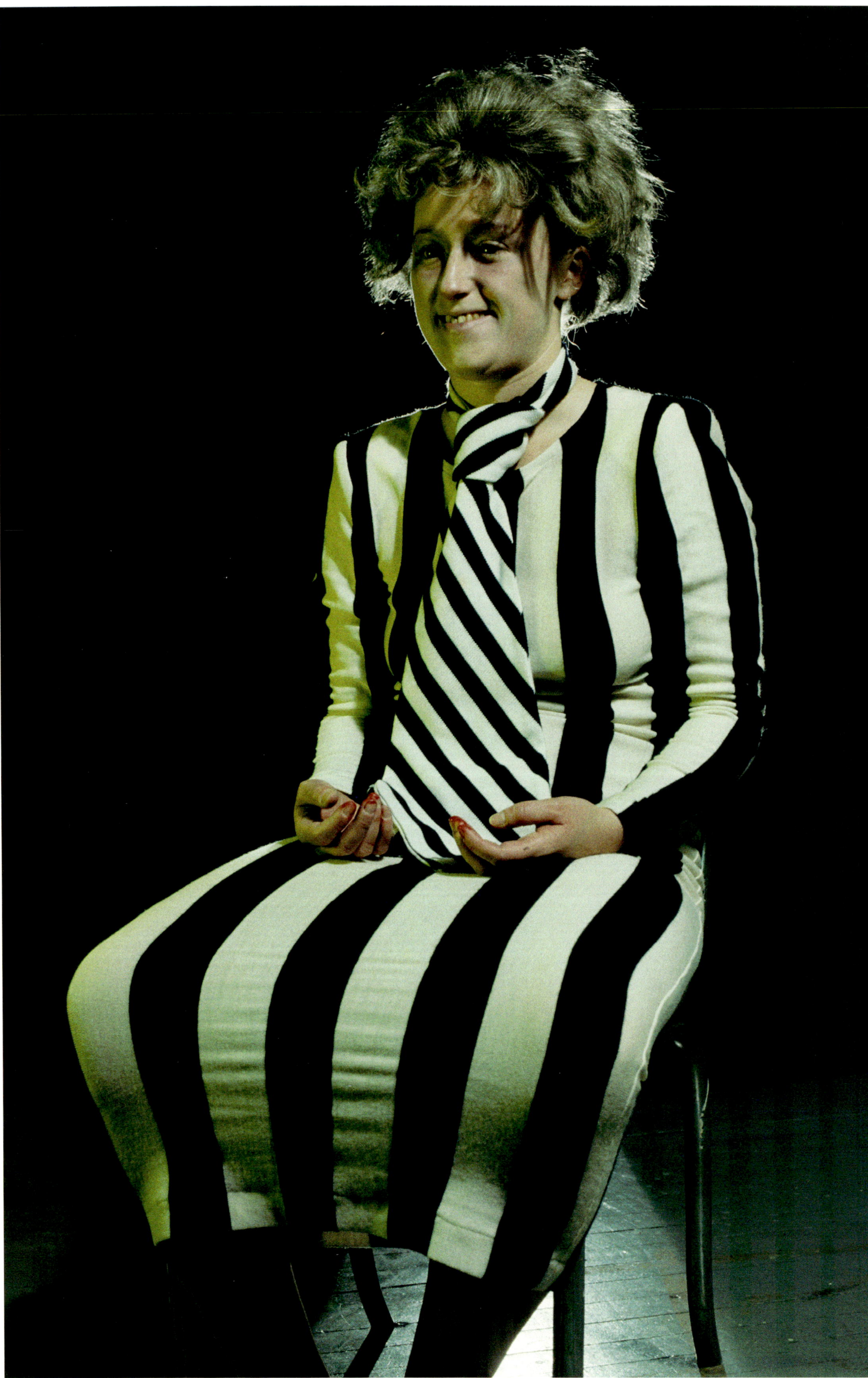

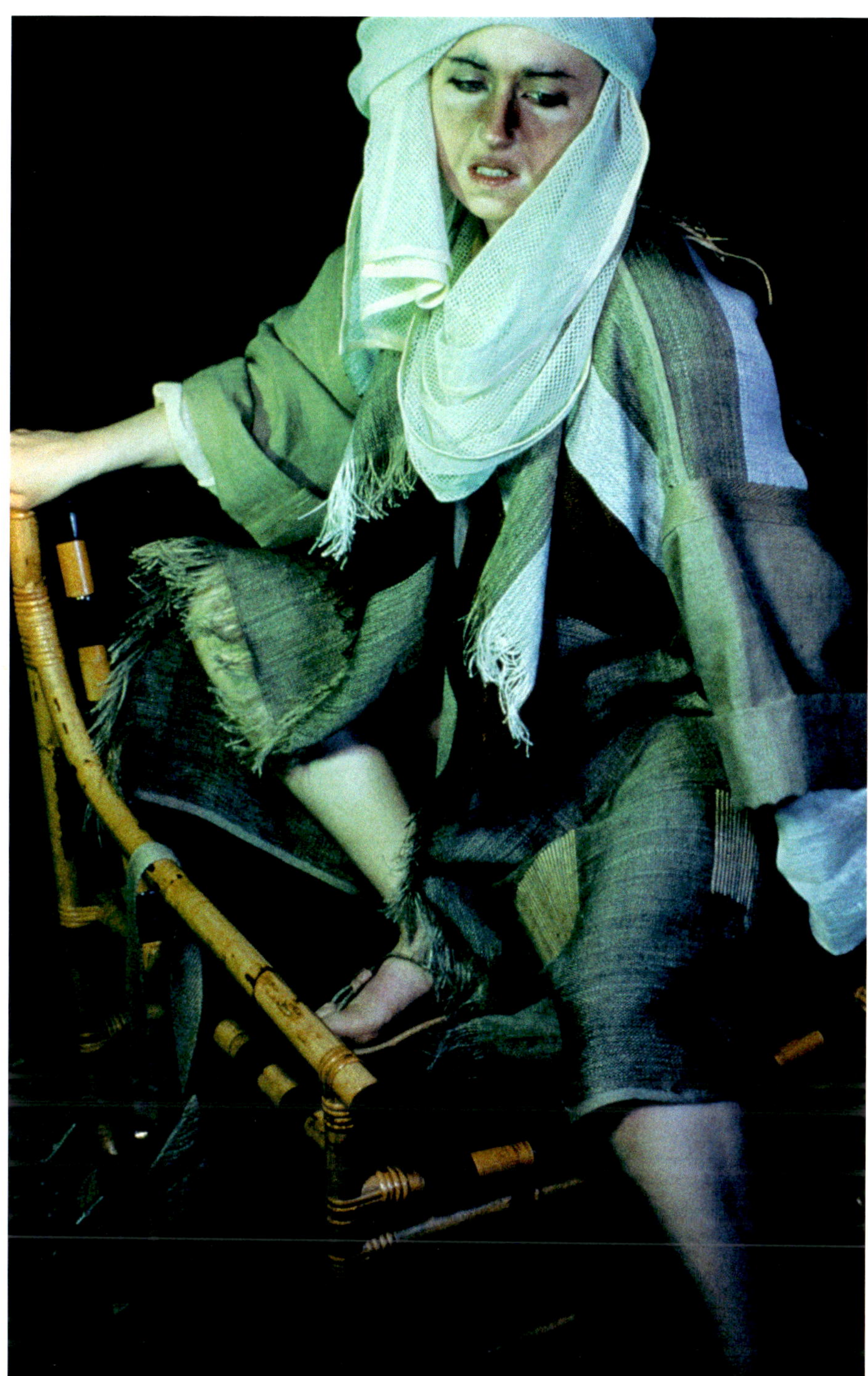

Untitled #145
Untitled #150
Untitled #146
Untitled #155
Untitled #156

1985

[Fairy Tales]

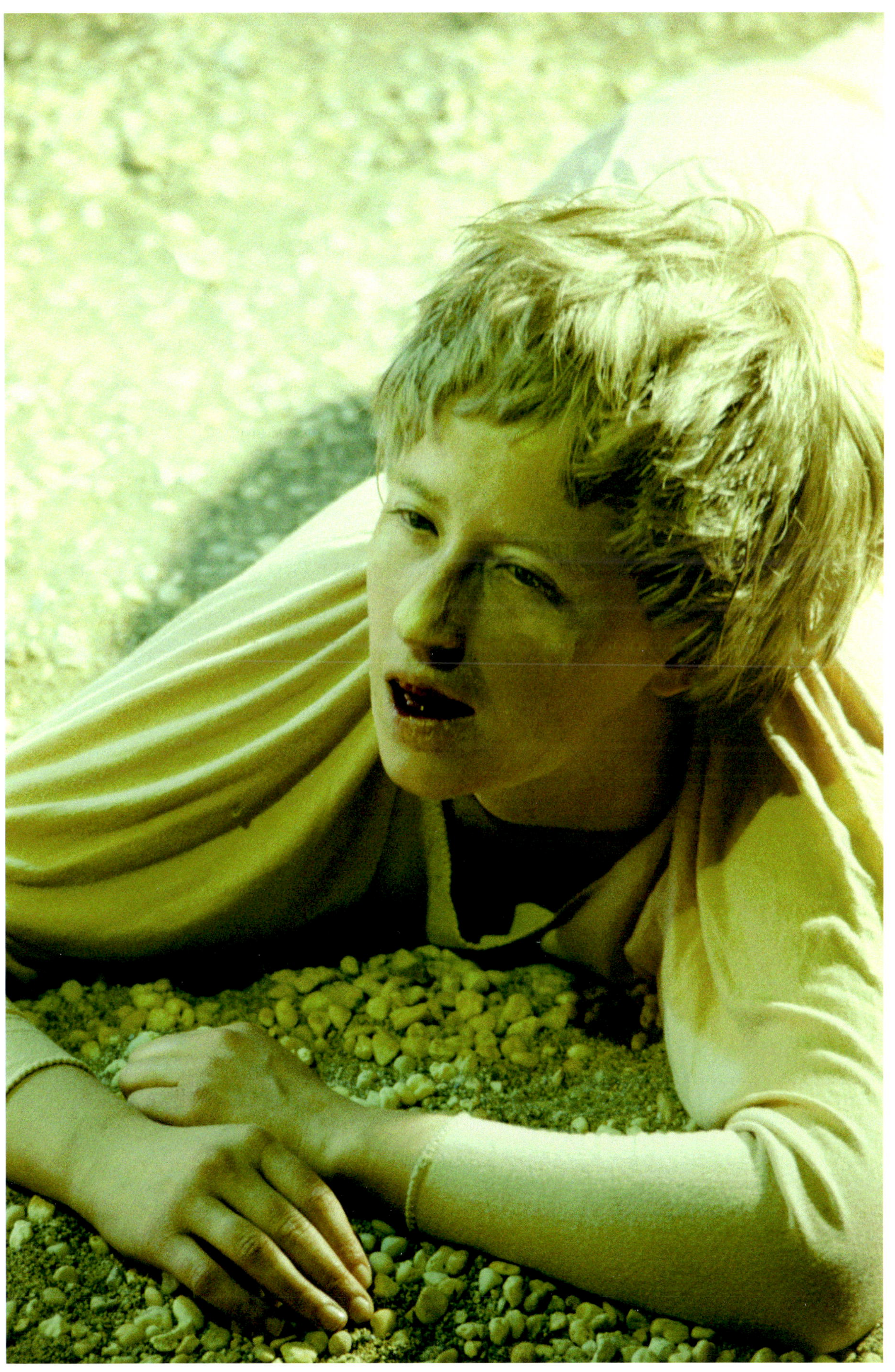

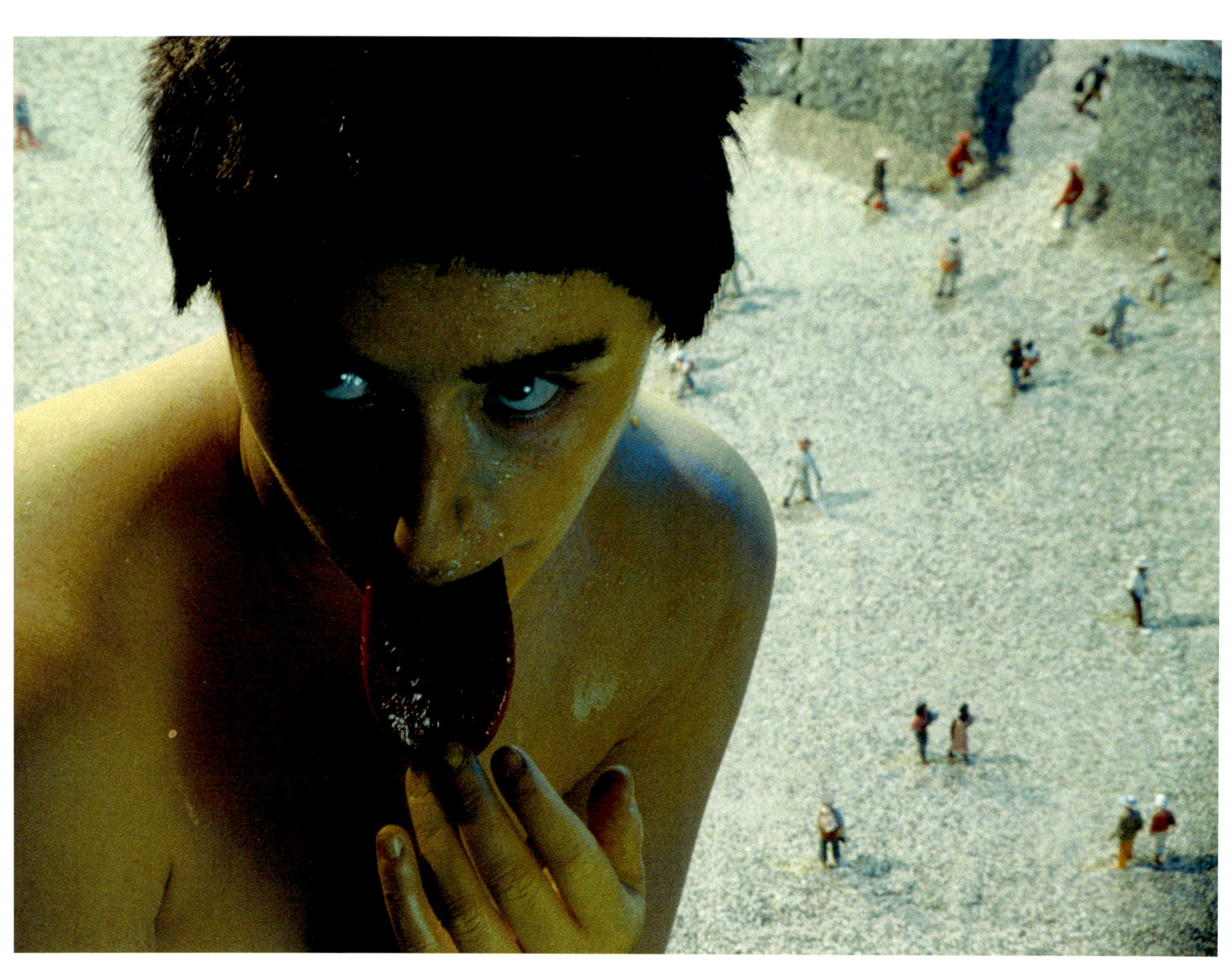

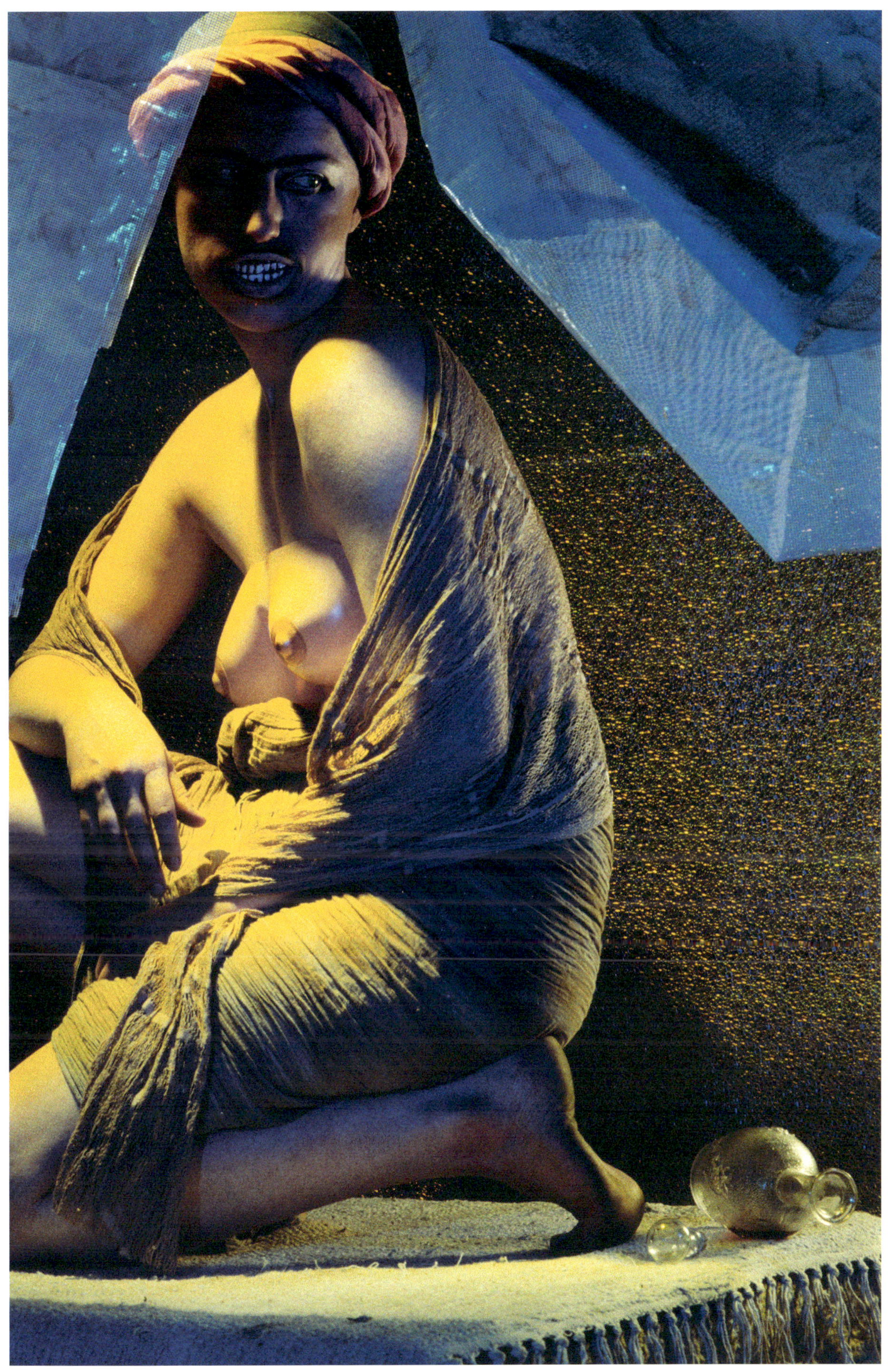

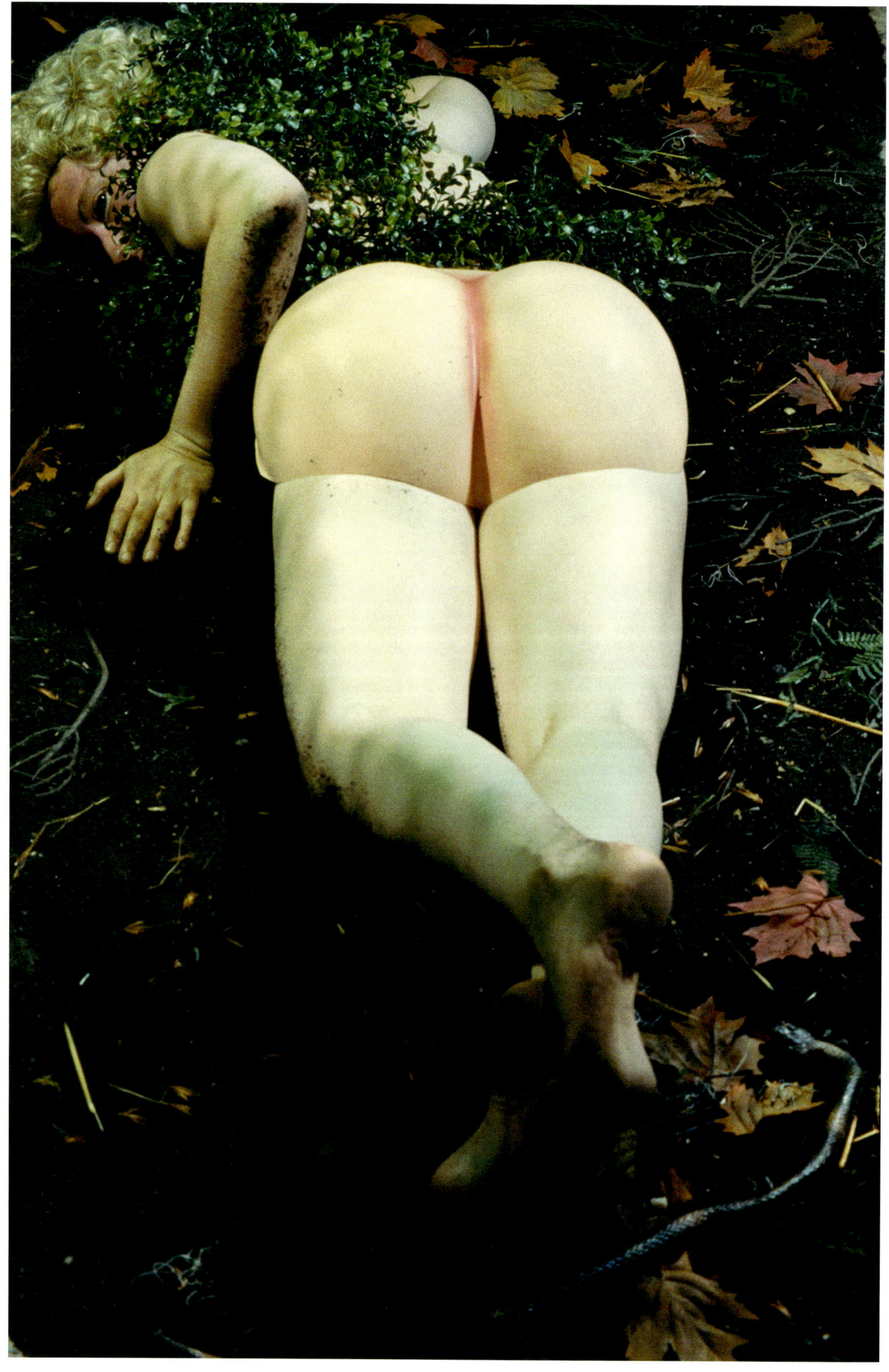

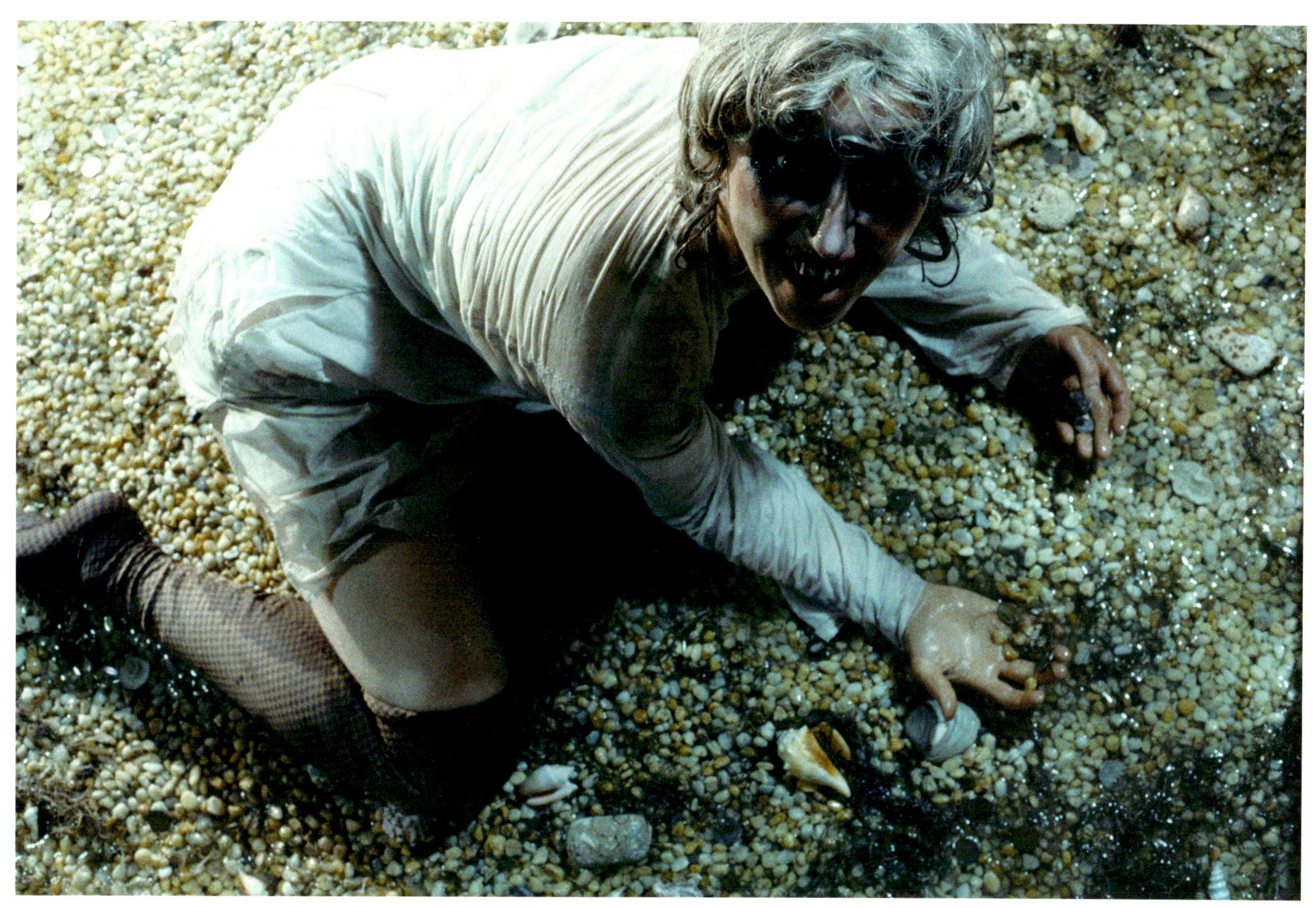

Untitled #168
Untitled #173
Untitled #175
Untitled #191
Untitled #188
Untitled #186
Untitled #174

1986—1989

[Disasters]

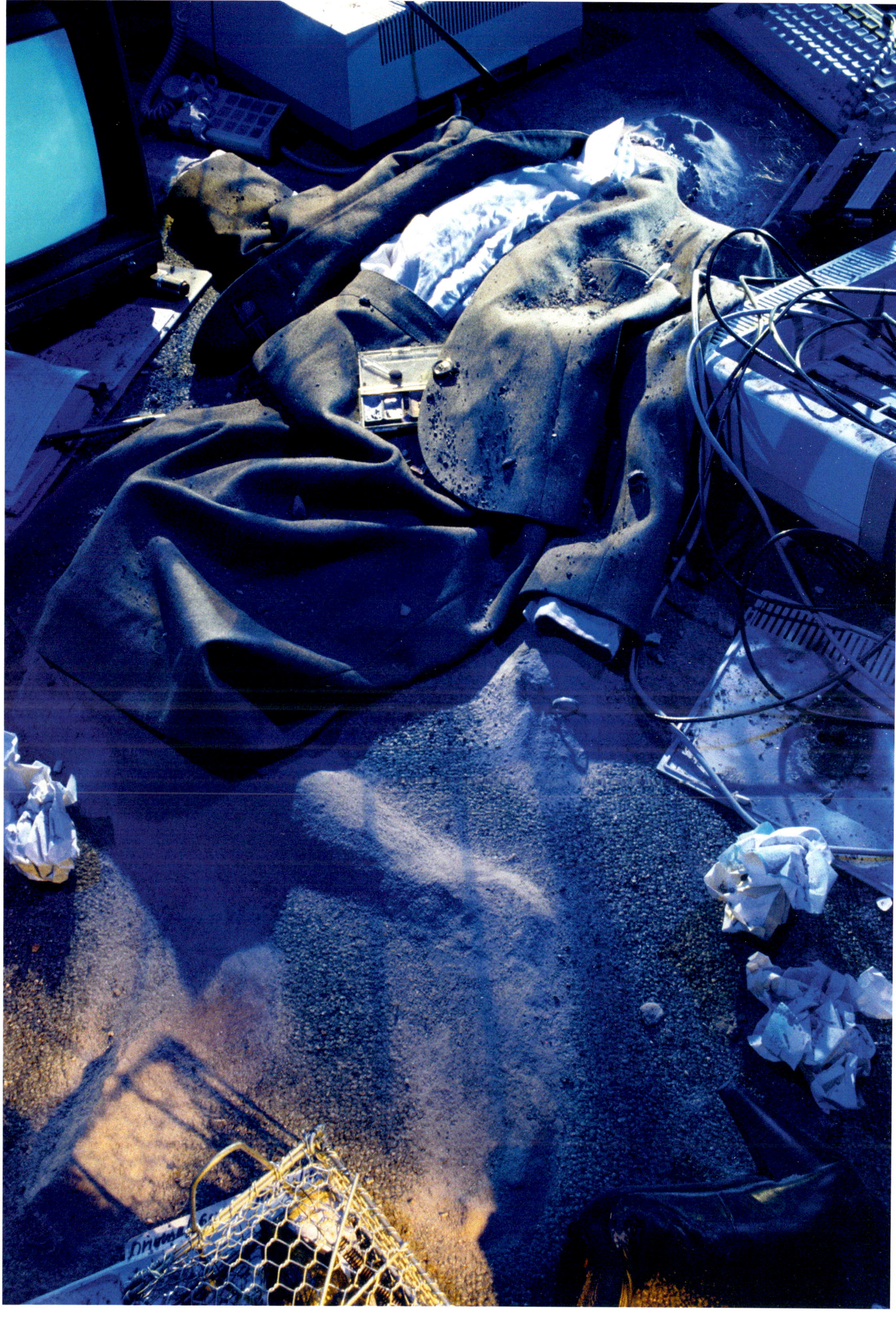

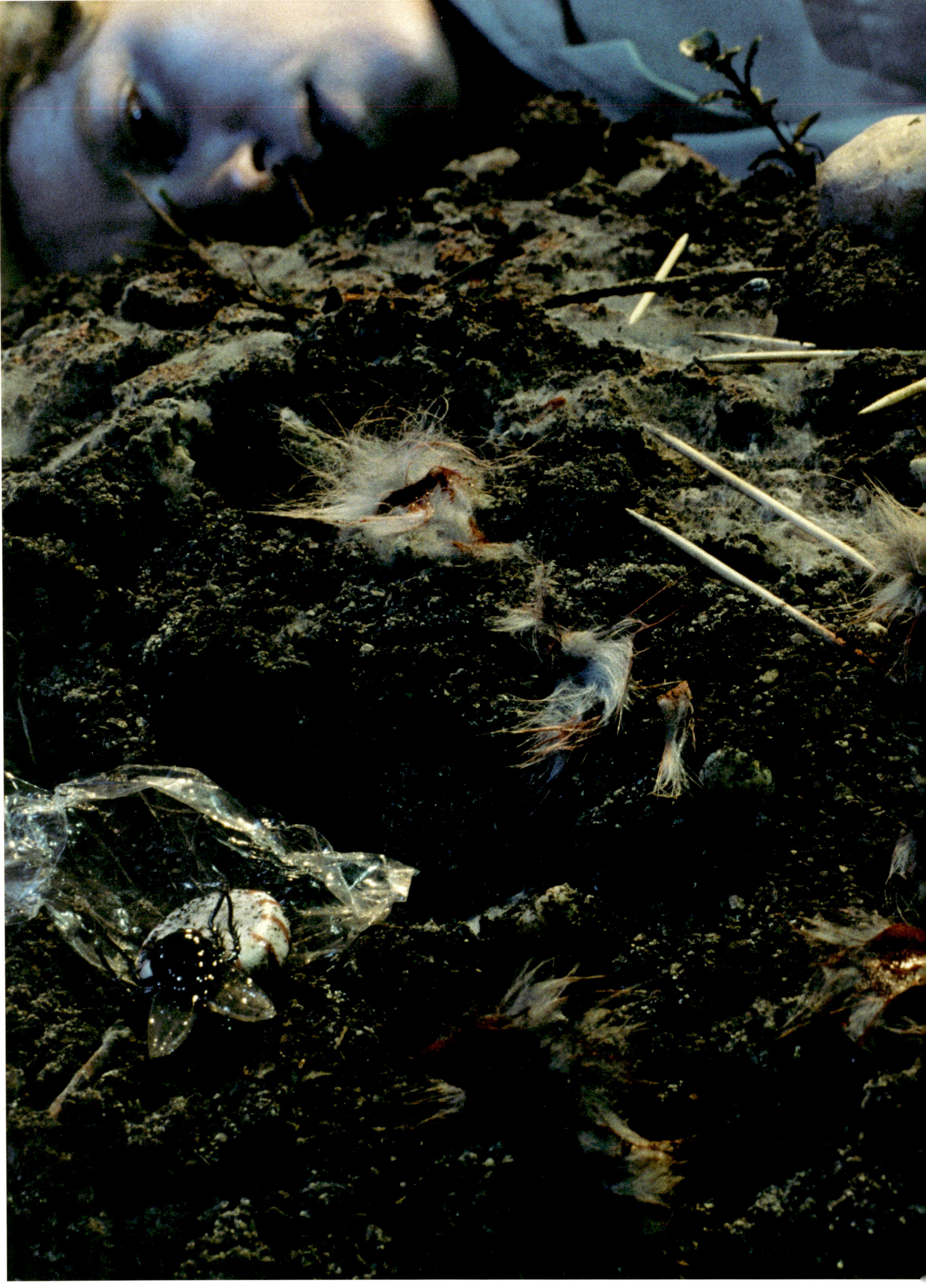

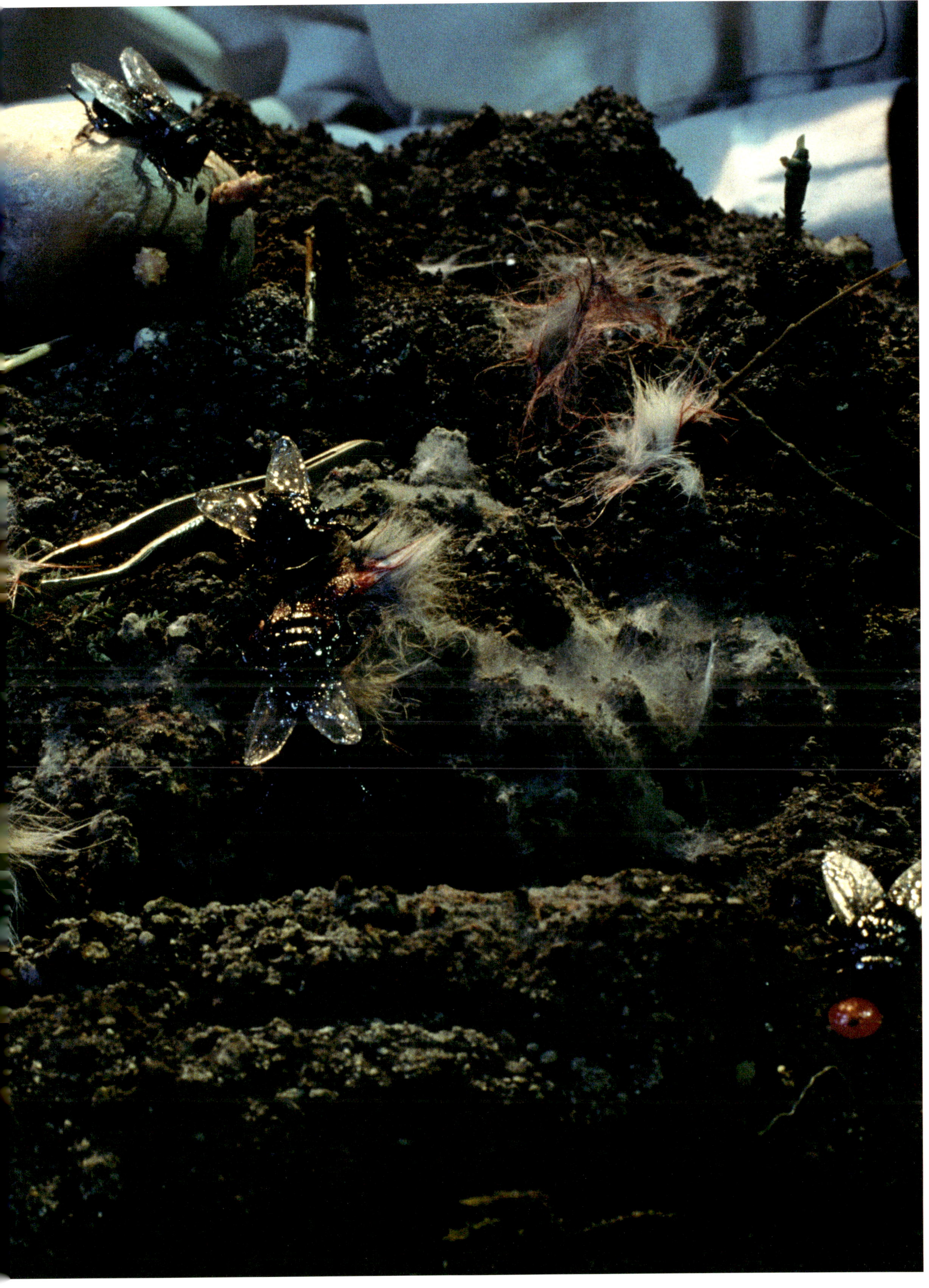

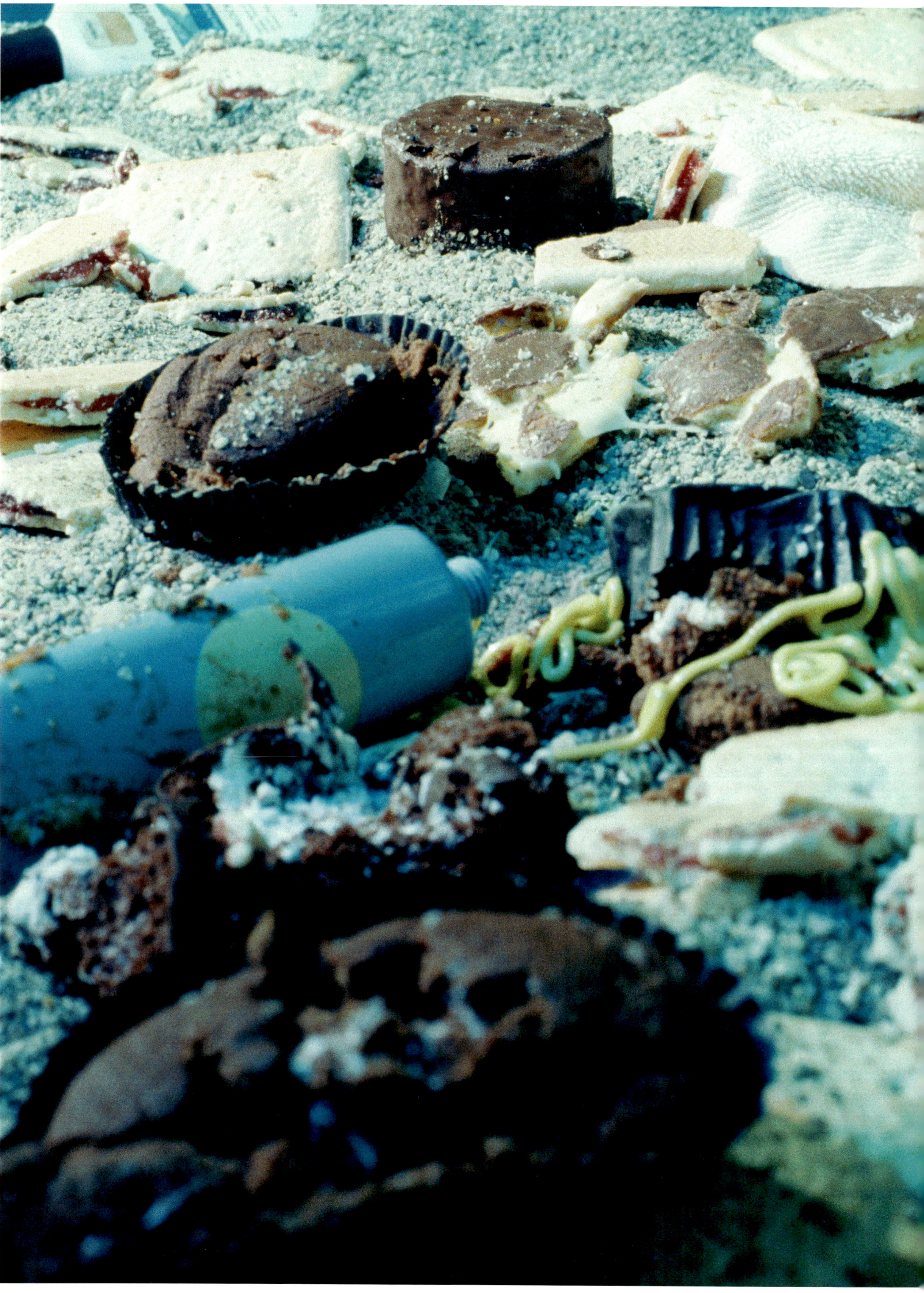

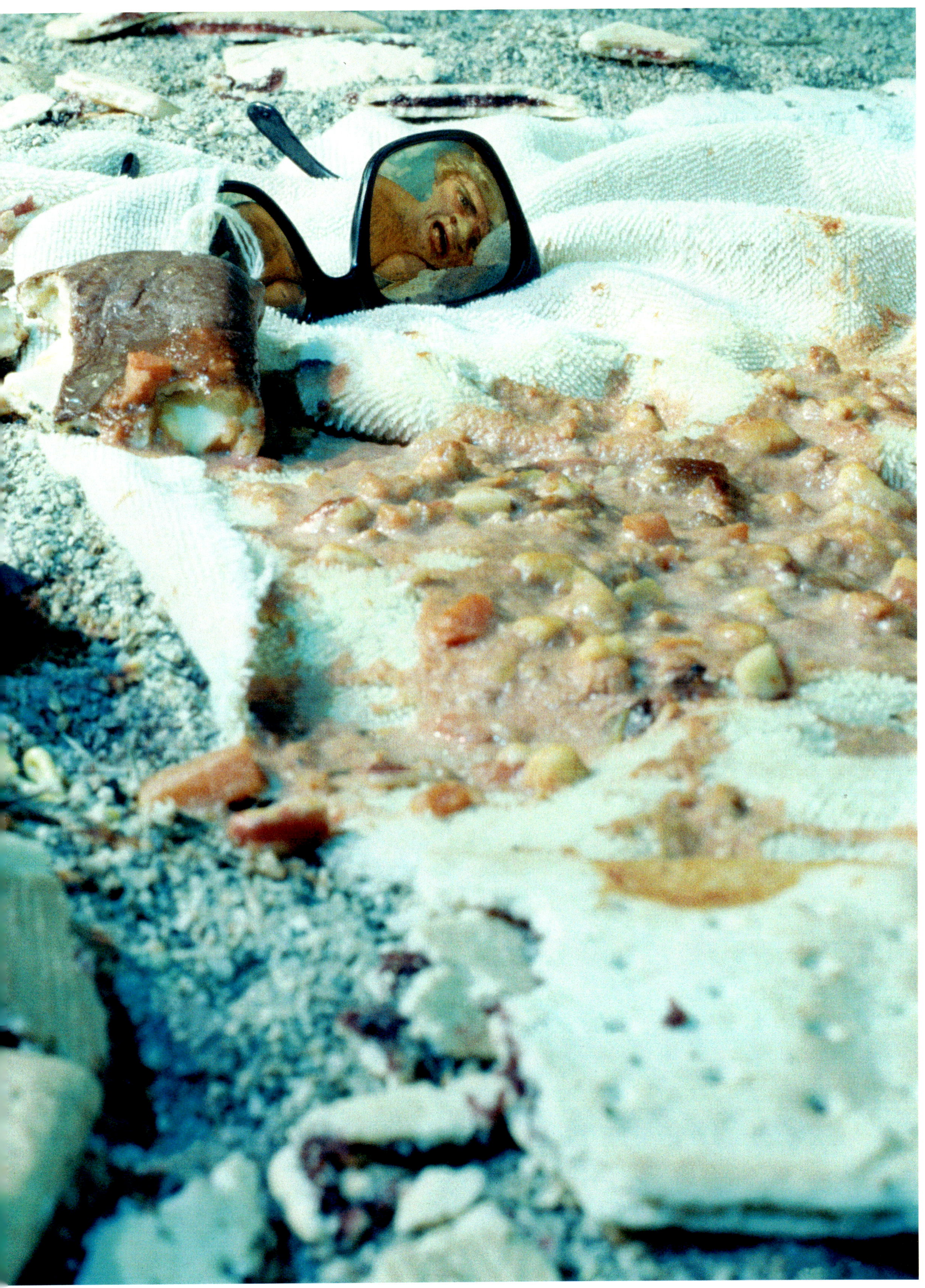

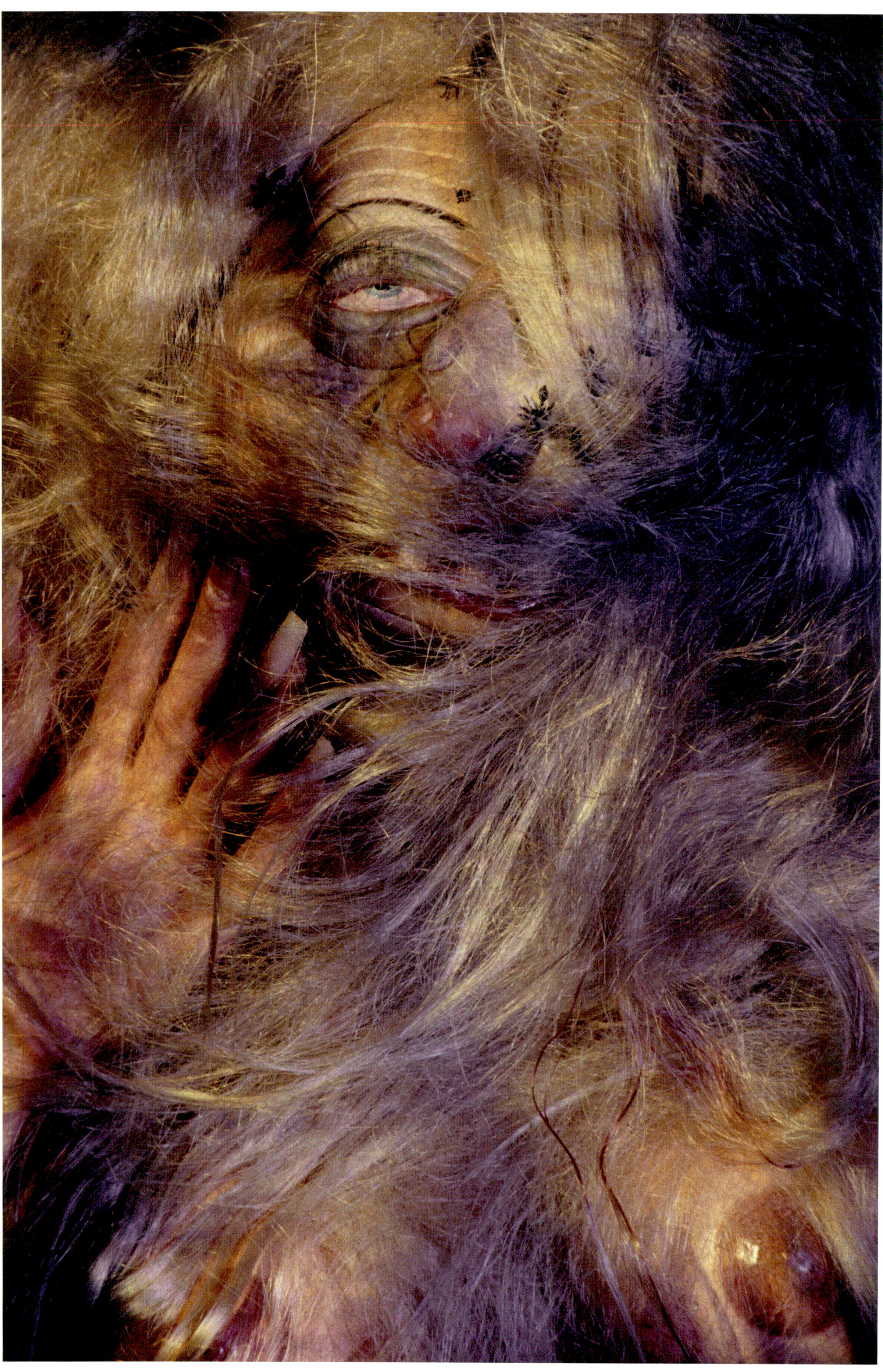

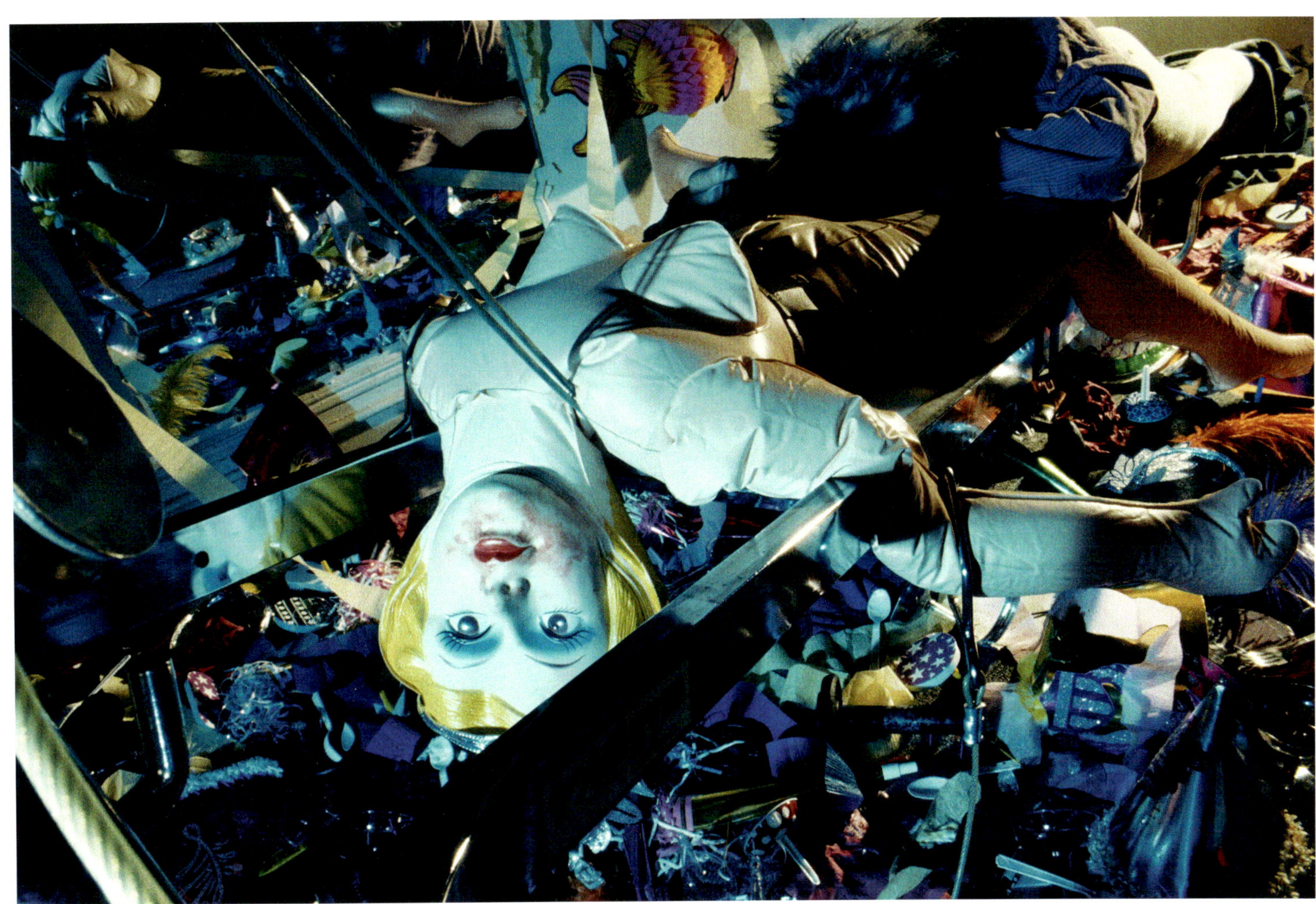

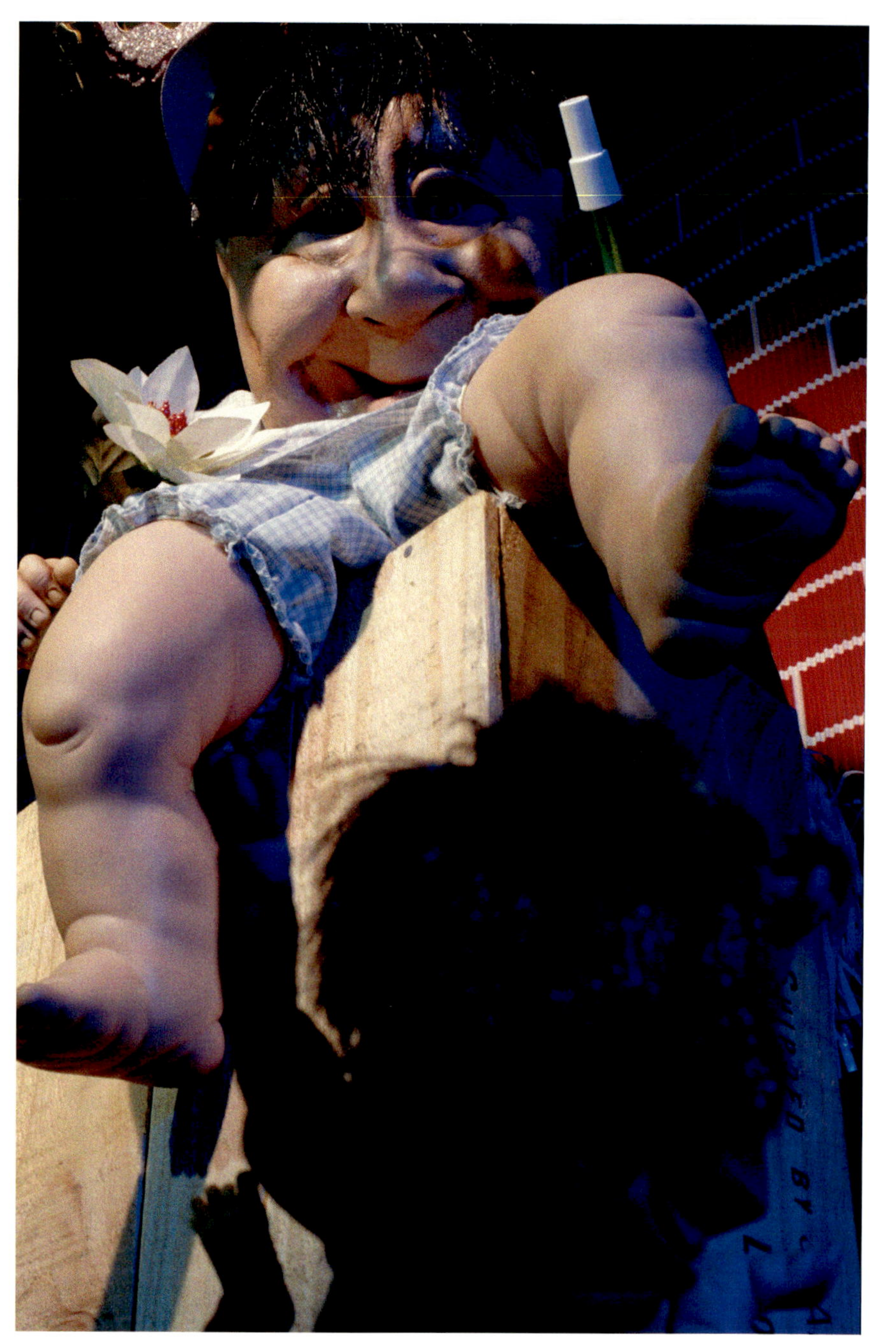

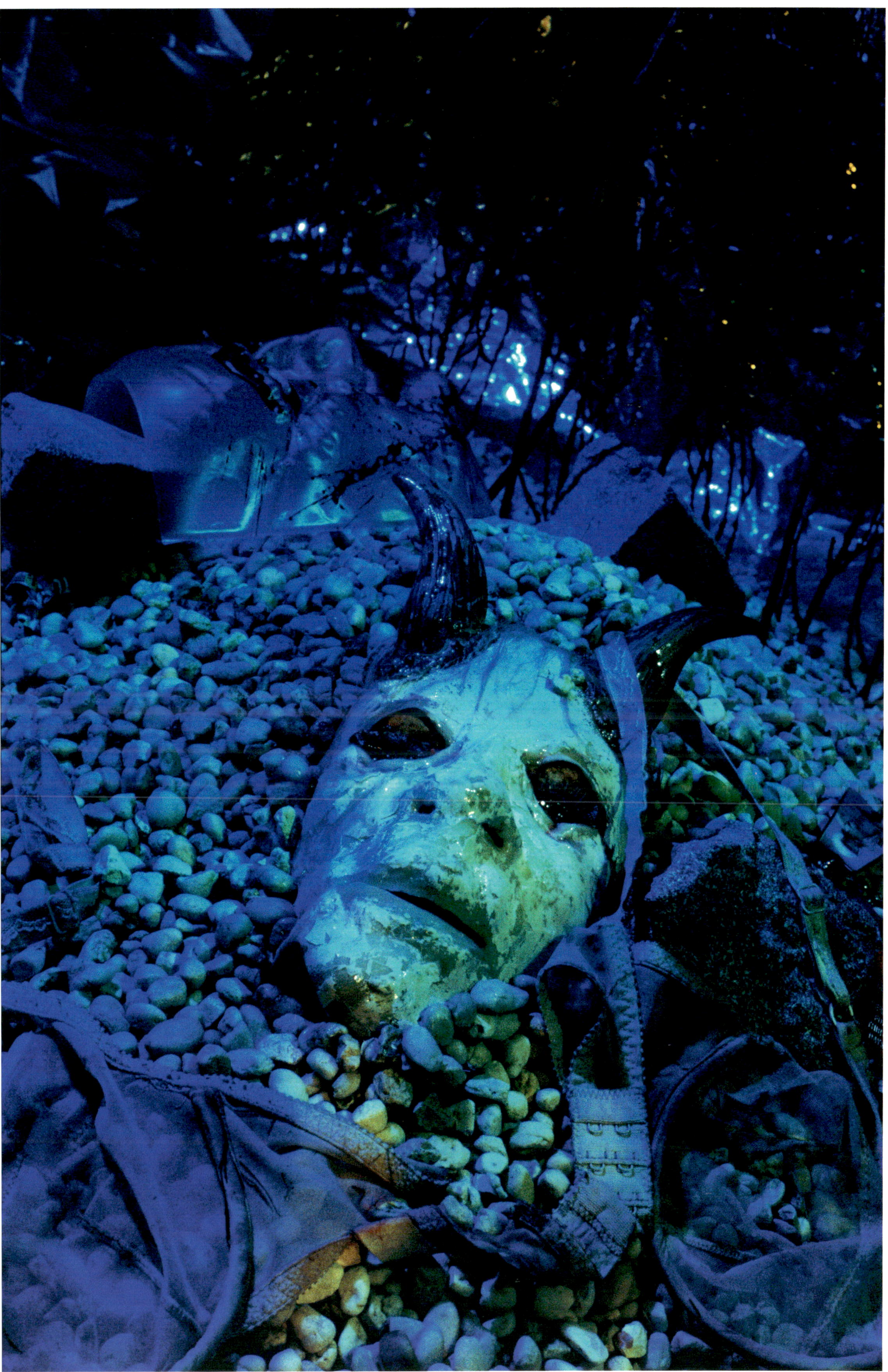

Untitled #193
Untitled #224
Untitled #198
Untitled #214
Untitled #210
Untitled #216
Untitled #194
Untitled #200
Untitled #212
Untitled #205
Untitled #226
Untitled #197
Untitled #228
Untitled #206
Untitled #211
Untitled #183
Untitled #195
Untitled #213
Untitled #221
Untitled #199
Untitled #222
Untitled #196
Untitled #215
Untitled #225
Untitled #209
Untitled #220

1988—1990

[History Portraits / Old Masters]

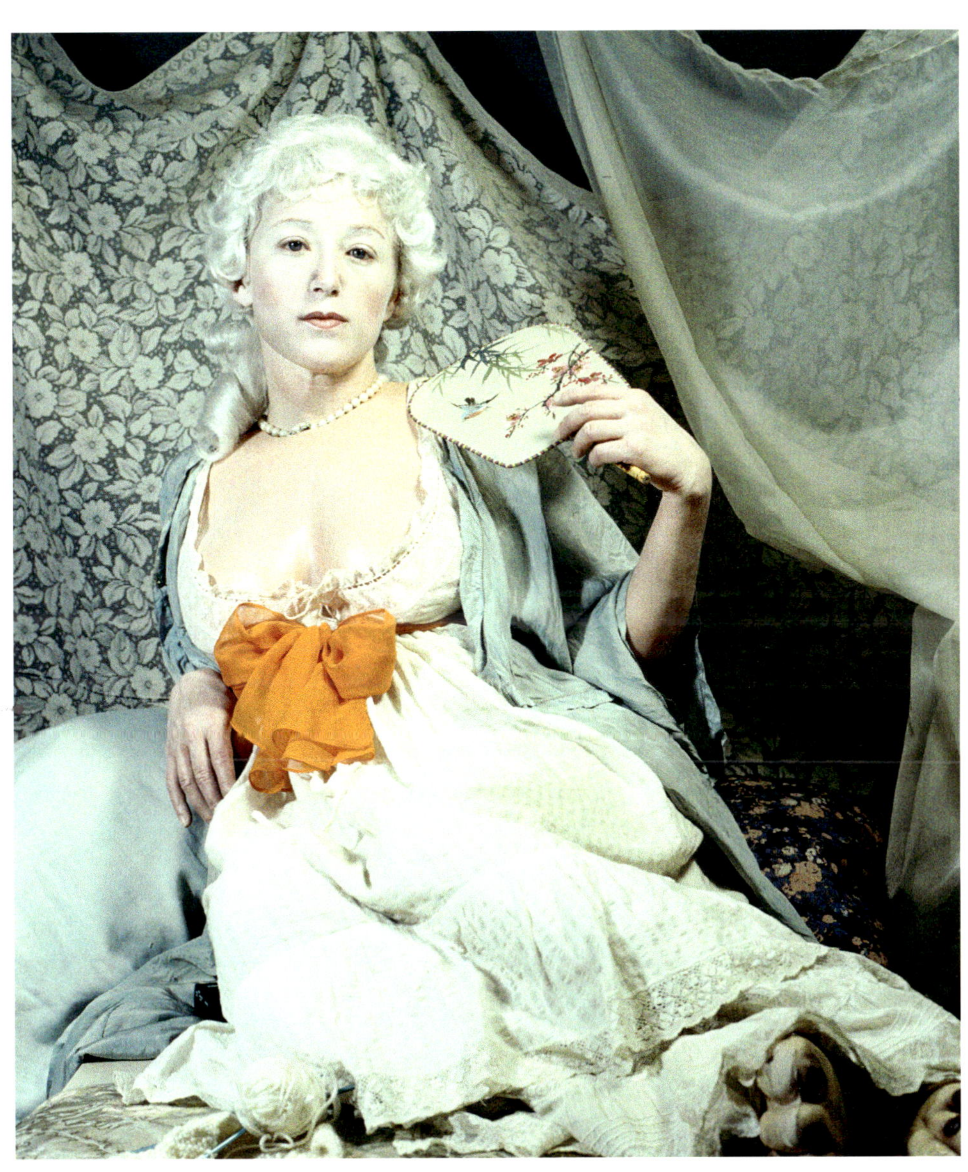

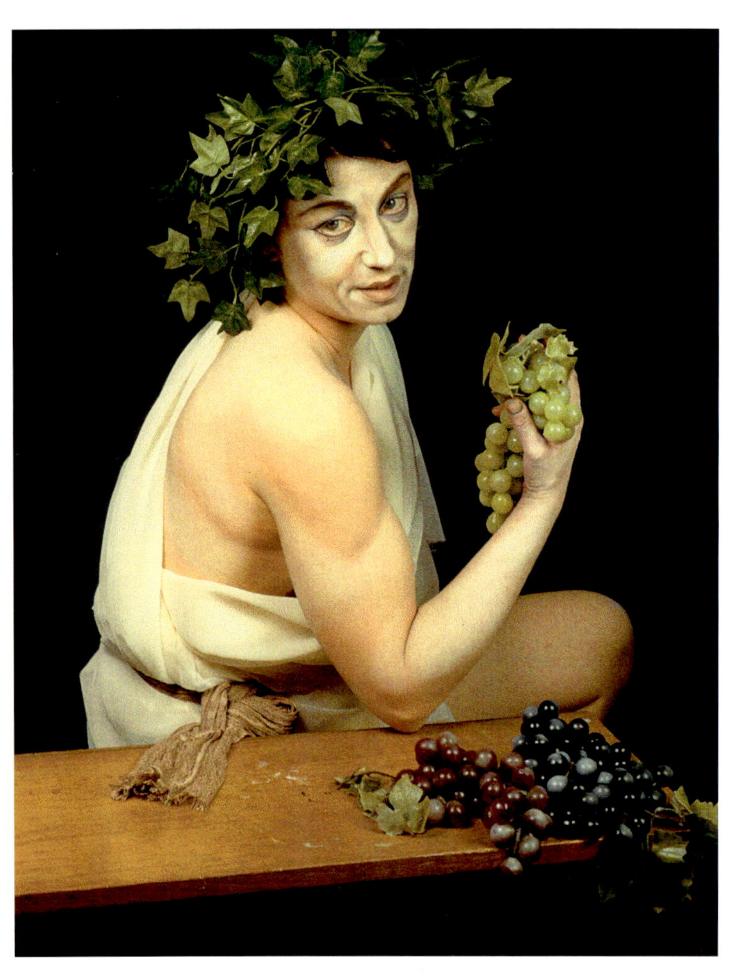

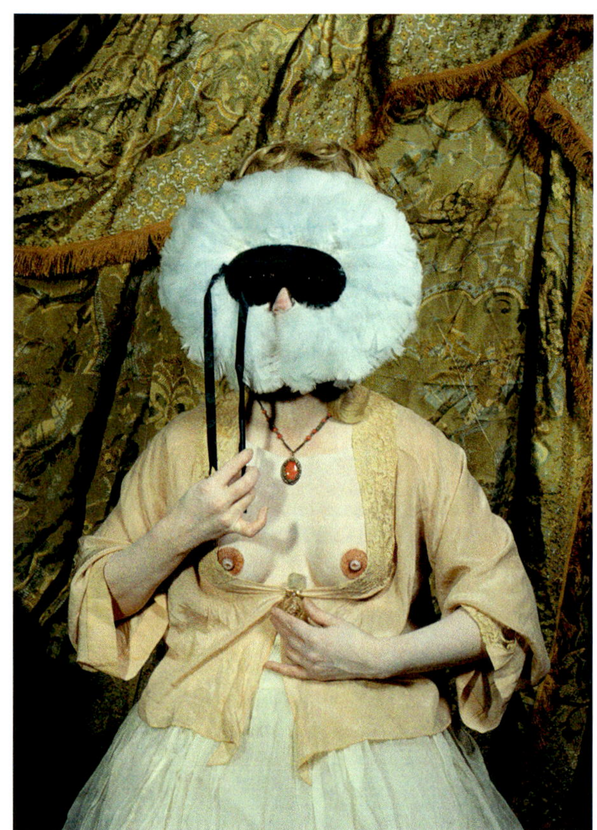

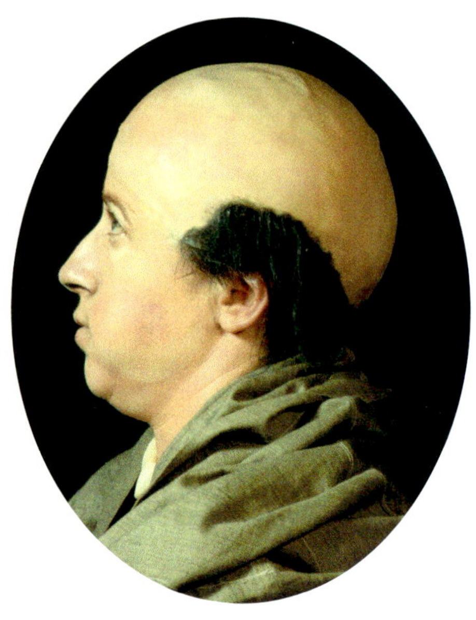

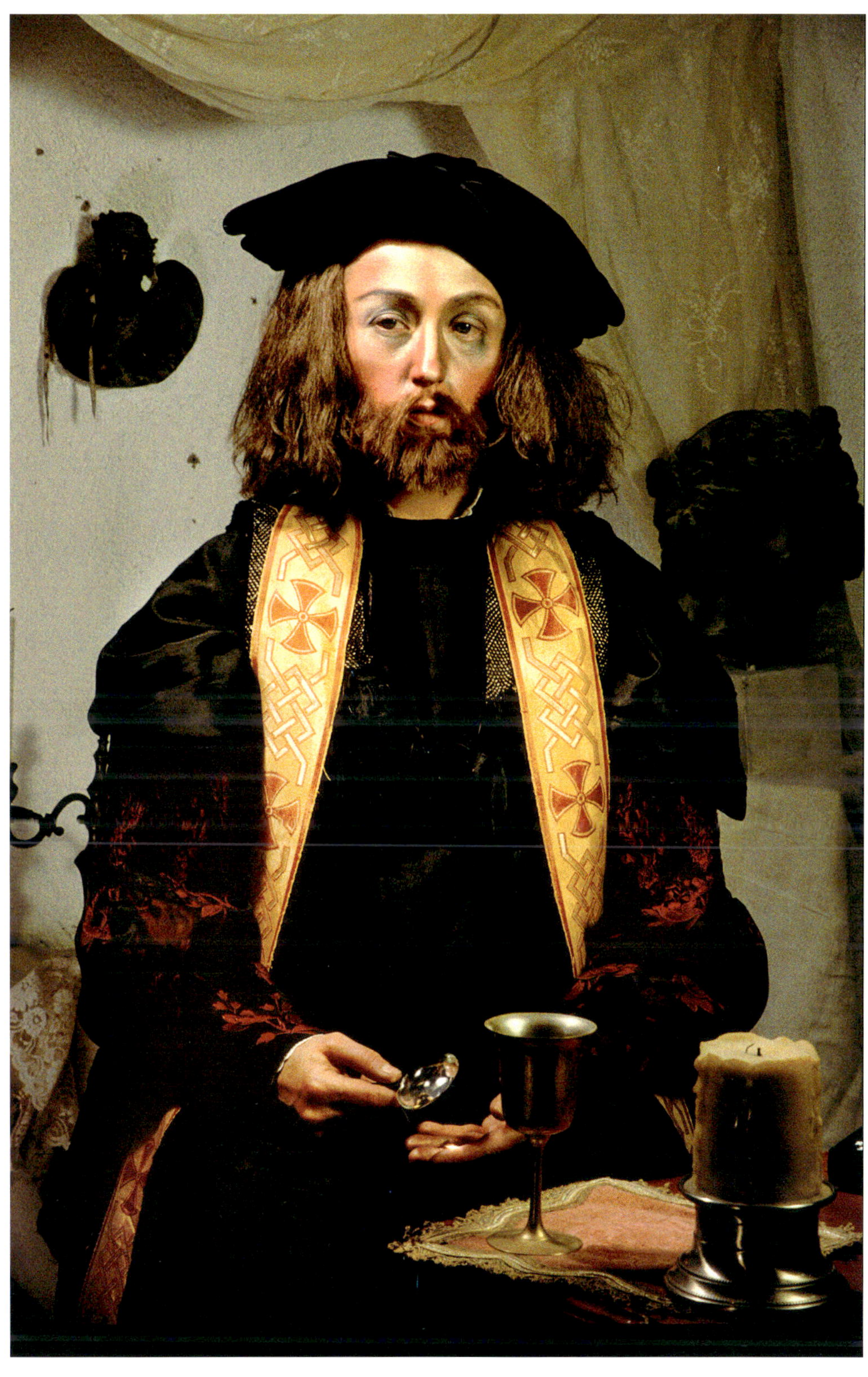

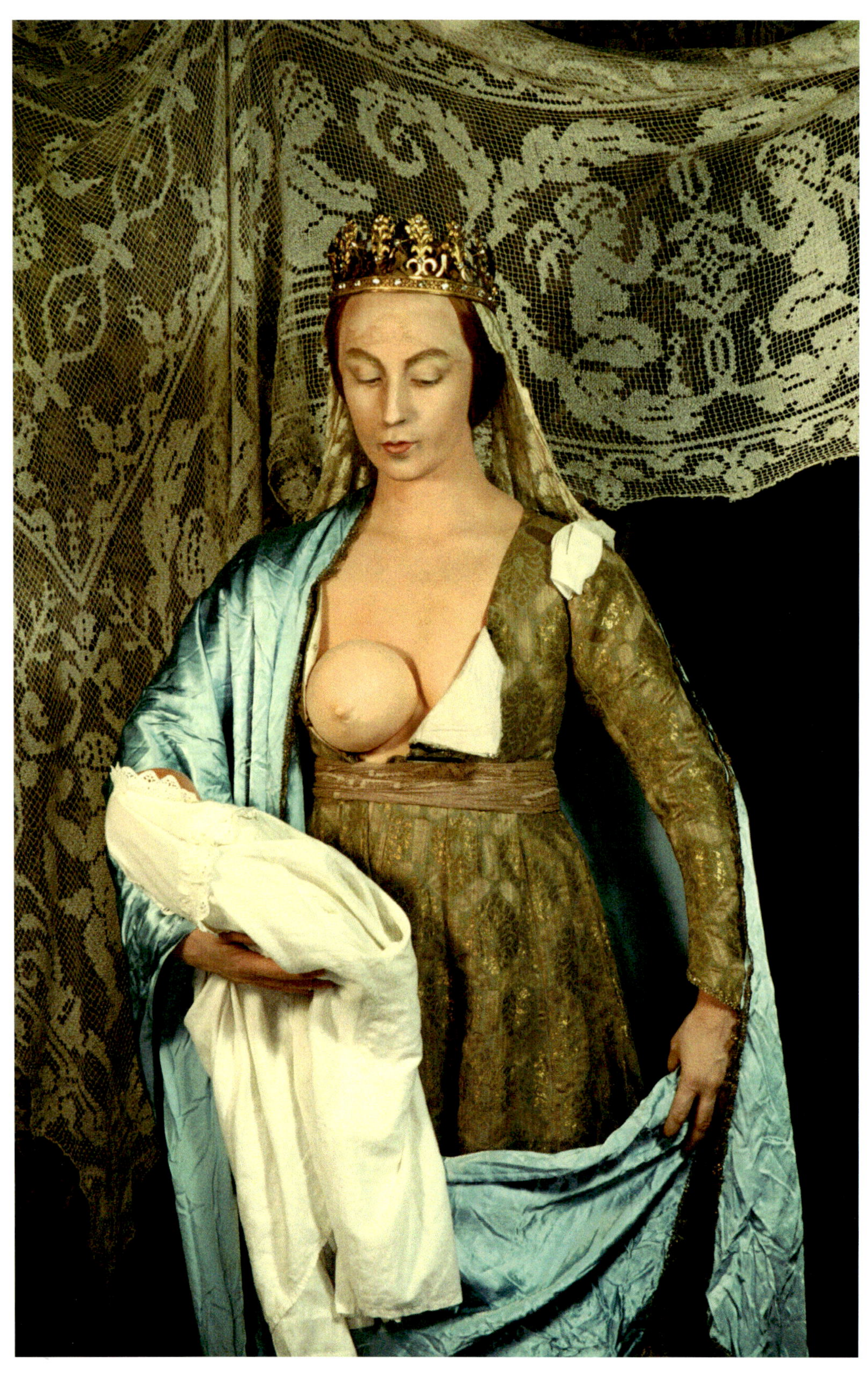

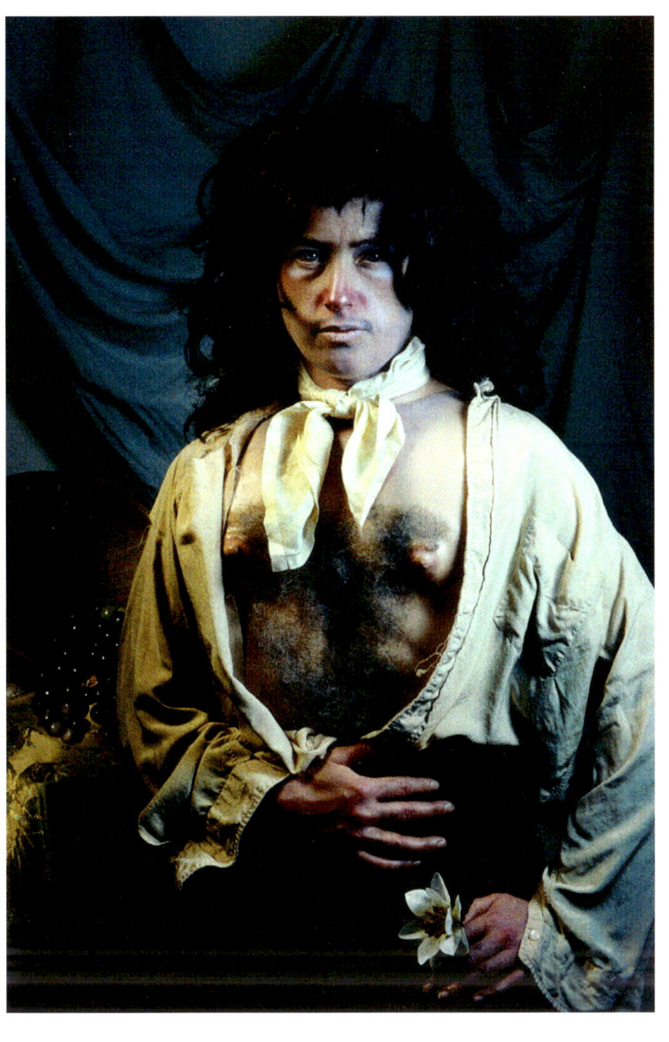
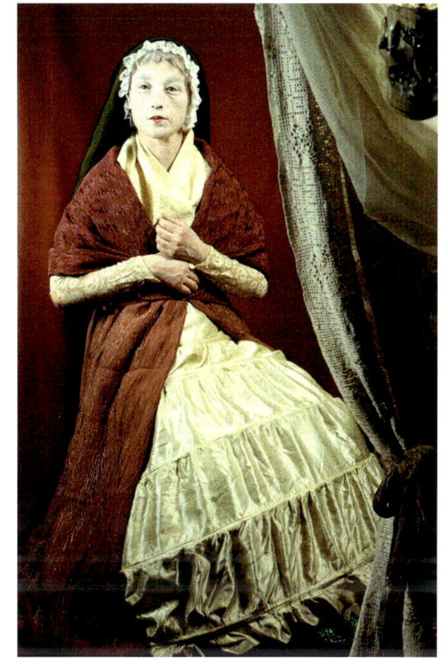
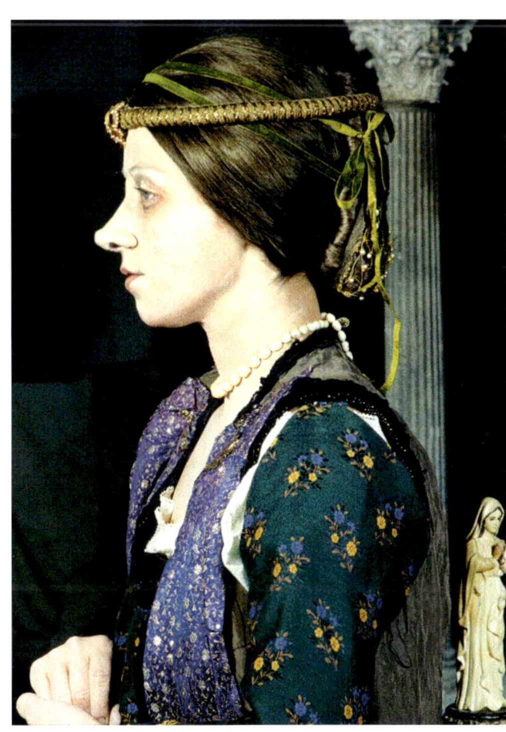

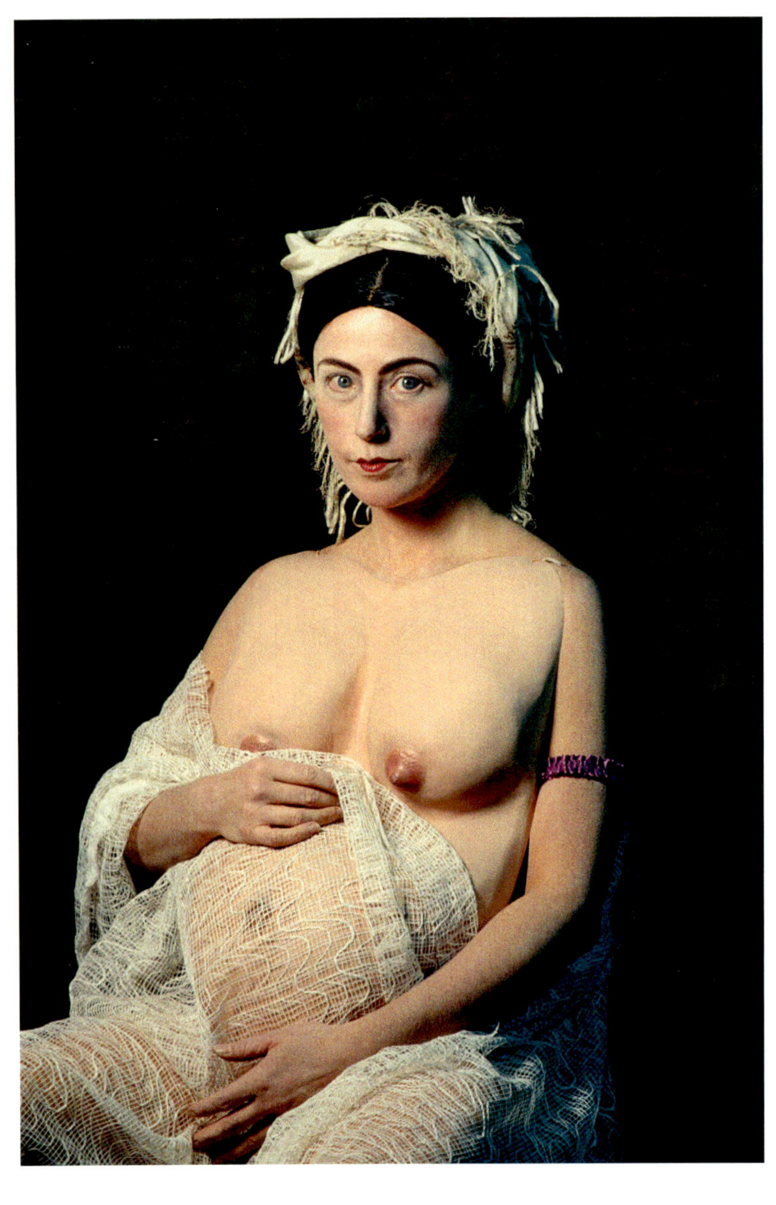

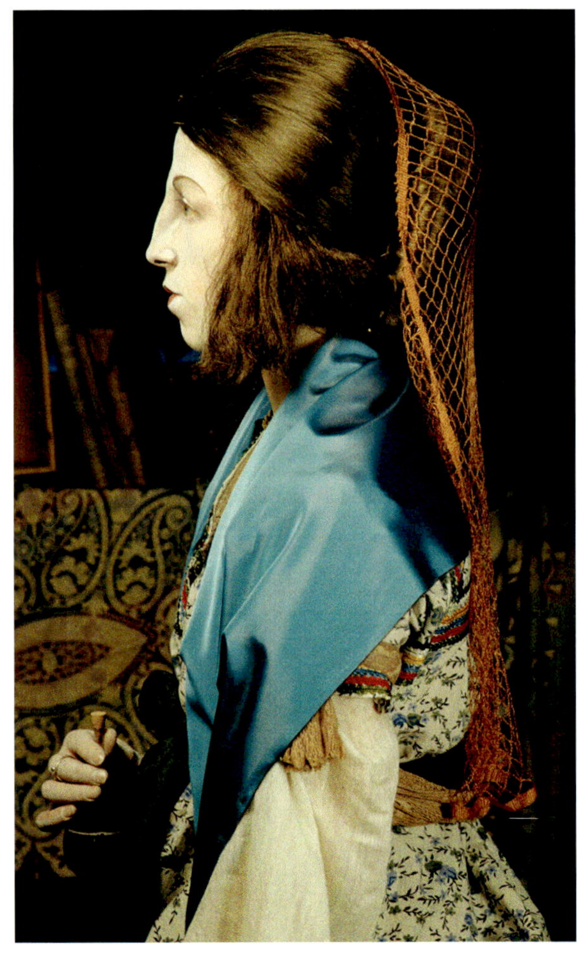

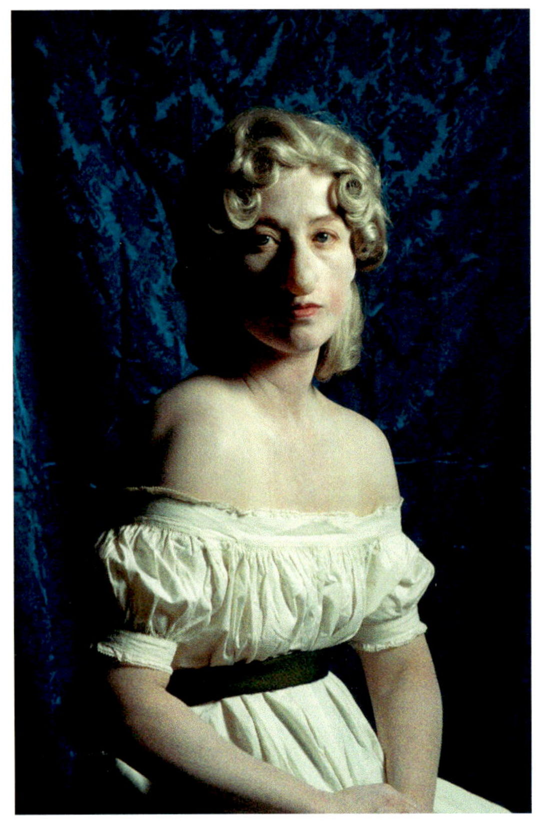

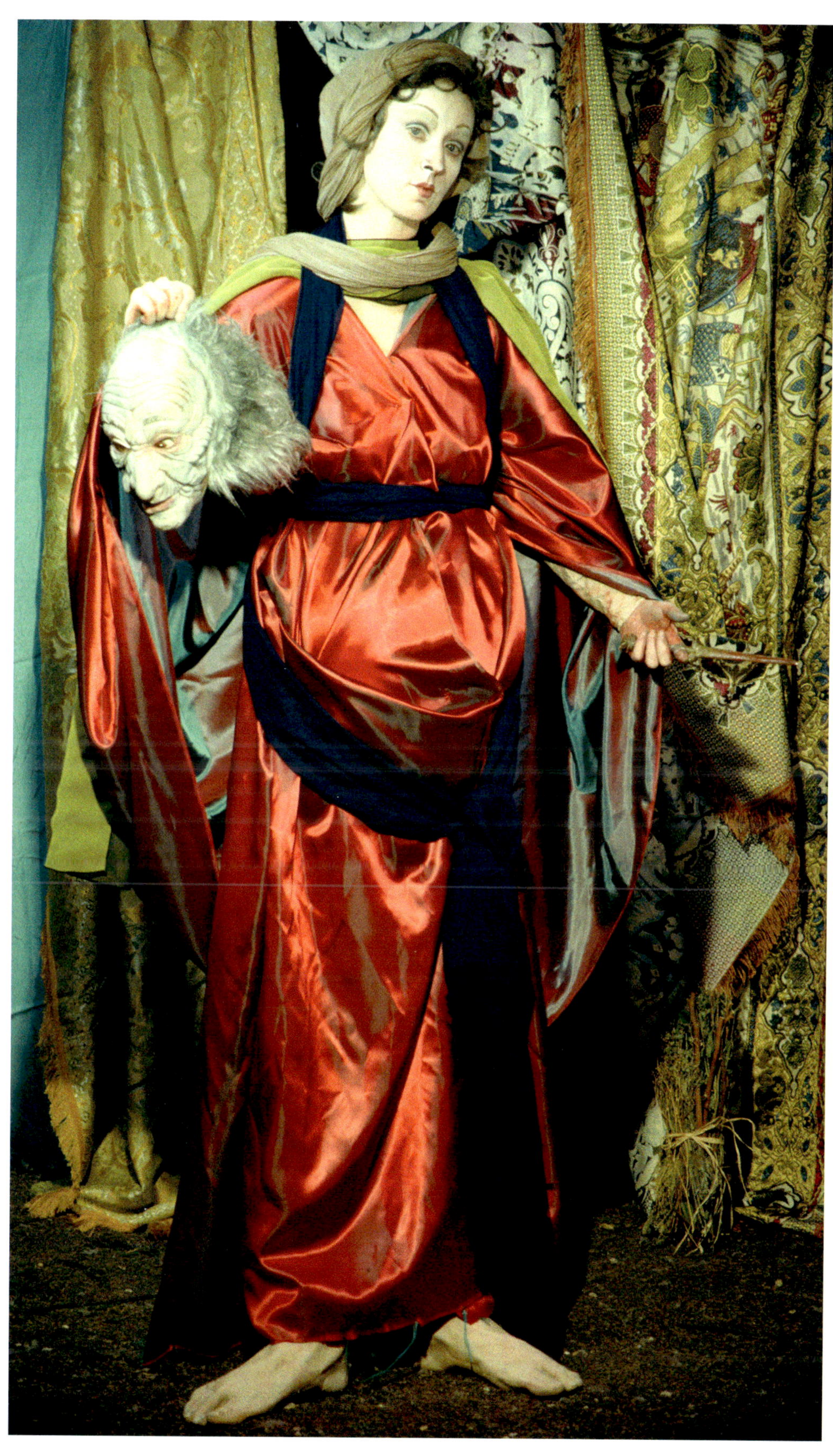

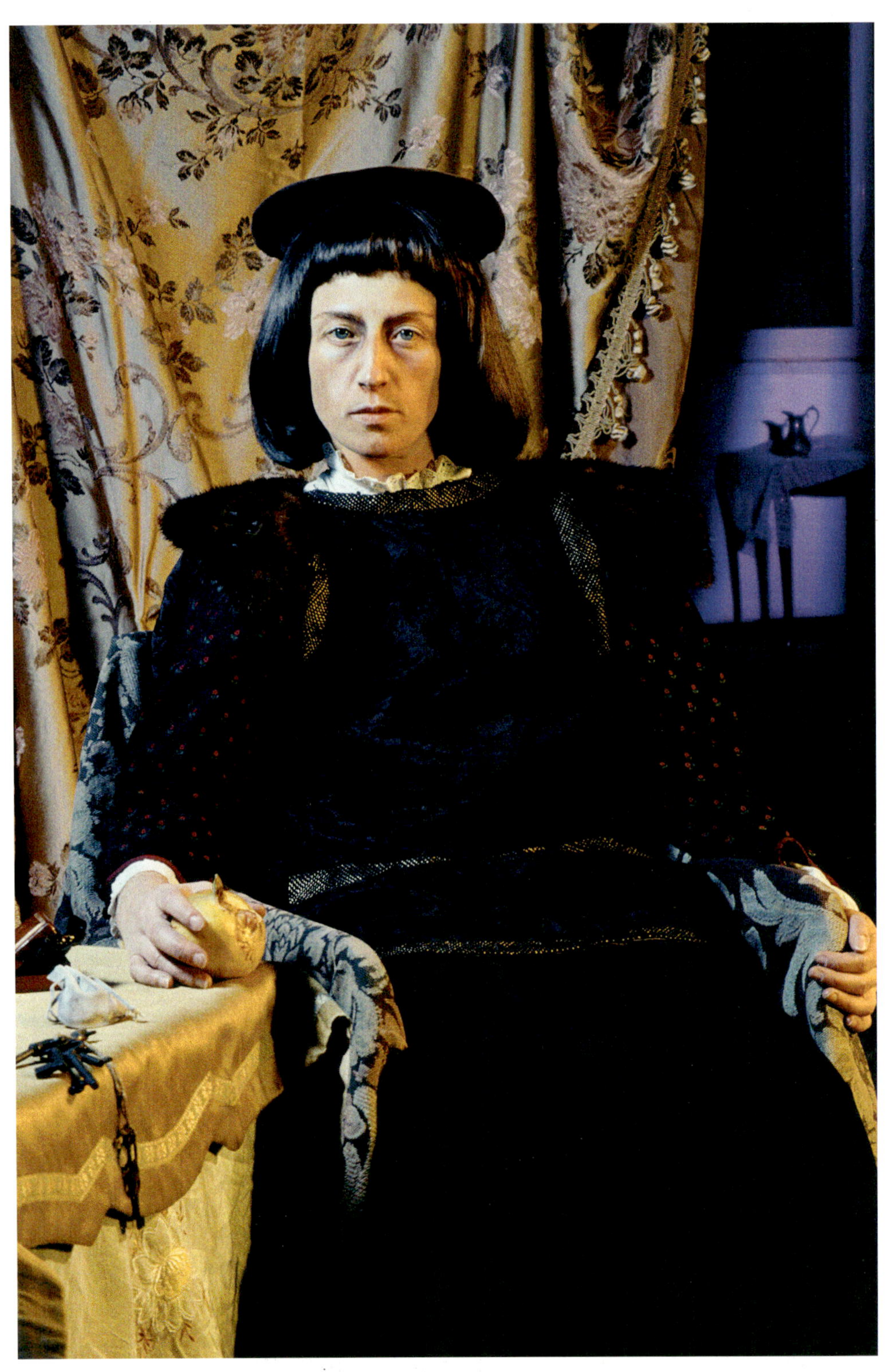

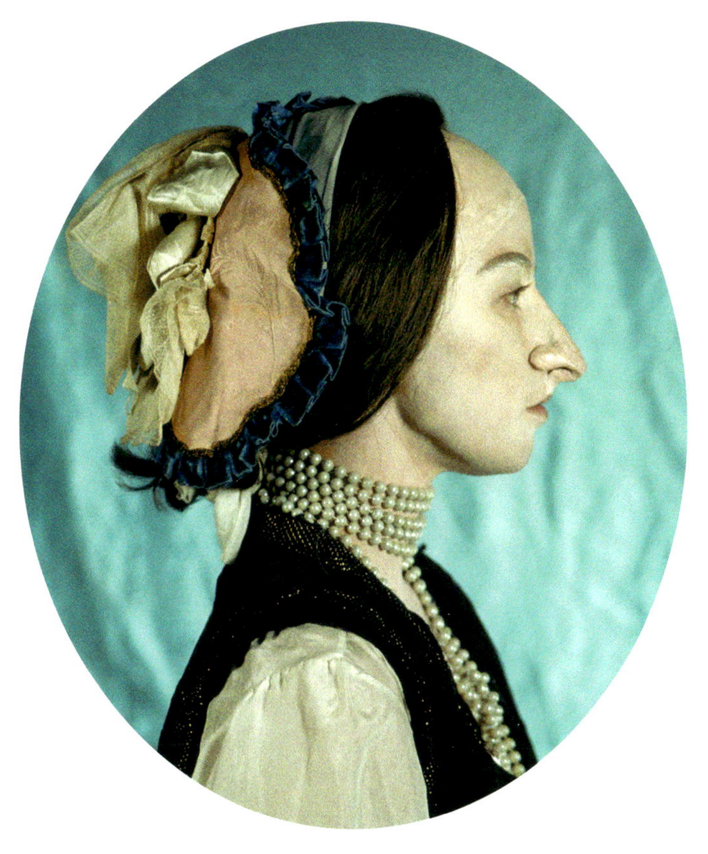

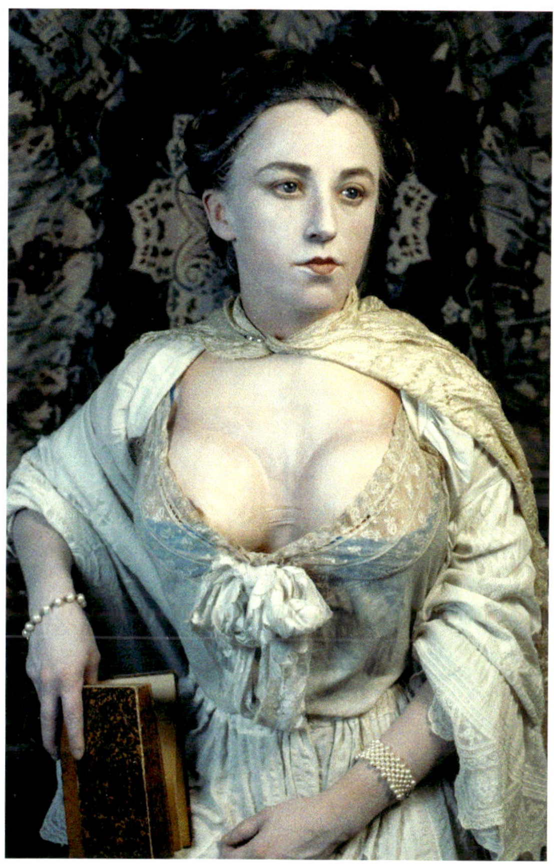

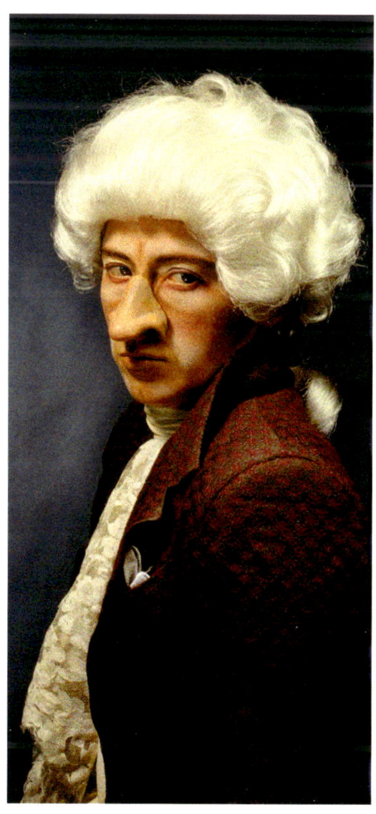

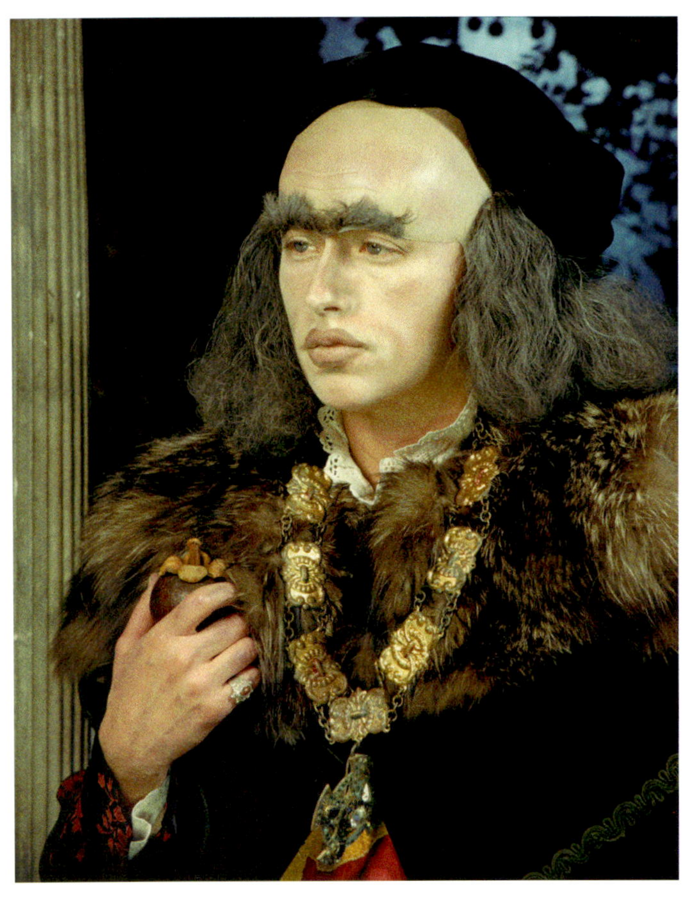
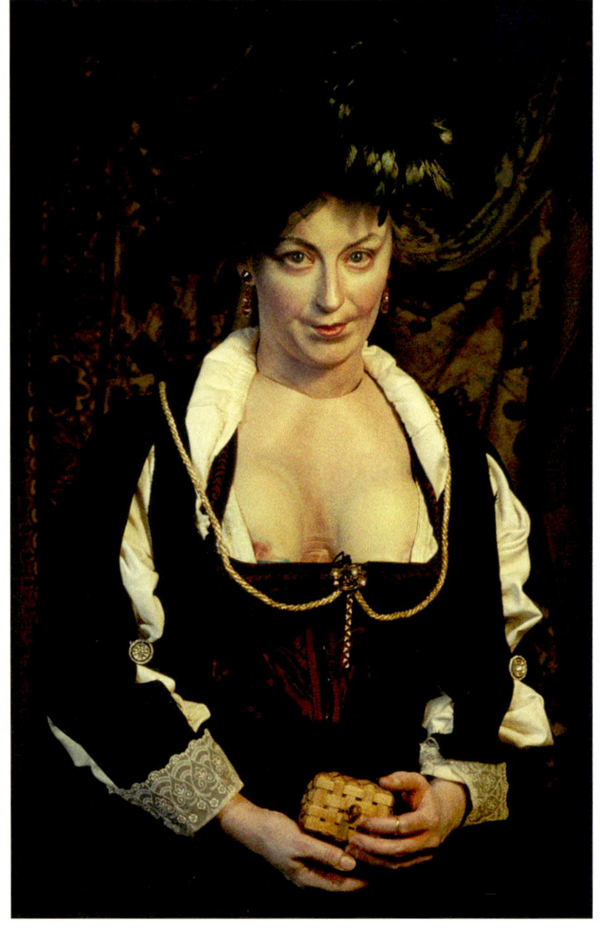
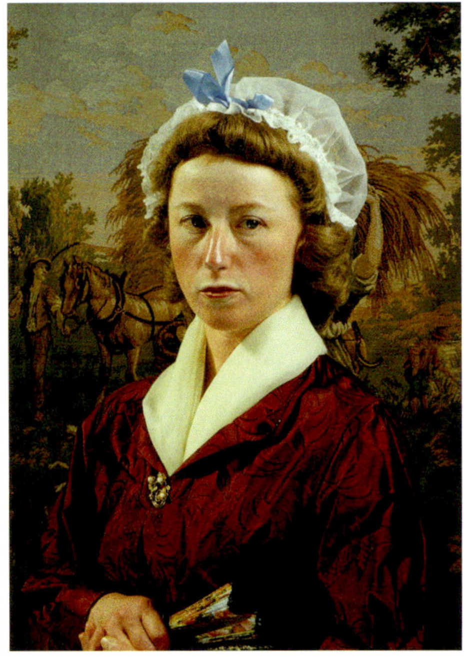

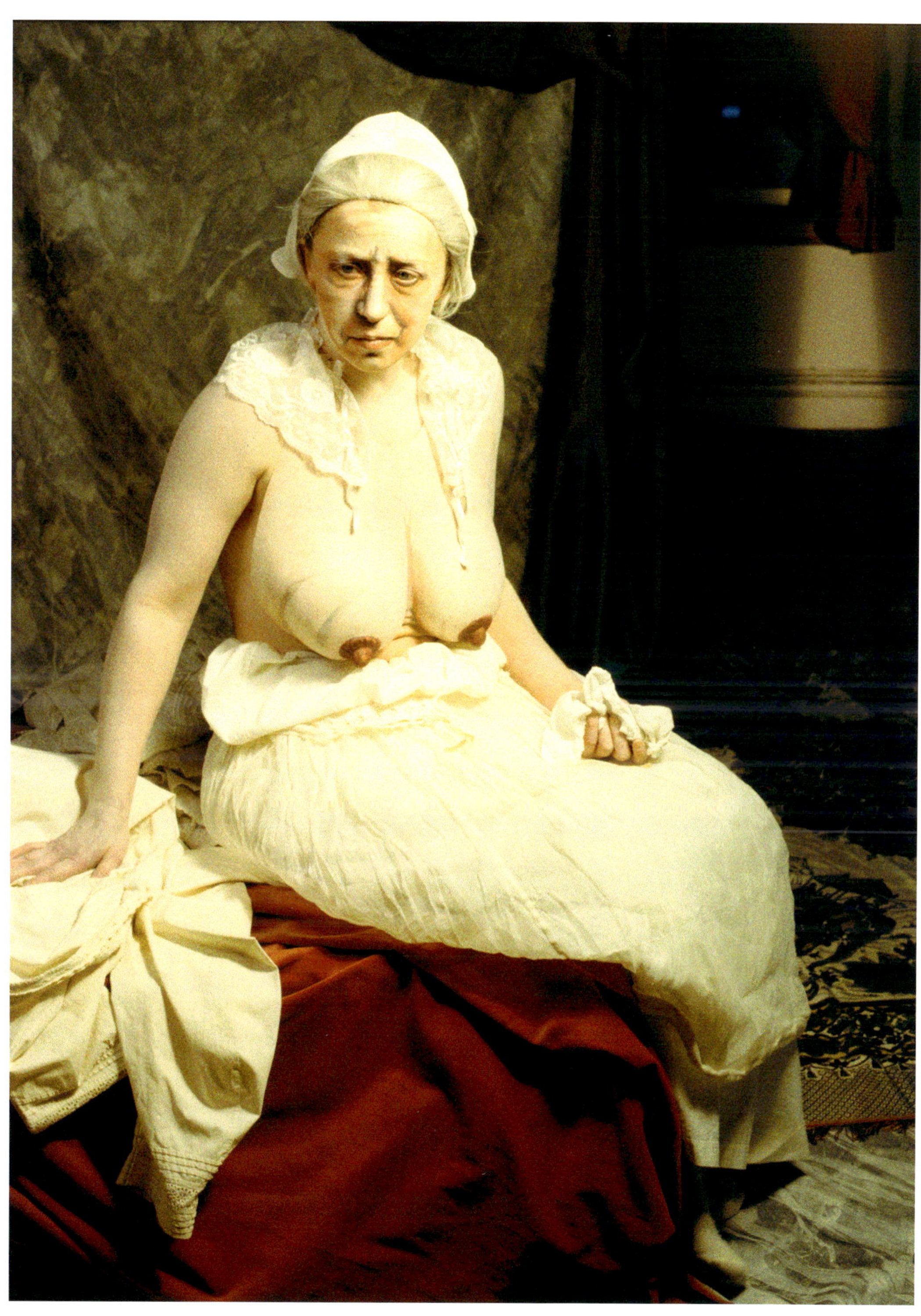

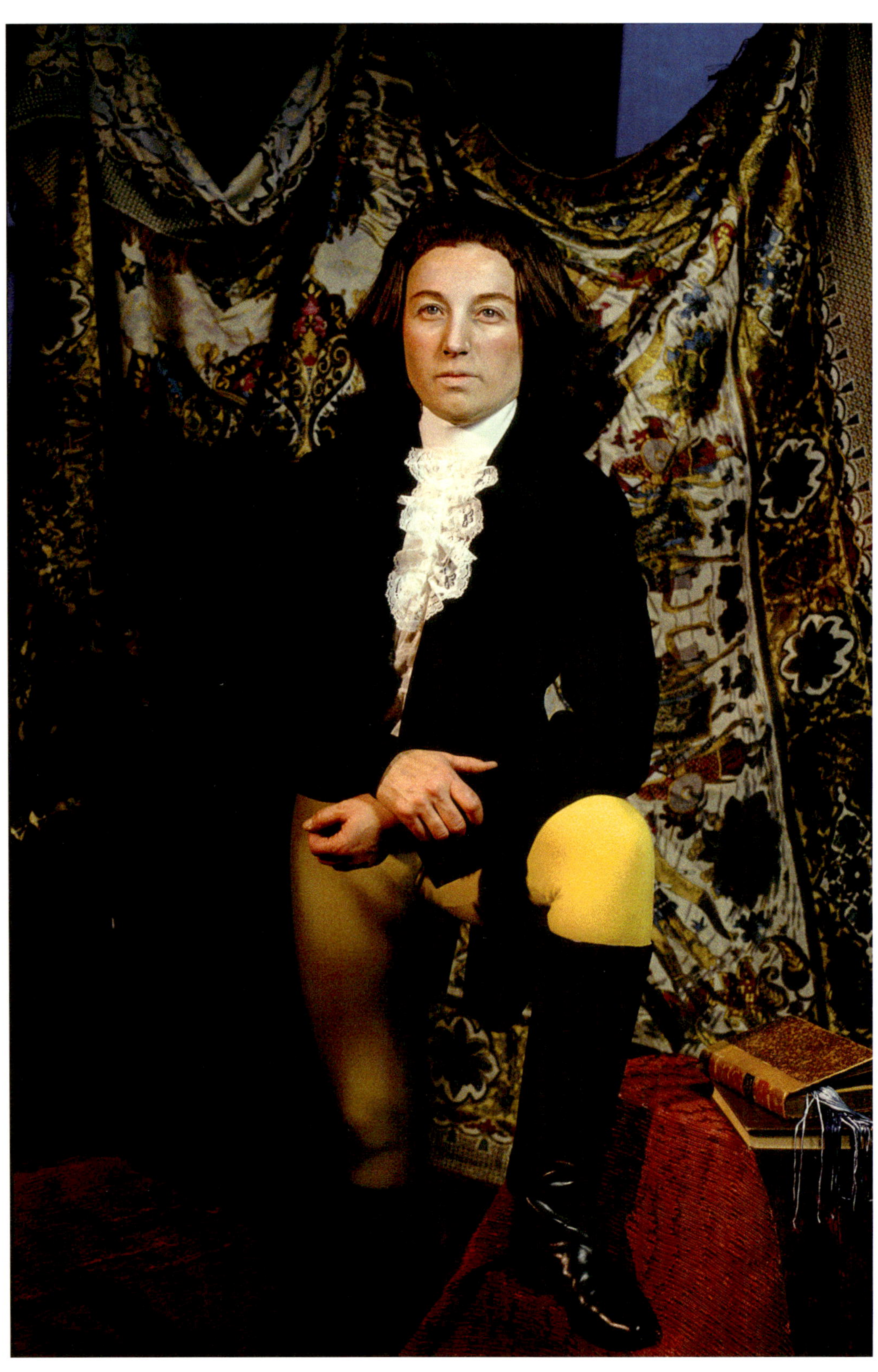

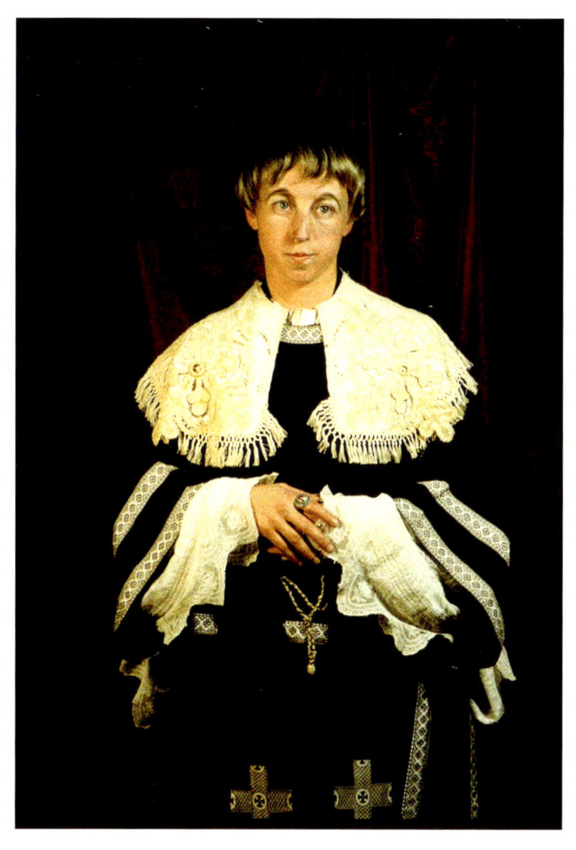
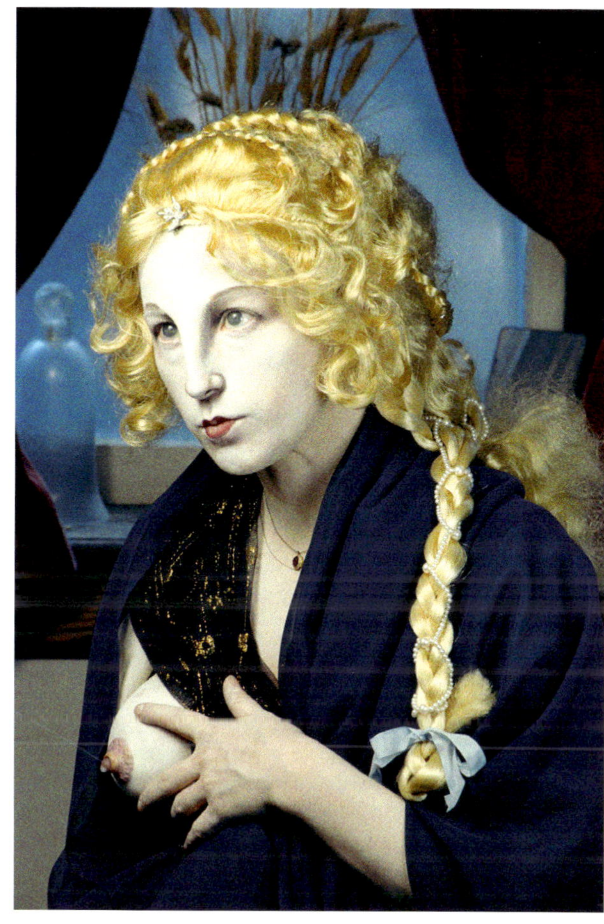
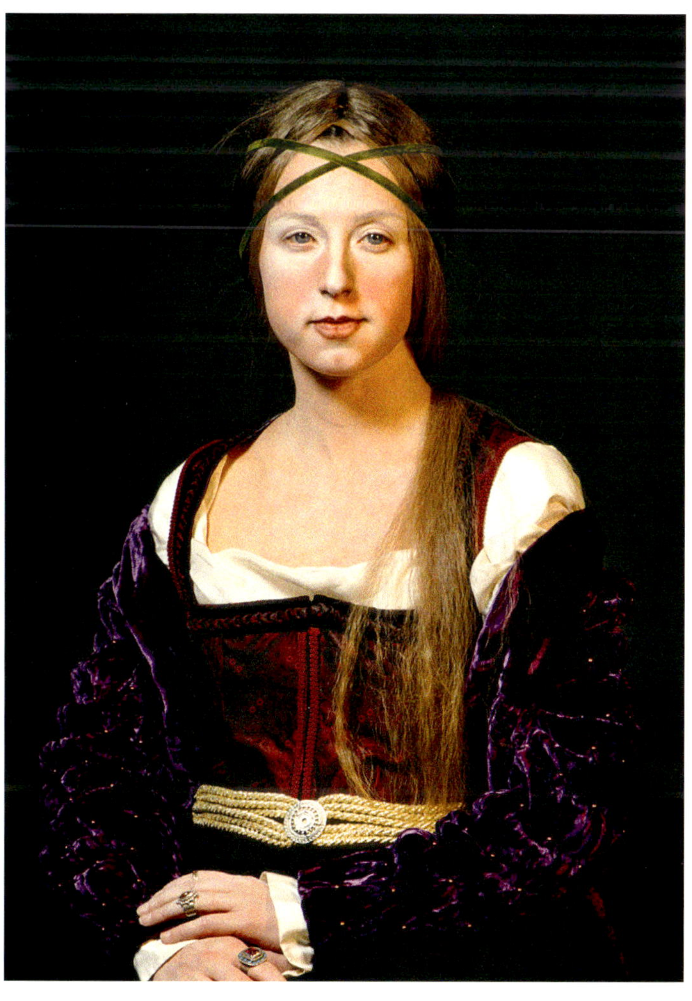

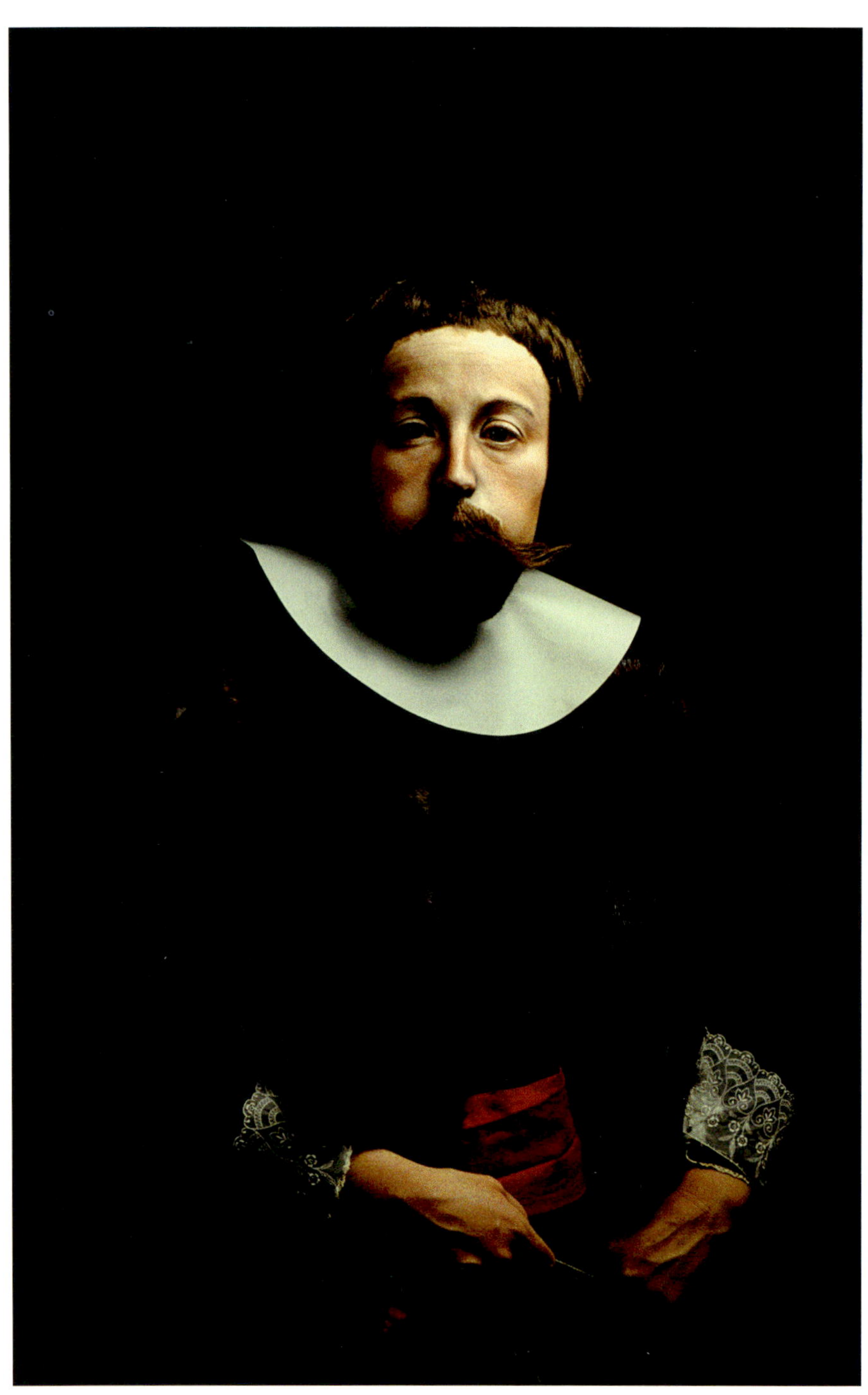

Untitled #240
Untitled #242
Untitled #243

1991

[Civil War]

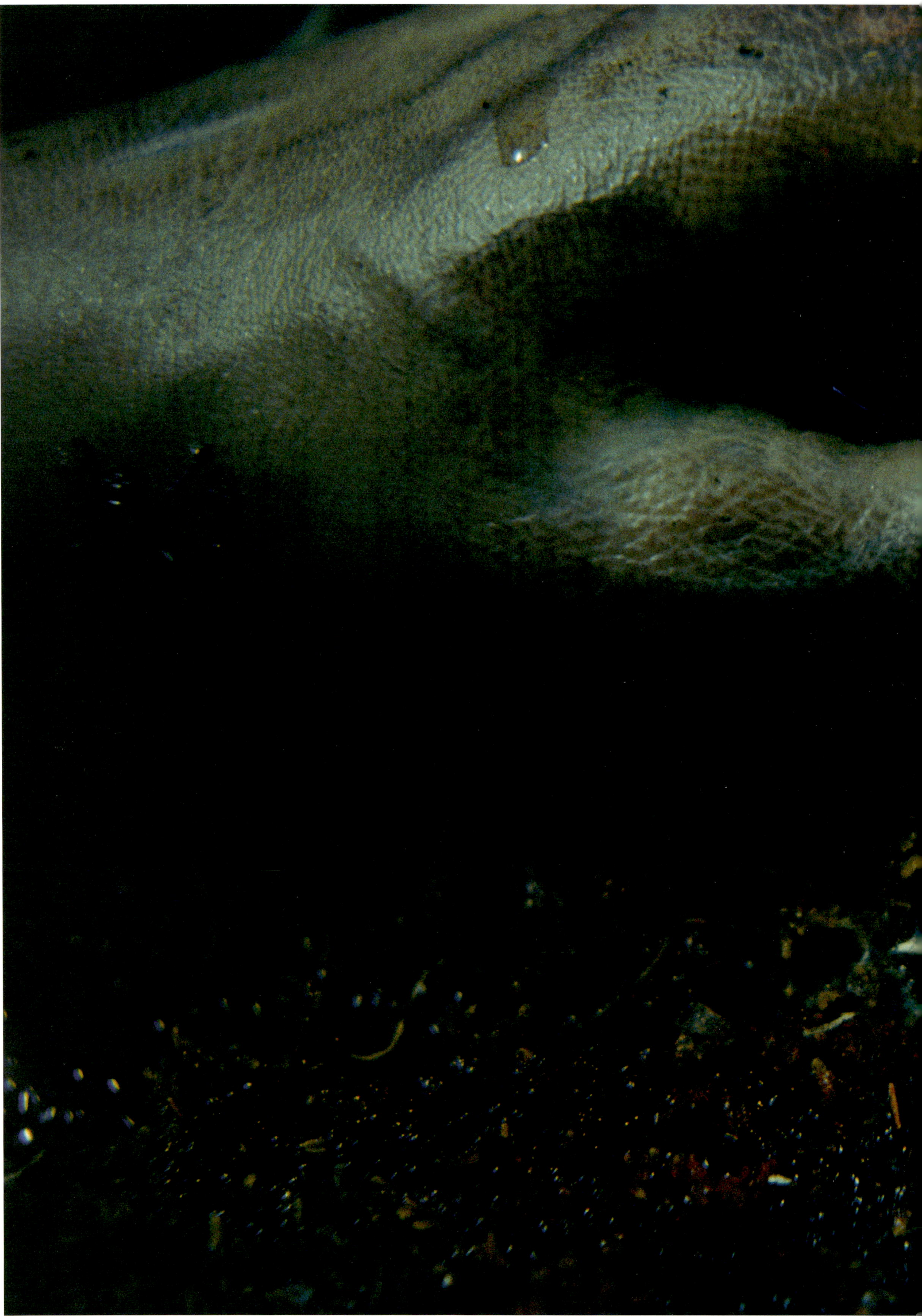

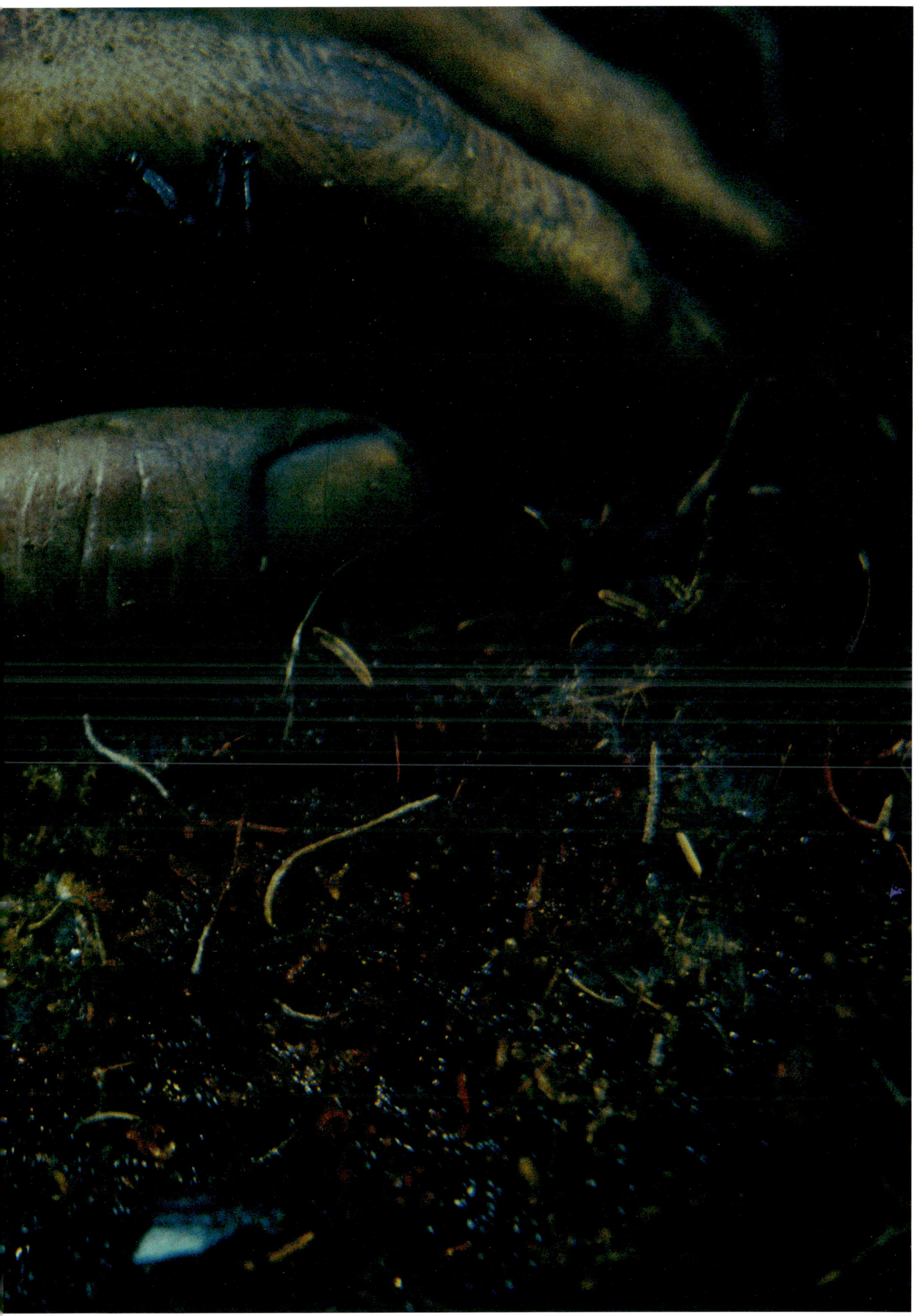

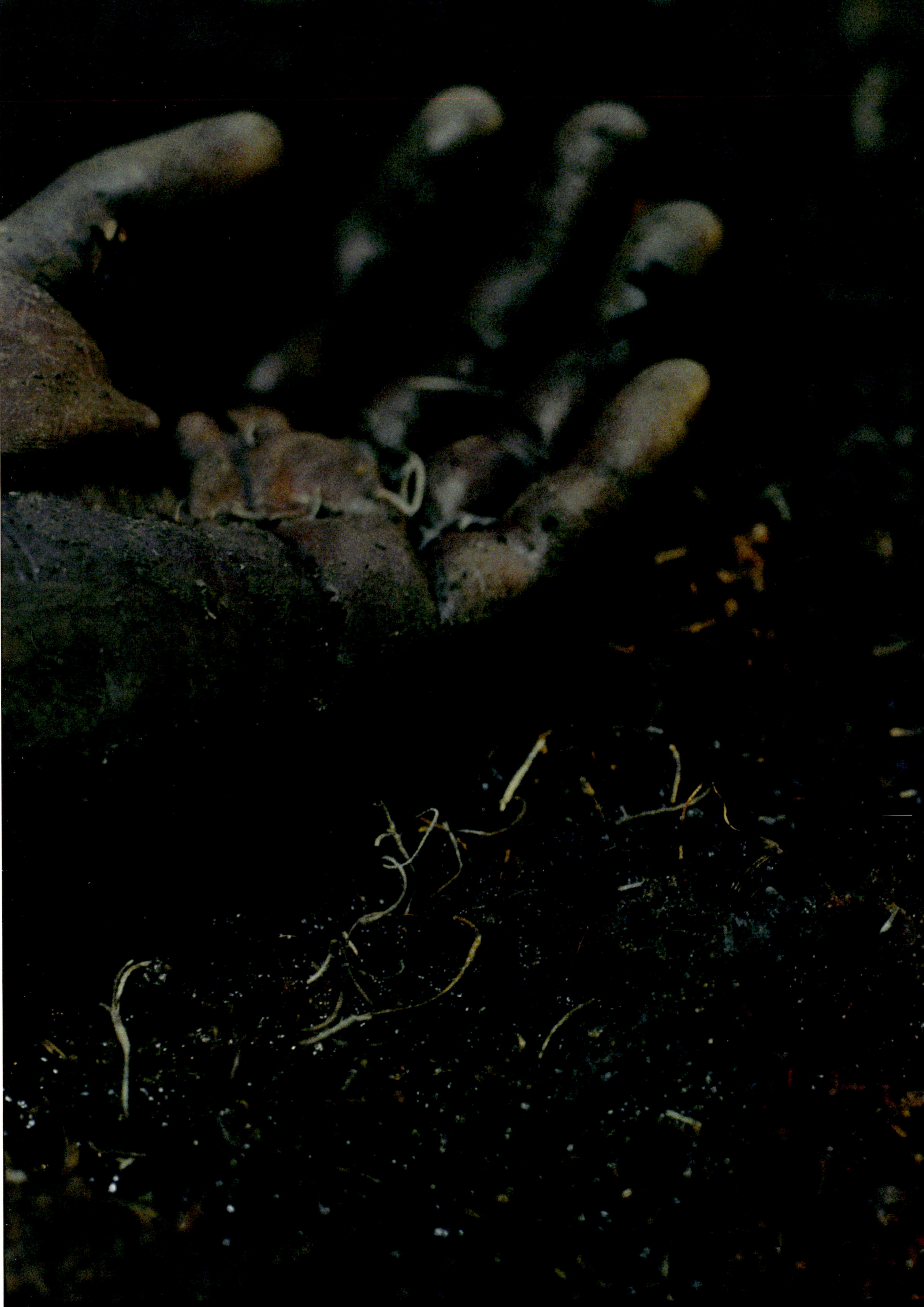

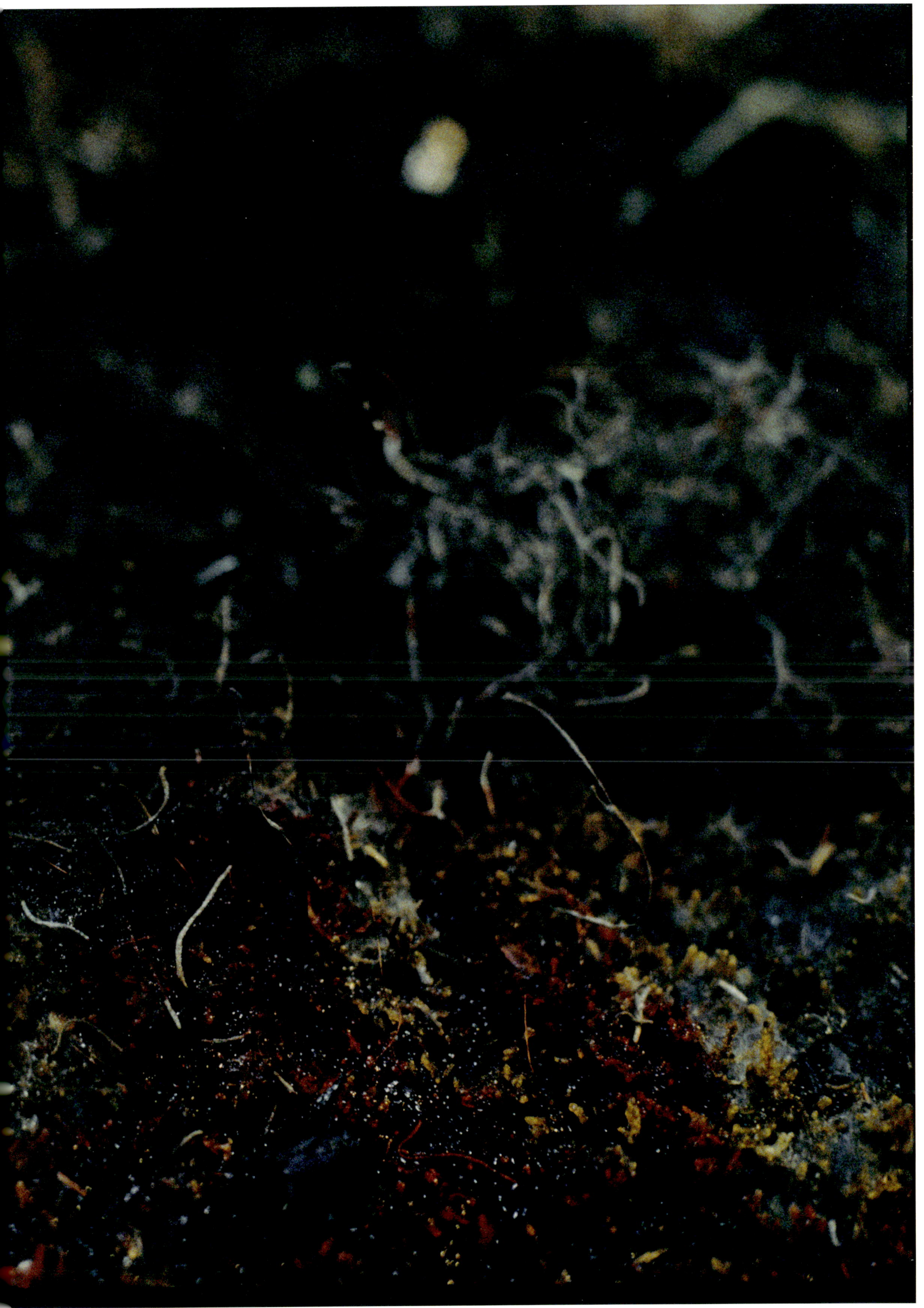

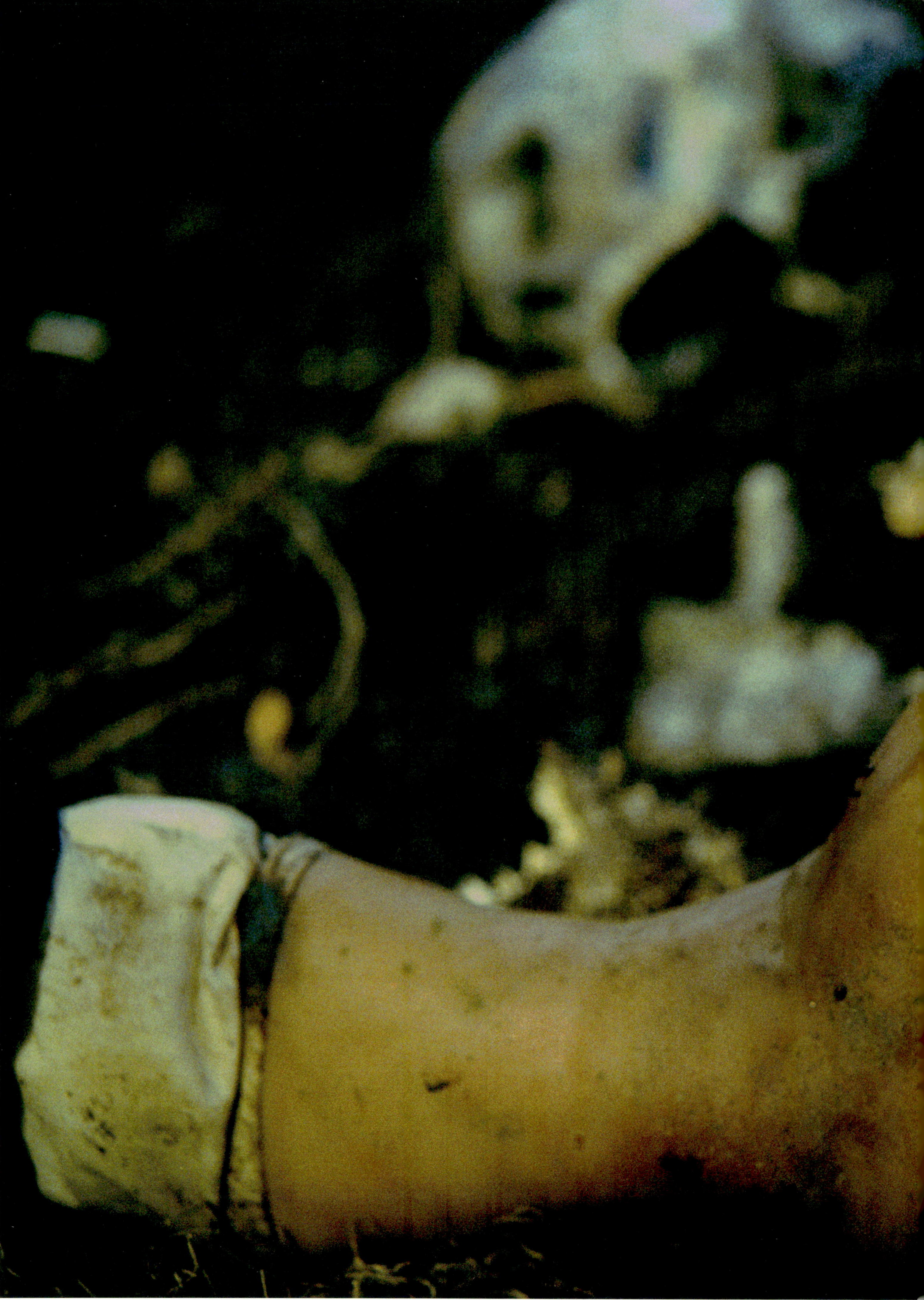

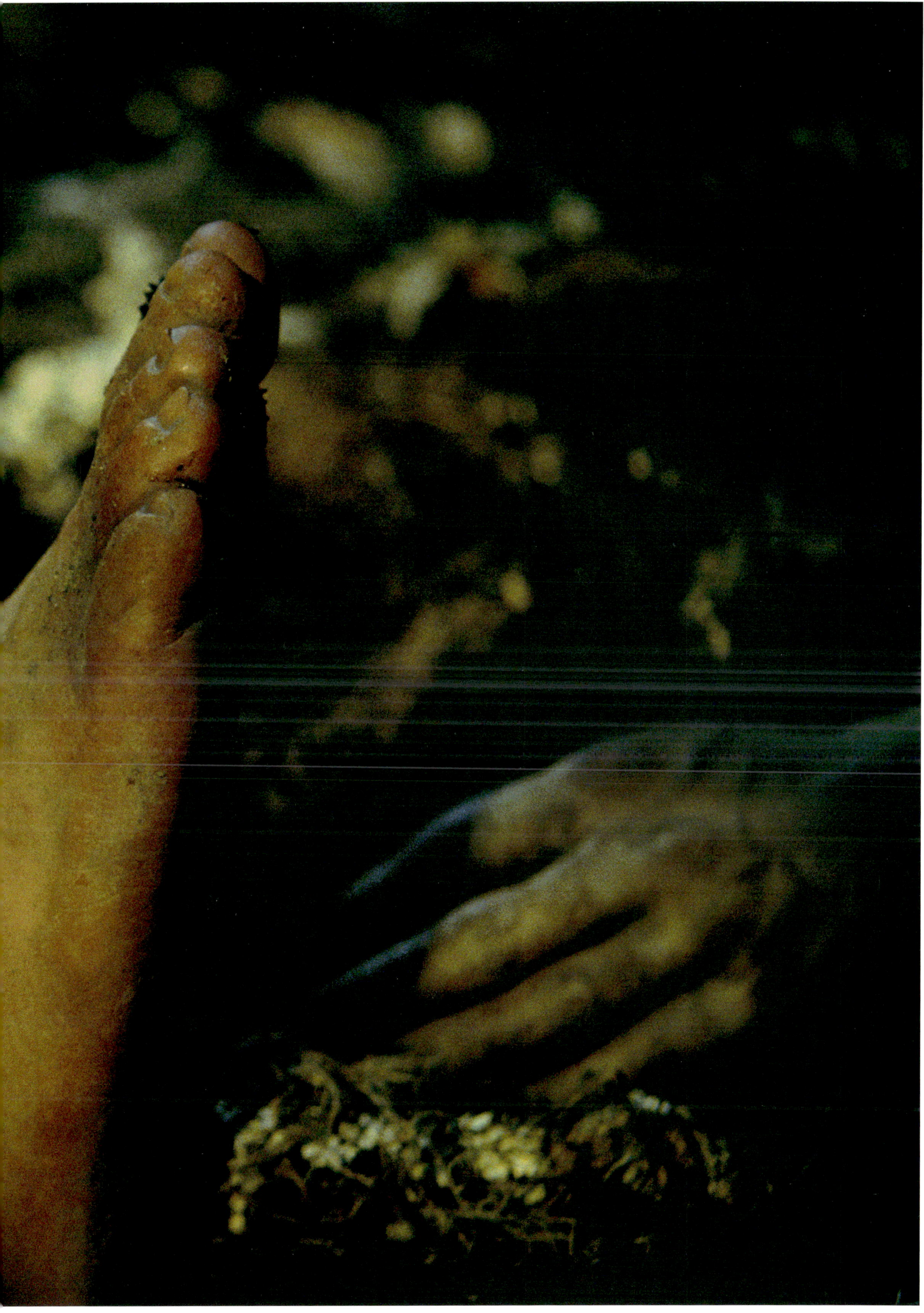

Untitled #253
Untitled #264
Untitled #251
Untitled #257
Untitled #256
Untitled #255
Untitled #259
Untitled #263
Untitled #258
1992

[Sex Pictures]

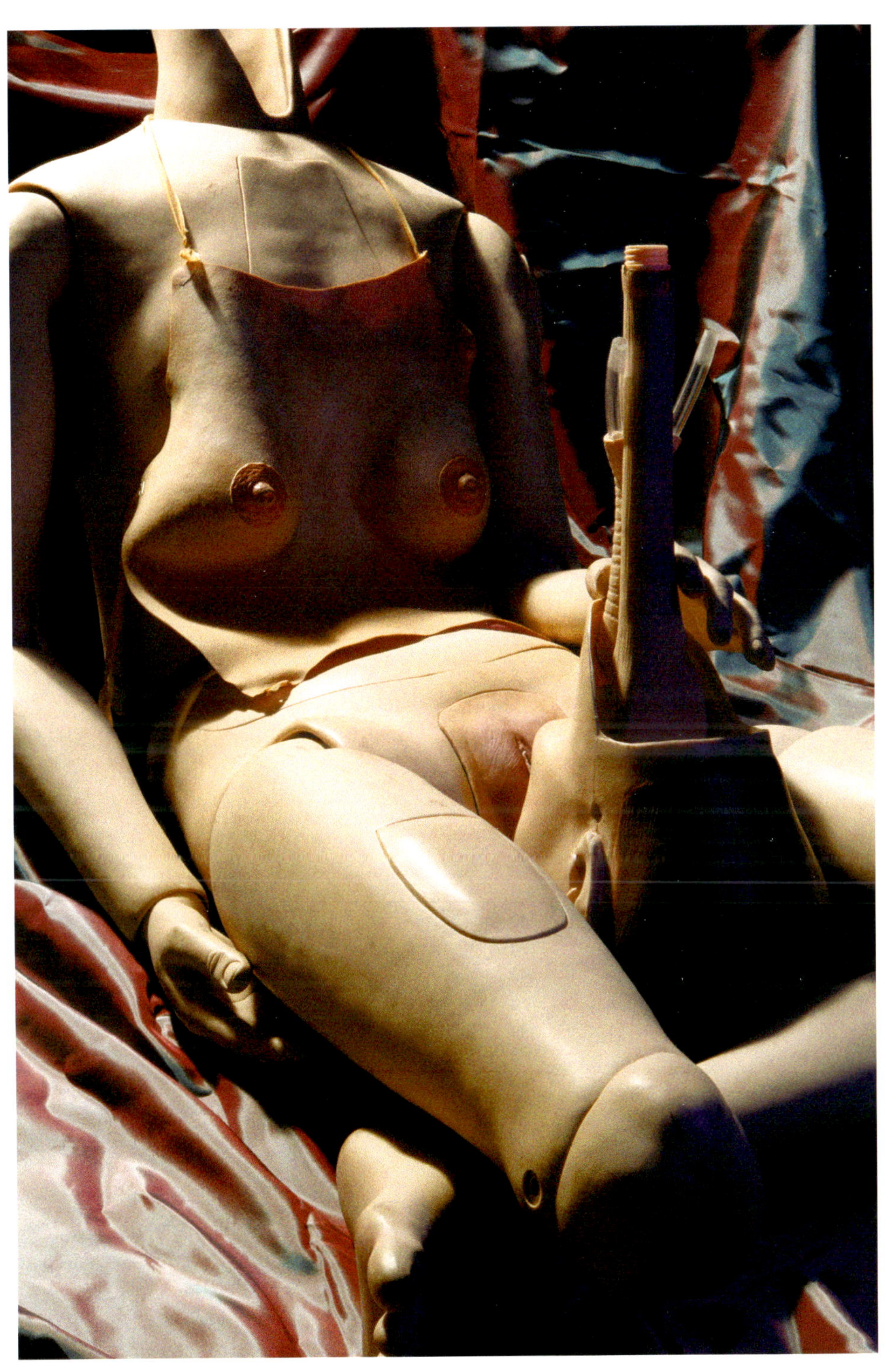

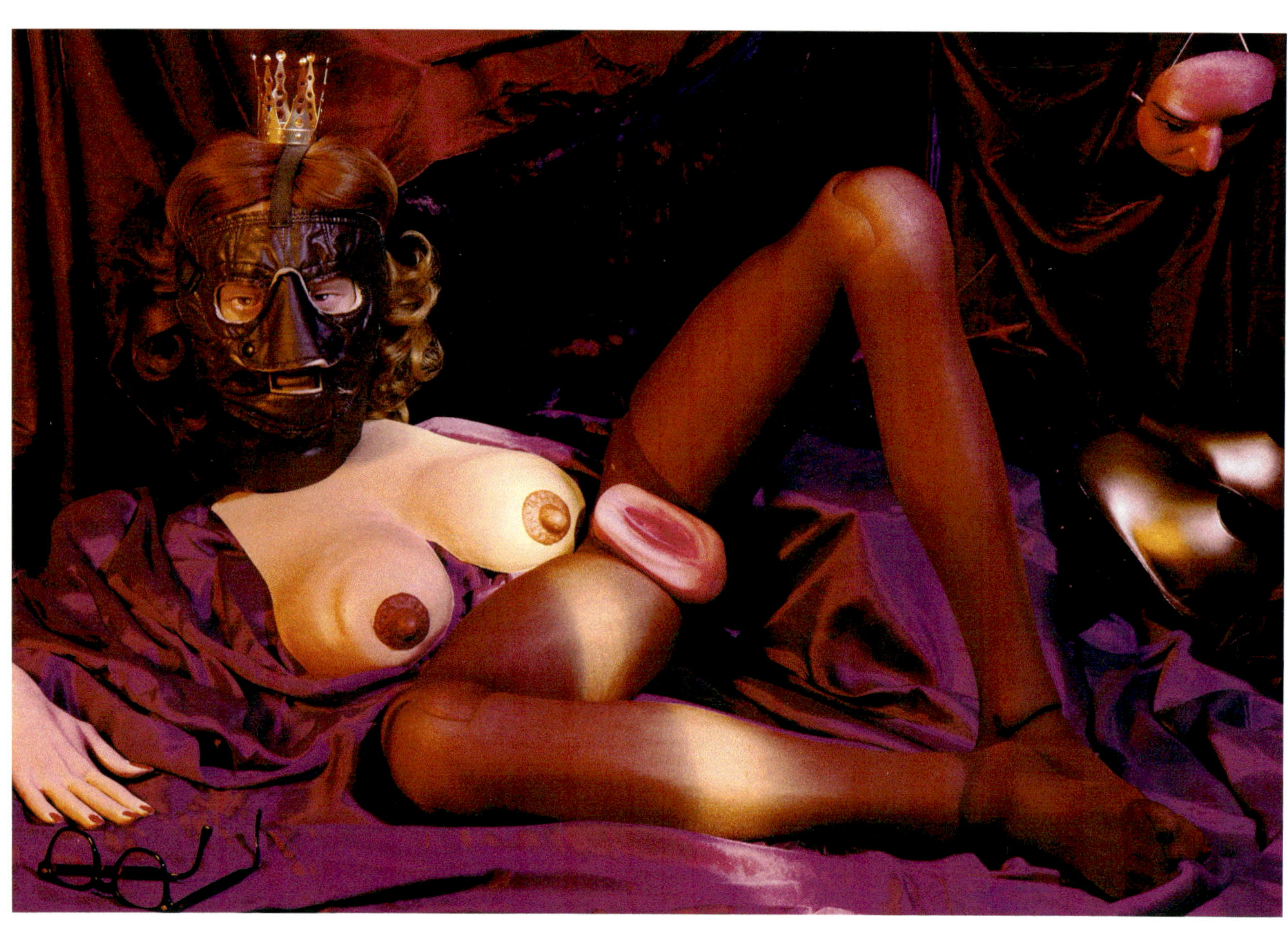

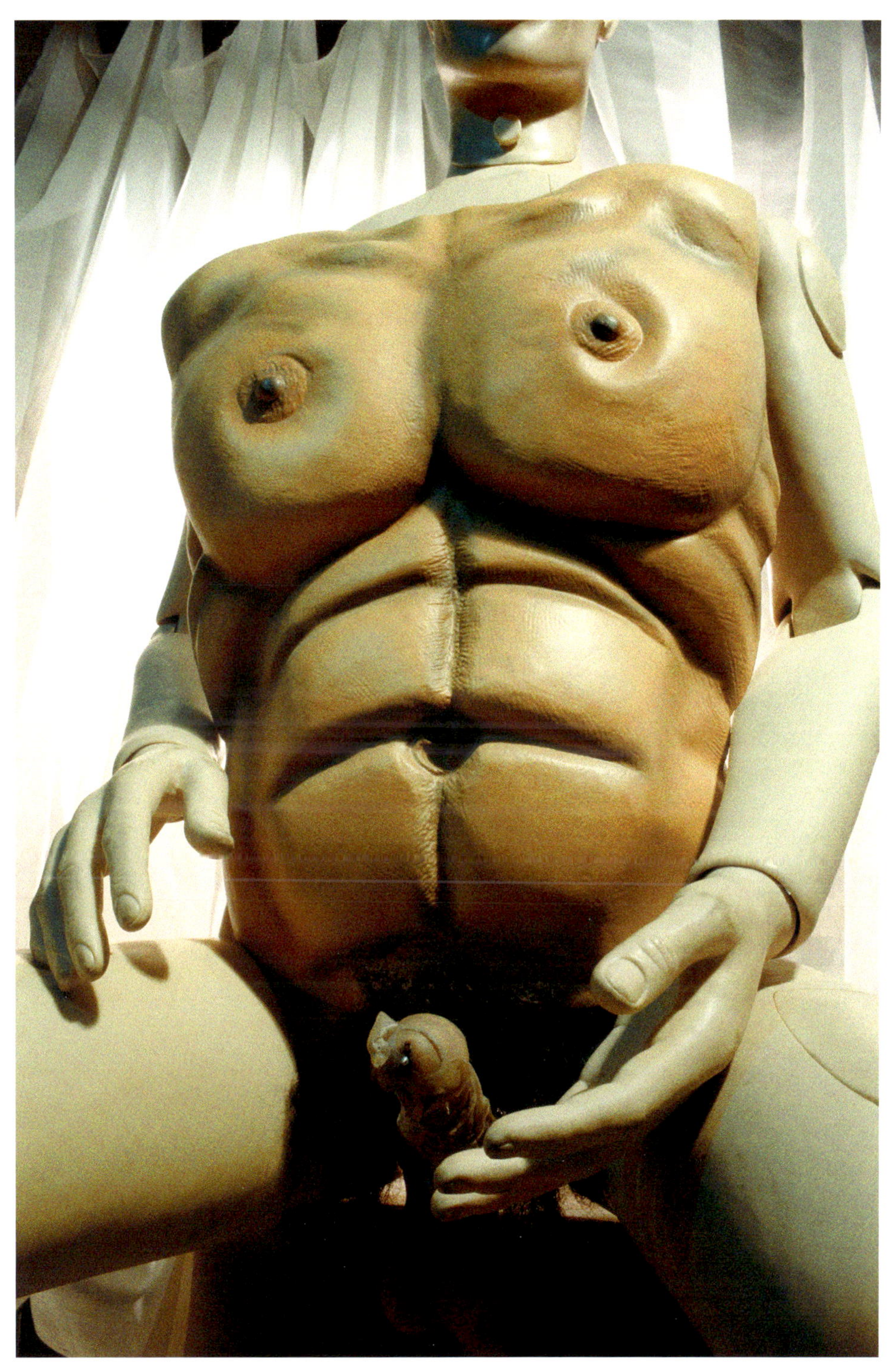

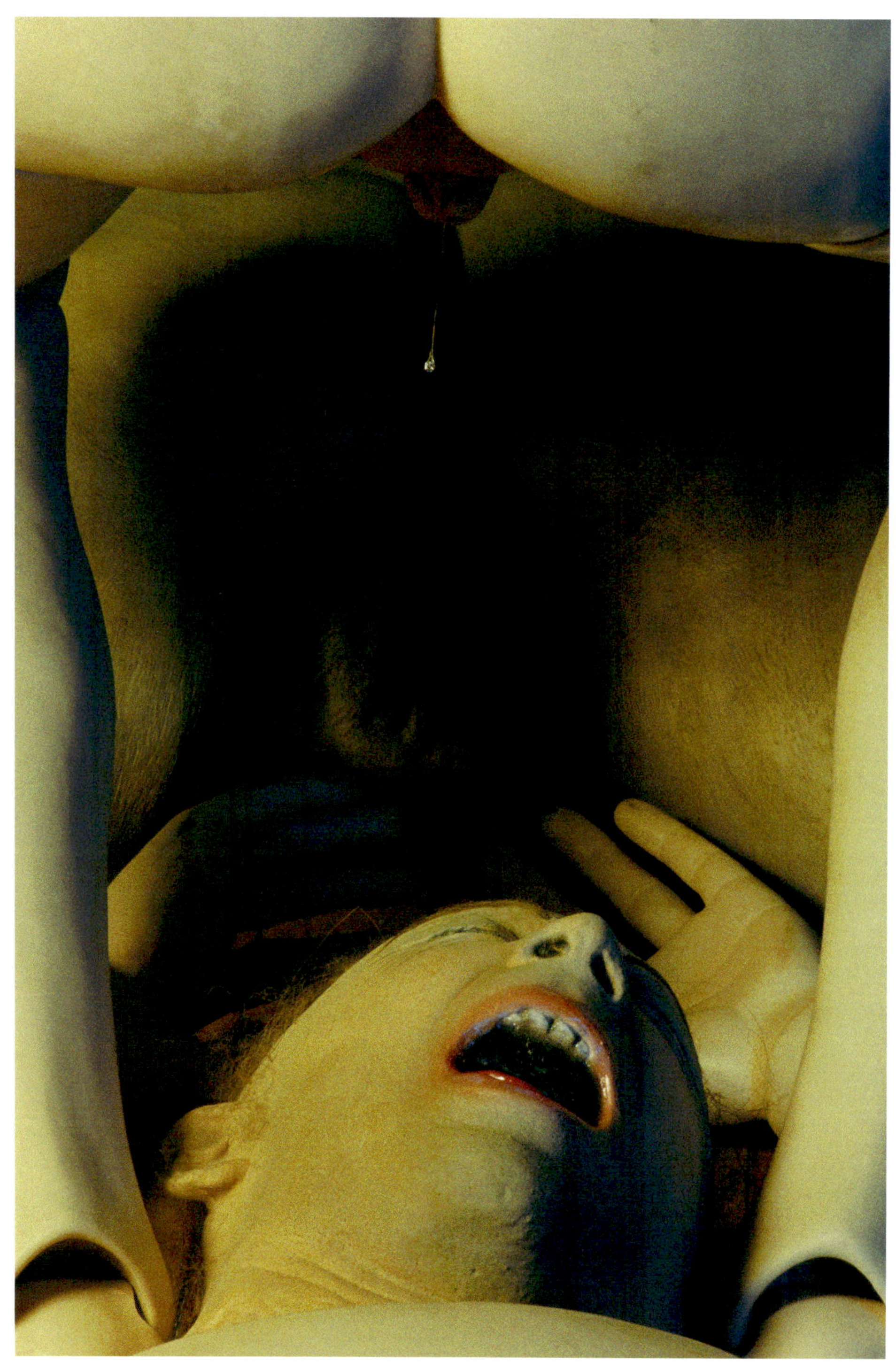

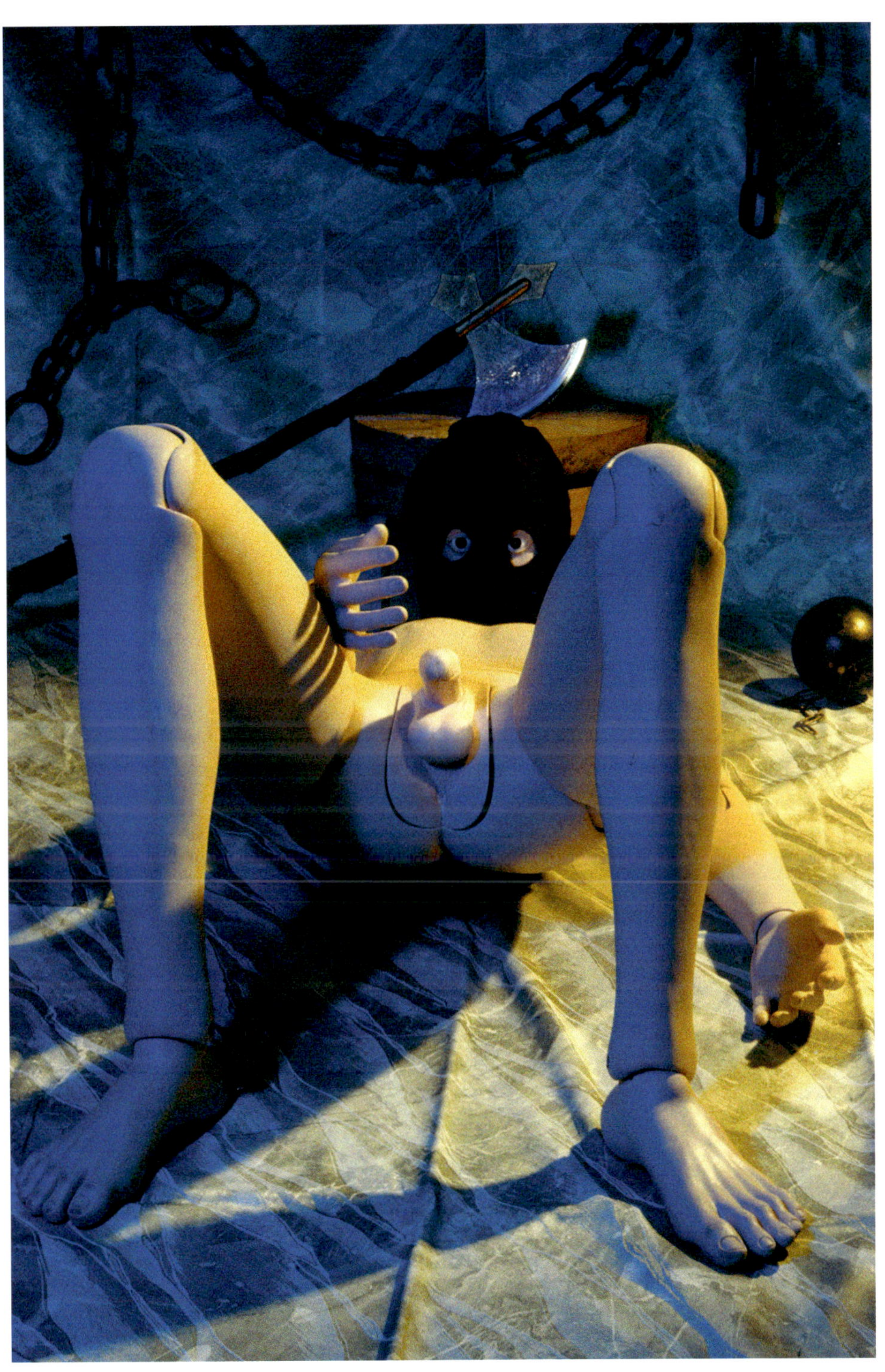

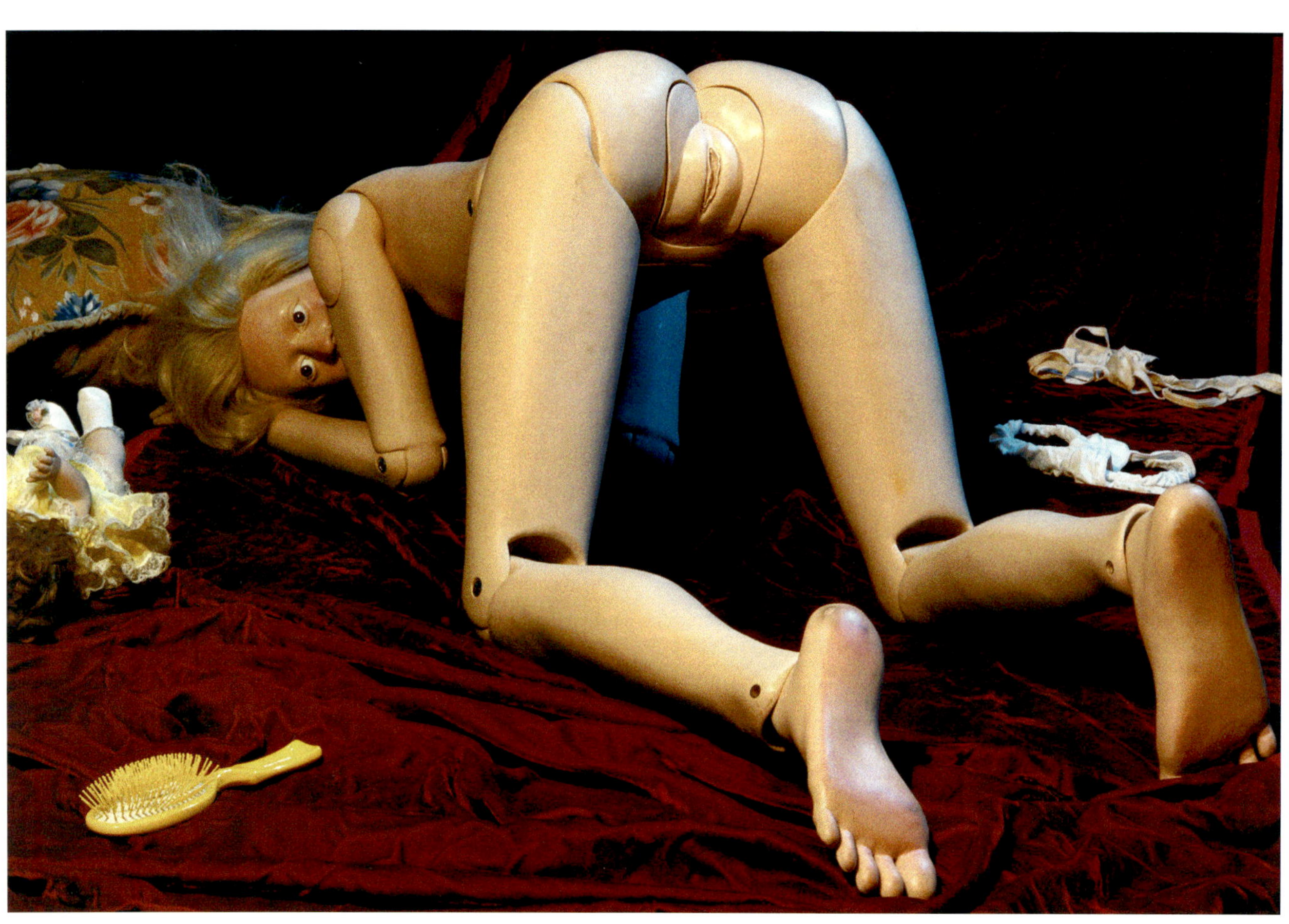

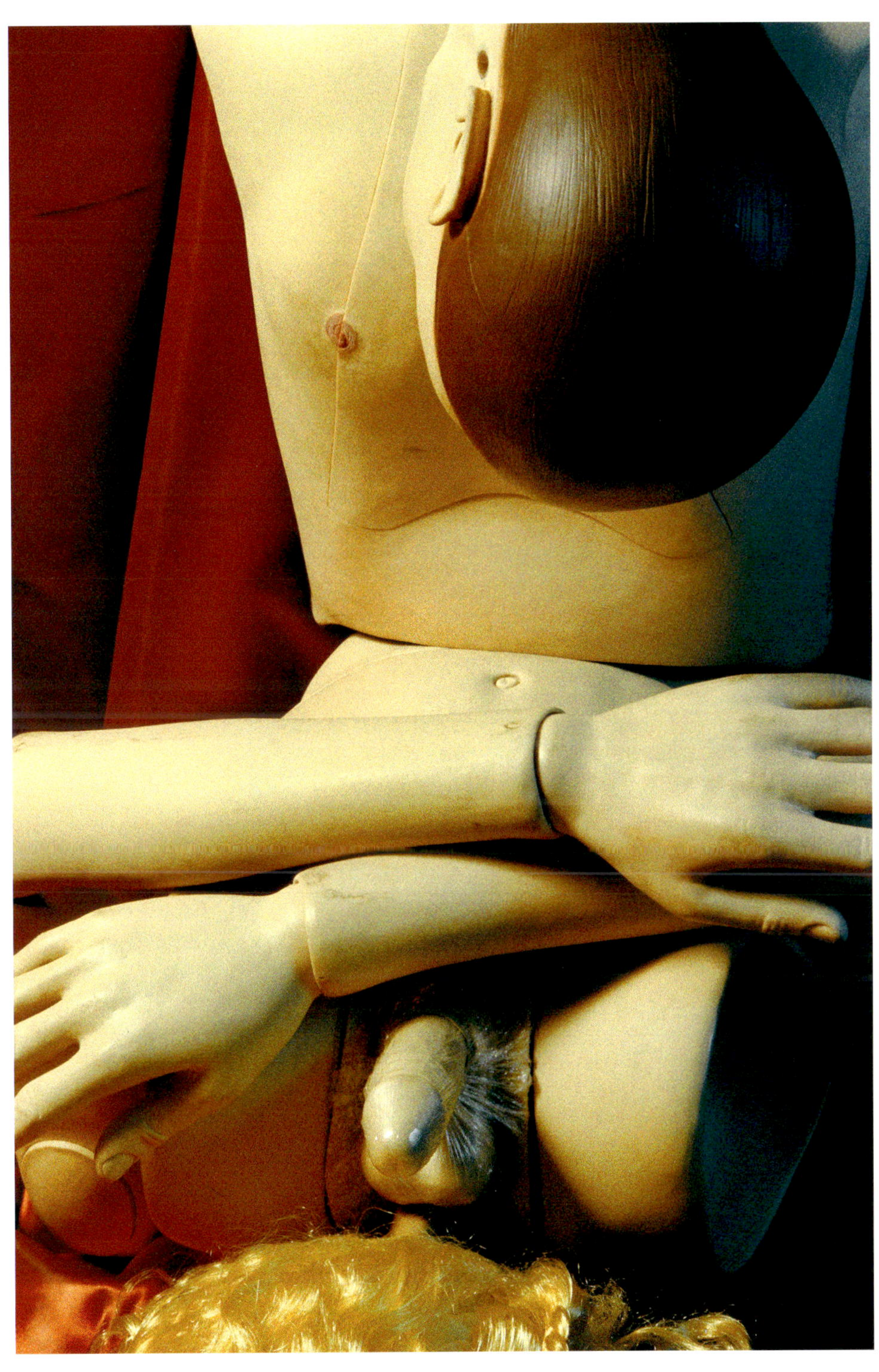

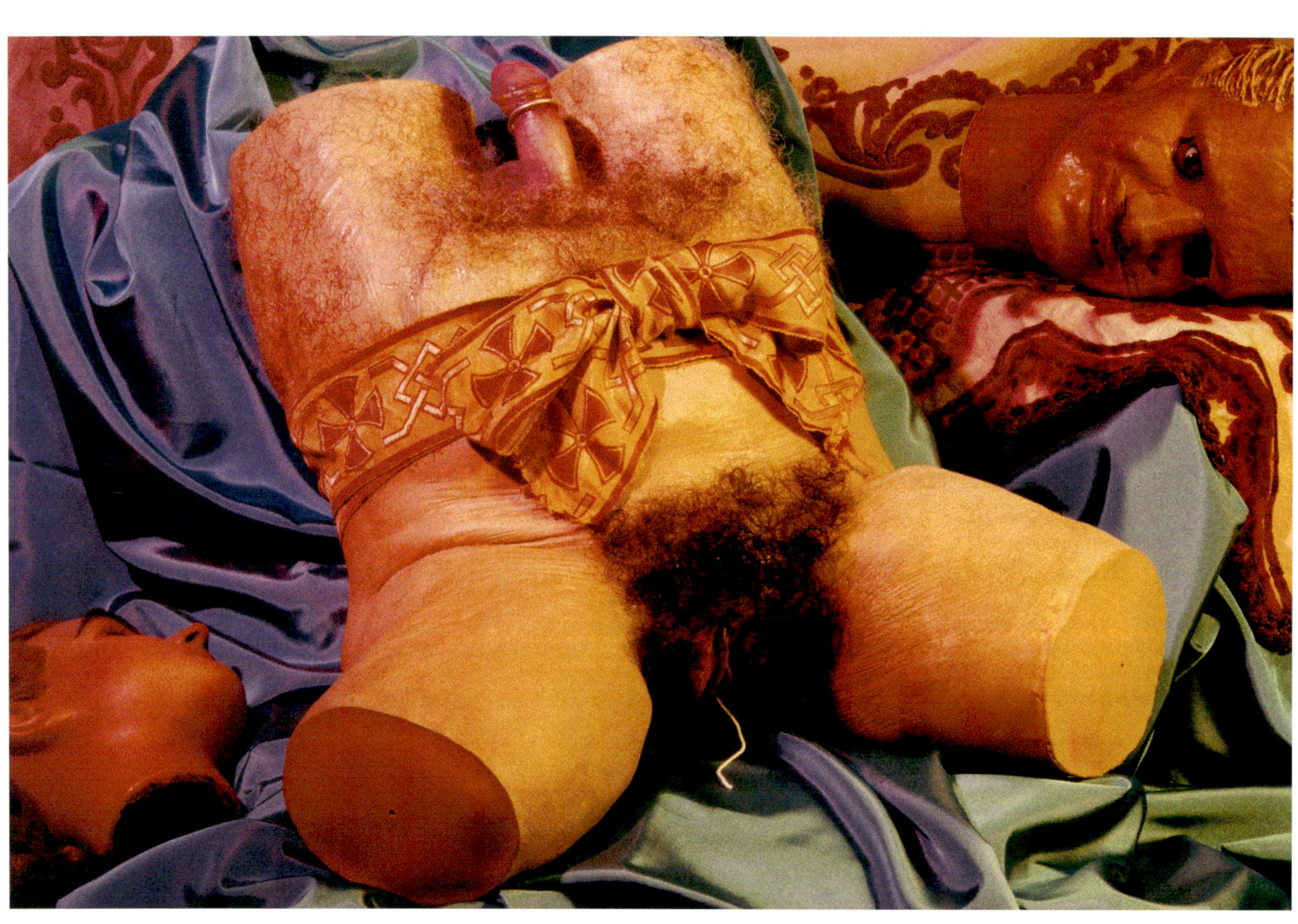

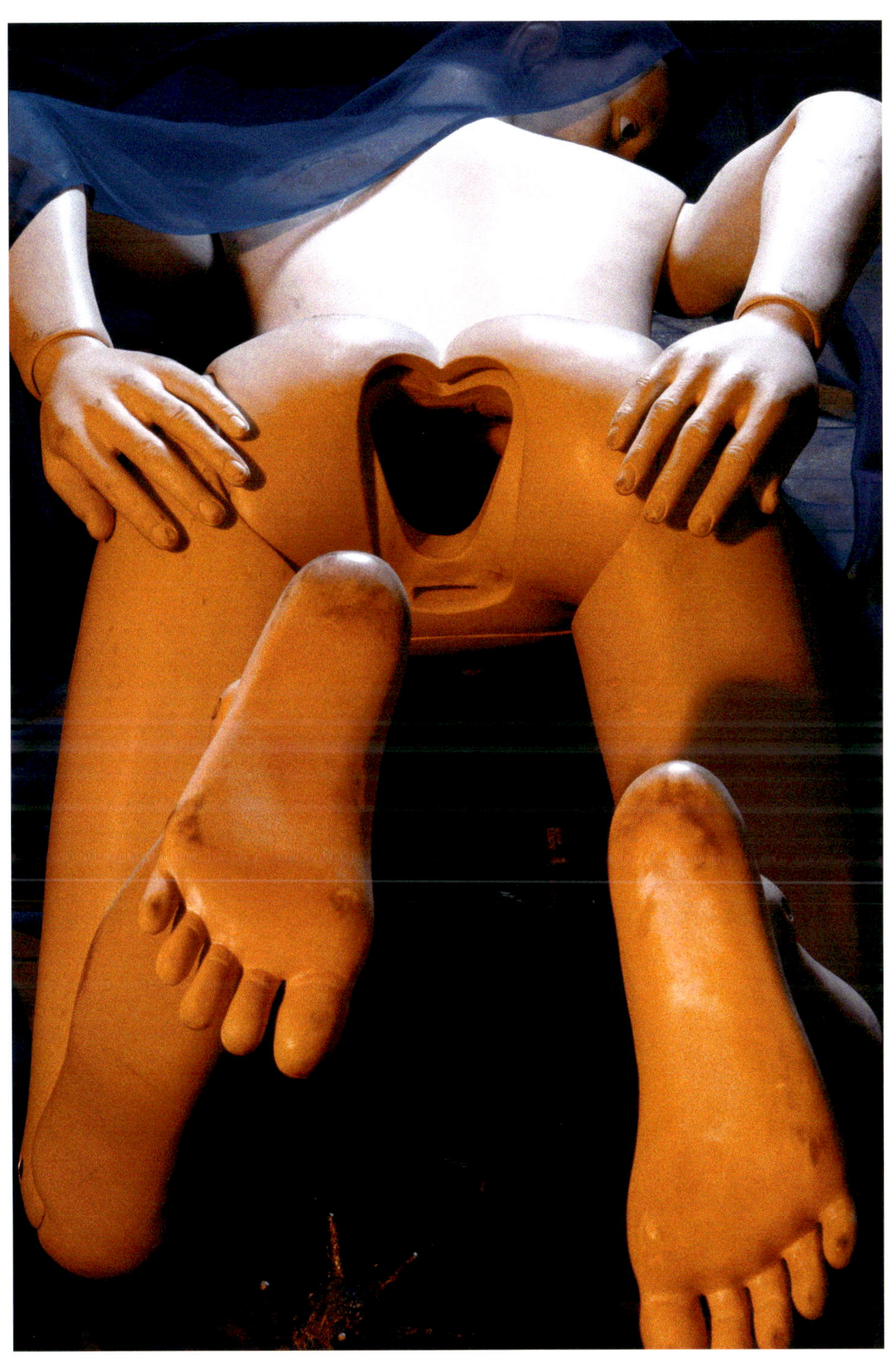

Untitled #278
Untitled #275
Untitled #299
Untitled #282
Untitled #280
Untitled #304
Untitled #302
Untitled #300
Untitled #303
Untitled #276
Untitled #279

1993—1994

[Fashion]

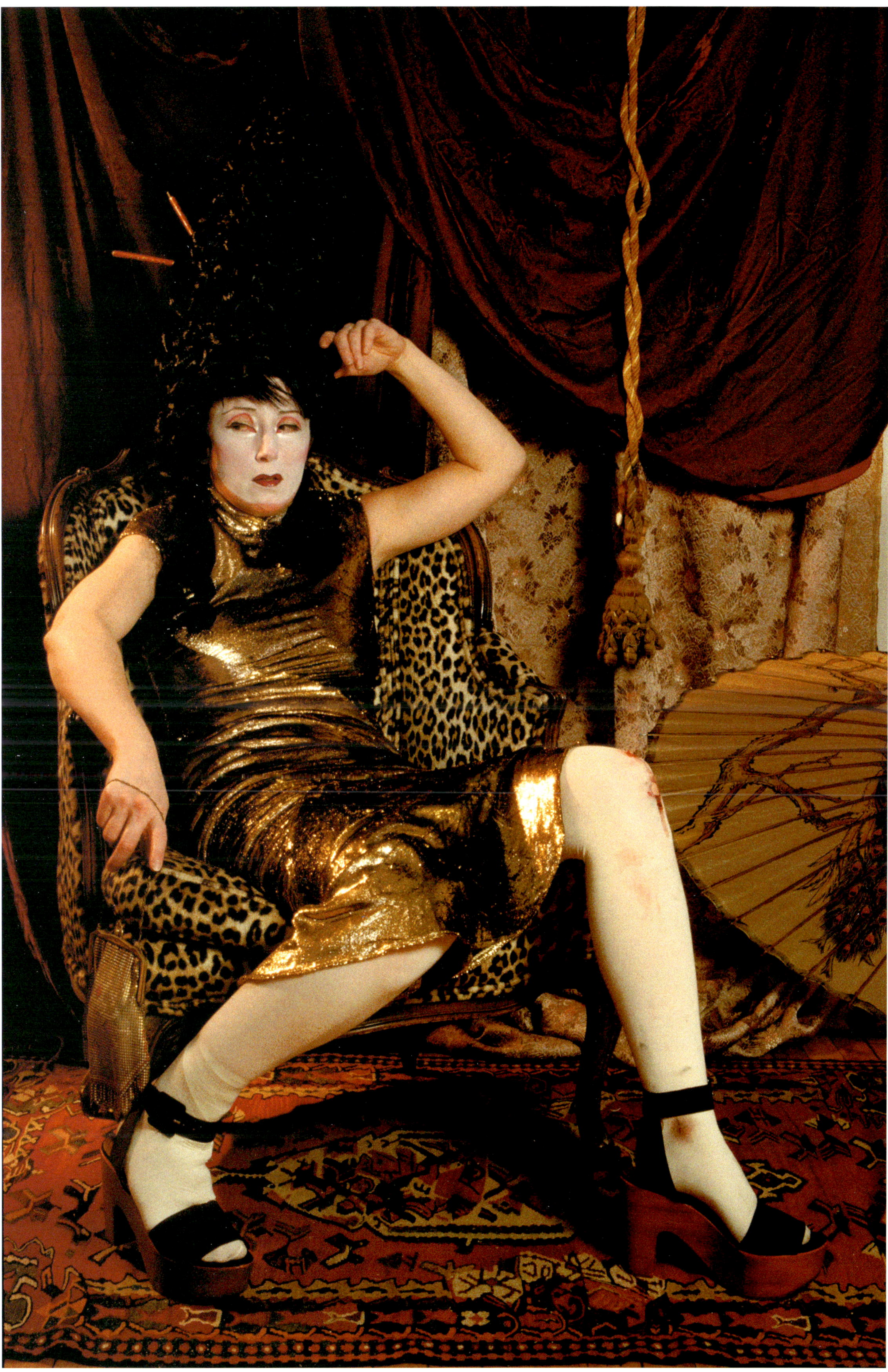

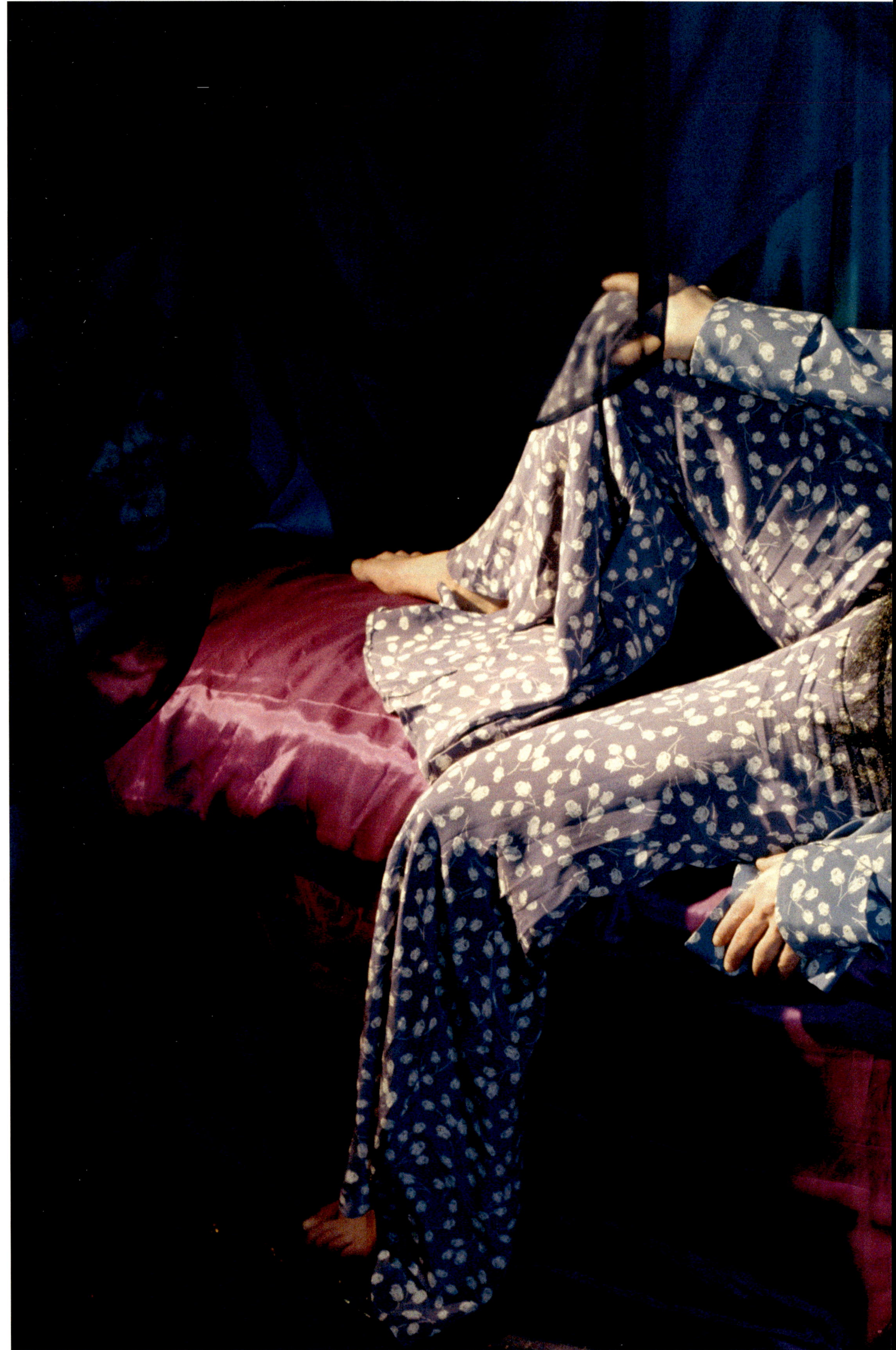

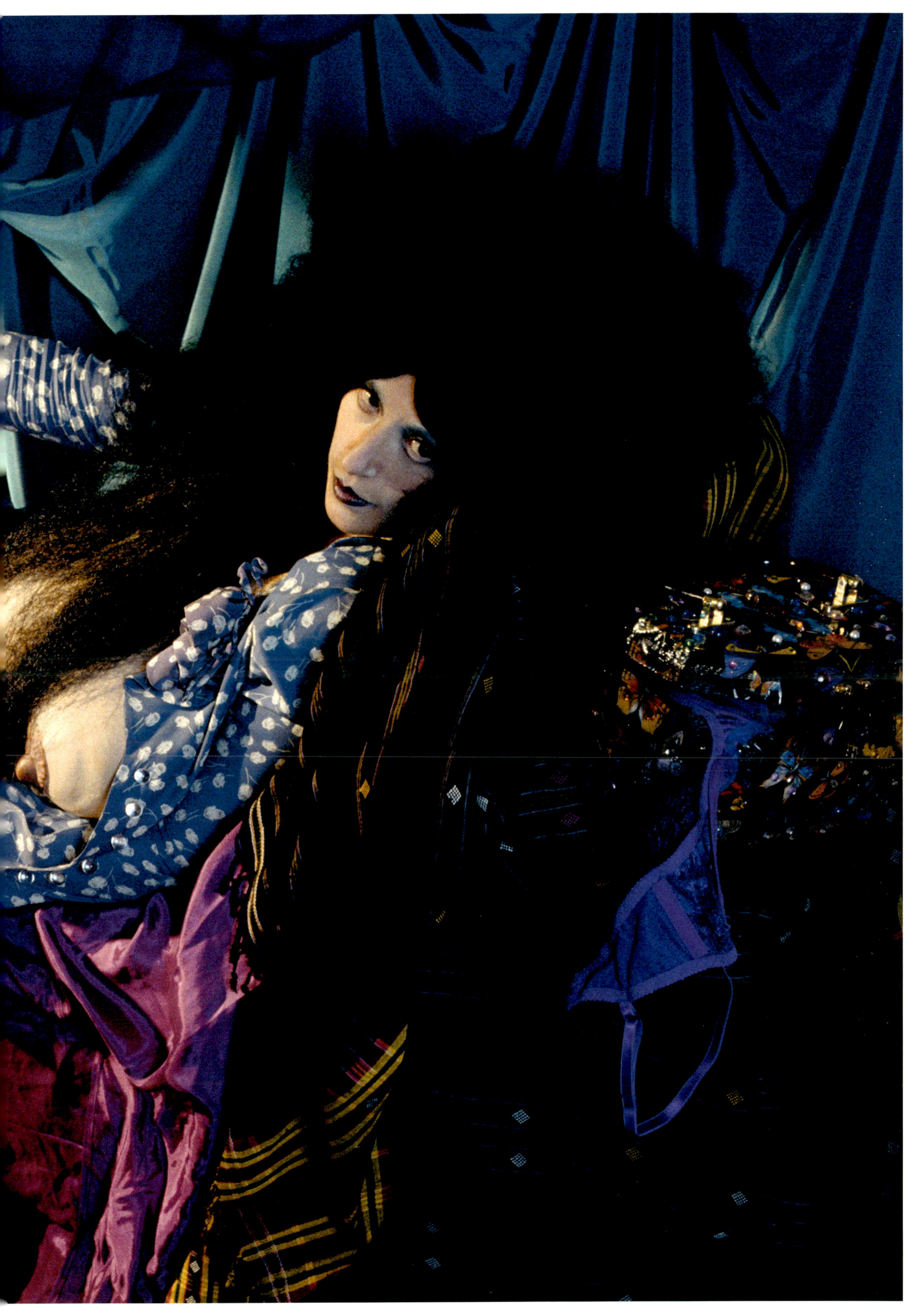

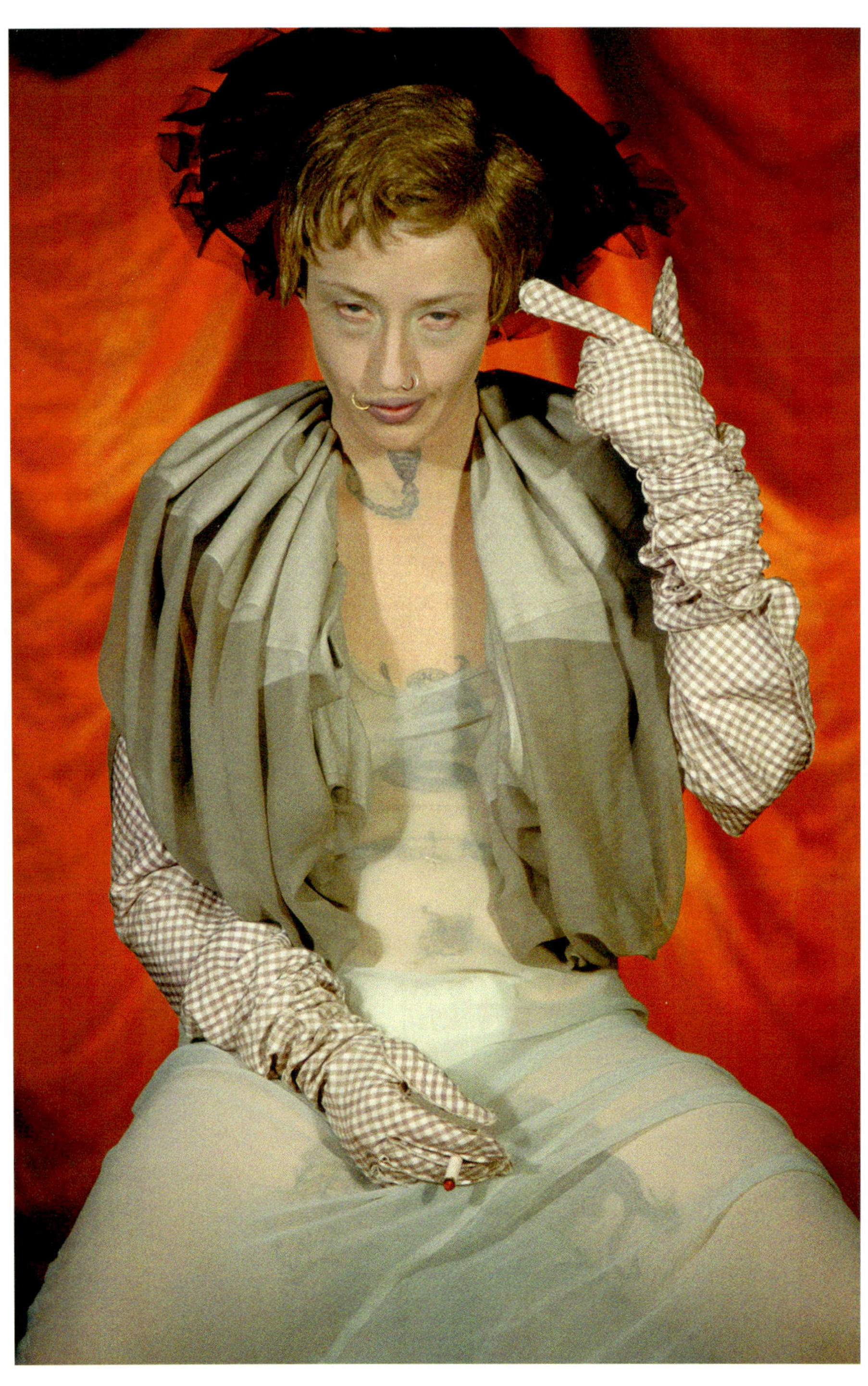

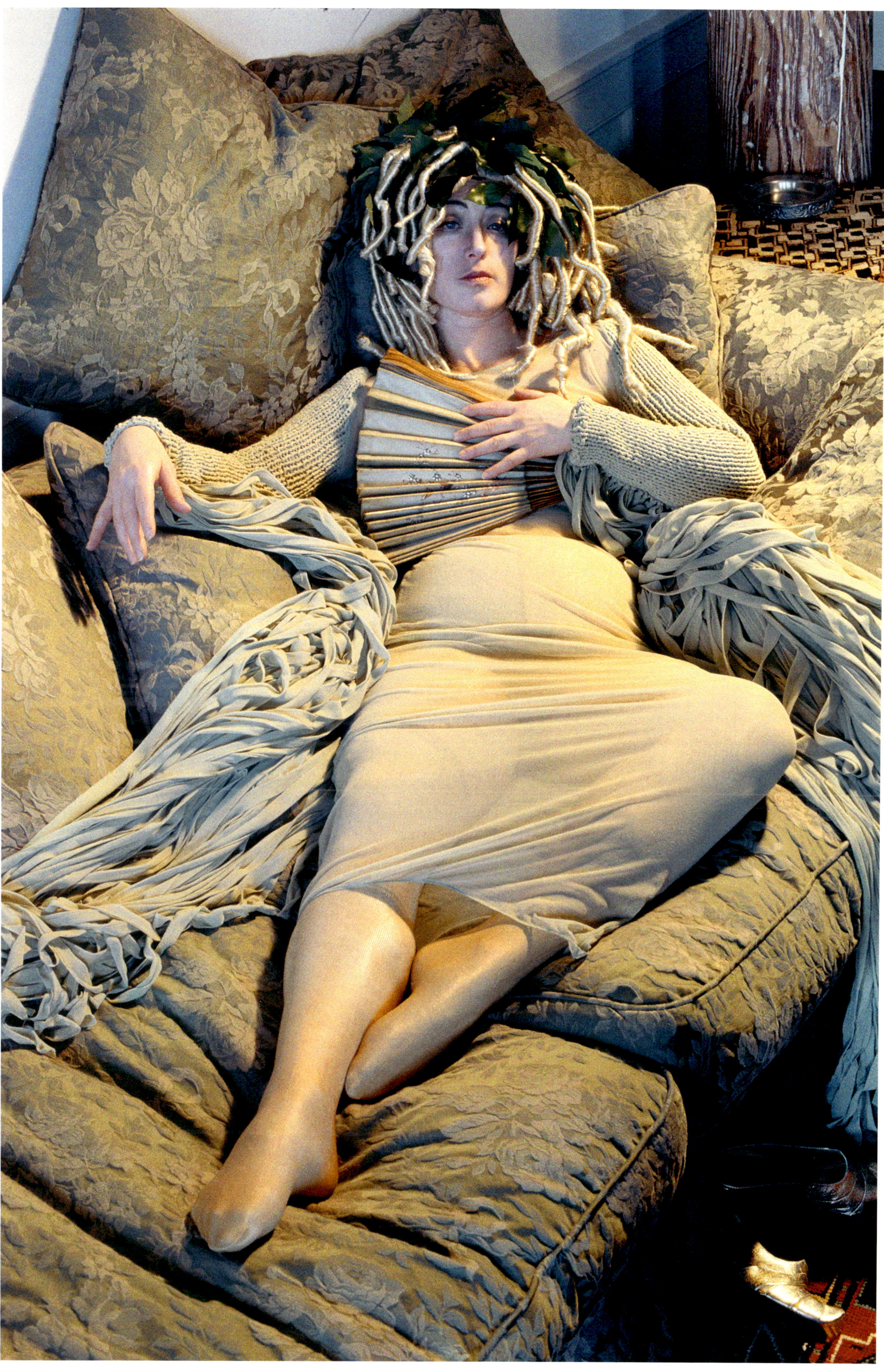

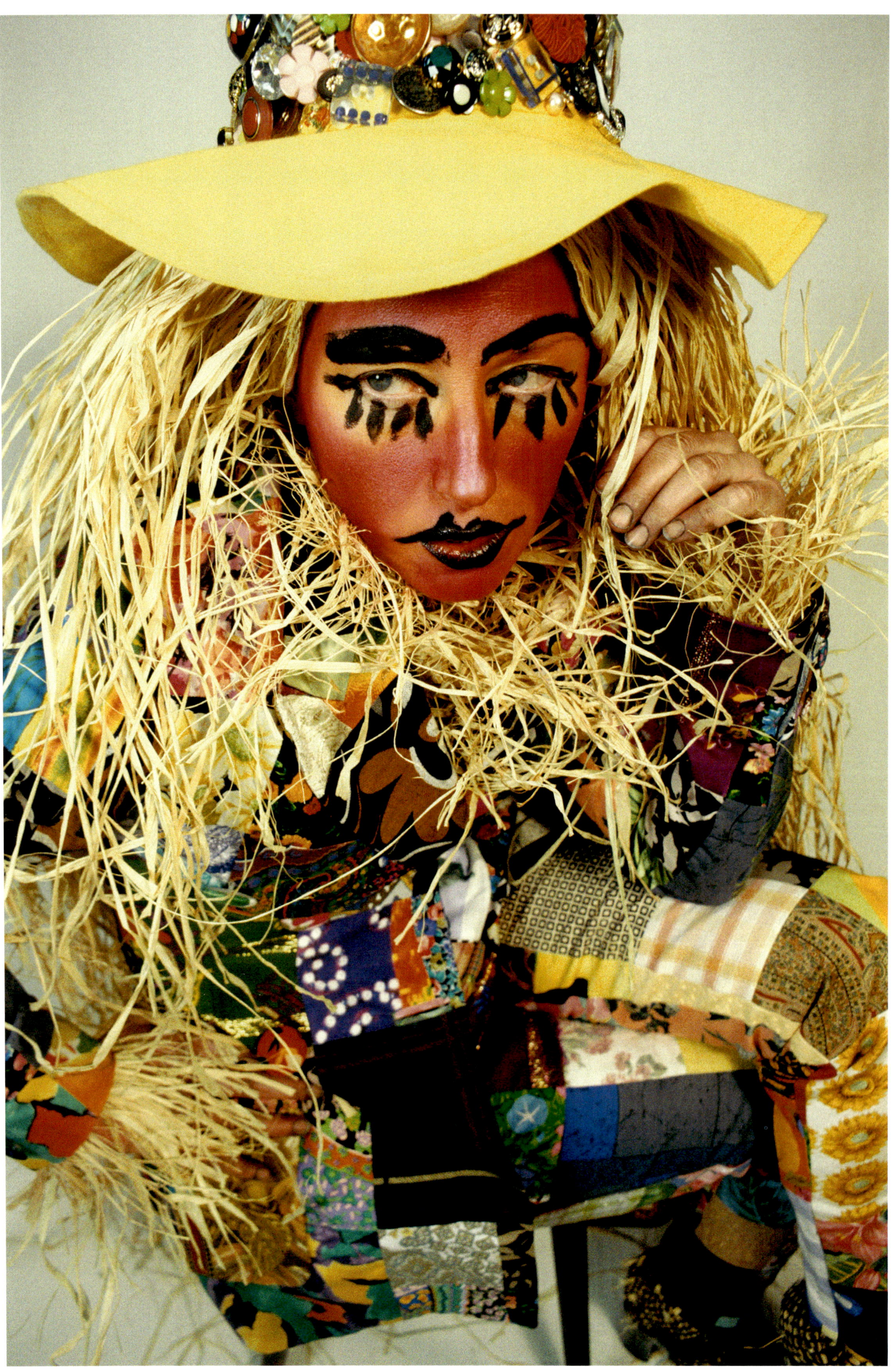

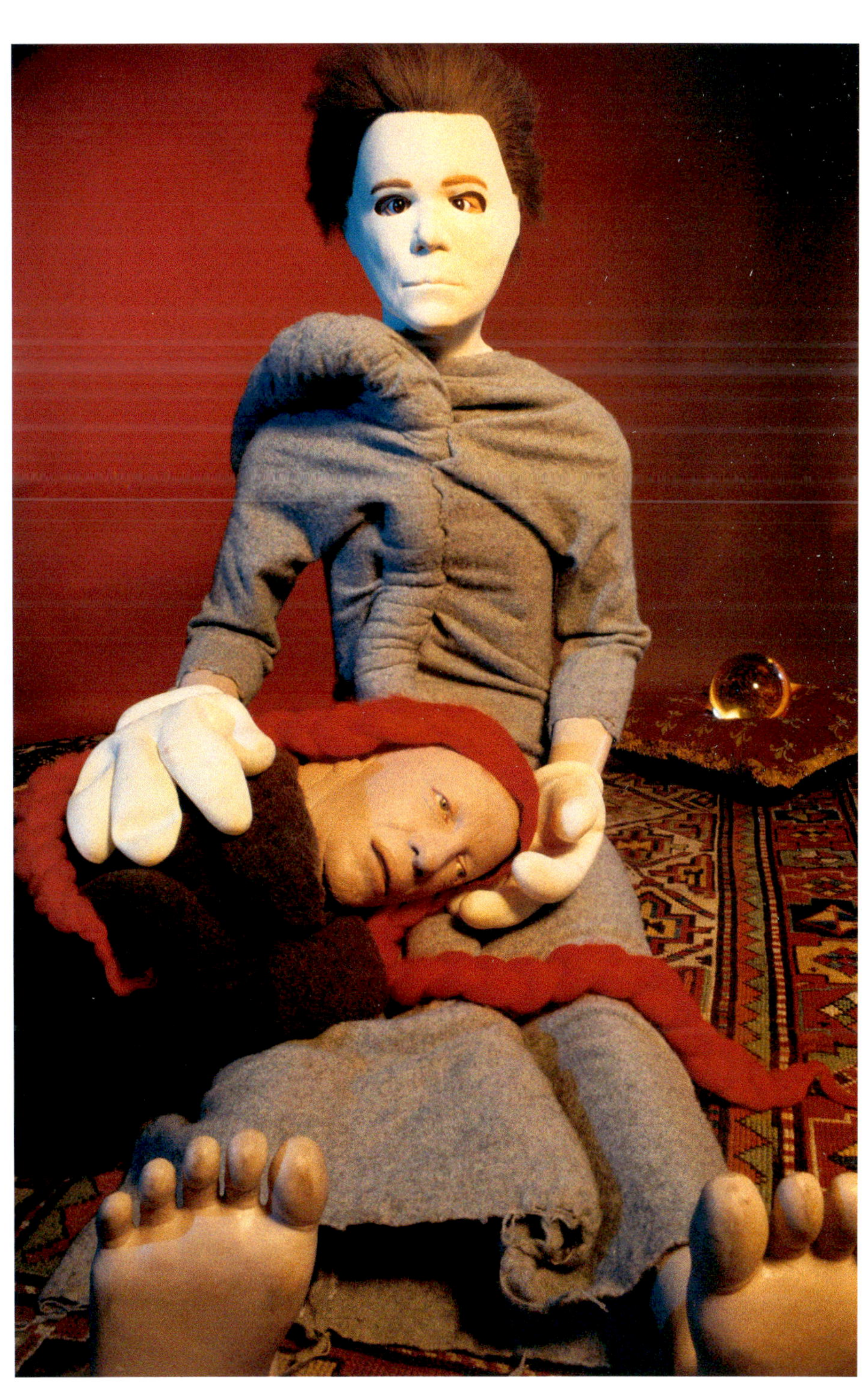

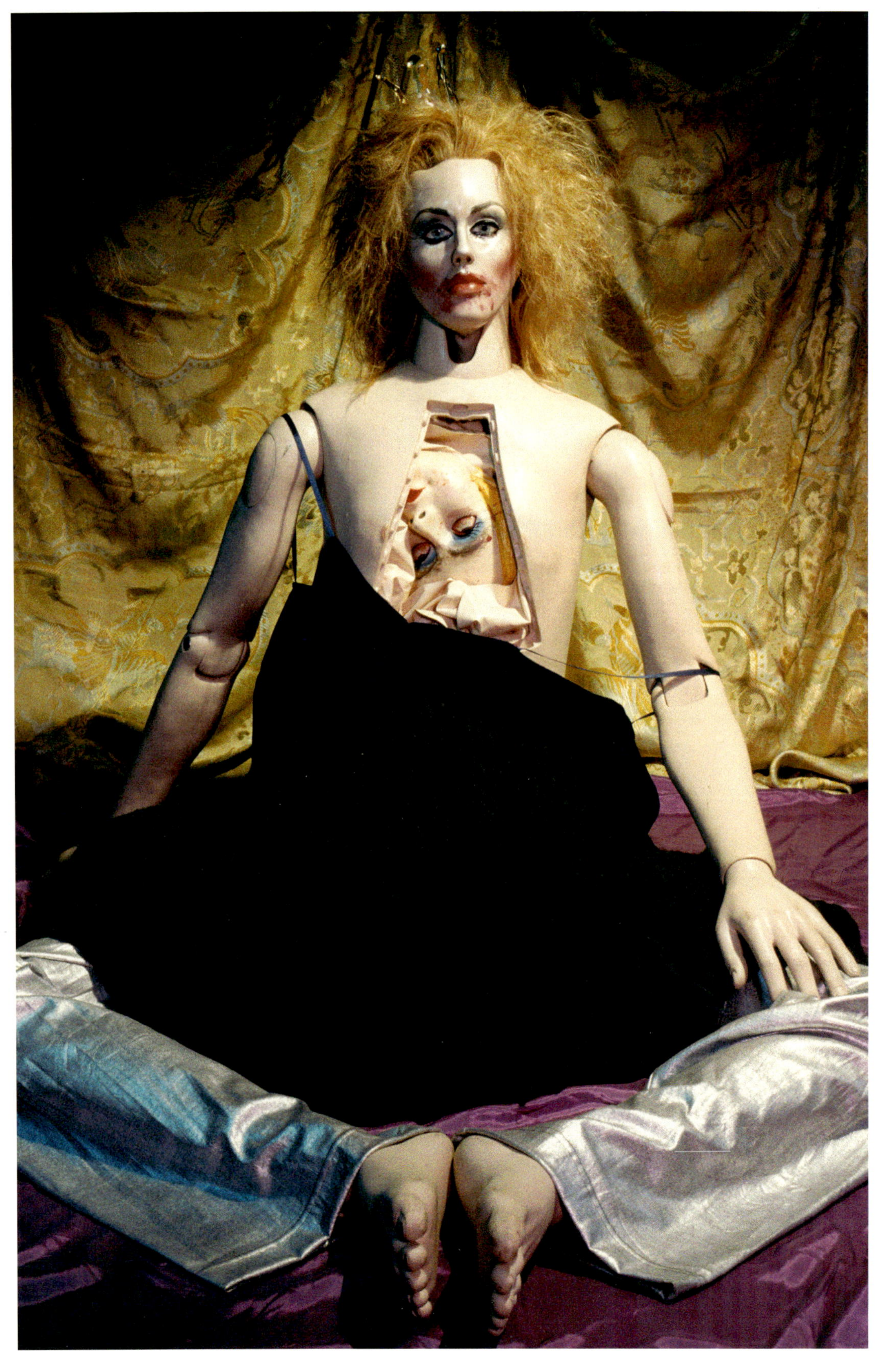

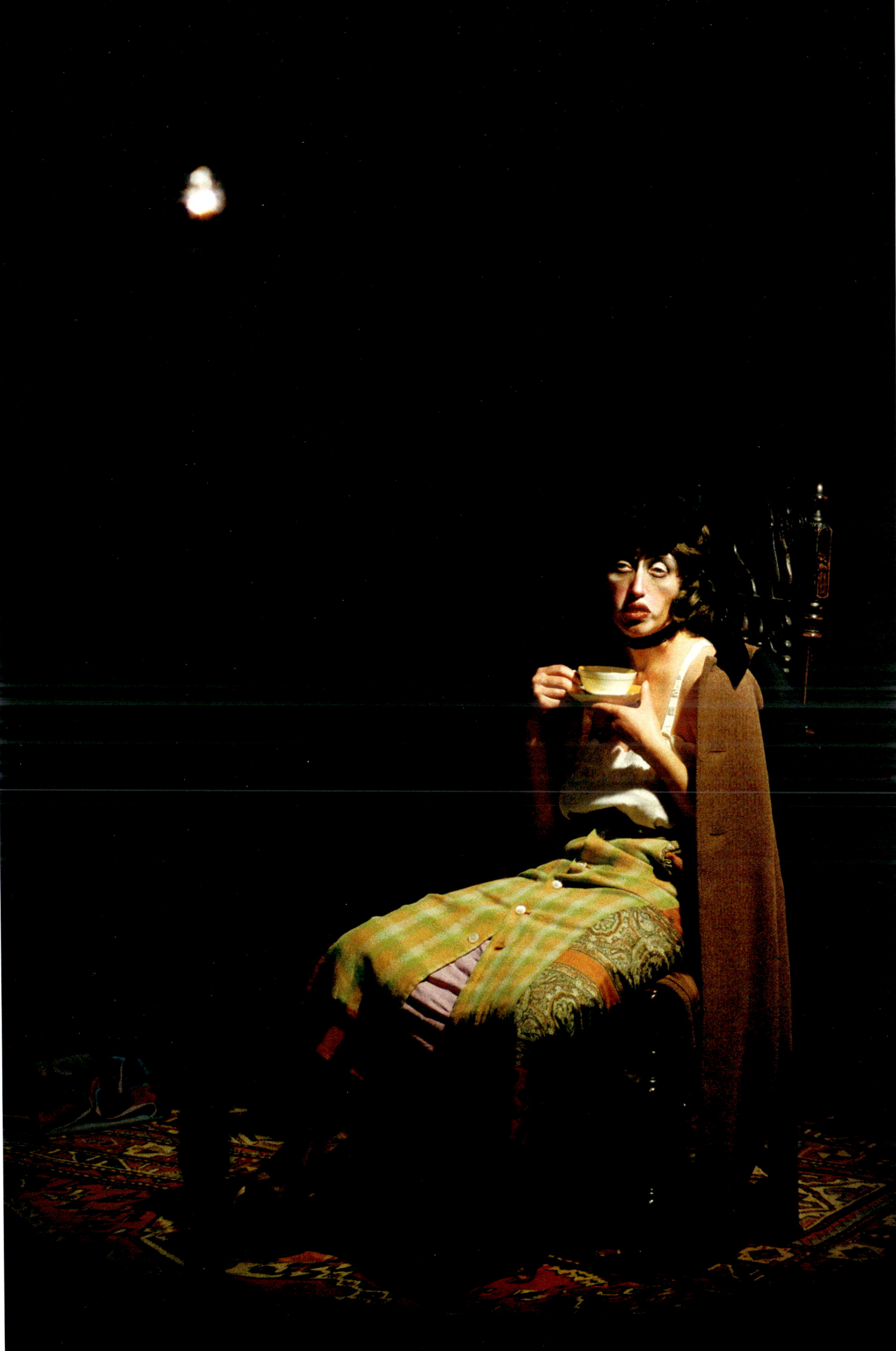

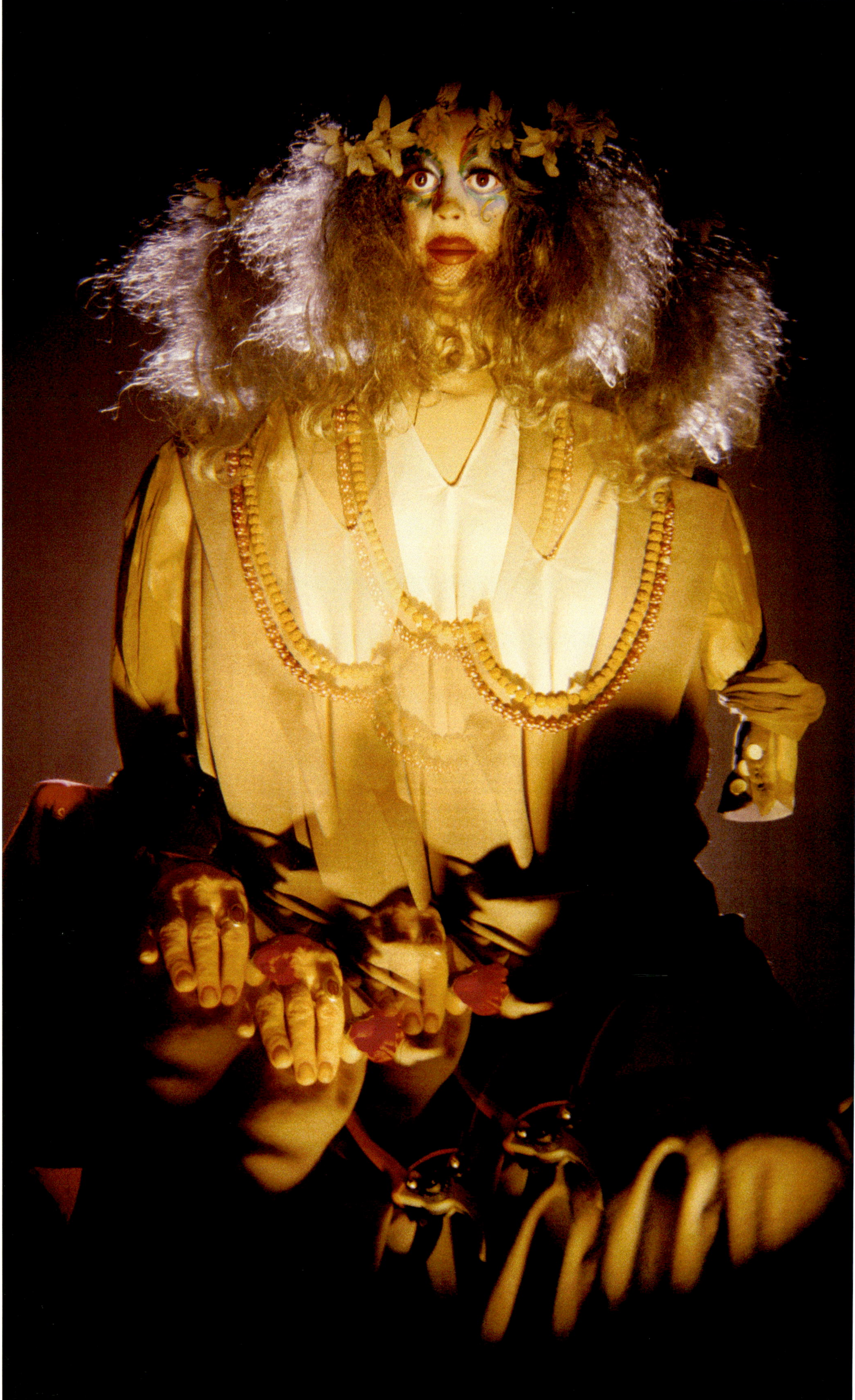

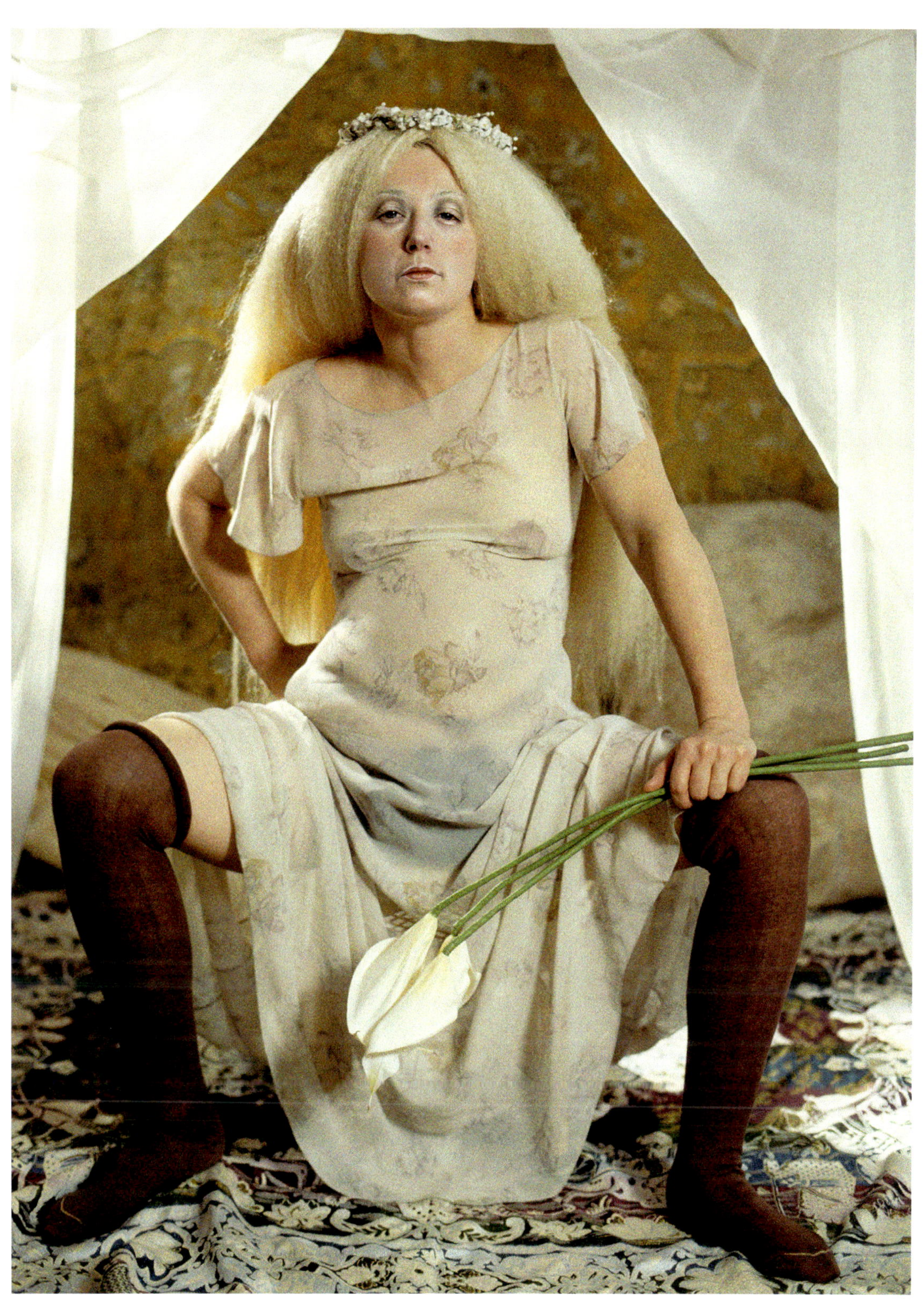

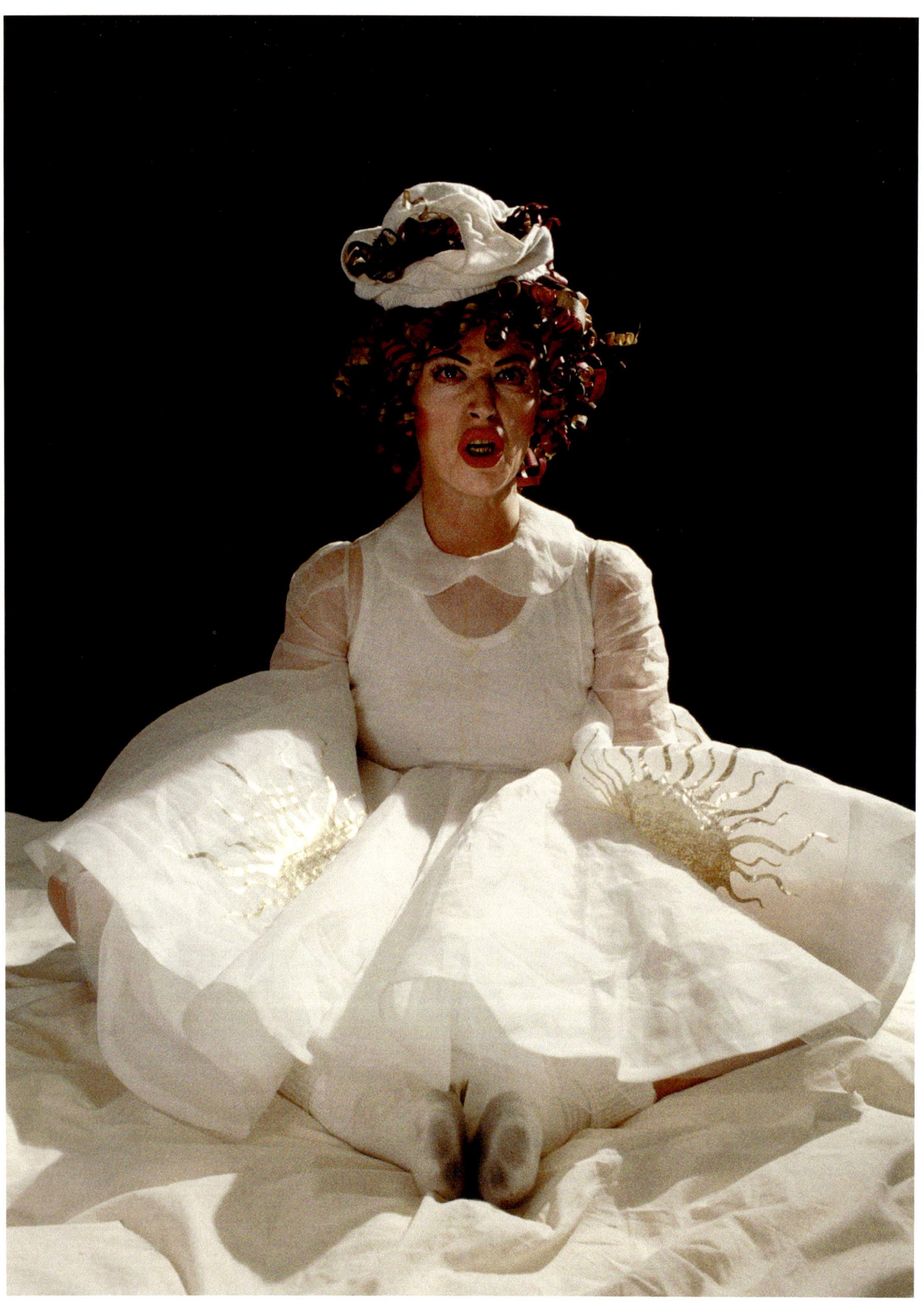

Untitled #305
Untitled #308
Untitled #310
Untitled #311
Untitled #307
Untitled #312

1994—1996

[Horror and Surrealist Pictures]

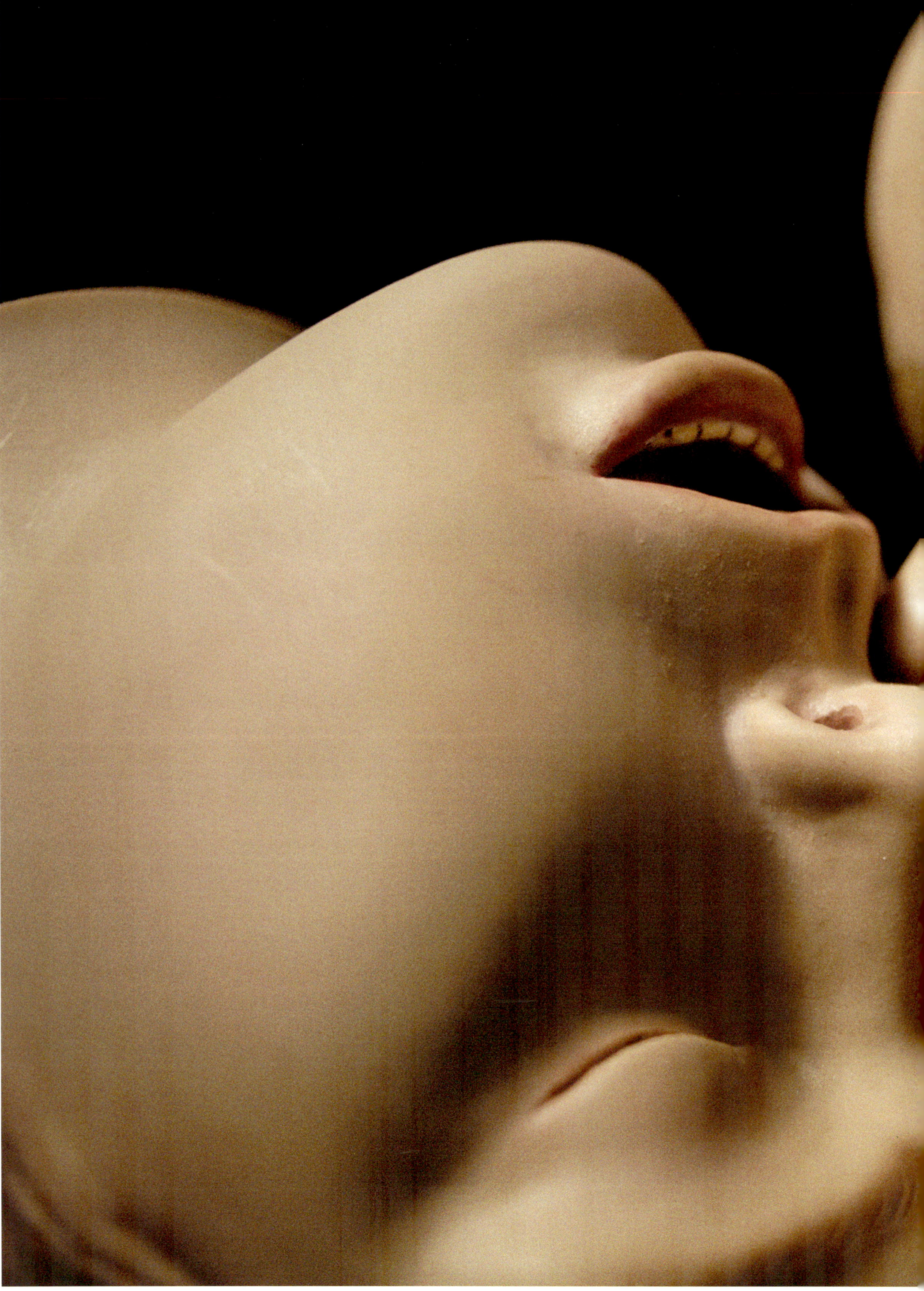

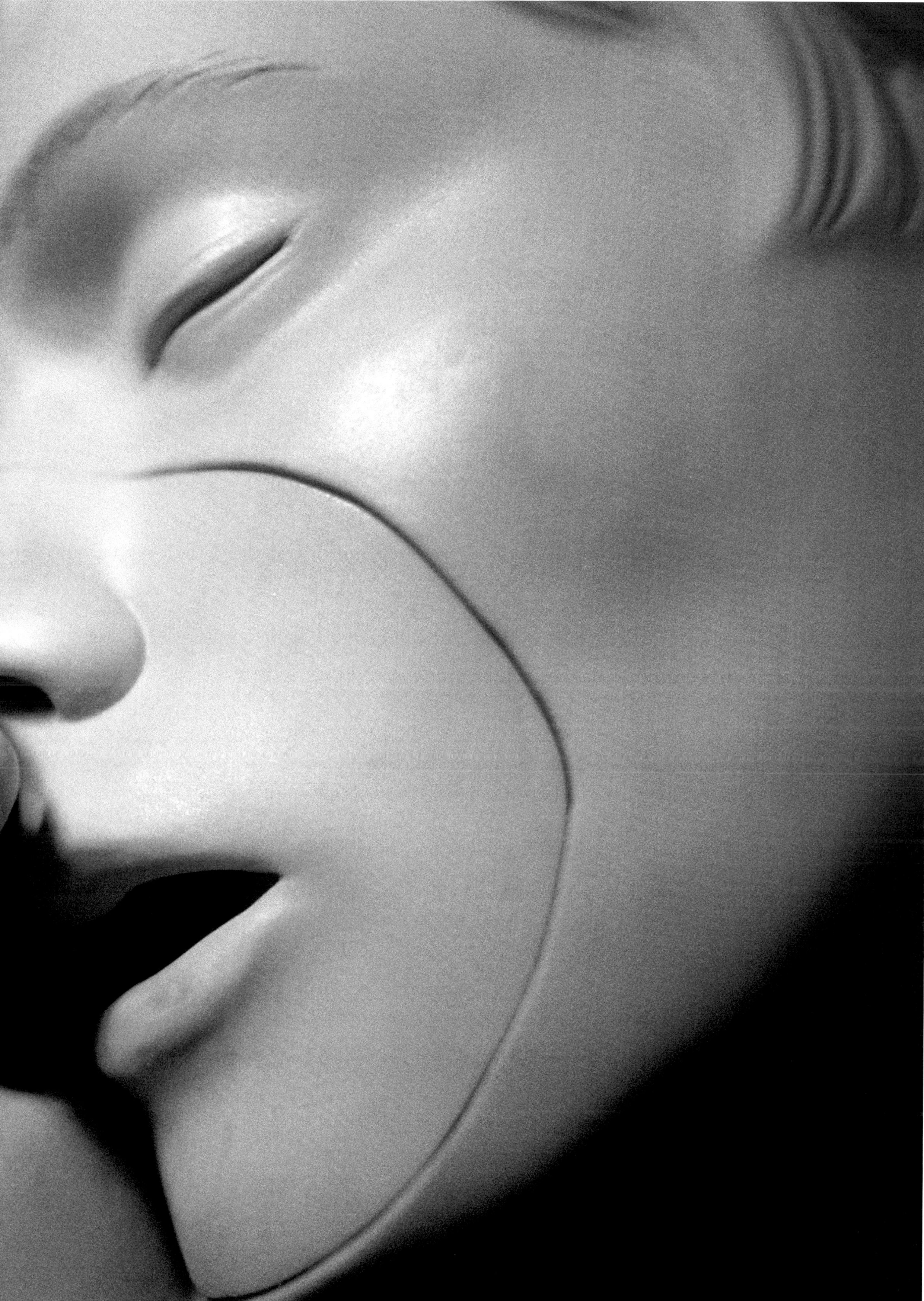

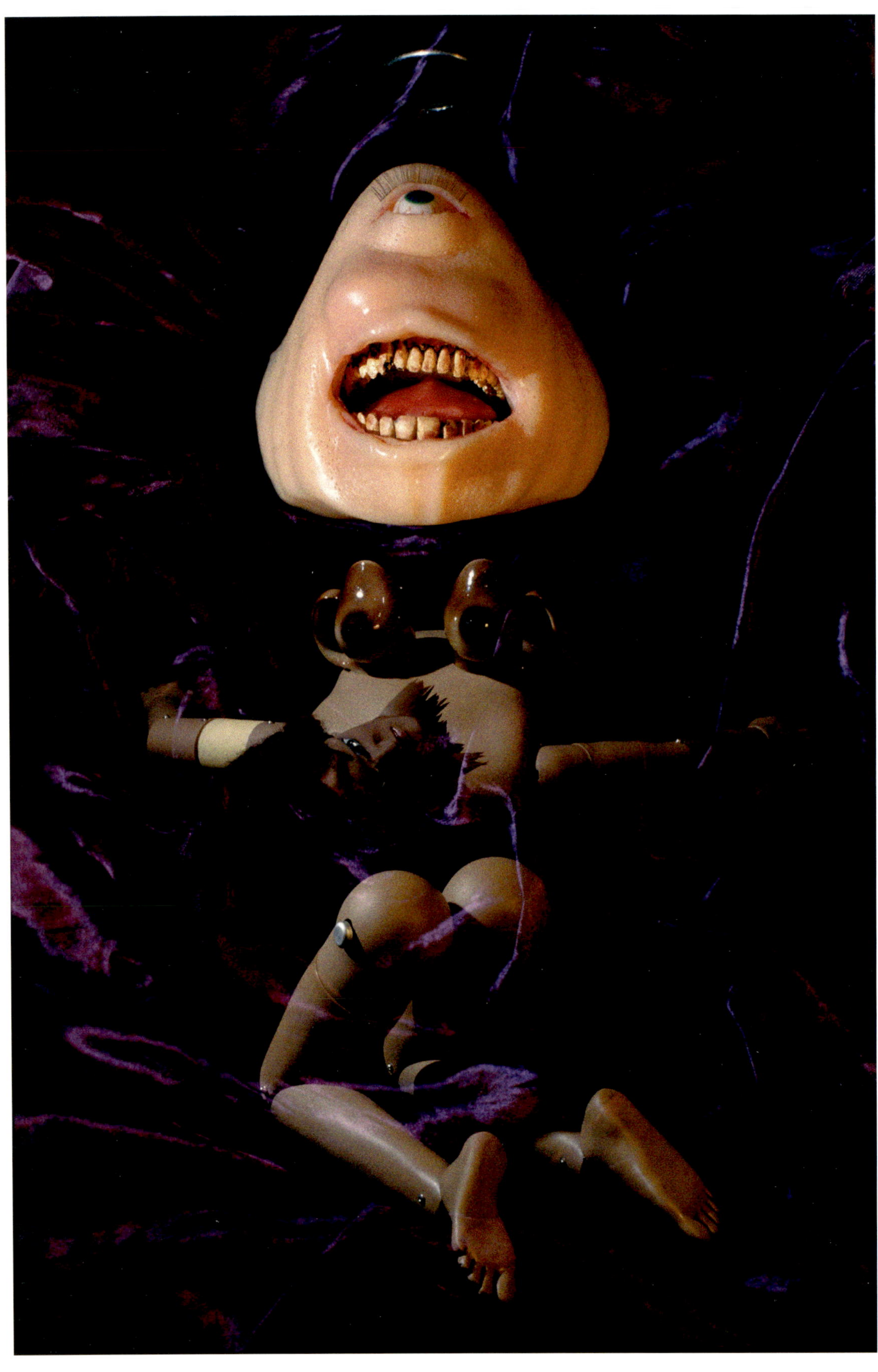

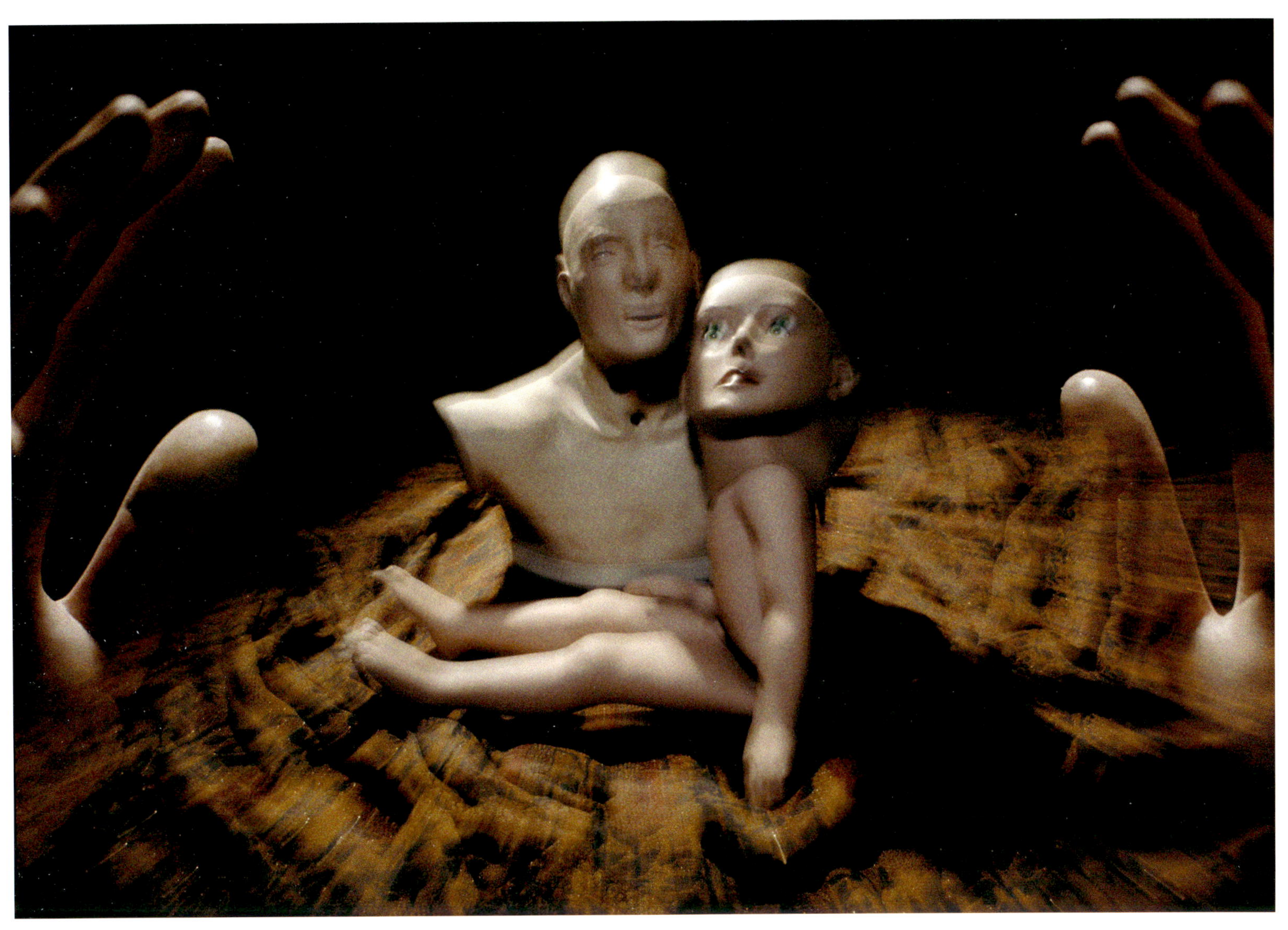

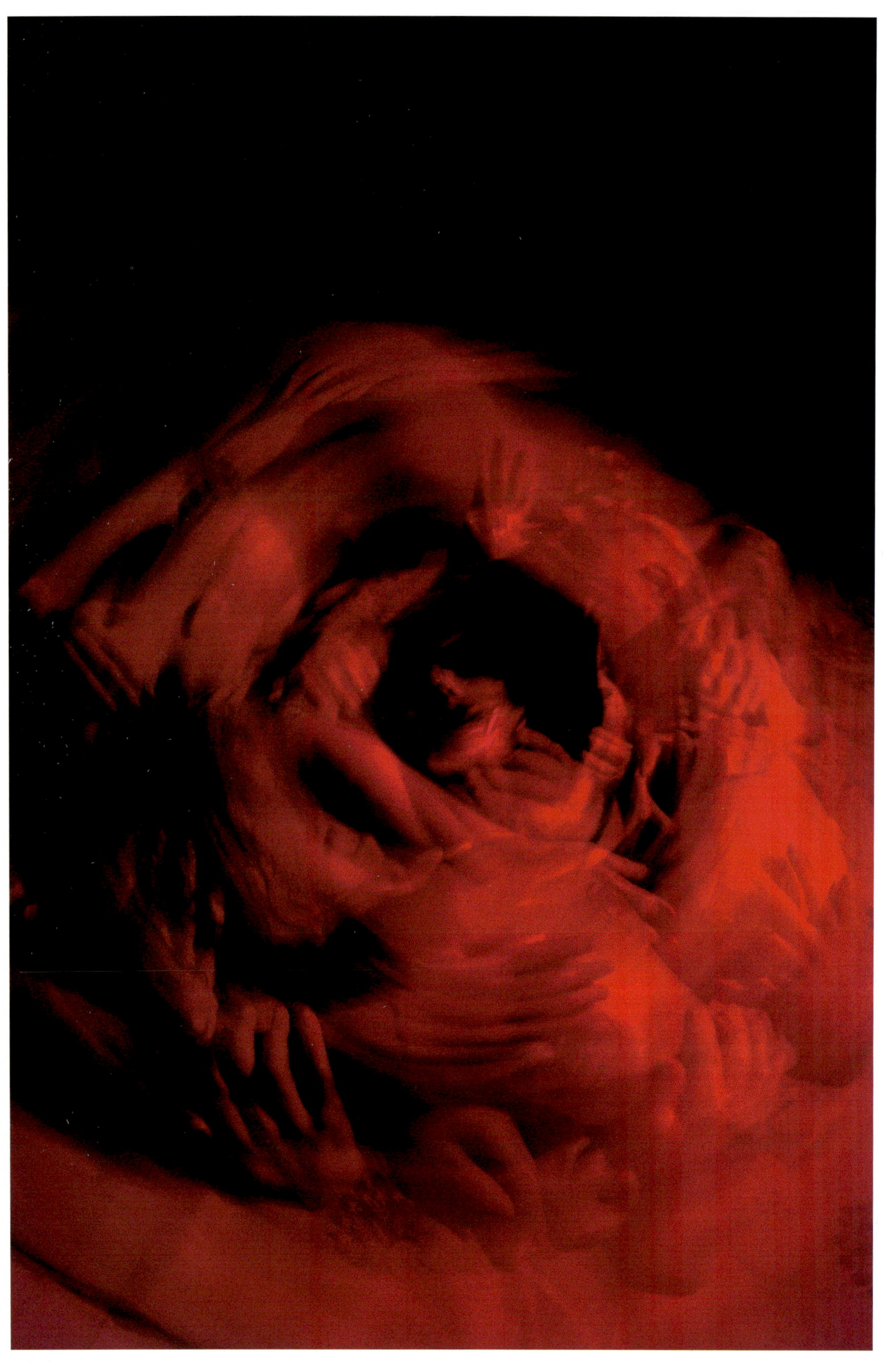

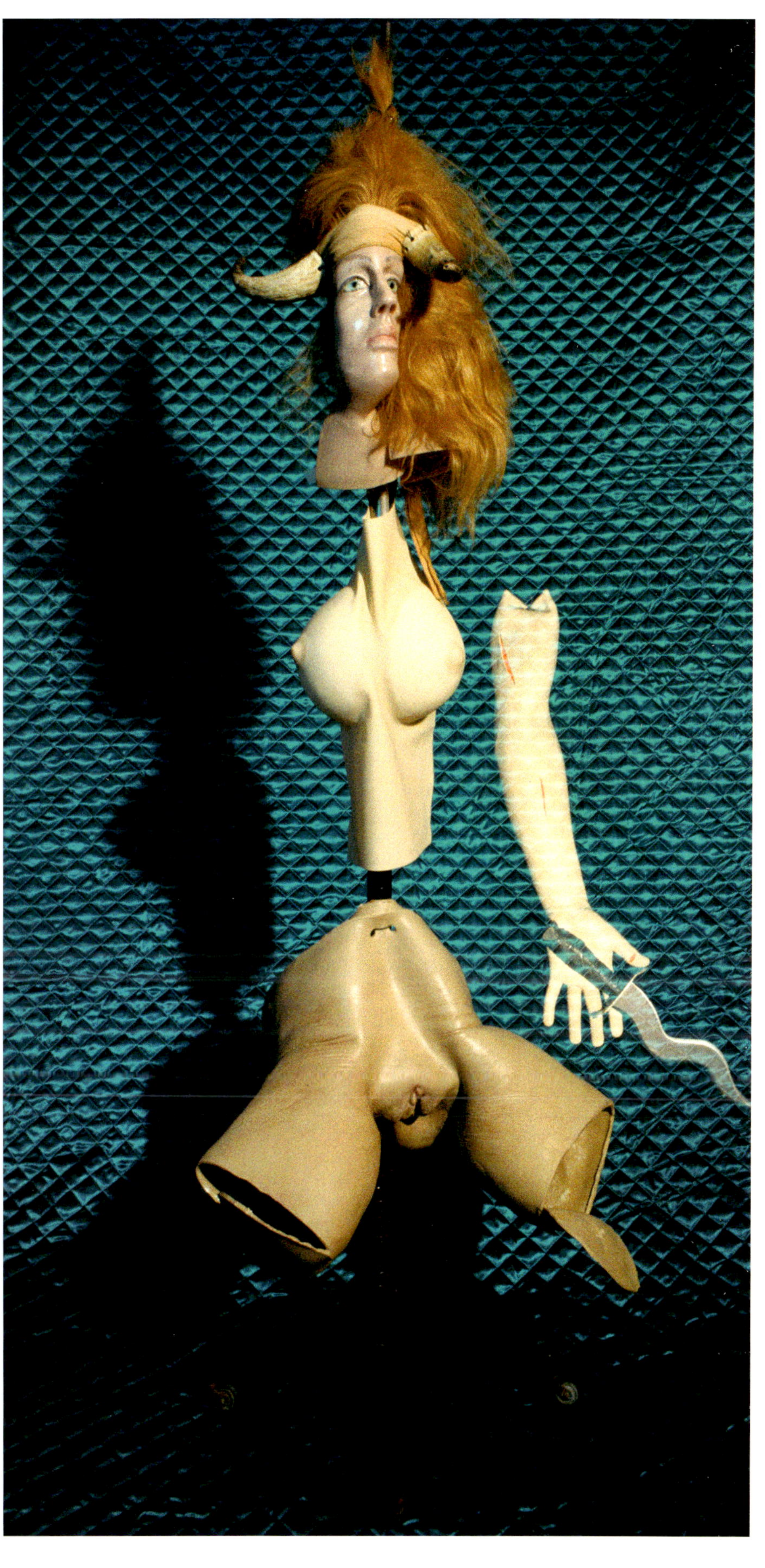

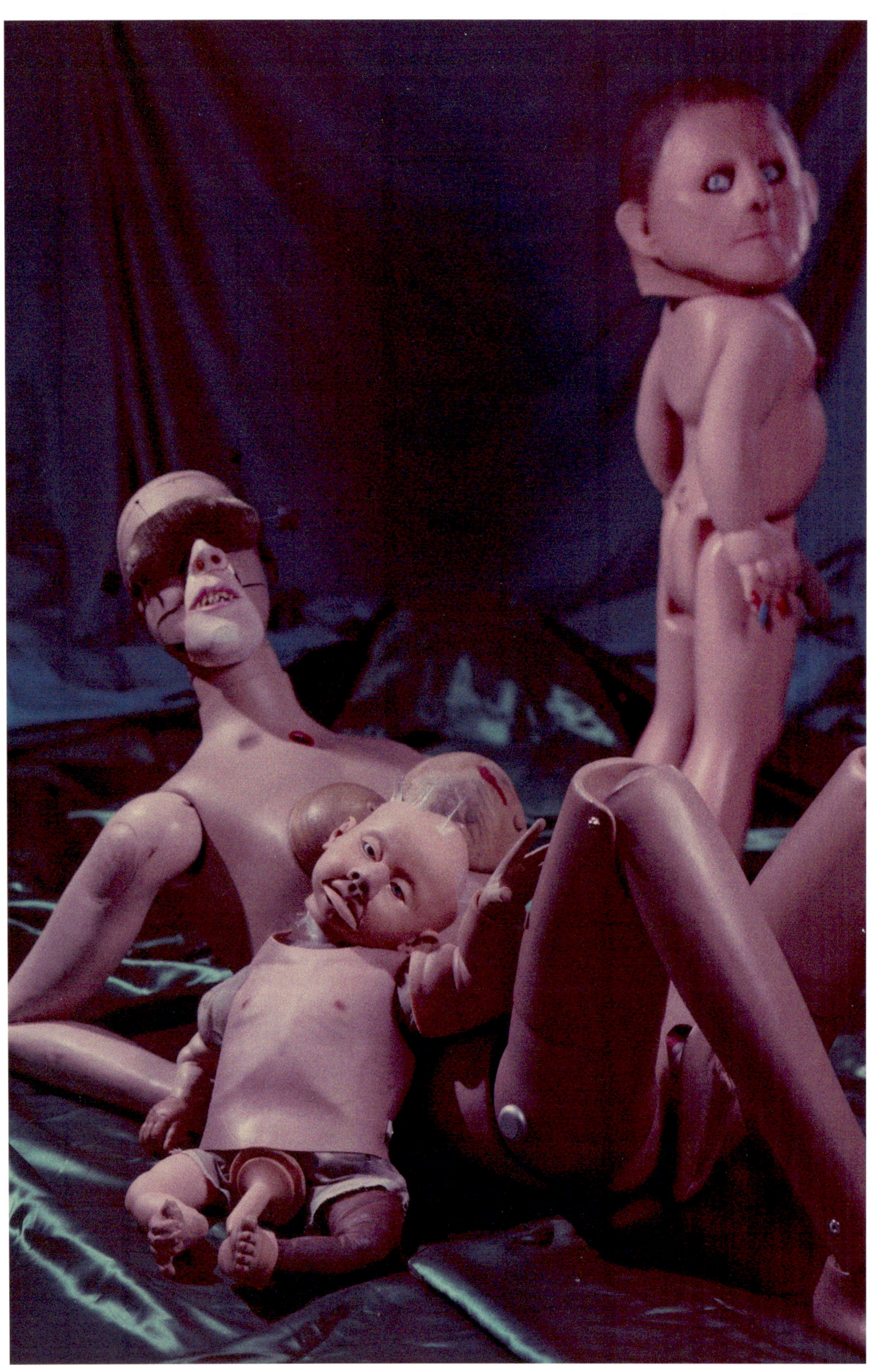

Untitled #314A
Untitled #314B
Untitled #314D
Untitled #314E
Untitled #314C
Untitled #314F
Untitled #324
Untitled #315
Untitled #323
Untitled #316

1994—1996

[Masks]

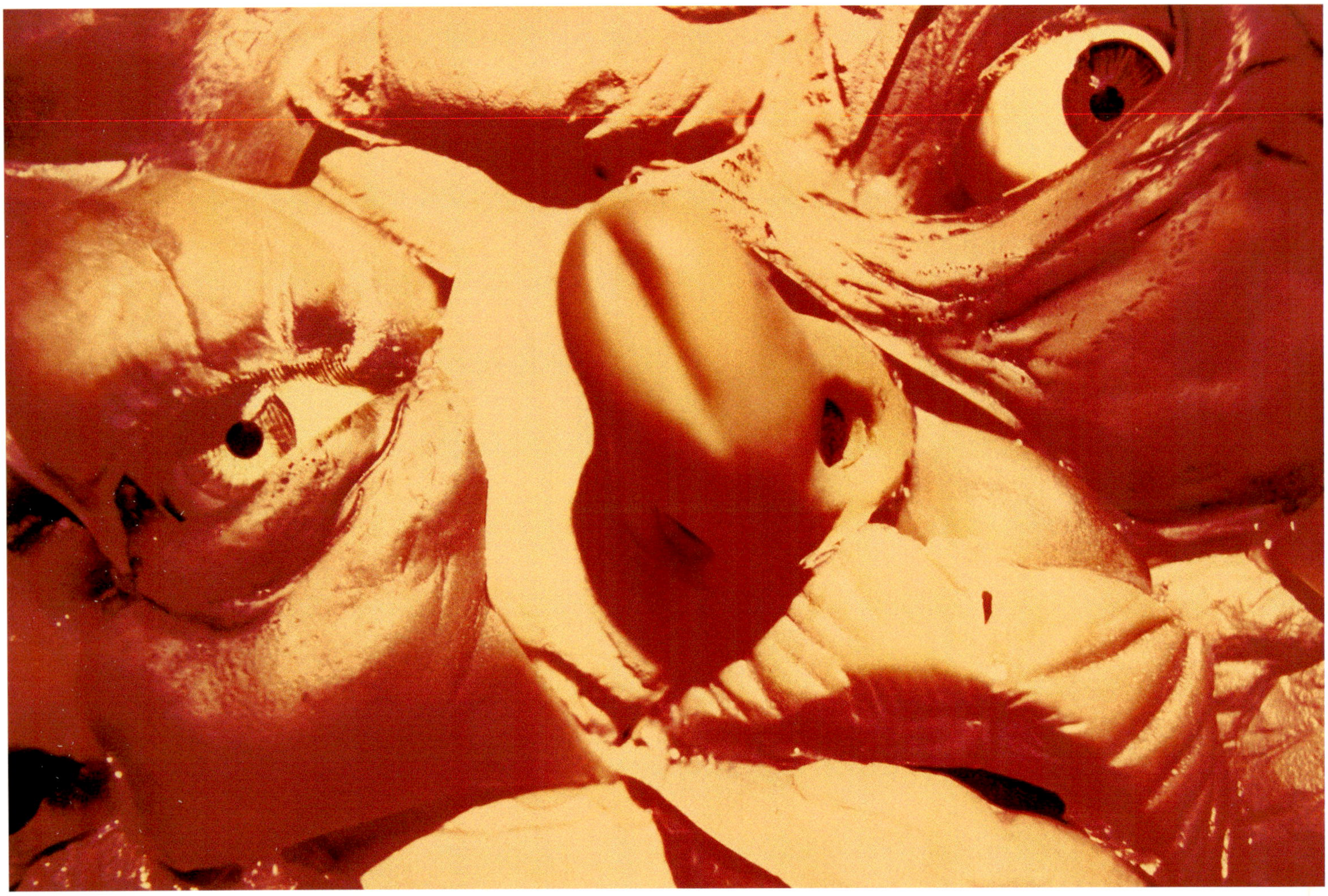

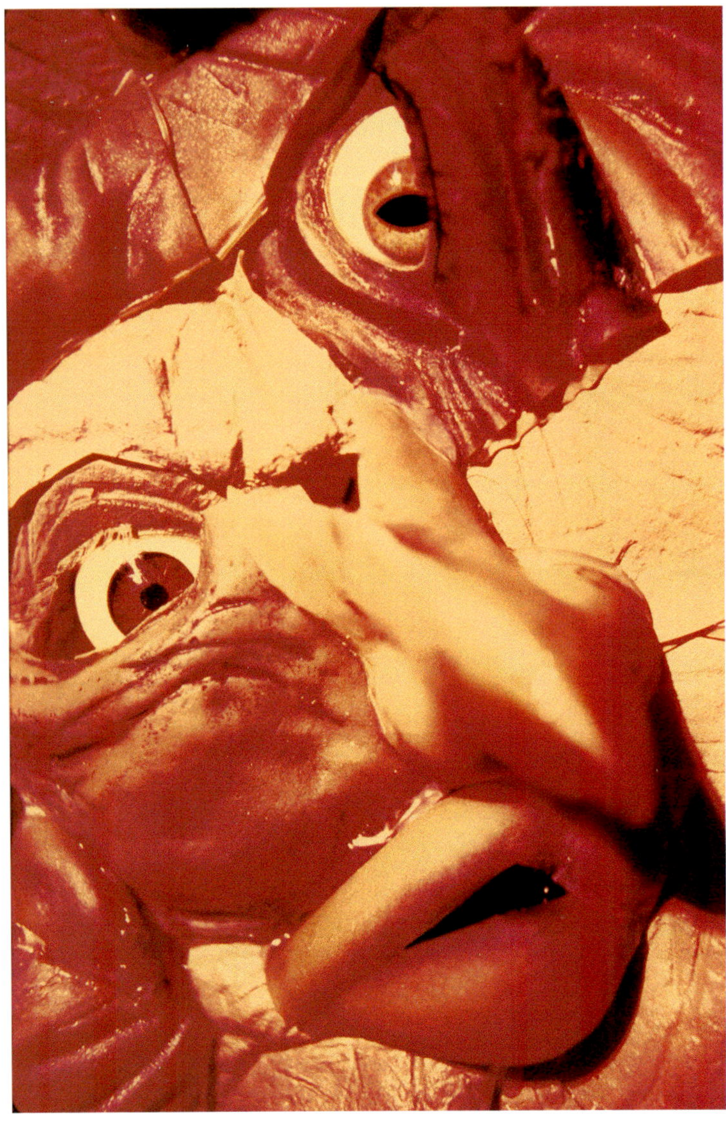

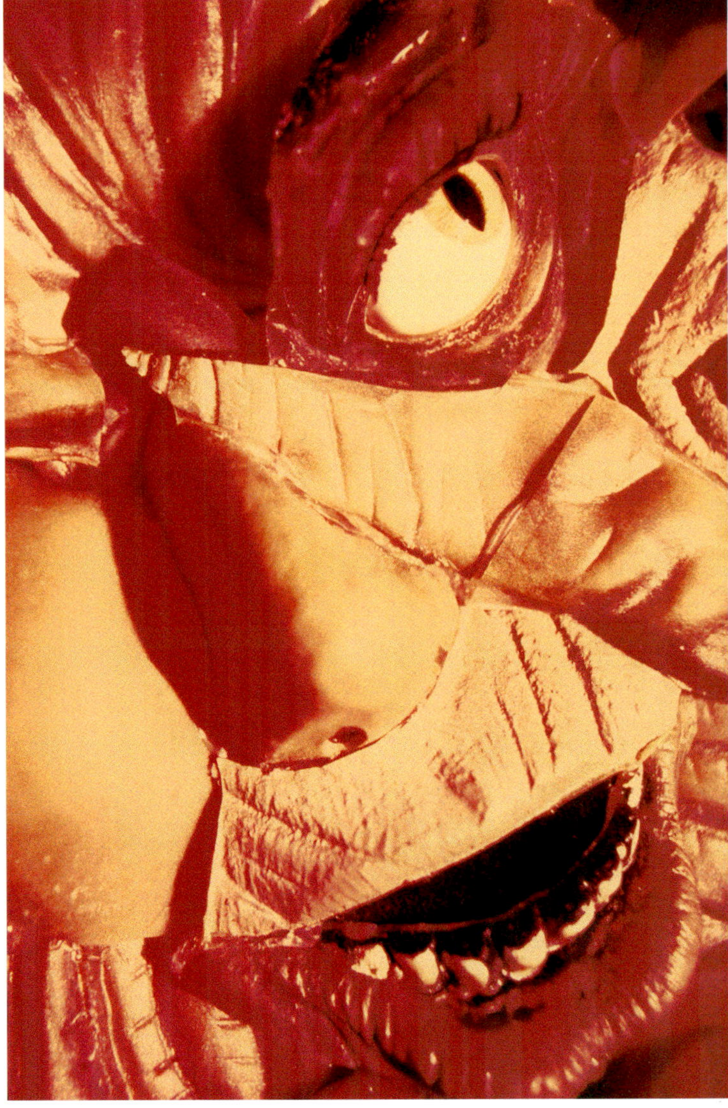

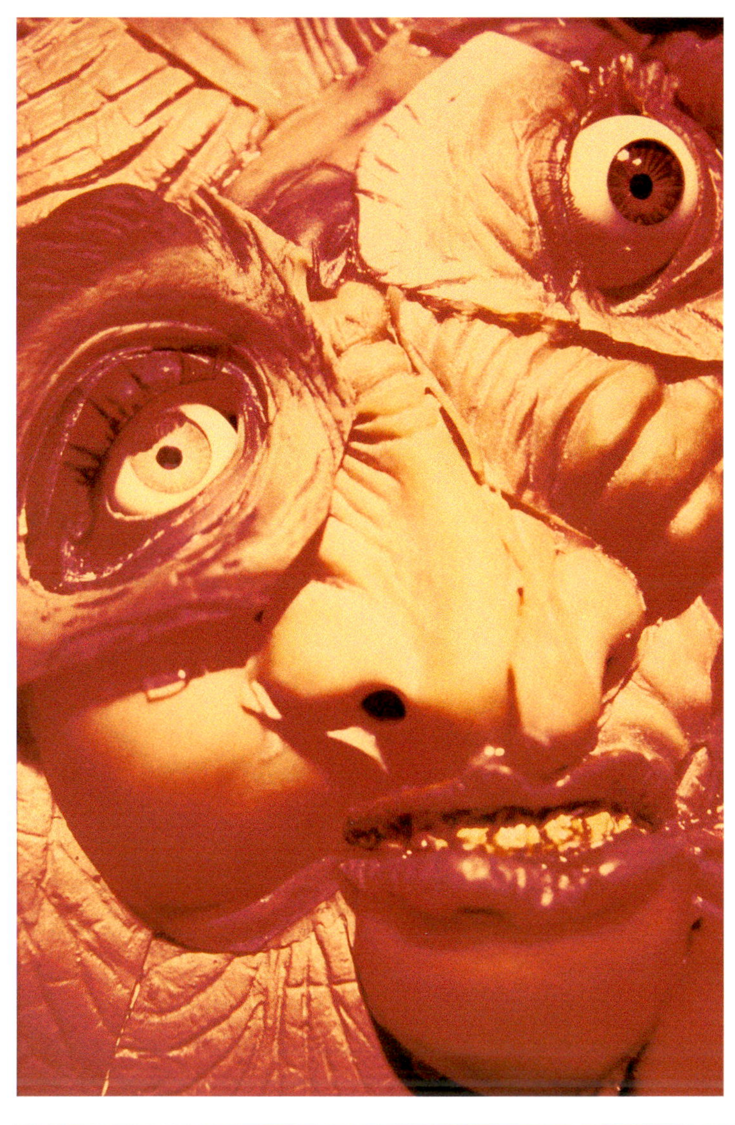

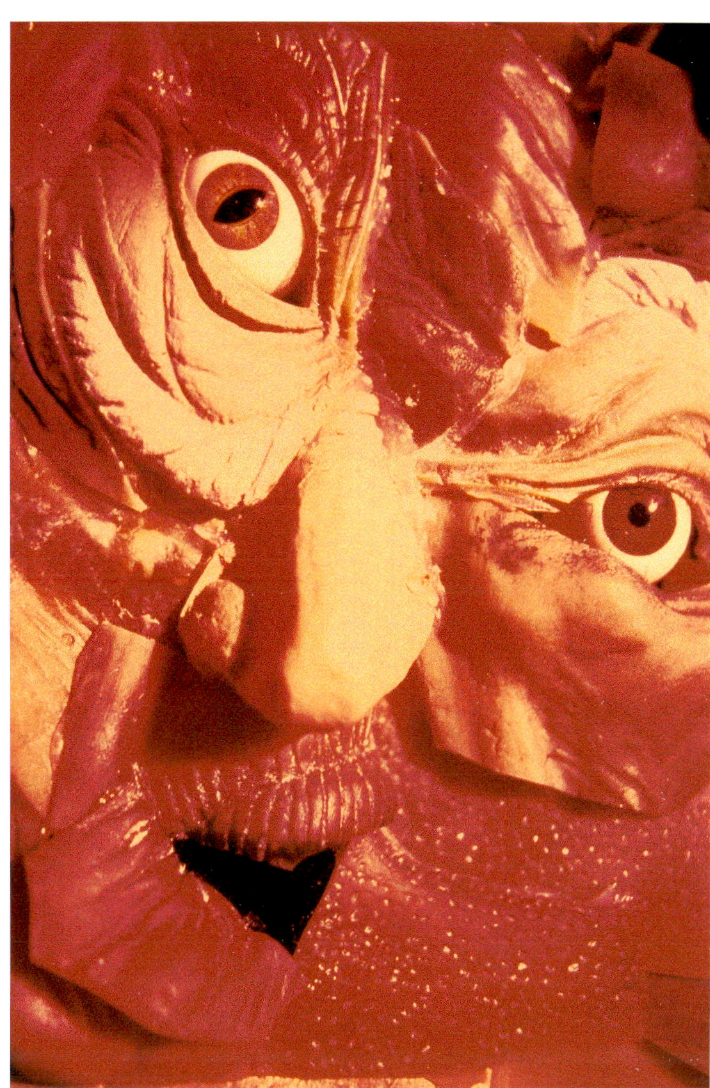

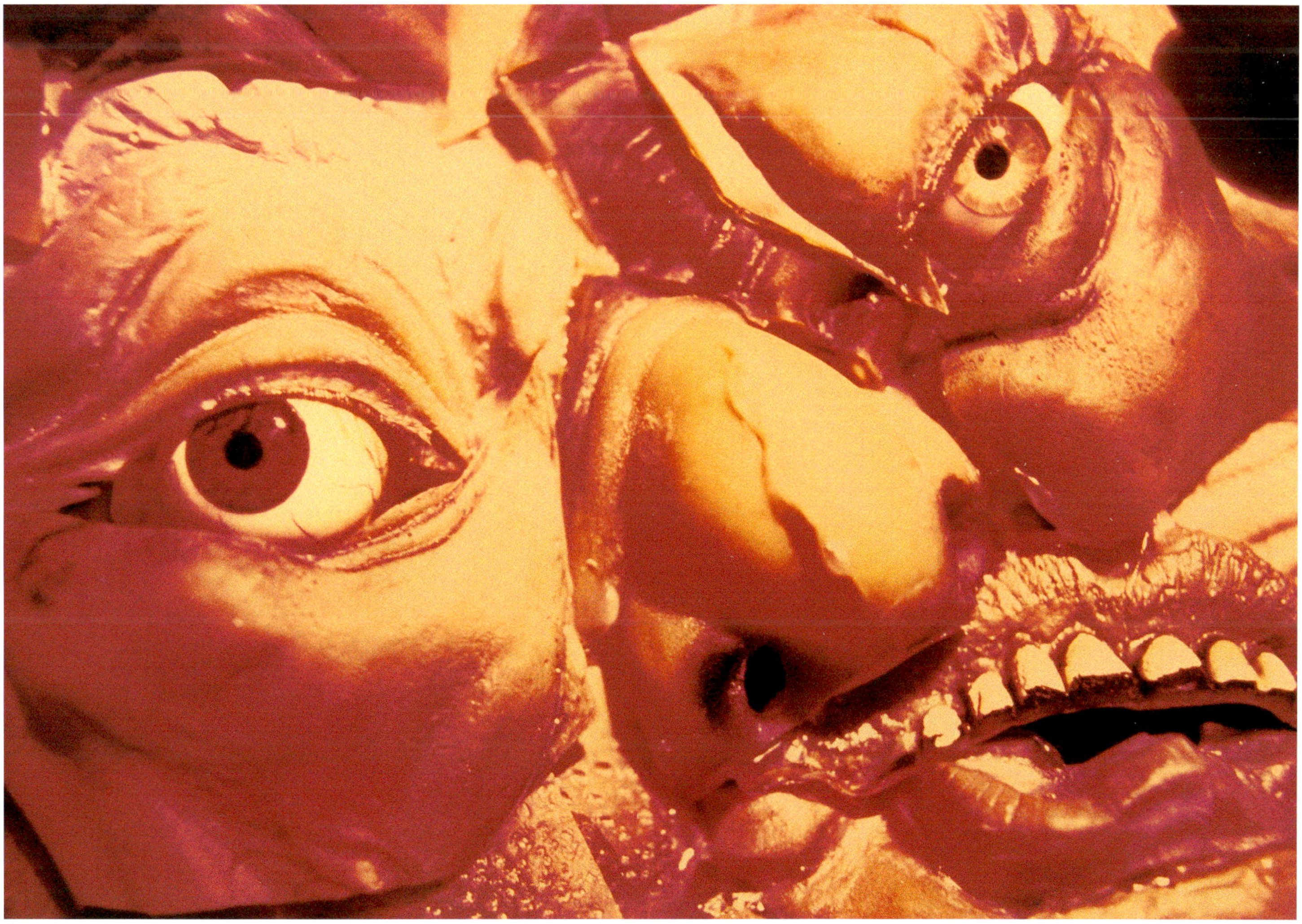

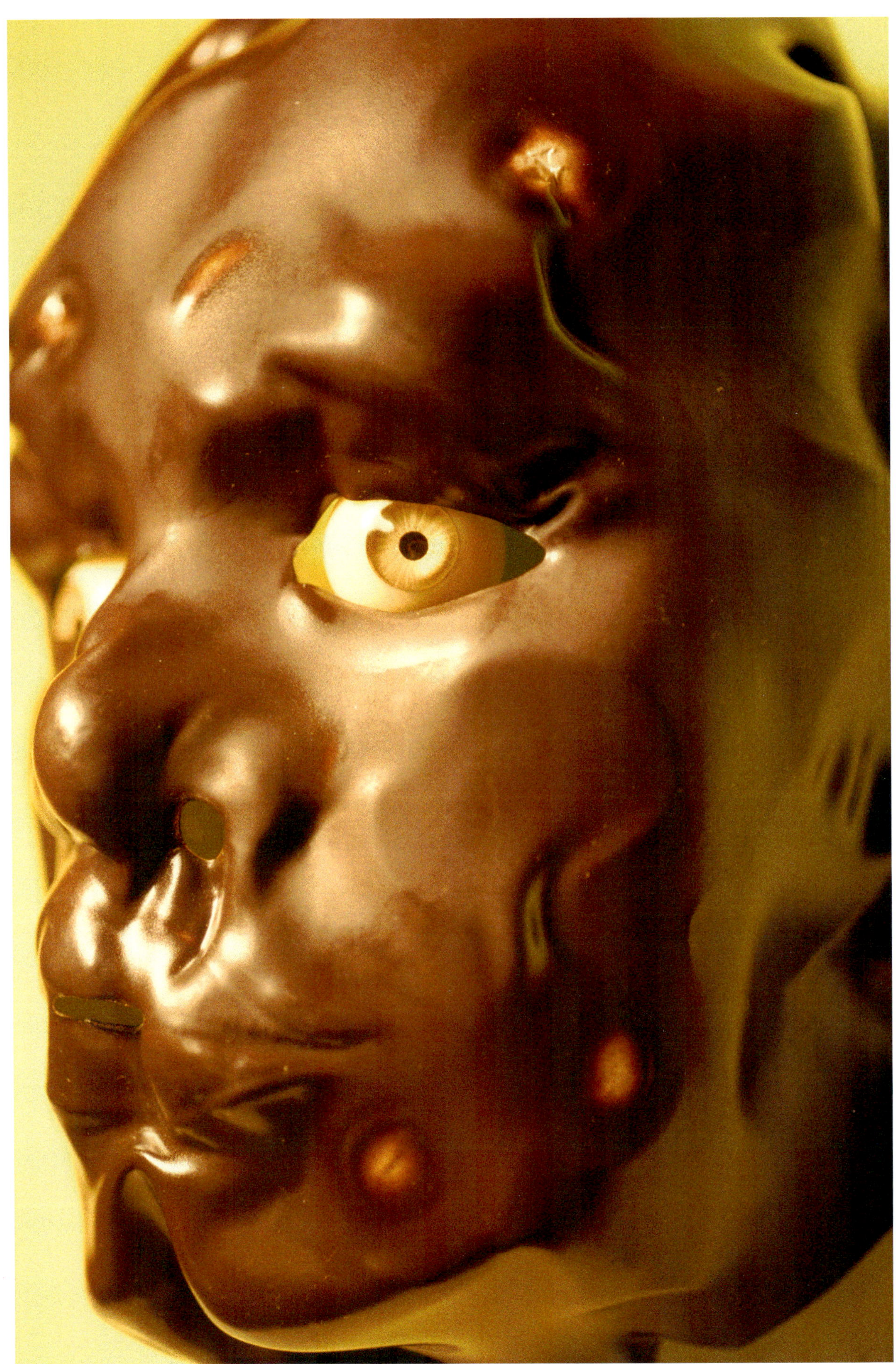

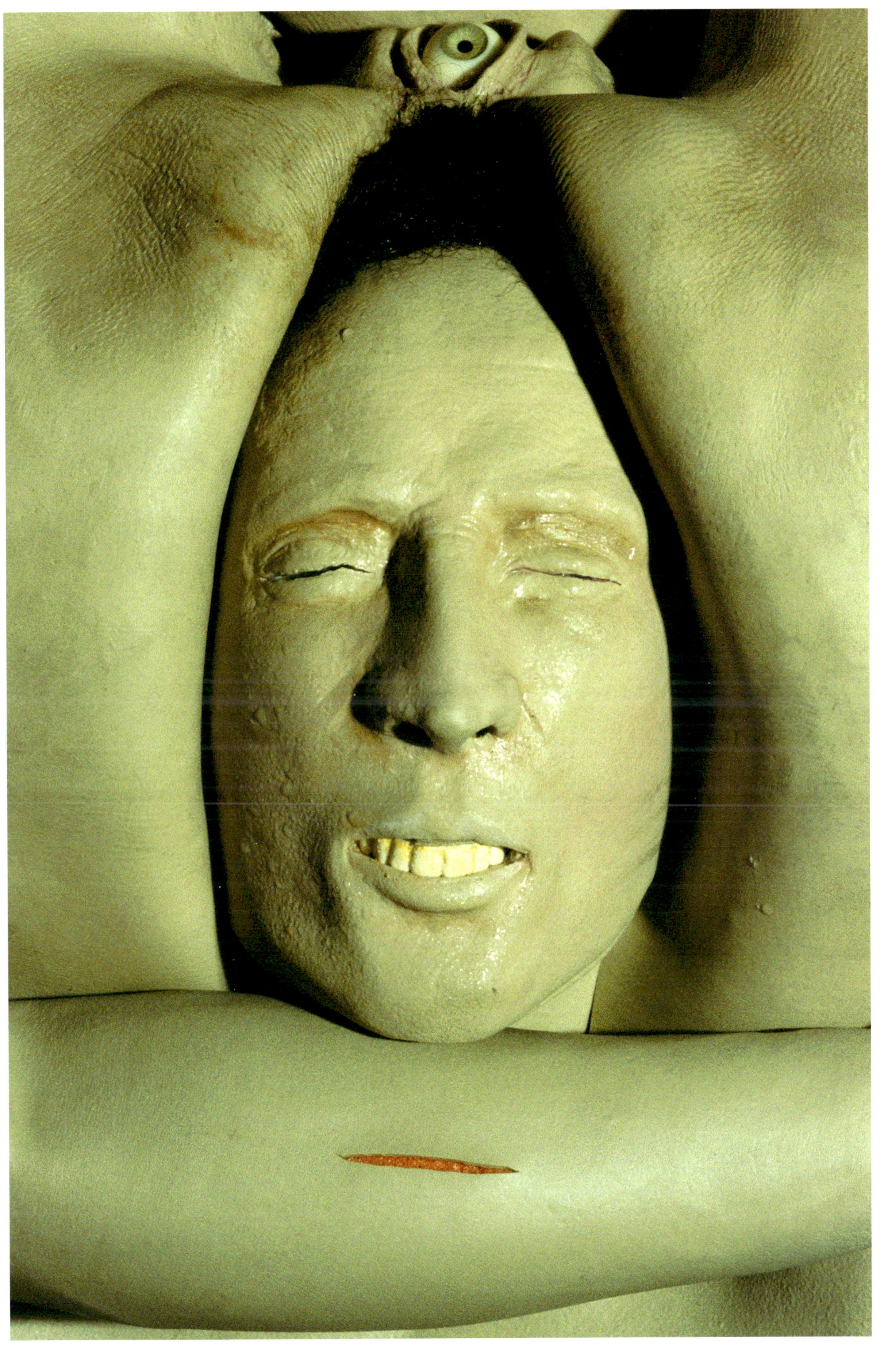

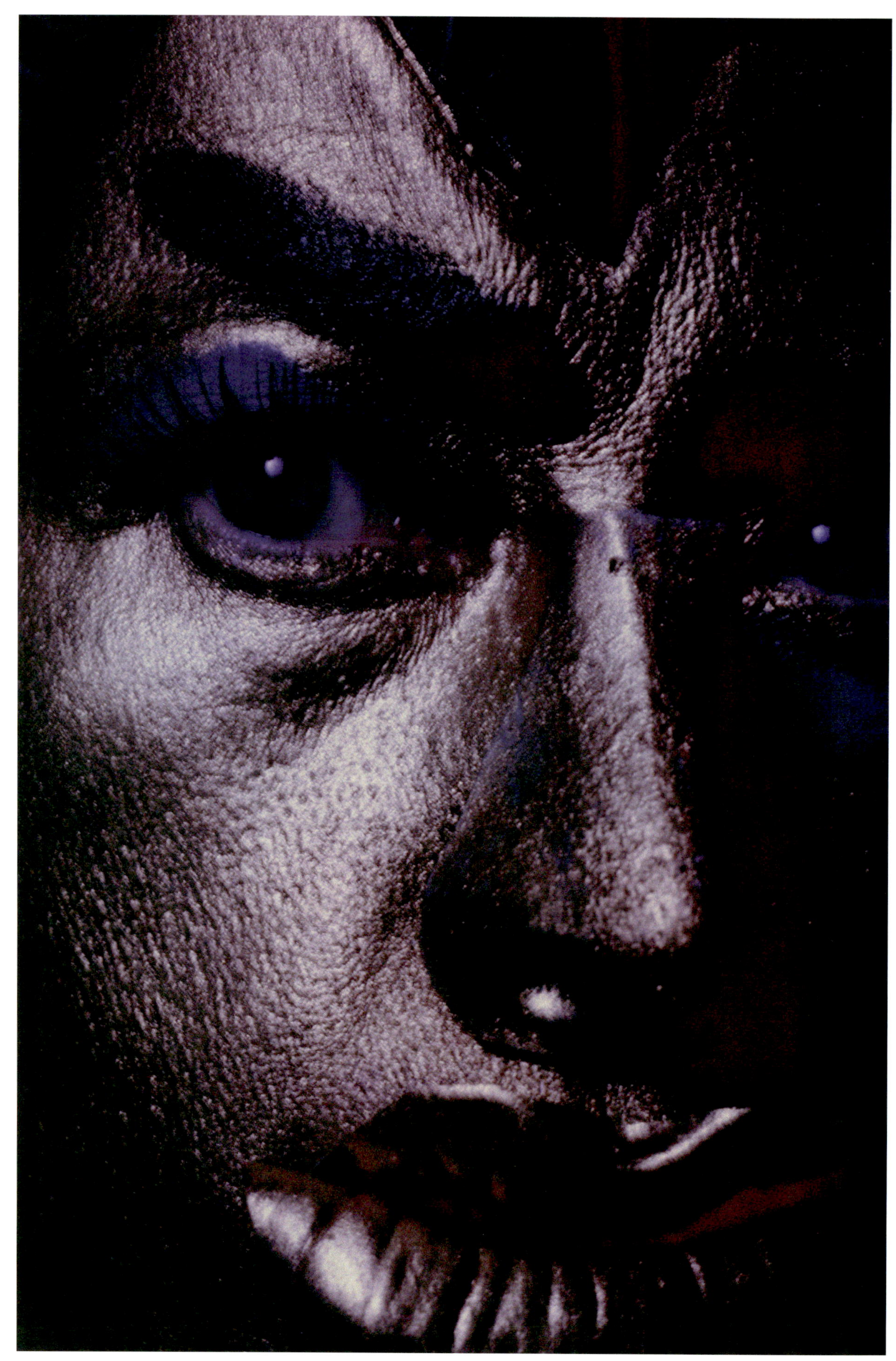

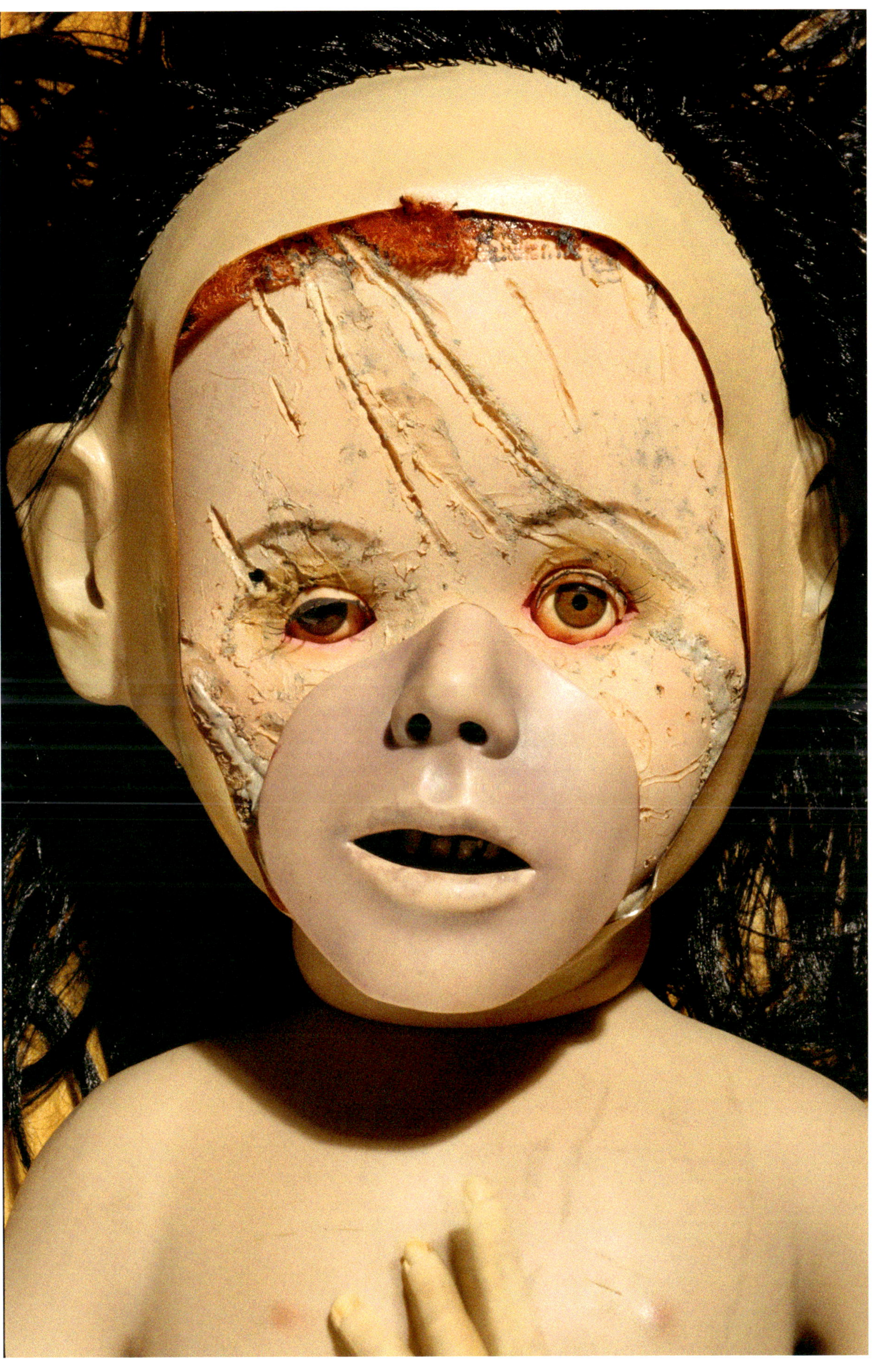

Untitled #335
Untitled #332
Untitled #343
Untitled #334
Untitled #348
Untitled #347
Untitled #337
Untitled #345

1999

[Broken Dolls]

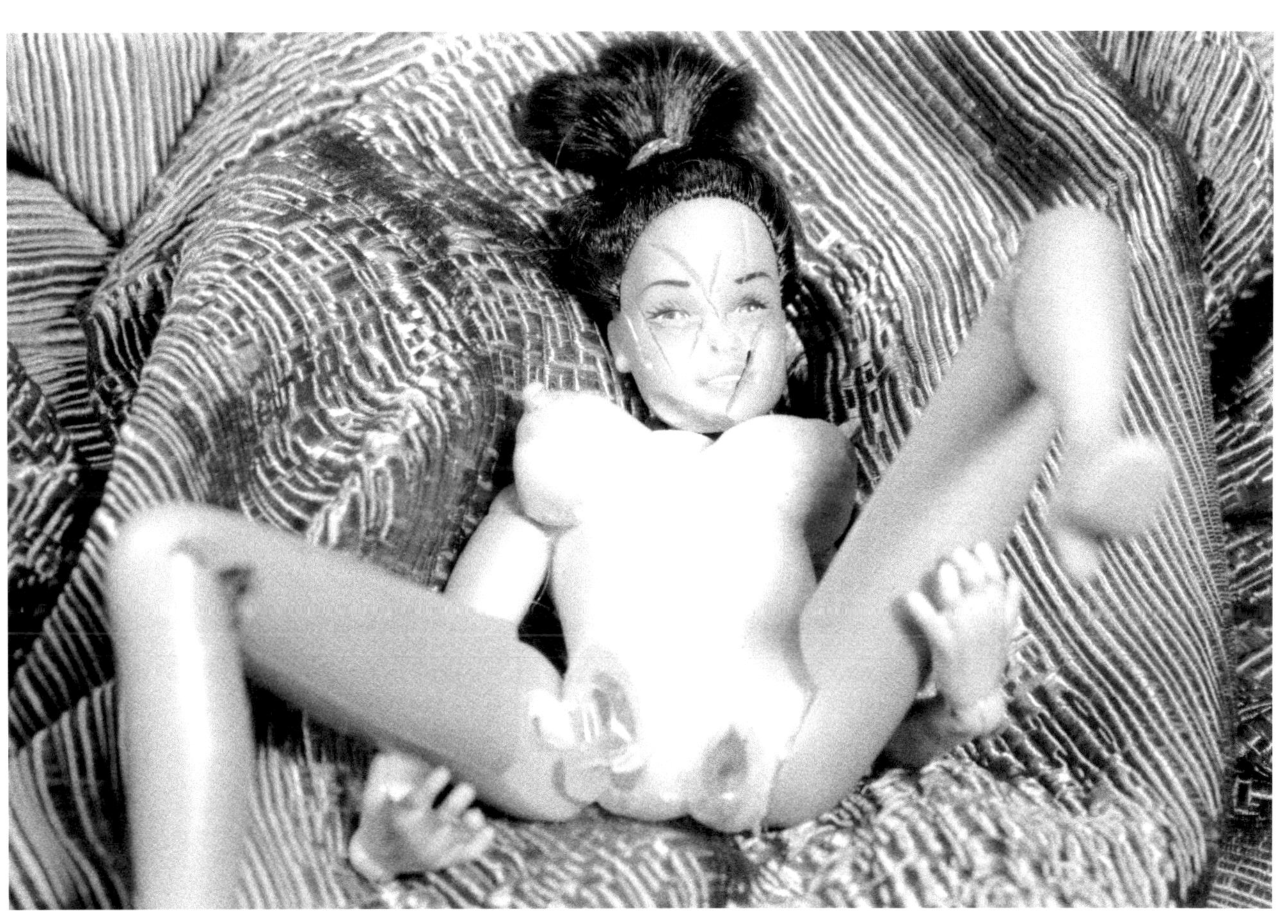

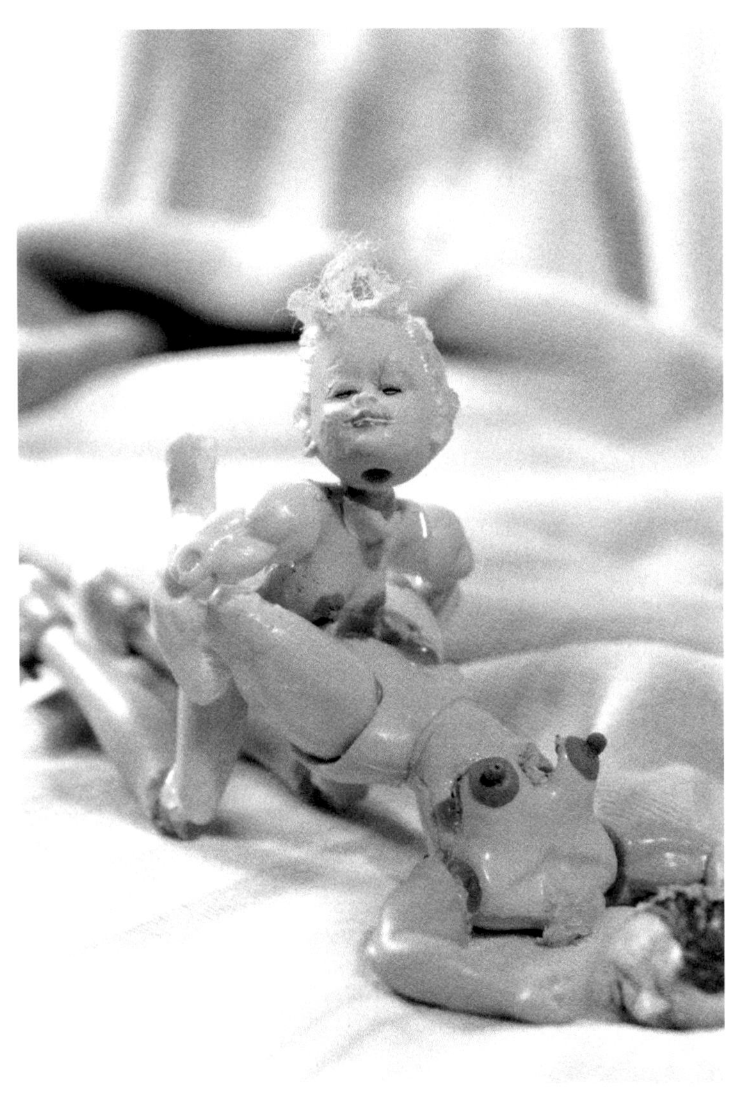

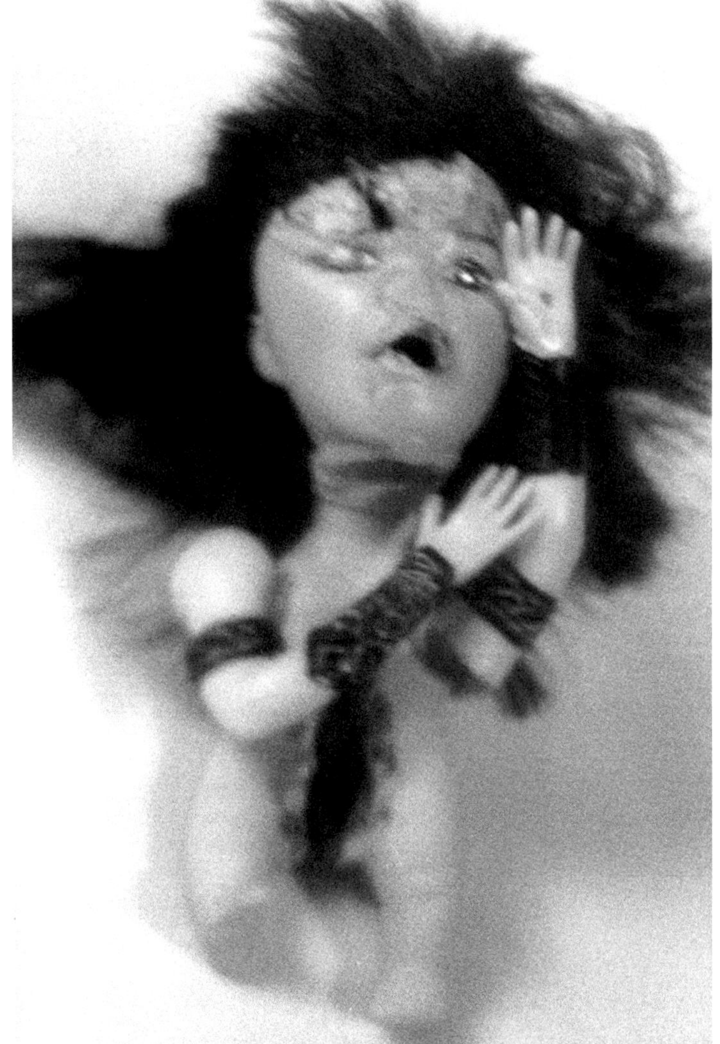

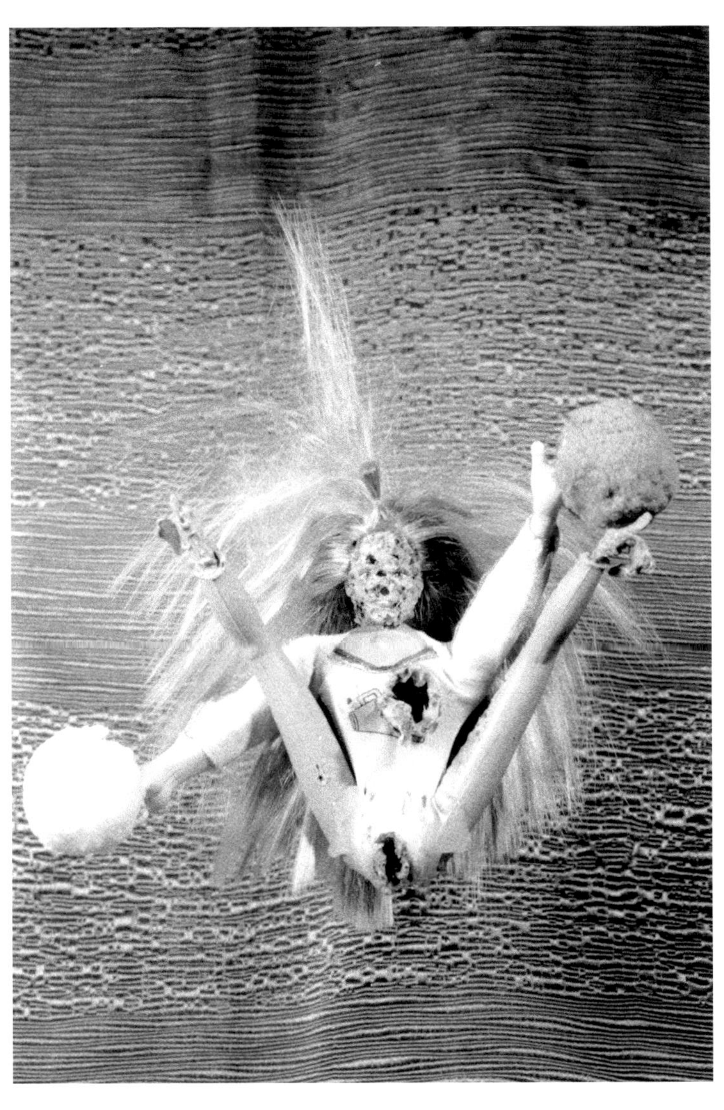

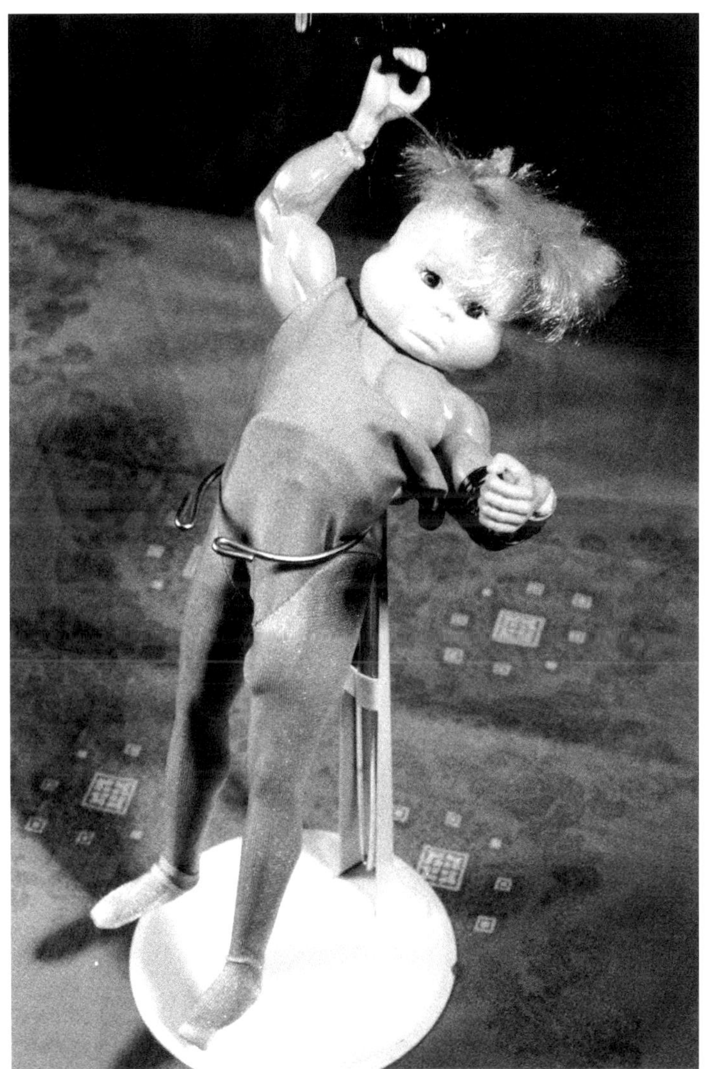

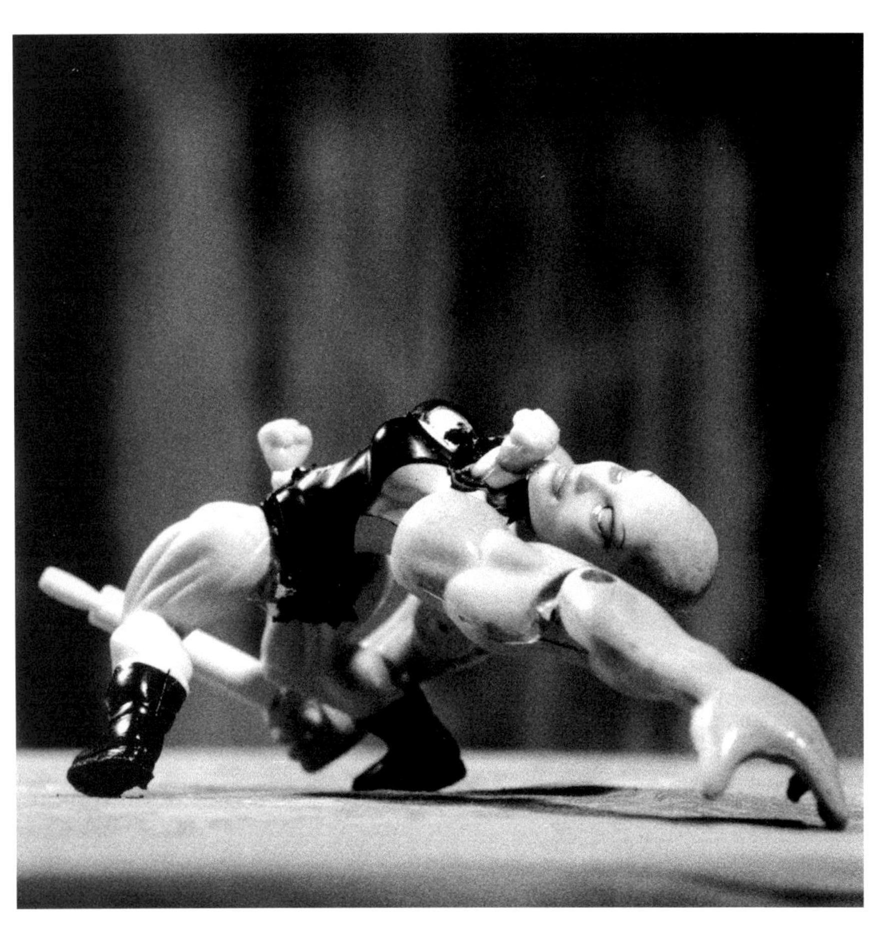

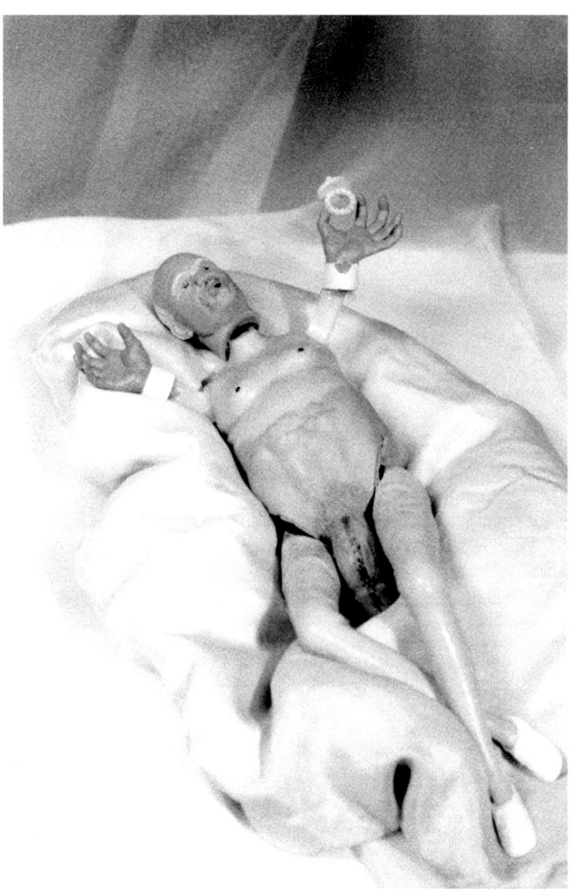

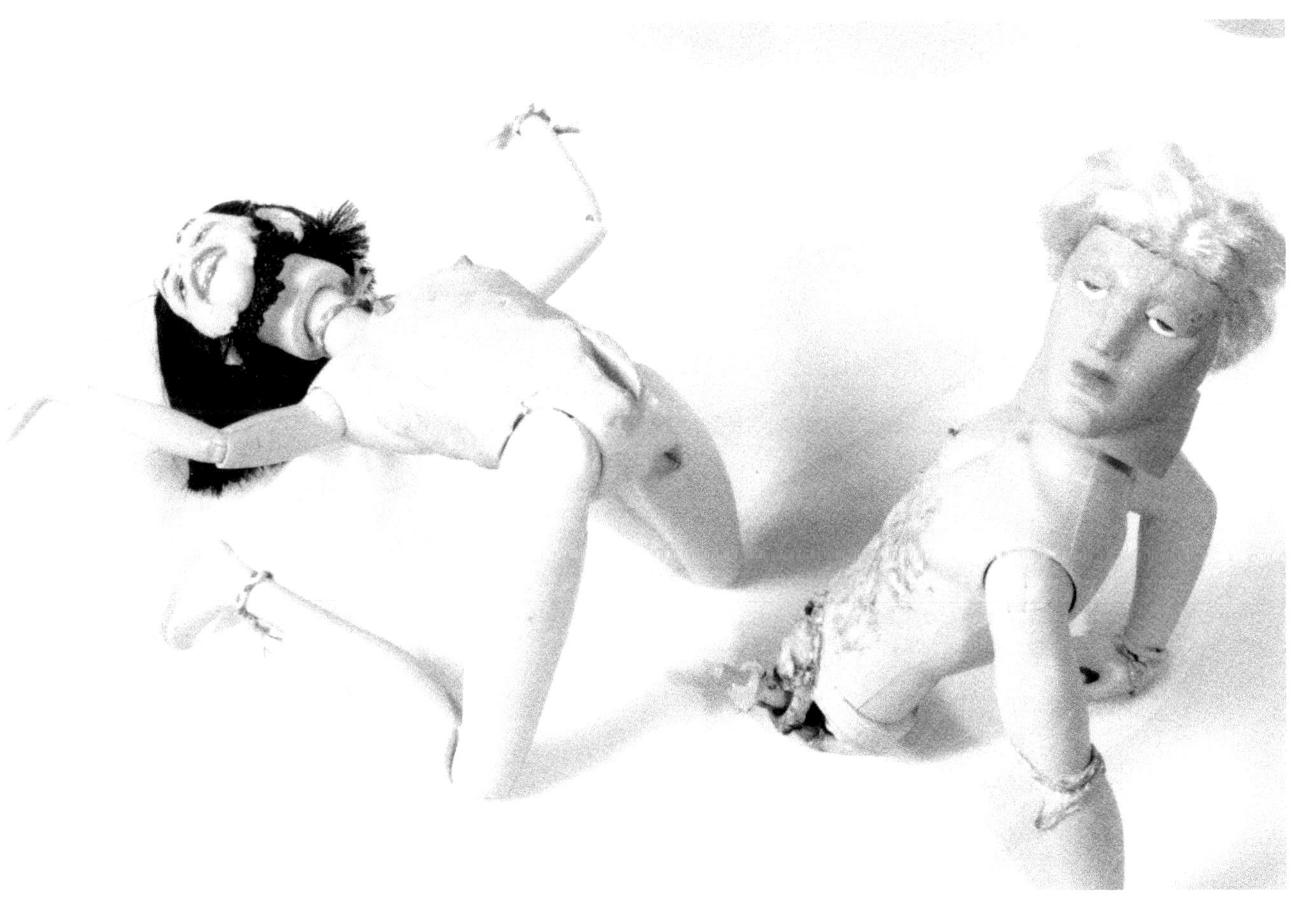

Untitled #352
Untitled #403
Untitled #402
Untitled #358
Untitled #359
Untitled #399
Untitled #400
Untitled #401
Untitled #351
Untitled #355
Untitled #360
Untitled #409
Untitled #408

2000 — 2002

[Hollywoods / Hampton Types]

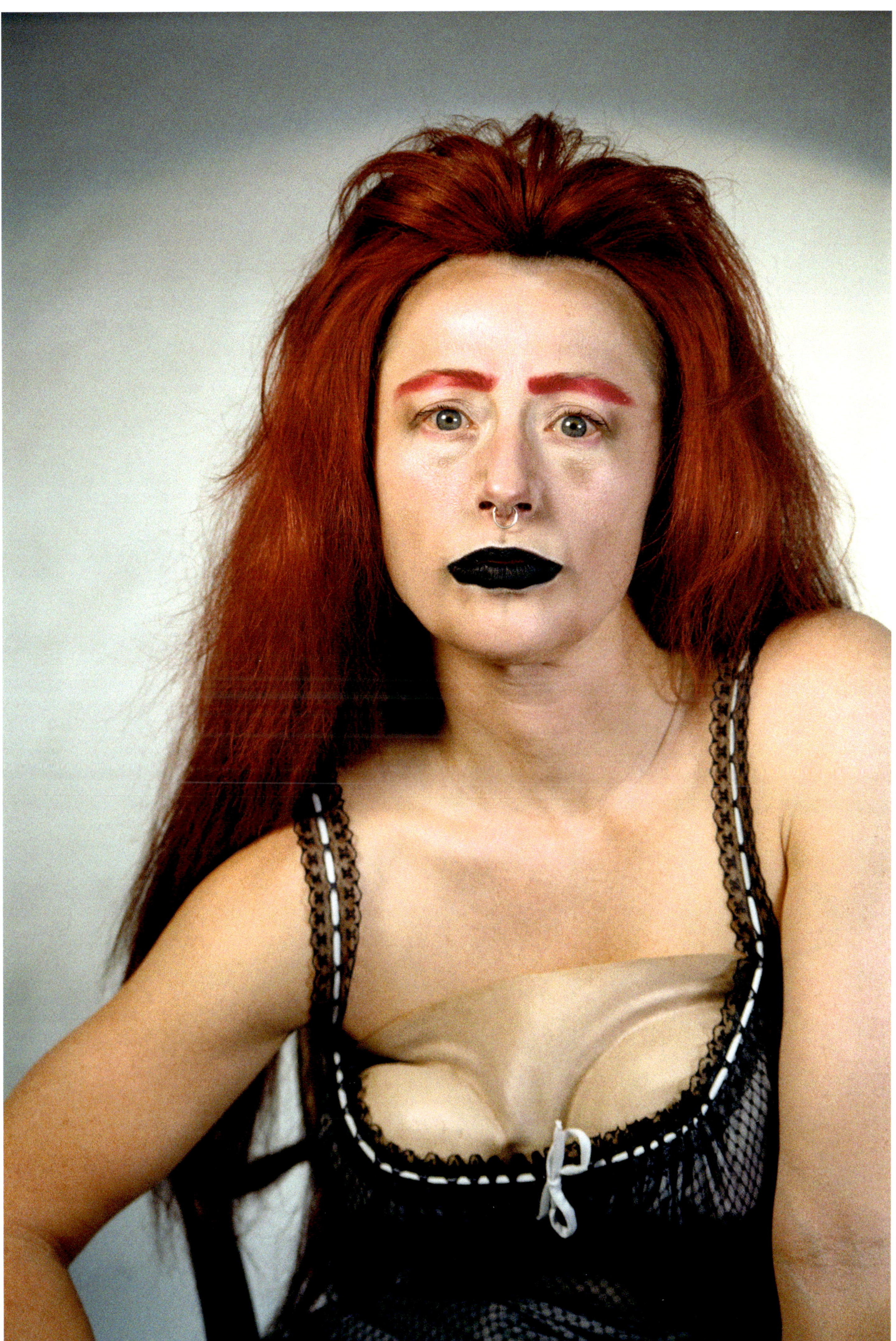

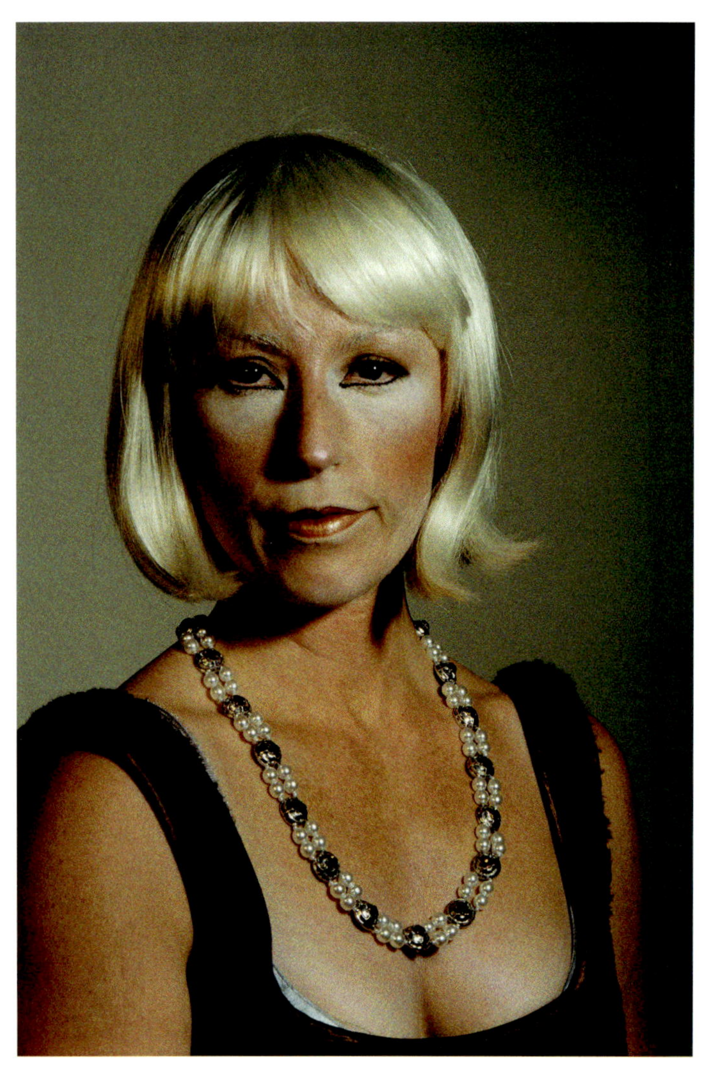
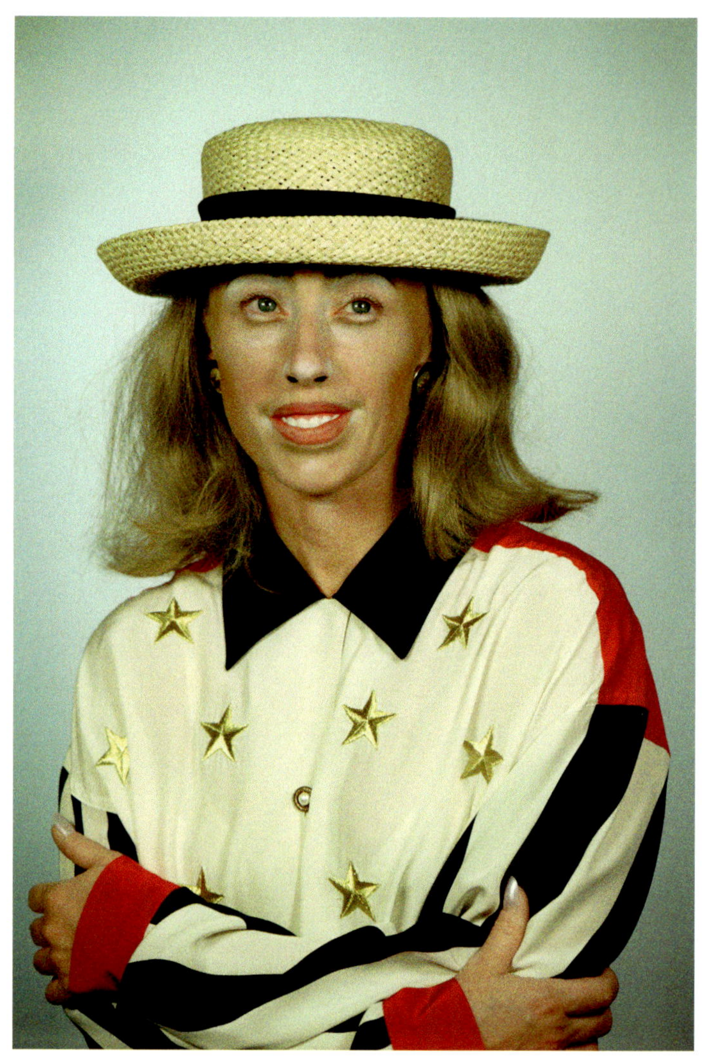
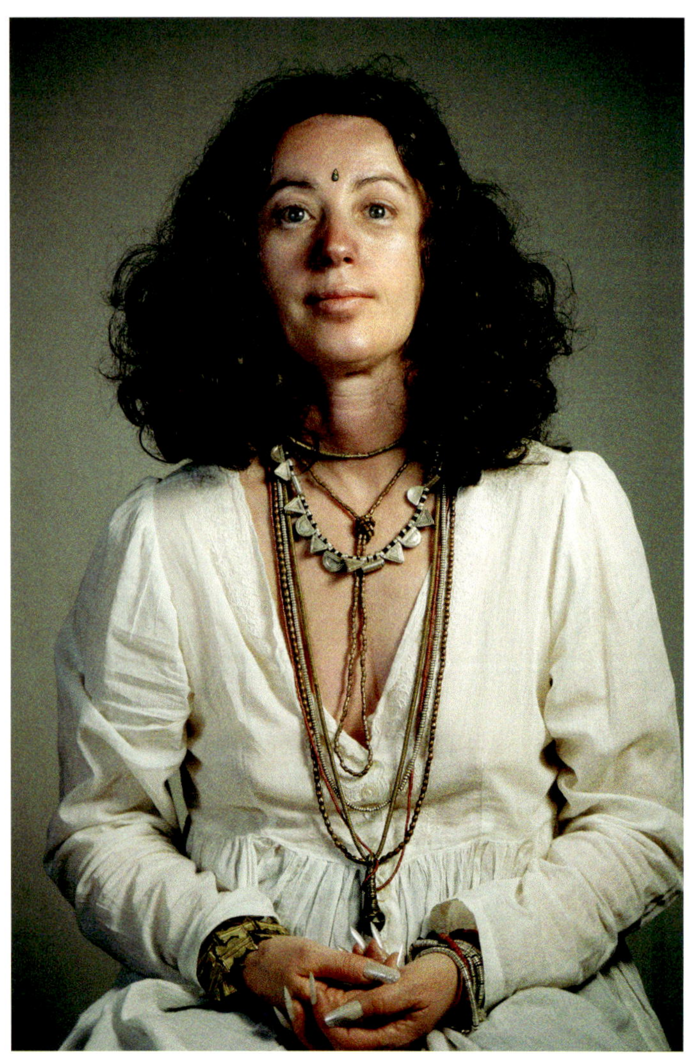
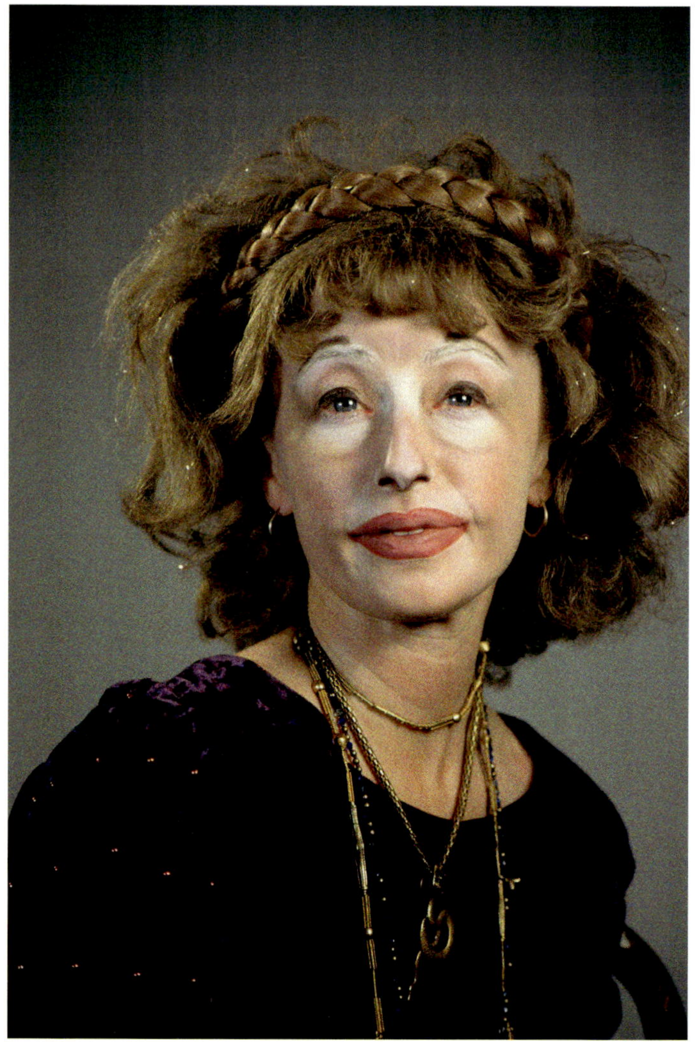

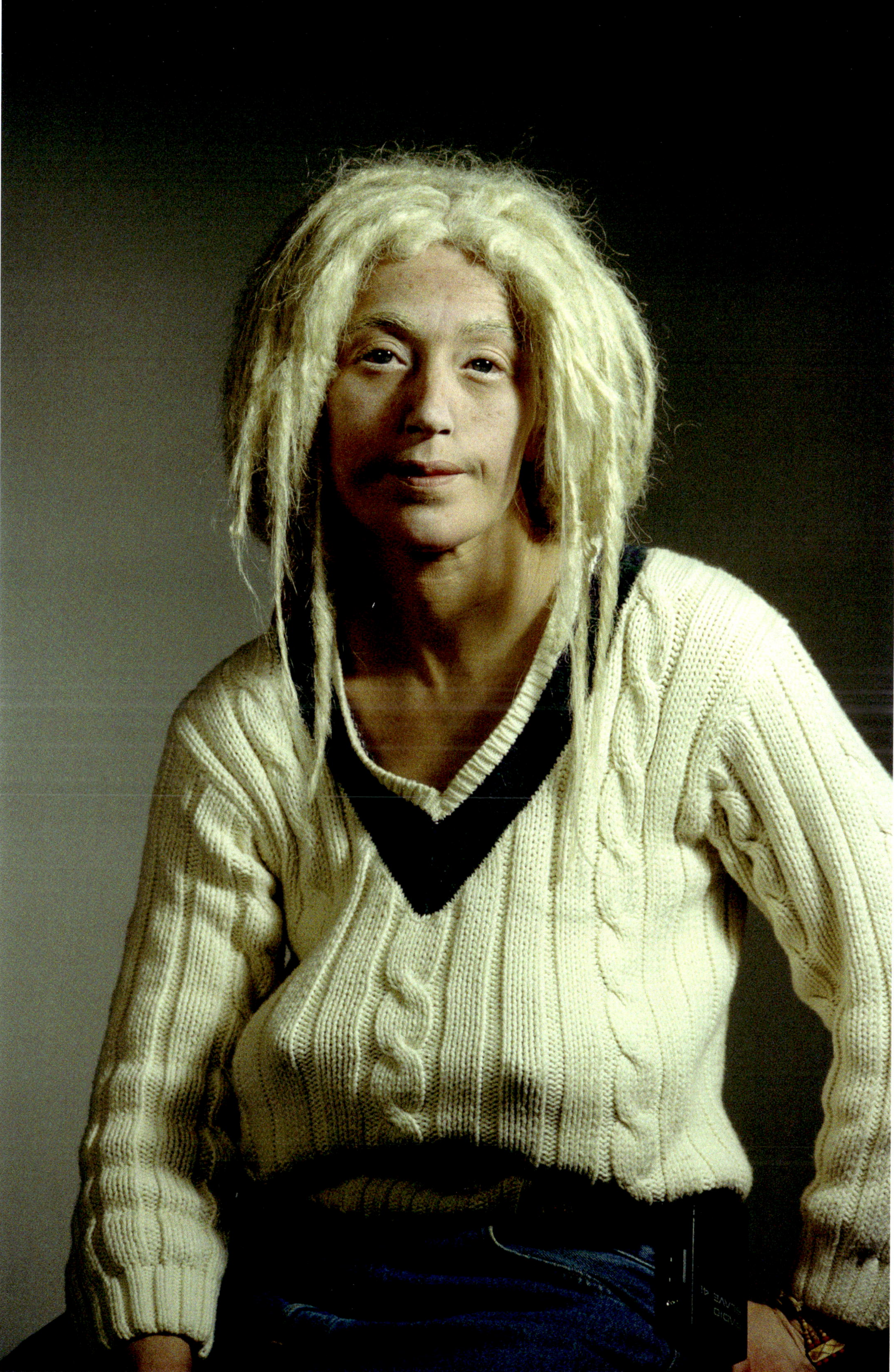

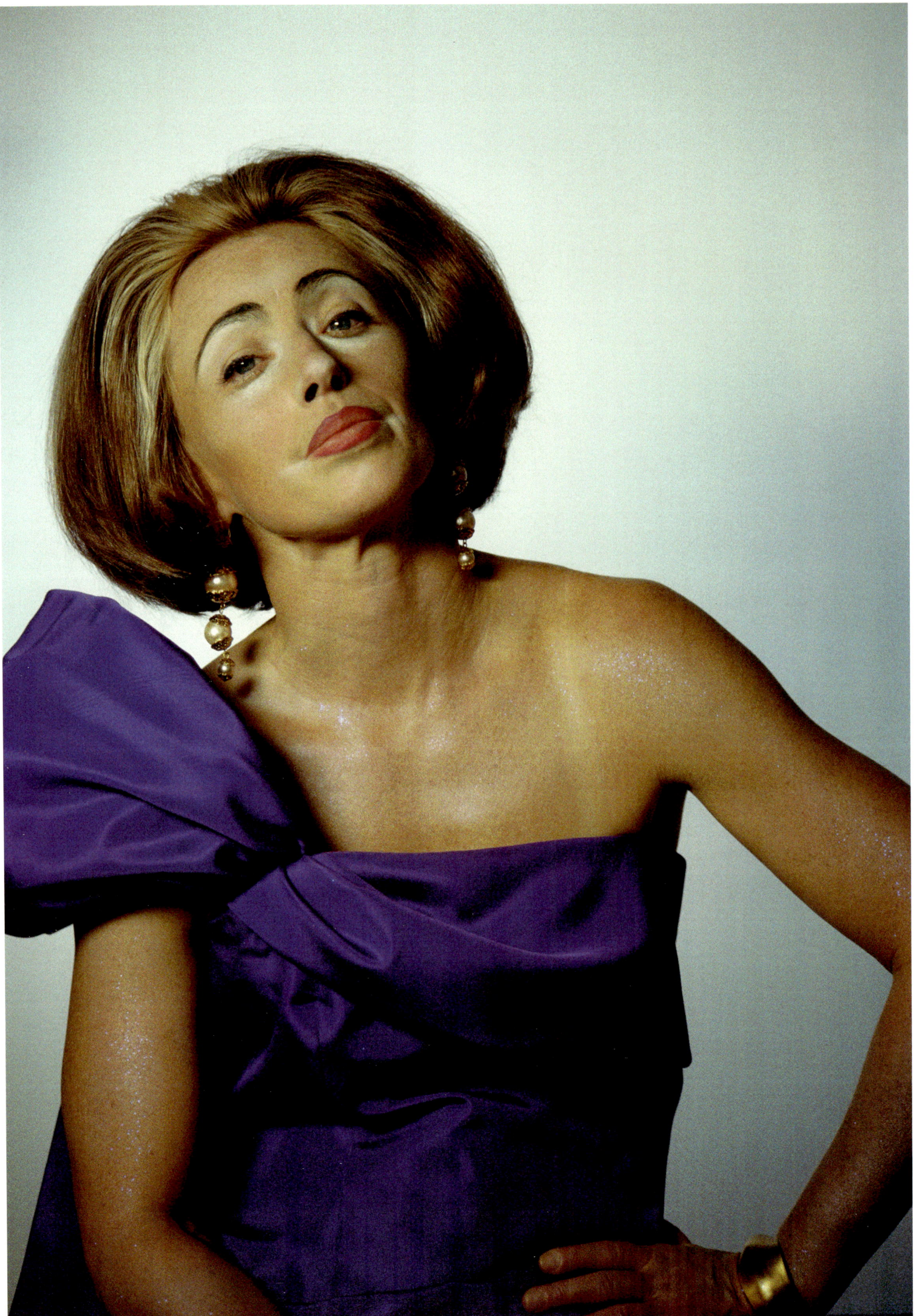

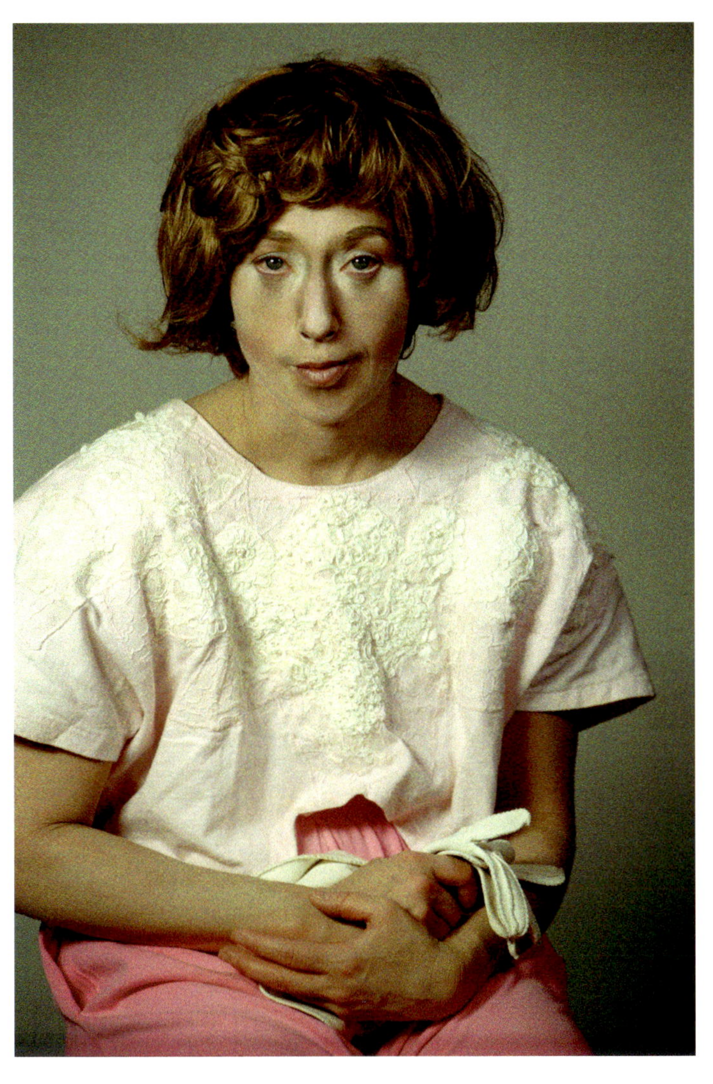
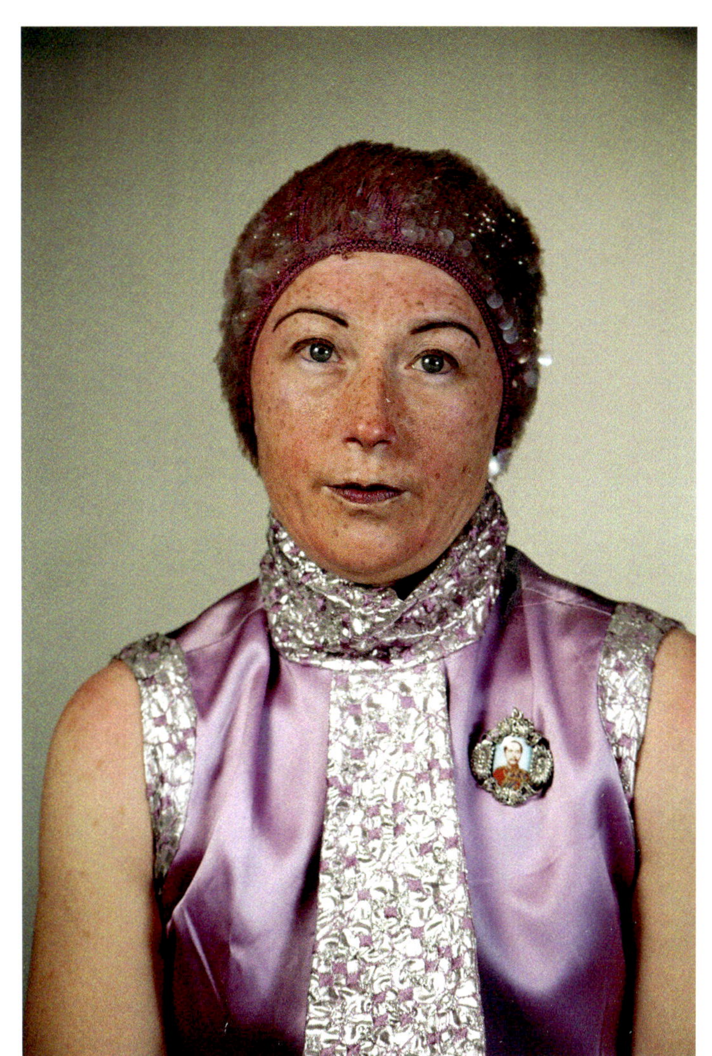
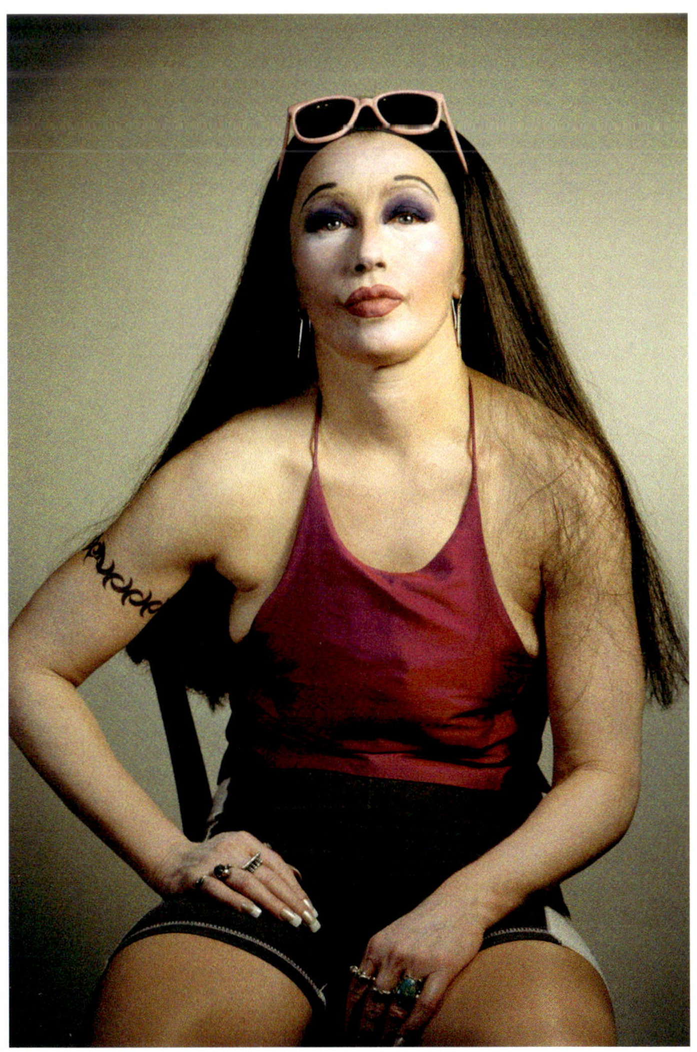
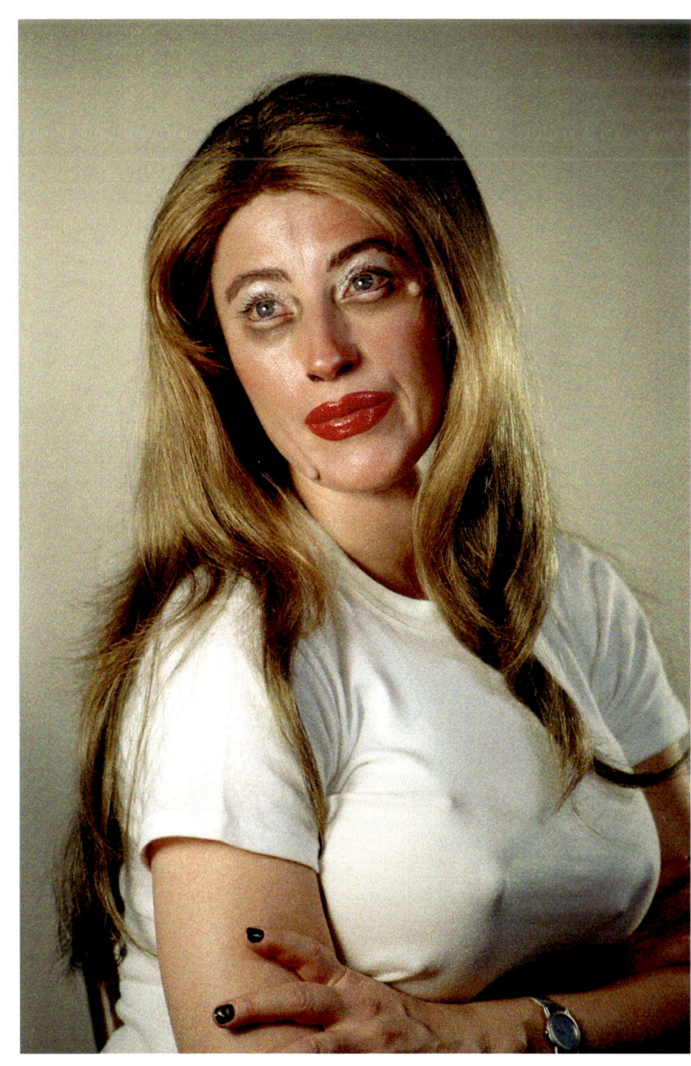

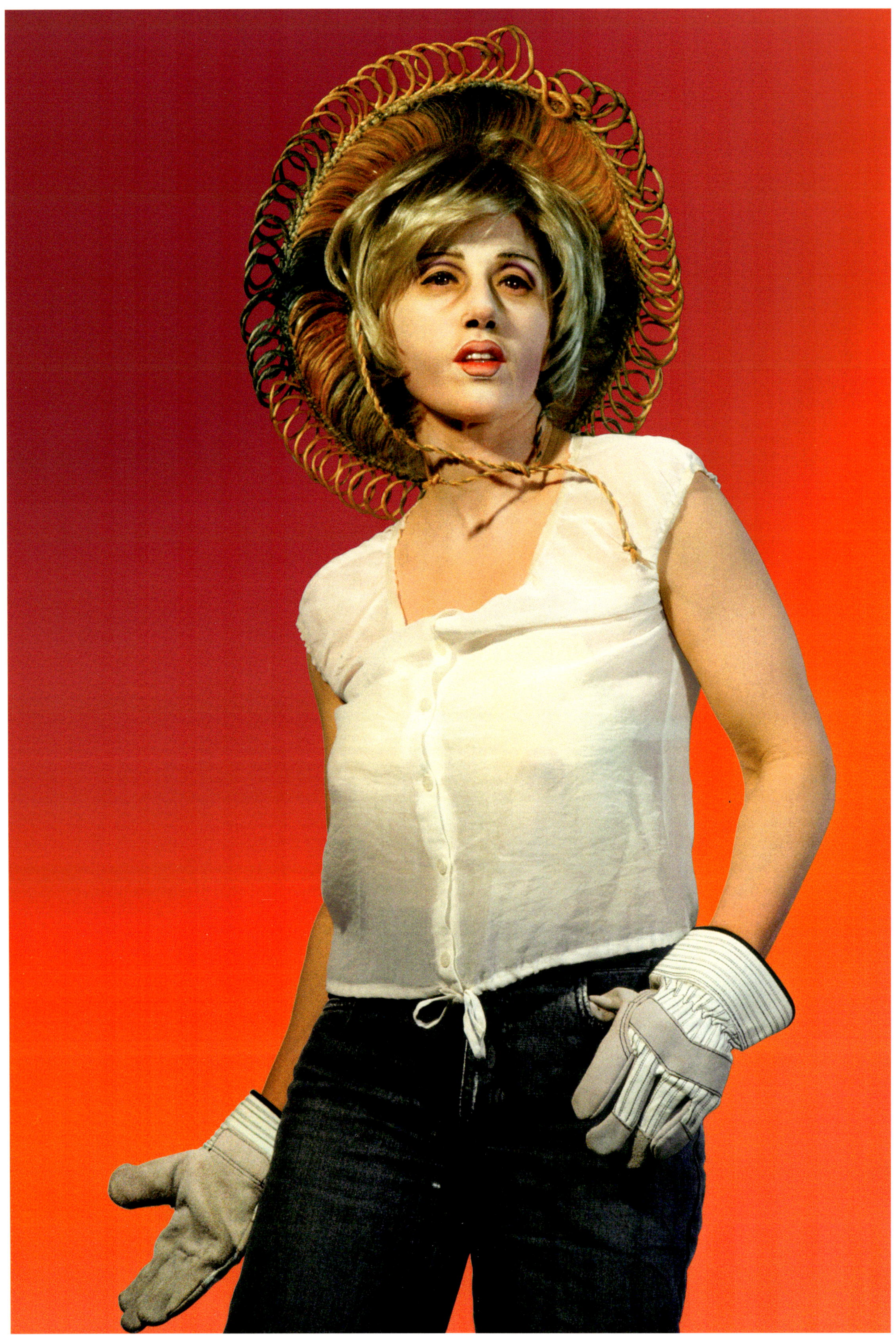

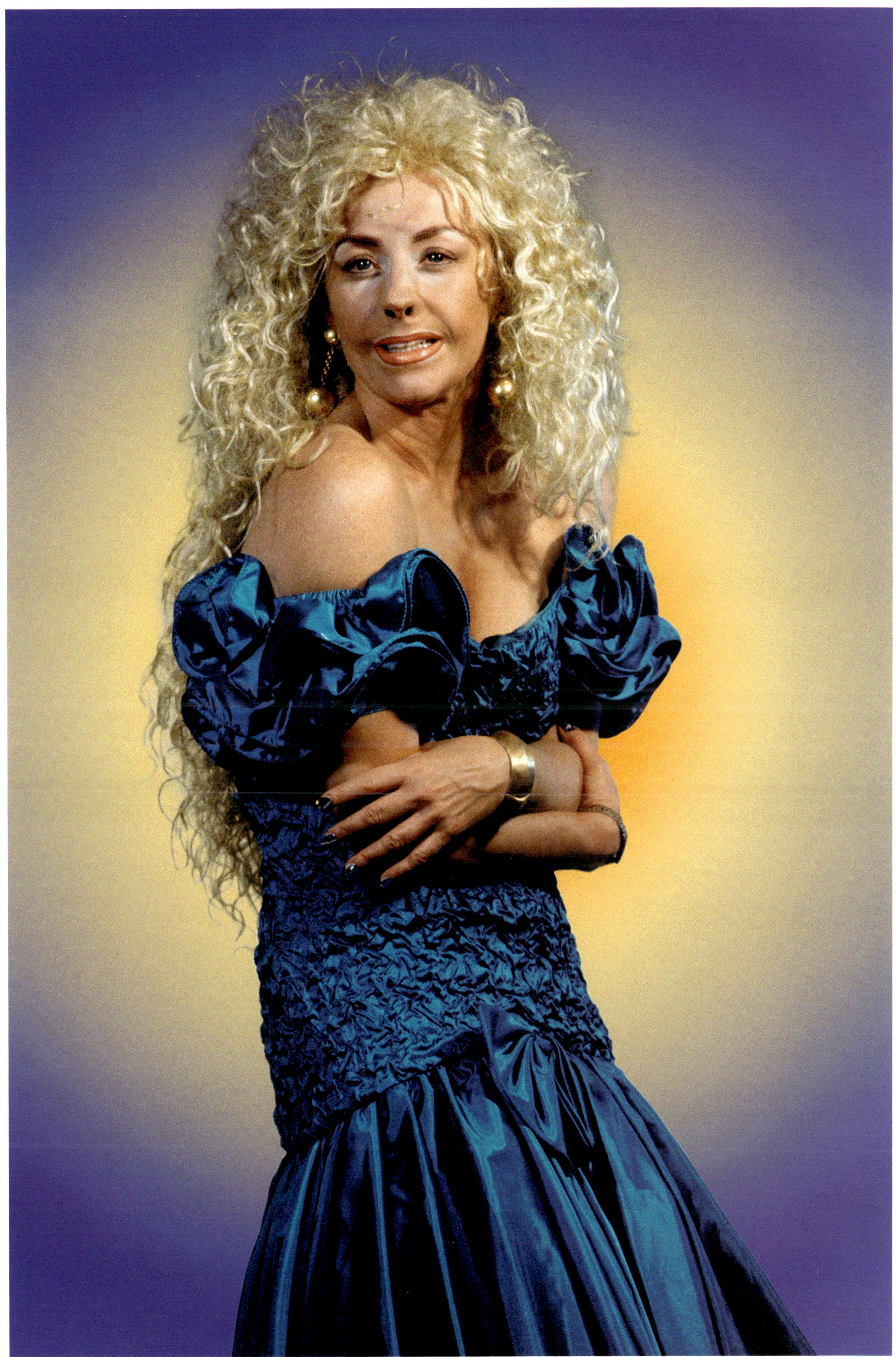

Untitled #412
Untitled #422
Untitled #421
Untitled #424
Untitled #416
Untitled #423
Untitled #417
Untitled #413
Untitled #419
Untitled #425
Untitled #426

2003 — 2004

[Clowns]

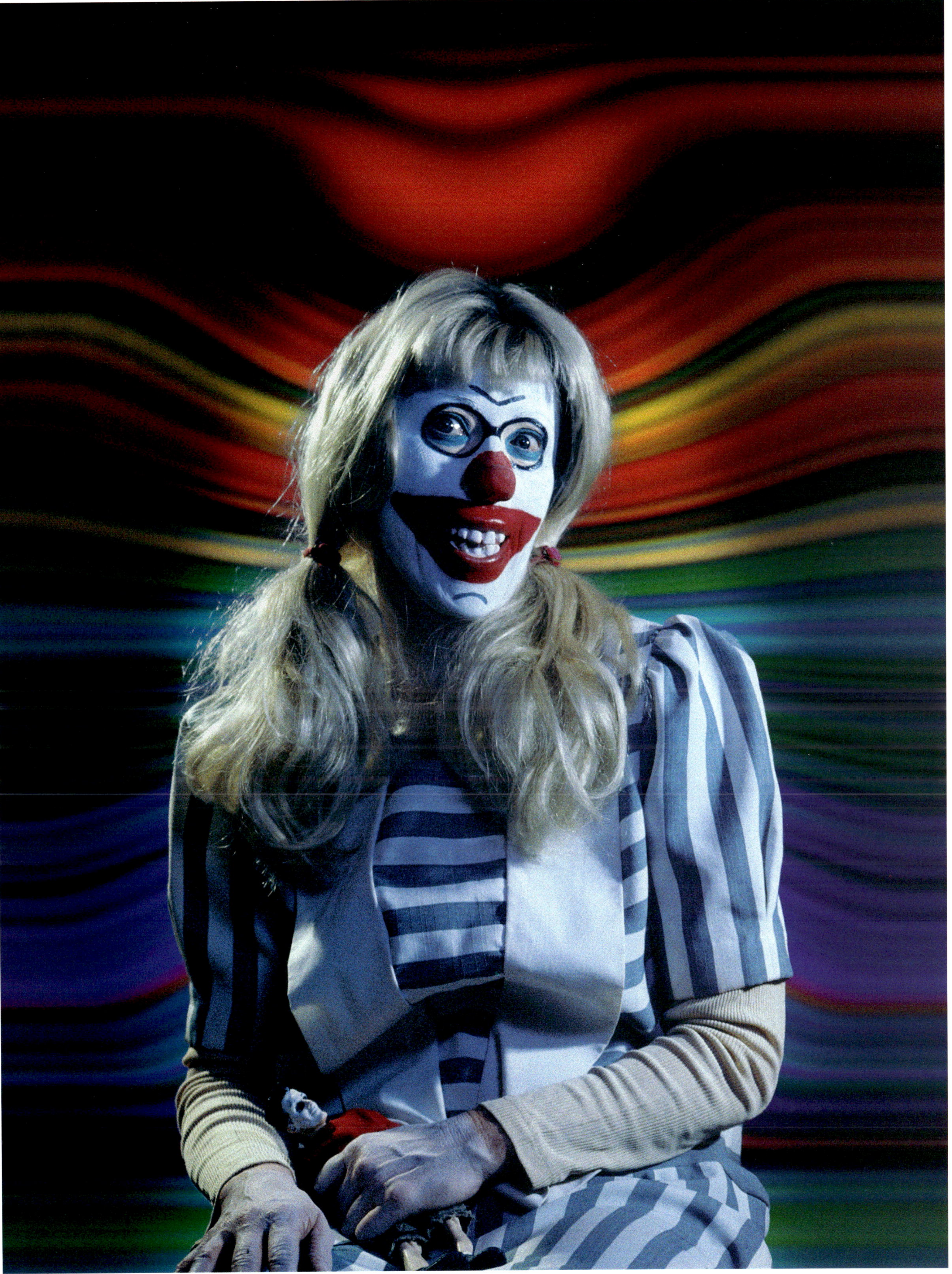

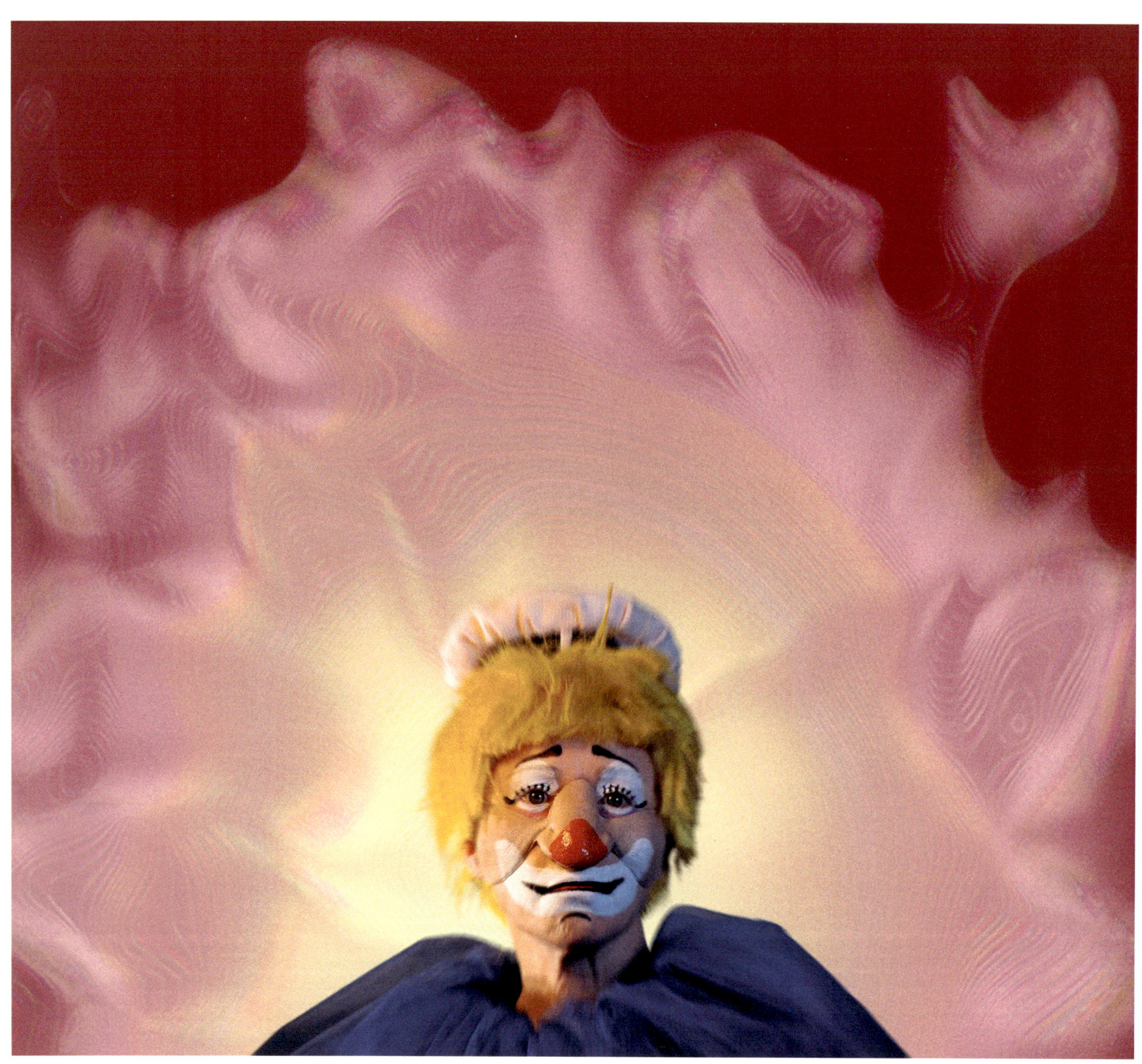

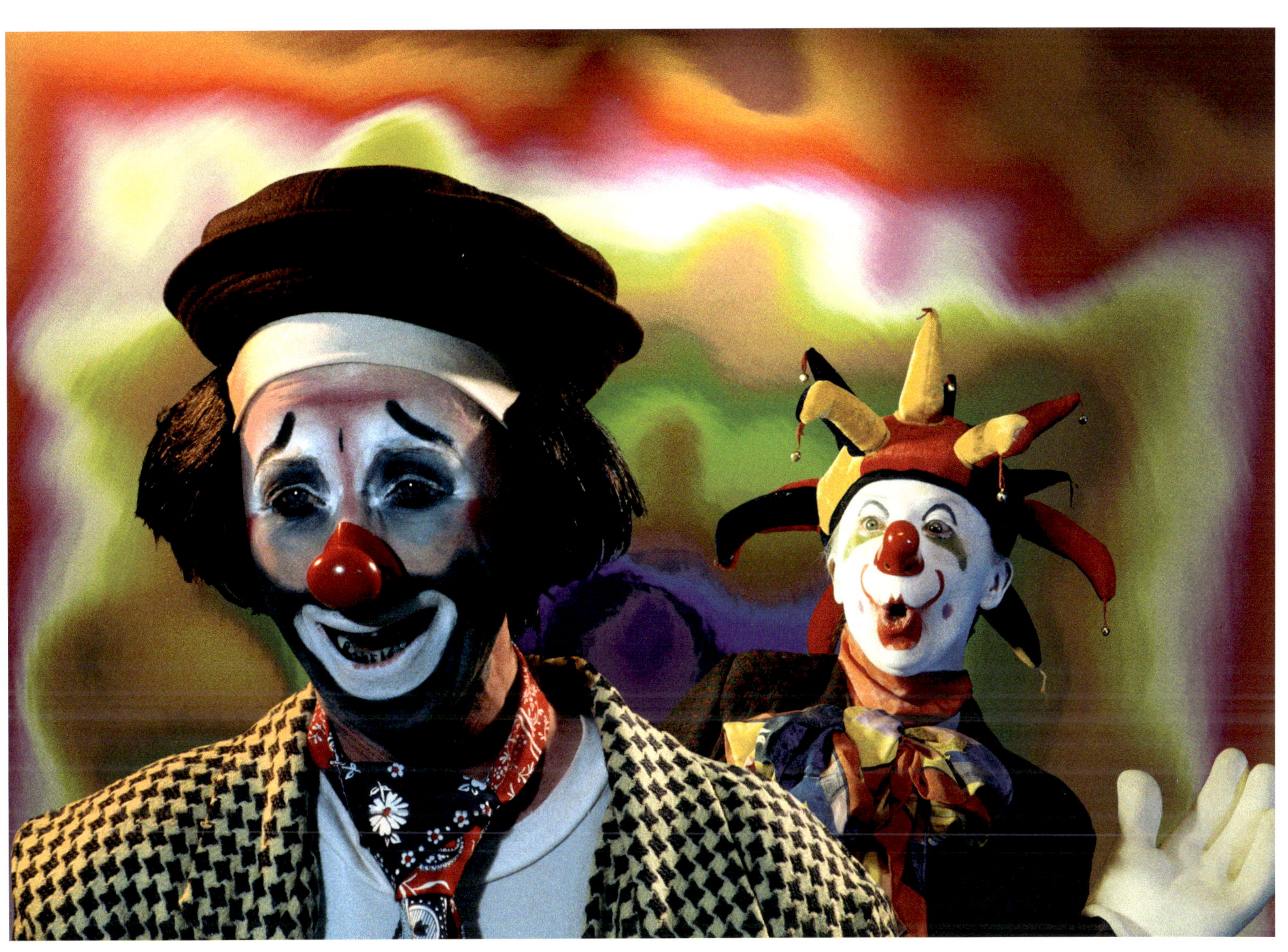

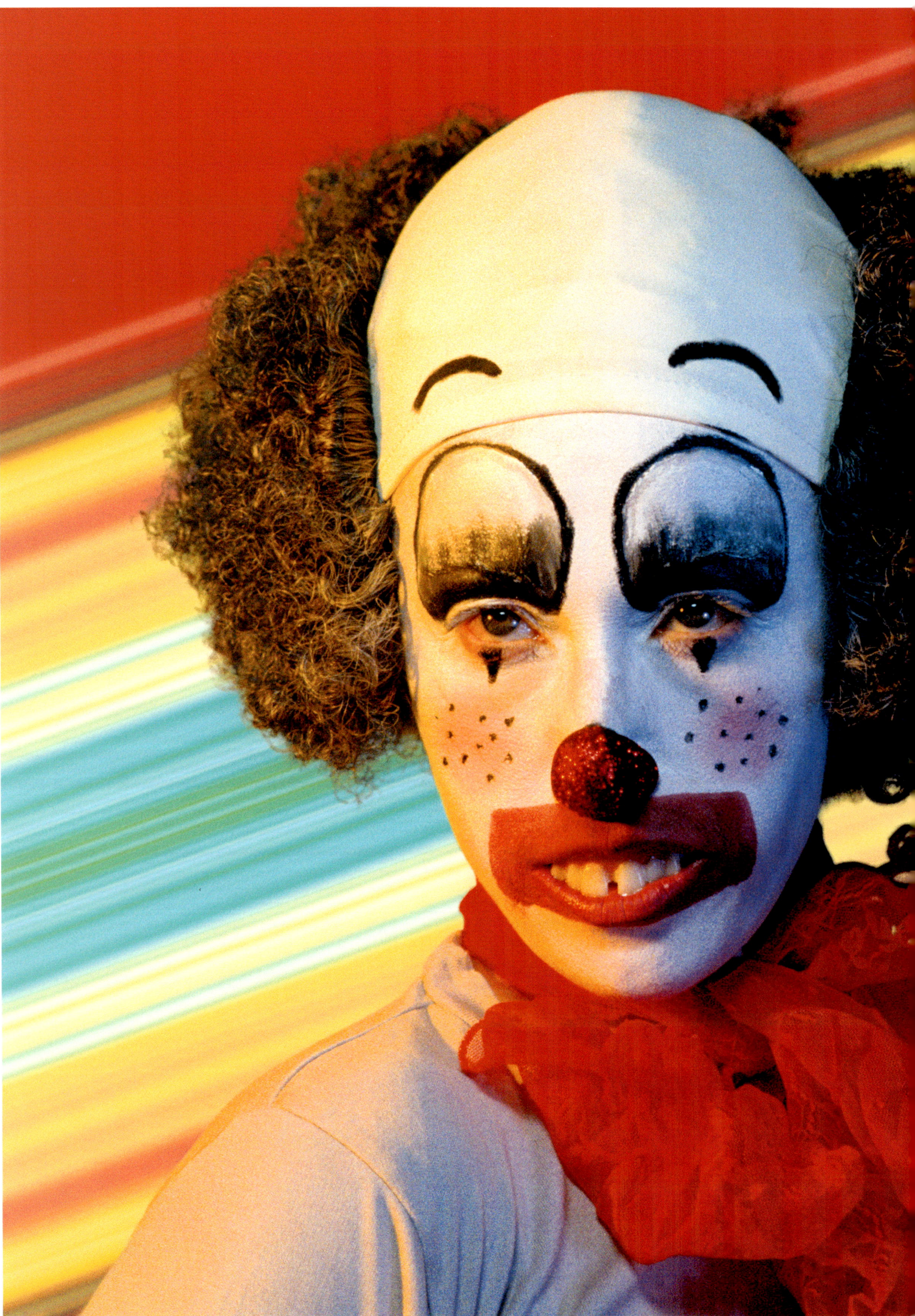

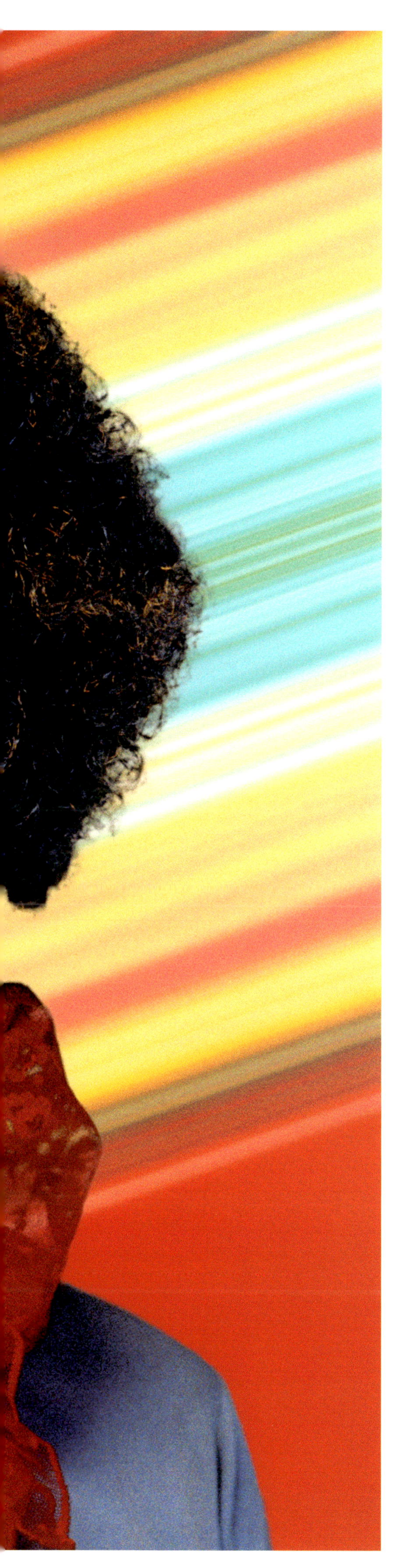

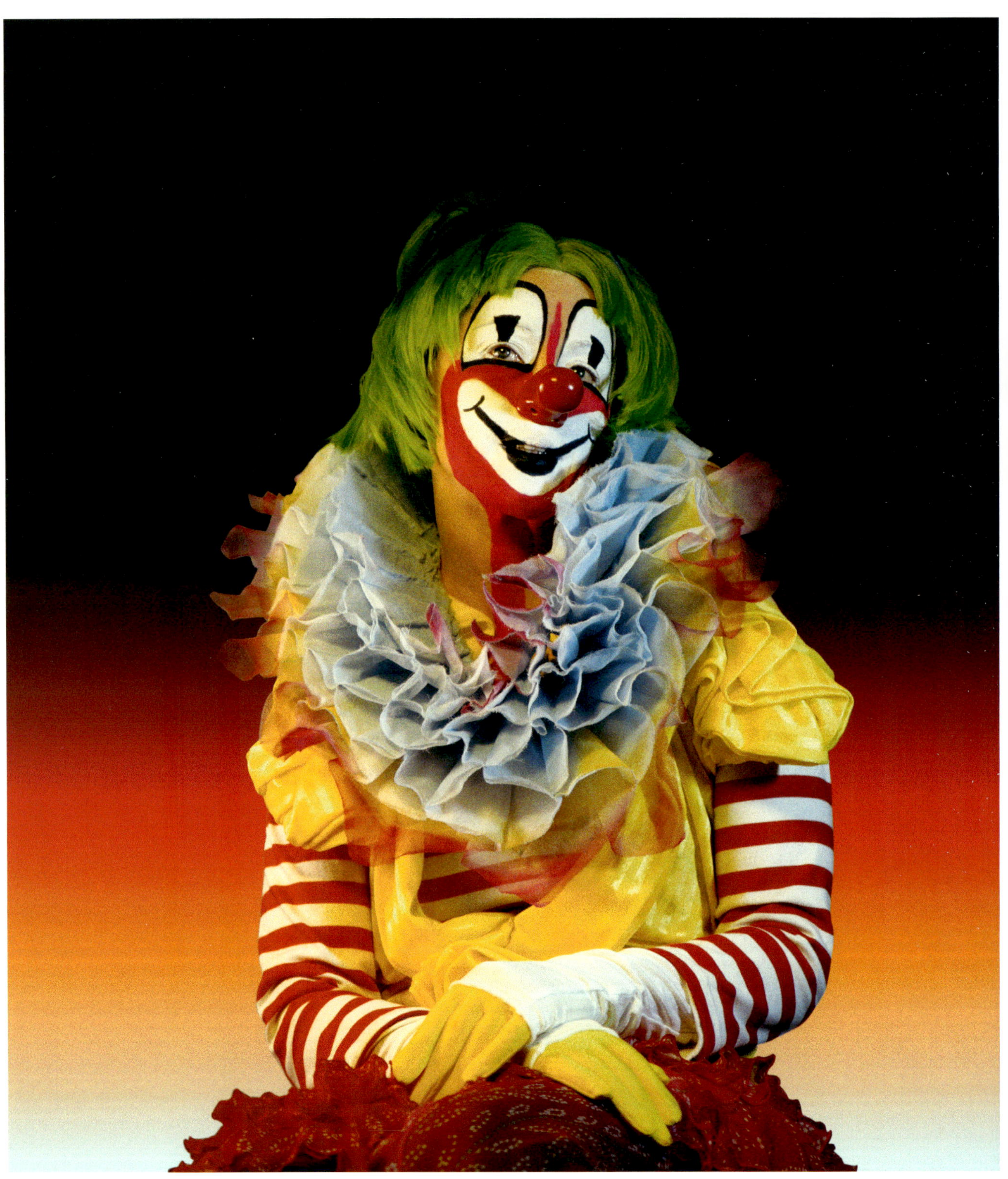

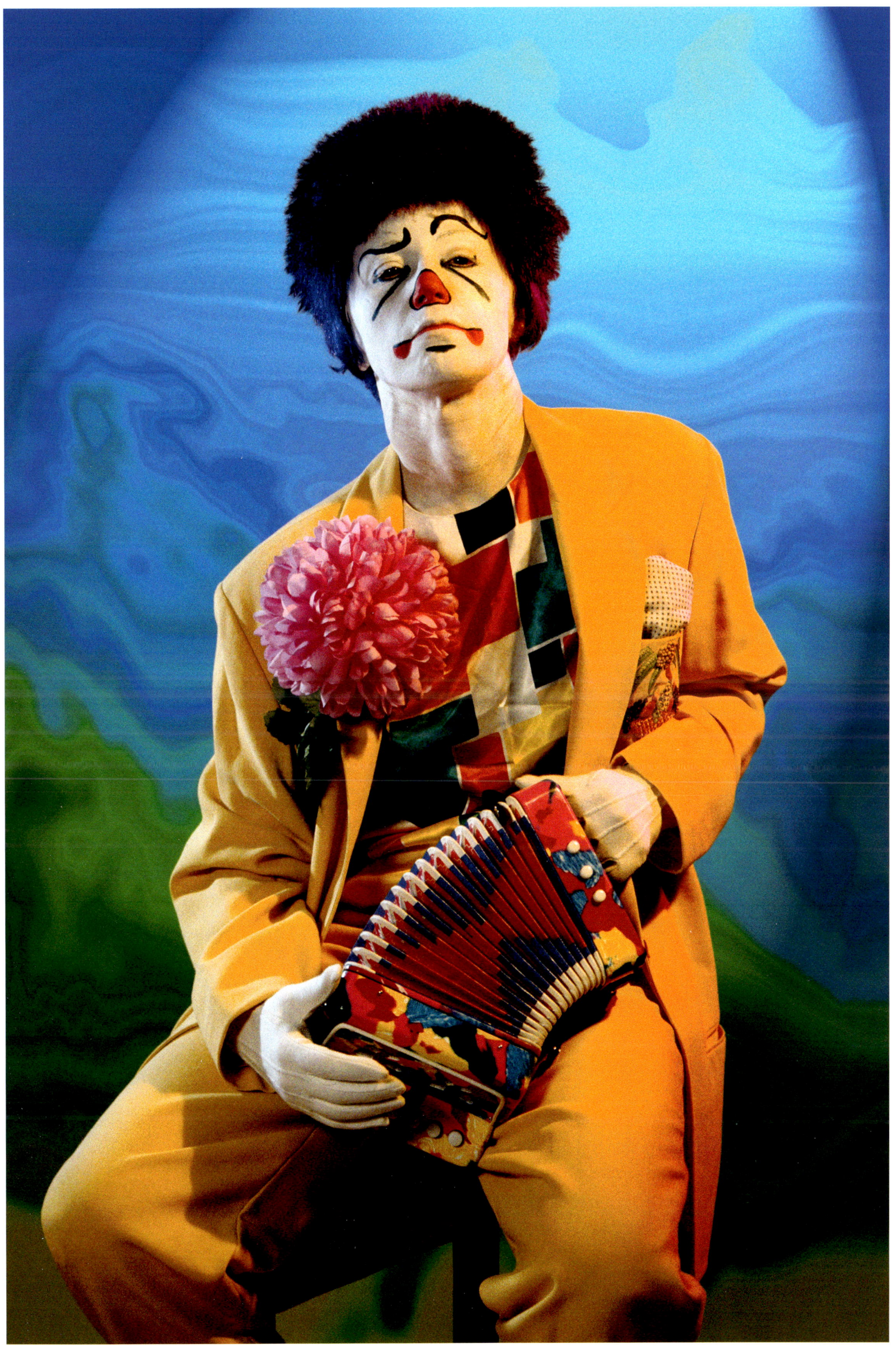

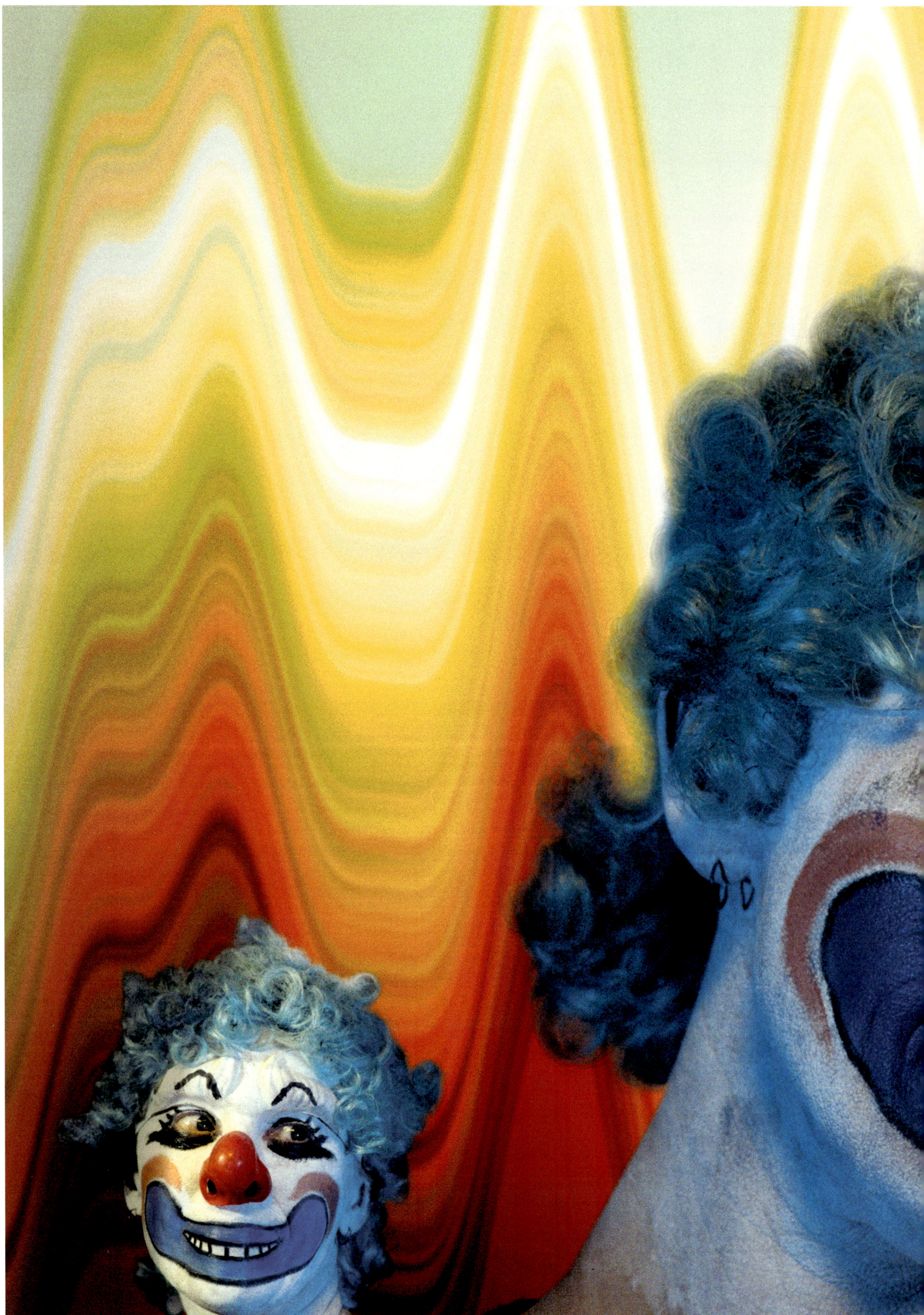

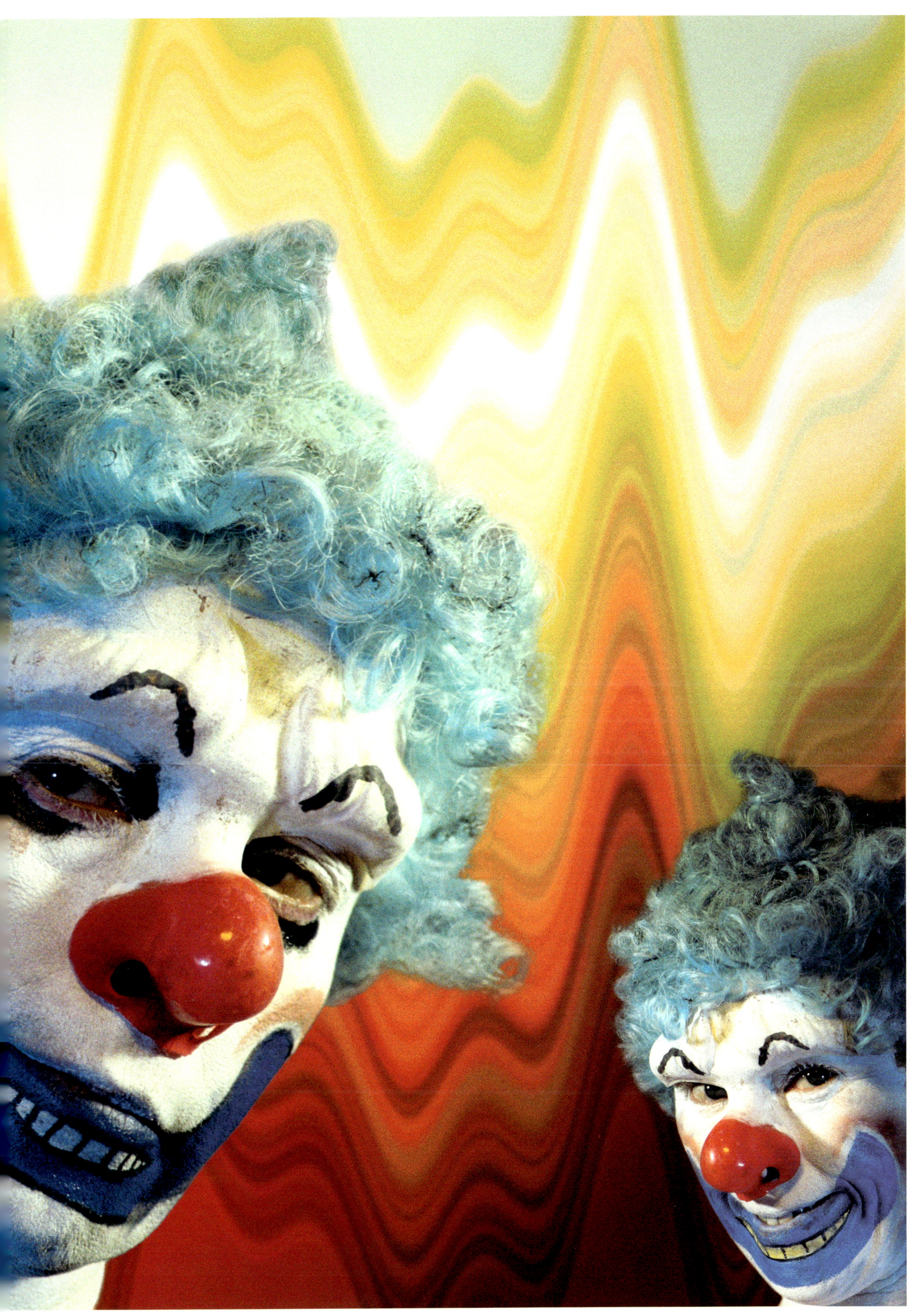

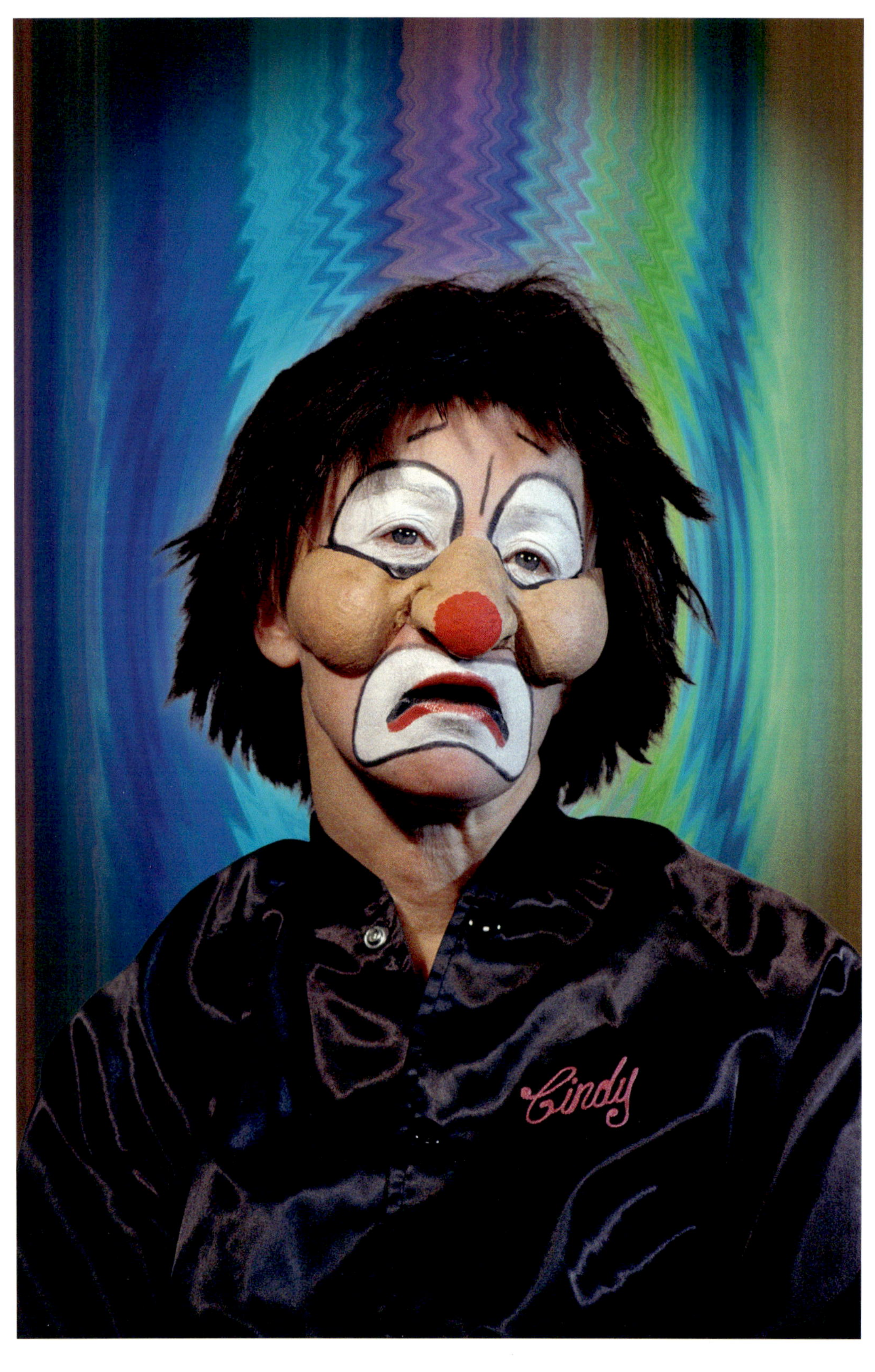
Cindy

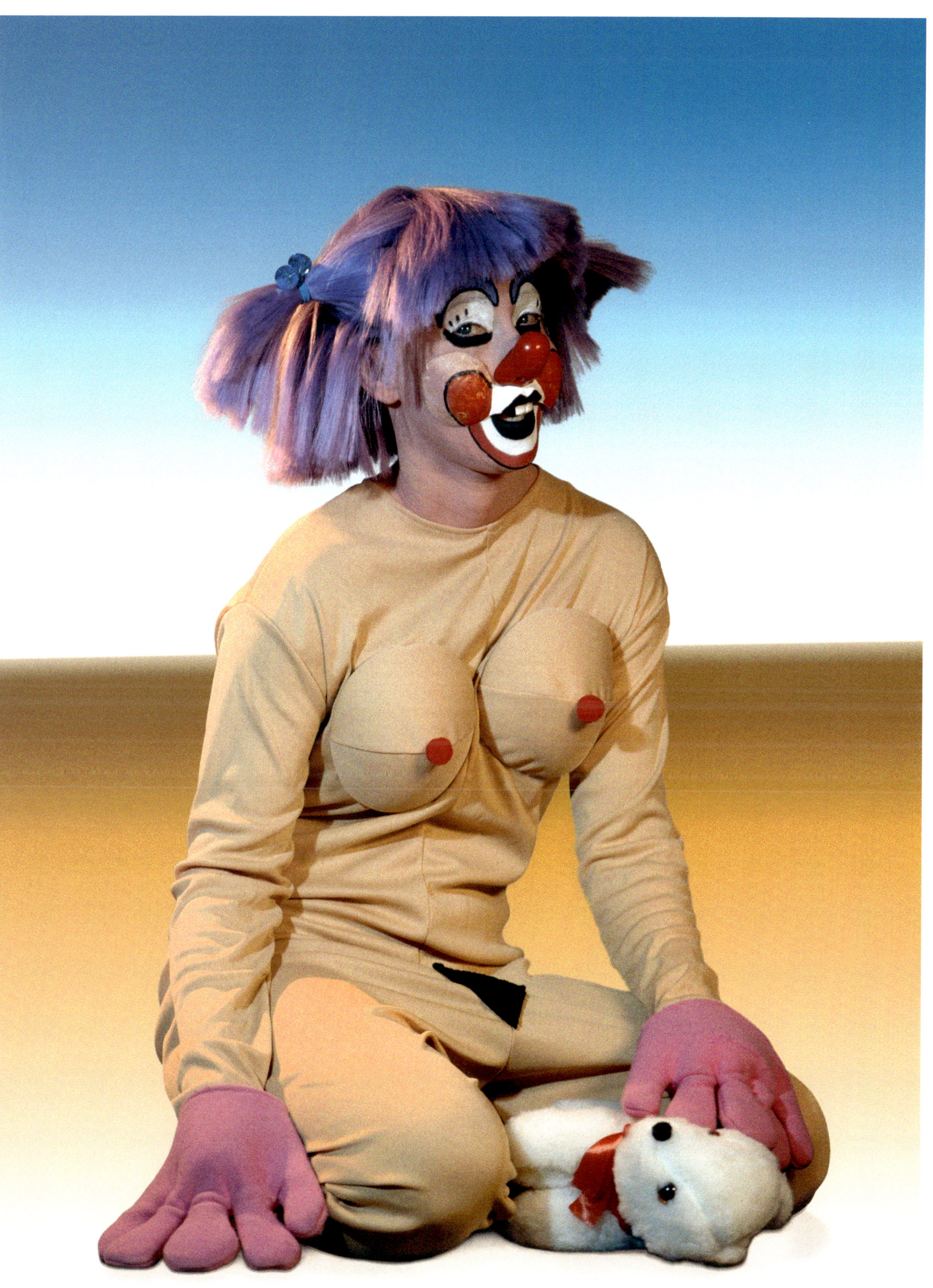

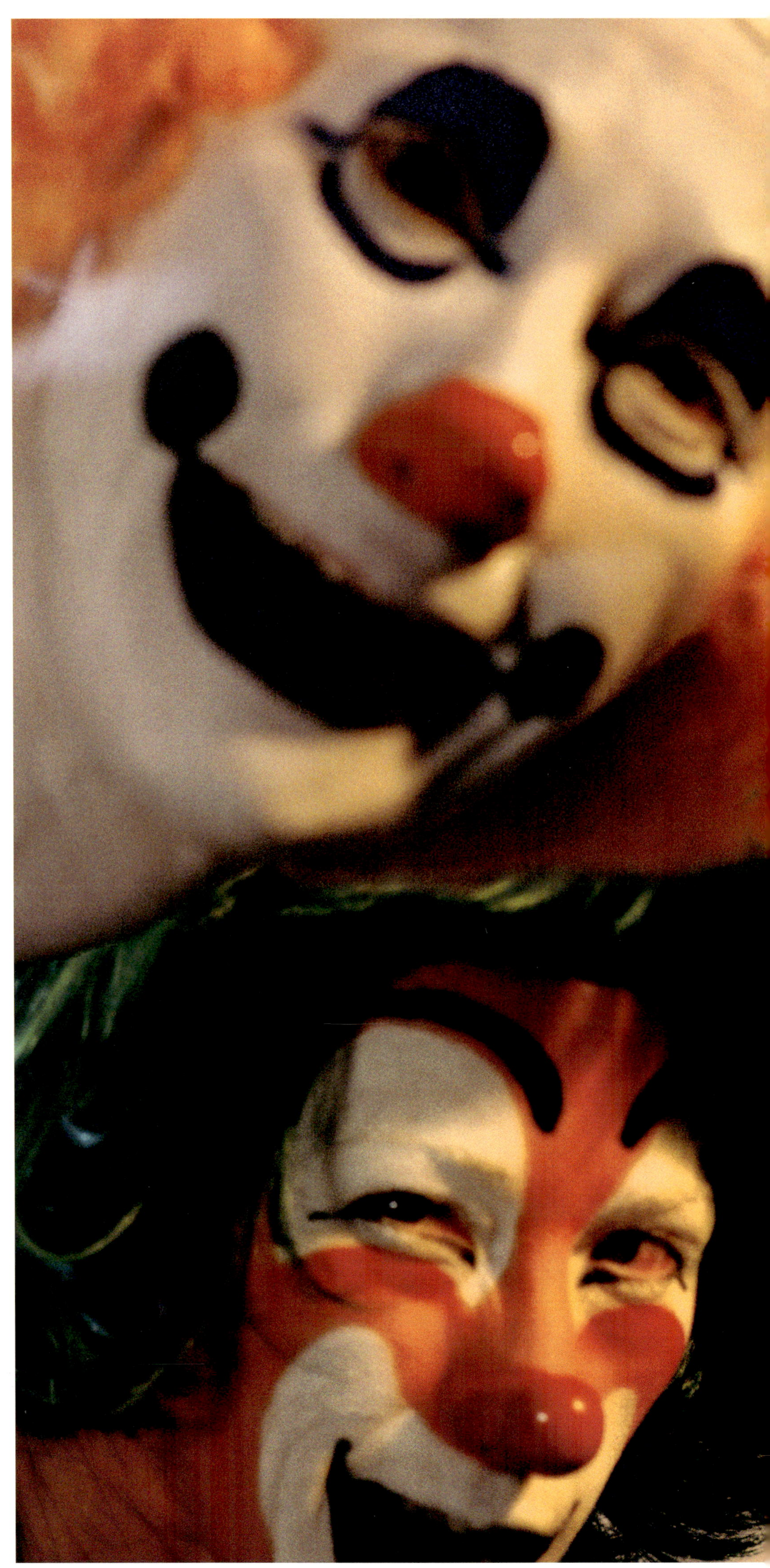

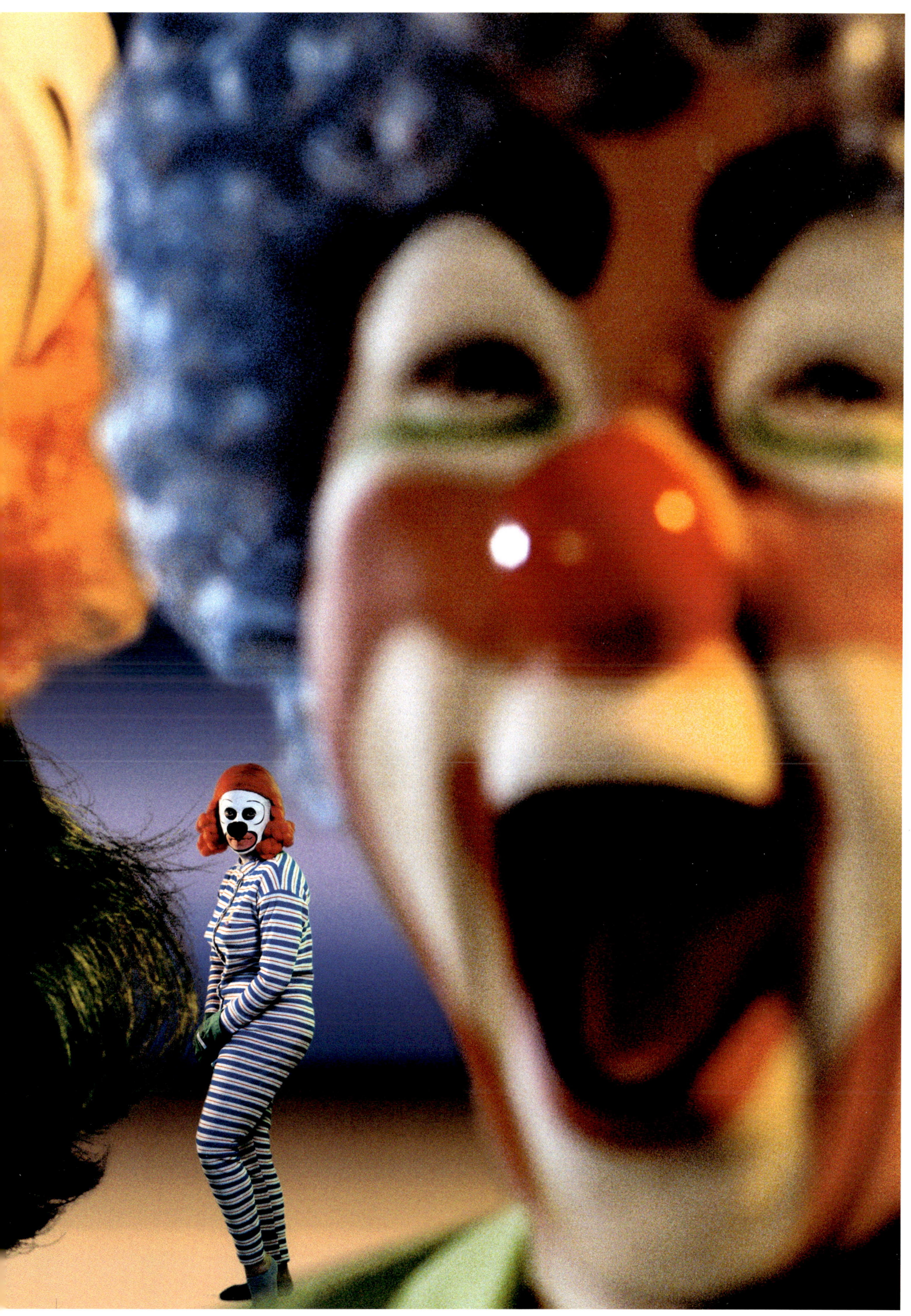

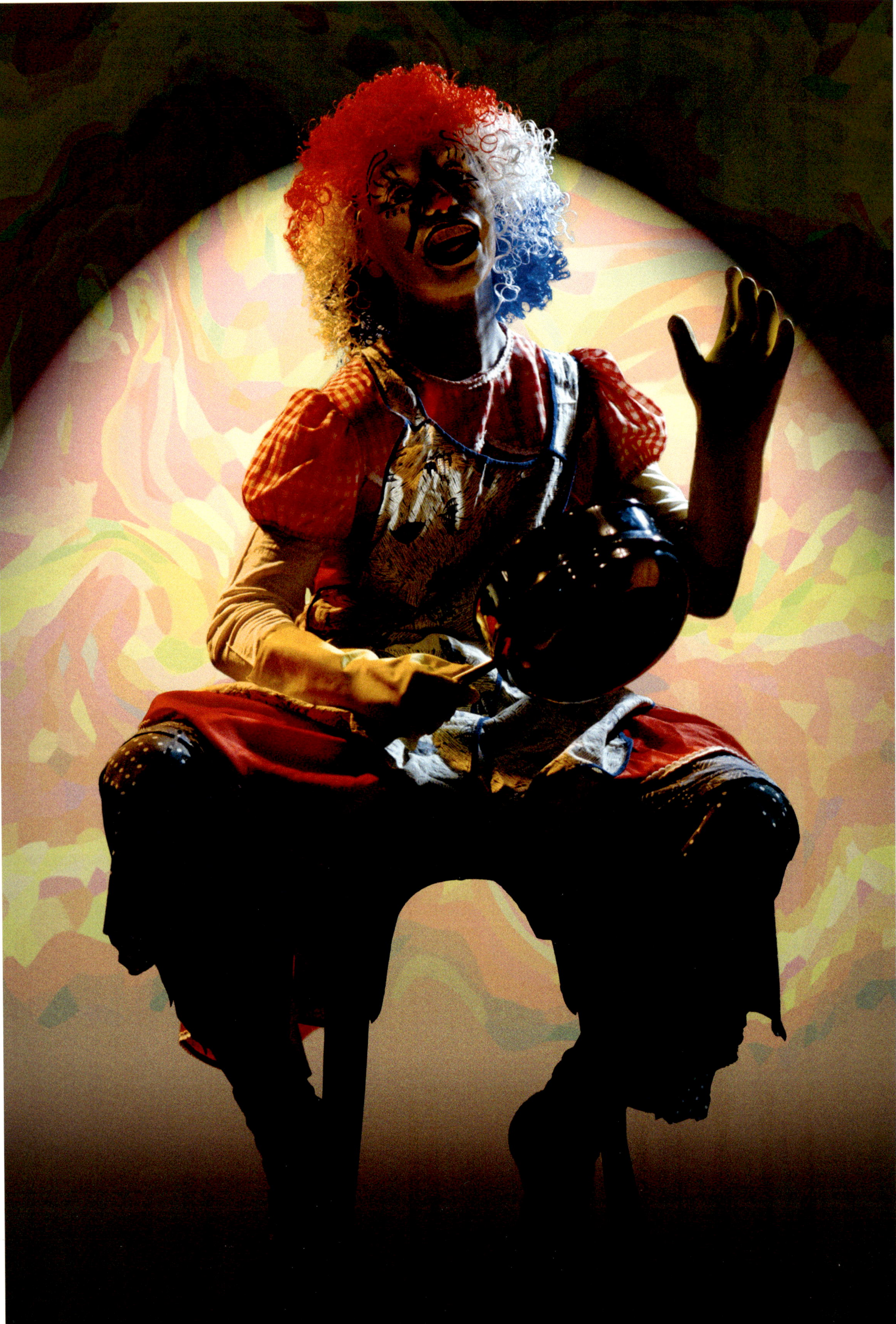

CINDY SHERMAN

Flammarion — JEU DE PAUME

The titles of the works and series in italics are the original ones given by the artist. To make it possible to identify the large series that make up Cindy Sherman's oeuvre, the titles used by critics and art historians are given in parentheses.

Régis Durand

A READING OF CINDY SHERMAN'S WORKS 1975–2006

With a few exceptions, Cindy Sherman's works are organized in this book, and in the exhibition, according to their respective series; the series themselves are arranged in chronological order. While acknowledging the potential for a number of transverse, thematic approaches (some are suggested below), and the occasional difficulties in determining precisely where each series begins and ends, this series/chronological approach is still the one that is most closely attuned to the evolution in Sherman's work, and the best adapted to an appreciation of its extraordinary internal coherence and successive developments.

Cindy Sherman's artistic journey impresses us with its remarkable rigor and inventiveness, its never-ending search for greater meaning and depth. Her work is also strikingly funny and extravagant, with darker elements touching on the impalpability of the self, and the omnipresence of illusion and death. At first glance all surface and sham, Sherman's images nonetheless succeed in retaining a compelling sense of mystery—a mystery that is unlikely to yield its darkness to the glare of better-informed or more systematic scrutiny. For the mysteries explored here are those of the nature of human identity, and our capacity to know or misread our true selves, to picture our own image, and invent parallel lives—a capacity that we share with no other living creature.

The notes and comments interspersed between the different sections simply punctuate the exploration, leaving Sherman's richly significant work to speak for itself. The photographs' sole protagonist is sometimes referred to here as "the subject," a descriptor indicating that we should not necessarily always interpret the images as representations of the artist herself (a straightforward psychological or autobiographical interpretation would be limiting indeed), nor as a succession of more or less "staged" depictions of characters, arrayed with the trappings of a particular social or psychological type that we would be forced to acknowledge, however briefly.

Roland Barthes uses the term "subject" in his 1977 work *Fragments d'un discours amoureux* (published in English as *A Lover's Discourse: Fragments*, trans. Richard Howard, Hill & Wang, 1979) to describe the generic, fictional character whose amorous transports he sought to analyze, and who was neither Barthes himself, nor one of the individual cases to which he referred, but a mixture of each. Used here, the term allows us to escape the limitations of a reductive, one-sided approach, and to apprehend the rich, diverse significance of Sherman's work.

Finally, the use of this sexually neutral term does not imply that we should in any way disregard Sherman's identity as a woman who has chosen to embody and dramatize mostly (but not exclusively) female figures in her work. This is a complex body of ideas which does not lend itself easily to reductive, schematized approaches and standpoints. The present exploration aims to do no more than suggest some possible points of reference.*

* This essay is indebted to *Cindy Sherman: Retrospective* published by Thames & Hudson in 1998, and in particular the chapter by Amanda Cruz entitled "Moves, Monstrosities and Masks: Twenty years of Cindy Sherman."

A Cindy Book

c. 1964 — 1975

The context and frame of reference within which Cindy Sherman's works are conceived were, it seems, already clearly defined in her juvenile album *A Cindy Book* (c. 1964–75), and the earliest works in the *Bus Riders* (1976–2006) or *Murder Mystery* (1976–2000).

A Cindy Book is an apparently typical adolescent photograph album: a sacred record of its creator's most important "life moments." However, there is a difference in that what seems to matter most is not the moment itself, but the subject's own image in the photograph. *That's me*, says the recurrent handwritten inscription—at different ages, on holiday in Maine, at my cousin's wedding, at my first dance. It is as if Sherman ("the subject") took perpetual delight in spotting herself among a group of other people, overjoyed by the fact of her own existence, the diverse situations in which she finds herself, and the plasticity of her being, allied to the continuity of a specific identity. Or could it be that the perpetually reiterated assertion (*That's me*) is in fact a sign of inner doubt ("Is that really me?")? We are, for the moment, outside the realm of art: the album is an undefined, narcissistic, ambivalent medium, the visual equivalent of an intimate journal, with the same relationship to art as the latter has to literature. The pictures are stuck into the same type of ruled exercise book that Sherman used in later years to record notes on works in progress, theoretical and technical questions, and the aims and strategies that shaped her thinking at successive stages in her career.

Perhaps the album's real distinguishing characteristic is the excessive repetition of the exclamation itself, an expression of mingled joy and anxiety. The images are, as the French autobiography specialist Philippe Lejeune has put it, *signes de vie* ("life signs"), collected here for their cumulative impact. Significantly, each reiterated *That's me* is followed by a comma (rather than, say, an exclamation mark)—a telling clue that points to the subject's awareness of the continuous plethora of selves, the potentially consecutive nature of the images, and perhaps even an emerging narrative. The "autobiographical pact" (in Lejeune's phrase) is vehemently asserted, but seems here to have been emptied of substance, reduced to its most spectral aspect. We are given no further information: it falls to the viewer to imagine what might fill the gaps between the pictures, or to project his or her own stories onto these "unattached" images of bachelor girlhood.

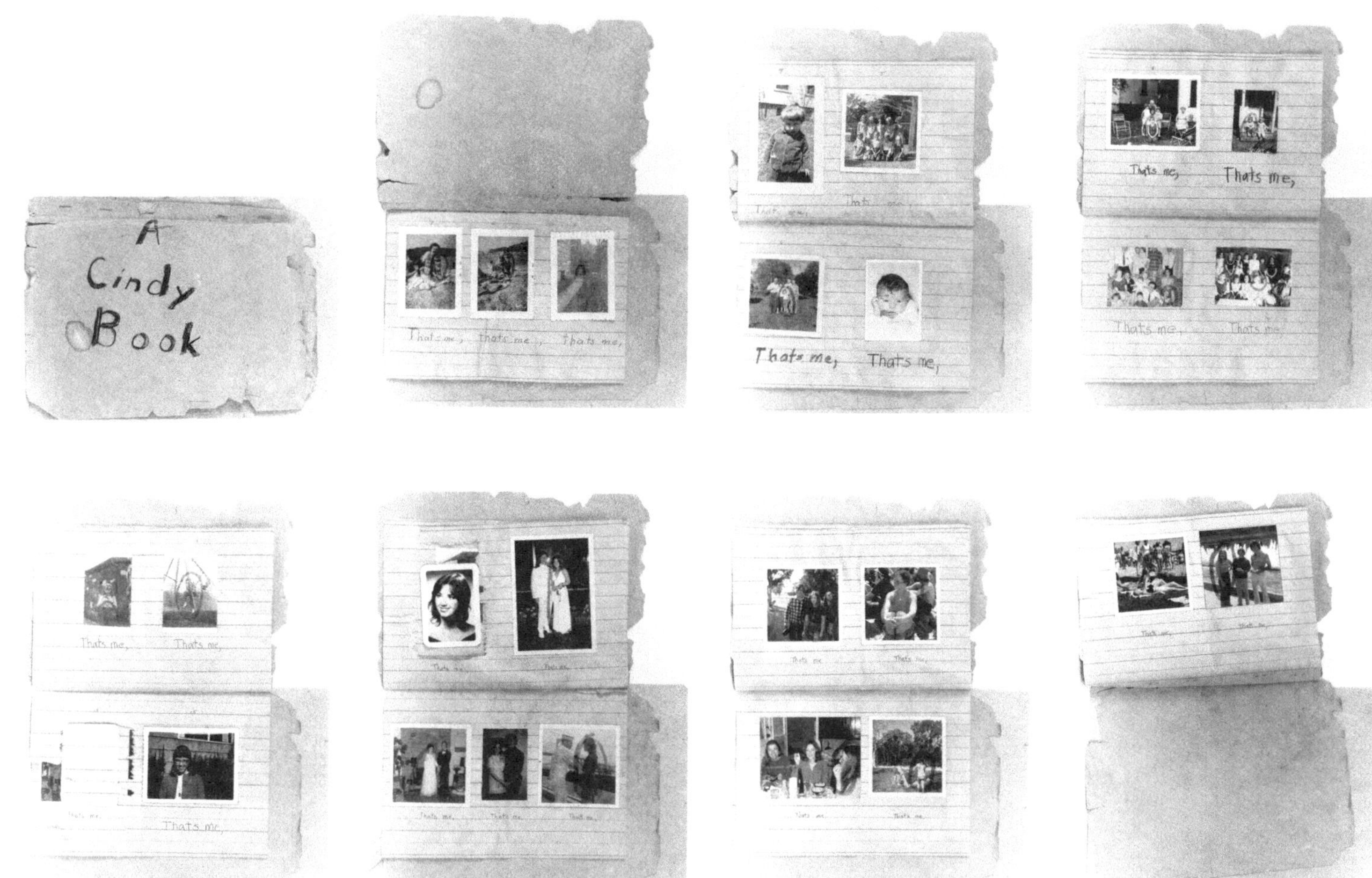

Pages taken from *A Cindy Book*, c.1964–75, 8 ¾ x 11 ¾ in. (22.5 x 29.8 cm)

Untitled A–E

1975

This short series of five works emerges, with hindsight, as a turning point in Sherman's work. The five images are all frontal portraits of young women, smiling at the camera. At the same time, the subject appears in a number of guises that go on to feature in later works (the clown, the young ingénue), treated here with the minimum of artifice, in a manner reminiscent of children's dressing-up games. The narrative dimension is relegated to the background, in favor of simpler, less anecdotal, forms: the images hint at potential fictions or worlds, rather than specific narratives. Here, in its simplest form, is an art of variations on a theme, which combine to produce an impression of both continuity (the subject, in a series of constantly changing forms) and discontinuity (each image is a fleeting glimpse of a fictional life).

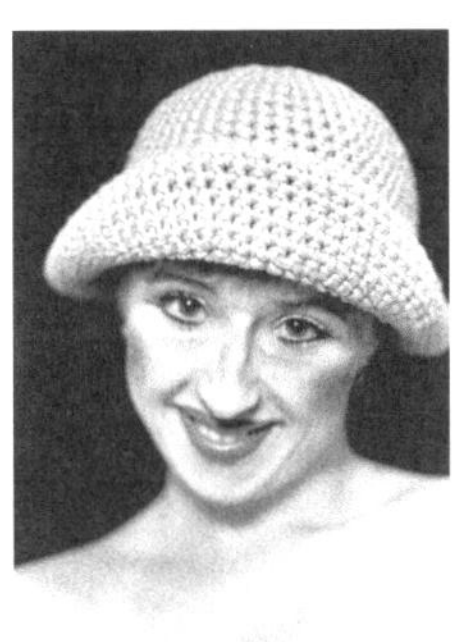

Untitled A, 1975
Black-and-white photograph
Edition of 10
20 x 16 in.
(50.8 x 40.6 cm)

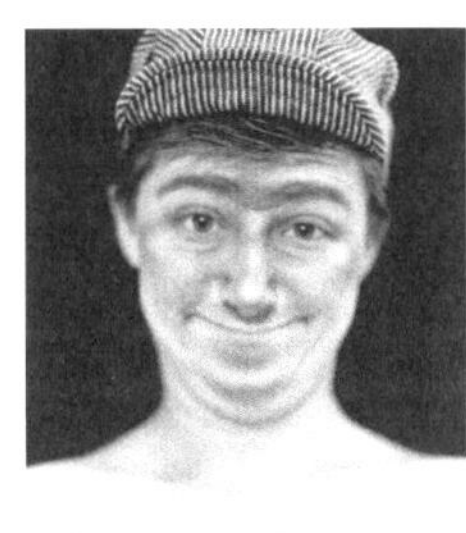

Untitled B, 1975
Black-and-white photograph
Edition of 10
7 ¾ x 6 ¼ in.
(20 x 16 cm)

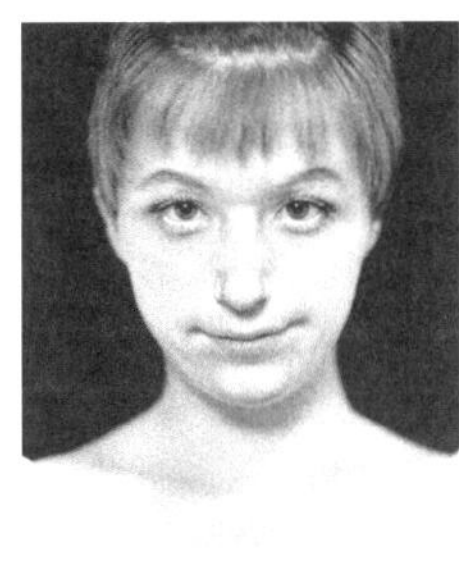

Untitled C, 1975
Black-and-white photograph
Edition of 10
20 x 16 in.
(50.8 x 40.6 cm)

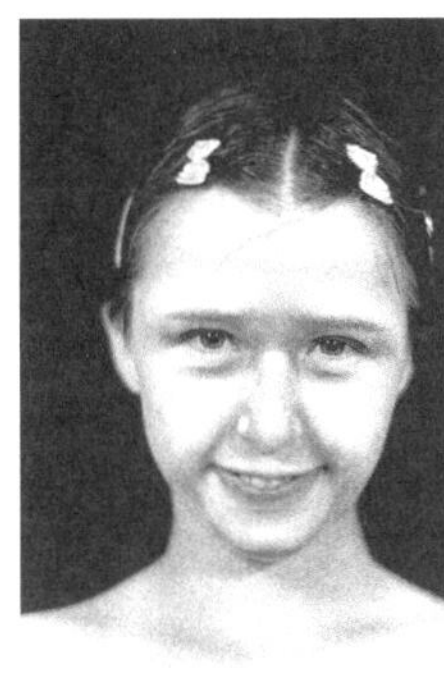

Untitled D, 1975
Black-and-white photograph
Edition of 10
20 x 16 in.
(50.8 x 40.6 cm)

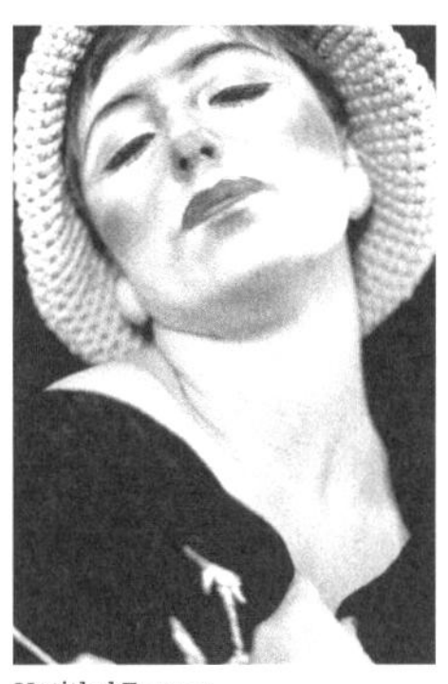

Untitled E, 1975
Black-and-white photograph
Edition of 10
20 x 16 in.
(50.8 x 40.6 cm)

Bus Riders

1976 — 2005

Bus Riders (1976–2005) marks the defining reversal in Sherman's work. The subject is no longer a somewhat hysterical "self" proclaiming its ubiquity and overweening desire for recognition amid a diverse array of appearances and situations. Now, through mimicry and playacting, the subject seeks instead to appropriate the multiple identities of those around her. Sherman deliberately exploits her natural changeability to impersonate a succession of bus passengers, representatives of a population that is itself, by definition, in a permanent state of flux. Using the simplest means (a chair placed in front of a white studio backdrop, a shutter release), the subject captures a series of incarnations embodying the multiplicity and anonymity of modern American society. We note that, deliberately or otherwise, Sherman has left the white studio floormarker clearly visible within the frame. As both actor and producer in this parade of simulacra, the subject's own identity (*That's me*) has been dissolved in favor of a gallery of social stereotypes.

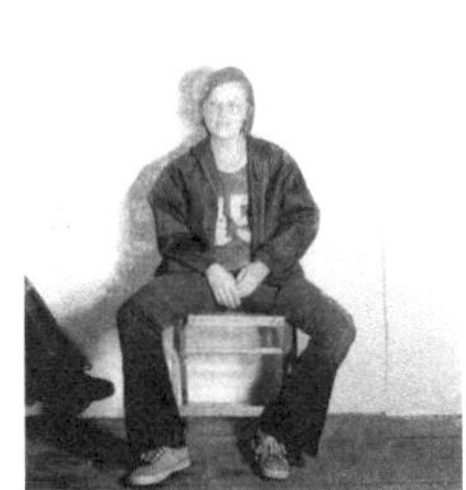

Untitled #363, 1976–2000
Black-and-white photograph
Edition of 20
7 ⅜ x 5 in. (18.9 x 12.7 cm)

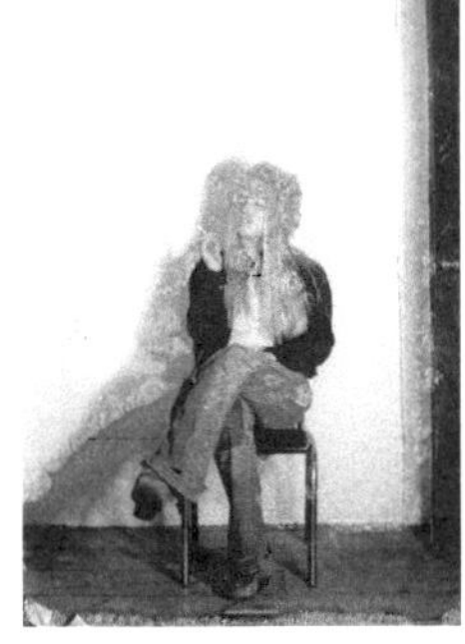

Untitled #364, 1976–2000
Black-and-white photograph
Edition of 20
7 ⅜ x 5 in. (18.9 x 12.7 cm)

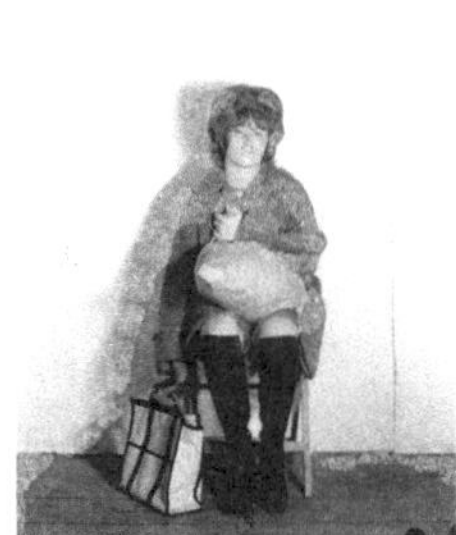

Untitled #365, 1976–2000
Black-and-white photograph
Edition of 20
7 ⅜ x 5 in. (18.9 x 12.7 cm)

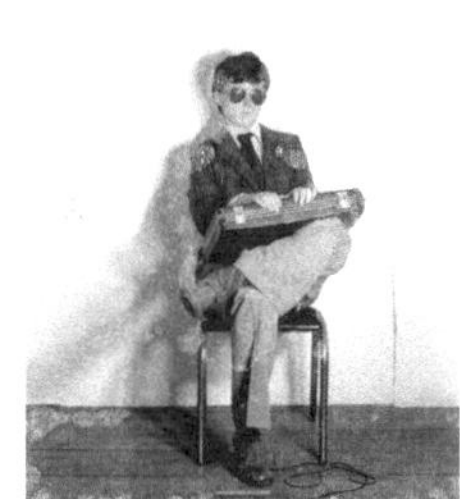

Untitled #366, 1976–2000
Black-and-white photograph
Edition of 20
7 ⅜ x 5 in. (18.9 x 12.7 cm)

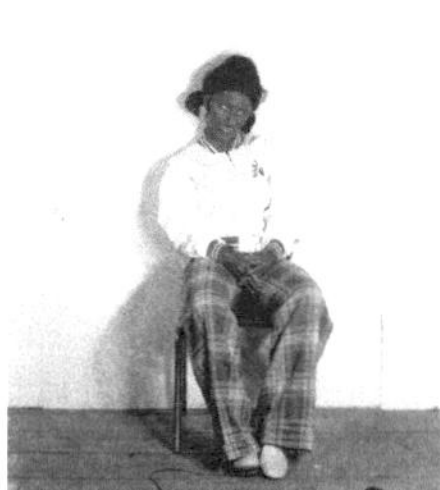

Untitled #367, 1976–2000
Black-and-white photograph
Edition of 20
7 ⅜ x 5 in. (18.9 x 12.7 cm)

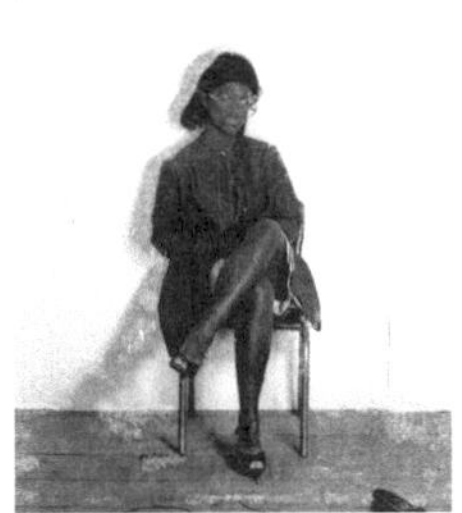

Untitled #368, 1976–2000
Black-and-white photograph
Edition of 20
7 ⅜ x 5 in. (18.9 x 12.7 cm)

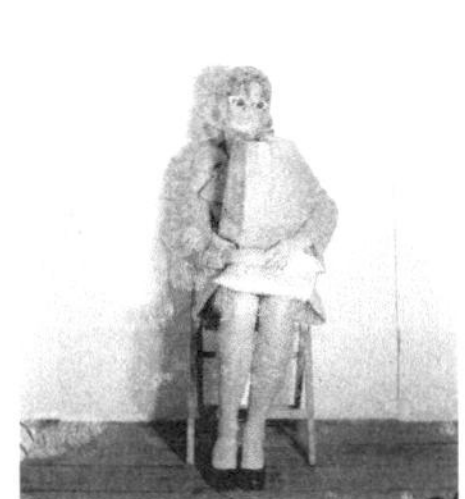

Untitled #369, 1976–2000
Black-and-white photograph
Edition of 20
7 ⅜ x 5 in. (18.9 x 12.7 cm)

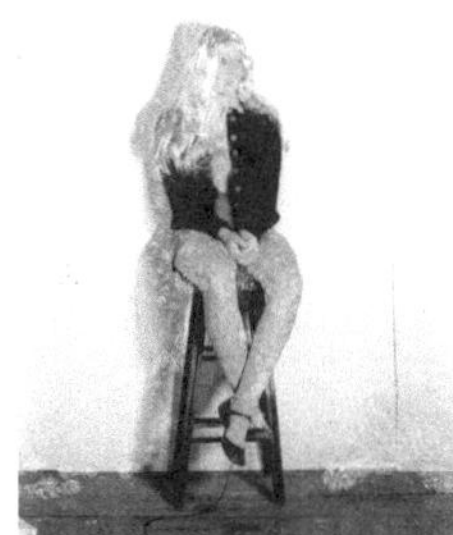

Untitled #370, 1976–2000
Black-and-white photograph
Edition of 20
7 ⅜ x 5 in. (18.9 x 12.7 cm)

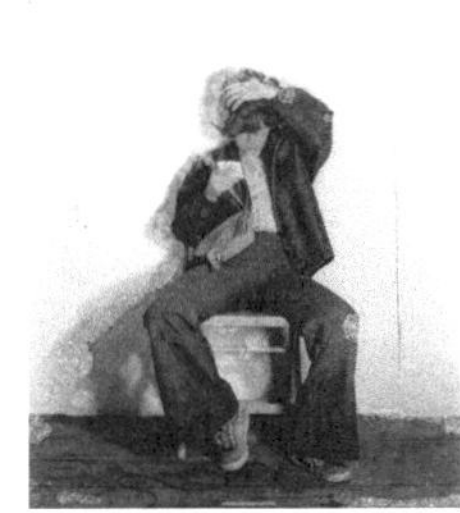

Untitled #371, 1976–2000
Black-and-white photograph
Edition of 20
7 ⅜ x 5 in. (18.9 x 12.7 cm)

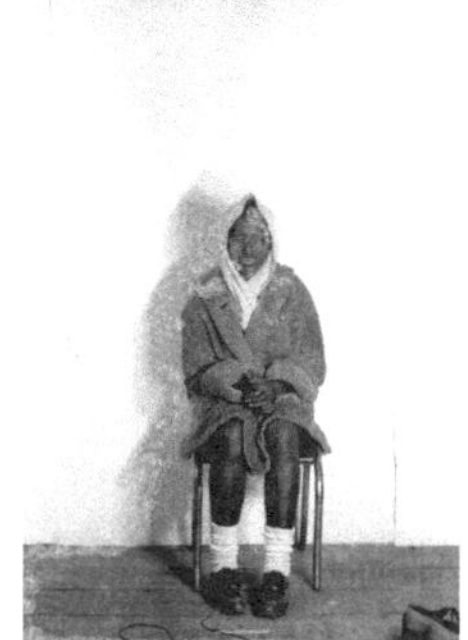

Untitled #372, 1976–2000
Black-and-white photograph
Edition of 20
7 ⅜ x 5 in. (18.9 x 12.7 cm)

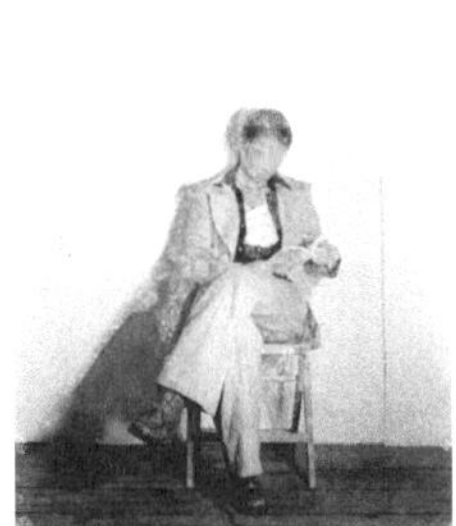

Untitled #373, 1976–2000
Black-and-white photograph
Edition of 20
7 ⅜ x 5 in. (18.9 x 12.7 cm)

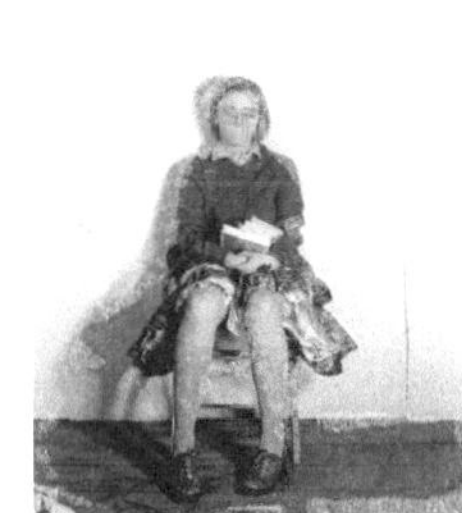

Untitled #374, 1976–2000
Black-and-white photograph
Edition of 20
7 ⅜ x 5 in. (18.9 x 12.7 cm)

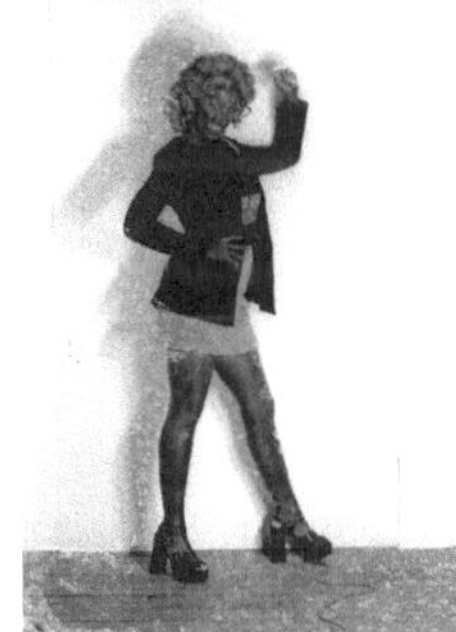

Untitled #375, 1976–2000
Black-and-white photograph
Edition of 20
7 ⅜ x 5 in. (18.9 x 12.7 cm)

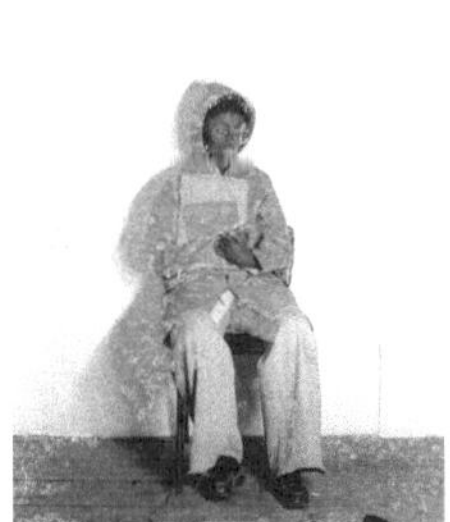

Untitled #376, 1976–2000
Black-and-white photograph
Edition of 20
7 ⅜ x 5 in. (18.9 x 12.7 cm)

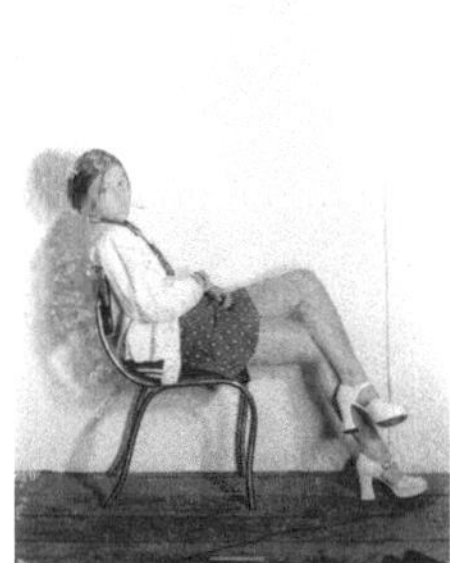

Untitled #377, 1976–2000
Black-and-white photograph
Edition of 20
7 ⅜ x 5 in. (18.9 x 12.7 cm)

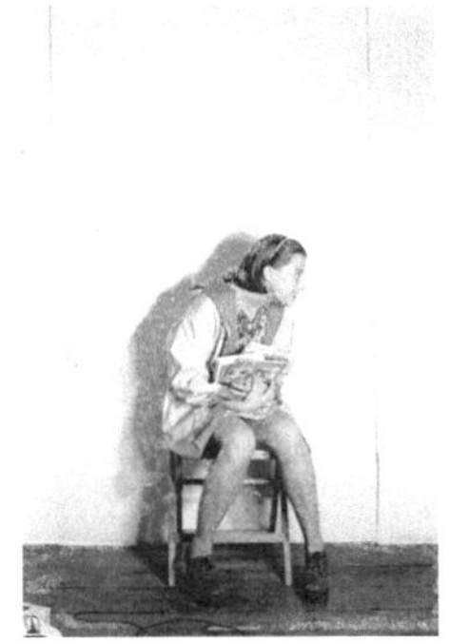

Untitled #430, 1976–2005
Black-and-white photograph
Edition of 20
7 ⅛ x 5 in. (18.3 x 12.7 cm)

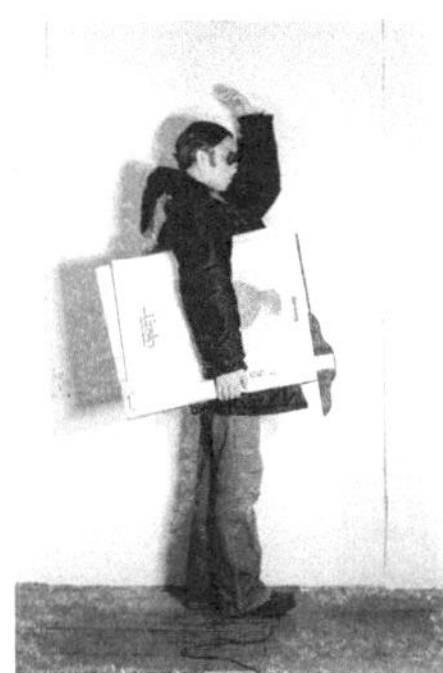

Untitled #431, 1976–2005
Black-and-white photograph
Edition of 20
7 ⅛ x 5 in. (18.3 x 12.7 cm)

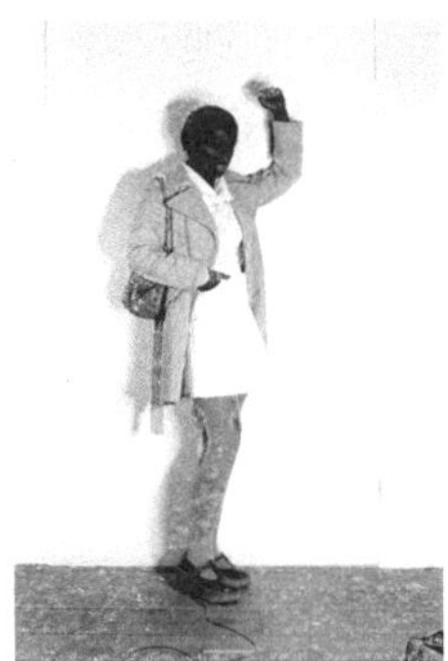

Untitled #433, 1976–2005
Black-and-white photograph
Edition of 20
7 ⅛ x 5 in. (18.3 x 12.7 cm)

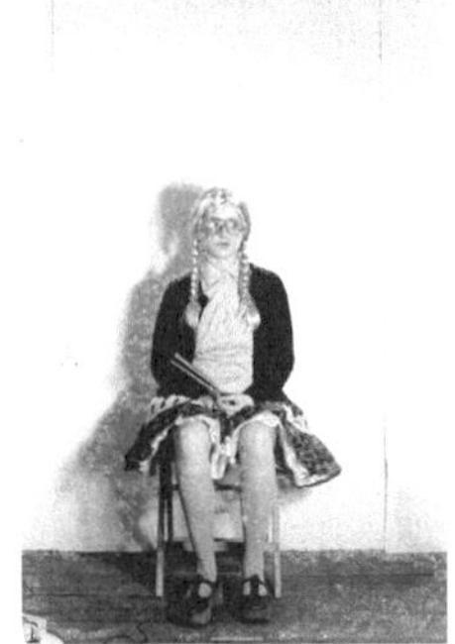

Untitled #434, 1976–2005
Black-and-white photograph
Edition of 20
7 ⅛ x 5 in. (18.3 x 12.7 cm)

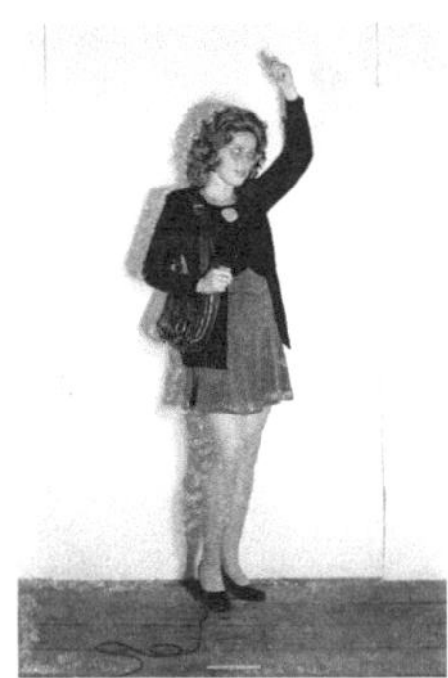

Untitled #439, 1976–2005
Black-and-white photograph
Edition of 20
7 ⅜ x 5 in. (18.9 x 12.7 cm)

Murder Mystery

1976 — 2000

In *Murder Mystery* (1976–2000) the gallery of roles is derived not from a fictional sociological context (passengers on a bus at a given moment in time), but from an imaginary narrative—a fictional murder mystery. The *Bus Riders* form a potentially limitless series of realist images (depictions of individuals in an anonymous city, whose paths might cross while riding on the same bus), while the *Murder Mystery* people create their own hermetically sealed, introspective, fictional universe. The characters represent the standard cast of protagonists in a fictional murder scenario, captured here by the subject/producer in a sequence of brief cameos for our prurient, omniscient scrutiny, just as they are by the author of a crime novel. We, the spectators/readers, are invited to spot the clues and construct our own theories as to "whodunit": the murder is clearly a high society crime (witness the maid and butler, the characters in riding clothes and evening dress). There is a photographer, a detective, a *femme fatale*, and the usual witnesses. As with the *Bus Riders*, the characters are staged against a plain, unchanging backdrop, with minimal props and a visible shutter-release cord. Here, the artful, virtuoso makeup and disguises used by the subject to appropriate each role convey a playful, childlike sense of jubilation. Significantly, both the *Bus Riders* and *Murder Mystery* seem to usher in two elements that feature in later works: a taste for types and stereotypes, and the presence of tiny, undeveloped clues that betray the fictive nature of the narrative scene.

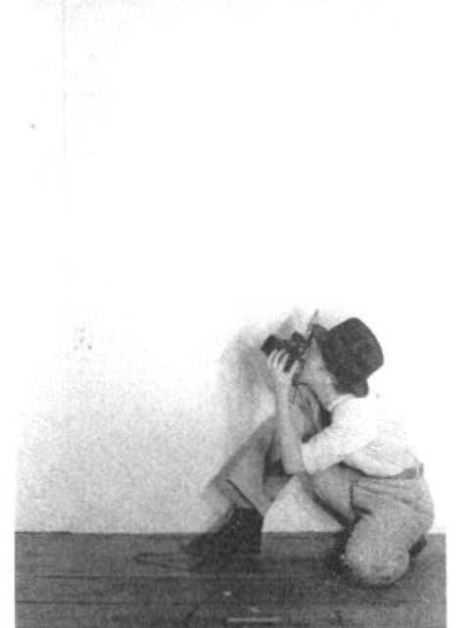

Untitled #378, 1976–2000
Black-and-white photograph
Edition of 20
10 x 8 in. (25.4 x 20.3 cm)

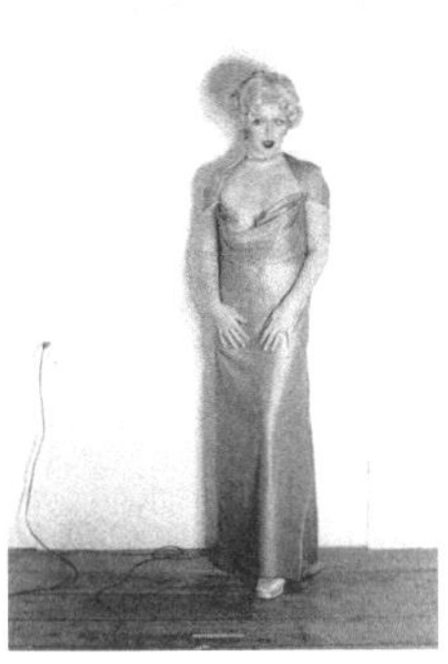

Untitled #379, 1976–2000
Black-and-white photograph
Edition of 20
10 x 8 in. (25.4 x 20.3 cm)

Untitled #380, 1976–2000
Black-and-white photograph
Edition of 20
10 x 8 in. (25.4 x 20.3 cm)

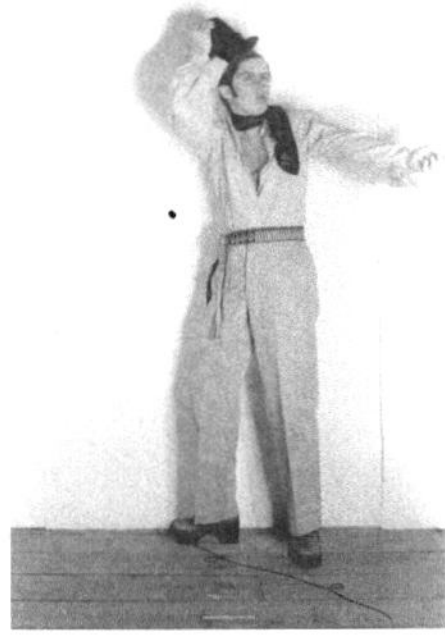

Untitled #381, 1976–2000
Black-and-white photograph
Edition of 20
10 x 8 in. (25.4 x 20.3 cm)

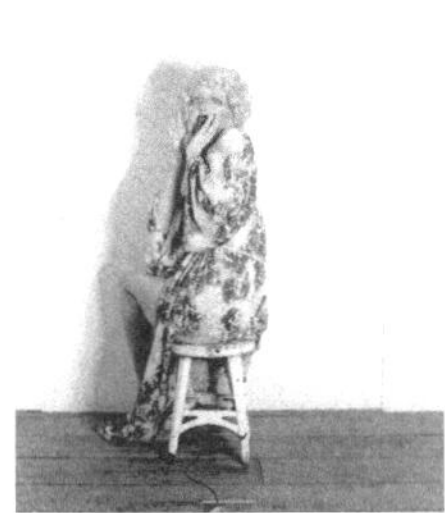

Untitled #382, 1976–2000
Black-and-white photograph
Edition of 20
10 x 8 in. (25.4 x 20.3 cm)

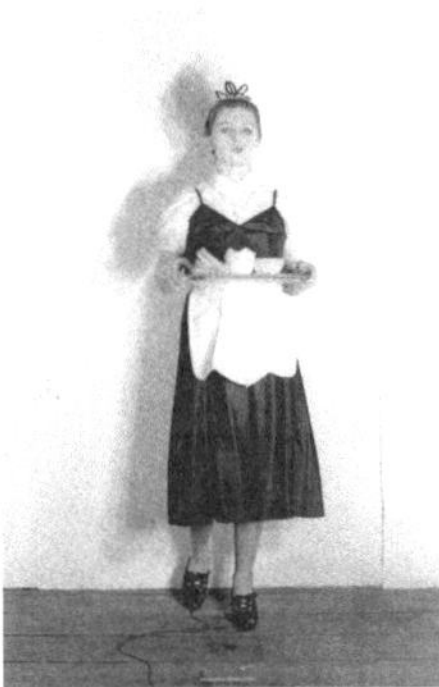

Untitled #383, 1976–2000
Black-and-white photograph
Edition of 20
10 x 8 in. (25.4 x 20.3 cm)

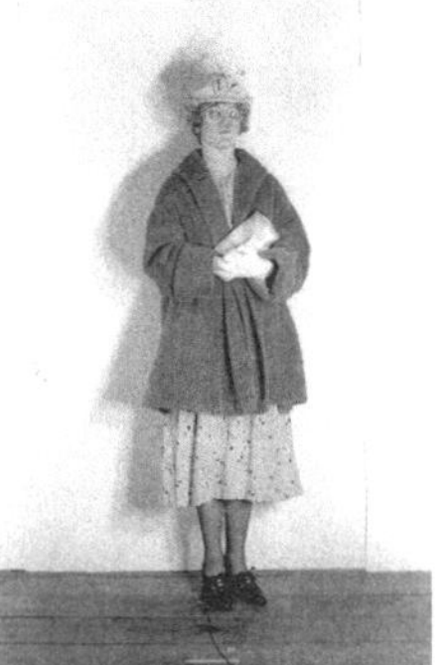

Untitled #384, 1976–2000
Black-and-white photograph
Edition of 20
10 x 8 in. (25.4 x 20.3 cm)

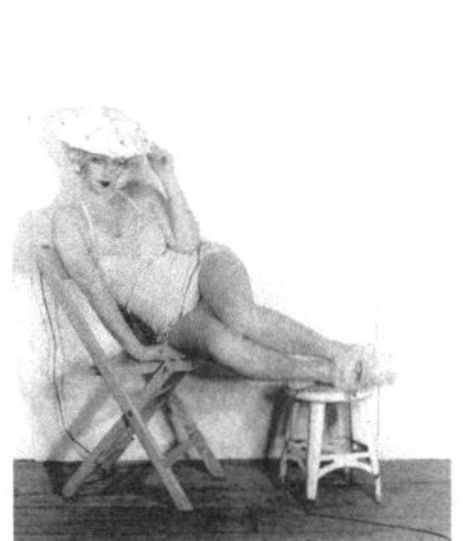

Untitled #385, 1976–2000
Black-and-white photograph
Edition of 20
10 x 8 in. (25.4 x 20.3 cm)

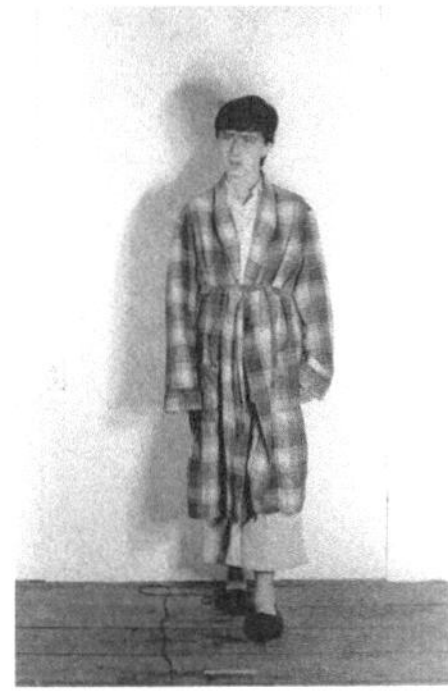

Untitled #386, 1976–2000
Black-and-white photograph
Edition of 20
10 x 8 in. (25.4 x 20.3 cm)

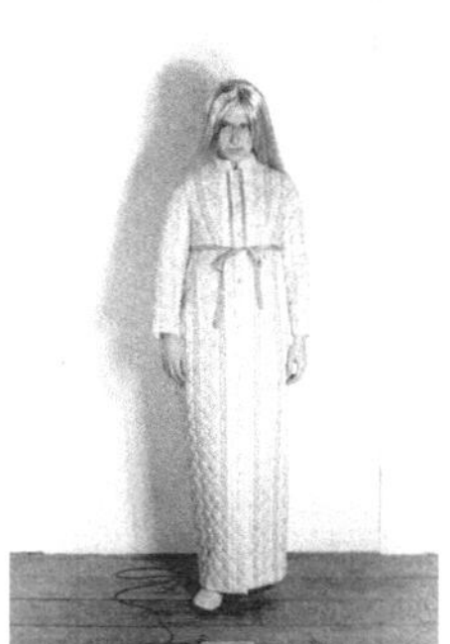

Untitled #387, 1976–2000
Black-and-white photograph
Edition of 20
10 x 8 in. (25.4 x 20.3 cm)

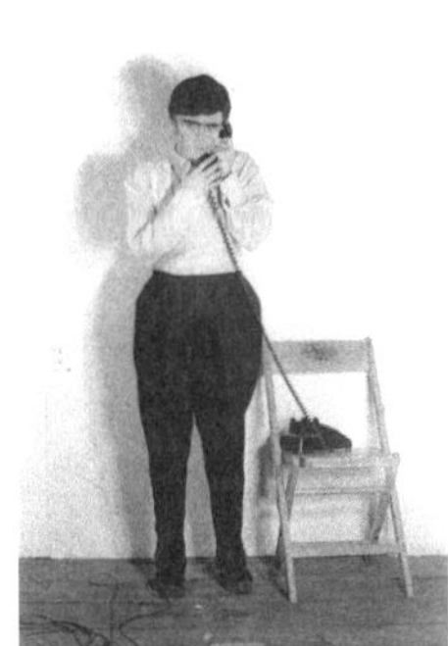

Untitled #388, 1976–2000
Black-and-white photograph
Edition of 20
10 x 8 in. (25.4 x 20.3 cm)

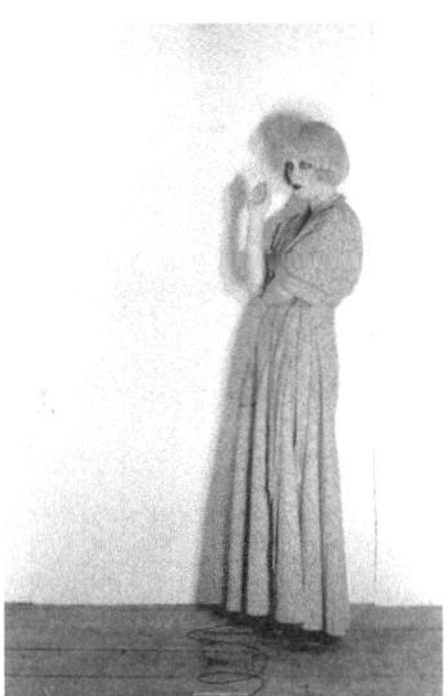

Untitled #389, 1976–2000
Black-and-white photograph
Edition of 20
10 x 8 in. (25.4 x 20.3 cm)

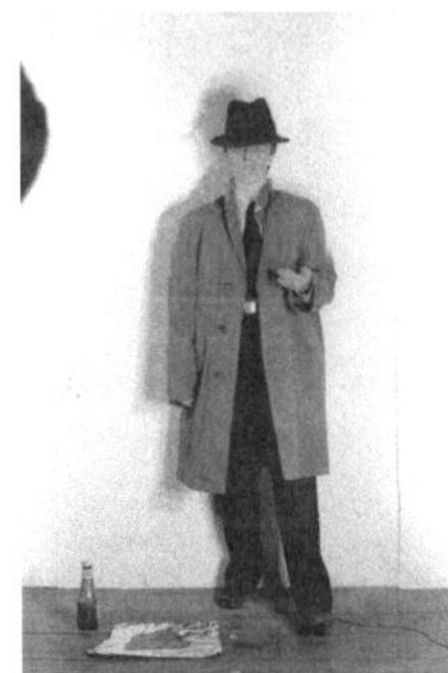

Untitled #390, 1976–2000
Black-and-white photograph
Edition of 20
10 x 8 in. (25.4 x 20.3 cm)

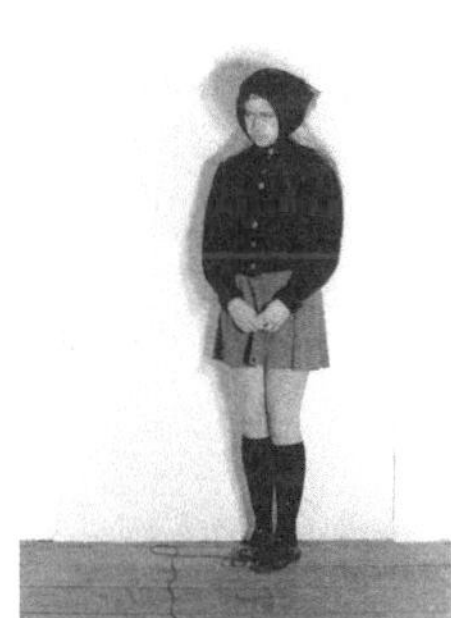

Untitled #391, 1976–2000
Black-and-white photograph
Edition of 20
10 x 8 in. (25.4 x 20.3 cm)

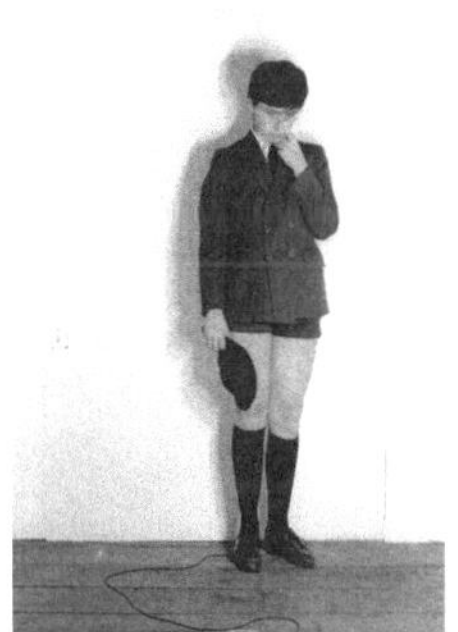

Untitled #392, 1976–2000
Black-and-white photograph
Edition of 20
10 x 8 in. (25.4 x 20.3 cm)

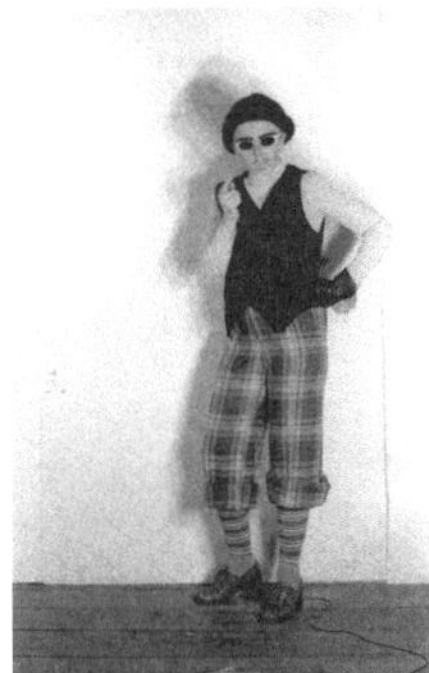

Untitled #393, 1976–2000
Black-and-white photograph
Edition of 20
10 x 8 in. (25.4 x 20.3 cm)

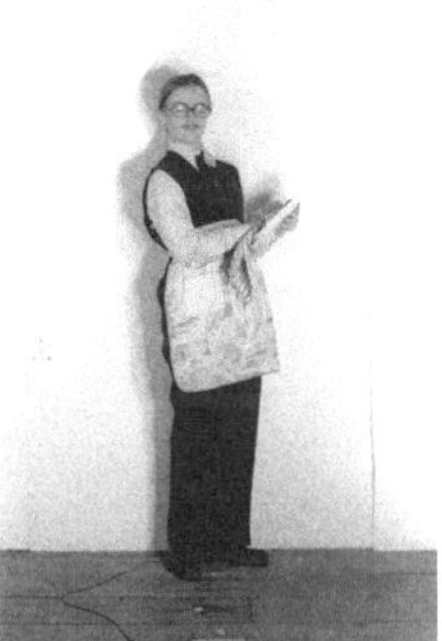

Untitled #394, 1976–2000
Black-and-white photograph
Edition of 20
10 x 8 in. (25.4 x 20.3 cm)

Untitled Film Stills

1977—1980

Without doubt the most important series in Cindy Sherman's early work, the seventy *Untitled Film Stills* create a metamorphic world in which the subject invents a succession of more elaborately constructed identities, complete with props and settings, but which are still not always necessarily entirely explicit. The subject's jubilant "chameleonism" appropriates a range of different worlds, ranging from the stereotypes of everyday life (the young housewife, the student) to literature, painting, and of course cinema (Italian Neorealism, or American *film noir*, for example).

These *Film Stills* recall the photographs taken on movie sets in the 1950s and 1960s, and used to advertise forthcoming motion pictures. Their *Untitled* status (in common with most of Sherman's work) leaves them open to multiple interpretations. The subject is generally seen in the foreground or middle ground of the picture, as one element of a theatricalized scene in which the setting, clothes, or pose combine to create a distinctive atmosphere. Here, and in Sherman's subsequent work, the artist alternates between detailed close-ups that reveal the components of the subject's "disguise" (makeup and prostheses), and wide-angle images in which the figure tends to "disappear." In both cases we witness a kind of self-effacement, as if the subject's natural destiny was to disappear beneath an array of artifacts, or to melt into the fictions created by those artifacts, according to some internal law of uncontrollable mutability, some kind of equilibrium being kept nonetheless by the sheer speed of the process.

One consequence of the size of this series is that the images have a tendency to form sub-groups centered around a particular character, or evoking another, similar or related figure (*Untitled Film Stills #1* to *#6*, for example, or *#45* and *#46*, *#17* to *#20*).

The series' success lies in the tension established by the artist between our immediate recognition of a reference or stereotype (with the inevitable danger that this becomes a somewhat superficial game), and the creation of a space onto which the viewer can project his or her fictional imaginings and desires. Each scene is constructed for the viewer alone; the images are the precursors of a fictional narrative. In this sense, they function exactly like "real" film stills, whetting the appetite and inviting the viewer to implicate him- or herself in the image, both visually and sexually. "Seductive, chameleonic subject wants to meet understanding, voyeuristic gaze:" a perfect match, if it weren't for the fact that everything is played out in a series of fantasy worlds that have, furthermore, been rigorously filtered by a strict set of artistic criteria.

The subject in this series appears like a dismembered body, torn between disparate aspirations, including a number of readily identifiable scenarios from the America of the 1970s. Many others are throwbacks to earlier periods (1950s cinema, the position of women in the 1960s). The series is also, perhaps, a nostalgic farewell to the idea of cinema as the sole vehicle for our great fictional role models, in a period that witnessed the definitive triumph of television.

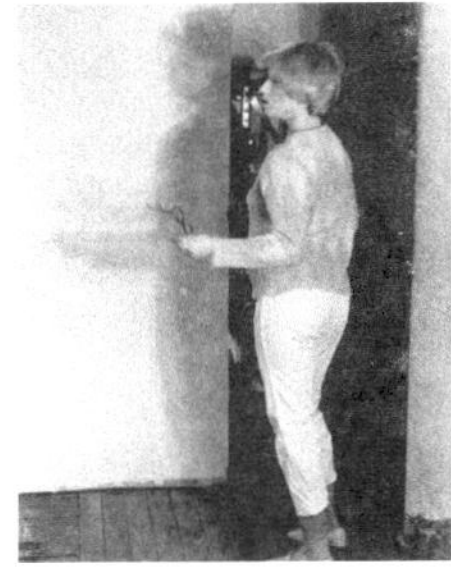

Untitled Film Still #1, 1977
Black-and-white photograph
Edition of 10

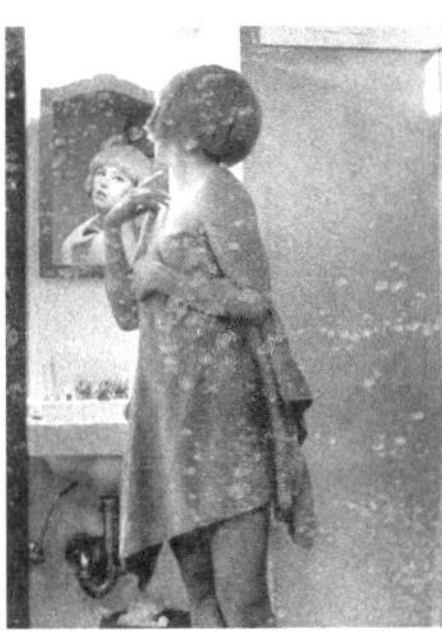

Untitled Film Still #2, 1977
Black-and-white photograph
Edition of 10

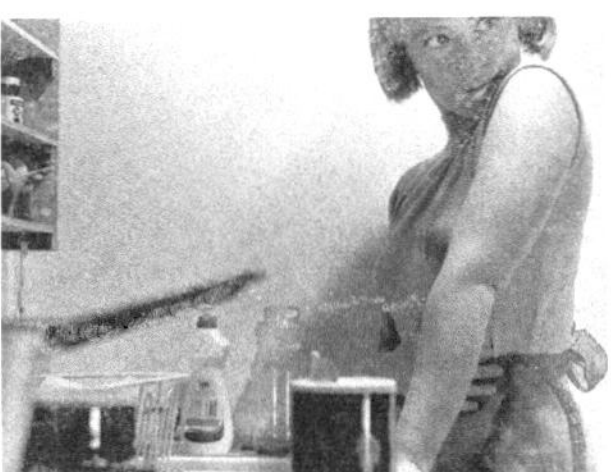

Untitled Film Still #3, 1977
Black-and-white photograph
Edition of 10

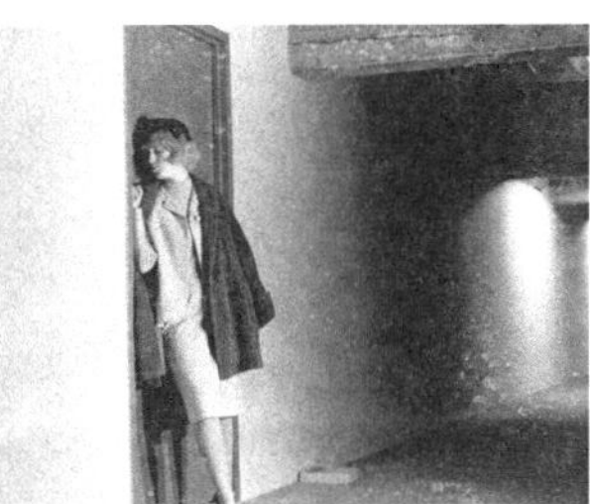

Untitled Film Still #4, 1977
Black-and-white photograph
Edition of 10

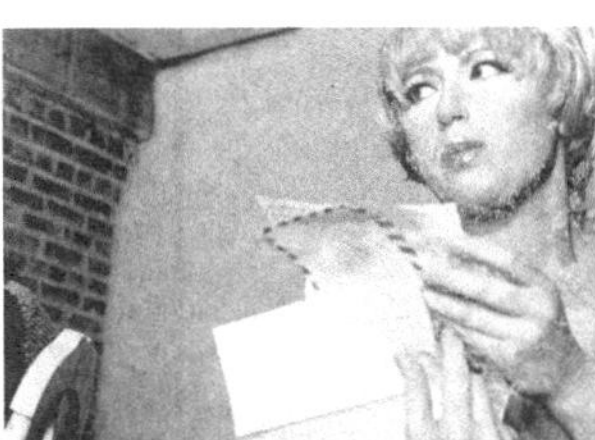

Untitled Film Still #5, 1977
Black-and-white photograph
Edition of 10

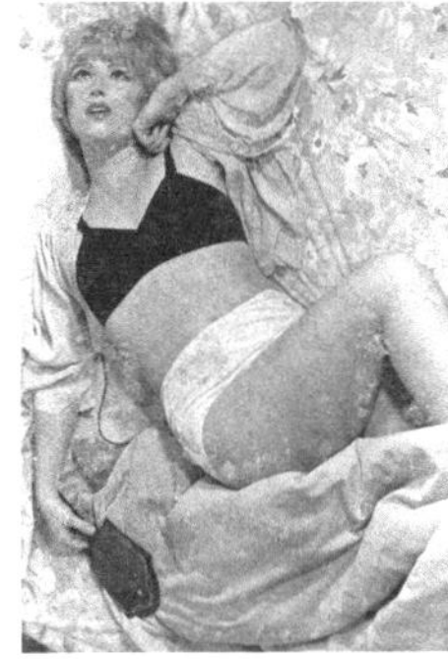

Untitled Film Still #6, 1977
Black-and-white photograph
Edition of 10

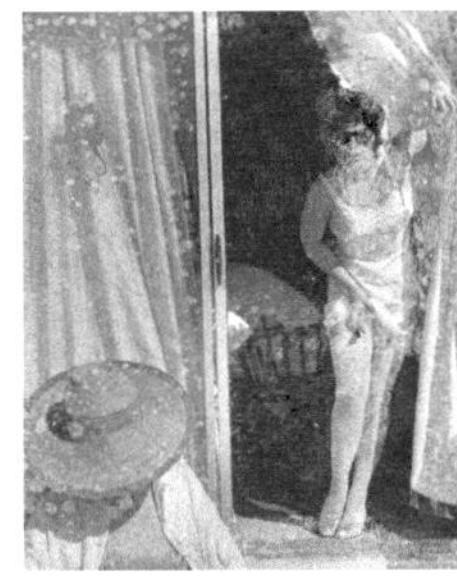

Untitled Film Still #7, 1978
Black-and-white photograph
Edition of 10

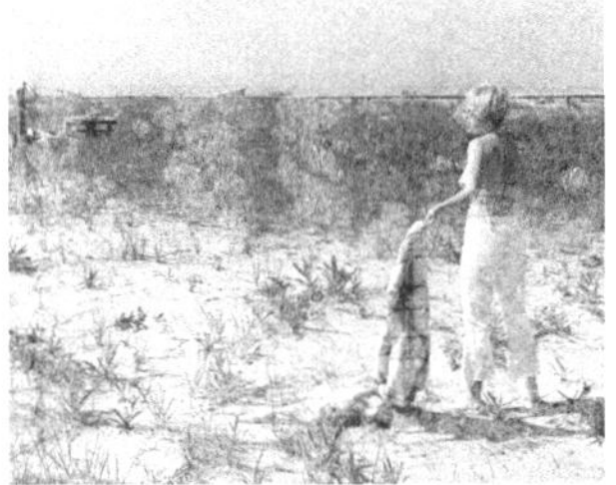

Untitled Film Still #8, 1978
Black-and-white photograph
Edition of 10

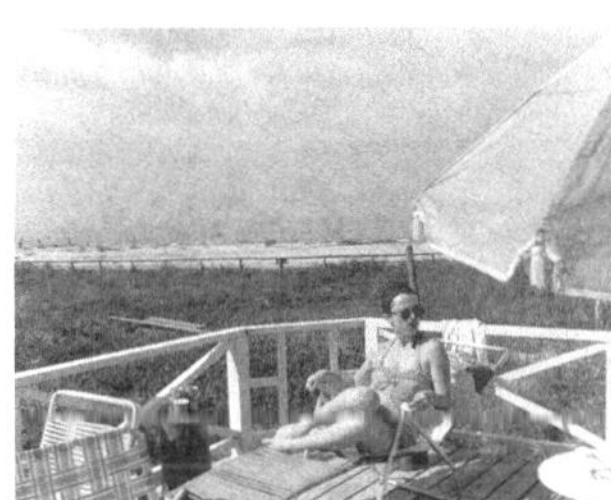

Untitled Film Still #9, 1978
Black-and-white photograph
Edition of 10

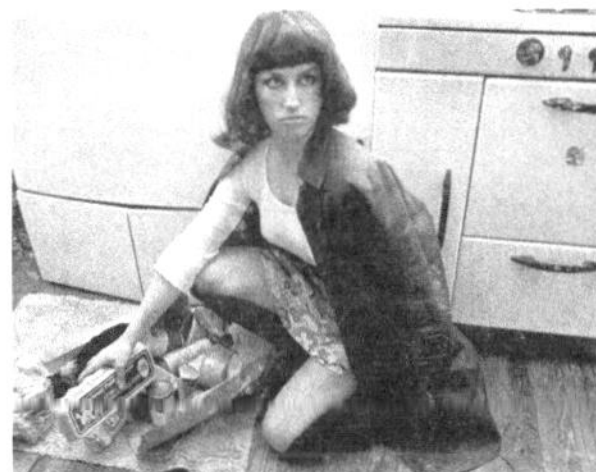

Untitled Film Still #10, 1978
Black-and-white photograph
Edition of 10

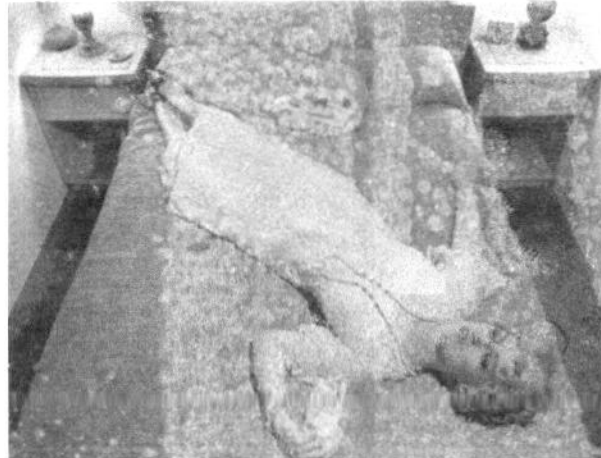

Untitled Film Still #11, 1978
Black-and-white photograph
Edition of 10

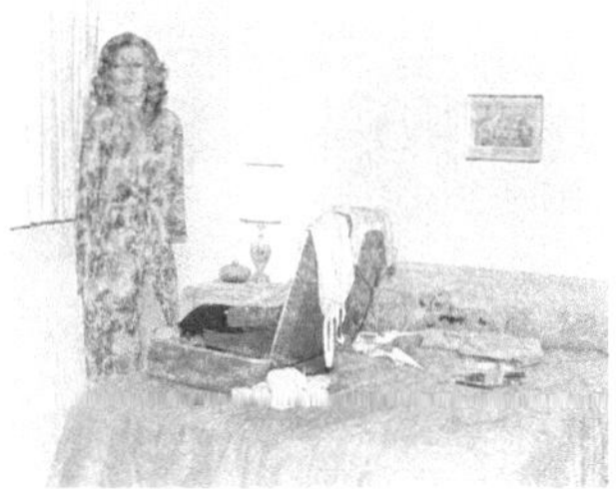

Untitled Film Still #12, 1978
Black-and-white photograph
Edition of 10

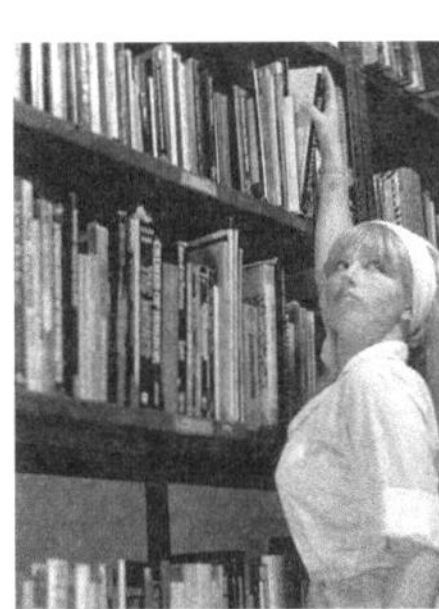

Untitled Film Still #13, 1978
Black-and-white photograph
Edition of 10

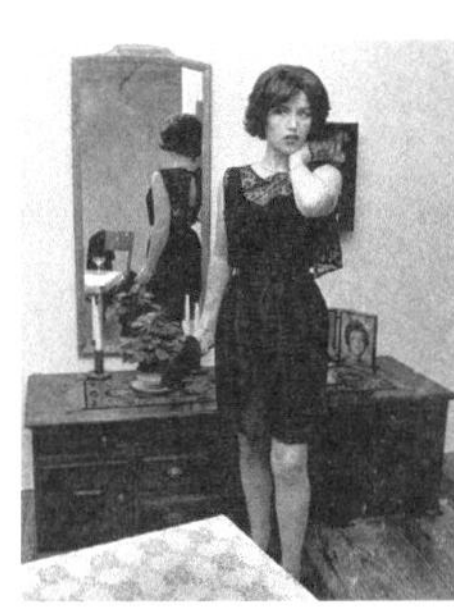

Untitled Film Still #14, 1978
Black-and-white photograph
Edition of 10

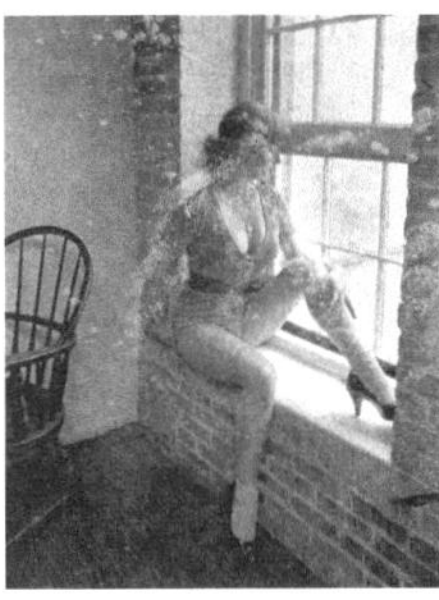

Untitled Film Still #15, 1978
Black-and-white photograph
Edition of 10

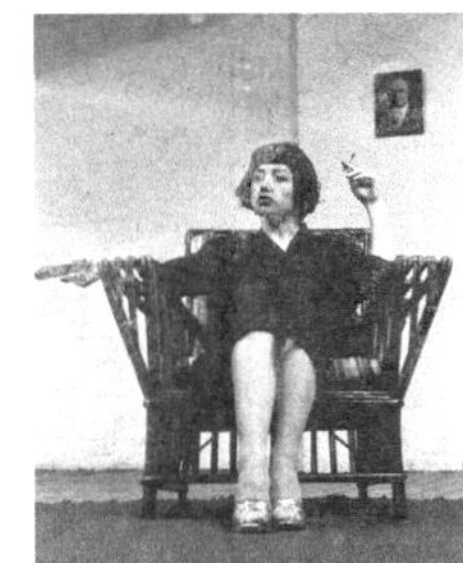

Untitled Film Still #16, 1978
Black-and-white photograph
Edition of 10

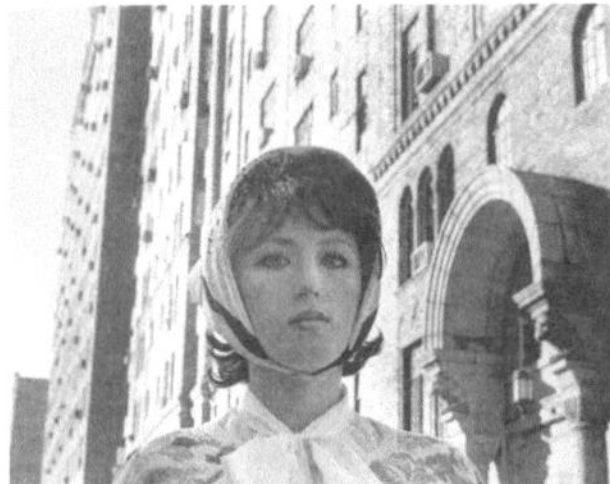

Untitled Film Still #17, 1978
Black-and-white photograph
Edition of 10

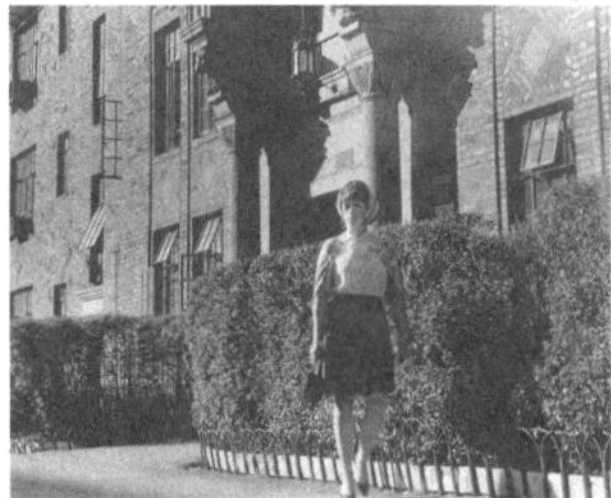

Untitled Film Still #18, 1978
Black-and-white photograph
Edition of 10

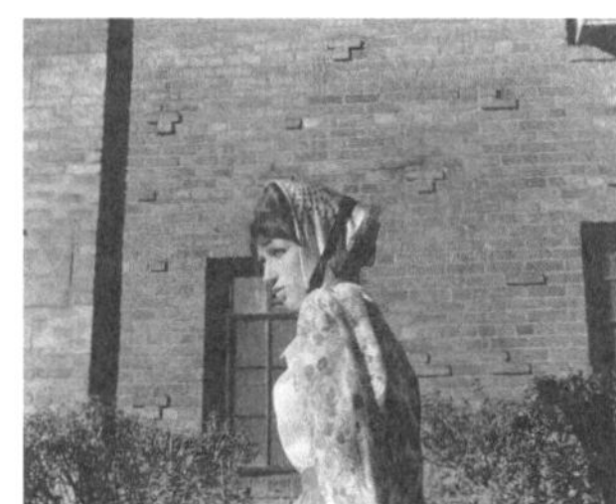

Untitled Film Still #19, 1978
Black-and-white photograph
Edition of 10

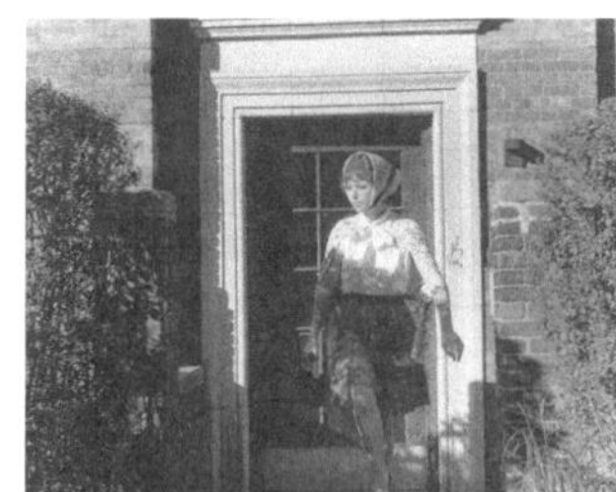

Untitled Film Still #20, 1978
Black-and-white photograph
Edition of 10

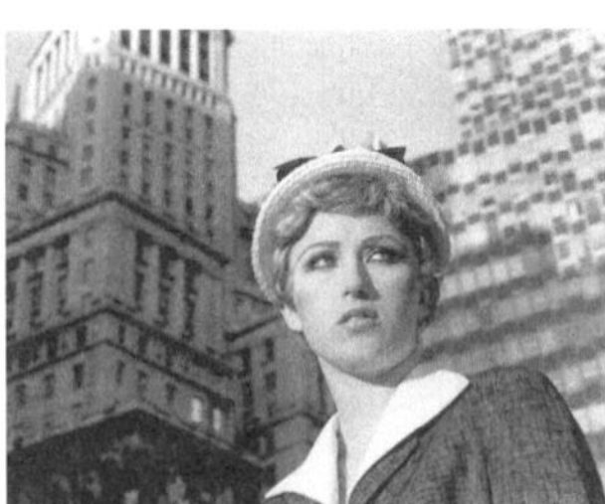

Untitled Film Still #21, 1978
Black-and-white photograph
Edition of 10

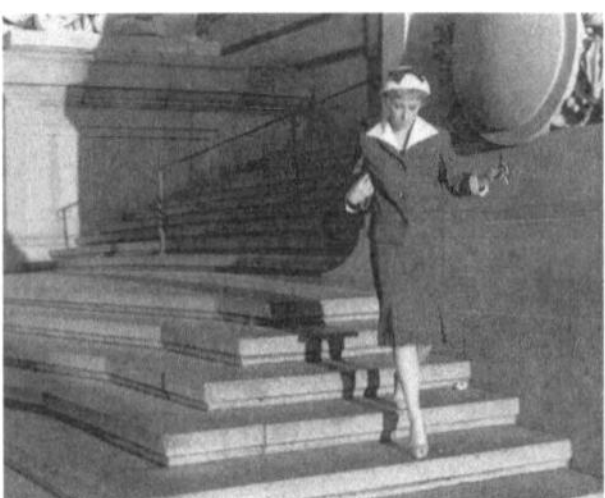

Untitled Film Still #22, 1978
Black-and-white photograph
Edition of 10

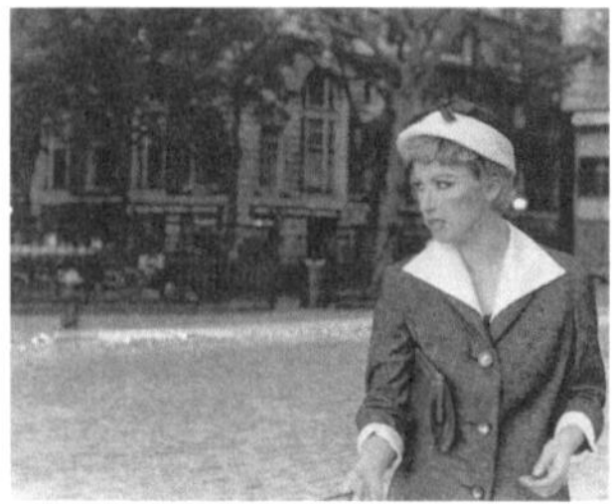

Untitled Film Still #23, 1978
Black-and-white photograph
Edition of 10

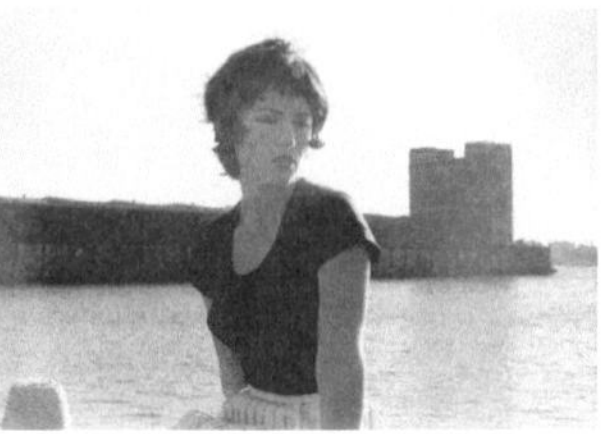

Untitled Film Still #24, 1978
Black-and-white photograph
Edition of 10

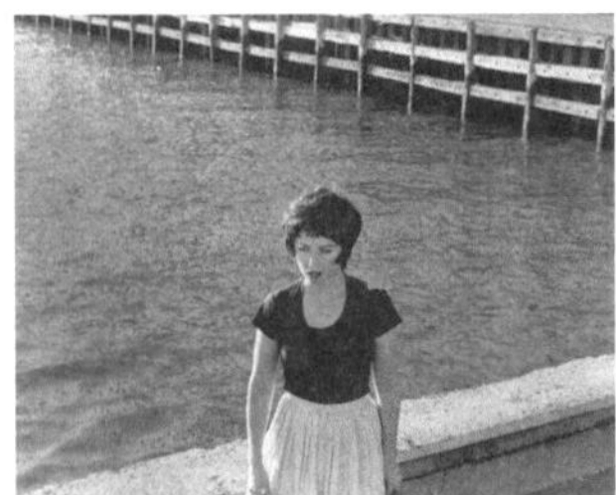

Untitled Film Still #25, 1978
Black-and-white photograph
Edition of 10

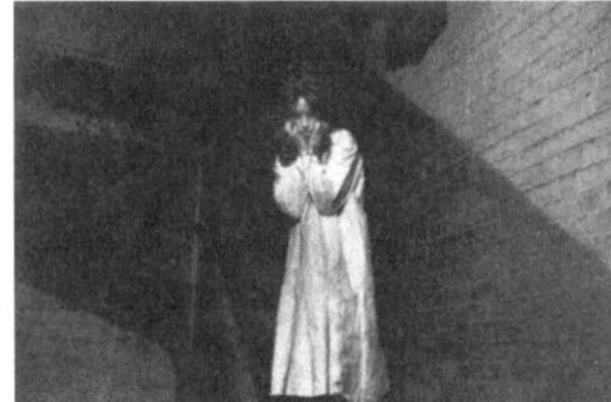

Untitled Film Still #26, 1979
Black-and-white photograph
Edition of 10

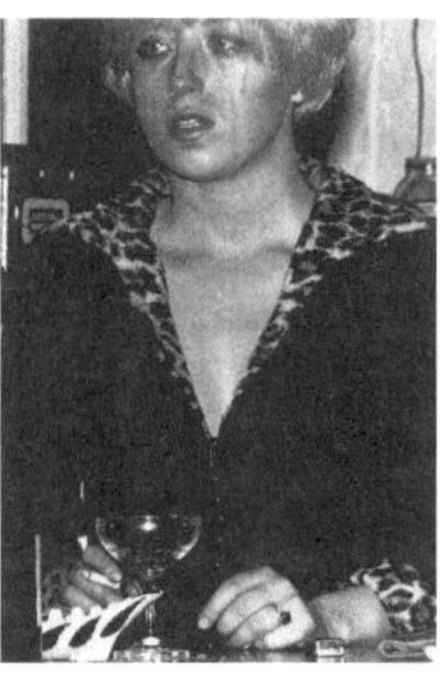

Untitled Film Still #27, 1979
Black-and-white photograph
Edition of 10

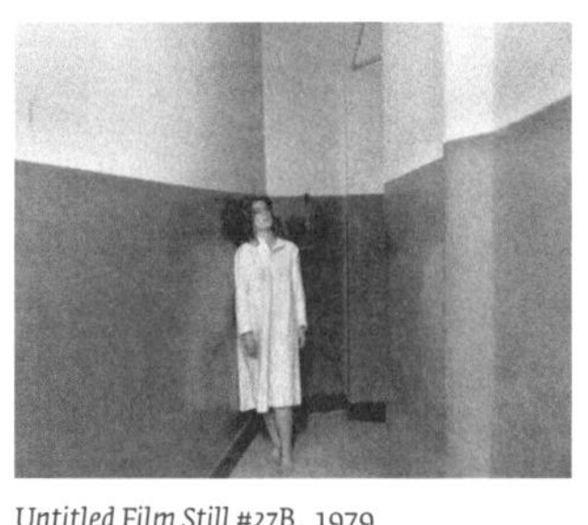

Untitled Film Still #27B, 1979
Black-and-white photograph
Edition of 10

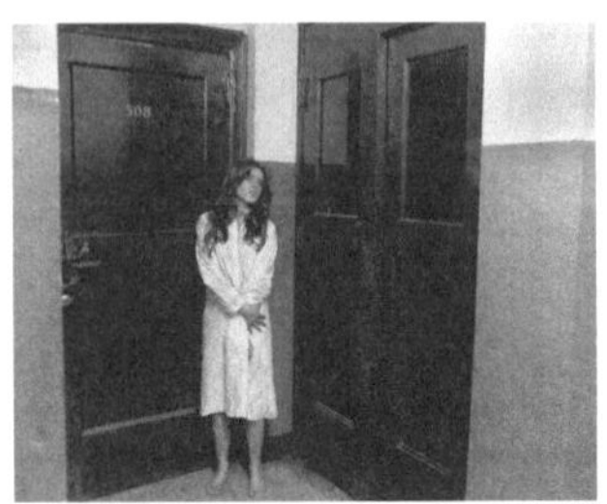

Untitled Film Still #28, 1979
Black-and-white photograph
Edition of 10

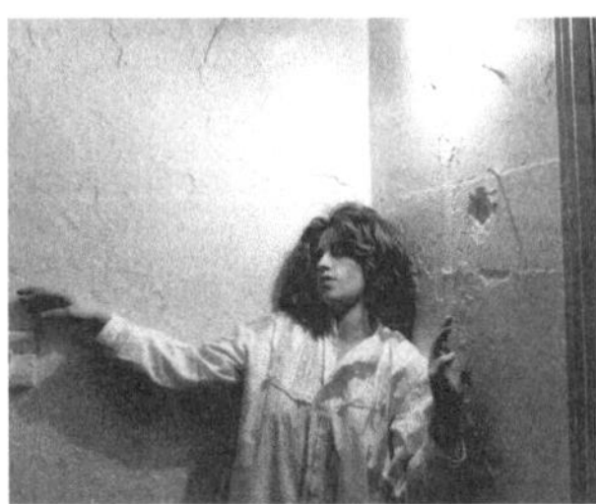

Untitled Film Still #29, 1979
Black-and-white photograph
Edition of 10

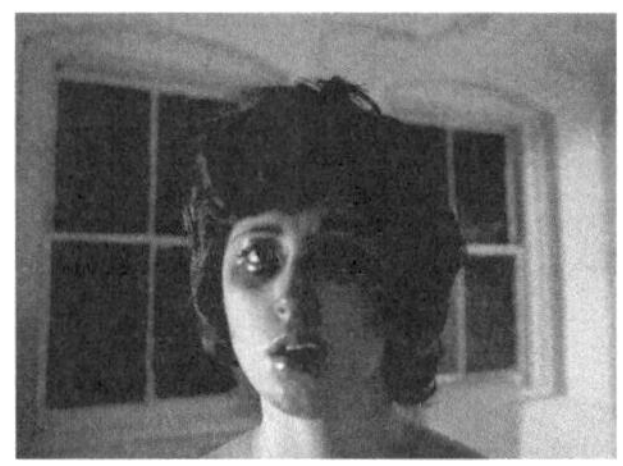

Untitled Film Still #30, 1979
Black-and-white photograph
Edition of 10

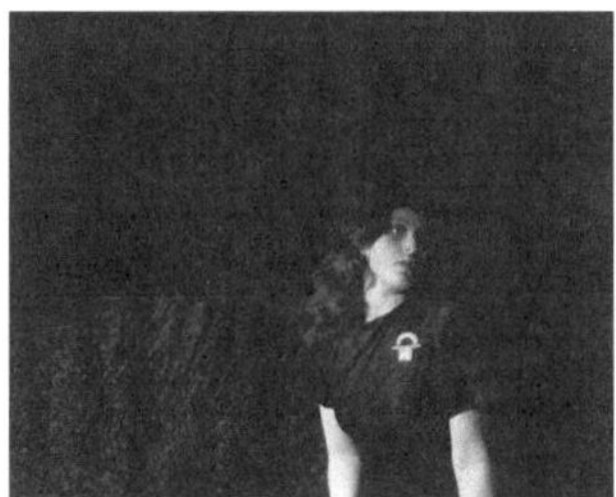

Untitled Film Still #31, 1979
Black-and-white photograph
Edition of 10

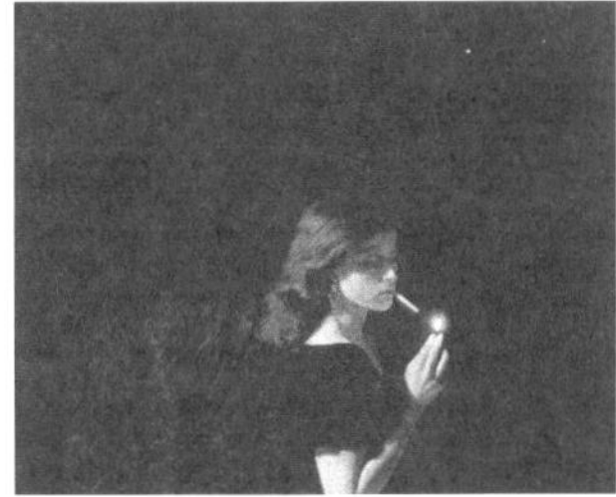

Untitled Film Still #32, 1979
Black-and-white photograph
Edition of 10

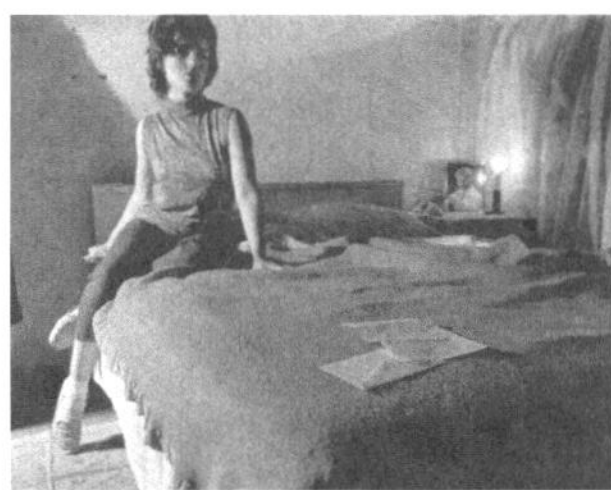

Untitled Film Still #33, 1979
Black-and-white photograph
Edition of 10

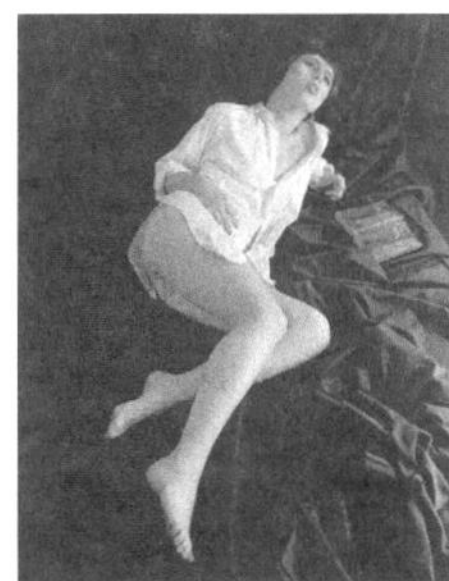

Untitled Film Still #34, 1979
Black-and-white photograph
Edition of 10

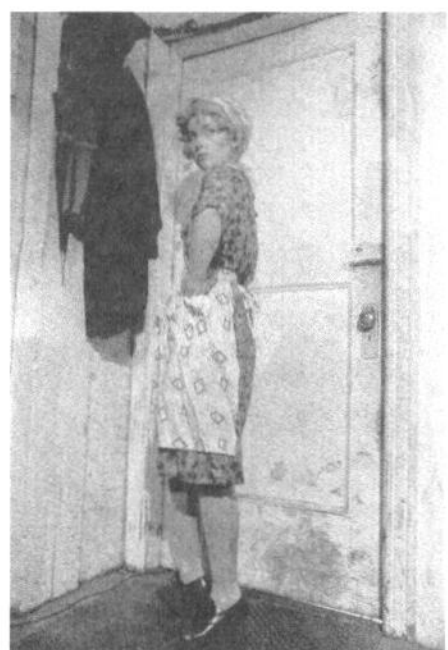

Untitled Film Still #35, 1979
Black-and-white photograph
Edition of 10

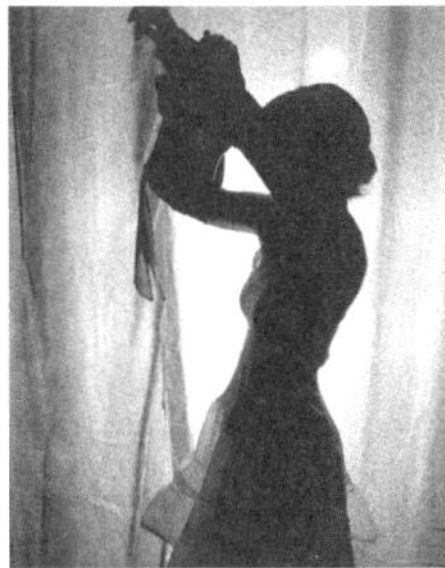

Untitled Film Still #36, 1979
Black-and-white photograph
Edition of 10

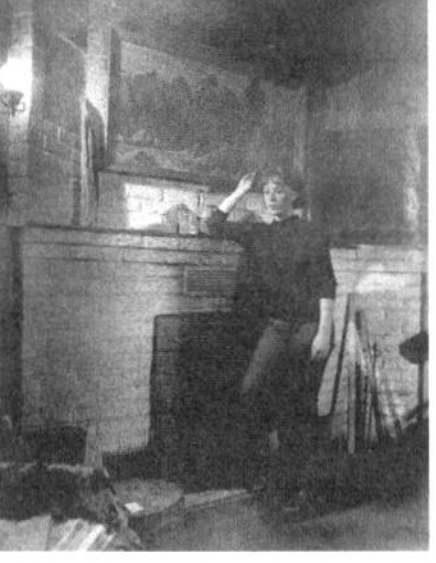

Untitled Film Still #37, 1979
Black-and-white photograph
Edition of 10

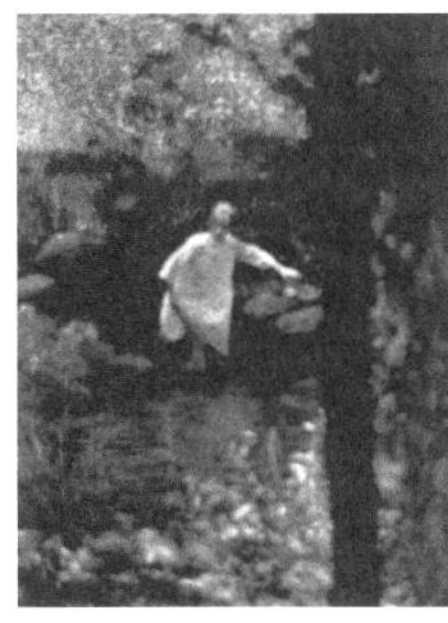

Untitled Film Still #38, 1979
Black-and-white photograph
Edition of 10

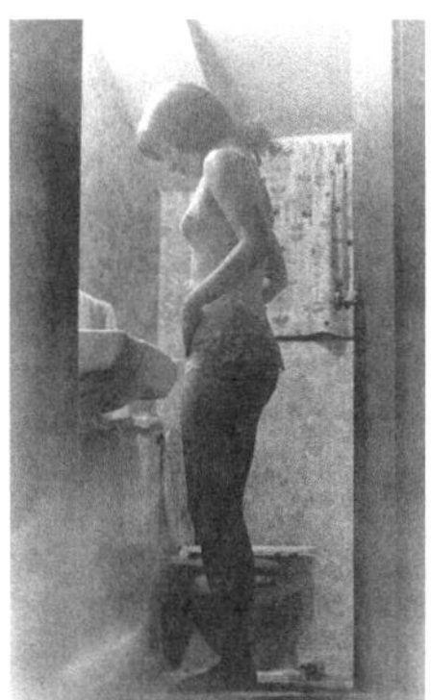

Untitled Film Still #39, 1979
Black-and-white photograph
Edition of 10

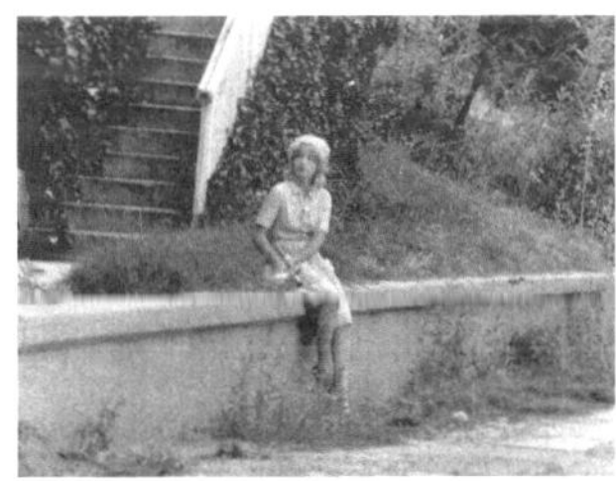

Untitled Film Still #40, 1979
Black-and-white photograph
Edition of 10

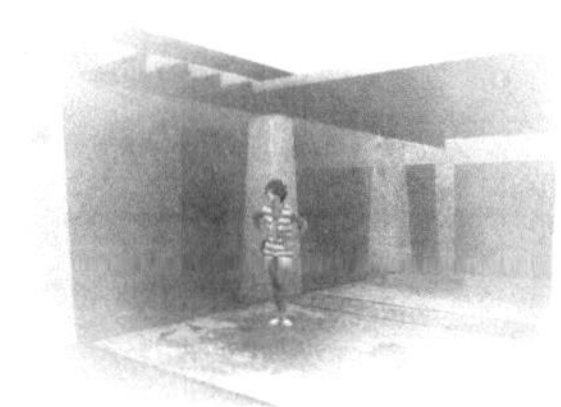

Untitled Film Still #41, 1979
Black-and-white photograph
Edition of 10

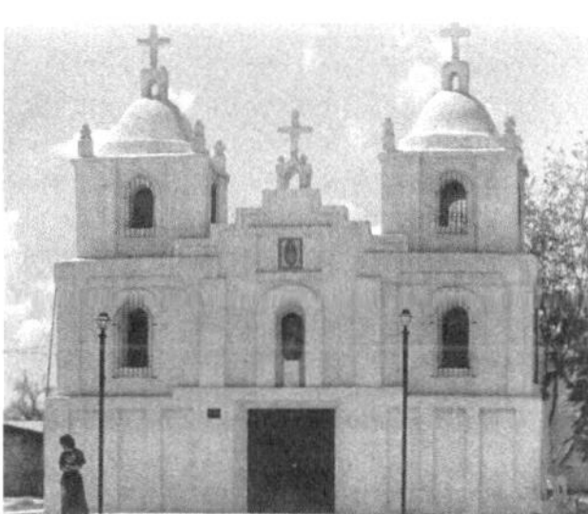

Untitled Film Still #42, 1979
Black-and-white photograph
Edition of 10

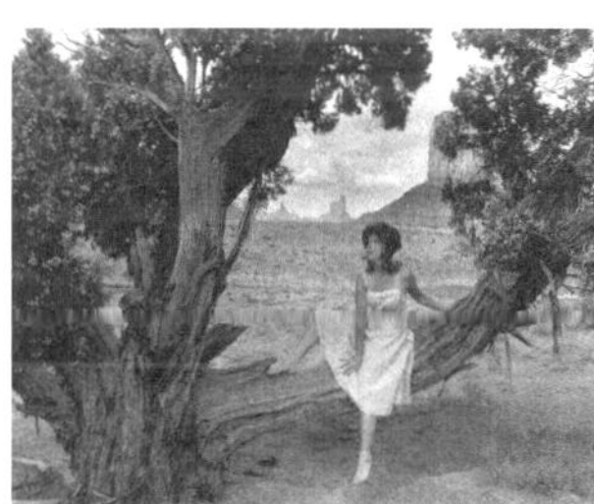

Untitled Film Still #43, 1979
Black-and-white photograph
Edition of 10

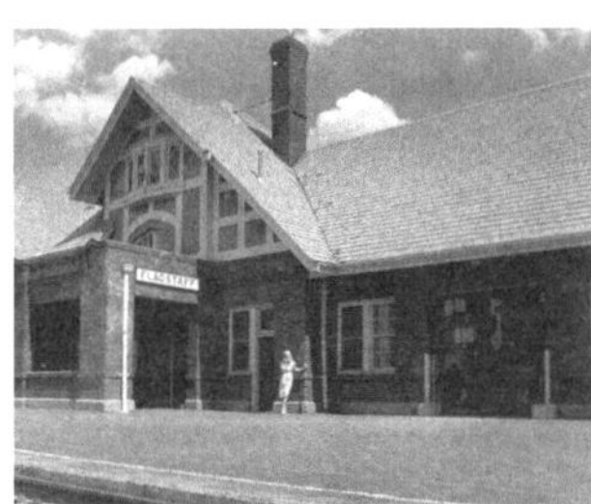

Untitled Film Still #44, 1979
Black-and-white photograph
Edition of 10

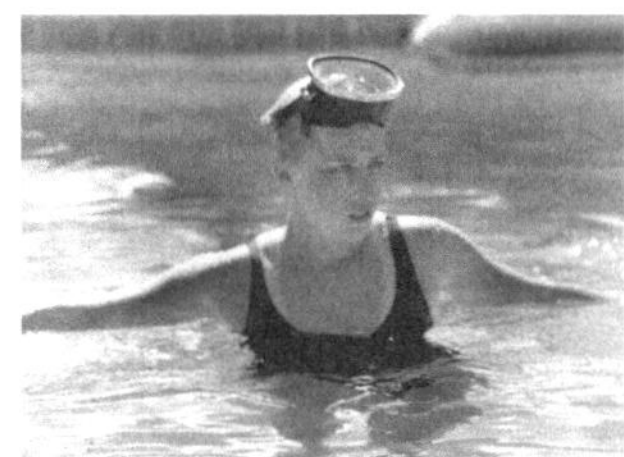

Untitled Film Still #45, 1979
Black-and-white photograph
Edition of 10

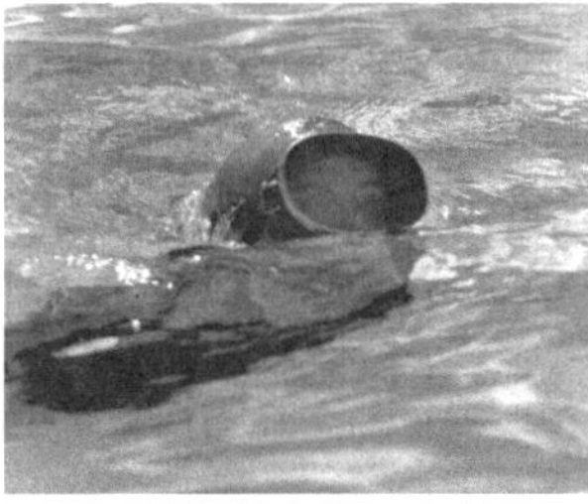

Untitled Film Still #46, 1979
Black-and-white photograph
Edition of 10

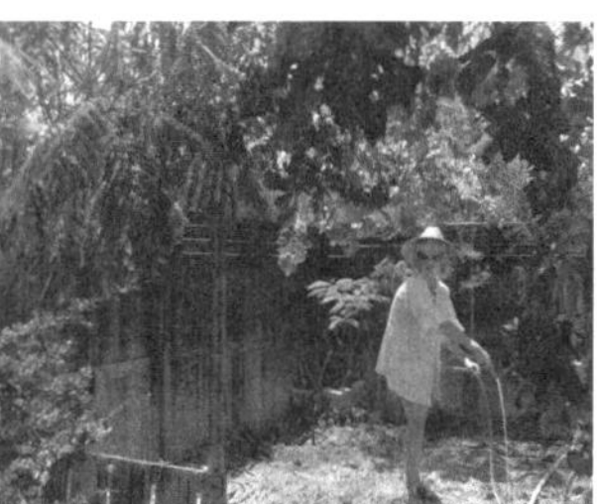

Untitled Film Still #47, 1979
Black-and-white photograph
Edition of 10

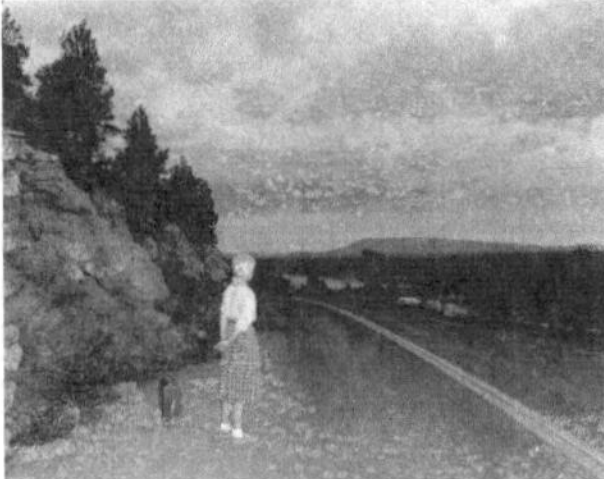

Untitled Film Still #48, 1979
Black-and-white photograph
Edition of 10

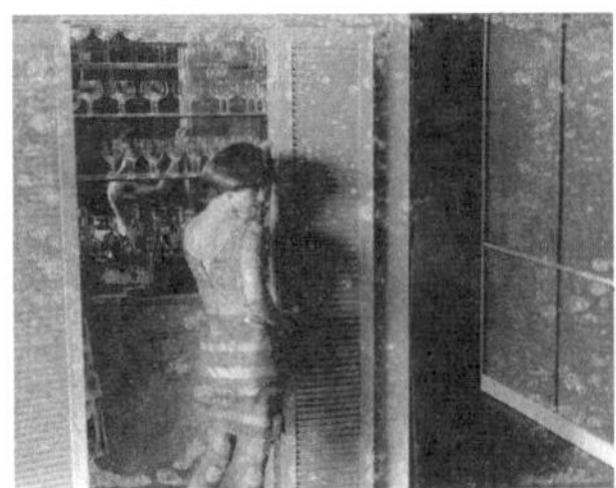

Untitled Film Still #49, 1979
Black-and-white photograph
Edition of 10

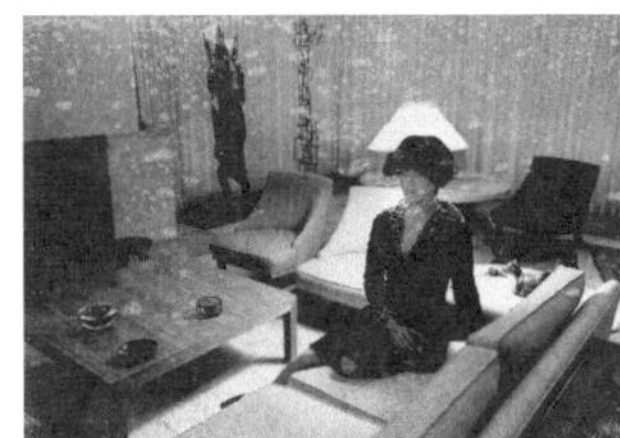

Untitled Film Still #50, 1979
Black-and-white photograph
Edition of 10

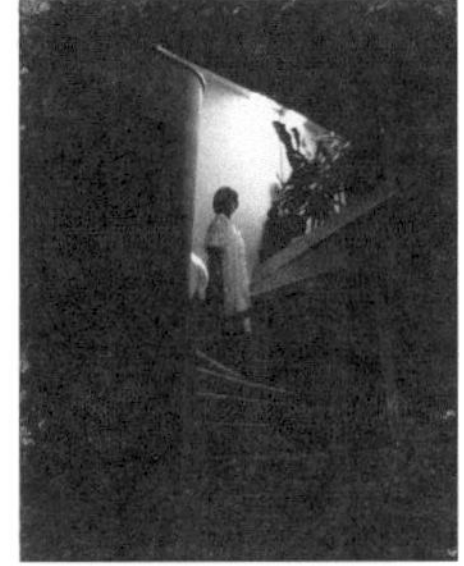

Untitled Film Still #51, 1979
Black-and-white photograph
Edition of 10

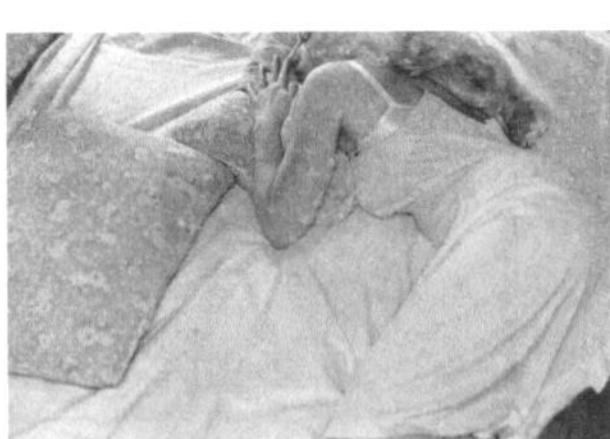

Untitled Film Still #52, 1979
Black-and-white photograph
Edition of 10

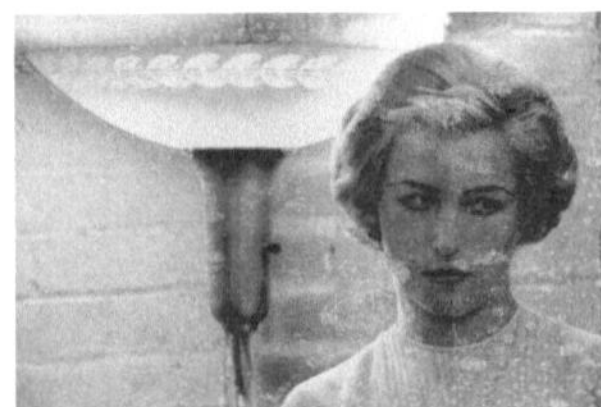

Untitled Film Still #53, 1980
Black-and-white photograph
Edition of 10

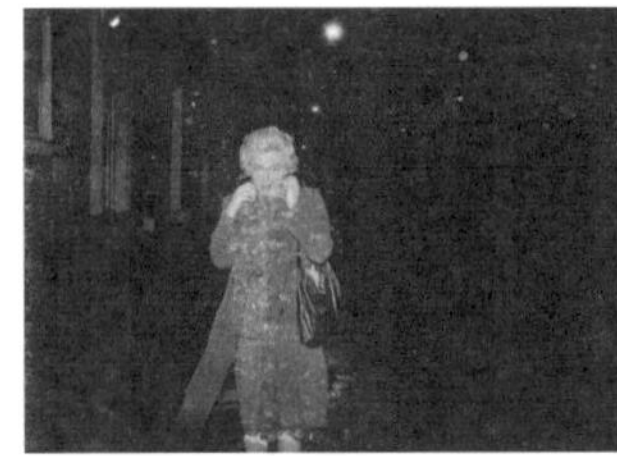

Untitled Film Still #54, 1980
Black-and-white photograph
Edition of 10

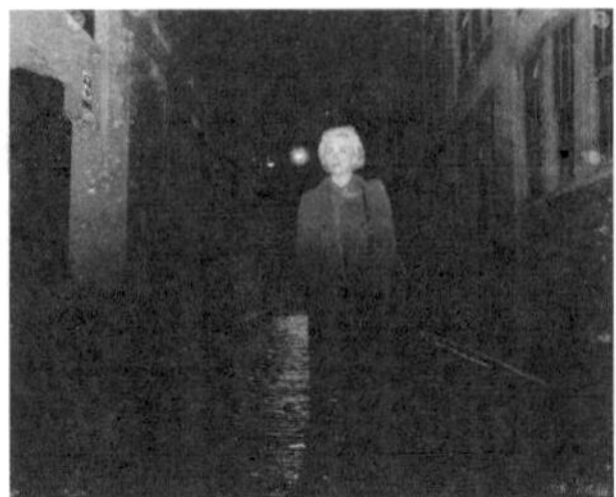

Untitled Film Still #55, 1980
Black-and-white photograph
Edition of 10

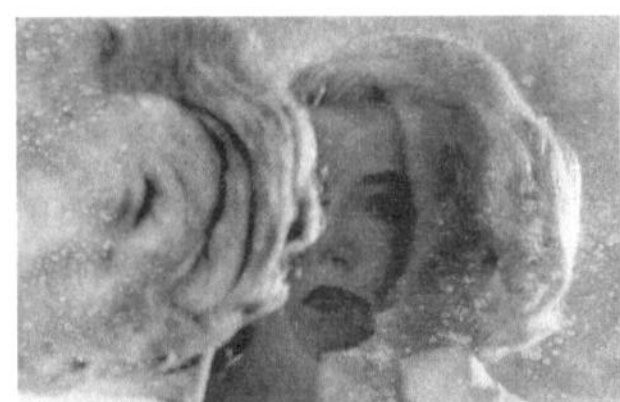

Untitled Film Still #56, 1980
Black-and-white photograph
Edition of 10

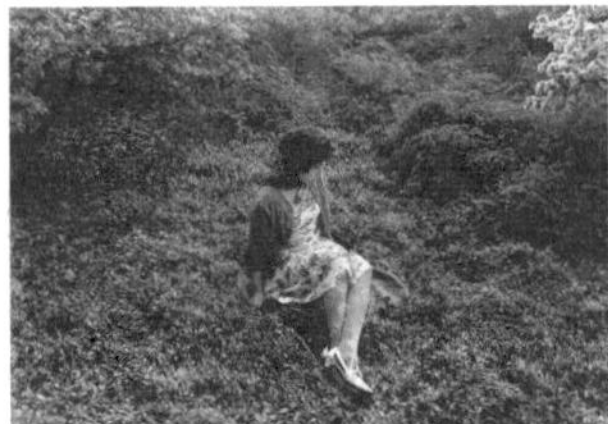

Untitled Film Still #57, 1980
Black-and-white photograph
Edition of 10

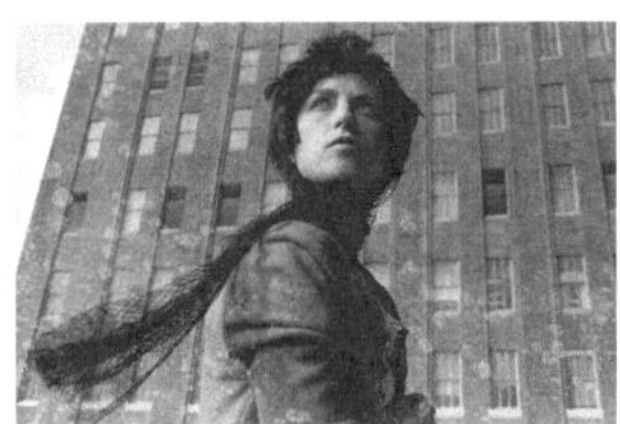

Untitled Film Still #58, 1980
Black-and-white photograph
Edition of 10

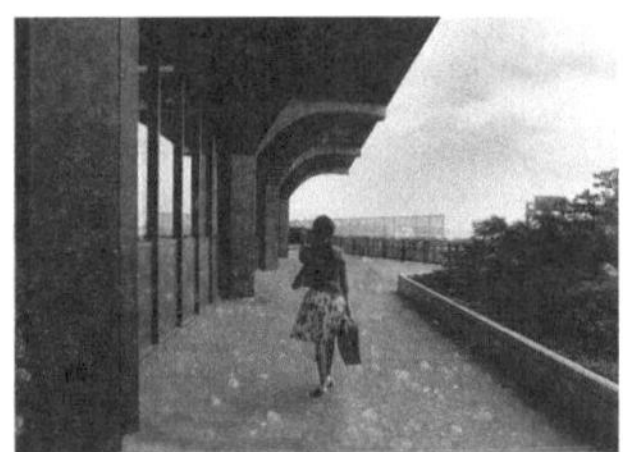

Untitled Film Still #59, 1980
Black-and-white photograph
Edition of 10

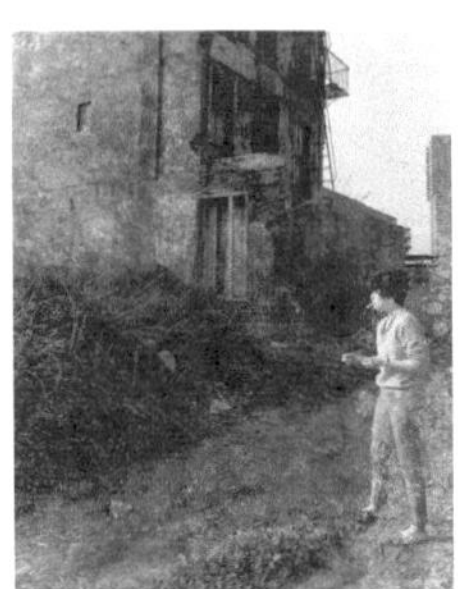

Untitled Film Still #60, 1980
Black-and-white photograph
Edition of 10

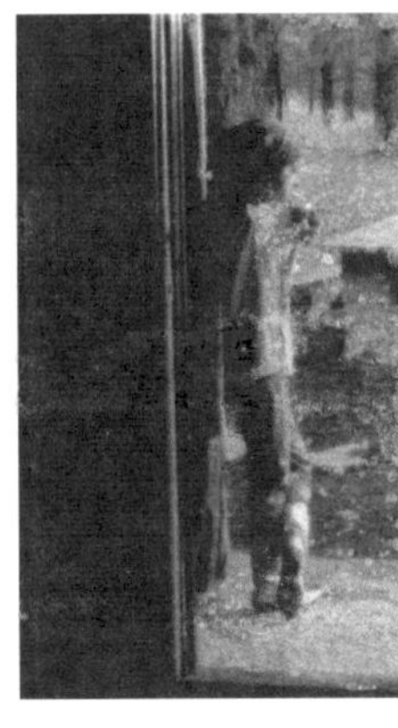

Untitled Film Still #61, 1979
Black-and-white photograph
Edition of 10

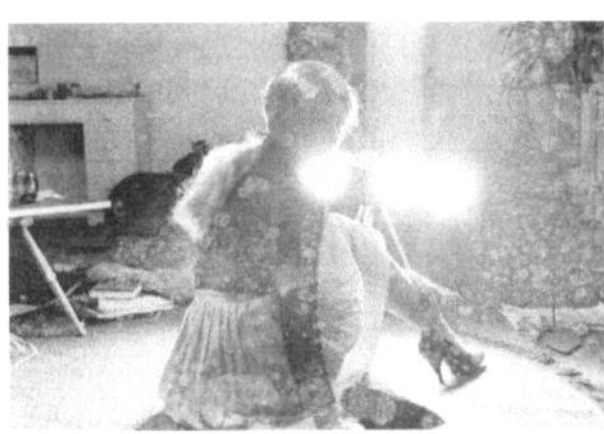

Untitled Film Still #62, 1977
Black-and-white photograph
Edition of 10

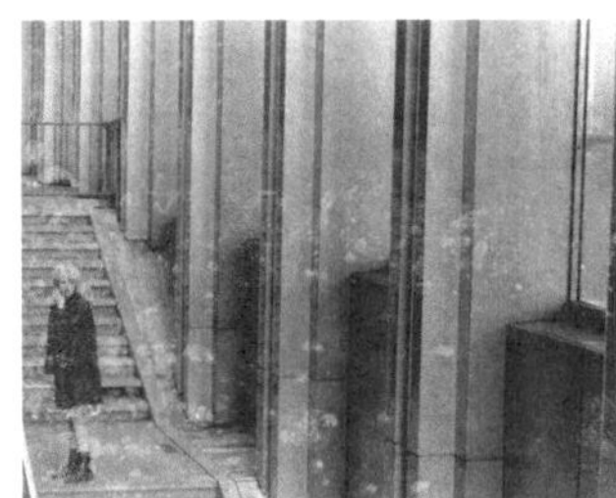

Untitled Film Still #63, 1979
Black-and-white photograph
Edition of 10

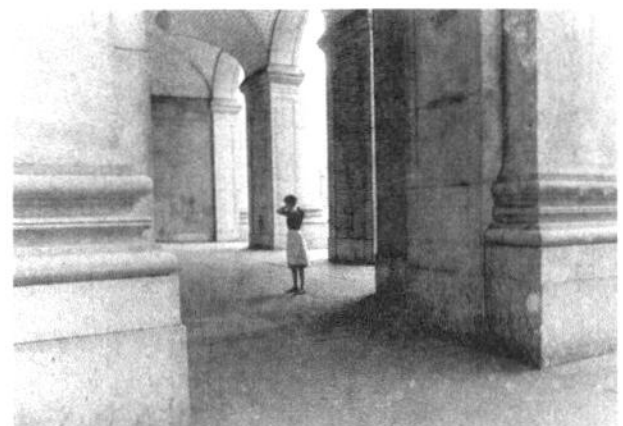

Untitled Film Still #64, 1980
Black-and-white photograph
Edition of 10

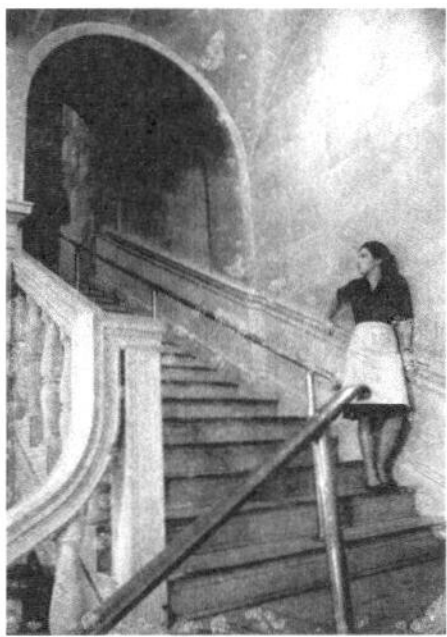

Untitled Film Still #65, 1980
Black-and-white photograph
Edition of 10

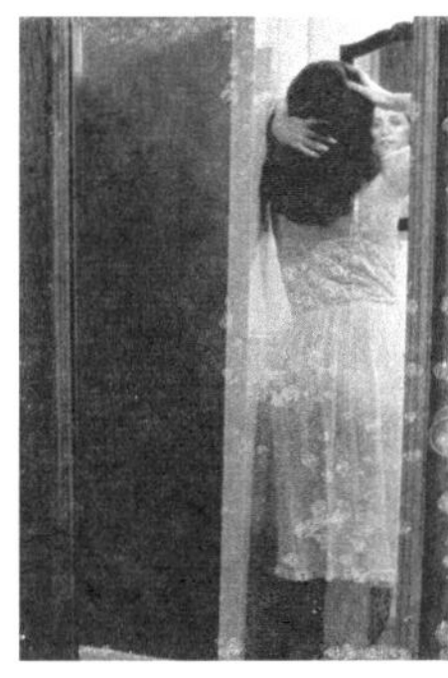

Untitled Film Still #81, 1978
Black-and-white photograph
Edition of 10

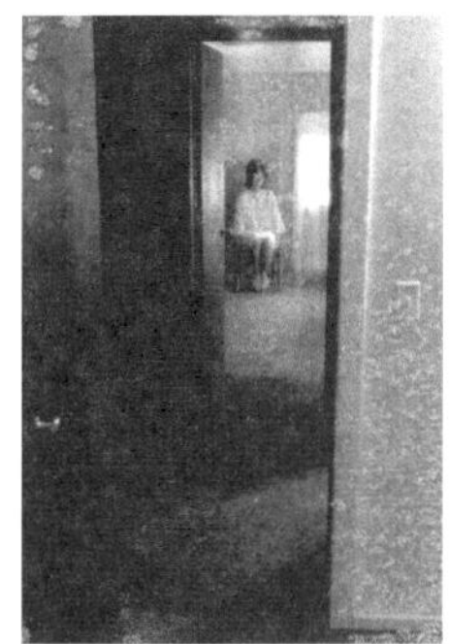

Untitled Film Still #82, 1979
Black-and-white photograph
Edition of 10

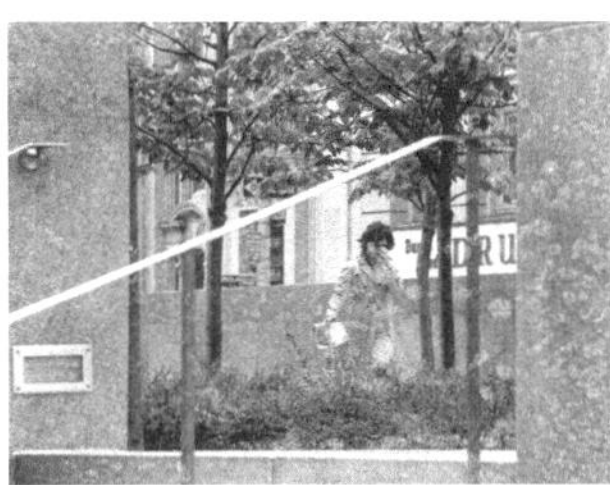

Untitled Film Still #83, 1980
Black-and-white photograph
Edition of 10

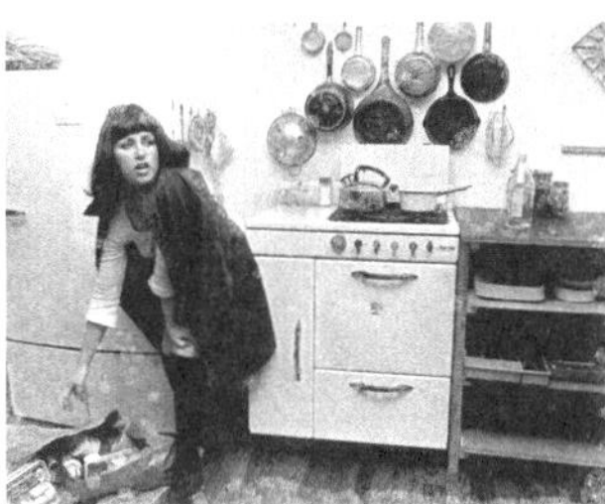

Untitled Film Still #84, 1980
Black-and-white photograph
Edition of 10

The measurements of *Untitled Film Stills* are between 5 ½ to 7 ½ in. and 8 ½ to 9 ½ in. (14 to 19.2 cm and 21.4 to 24.1 cm)

[Rear Screen Projections]

1980

This series marks Cindy Sherman's passage from black-and-white to color images, and significantly larger formats (up to 20 x 24 in./50.8 x 61 cm). The series also introduces a new approach and technique: the figure is now photographed in front of a screen featuring a projected image that serves as a "setting." The effect is cinematographic (albeit in a technically rudimentary way): a significant departure from the overt cinephilia of the earlier series, and a step forward from the world of the 1950s and 1960s (the childhood years) to the present of the artist's own time.

The subject appears as a more everyday figure, less overtly linked to specific cultural or social references. Young, modern-looking women are captured against a projected background (interior or exterior), in close-up or in the middle distance, sometimes positioned off-center within the frame, and apparently caught unawares in the course of a narrative situation, the exact nature of which is not immediately apparent.

The impression is of an open-ended series of photograms, created using projected "stock" cinematic backdrops, whose multiple permutations suggest narratives with any number of possible beginnings or endings The pictures are united by their characteristic play on the subject's gaze (an emerging theme in some of the *Untitled Film Stills*). The subject, and the image she creates, are characterized by their self-absorption (to use the term of the American art critic Michael Fried, in *Absorption and Theatricality: Painting and Beholder in the Age of Diderot*, Chicago: University of Chicago Press, 1980). The subject looks out of the frame, not at the viewer but at something or somebody else (with the exception of *#69*, in which the young woman gazes downward, in profile). We may imagine that the subject is being watched by another person apart from the viewer—the tension lies in our perception of our status as spectators of a scene that does not concern us, and which is, at the same time, not real, but a cleverly constructed artistic composition. The spectator has a heightened sense of his or her role in this circular interplay of gazes. We feel entitled to suppose that the scene being played out in each case is one of sexual seduction, or sexual violence. The different scenarios seem, in each case, to embody the dominating male gaze and the passive female subject in photography and cinematography, or (at least) "the positioning of the female subject as an effect of the projective eye."[1] This series marks a departure from the pleasing security that emanates from reference to the familiar, and denotes an engagement with the open-ended game of violence that is about to ensue.

As described by Amelia Jones in her very useful essay "Tracing the Subject with Cindy Sherman" in *Cindy Sherman: Retrospective*, Thames & Hudson, 1998. And as demonstrated by a number of theorists (both male and female) from the 1970s onwards, notably Laura Mulvey, in her celebrated 1975 essay "Visual Pleasure and Narrative Cinema," together with Judith Butler, Mary Ann Doane, Abigail Salomon-Godeau, and many others.

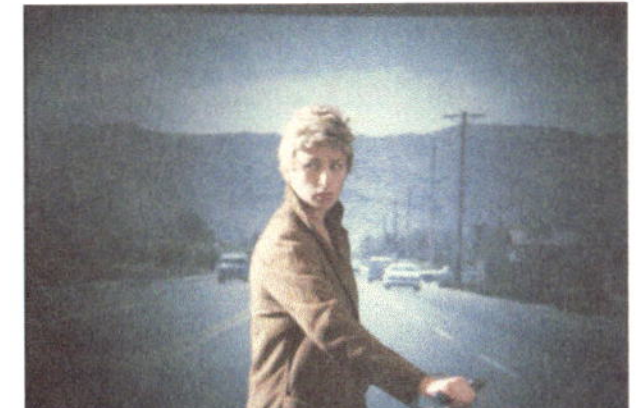

Untitled #66, 1980
Color photograph
Edition of 5
16 x 24 in.
(40.6 x 61 cm)

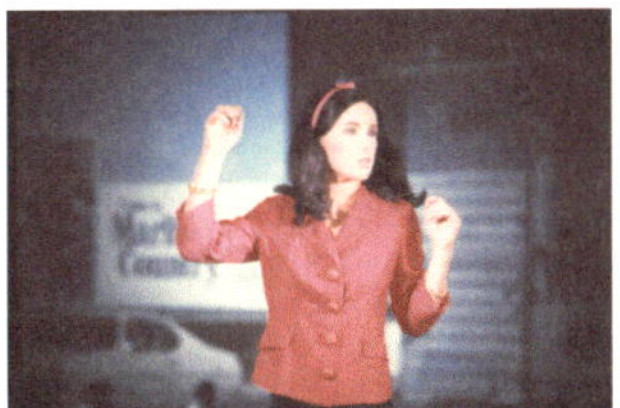

Untitled #67, 1980
Color photograph
Edition of 5
20 x 24 in.
(50.8 x 61 cm)

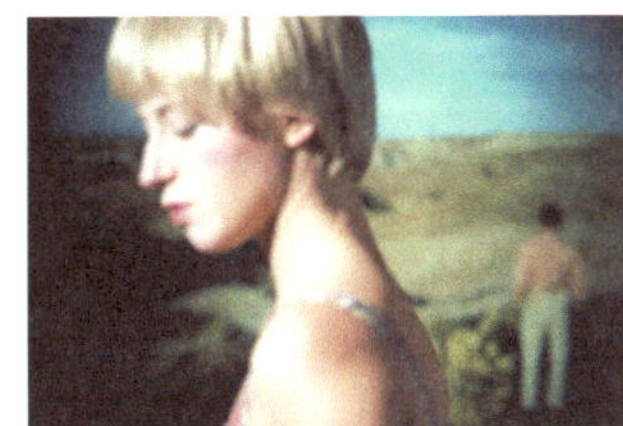

Untitled #69, 1980
Color photograph
Edition of 5
20 x 24 in.
(50.8 x 61 cm)

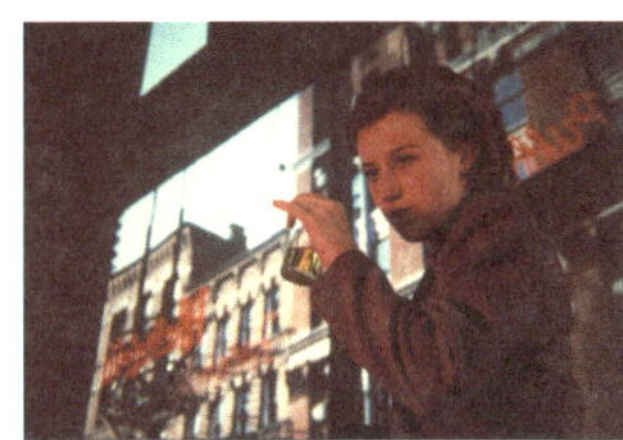

Untitled #70, 1980
Color photograph
Edition of 5
20 x 24 in.
(50.8 x 61 cm)

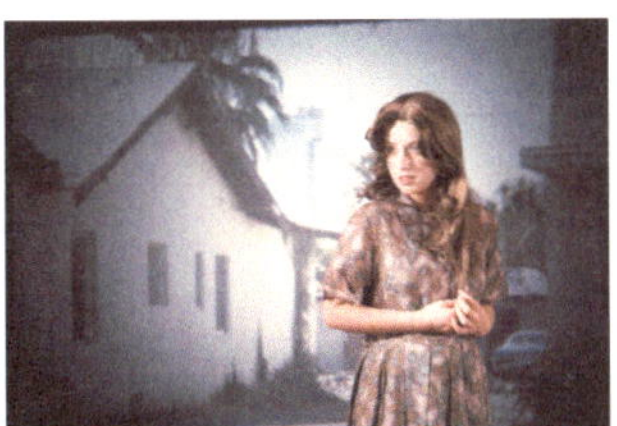

Untitled #71, 1980
Color photograph
Edition of 5
20 x 24 in.
(50.8 x 61 cm)

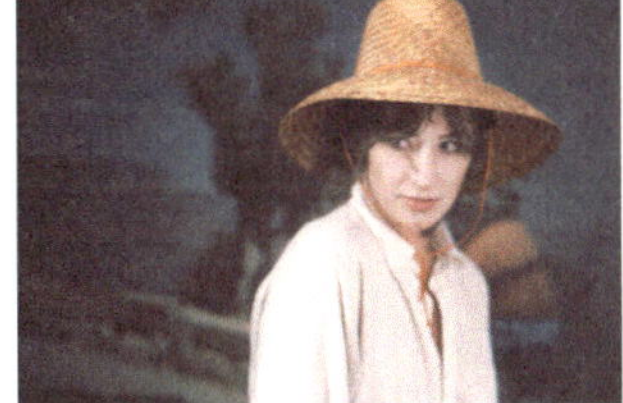

Untitled #72, 1980
Color photograph
Edition of 5
20 x 24 in.
(50.8 x 61 cm)

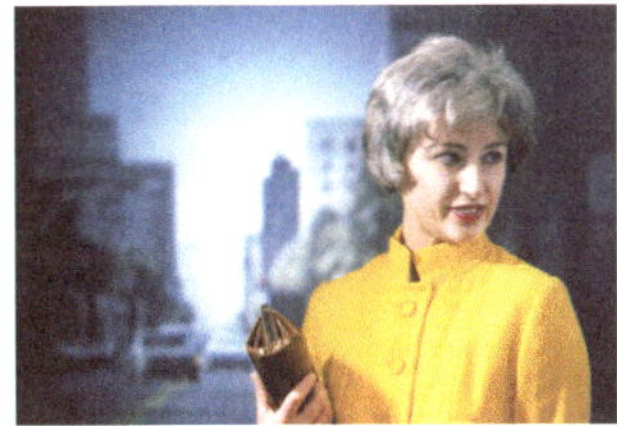

Untitled #74, 1980
Color photograph
Edition of 5
20 x 24 in.
(50.8 x 61 cm)

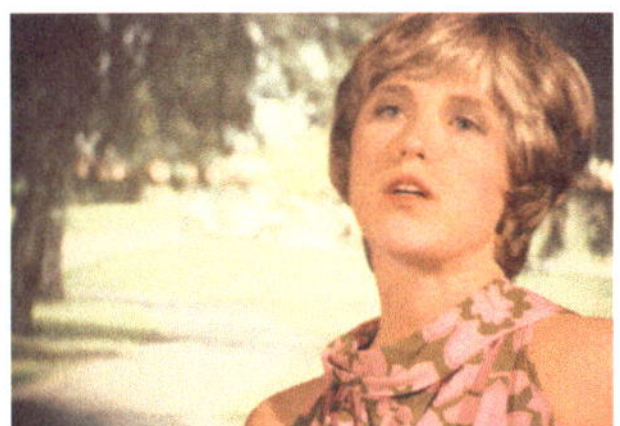

Untitled #75, 1980
Color photograph
Edition of 5
20 x 24 in.
(50.8 x 61 cm)

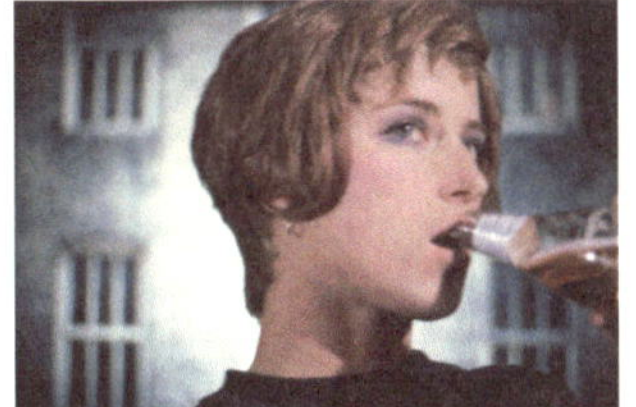

Untitled #76, 1980
Color photograph
Edition of 5
20 x 24 in.
(50.8 x 61 cm)

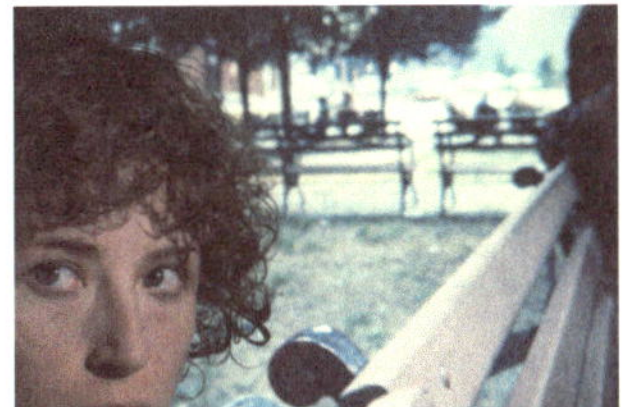

Untitled #77, 1980
Color photograph
Edition of 5
20 x 24 in.
(50.8 x 61 cm)

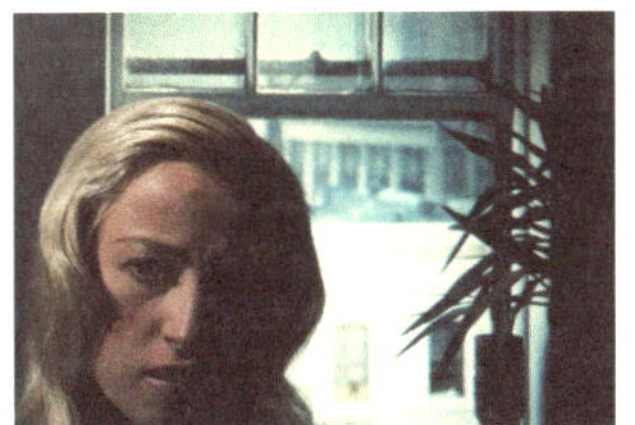

Untitled #78, 1980
Color photograph
Edition of 5
20 x 24 in.
(50.8 x 61 cm)

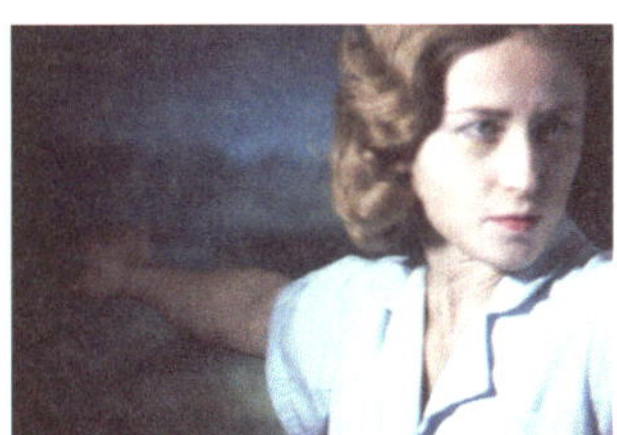

Untitled #79, 1980
Color photograph
Edition of 5
20 x 24 in.
(50.8 x 61 cm)

[Centerfolds/Horizontals]

1981

These horizontal, large-format images (24 x 48 in./61 x 122 cm) evoke the double-page spreads of fashion or "adult" magazines. They were originally commissioned by the magazine *Artforum*, which ultimately refused to publish them. The protagonist is viewed in extreme close-up, generally seated or reclining. The figure is photographed from above, heightening our impression of a narrative in progress: something has happened, or is about to happen, almost as if the events foreshadowed in the preceding series of *Rear Screen Projections* were now coming to pass. The woman appears by turns defeated, martyred, or gripped by anxiety or terror, as if the narrative hypotheses suggested in the earlier series had turned out badly, or failed to live up to their promise, leaving these women, once again, in the position of the victim. And (once again) leaving the situation as a whole in an ambivalent, circular relationship to the stereotype. Why does this relationship continue to exert such a powerful attraction, at once psychological and theatrical? Because it is still, and will always be, relevant to real events? To our fantasies, our source of ultimate pleasure?

What seems important in this series is the close focus on the protagonist (to the detriment of the setting, props, or background), and hence on the detailed transformations in her appearance, through the use of makeup, hair, and clothes. The clothes are especially important here, to the point where they become the setting into which the protagonist is introduced. The overall flavor remains markedly cinematographic. These images are, it seems to me, just as evocative of the CinemaScope format (if not more so), as they are of the magazines to which they are most often linked.

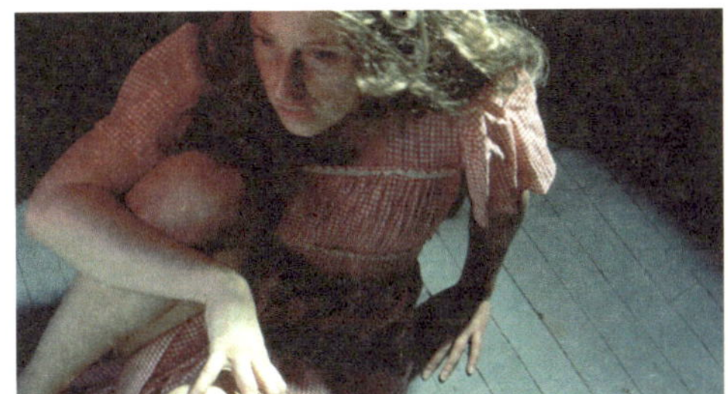

Untitled #85, 1981
Color photograph
Edition of 10
24 x 48 in.
(61 x 121.9 cm)

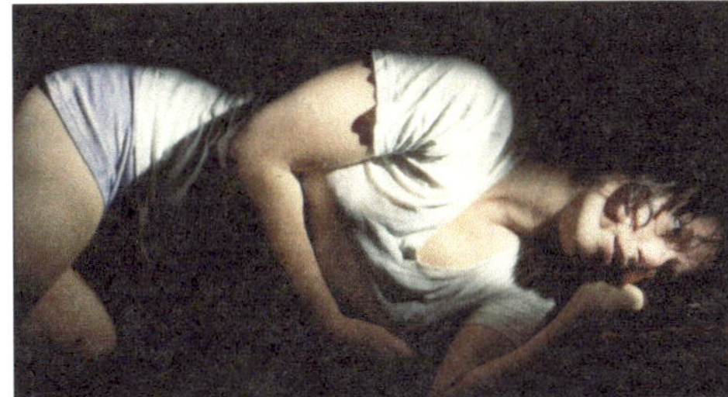

Untitled #86, 1981
Color photograph
Edition of 10
24 x 48 in.
(61 x 121.9 cm)

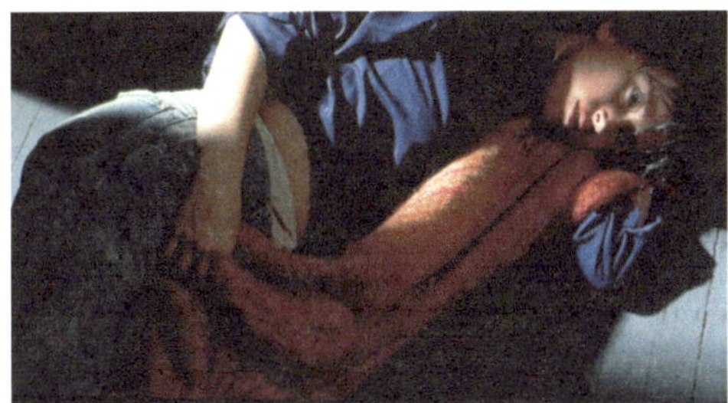

Untitled #87, 1981
Color photograph
Edition of 10
24 x 48 in.
(61 x 121.9 cm)

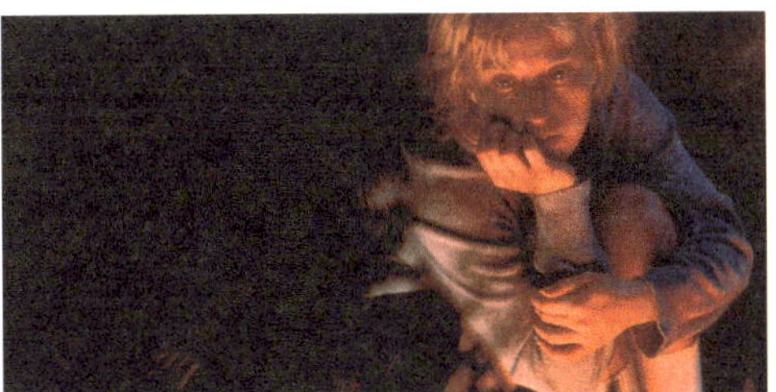

Untitled #88, 1981
Color photograph
Edition of 10
24 x 48 in.
(61 x 121.9 cm)

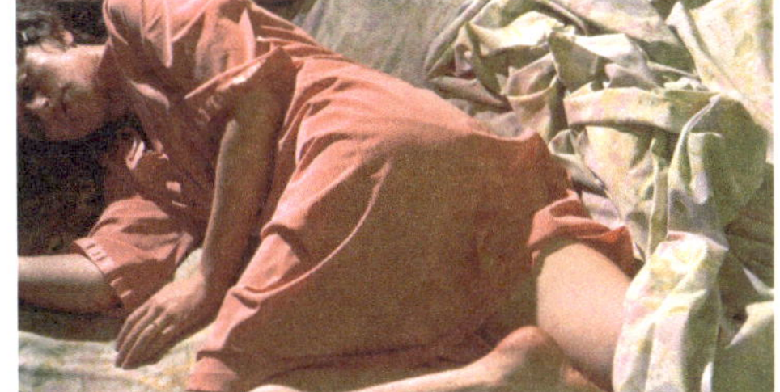

Untitled #89, 1981
Color photograph
Edition of 10
24 x 48 in.
(61 x 121.9 cm)

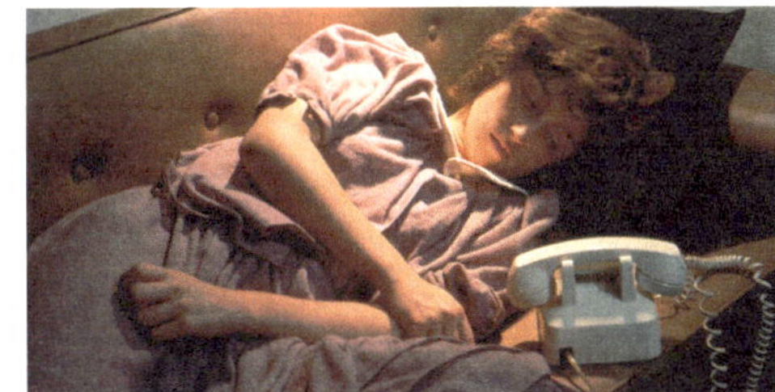

Untitled #90, 1981
Color photograph
Edition of 10
24 x 48 in.
(61 x 121.9 cm)

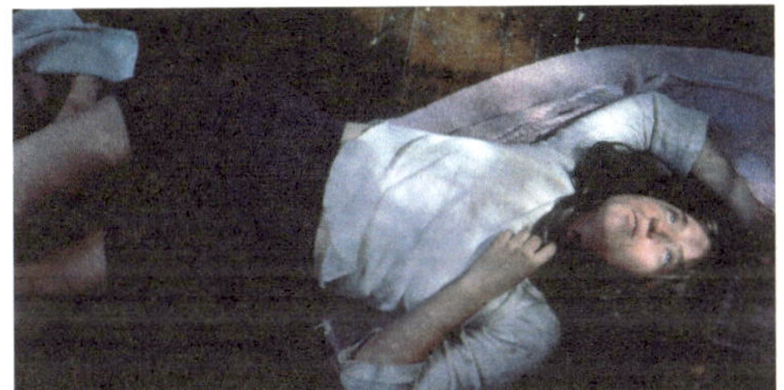

Untitled #91, 1981
Color photograph
Edition of 10
24 x 48 in.
(61 x 121.9 cm)

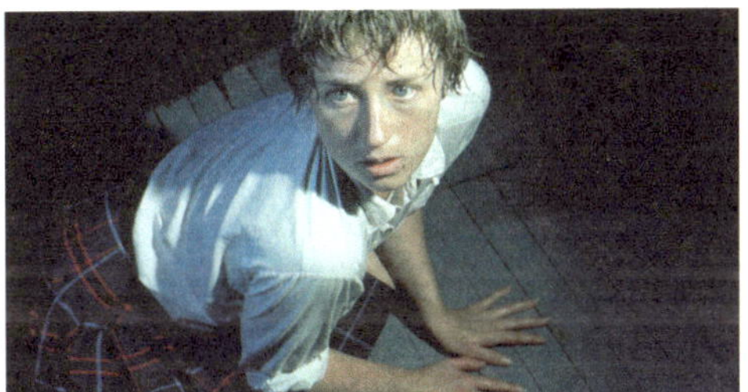

Untitled # 92, 1981
Color photograph
Edition of 10
24 x 48 in.
(61 x 121.9 cm)

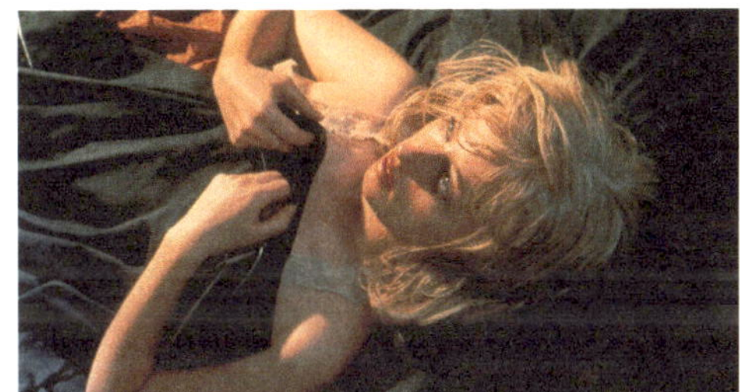

Untitled #93, 1981
Color photograph
Edition of 10
24 x 48 in.
(61 x 121.9 cm)

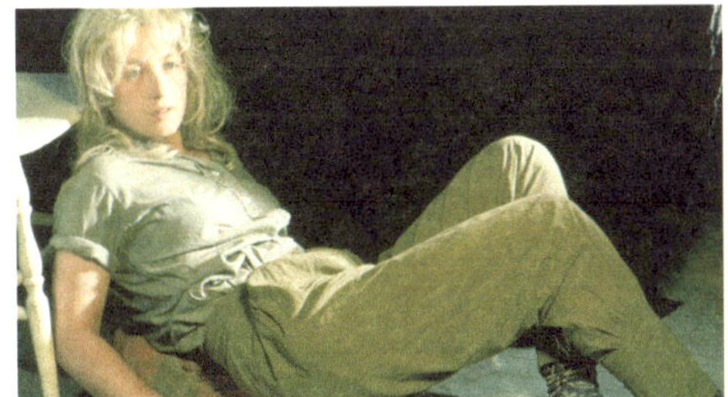

Untitled #94, 1981
Color photograph
Edition of 10
24 x 48 in.
(61 x 121.9 cm)

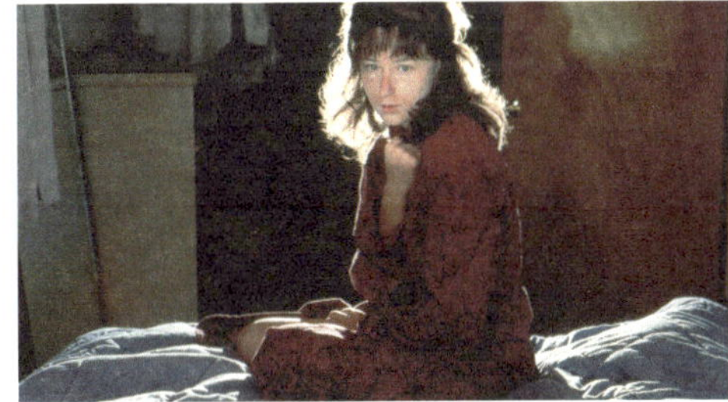

Untitled #95, 1981
Color photograph
Edition of 10
24 x 48 in.
(61 x 121.9 cm)

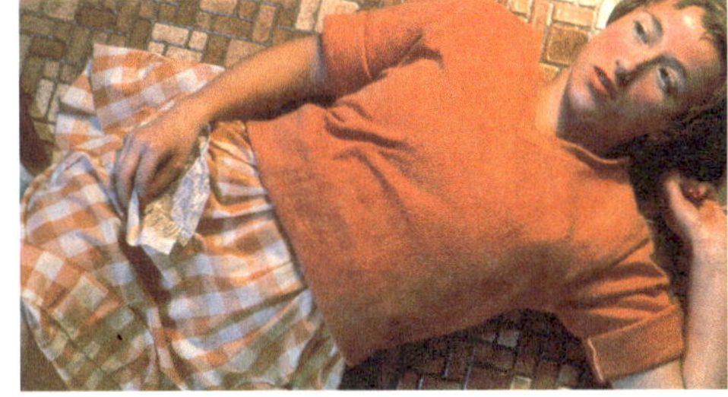

Untitled #96, 1981
Color photograph
Edition of 10
24 x 48 in.
(61 x 121.9 cm)

[Pink Robes]
1982

[Untitled #102–#116]
1982

[Fashion]
1983 — 1984

[Fashion]
1993 — 1994

The importance of fabrics and clothes becomes apparent in these four series (one of which was created ten years after the others), whose basic subject matter they are. In the *Pink Robes* series, the protagonist appears to adopt a completely unstaged, unaffected pose, staring straight at the camera, in total contrast to Sherman's earlier works, with their emphasis on dressing up and playacting—as if Cindy Sherman was seeking to prove, ironically, that "naturalism" is simply another layer of disguise, and perhaps the most enigmatic of all. The subject's facial expression and general appearance suggest someone caught unawares while getting out of bed, or the bath, modestly holding their robe against their body. The series evolves through a sequence of subtle chromatic and stylistic variations, like a suite of old-fashioned studies based on the nuances of a particular color, or the drapery of a figure's clothing, but suffused and perverted here by a troubling sense of intimacy.

This pivotal series develops in two different directions: on the one hand (in *Untitled #102* to *#116*) we have a succession of tightly cropped images of women with hardened expressions, characterized by strong contrasts of light and shade; on the other are two series of so-called *Fashion* photographs created ten years apart, but linked by their prominent use of haute-couture clothes, which are given Sherman's "traditional" treatment as items for dressing up or disguise.

In *Untitled #102* to *#116* the lighting, and the position of the body, herald the complex postures of later works, and the progressive elimination of the subject in favor of more indistinct forms. As if, after coming as close as possible to her "naked" truth (or at least pretending to), the subject had now decided to allow herself to move further and further away from it. The alternating, twin themes of appearance and disappearance become still more amplified. Or perhaps the subject is indirectly communicating more and more about herself, as she becomes less and less visible.

...

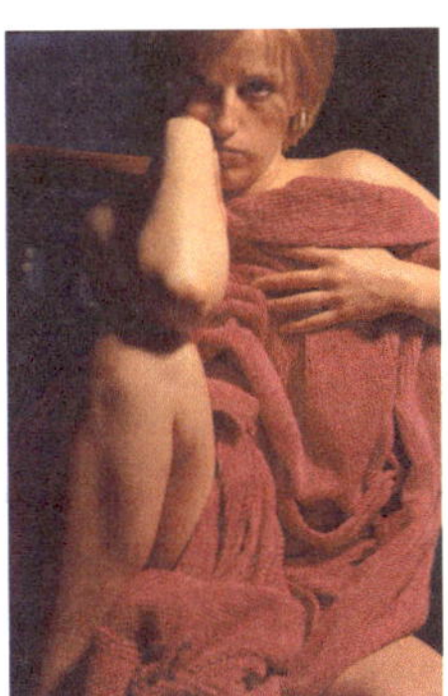

Untitled #97, 1982
Color photograph
Edition of 10
45 x 30 in.
(114.3 x 76.2 cm)

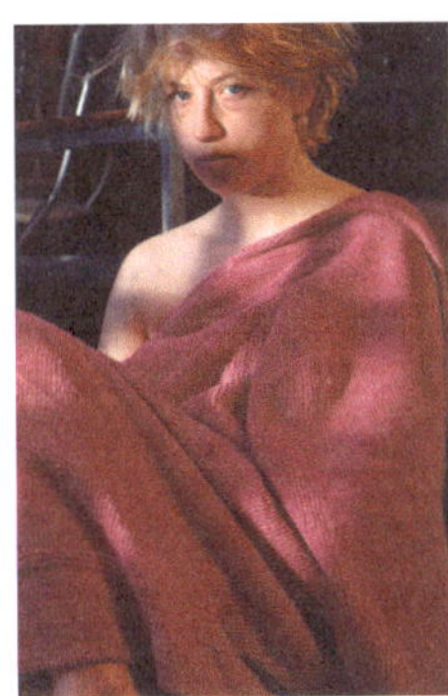

Untitled #98, 1982
Color photograph
Edition of 10
45 x 30 in.
(114.3 x 76.2 cm)

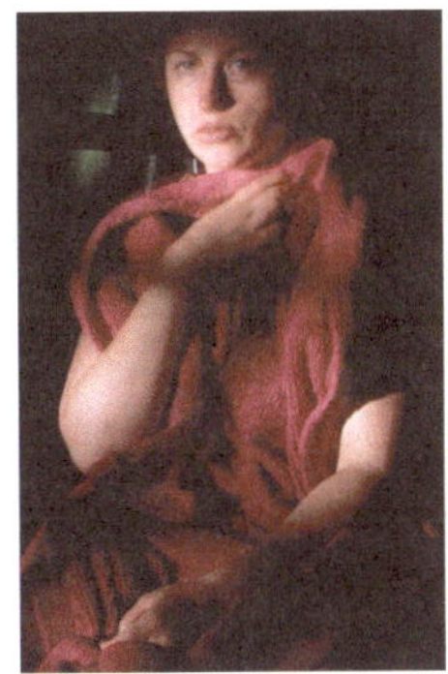

Untitled #99, 1982
Color photograph
Edition of 10
45 x 30 in.
(114.3 x 76.2 cm)

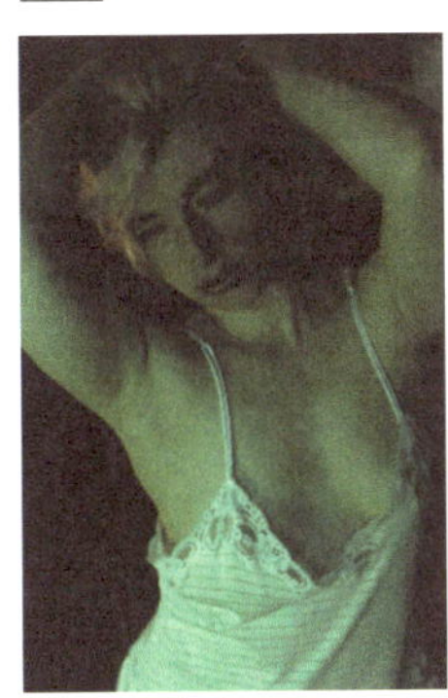

Untitled #103, 1982
Color photograph
Edition of 10
30 x 19 ½ in.
(76.2 x 50.2 cm)

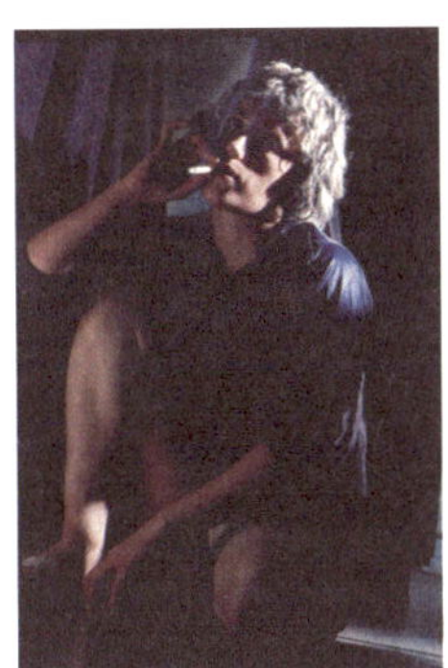

Untitled #113, 1982
Color photograph
Edition of 10
48 x 24 in.
(122 x 61 cm)

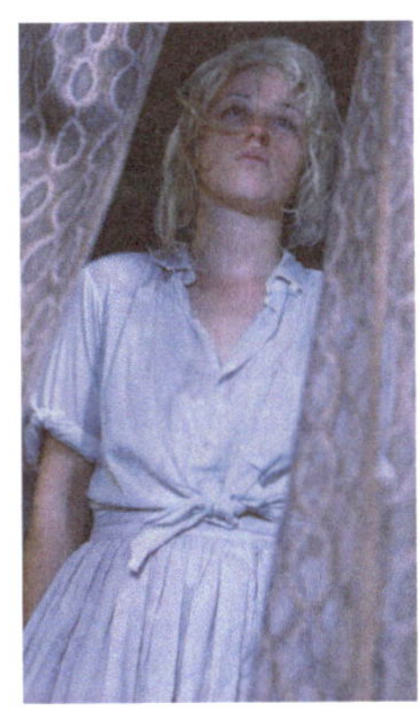

Untitled #114, 1982
Color photograph
Edition of 10
49 x 30 in.
(124.5 x 76.2 cm)

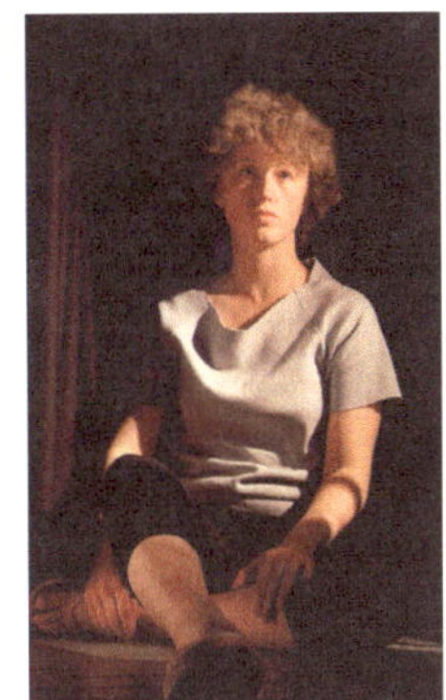

Untitled #116, 1982
Color photograph
Edition of 10
45 ½ x 30 in.
(114.9 x 76.2 cm)

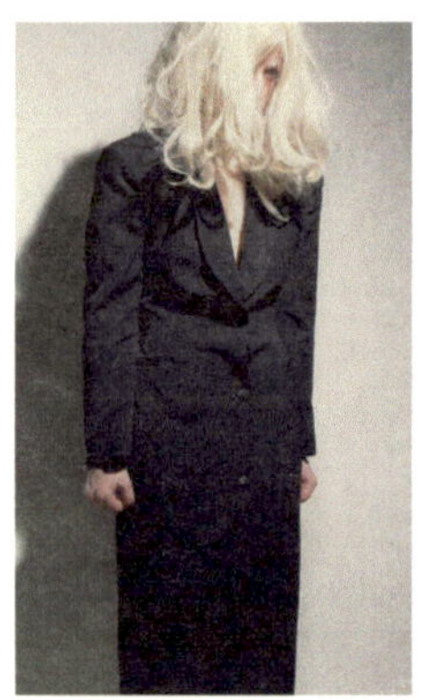

Untitled #122, 1983
Color photograph
Edition of 18
35 ½ x 21 ¼ in.
(89.5 x 54 cm)

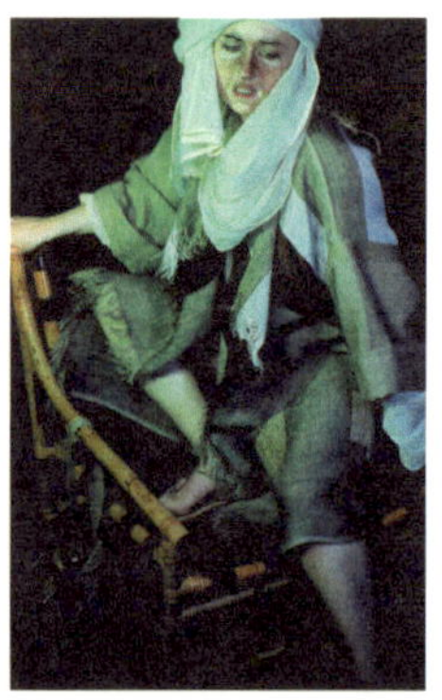

Untitled #126, 1983
Color photograph
Edition of 18
34 ½ x 22 ¾ in.
(87.6 x 57.6 cm)

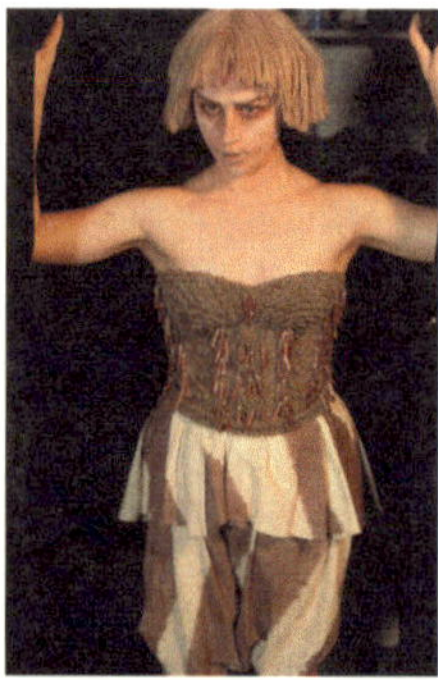

Untitled #127, 1983
Color photograph
Edition of 18
34 x 23 in.
(86.4 x 58.4 cm)

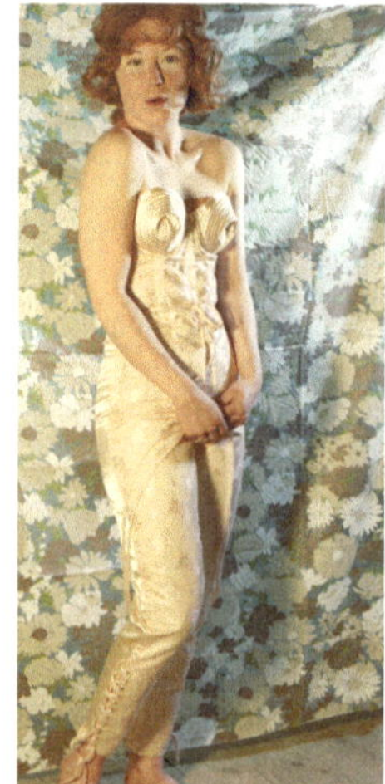

Untitled #131, 1983
Color photograph
Edition of 18
34 ½ x 16 ½ in.
(88.3 x 41.9 cm)

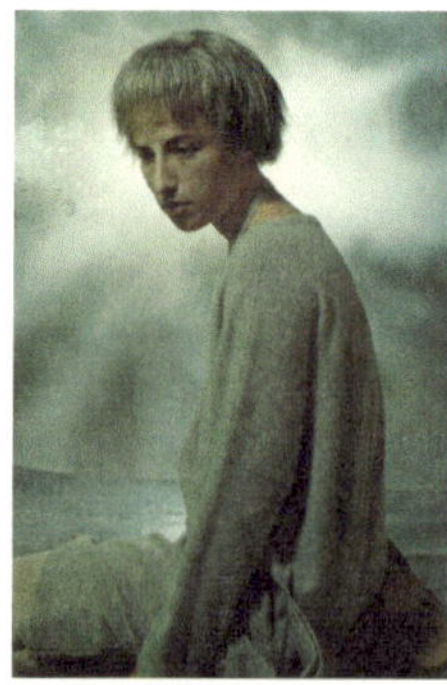

Untitled #133, 1984
Color photograph
Edition of 5
71 ¼ x 47 ½ in.
(181 x 120.7 cm)

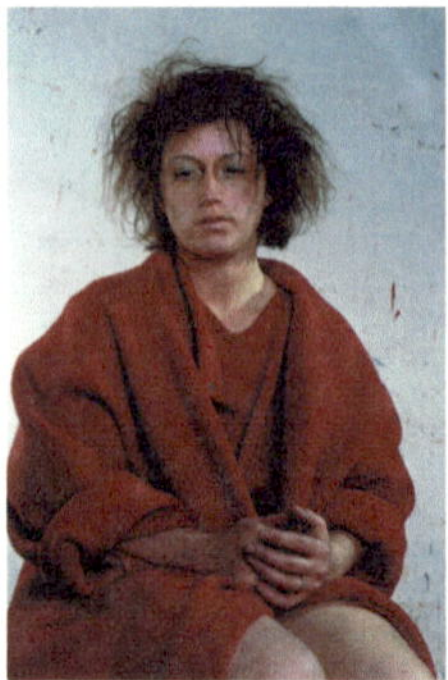

Untitled #137, 1984
Color photograph
Edition of 5
70 ½ x 47 ¾ in.
(179.1 x 121.3 cm)

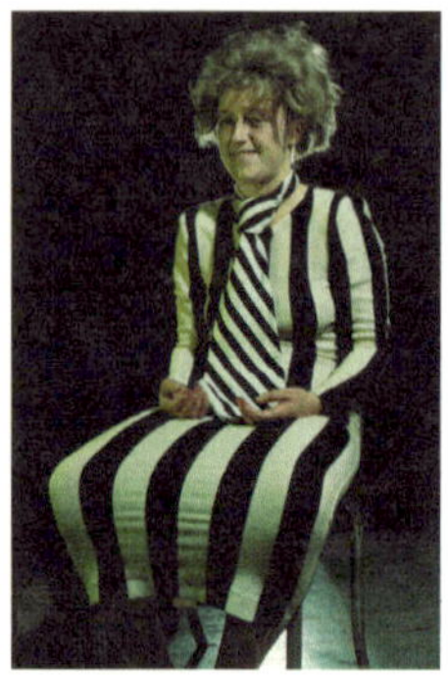

Untitled #138, 1984
Color photograph
Edition of 5
71 x 48 ½ in.
(180.3 x 123.2 cm)

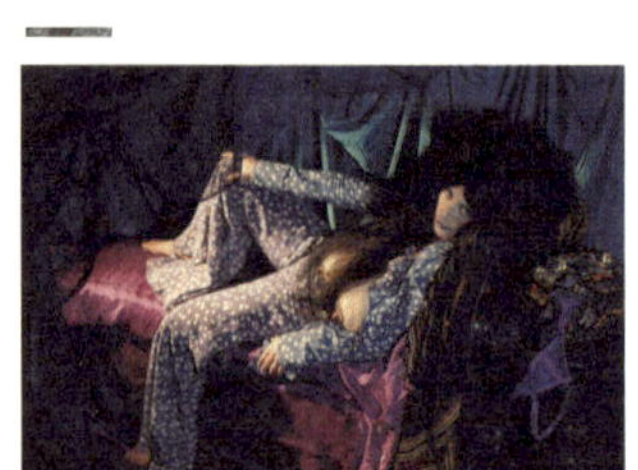

Untitled #275, 1993
Color photograph
Edition of 6
63 x 88 in.
(160 x 223.5 cm)

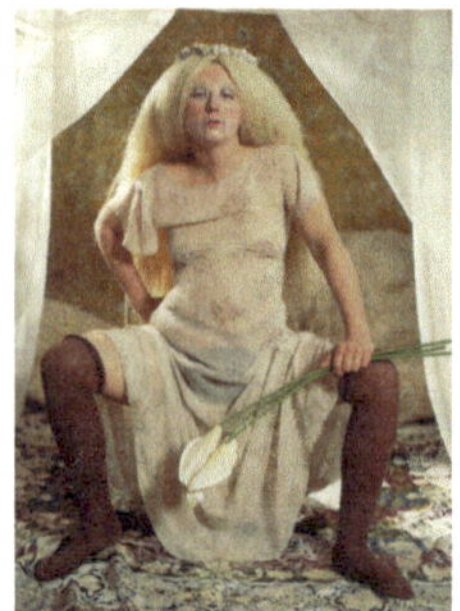

Untitled #276, 1993
Color photograph
Edition of 6
78 ½ x 59 in.
(199.4 x 149.9 cm)

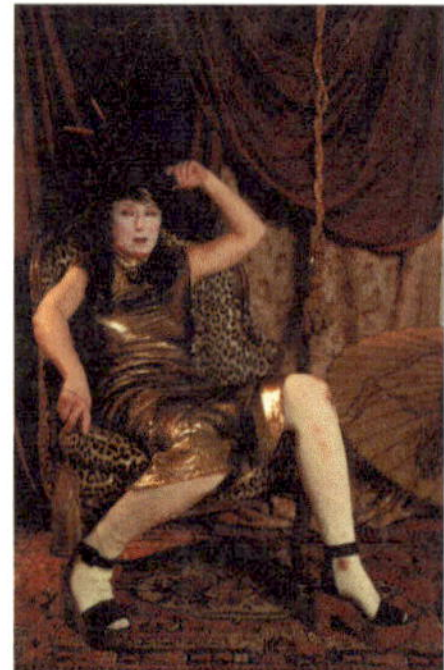

Untitled #278, 1993
Color photograph
Edition of 6
73 x 49 in.
(185.4 x 124.5 cm)

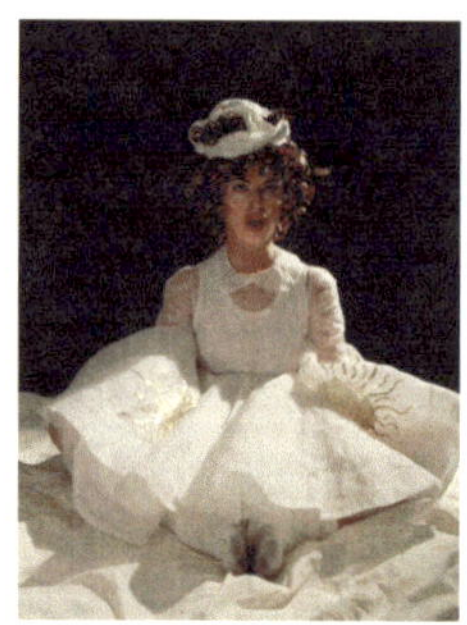

Untitled #279, 1993
Color photograph
Edition of 6
65 x 49 in.
(165.1 x 124.5 cm)

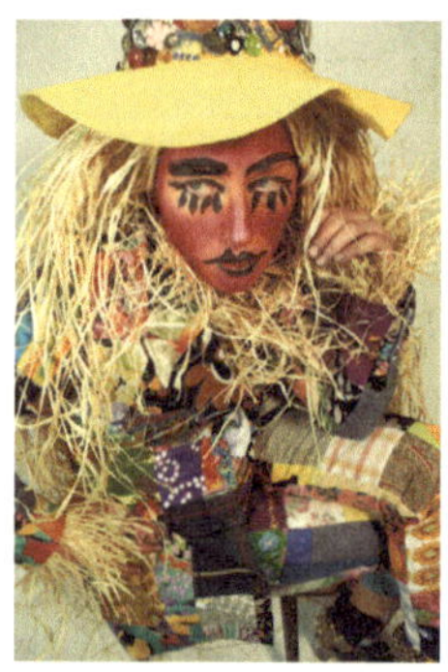

Untitled #280, 1993
Color photograph
Edition of 6
53 x 35 in.
(134.6 x 88.9 cm)

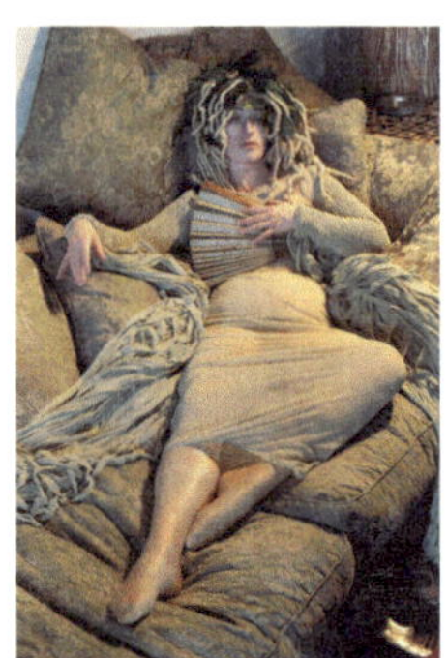

Untitled #282, 1993
Color photograph
Edition of 6
90 x 60 in.
(228.6 x 152.4 cm)

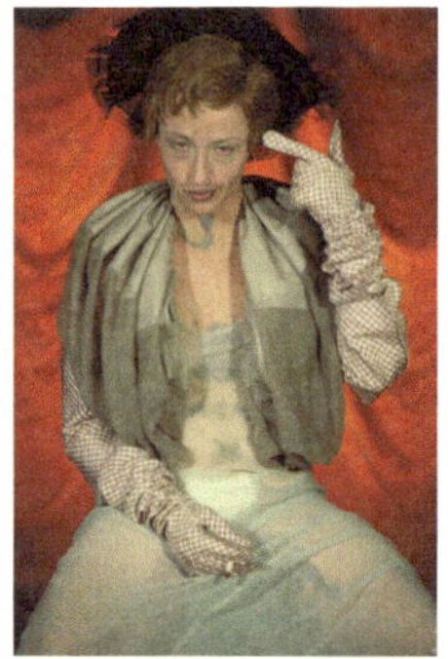

Untitled #299, 1994
Color photograph
Edition of 6
48 x 31 ⅞ in.
(122 x 81 cm)

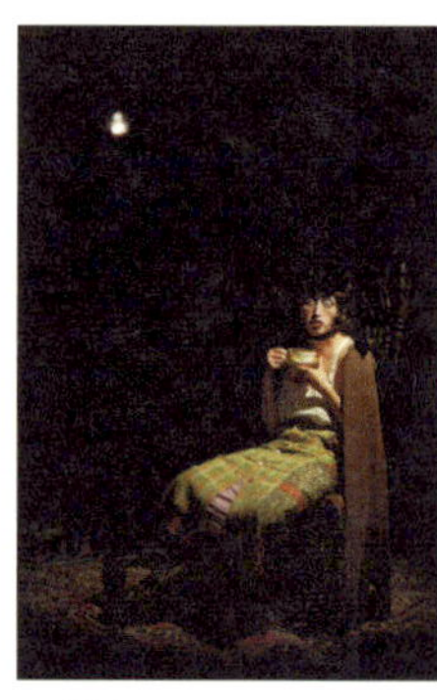

Untitled #300, 1994
Color photograph
Edition of 6
78 x 53 in.
(198.1 x 134.6 cm)

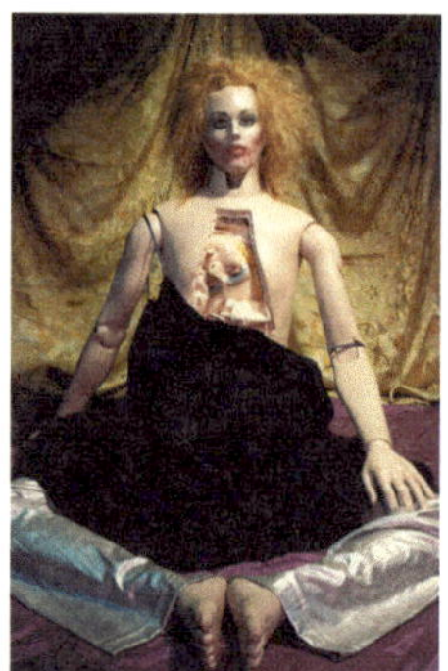

Untitled #302, 1994
Color photograph
Edition of 6
67 ½ x 45 in.
(172 x 114.3 cm)

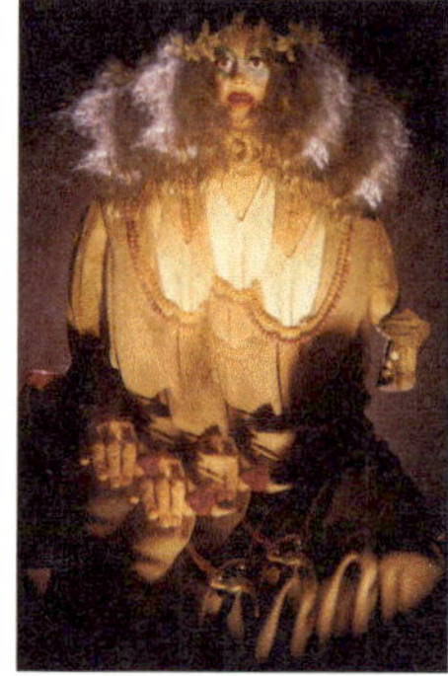

Untitled #303, 1994
Color photograph
Edition of 6
67 ½ x 43 in.
(172 x 109.2 cm)

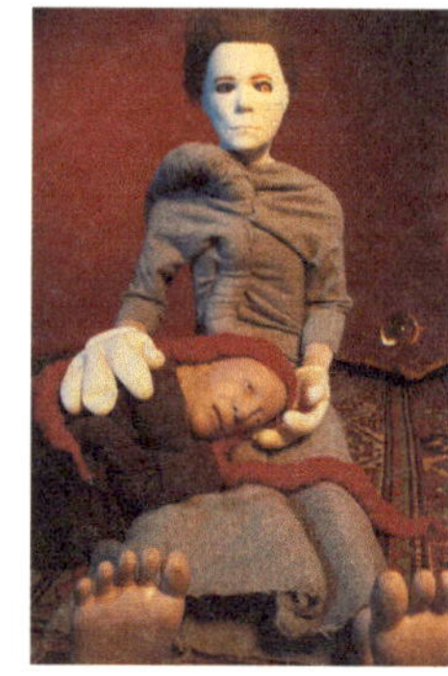

Untitled #304, 1994
Color photograph
Edition of 6
61 x 41 in.
(155 x 104 cm)

In *Fashion* (1983–1984), as with *Centerfolds*, Cindy Sherman revisits a classic genre (full-page or double-page fashion photographs in magazines), and gives it a new twist. She also succeeds in hijacking the basic purpose of fashion itself, namely beautification and the incitement to dream (perhaps these notions were increasingly passé in the fashion world, too: this period coincided with the rise of the "trash" tendency). Sherman uses her own phantasmagoric wardrobe as a source of props, and systematically debases the items she has chosen. The items of clothing are always clearly presented, but they are worn by grotesque, caricatural figures. As her notebooks of the period confirm, Sherman is seeking to express her loathing of the fashion industry and the clothes it produces: the outfits are too rigidly categorized, too "perfect" to be of any use to the artist, or to enter into her imaginary world. In a brilliant reversal of her usual strategy, Sherman—faced with the difficulty of appropriating the garments themselves—uses the clothes "as they stand" and transforms the figures that are supposed to show them off.

In her "fashion" photographs of 1993–94, Sherman reaches beyond this basic reversal, to create images of exuberant theatricality drawing on elements seen in some of her earlier works, such as prostheses (#275) and variations on the grotesque (#275 and #299). The pictures may be read as a strident critique of the drastic criteria imposed by the fashion world on its professional models, and which it tries to impose on the ordinary individuals for whom the clothes are ultimately destined: namely youth, slenderness, and beauty. Sherman's outrageous images use caricature to rehabilitate alternative feminine types, which fashion has also tried (periodically and without much conviction) to reappropriate for itself.

Furthermore, some of these photographs clearly anticipate the themes which later appear in *Horror and Surrealist Pictures*. Such is the case for #302, #303, and #304 which, although the result of a commission from the Comme des Garçons designers, show humanoid mannequins with a disturbing appearance, whose faces and bodies are deformed or mutilated. The torso of the female figure in #302 has been opened to reveal a face lodged inside. The blood spattered across her lips and cheek suggests an act of cannibalism.

[Fairy Tales]
1985

[Disasters]
1986 — 1989

Cindy Sherman's *Fairy Tales* are the stuff of nightmares (but then fairy tales often are): fantasy cohabits dangerously with elements of the macabre, and a strange, troubling quality. All trace of realism is expunged here in favor of the artificial and the nonhuman. For the first time, the artist makes undisguised use of prostheses and dummies, creating scenes that are both grotesque and mysterious. In *Untitled #156*, the subject scrabbles feverishly at the ground, as if possessed, while in *#145* she seems to be gifted with mimetic powers, enabling her to melt into the soil. In *#146*, she seems to be acting under the influence of drugs or demonic powers. In *#150* we see a giantess-like figure sticking out an enormous scarlet tongue (and demonstrating, as she does so, the artistic distance covered since the *Rear Screen Projections*). In *#155* we see a half-flesh, half-prosthetic figure recumbent on the ground, becoming gradually overgrown and invaded by vegetation. The images are sometimes unidentifiable in relation to particular fairy tales or traditional stories. More importantly, however, they should be seen as invitations to the viewer to project his or her own memories or unspecified fantasies. The pictures explore the world of fairy tales in general: the realm of fantasy, shown here at its most troubling and grotesque.

As if to highlight this, one image in the *Fairy Tales* series (*#155*) is directly linked to *#173* in the subsequent *Disaster* series. The continuity is total: nothing seems to have changed, except the angle of vision. The ground upon which the prosthetic figure lies in *Fairy Tales #155* is seen in close-up in *Disaster #173*, filling the picture's foreground. The figure's face, with eyes open, is now partly visible at the top of the frame. In this series, the face and body tend to dematerialize, existing only as masks (*#174*), imprints, or skeletons (*#168*), or as a sinister, reflected grimace in the lens of a pair of glasses, discarded on a carpet of filth (*#175*). The body becomes a blow-up doll stretched out on a bed of rubble and debris (*#188*), or a deformed monstrosity perched on a plywood packing case (*#186*). In *#191*, all that remains is a magma of hair and flesh, in the midst of which a bloodshot, rolled-back eye is the last remnant of what was once a face (this picture, it should be noted, is closely similar to *#311* of the *Horror and Surrealist Pictures*, one of Sherman's rare images obtained using strictly photographic techniques—the superimposing of a number of different exposures—rather than by means of a staged, surrealistic composition.)

What disasters have given rise to these grotesque scenes? As with the *Fairy Tales*, it is impossible for us to say. Sherman herself has doubtless no intention of venturing any more or less rational explanation. Clearly, we are presented with a dark vision—perhaps the hidden face of our society's cult of beauty and normality, and the soothing, idealized images (from the world of advertising, in particular) that fill our daily lives. These "monsters" have not, then, risen from the depths of "the sleep of reason." Sherman implies that they are always there, barely concealed behind the thin veil of illusion and appearances.

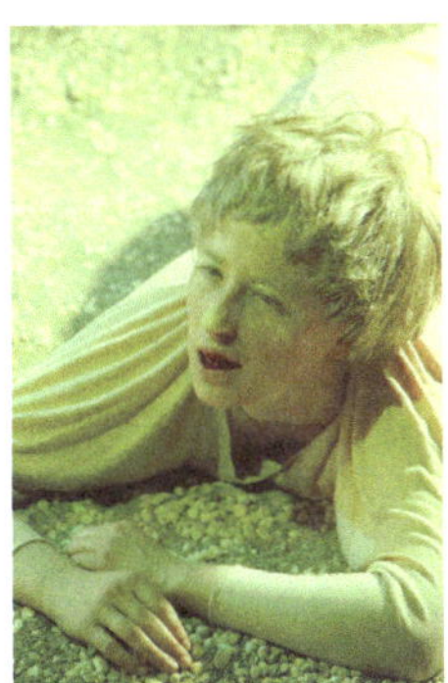

Untitled #145, 1985
Color photograph
Edition of 6
70 x 47 ¼ in.
(178 x 120 cm)

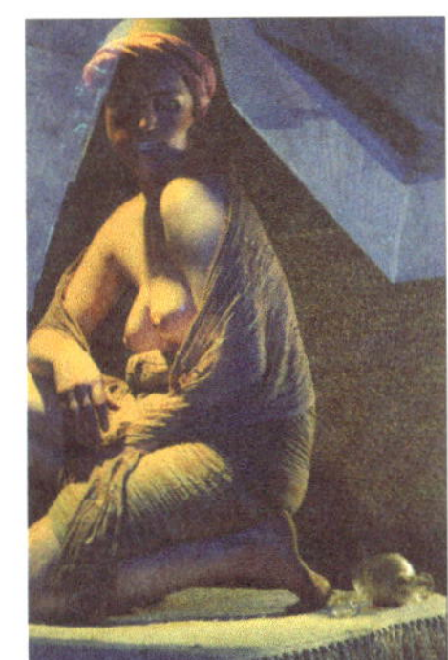

Untitled #146, 1985
Color photograph
Edition of 6
72 ½ x 49 ½ in.
(184.2 x 125.4 cm)

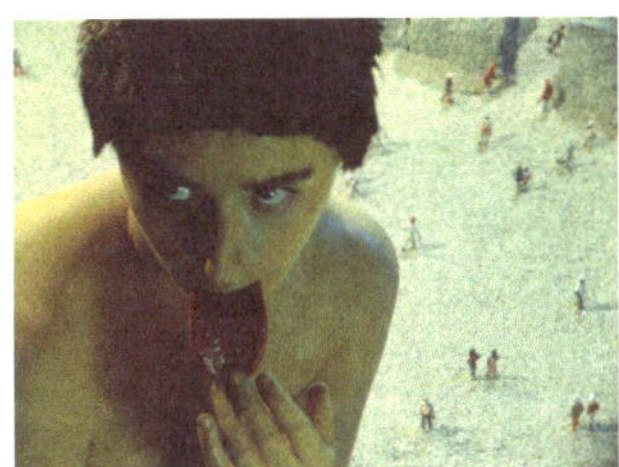

Untitled #150, 1985
Color photograph
Edition of 6
49 ½ x 66 ¾ in.
(125.7 x 169.5 cm)

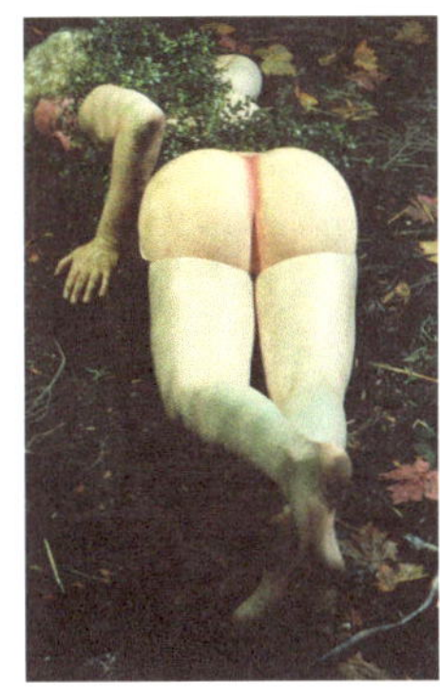

Untitled #155, 1985
Color photograph
Edition of 6
72 ½ x 49 ½ in.
(184.2 x 125 cm)

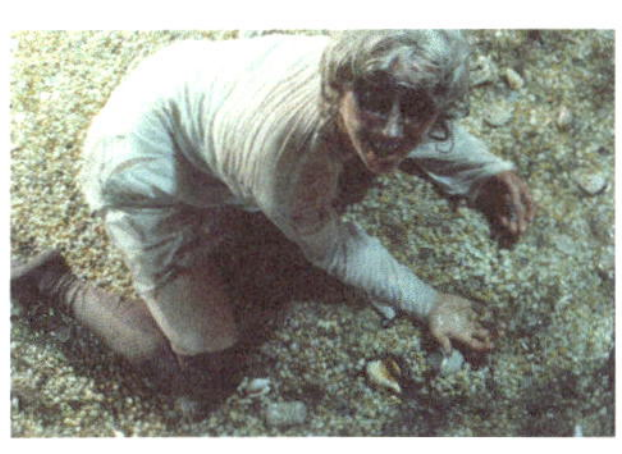

Untitled #156, 1985
Color photograph
Edition of 6
49 ⅝ x 72 ½ in.
(126 x 184 cm)

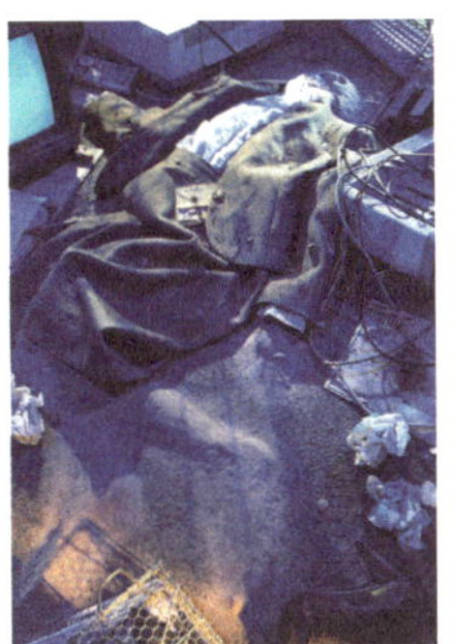

Untitled #168, 1987
Color photograph
Edition of 6
85 x 60 in.
(215.9 x 152.4 cm)

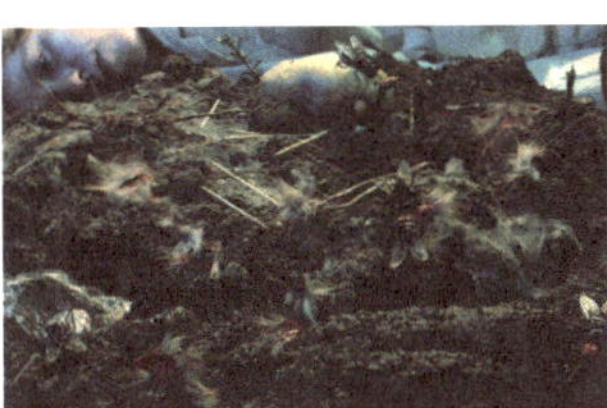

Untitled #173, 1986
Color photograph
Edition of 6
60 x 90 in.
(152.4 x 228.6 cm)

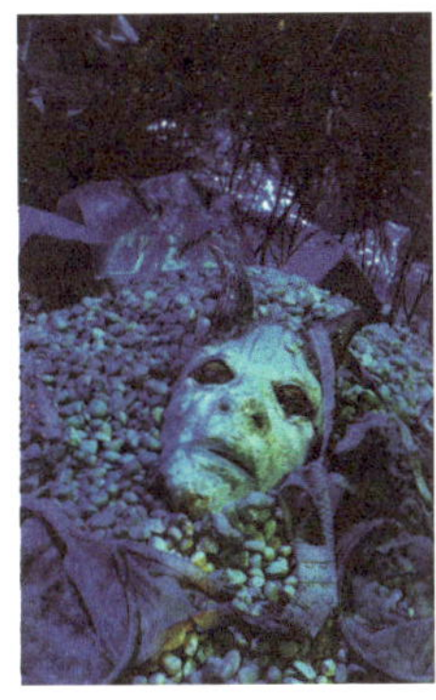

Untitled #174, 1986
Color photograph
Edition of 6
71 x 47 ½ in.
(180.3 x 120.6 cm)

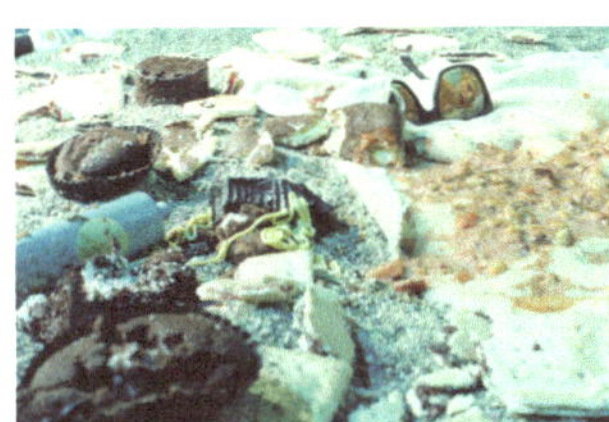

Untitled #175, 1987
Color photograph
Edition of 6
47 ½ x 71 ½ in.
(120.7 x 181.6 cm)

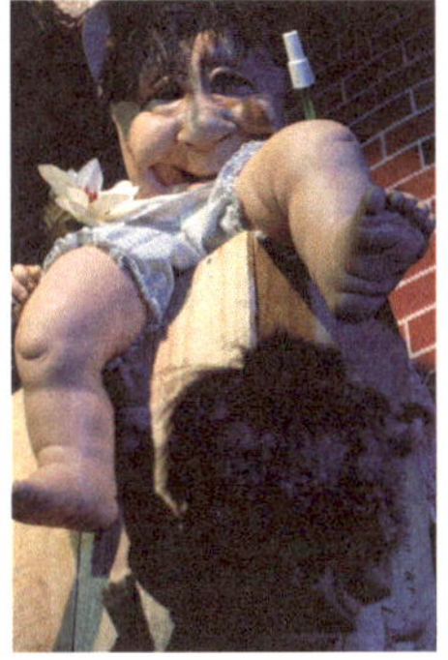

Untitled #186, 1989
Color photograph
Edition of 6
44 ¾ x 29 ½ in.
(113.7 x 74.3 cm)

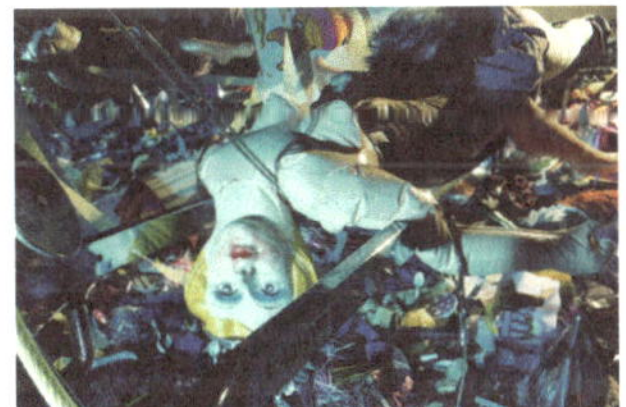

Untitled #188, 1989
Color photograph
Edition of 6
43 ½ x 65 ½ in.
(110.5 x 166.4 cm)

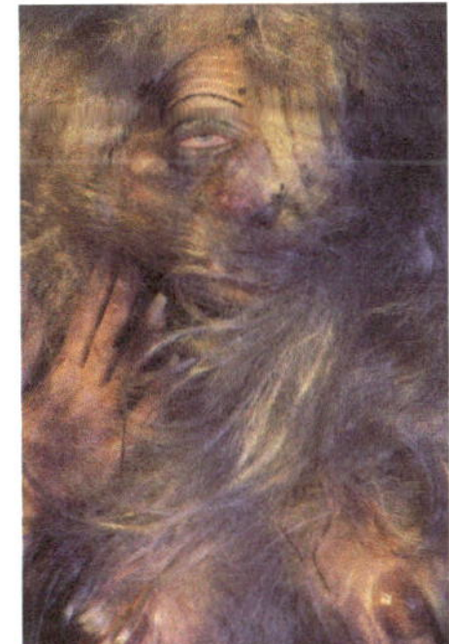

Untitled #191, 1989
Color photograph
Edition of 6
90 x 60 in.
(228.6 x 152.4 cm)

[History Portraits/Old Masters]

1988 — 1990

[Sex Pictures]

1992

The grotesque vein that emerges in the preceding series continues to flourish here in comic mode. (Comedy is never far from the surface in Cindy Sherman's work. There is jubilation in her excesses, and her sheer sense of pleasure in playacting, theatricality, and props is evident throughout her work, even in the "darkest" images.)

The first and most striking aspect of the *History Portraits* is their very nature as portraits in the classic sense of the term. The subject poses with a range of props, costumes, and prostheses, which are themselves often explicit references to Old Master paintings: the character portrayed is by turns an androgynous, Caravaggesque figure (#224), a Botticelli blonde, a Renaissance-style grand dignitary (#213), an English aristocrat straight out of a painting by Reynolds or Gainsborough (#195), and a Flemish burgher.

The references are by no means all explicit, but every image in the series evokes the art of painting. What does the artist hope to achieve by focusing on color and style in this way? Should we interpret the series as a masterly deconstruction of the norms of easel painting at different periods in the history of art, decomposed and retranscribed into her personal plastic vocabulary? Perhaps even as a parody of painting itself? Has Sherman sought to appropriate and pay homage to a bygone form of expression, to express her own fascination for a particular order of representation, itself the product of a particular social order? It is an acknowledgment, perhaps, that parody, imitation (at best), and envy (in any event) are all that is left to us today. Beyond a certain mocking quality, there is a critical intelligence at work in these portraits. By taking as her subject the pantheon of Western art, Cindy Sherman is undermining these pictures' immutable, "frozen" character, and wrecking the arrogant assurance of a set of icons that have been thoroughly hijacked by the commercial world. Even devalued and transformed into graven idols, these Old Master portraits overflow with life, significance, and symbols. Sherman seems to be striving to undermine their self-satisfied complacency, to attack the traditional relationship between the painter and his model, and the unchallenged dominance of a particular form of representation that has stayed ahead of the rest.

...

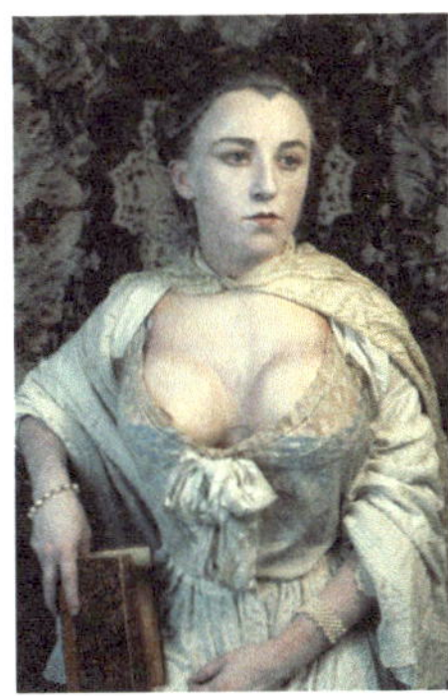
Untitled #183, 1988
Color photograph
Edition of 6
42 ½ x 28 ½ in.
(108 x 72.4 cm)

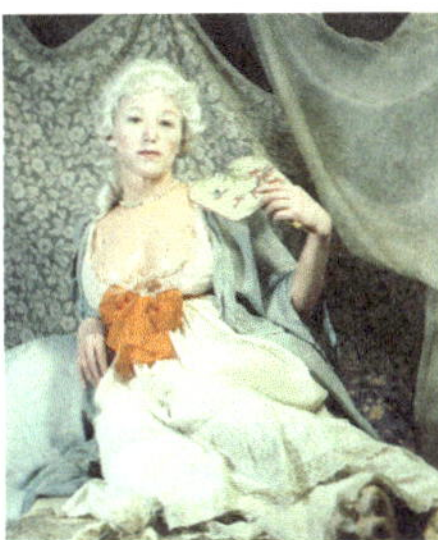
Untitled #193, 1989
Color photograph
Edition of 6
48 ⅞ x 42 in.
(124.1 x 106.5 cm)

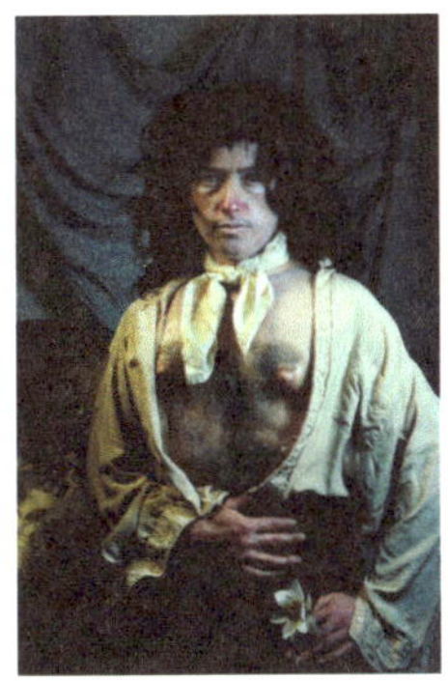
Untitled #194, 1989
Color photograph
Edition of 6
42 x 28 in.
(106.7 x 71.2 cm)

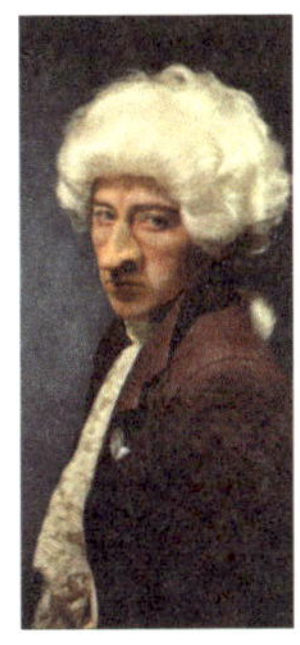
Untitled #195, 1989
Color photograph
Edition of 6
21 x 14 in.
(77.2 x 52.1 cm)

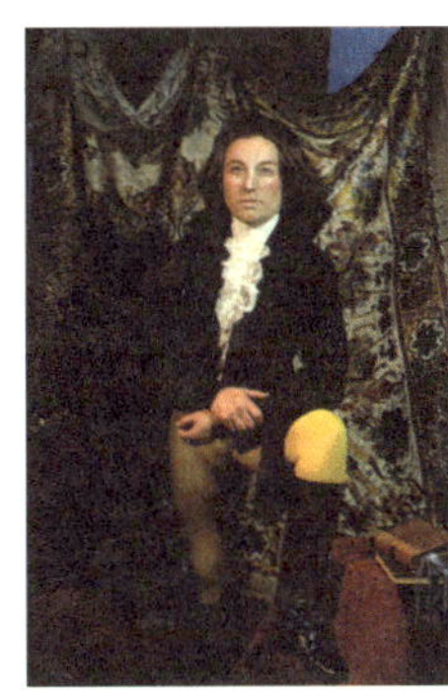
Untitled #196, 1989
Color photograph
Edition of 6
66 x 44 in.
(167.6 x 111.8 cm)

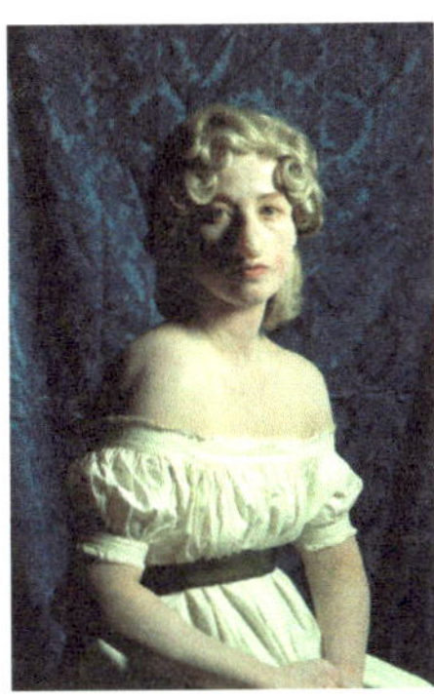
Untitled #197, 1989
Color photograph
Edition of 6
31 ½ x 21 in.
(80 x 53.3 cm)

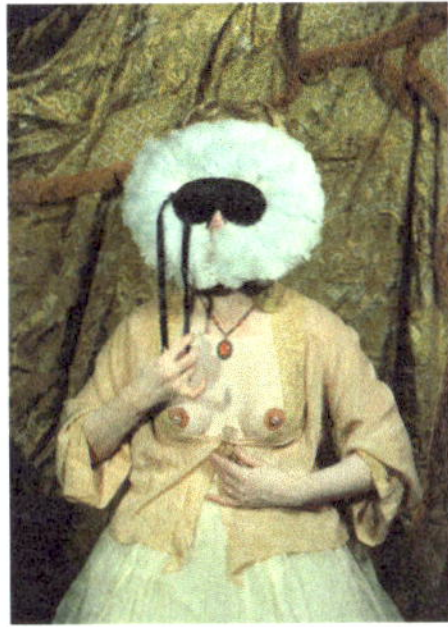
Untitled #198, 1989
Color photograph
Edition of 6
38 ⅜ x 27 ¾ in.
(97.5 x 70.8 cm)

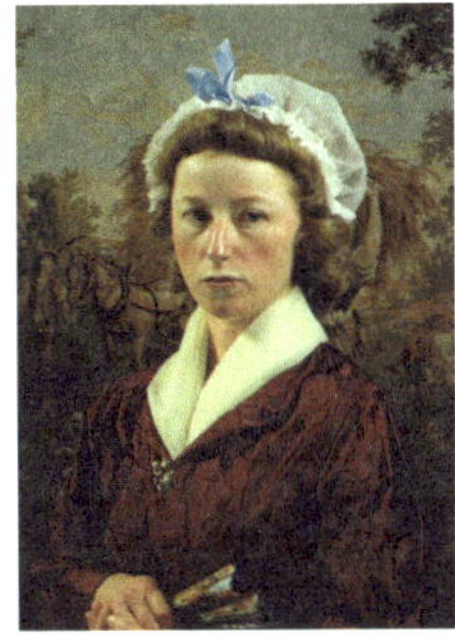
Untitled #199, 1989
Color photograph
Edition of 6
25 x 18 in.
(63.5 x 45.7 cm)

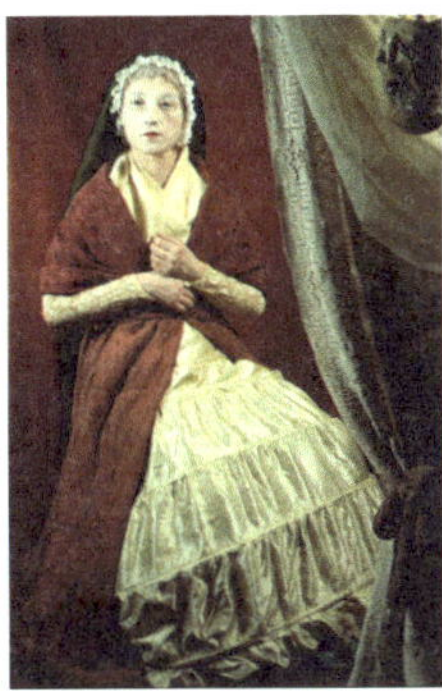
Untitled #200, 1989
Color photograph
Edition of 6
31 x 20 ¾ in.
(78.6 x 53 cm)

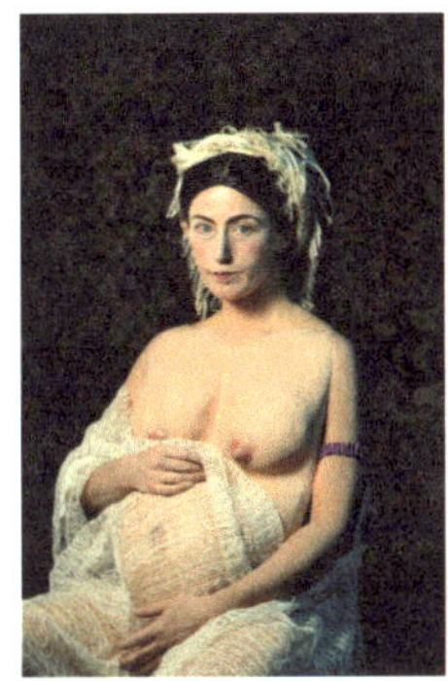
Untitled #205, 1989
Color photograph
Edition of 6
53 ½ x 40 ½ in.
(136 x 102.2 cm)

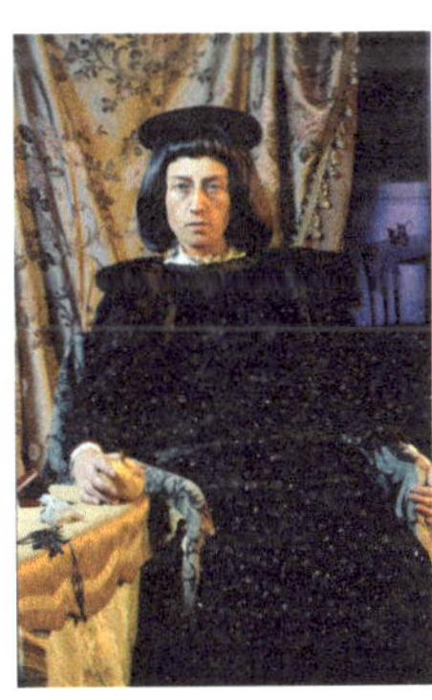
Untitled #206, 1989
Color photograph
Edition of 6
67 ½ x 45 in.
(171.4 x 114.3 cm)

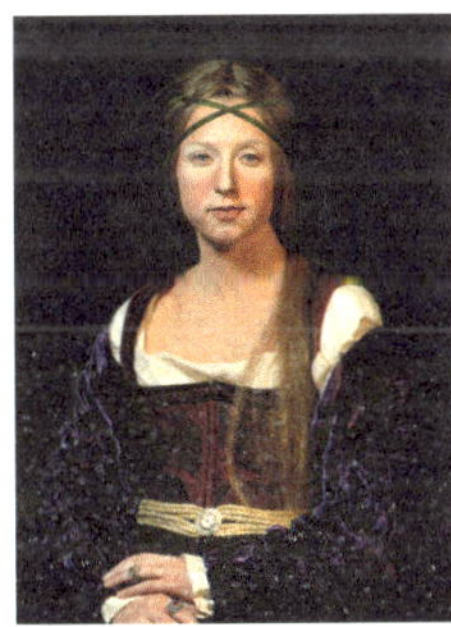
Untitled #209, 1989
Color photograph
Edition of 6
57 x 41 in.
(144.8 x 104.1 cm)

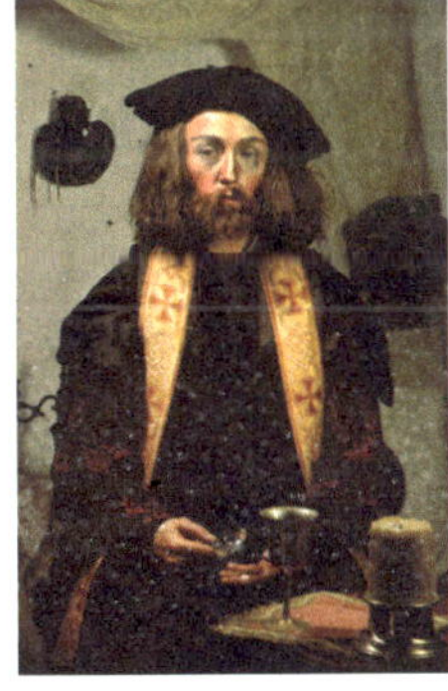
Untitled #210, 1989
Color photograph
Edition of 6
67 x 45 in.
(170.2 x 114.3 cm)

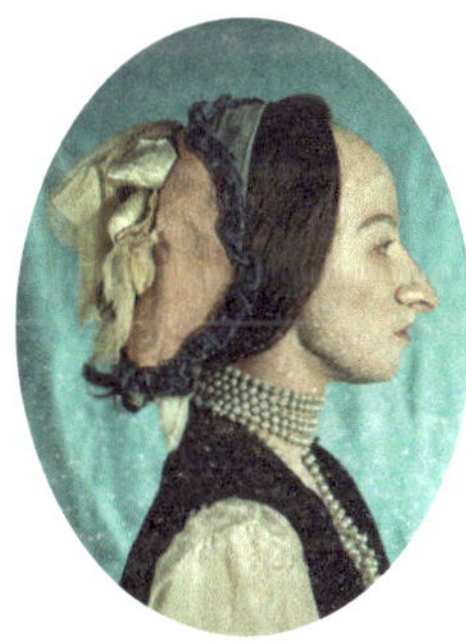
Untitled #211, 1989
Color photograph
Edition of 6
37 x 31 in.
(94 x 78.7 cm)

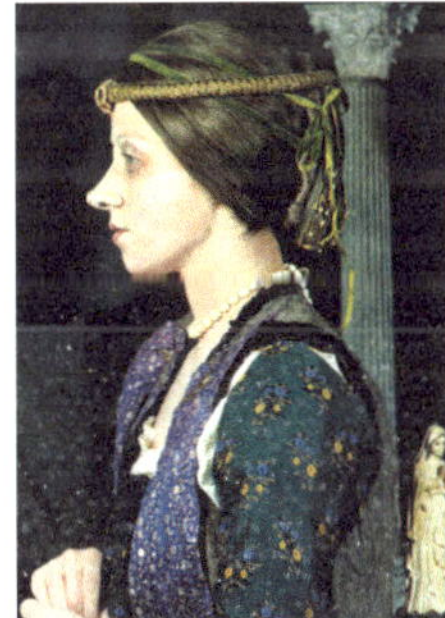
Untitled #212, 1989
Color photograph
Edition of 6
33 x 24 in.
(83.8 x 61 cm)

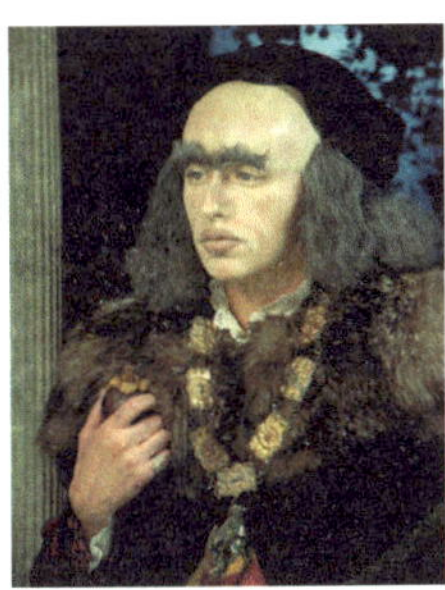
Untitled #213, 1989
Color photograph
Edition of 6
29 ½ x 25 in.
(74.9 x 63.5 cm)

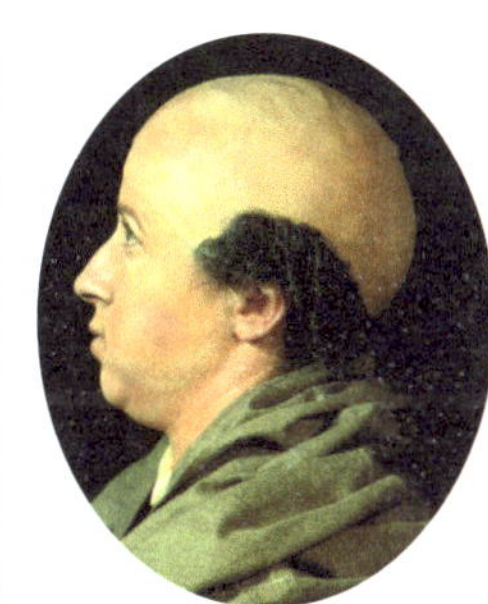
Untitled #214, 1989
Color photograph
Edition of 6
29 ½ x 24 in.
(74.9 x 61 cm)

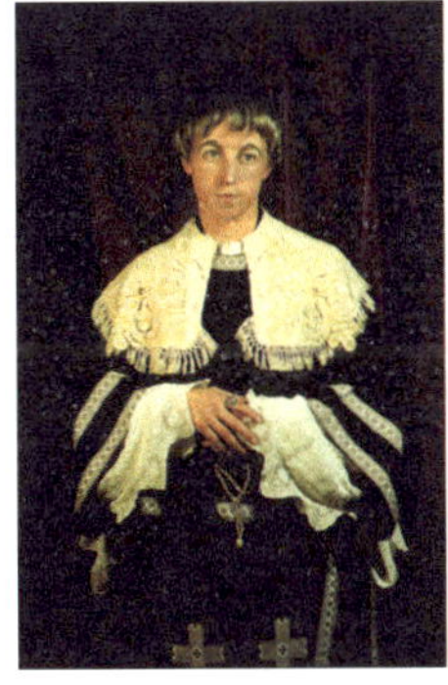
Untitled #215, 1989
Color photograph
Edition of 6
74 ¼ x 51 in.
(188.6 x 129.5 cm)

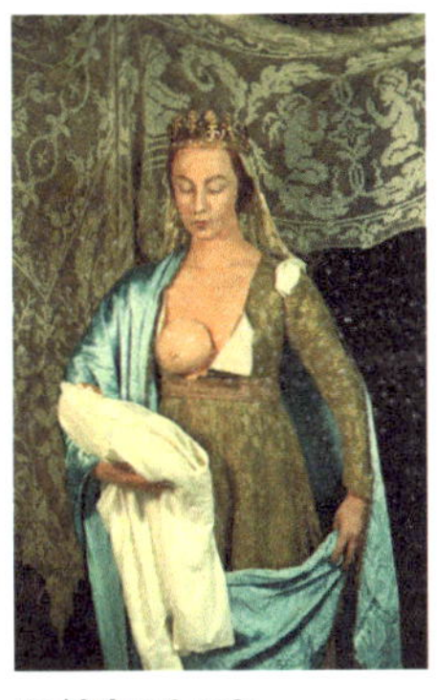
Untitled #216, 1989
Color photograph
Edition of 6
87 x 56 in.
(221 x 142.2 cm)

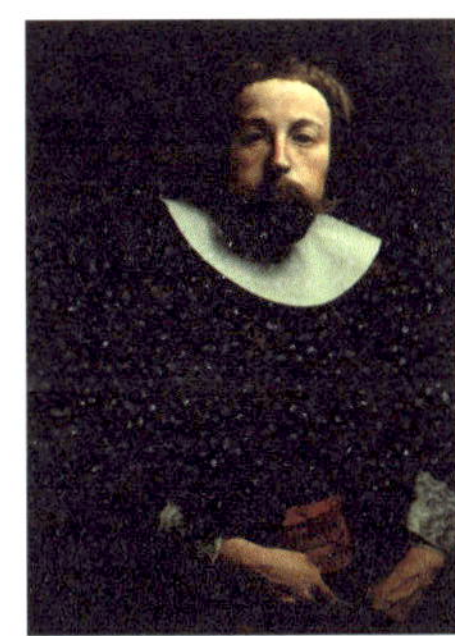
Untitled #220
Color photograph
Edition of 6
64 x 40 in.
(162.6 x 101.6 cm)

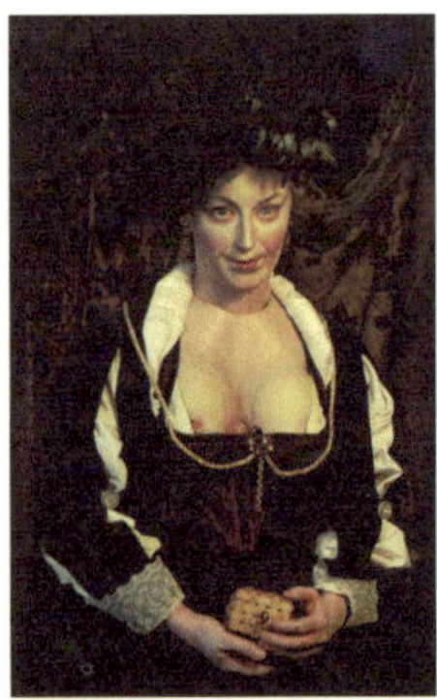

Untitled #221, 1990
Color photograph
Edition of 6
48 x 30 in.
(121.9 x 67.2 cm)

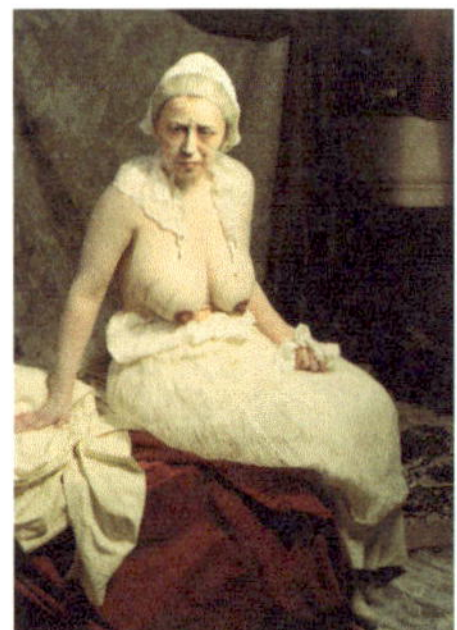

Untitled #222, 1990
Color photograph
Edition of 6
59 ½ x 43 ½ in.
(151 x 110.3 cm)

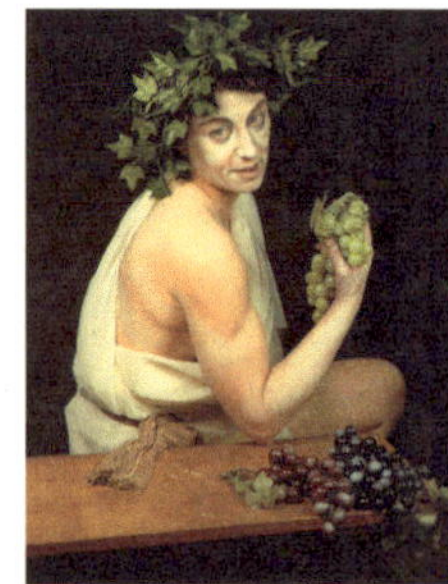

Untitled #224, 1990
Color photograph
Edition of 6
48 x 38 in.
(121.9 x 96.5 cm)

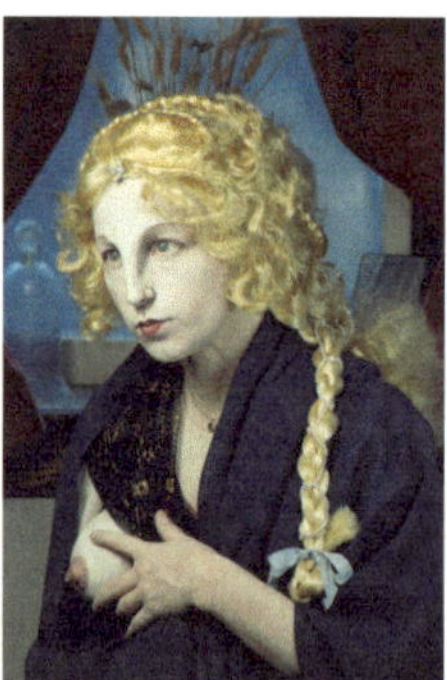

Untitled #225, 1990
Color photograph
Edition of 6
48 x 33 in.
(121.9 x 83.8 cm)

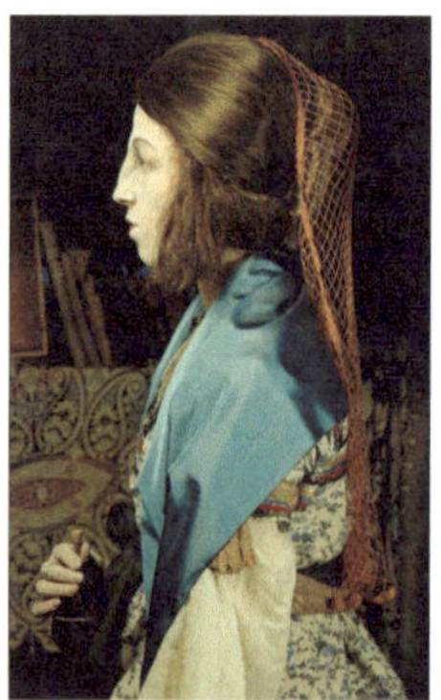

Untitled #226, 1990
Color photograph
Edition of 6
48 x 30 in.
(121.9 x 76.2 cm)

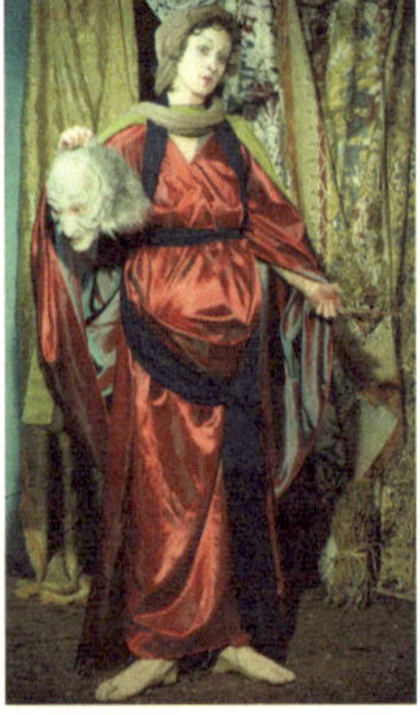

Untitled #228, 1990
Color photograph
Edition of 6
82 x 48 in.
(208.4 x 122 cm)

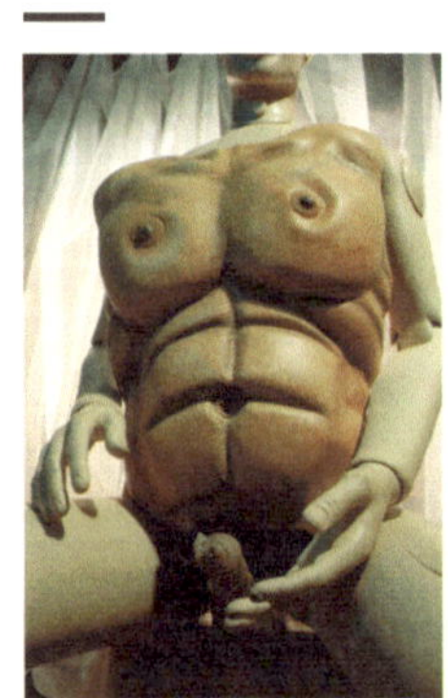

Untitled #251, 1992
Color photograph
Edition of 6
68 x 45 in.
(172.7 x 114.3 cm)

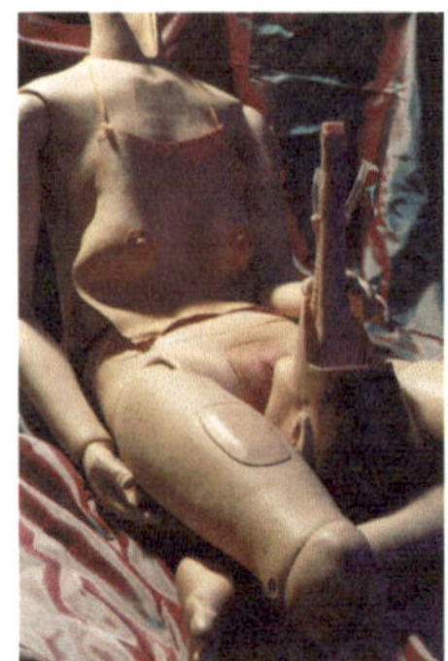

Untitled #253, 1992
Color photograph
Edition of 6
75 x 50 in.
(190.5 x 127 cm)

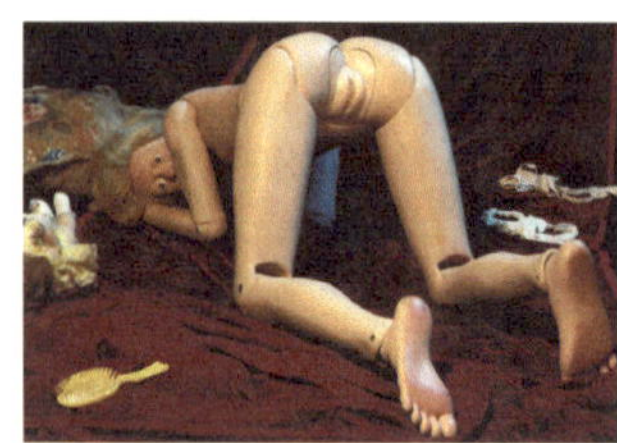

Untitled #255, 1992
Color photograph
Edition of 6
46 ¼ x 69 ¼ in.
(117.5 x 176 cm)

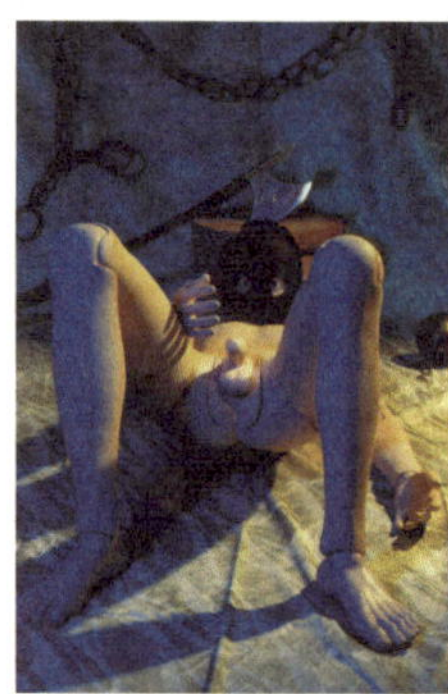

Untitled #256, 1992
Color photograph
Edition of 6
68 x 45 in.
(172.7 x 114.3 cm)

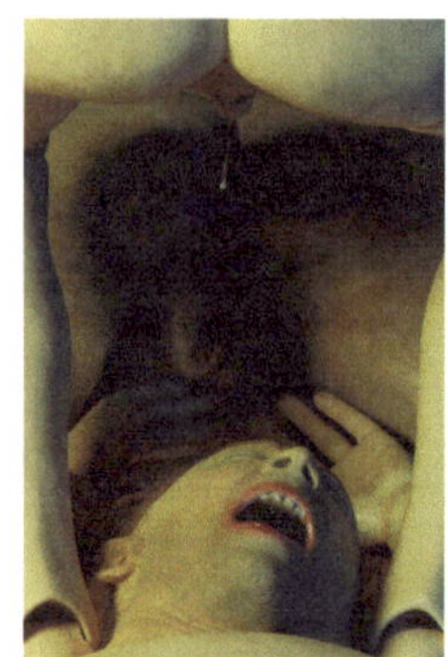

Untitled #257, 1992
Color photograph
Edition of 6
69 ¼ x 46 ¼ in.
(176 x 117.5 cm)

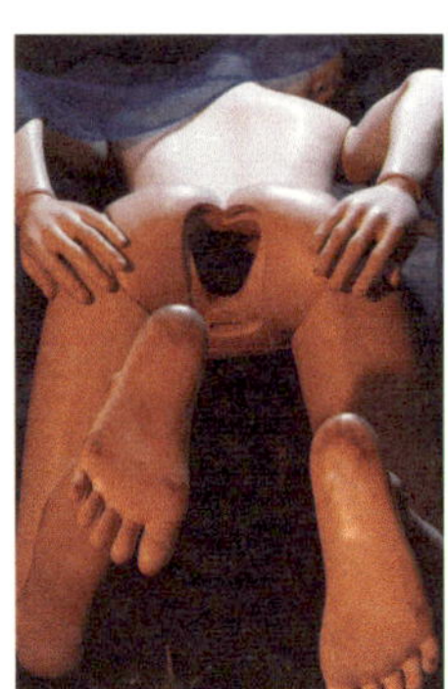

Untitled #258, 1992
Color photograph
Edition of 6
68 x 45 in.
(172.7 x 114.3 cm)

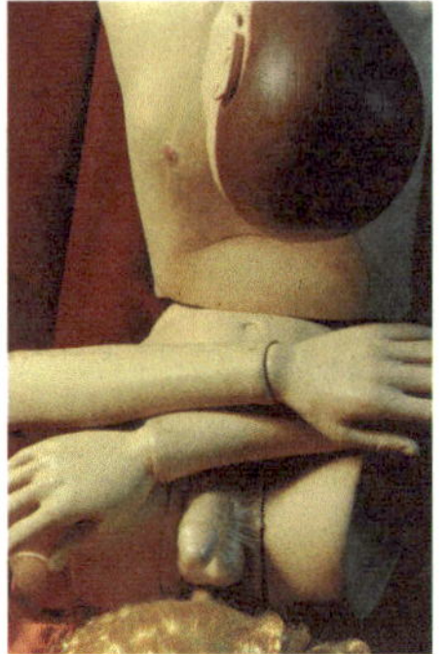

Untitled #259, 1992
Color photograph
Edition of 6
60 x 40 in.
(152.4 x 101.6 cm)

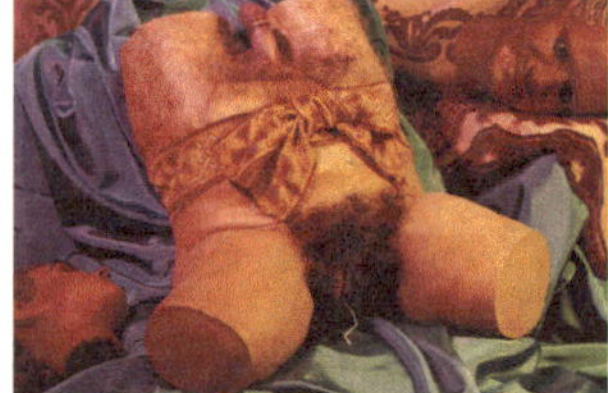

Untitled #263, 1992
Color photograph
Edition of 6
39 ½ x 45 ¼ in.
(100 x 115 cm)

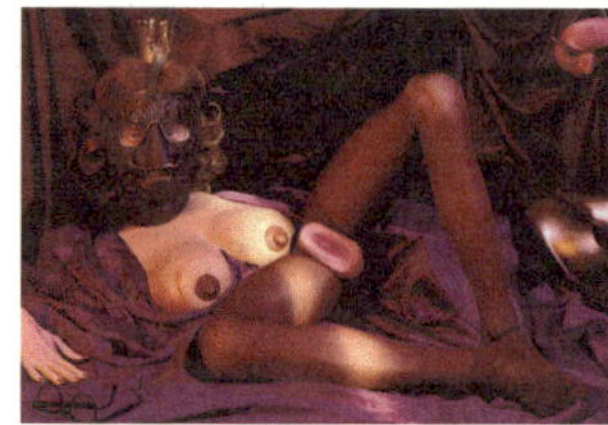

Untitled #264, 1992
Color photograph
Edition of 6
50 x 75 in.
(127 x 190.5 cm)

Sherman's attack is perhaps all the more impassioned for the fact that virtually all of the Old Masters were, of course, men. In this context, the series is all the more remarkable for its vehement denunciation of the particular hubris of fine painting. Icons and echoes from the history of Western art are here reduced to their humblest constituent parts—a few bits of tatty drapery, makeup, a model posing in isolation. The resulting images are probably not that far removed from the daily reality of the workshops of many painters: the rather tawdry, staged compositions that subsequently entered the cultural pantheon. Where the finished paintings convey an illusion of power and life, Sherman presents a crude assemblage of signs and signifiers. In that sense, these painterly photographs are truly the debased heirs of the Vanitas tradition.

The *History Portraits* depict their inanimate subjects (the paintings themselves) by means of a discordant amalgam of living and artificial elements (the artist herself, as the "painter's model" in each portrait, and the prostheses and costumes in which she is arrayed). The object represented (and re-presented) in each case is not the real world, but art itself. And yet, in a certain sense, the series may be seen as part of an unbroken chain of representations, a logical extension of Sherman's work prior to this period. The *Sex Pictures* mark another important step forward: sex, the preserve of life and living creatures, is depicted (with, perhaps, one exception) using inanimate dummies. The subject in this series has, in a manner of speaking, absented herself in person.

How should we interpret this? Has Cindy Sherman tired momentarily of appearing in her own work, and chosen instead to delegate her role to dolls and dummies, masked and accessorized like living beings? Or should we see the pictures as another step on the path to our own dehumanization, as if the images that surround us had relinquished their nourishing, enriching function (in painting and cinema), becoming progressively debased and degraded to the status of by-products and loud, intrusive parodies (TV series, advertising) until finally all that remains is the grinding mechanism of pornography—pornography as our only abiding source of universal imagery and entertainment.

The *Sex Pictures* are, in fact, not exclusively pornographic, but alternate between obscene visions of the body and "straightforward" illustrations of specific practices. The details of the poses and actions are relatively unimportant, however. What matters is the pictures' disturbing dehumanization of sexual desire: the fact that the sex act has, in a sense, been delegated to be carried out by plastic dummies whose obscene exhibitionism is itself horribly humanizing. This is a troubling world, midway between the human and the nonhuman, where transgressions of every sort are permissible—as in the phantasmagorical works of Bosch. An androgynous torso-being (#267), a criss-crossed mass of plastic limbs or severed heads, seem to offer themselves to us, inviting us to join in their "carnal" games. The bodies, if we can call them that, are reduced to gaping orifices (#275, #264). And yet, in this grotesque garden of delights, there is the promise of climactic joy, as seen in #257, one of the series' rare inclusions of a living human subject.

[Civil War]

1991

[Horror and Surrealist Pictures]

1994 — 1996

These two series are a logical extension of the *Sex Pictures*, featuring bodies that have been dismembered or reduced to the status of incomplete objects. The pictures of *Civil War* appear to be details of cadavers, mostly feet and hands, strewn upon the earth with which they will soon be mingled. These *membra disjecta* are all that remain of the body: grim, metonymous signifiers of its former state of wholeness. The title is, of course, a reference to the conflict between the northern and southern American states between 1861 and 1865, which provoked extraordinary carnage, recorded in a horrifying body of contemporary photographic evidence. But it is also the war that continues to rage throughout the modern world, the anonymous, everyday violence whose consequences are seen in tiny "forgotten" wars, news reports and morgues all over the world. Cindy Sherman's style in these pictures is expressionistic, characterized by the extreme elongation or magnification of the hands and feet. Her use of these motifs and devices remains indirect, however. The horror is barely hinted at, and submerged in the pictures' dominant dark gray palette.

In the *Horror and Surrealist Pictures*, the artist's fantastical, gothic vision pulls back from its tight focus on the incomplete object, the genitalia or scattered limbs, to encompass the whole body—a body that has, it seems, been dismembered and recomposed, and whose different parts appear to be living separate, monstrous lives, like the components of some sinister golem. In *#305*, the enraptured profiles of two shop-window dummies are placed close together, like post-coital lovers. Photograph *#308* shows a monstrous figure: an assemblage of disproportionate, inverted body parts. A Cyclopean eye opens in the chin of a giant face, dominating the disjointed body of a puppet. In *#312*, we see a whole family of dummies with monstrous faces. As in *#304*, the tender family pose only serves to heighten the sense of malaise generated by these double masks, which seem to spring from a different, nonhuman order of creation. As already noted by several contemporary commentators, Cindy Sherman is attacking whatever last remnants of idealized womanhood and female beauty might still be found lodged in the surrealist imagination. As if her modern female consciousness could no longer accept the surrealists' mythologizing use of the female form, and now sought to bring such practices to an end once and for all through the symbolic destruction, by a magical process close to that of exorcism, of all the world's remaining beauty and idealism.

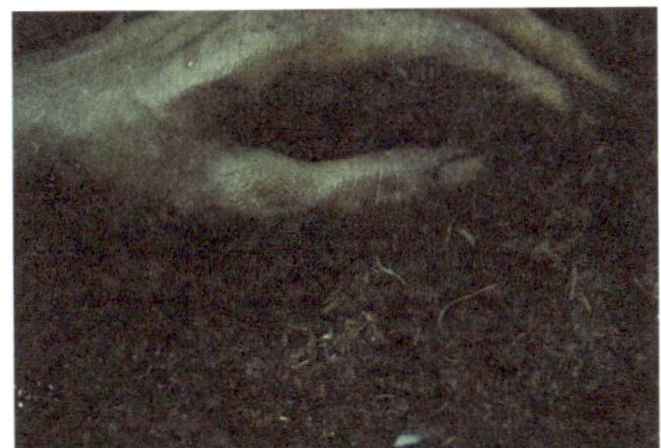

Untitled #240, 1991
Color photograph
Edition of 6
49 x 72 in.
(124.5 x 182.9 cm)

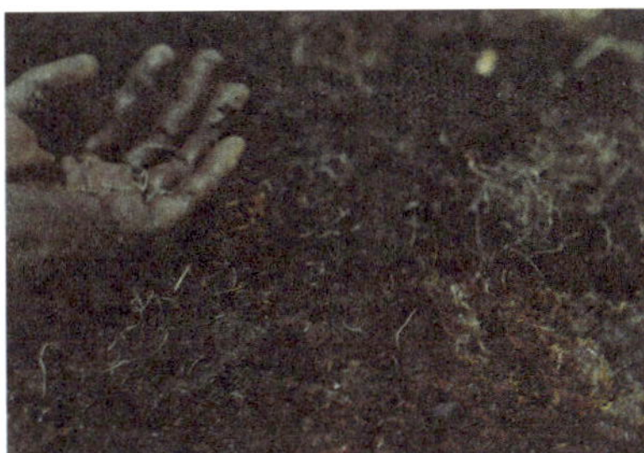

Untitled #242, 1991
Color photograph
Edition of 6
49 x 72 in.
(124.5 x 182.9 cm)

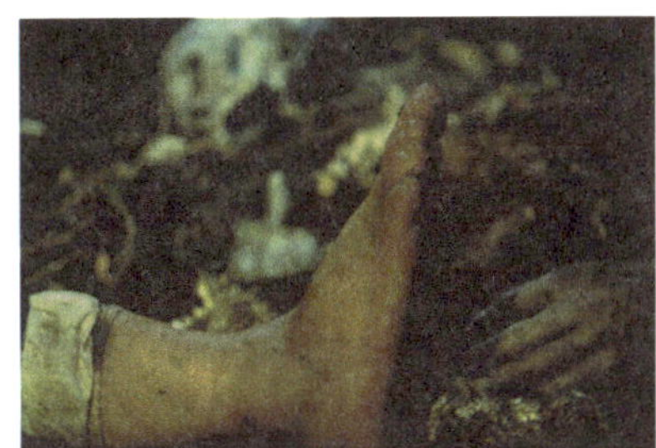

Untitled #243, 1991
Color photograph
Edition of 6
49 x 72 in.
(124.5 x 182.9 cm)

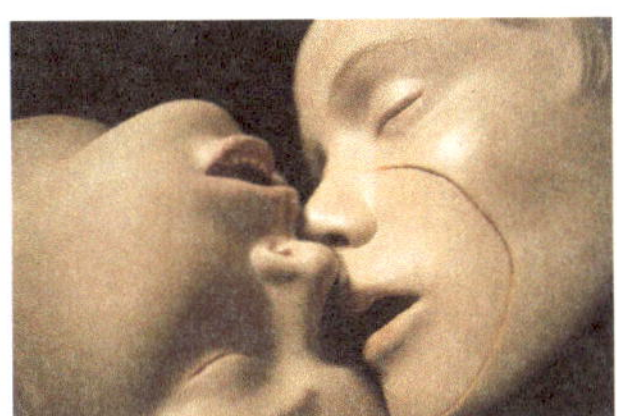

Untitled #305, 1994
Color photograph
Edition of 6
49 ¾ in x 73 ½ in.
(126.4 x 186.7 cm)

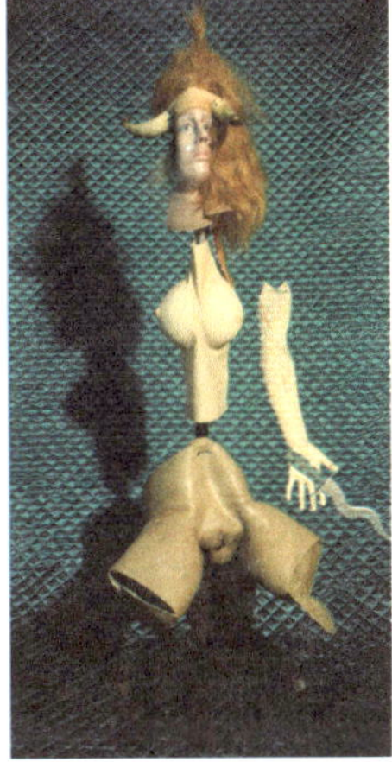

Untitled #307, 1994
Color photograph
Edition of 6
79 x 42 ½ in.
(200.7 x 108 cm)

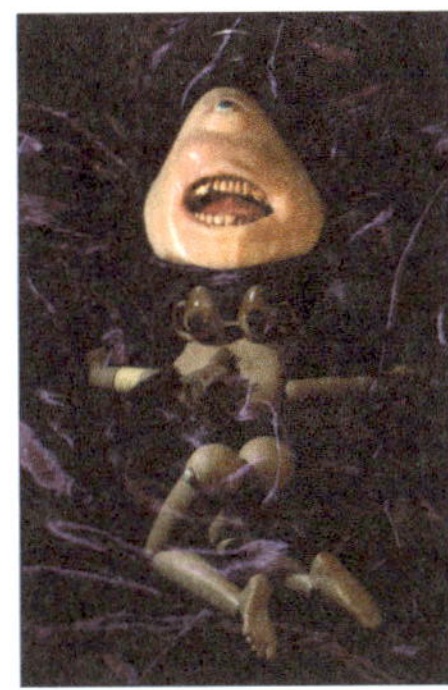

Untitled #308, 1994
Color photograph
Edition of 6
69 ½ x 47 in.
(176.5 x 119.4 cm)

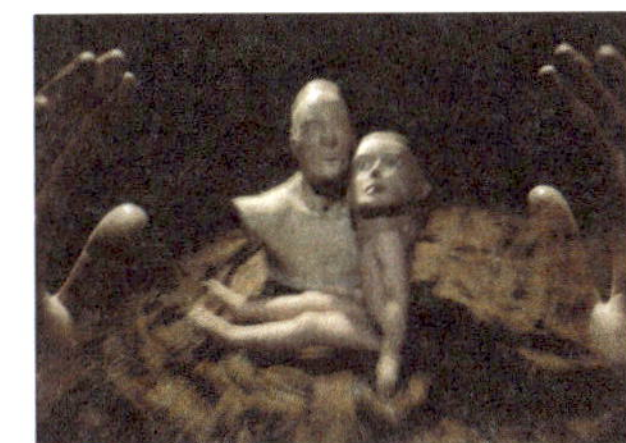

Untitled #310, 1994
Color photograph
Edition of 6
44 x 63 ½ in.
(111.7 x 161.3 cm)

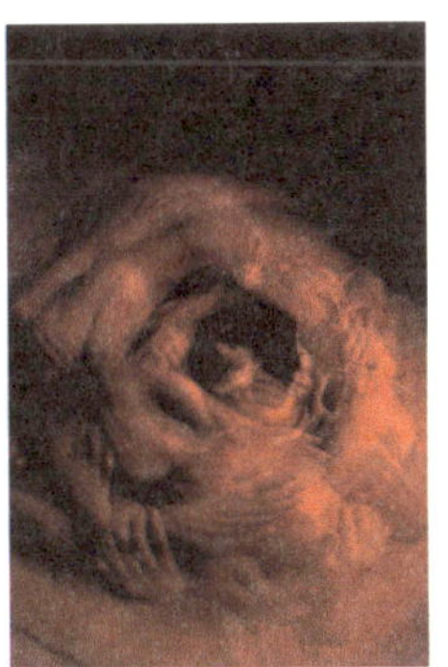

Untitled #311, 1994
Color photograph
Edition of 6
76 x 51 in.
(193 x 129.5 cm)

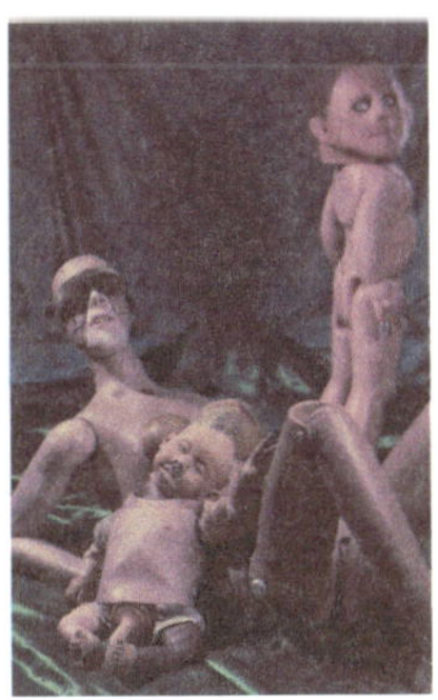

Untitled #312, 1994
Color photograph
Edition of 6
61 x 41 ½ in.
(154.9 x 105.4 cm)

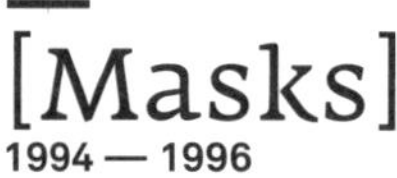

[Masks]

1994 — 1996

Masks are a growing, insistent presence in the *Sex Pictures* and the *Horror and Surrealist Pictures*. Their increasingly frequent use may be explained by Sherman's desire to stop using herself as the "model" in her pictures, and to delegate the onerous task of dressing up and performing to a cast of inanimate substitutes. Hence the masks, then, but also the dummies and shadow silhouettes, and the complete absence of any identifiable figure.

In the *Masks* series, the mask becomes the subject of the picture (replacing the human subject of earlier works), and seems to acquire an autonomous life of its own. Photographed in extreme close-up (as in *#314 A* to F), then cut up and reassembled into grotesque forms, the features create their own nightmarish topography, reinforced by the predominant use of red.

In *#315*, the "mask" is set in a gray plaster-like coating, and seems to emerge from a uterine orifice, surmounted by a single eye, in a new take on the dysfunctional physionomical vocabulary and grammar that is so characteristic of this series.

In *#316* the mask has been slashed and wounded, and seems to be made up of several layers or skins, at the frontier between the living and the inorganic. In *#324*, on the other hand, the mask appears molten and smooth, molding and sealing the face that it covers completely, with the exception of two glassy eyes, lit with the flame of inner life. It is impossible here to distinguish between the face and the mask. The latter is no longer indicative of some secret identity or ceremony, as it was earlier. It can no longer be removed to reveal the living face beneath. As in so many fantastical stories, the mask has assumed an identity of its own, and brought the living flesh under its controlling power.

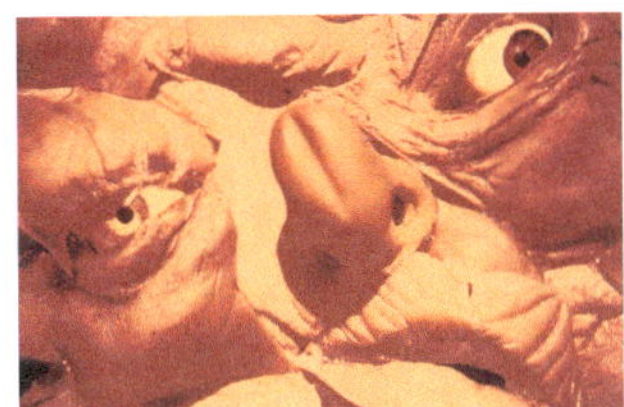

Untitled #314A, 1994
Color photograph
Edition of 6
30 x 44 in.
(76.2 x 111.8 cm)

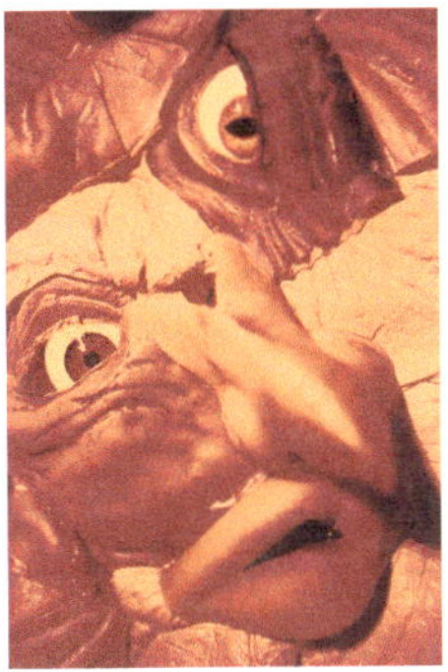

Untitled #314B, 1994
Color photograph
Edition of 6
44 x 30 in.
(111.8 x 76.2 cm)

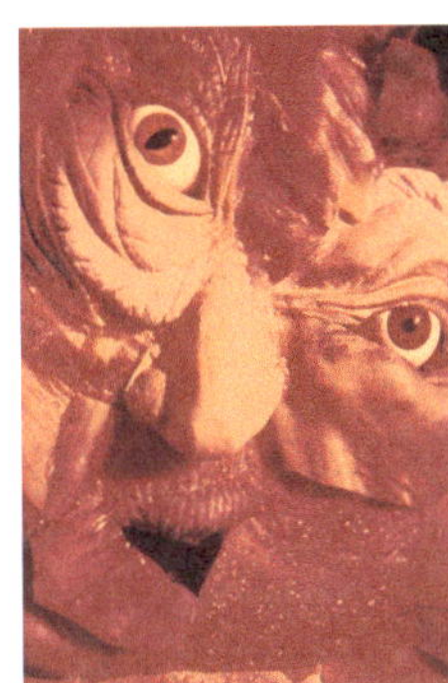

Untitled #314C, 1994
Color photograph
Edition of 6
44 x 30 in.
(111.8 x 76.2 cm)

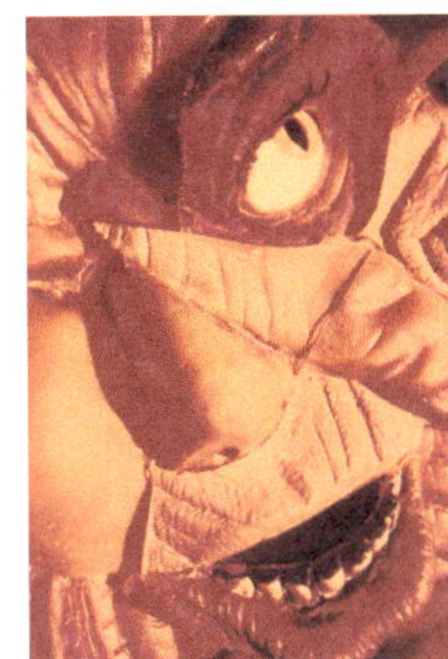

Untitled #314D, 1994
Color photograph
Edition of 6
44 x 30 in.
(111.8 x 76.2 cm)

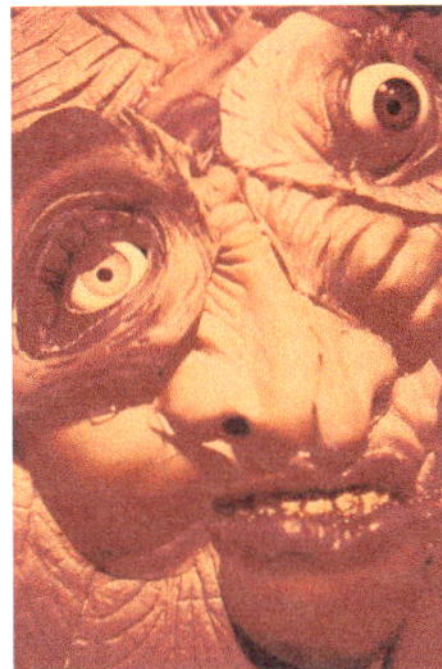

Untitled #314E, 1994
Color photograph
Edition of 6
44 x 30 in.
(111.8 x 76.2 cm)

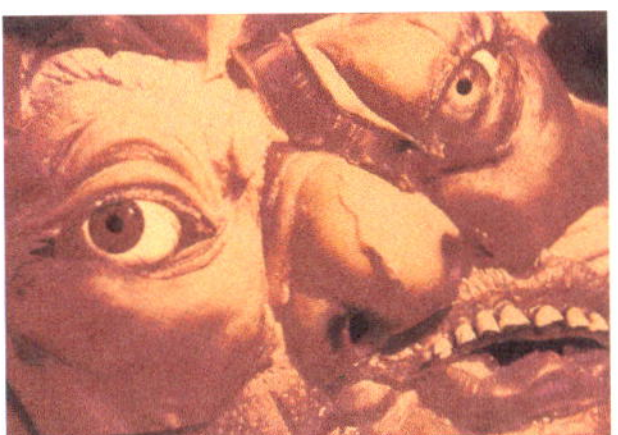

Untitled #314F, 1994
Color photograph
Edition of 6
30 x 44 in.
(76.2 x 111.8 cm)

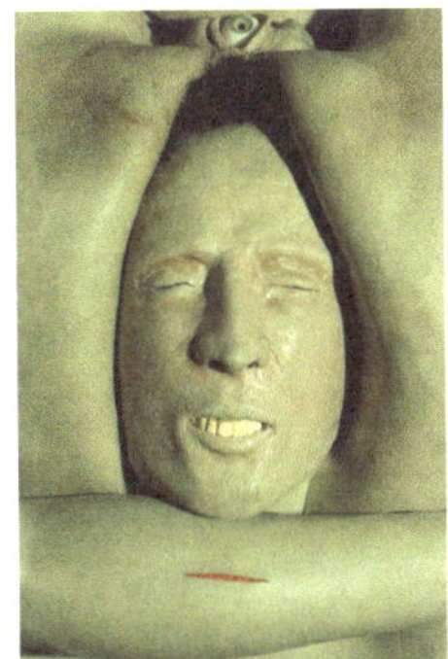

Untitled #315, 1995
Color photograph
Edition of 6
60 x 40 in.
(152.4 x 101.6 cm)

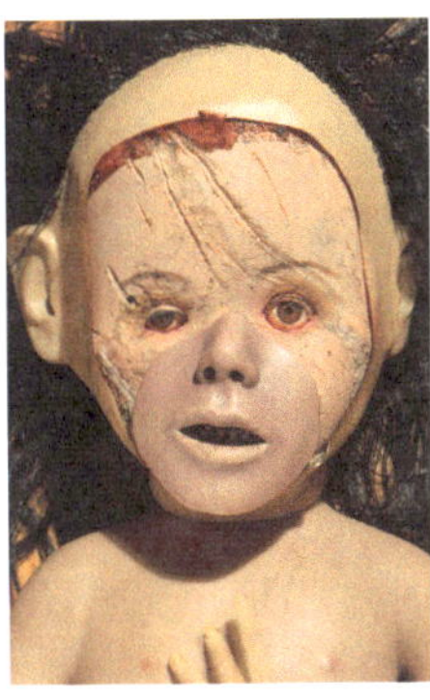

Untitled #316, 1995
Color photograph
Edition of 6
48 x 32 in.
(121.9 x 81.3 cm)

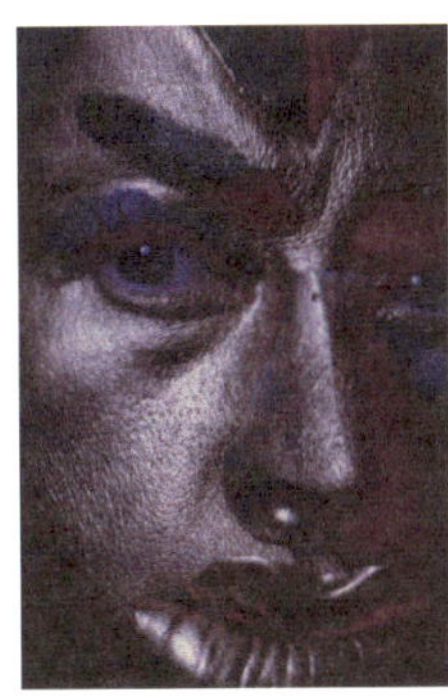

Untitled #323, 1995
Color photograph
Edition of 6
57 ⅞ x 39 in.
(147 x 99.1 cm)

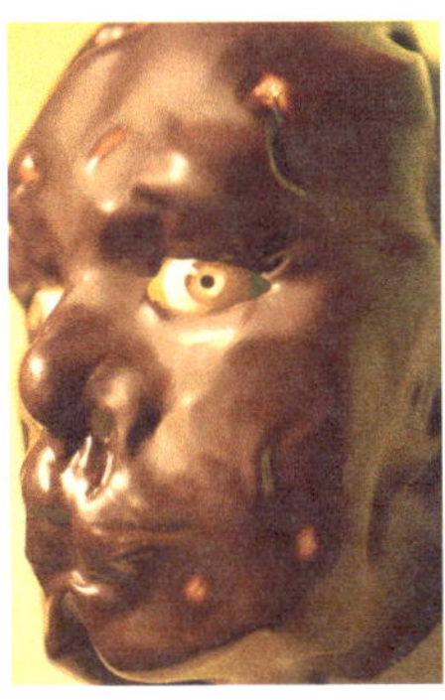

Untitled #324, 1996
Color photograph
Edition of 6
57 ⅞ x 39 in.
(147 x 99.1 cm)

[Broken Dolls]

1999

In this series of black-and-white photographs all trace of a human presence (the male or female figure previously referred to as "the subject") has disappeared, replaced by mutilated dolls that have been torn apart and placed in a variety of obscene postures, in settings reminiscent of those seen in the *Sex Pictures* and, sometimes, the *Horror Pictures*. The series' most striking aspect is the remarkable intensity and expressiveness of the figures created using these damaged, degraded objects. The bodies in #345 and #347 writhe in the grip of pain or pleasure; those in #334, #335, and #337 offer themselves to us with almost monstrous obscenity. The series takes us to the dark side of childhood, with its amorality and "polymorphic perversion" (tendencies which will be gently mastered or buried through the gradual inculcation of social and moral codes), and its burden of violence—the violence that children often show so readily toward their "transitional objects."

The doll, that emblematic symbol of female childhood, is mistreated and desecrated while at the same time revealing its capacity to retain some form of residual life, to continue to embody something of its owner's inner desires, even over long stretches of time. There is something deeply troubling about the sadistic energy with which these dolls have been mutilated, their lively, seemingly autonomous participation in the scenes depicted. The dolls are the apotheosis of the evolving use of props in Sherman's earlier series, their tendency to live their own autonomous lives, to embody the urges of the people manipulating them by appropriating a part of their being, and by looking ahead, perhaps, to their imminent annihilation.

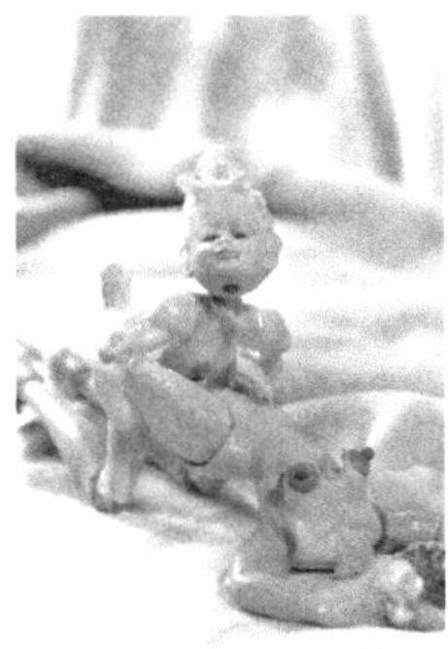

Untitled #332, 1999
Black-and-white photograph
Edition of 10
38 ½ x 25 ½ in.
(97.8 x 64.8 cm)

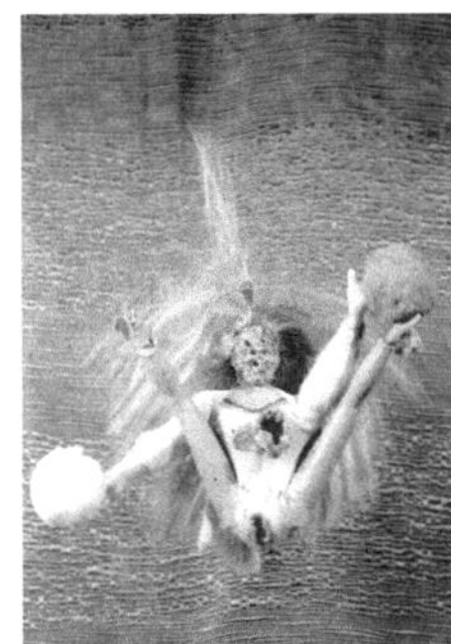

Untitled #334, 1999
Black-and-white photograph
Edition of 10
47 ½ x 31 ½ in.
(120.6 x 80 cm)

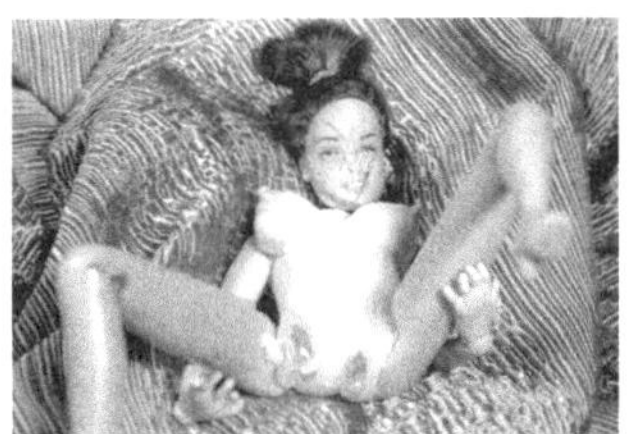

Untitled #335, 1999
Black-and-white photograph
Edition of 10
21 ½ x 32 ½ in.
(54.6 x 82.6 cm)

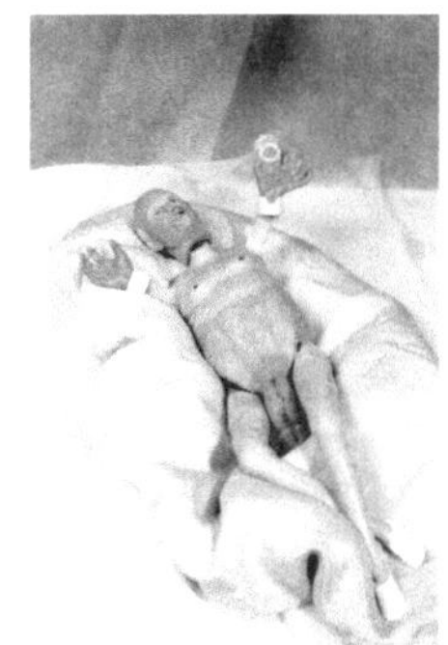

Untitled #337, 1999
Black-and-white photograph
Edition of 10
35 ½ x 25 ½ in.
(90.2 x 64.8 cm)

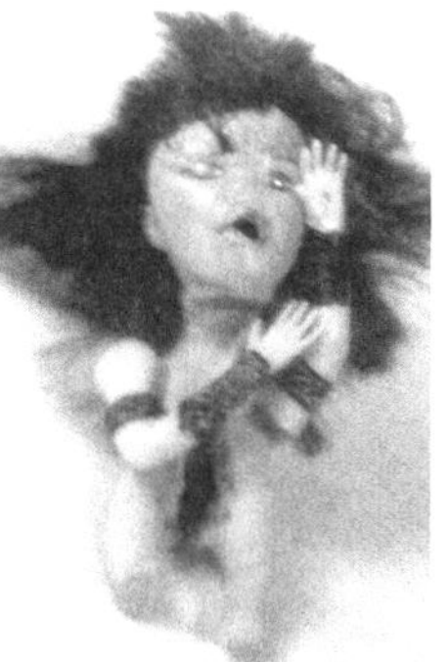

Untitled #343, 1999
Black-and-white photograph
Edition of 10
38 ½ x 25 ½ in.
(97.8 x 64.8 cm)

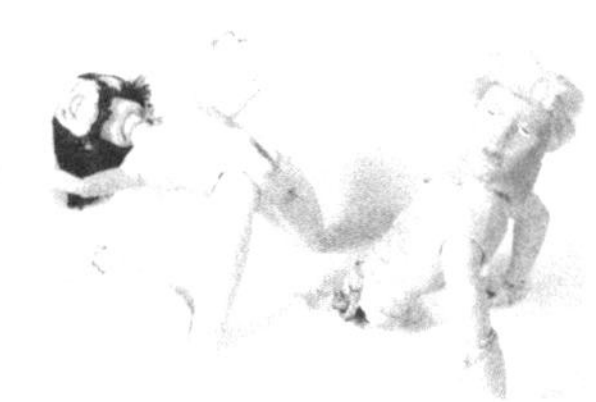

Untitled #345, 1999
Black-and-white photograph
Edition of 10
25 ½ x 38 ½ in.
(64.8 x 97.8 cm)

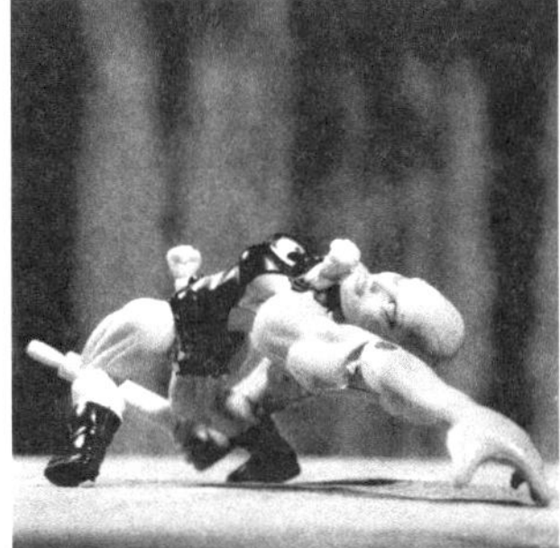

Untitled #347, 1999
Black-and-white photograph
Edition of 10
22 x 22 in.
(55.9 x 55.9 cm)

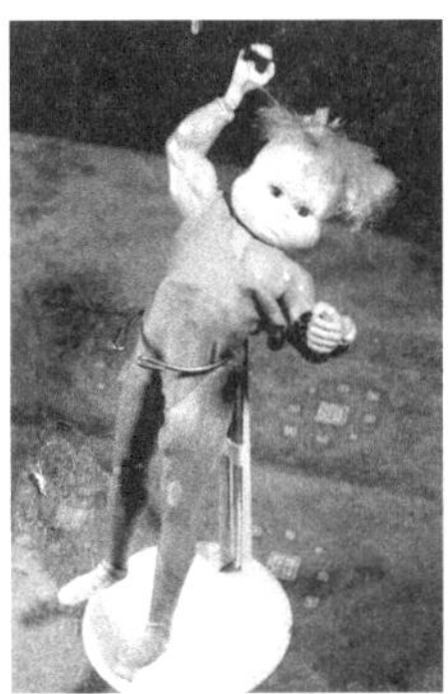

Untitled #348, 1999
Black-and-white photograph
Edition of 10
38 ½ x 26 in.
(97.8 x 66 cm)

[Hollywood/Hampton Types]

2000 — 2002

Cindy Sherman has compared the figures in these portraits to failed or fallen actors: people who are working as secretaries, cleaners, or gardeners to make ends meet, but who are posing here for casting pictures.[2] They are trying to sell themselves as best they can, imploring the viewer to give them a break. This is indeed the basic idea behind the series, but we know—as with the *Clowns*—that the different "types" are often also inspired by the chance discovery of an item of clothing or a prop. Whatever its superficial context, this succession of frontal portraits is both humorous and pathetic. Inevitably, these people—fallen by the wayside of the Hollywood dream—turn the spotlight on our own illusions, our incessant craving for attention and recognition. They are caricatural, but scarcely any more so than the "real-life" stories and situations they evoke.

A prosthesis is clearly visible in #352, but most of the images depend solely on makeup and costumes, marking a significant return to the use of the human figure in Sherman's work following a period in which it disappeared almost entirely in favor of a range of substitutes. Certain images, such as #359, anticipate the clown figures of the later series. Both series explore the "flip side" of their superficial subject matter. While the *Clowns* evoke the dark, disturbing side of childhood and laughter, the *Hampton Types* speak to us of lost illusions, growing old, and the individual's battle to find his or her place on the gameboard of accepted, predetermined identities that make up modern society: advertising shots in a human marketplace that strives to conceal its brutality beneath a superficial attention to questions of style and appearance. And yet the fixed, stereotypical style adopted by the people in these photographs is precisely what condemns them to the Hollywood scrap heap. Only a polymorphous actor of no particular "type," one who has no visible identity of his or her own but is capable of assuming every identity, stands a chance of making it, leaving the rest to fight over bit parts and dead-end catering jobs. Just like the artist? Or, perhaps, the viewer? We all strive ceaselessly for some small recognition, some validation of the role we have chosen for ourselves, forsaking all others; forsaking, too, the polymorphous potential that we may all have had within us, once upon a time.

And so this series, taken as a whole, reads as a kind of allegory of identity itself, and of the harnessing of identity to the demands of one single role. The images read, too, as a commentary on the post-industrial society in which we live, a society where images (rather than beings) and people trafficking reign supreme. A Kafkaesque society governed by opaque, contradictory laws. A society that forces us to make choices and take risks that lead, almost inevitably, to defeat and loss.

2
"No Make-Up," an interview with Isabelle Graw in the catalog *Cindy Sherman: Clowns*, Schirmer/Mosel, 2002.

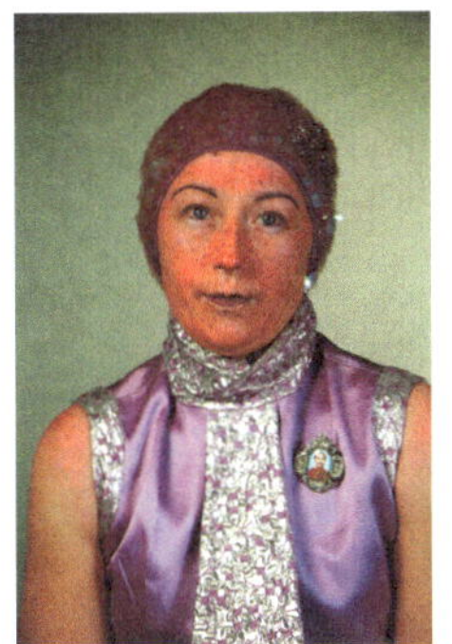

Untitled #351, 2000
Color photograph
Edition of 6
30 x 20 in.
(76.2 x 50.8 cm)

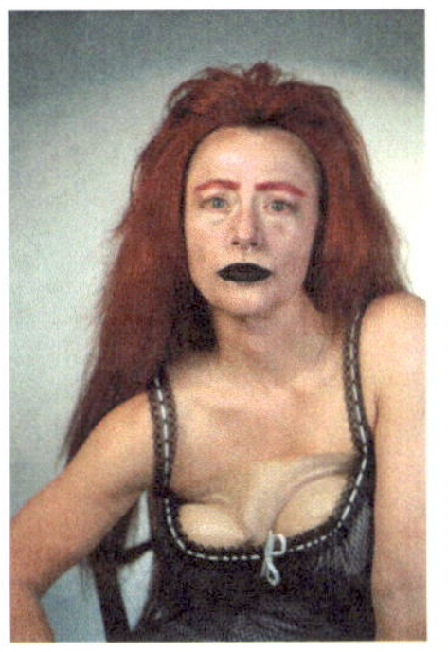

Untitled #352, 2000
Color photograph
Edition of 6
27 x 18 in.
(68.6 x 45.7 cm)

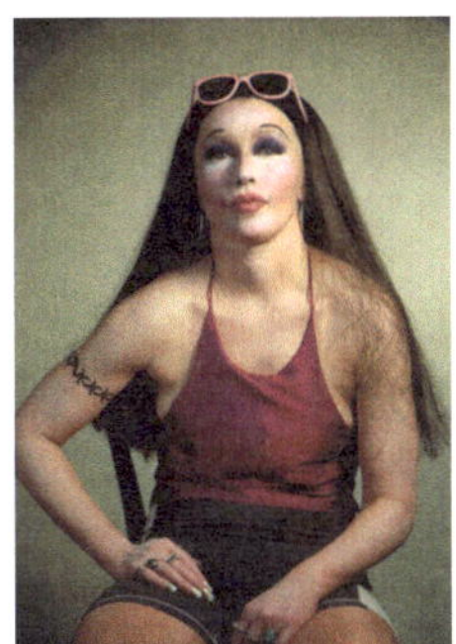

Untitled #355, 2000
Color photograph
Edition of 6
36 x 24 in.
(91.4 x 61 cm)

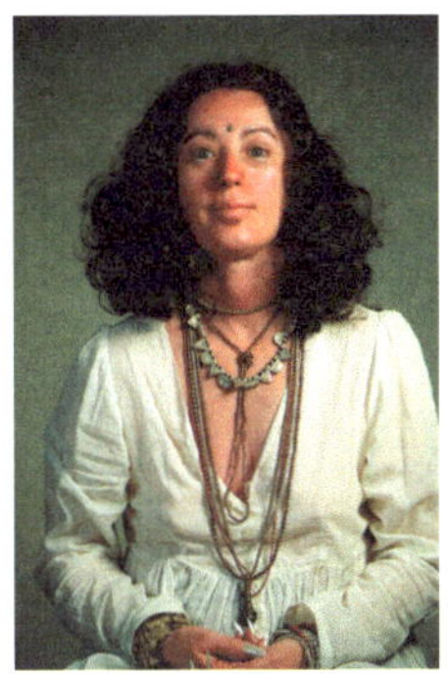

Untitled #358, 2000
Color photograph
Edition of 6
30 x 20 in.
(76.2 x 50.8 cm)

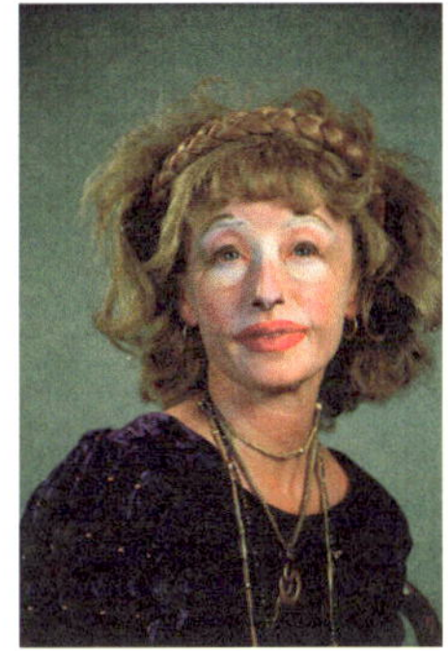

Untitled #359, 2000
Color photograph
Edition of 6
30 x 20 in.
(76.2 x 50.8 cm)

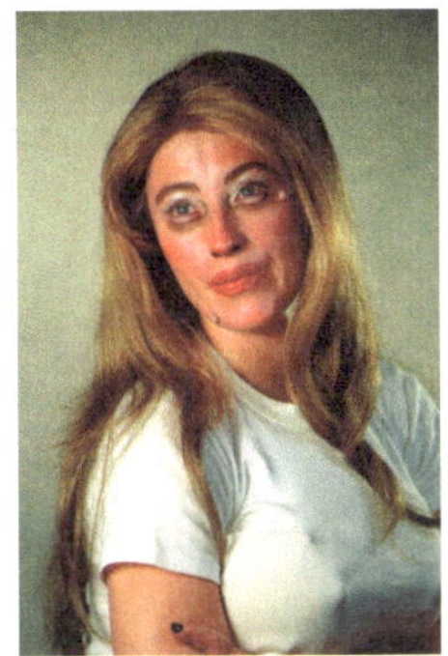

Untitled #360, 2000
Color photograph
Edition of 6
30 x 20 in.
(76.2 x 50.8 cm)

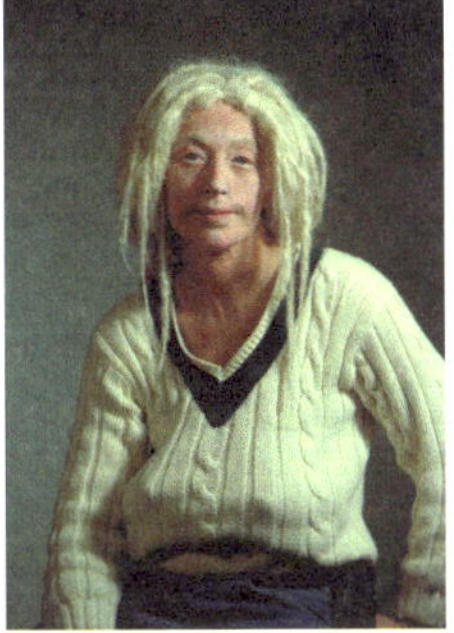

Untitled #399, 2000
Color photograph
Edition of 6
39 x 26 in.
(99.1 x 66 cm)

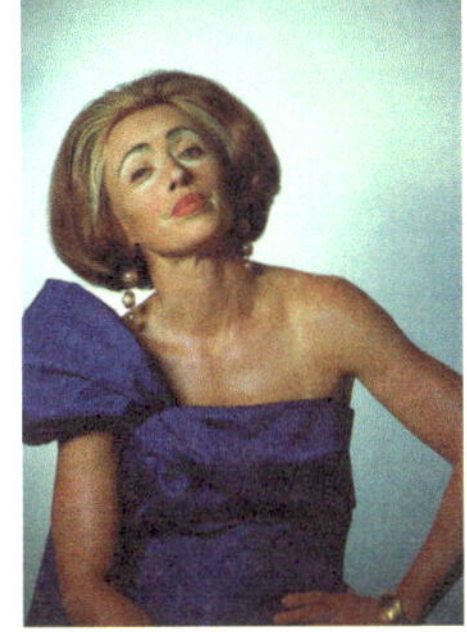

Untitled #400, 2000
Color photograph
Edition of 6
36 ¾ x 26 in.
(93.3 x 66 cm)

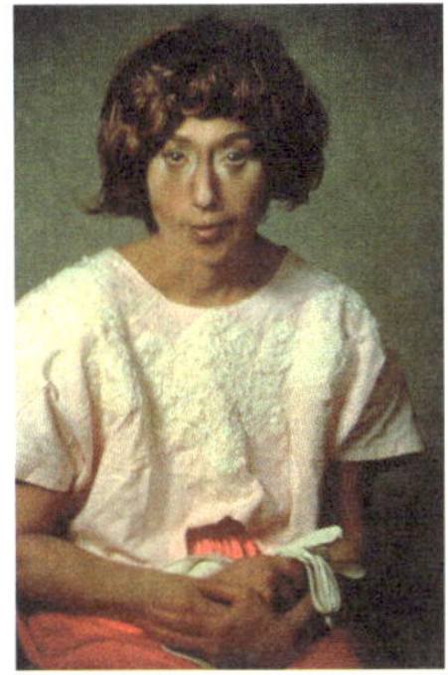

Untitled #401, 2000
Color photograph
Edition of 6
36 x 24 in.
(91.4 x 61 cm)

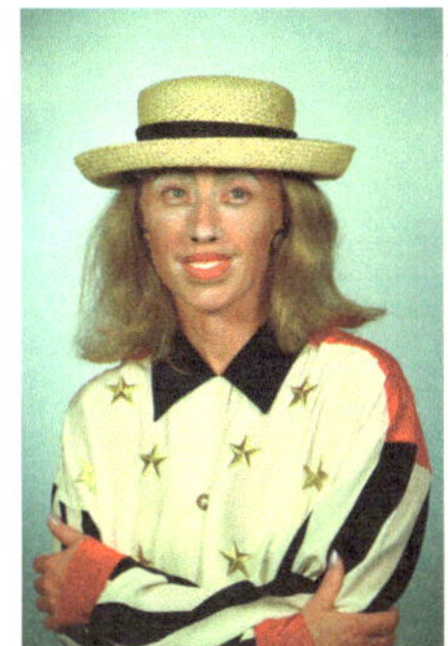

Untitled #402, 2000
Color photograph
Edition of 6
36 x 26 in.
(91.4 x 66 cm)

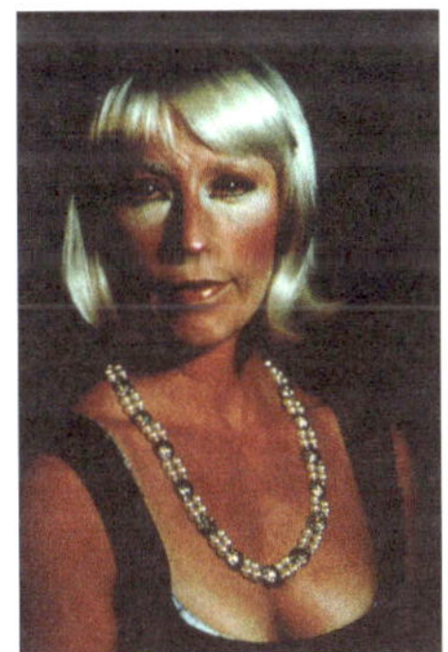

Untitled #403, 2000
Color photograph
Edition of 6
22 x 15 in.
(55.9 x 38.1 cm)

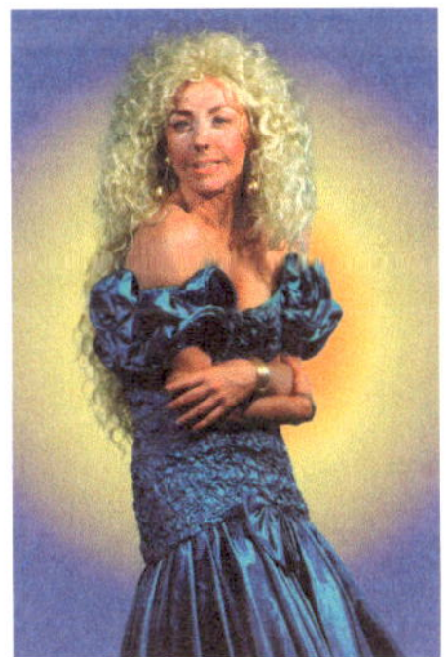

Untitled #408, 2002
Color photograph
Edition of 6
54 x 36 in.
(137.2 x 91.4 cm)

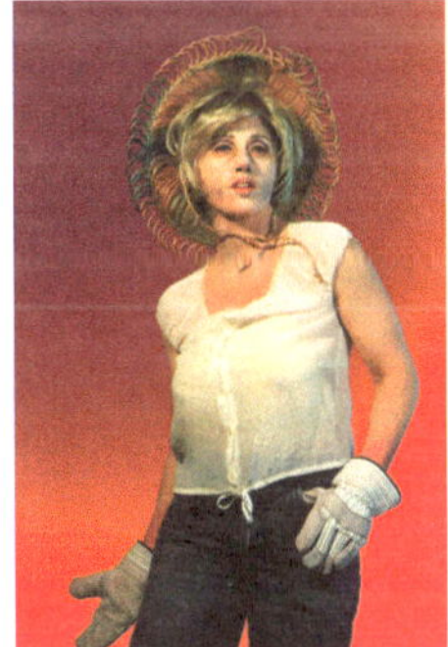

Untitled #409, 2002
Color photograph
Edition of 6 .
54 x 36 in.
(137.2 x 91.4 cm)

[Clowns]

2003 — 2004

The appearance of the clown in Cindy Sherman's work was, without doubt, inevitable. Sherman's taste for masquerades and dressing up, the mixture of the grotesque and the serious, her hysterical chameleonism, all combine to conjure the essence of clowns and clowning, hinted at in early works such as the *Untitled A* and *B* portraits, or (much later) photograph *#359* in the *Hollywood Types* series.

The clown is the logical extension of many fundamental themes in Cindy Sherman's work. But Sherman is now no longer interested in exploring the infinite potential of dressing up, disguise, and impersonation, the virtuoso game of borrowed identities that has unfolded so far. On the contrary, the *Clowns* series adopts a single, universally familiar type whose attributes remain more or less constant. Sherman's purpose is to suggest the range of physiognomies and facial expressions of emotion that may be glimpsed via the stereotype itself. The clown figures are the quintessential expression of the carnivalesque quality of Cindy Sherman's work, with its attendant load of contradictions and excess.

The disturbing quality of the traditional clown's makeup is widely acknowledged—there is an inescapable hint of ambivalence, depression, even perversity, beneath the cheery mask. Inevitably, too, clowns are associated with childhood, and the ambivalence of childhood. Cindy Sherman's clowns step outside the boundaries of convention governing their traditional costumes and makeup. The long, painted teeth in *#412* and *#424* suggest vampirism, while some of the faces sport disturbing expressions of bitterness and cruelty (such as *#413*, wearing a clown suit embroidered with the name "Cindy"), or sexual enticement (the figure in *#417*).

The occasional inclusion of several clowns in the same picture hints at a perverse, lecherous community of individuals, while the figure in *#426* suggests echoes of witchcraft, a black Sabbath, or shamanism. The extravagance of the costumes is heightened by the digitally produced backdrops, which accentuate the pictures' troubling, acid atmosphere. It is as if we were being sucked into an endless, dizzying spiral where bestiality, lust, and psychotic regression are increasingly apparent beneath the psychedelic veneer (as in *#419*). The clown, almost always a male figure in the traditional circus, is frequently feminized here, in keeping with Sherman's recurring reappropriation of sexual and social roles. But while the clown remains an explicitly sexual figure in this series (the breasts in *#419*, or the hairpiece and wig in *#424*), the overall impression is of a hybrid creature, a kind of transgender mutant: our escort and guide as we plunge into the world of the grotesque. The clown may also represent a version of the "complete" artist: an actor/producer, equally at home with music, speech, or mime. Unlike Sherman's earlier series, the narrative element is completely absent here. The clown figure is highly expressive and communicative, but we are given no clue as to any other existence beyond the comic, unpredictable, "crazy" character revealed in the photographs. The clown makes no attempt to take the viewer back to his or her past, and plays no part in the recreation (or invention) of narrative events of any kind. We stand, with the clown, on the brink of infinite possibilities, waiting expectantly for the unimaginable performances that are still to come.

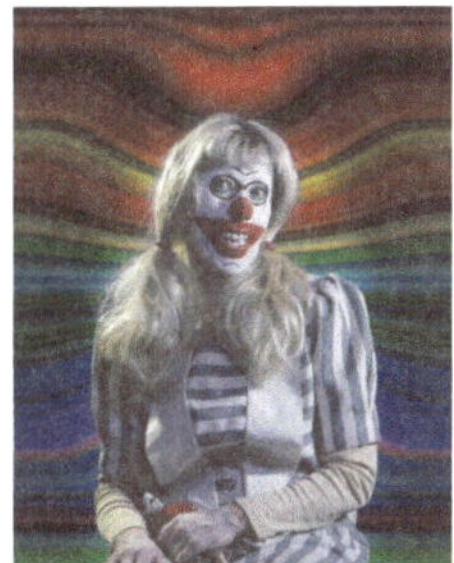

Untitled #412, 2003
Color photograph
Edition of 6
51 ¼ x 41 ¾ in.
(130.2 x 104.8 cm)

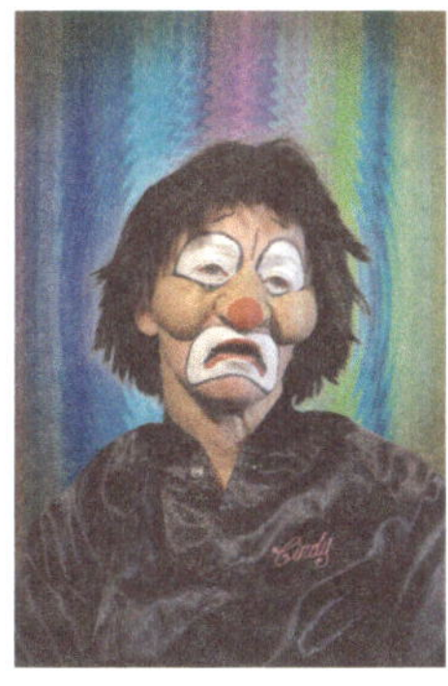

Untitled # 413, 2003
Color photograph
Edition of 6
46 x 31 in.
(116.8 x 79.1 cm)

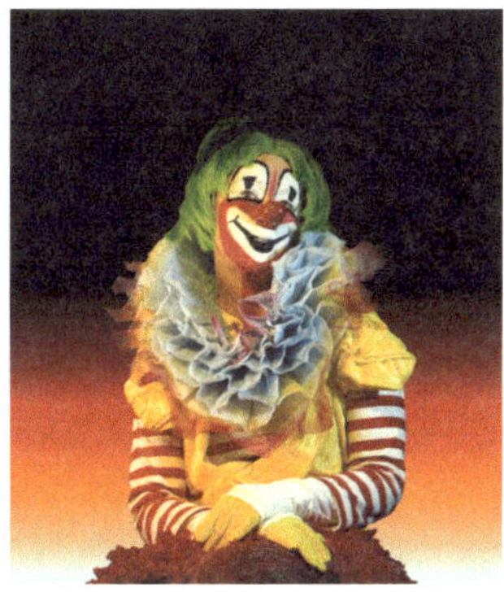

Untitled # 416
Color photograph
Edition of 6
55 x 48 ½ in.
(139.7 x 123.2 cm)

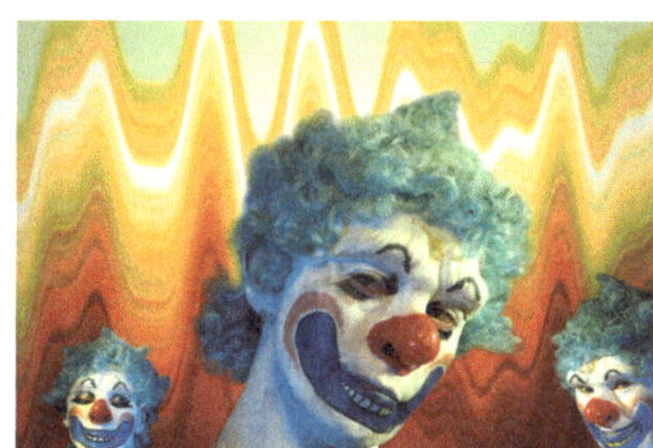

Untitled # 417, 2004
Color photograph
Edition of 6
60 x 90 in.
(152.4 x 228.6 cm)

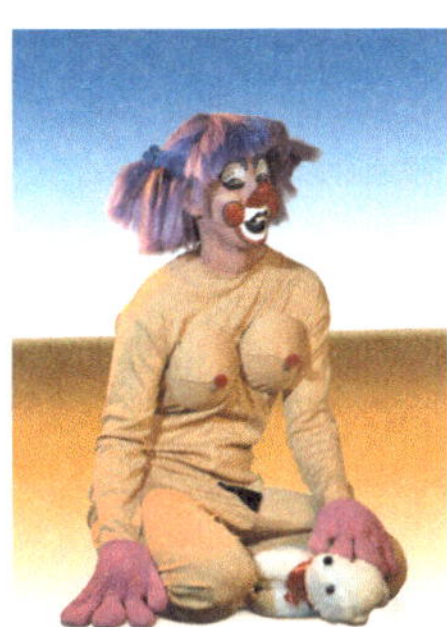

Untitled #419, 2004
Color photograph
Edition of 6
55 ½ x 48 ¼ in.
(141 x 122.6 cm)

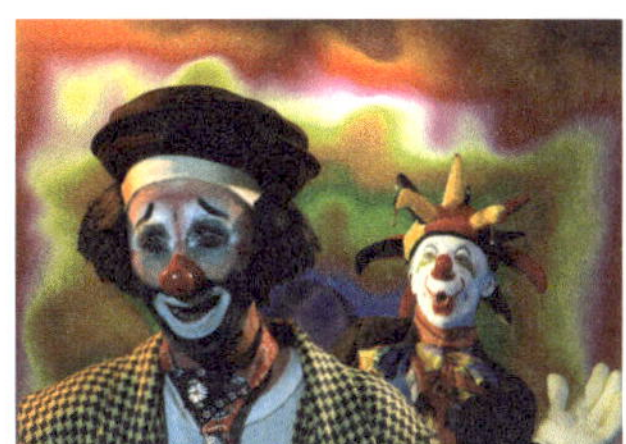

Untitled #421, 2004
Color photograph
Edition of 6
54 ⅞ x 78 ⅞ in.
(139.4 x 200.3 cm)

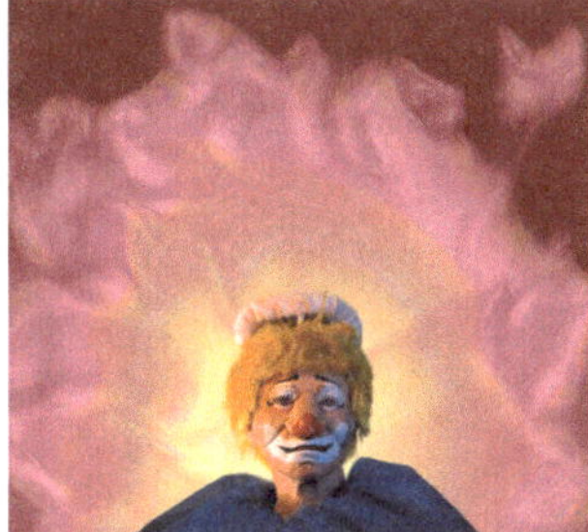

Untitled #422, 2004
Color photograph
Edition of 6
48 x 54 in.
(121.9 x 137.2 cm)

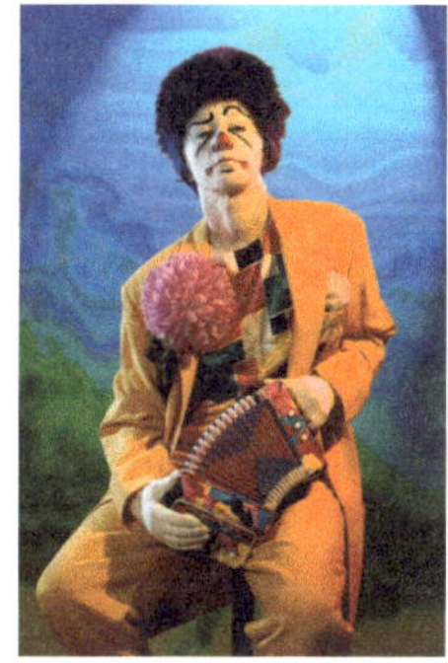

Untitled #423, 2004
Color photograph
Edition of 6
71 ¾ x 48 ½ in.
(182.2 x 123.2 cm)

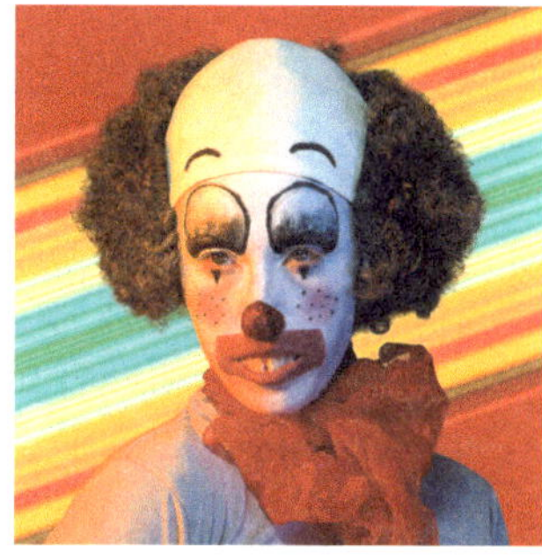

Untitled #424, 2004
Color photograph
Edition of 6
53 ½ x 54 ½ in.
(135.9 x 138.4 cm)

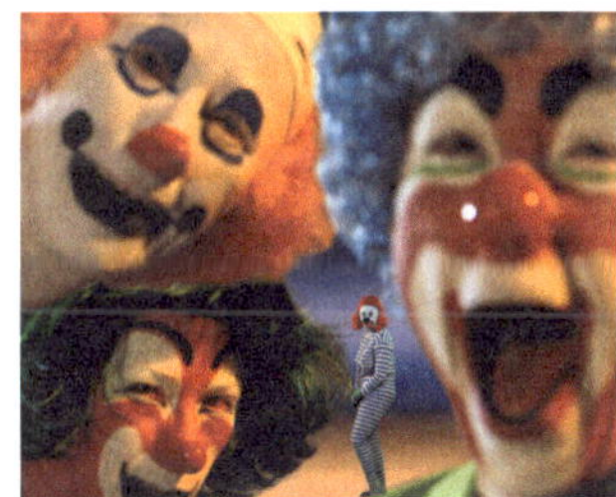

Untitled #425, 2004
Color photograph
Edition of 6
70 ½ x 89 ½ in.
(179.1 x 227.3 cm)

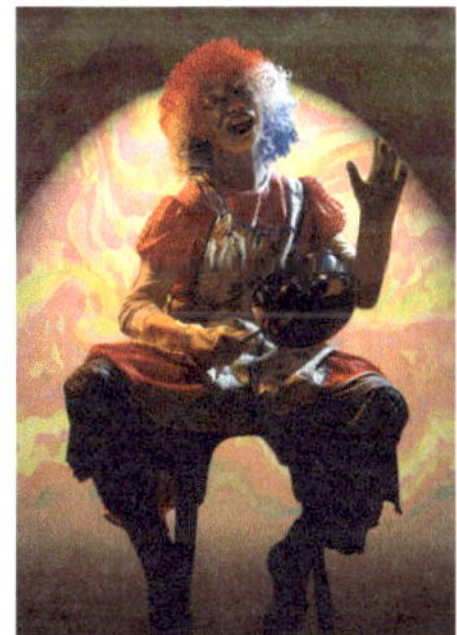

Untitled #426, 2004
Color photograph
Edition of 6
79 ½ x 54 in.
(201.9 x 137.2 cm)

JEAN-PIERRE CRIQUI

THE LADY VANISHES

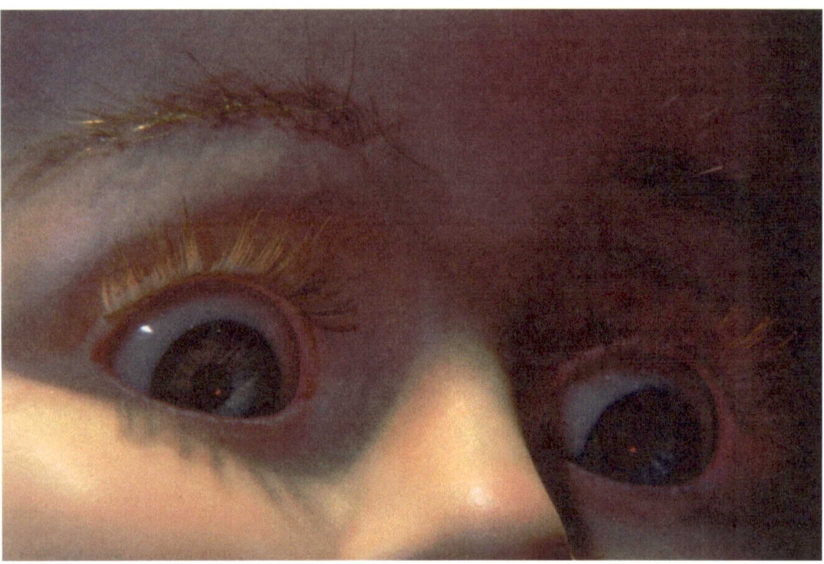

Untitled #267, 1992
Color photograph
26 ½ x 40 in.
(67.3 x 101.6 cm)

Untitled #267 (1992) is an image of extreme simplicity, filled almost completely by a pair of eyes trained on an unknown object situated beneath them, outside the picture frame. The picture features dramatic contrasts of light and shade that leave the fascinated gaze in shadow. "*Regarde de tous tes yeux, regarde!*" ("Look with all the power of your eyes, look!"). In Jules Verne's novel *Michel Strogoff*, the eponymous hero's order not to avert his gaze from the spectacle laid on for him by the dancers of Nijni-Novgorod foreshadows his imminent blinding with the white-hot blade of a saber.[1] Similarly, in Sherman's picture, we cannot fail to be struck by the dual nature of the gaze represented, at once vibrant and intense yet utterly disembodied. It constitutes a curious theater of vision, which is in a sense turned against itself, where we are given to see only that which, itself, sees nothing: the luscious lashes of a shop-window dummy or a doll, transfixed by a scene that we cannot justifiably say has been concealed from our own view, since it does not exist. *Untitled #267*—with its play on the living and the inanimate, concealment and display, the idea of "everything to see" and "nothing to be seen," and its reminder of the barely voiced connection between curiosity, prurience, and sexuality—is the closing image in the *Sex Pictures* series created by Cindy Sherman in 1992. Sherman's successful demonstration of this connection, by such strongly alienating and mildly ironic

1
Following this incident, Michel Strogoff miraculously recovers his sight. The phrase *Regarde de tous tes yeux, regarde!* is also the title of the French literary historian Jean-Yves Tadié's recent study of Jules Verne (Paris: Gallimard, 2005). It was quoted by Georges Perec as the epigraph to his 1978 novel *La Vie: Mode d'Emploi*, published in English as *Life: A User's Manual*, translated by David Bellos (Boston: D.R. Godine, 1987).

means, should come as no surprise. Throughout her work, Sherman (who, while still a student, represented herself in a short film as a paper doll coming to life),[2] has indeed engaged in an unceasing quest to combine a desperate urge to probe and devour, with a kind of reticence, or absence, rendered paradoxical by her near-constant recourse to the use of her own body as an element or central focus in her compositions. *Untitled #267* nonetheless falls into that small (but not, since the later 1980s, especially unusual) category of works in which Sherman herself does not appear. As such, the picture enacts all the more clearly this conscious attempt to disappear, the willful self-oblivion that seems to me to characterize Sherman's artistic endeavor, and which should be borne in mind as a kind of *basso continuo* to a reading of the remarks that follow.

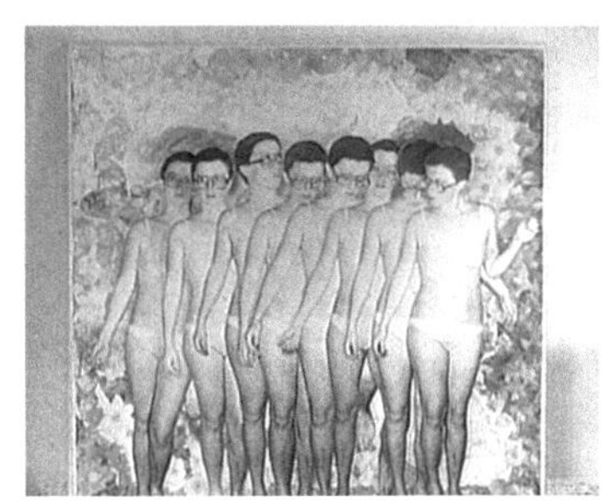

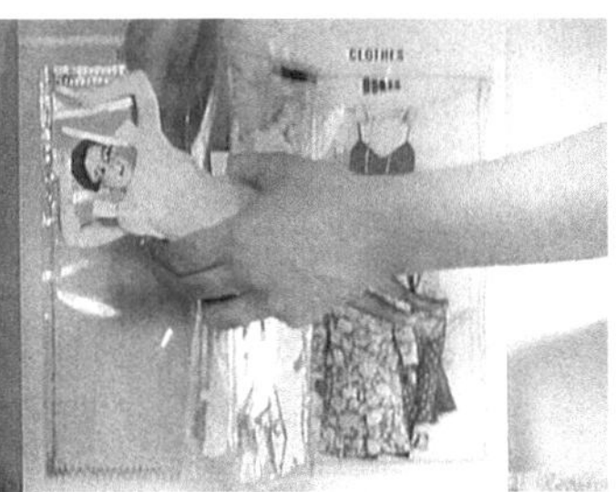

*

There is not a single image in Cindy Sherman's work that does not explore concepts of pretense and fabrication, staginess and simulation. She has succeeded quite conclusively in bringing photography into the realm of fiction. This is a radical relocation, of which Sherman's close contemporary Jeff Wall is the other noted exponent. Both artists have made parallel, significant contributions to the promotion of photography as a contemporary art form. For Sherman, the use of the photographic medium is inseparable from her decision to make herself the main instrument in her work, chiefly for practical purposes, as she has pointed out on several occasions:[3] never particularly authoritarian by nature, Sherman cannot envisage subjecting others to the sort of control which she feels is essential. As her own "model" she has also, she says, found the ideal solution to the problems of availability and autonomy experienced by so many artists when working with other people. She is free to work whenever and however she pleases. Clearly, then, the issue of identity—regarding the woman whose name guarantees only the *identification* of these works—may not be as crucial as some commentators would have us believe. *Cum grano salis*, we might even suggest that interpretations highlighting Sherman's apparent exploration of the nature of identity are shaped in part by a simplistic, "faithful," even credulous reading of her works. To take a random example: faced with the menacing stare of the

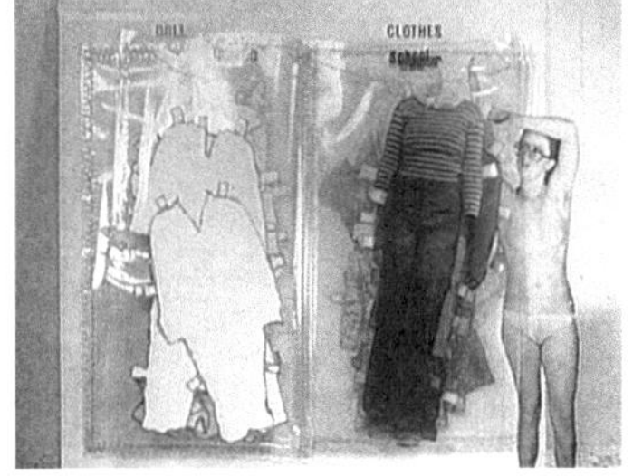

Doll Clothes, 1975
Super 8 film,
black and white, no sound,
2 minutes 22 seconds

2
Cindy Sherman, "The Making of *Untitled*," in *Cindy Sherman: The Complete Untitled Film Stills* (New York: The Museum of Modern Art, 2003): 5.

3
For example: "I wanted too much control to use someone else as a model" Xavier Douroux and Franck Gautherot, *"Conversation avec Cindy Sherman,"* in *Cindy Sherman, Succès du Bedac* 1, Dijon (1982): n.p. Or: "I wanted to work alone, because otherwise I acquiesce too easily" in "The Making of *Untitled*," in *Cindy Sherman: The Complete Untitled Film Stills* (New York: The Museum of Modern Art, 2003): p.11.

shady hoodlum in *Untitled #141*, our only comfort is a kind of collective "folk" awareness, almost at the level of a received idea, that Cindy Sherman herself is "under there somewhere," if I may be permitted an echo of the exclamation of Balzac's artist hero Frenhofer ("There's a woman under there!"; many aspects of Balzac's novel *The Unknown Masterpiece* seem to point to its interpretation as the story of a disappearance.) Above all, what difference would it make if we were not granted this comforting reassurance? If the model had not been Sherman herself? The image would remain the same; and it would still be a photograph *by* Cindy Sherman. Sherman admits no living model other than herself into her work. In so doing, she is far from engaging in some record-breaking shape-shifting marathon. Rather, she succeeds in gradually diminishing the importance of this type of inquiry. As has often been noted, there is no substitute for Cindy Sherman herself in her work, except in her "still lifes." In accordance with a process that has doubtless been at work since her earliest pictures, but which has become increasingly apparent in recent years, Sherman's very ubiquity has tended to neutralize the impact of her presence. Who could fail to see that this constraint, to which the artist has so willingly and graciously submitted, is the very characteristic (in the context of her work as a whole) that facilitates the remarkable diversity of Sherman's images; that her ostensibly limiting use of her self as the sole model in her work in fact provides the constant against which the dazzling panoply of variations is measured?

Like all works of fiction, Sherman's soliloquy suspends the distinction between what is true and what is false. In other words, the *pseudos*—the "falsehood" so roundly condemned by Plato and Aristotle—reigns supreme, allied to what the Second Sophistic referred to as *plasma* (from the verb *plassô*, meaning to shape, model, imagine, or feign), namely an assertion of the image's existence as a work of brilliant artifice, emphasizing its essential nature as an artificial construct.[4] A literary aesthetic shared in the visual arts, for example, by sixteenth-century mannerism and, in the twentieth century, by an entire branch of postmodernism to which Sherman has made a decisive contribution. One of the most notable aspects of Sherman's contribution is the way in which she has sought to make the fictional basis of her work more and more visible. In this context, the recent *Clowns* series (2003–04) is something of a manifesto. An outrageous

4
For more on the elaboration, usage, and implications of these concepts, see the remarkable book by Barbara Cassin, *L'Effet sophistique* (Paris: Gallimard, 1995): 470–87.

emblem of makeup and disguise (the two cardinal driving forces in Sherman's work), the clown is above all the pretext for a riot of color and form, emphasized still further by the gaudy backdrops featuring computer-generated designs and patterns (a technique first seen in Sherman's photographs of 2002, used here in combination with digital montage, which allows her to introduce group portraits into her work for the first time, for example *Untitled #417*, *#421* or *#425*). At the same time, as indicated in a revealing study by Jean Starobinski, "the choice of the clown image implies not only the endorsement of a pictorial or poetic motif, but also an alternative, parodic way of addressing the question of art itself . . . The artist's ironic game is an interpretation of the self, by the self: a mocking revelation of the true nature of art and the artist."[5] Hence our intimation that the *Clowns* series brings Sherman closer than ever before to a commentary on her existence *as an artist*. The clown in *Untitled #413*, wearing a top embroidered with the word "Cindy," adds nothing that has not already been insinuated by its fellows, unless we take it that the figure is making explicit (in the manner of an "open secret") the short-circuited, self-reflexive nature of the series as a whole (an oblique reminder of the Warholian apology for surface and seeming).[6] Because, in the final analysis, we are dealing with invented images, nothing more, nothing less: "Nothing has to make sense, you can just mix things up because they just look good together."[7]

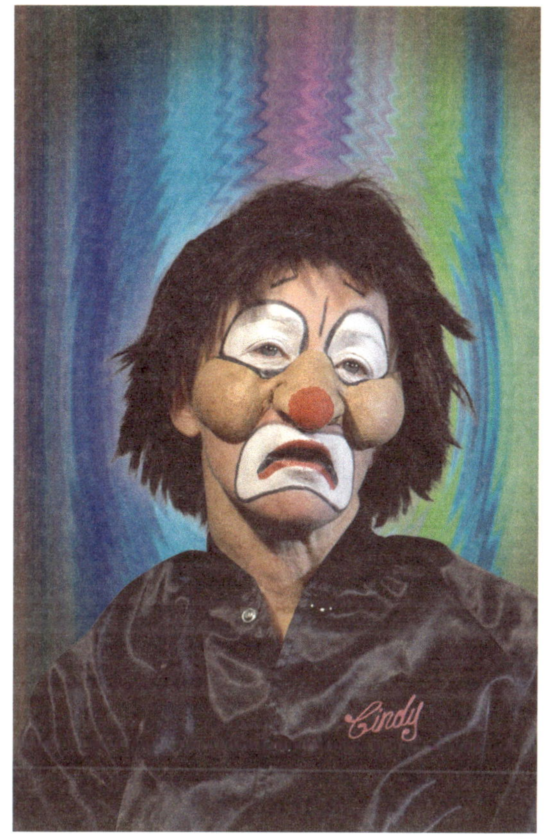

Untitled #413, 2003
Color photograph
Edition of 6
46 x 31 in. (116.8 x 79.1 cm)

Faced with an "image factory" of such proportions, the viewer's response is similar to that provoked by the Latin elegies of Tibullus, Propertius, or Ovid. As the French historian Paul Veyne has shown, their markedly ambiguous model of what constitutes fiction follows in the wake of the Hellenistic Greek poet Callimachus. The "I" of Callimachus' ancient hymns had already been appropriated to create a network of infinite reflections: "[Callimachus] profits from the apparent polyvalence of the hymnic 'I' to draw a literary procedure from it

5 Jean Starobinski, *Portrait de l'artiste en saltimbanque*, new edition, revised and corrected by the author (Paris: Gallimard, 2004): 8–9.

6 An apology which is brilliantly condensed in Jean-Claude Lebensztejn's text on Warhol, "*Braille Mental*" (Mental Braille) in *Critique*, 522, November 1990: 875-890. Among his sources, Lebensztejn cites the German Romantic poet Novalis (Friedrich von Hardenberg), who put it, "The exterior is really only . . . a higher level of interiority." We might also remember Paul Valéry's aphorism, that man's skin is his greatest depth.

7 Cindy Sherman in conversation with Isabelle Graw: "No Make-Up," in *Cindy Sherman: Clowns*, catalog of an exhibition at the Hanover Kestnergesellschaft (Munich: Schirmer/Mosel, 2004): 60.

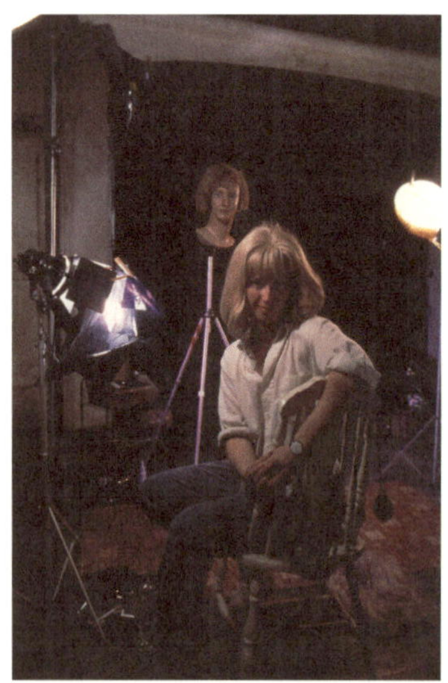

Untitled, 1983
Color photograph
20 x 16 in.
(50.8 x 40.6cm)

that will allow him to place himself, as an artist, apart from other men. He makes himself a ventriloquist. The chorus, its leader, the crowd, everybody speaks; reality breaks up into exclamations, orders, and interrogations. . . . This absence of a coherent point of view decenters what the text says."[8] The "Cindy" that we contemplate here is of the same stuff as Propertius' Cynthia, whose loves were hymned at the end of the first century B.C. This is art indeed, a decoy by which we are only half-deceived, which never forgets to signify its artificial nature, and which is similar, in this regard, to the decoy assembled by the poet for his readers: "Roman erotic elegy is a photomontage of feelings and typical situations of the life of passion outside of the everyday forms, presented in the first person."[9] This is why the question "Who Does Cindy Sherman Think She Is?" posed on the cover of *Art News* in September 1983, will always ring hollow. The question was, in any case, completely (even somewhat comically) undermined by the accompanying photograph, taken by the artist herself, showing Sherman sitting in her studio with her shirt-sleeves rolled up, gazing into the lens, flanked by two powerful arc-lamps trained on her figure, and a hairdresser's dummy placed on a tripod. But how does this improvised self-portrait differ from the *Untitled Film Stills* or the *Centerfolds* with which Sherman first made her name as an artist? What does the image tell us about its subject, beyond the fact that her work is comprised of lighting, wigs, and a spotlight on her own metamorphic abilities? Cindy Sherman the artist has made her work in her own image: each picture relates only to itself, and to the circumstances and processes of its creation. The images never open a door onto some other life or inner world that predates or lies beyond the world of the picture. Photographic work of this kind is, then, diametrically opposed to the world of photoreportage, which stakes its existence on its transparency and honesty. Nor are we in any way close to the work of Nan Goldin, another American woman photographer of Sherman's generation, whose vocation to record ostensibly non-mediatized

8
Paul Veyne, *Roman Erotic Elegy: Love, Poetry and the West*, translated by David Pellauer (Chicago: University of Chicago Press, 1988): 22.

9
Ibid., p. 36.

10
For an initial analysis of the "realist" hypotheses underpinning Goldin's pictures, and the ways in which these have influenced commentaries on her work, see Marie Bottin, "*La critique en dépendance. La réception de l'œuvre de Nan Goldin en France*," *Études photographiques* 17 (November 2005): 67–85.

glimpses of her subjects' lives presupposes a certain rhetoric of "truth" and a belief in the possibility of breaking out of the cycle of representation.[10]

*

Sherman's work is an extension and intensification of childhood through art: "As a kid I would play 'dress-ups' and even at SUNY I had all this makeup. I just wanted to see how transformed I could look. It was like painting in a way: staring at my face in a mirror, trying to figure out how to do something to this part of my face, how to shade another part."[11] We are reminded of Bruce Nauman's *Art Make-Up* (1967–68), the simultaneous projection of four films recording his own gradual transformation into black-and-white, using a mirror. In the same way, all of Sherman's early images (and a large part of her later work) are the result of a process of "self painting" rather than self-portraiture as such.[12] Added to this is the artist's quite remarkable "fictional skill," to borrow a phrase from Jean-Marie Schaeffer's study *Pourquoi la Fiction?* ("Why Fiction?"). Schaeffer reminds us of how far an adult talent for fiction stems from childhood games and how, most significantly, it is constructed from a common fund of images and representations:

> If the representational skills at my disposal are indeed my own, I am—on the other hand—only very marginally responsible for the sources of the content of my representations. This is a corollary of the fact that the first things we learn (and hence the representations that inform our learning) are only partly the result of our tentative empirical experiments, based on trial and error. In truth, they are absorbed mostly through the assimilation (which may be mimetic but also, of course, verbal) of existing representations in the public domain . . . From this standpoint, even the most solitary form of fictional activity inevitably falls short of solipsism: based on representational materials that, for the most part, fall within the established cultural repertoire, it is, from the outset, a partially shared reality.[13]

A photograph taken in 1977 by Helene Winer, showing "the secretary at Artists Space" (an alternative art space in SoHo, New York, where Sherman worked) testifies to the persistence of a taste

11
In conversation with Gerald Marzorati, "Imitation of Life," in *Art News* (September 1983): 85. This article remains one of the most useful sources for an understanding of Sherman's work.

12
See the author's own article *"Pour un Nauman,"* in *Un trou dans la vie. Essais sur l'art depuis 1960* (Paris: Desclée de Brouwer, 2002), especially pp.170–72.

13
Jean-Marie Schaeffer, *Pourquoi la fiction?* (Paris: Seuil, 1999): 232–33. Later in the book, Schaeffer makes a brief reference to Sherman and emphasizes her role in establishing photography within the world of fiction. One of the "attractions" of her work lies, he says, in the fact that "in reality, we are constantly invited to alternate between a posture of fictional immersion and the classic 'referentialist' attitude." (p. 294). Obviously, the indexical nature of the medium itself makes this alternation inevitable. However, it seems to me that Sherman's increasingly frequent and wholescale transformations, and the self-effacement which they induce, work continuously, and quite deliberately, to reduce the extent and impact of simple "indication" in her photography. The to-ing and fro-ing described by Schaeffer (and which is inherent in all the recording-based arts) is far more noticeable in other contexts: in Mankiewicz's film *The Barefoot Contessa*, for example, we are every bit as engrossed in Ava Gardner's personal beauty as we are in the story of the checkered career of her character, Maria Vargas. Sherman's images do not, it seems to me, work in at all the same way.

14
Winer's photograph is reproduced in *Cindy Sherman: The Complete Untitled Film Stills* (New York: The Museum of Modern Art, 2003): 11.

for dressing up as part of everyday life, long after her childhood, and even after her student years. The picture was taken at the around the same time as the first *Untitled Film Stills*, and clearly highlights the sliding scale that operates between Sherman's real-life "roles" and her pictures.[14]

On the subject of Sherman's working method, in particular the use of the camera to take shots at regular intervals while adopting a range of poses and "mimes" in front of the mirror, Sherman has said: "I don't feel that I *am* that person. I may be thinking about a certain story or situation, but I don't *become* her. There's this distance. The image in the mirror becomes her—the image the camera gets on the film. And the one thing I've always known is that the camera lies."[15] These last words are thrown into even greater relief when we consider them in light of the cinematographic (and, of course, photographic) intertext favored by the artist, whose work, like an untruth told about another untruth, emerges as a construct founded on representations that are wholly traversed by the "power of falsehood" in which she exalts. Part of the debate over the relationship between the *Untitled Film Stills* and the world of cinema has focused on the extent and depth of the pictures' cinematic references. In her extended essay on Sherman's work, Rosalind Krauss—faithful to the postmodernist art theory of which she herself was the principal architect—defends the idea of the *Untitled Film Stills* as "copies without originals," and prefaces her text with the following quote from the artist herself: "Some people have told me that they remember the film that one of my images is derived from, but in fact I had no film in mind at all."[16] I agree with Krauss, but at the same time we should remember that Sherman has often gone on the record with quite contradictory statements, as here, in a comment on the *Untitled Film Still #35* (1979): "For the woman standing in front of my studio, I thought of a film with Sophia Loren, *Two Women*."[17] Ultimately, the distinction is of little importance. Given the process-based aspect of Sherman's work, in which her pictures emerge as the product of an extended game of poses and props, it becomes clear that she has never set out simply to "transfer" a series of

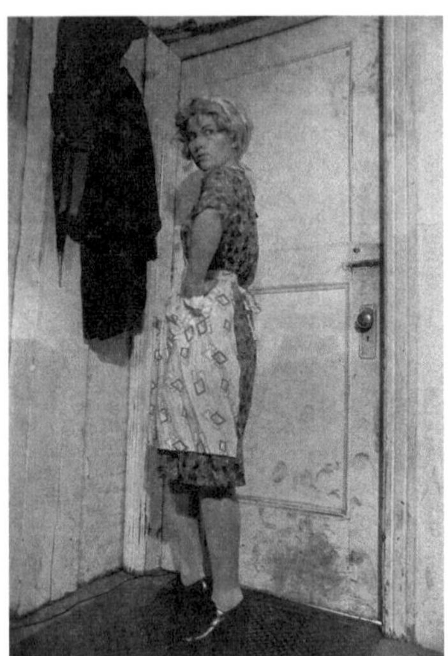

Untitled Film Still #35, 1979
Black-and-white photograph
10 x 8 in.
(25.4 x 20.3 cm)

15
In conversation with Gerald Marzorati, "Imitation of Life," in *Art News* (September 1983): 81. In *The Notebooks of Malte Laurids Brigge*, the German poet Rainer Maria Rilke gives a magnificent description of this mixture of distance and equivocal malaise, experienced by a child in fancy dress gazing at its reflection in a mirror: "Ah, how one trembled to be in there, and how ravishing when one was. When out of the dimness something drew near, more slowly than oneself, for the mirror did not, so to speak, believe it, and did not want, sleepy as it was, to repeat promptly what had been said to it. But naturally, it had to in the end. And now it was something very surprising, strange, altogether different from one's expectation, something sudden, independent, which one rapidly surveyed, only in the next instant to recognize oneself after all, not without a certain irony which came within a hairsbreadth of spoiling all the fun. But if one promptly began to talk, to bow, if one nodded to oneself, walked away, constantly looking round, and then came back, brisk and determined, one had imagination siding with one as long as one liked," translated by M. D. Herter Norton (New York: W.W. Norton & Co. Inc., 1940): 91.

16
See Rosalind Krauss, "Cindy Sherman: Untitled," in *Cindy Sherman 1975–1993* (New York: Rizzoli, 1993): 17. Sherman's quote was first published in an interview with Lisbet Nilson in *American Photographer*, September 1983.

17
The film's original title is *La Ciociara*, by Vittorio De Sica. The quote appears in an interview with Else Barent in *Cindy Sherman, Clowns* (Munich: Schirmer/Mosel, 1984): 8. Talking to Marzorati about *Untitled #118* (1983), Sherman refers to "a Judy Garland and Mickey Rooney movie," in conversation with Gerald Marzorati, "Imitation of Life," in *Art News* (September 1983): 79.

18
The term "library of stereotypes" is used by Victor Burgin to describe the repertoire of images and narratives left us by the world of cinema, before we are even aware of it. See *The Remembered Film* (London: Reaktion Books, 2004): 17.

pre-established characters or situations into her photographs. Rather, the library of stereotypes from which she borrows (and to which she contributes) inevitably revives often quite unconnected, and more or less clearly defined, memories and associations in both the artist and viewer.[18]

The "perfume of cinema" that suffuses Sherman's earliest photographs is what the critic Roland Barthes termed "filmic": a fugitive emanation as far removed from film itself as the novelistic is from the novel, and for which the "film still" is indeed the ideal vehicle.[19] Because they do not refer to any specific film, the *Untitled Film Stills* are a marvelous demonstration of what Barthes has already observed in "real" film stills: they are both "parodic" and calculated to communicate a message. They should not be seen as "samples," but rather as "quotations."[20] The series comes closest to parody in images that hint at autobiographical as well as cinematographic references—the "student" in *#13* (1978) for example, surrounded by books such as *The Structure of Art*, *American Art Since 1900*, or even *The Movies*. In a similar, albeit more coded, vein, Sherman has indicated that she is wearing her mother's wedding dress in *#11* (1978), and that the photograph of the "young man" on the bedside table in *#33* (1979) is another of her many transformations, just like the young woman sitting on the bed.[21] A closer look at *#34* (1979) reveals that the book on the bed beside the would-be femme fatale is the novel *A Prologue to Love* (1962) by Taylor Caldwell (1900–85), a well-known woman writer and a familiar local personality in the town of Buffalo, where Sherman studied and produced her early works. The communicative, "broadcast" power of the film still, through which each of us invests the diegetic horizon suggested by the picture with our own imaginings, is allied here to the desire to create art that is rooted in a wide-ranging shared culture. Asked about her beginnings, Sherman explained: "I didn't want to make 'high' art. I had no interest in using paint. I wanted to find something that anyone could relate

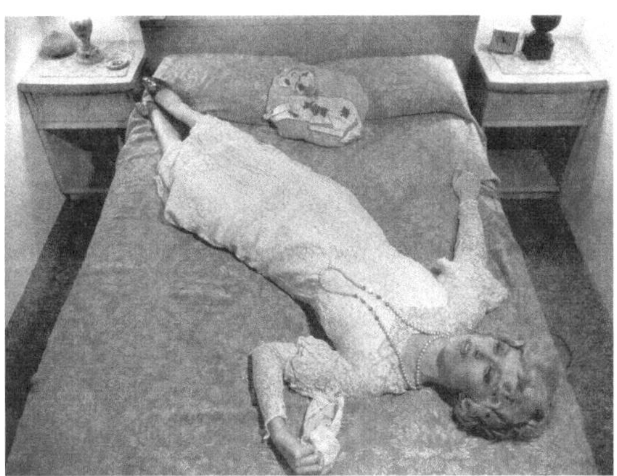

Untitled Film Still #11, 1978
Black-and-white photograph
8 x 10 in.
(20.3 x 25.4 cm)

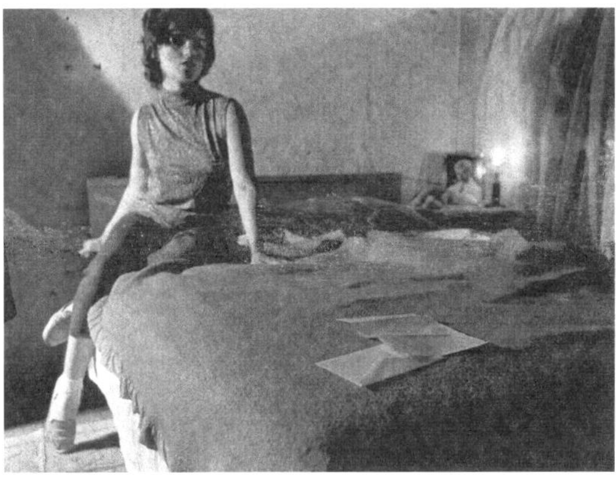

Untitled Film Still #33, 1979
Black-and-white photograph
8 x 10 in.
(20.3 x 25.4 cm)

19
Roland Barthes, *The Third Meaning* (1970) and *L'obvie et l'obtus* (Paris: Seuil, 1982): 59–61.

20
Ibid., p. 60.

21
See "The Making of *Untitled*," in *Cindy Sherman: The Complete Untitled Film Stills* (New York: The Museum of Modern Art, 2003): 11 and 10.

22
"Cindy Sherman Talks to David Frankel," *Artforum*, March 2003, p. 54.

23
See, for example, Cindy Sherman's own untitled preface in *Cindy Sherman, Succès du Bedac 1*, Dijon (1982): "Recently, music has become more of a stimulation to me, as it leaves the imagination to conjure up all sorts of images, not unlike how I'd want my photos to function."

to without knowing about contemporary art."[22] Sherman is alluding here to her "pop" ambitions (in the double sense of Pop Art, and "pop" music). Indeed, the important influence of British and American punk and New Wave music on the visual arts has gone largely unnoticed, despite one or two explicit statements from Sherman herself.[23] This affinity with punk is also noticeable when we look at Sherman's description of her state of mind for some of the photographs (such as those using clothes by Dorothée Bis, the quintessential "punk" fashion designer), in which she spontaneously presents herself as a member of the "blank generation" hymned a few years earlier by Richard Hell: "I wanted to get rid of the idea that these clothes would make me look beautiful. I wanted to go blank."[24]

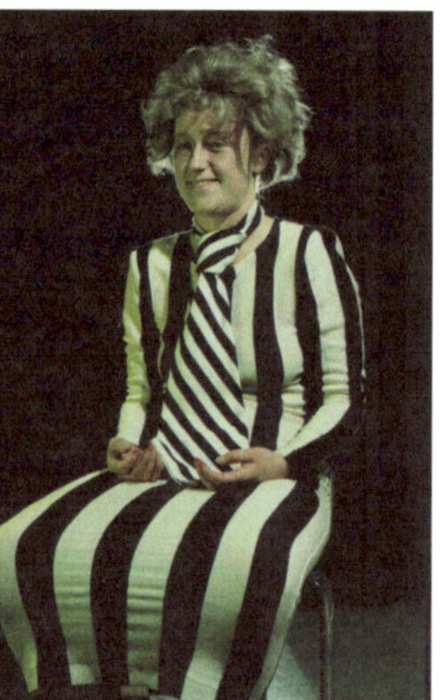

Untitled #137, 1984
Color photograph
70 ½ x 48 in.
(179.1 x 121.3 cm)

Untitled #138, 1984
Color photograph
71 x 48 ½ in.
(180.3 x 123.2 cm)

This wholesale rejection of beauty quickly progressed to an exploration of the morbid and disturbing. From 1984, the seemingly autistic, withdrawn, defeated figure in green, in *Untitled #133*, or the two crazed characters in *#137* and *#138* (both with blood on their hands, one smiling, the other not) are a foretaste of things to come. Increasingly, Sherman's pictures go on to feature the lurid tonalities of nightmare or Grand Guignol. I find these images—completely lacking the seductive quality of the *Untitled Film Stills*, the *Centerfolds*, or the dreamy young women of 1982—extremely difficult and challenging. They have, it seems to me, gradually "fallen out of love" with the viewer, heaping scorn and ridicule on the latter's aspiration to any form of empathy or enjoyment. They herald the omnipresence of death, and its attendant signs and symbols.

*

Sherman's work charts one of the most astonishing journeys in Western art of the past three decades. The transition from her somewhat severe early images in black-and-white, to the excesses of color and "special effects" in her later works, parallels that seen in the work of Frank Stella, from his *Black Paintings* onward (the similarities are structural, rather than content-based, but this serves to heighten their common urge for

24
Reported by Marzorati, "Imitation of Life," in *Art News* (September 1983): 81. Later in the same article, Sherman states that she bought about twelve music albums per week, and that she frequently listened to the British group The Gist during the sessions for these pictures. The album *Blank Generation* by Richard Hell and The Voivoids dates from 1977: "I belong to the blank generation and / I can take it or leave it each time" says the refrain of the New York punk anthem of the same name, in which Hell also states: "It's such a gamble when you get a face / It's fascinating to observe what the mirror does / But when I dine it's for the wall that I set a place." A few lost souls may remember that the New York Dolls' 1973 debut album opened with the song "Personality Crisis" and the words: "And you're a prima ballerina on a spring afternoon / Change on into the wolfman howlin' at the moon."

renewal). Stella's plainly evident, growing taste for the shocking, violent, and traumatic also mimics the path taken by cinema itself: Cindy Sherman, from George Cukor to Wes Craven.[25] By "mimics," I also mean to imply "rails against": a derisive polemic is permanently at work in these pictures. Like the motley, red-nosed Auguste clown, whose every action is guaranteed to undermine the poise and solemnity of his partner, the Whiteface clown, Sherman's work, whatever its apparent avowed intent, always seems to be simultaneously throttling the life out of some established "monument." Take, for example, her exploration of photography in the *Bus Riders* series (1976–2005), comprising fifteen pictures from her earliest period, in which the artist plays a succession of types (male and female) observed on public transportation in her home city of Buffalo. We are reminded, above all, of Walker Evans's photographs of passengers taken unawares on the New York subway, between 1938 and 1941.[26] However, Sherman, by placing herself both behind and in front of the camera, drains her images of any impression of reality, and offers in exchange a half-amused, half-sardonic representation of the characteristics that make each person a representation in themselves.

In the *History Portraits*, created in 1989–90 on the theme of Old Master paintings, Sherman unleashes the full blast of her iconoclastic verve. False noses, false breasts, cheap costume jewelry, everyday fabrics, and thickly plastered makeup are assembled under dazzling, bright light: the joke shop takes its revenge on the museum. As in the *Untitled Film Stills*, the references are precise in some cases, and more fragmented in others (although such judgments are, of course, always dependent on the viewer's personal cultural baggage). The overall impression is of an unsavory cultural minestrone, floating with bits of Fouquet, Raphael, Rubens, Fragonard, and Ingres. Paradoxically, *Untitled #224* (1990), a direct recasting of Caravaggio's *Bacchino Malato* ("Sick Little Bacchus") is one of the least caricatural pictures in the series. Sherman's figure is unaffected by the sallow, jaundiced complexion that is so suggestive of sickness in the original, and is further distinguished by the omission of two peaches from the foreground of the picture—

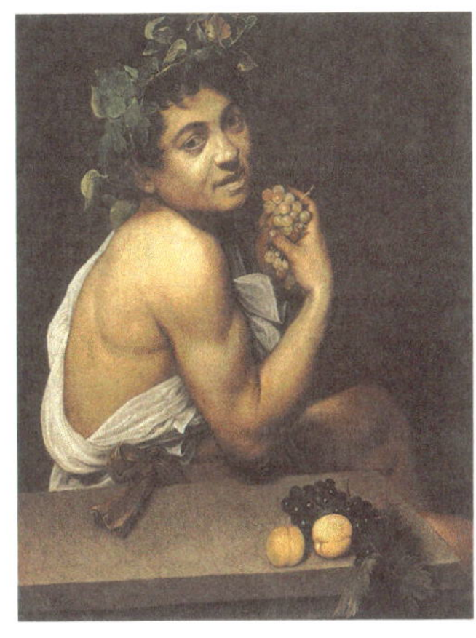

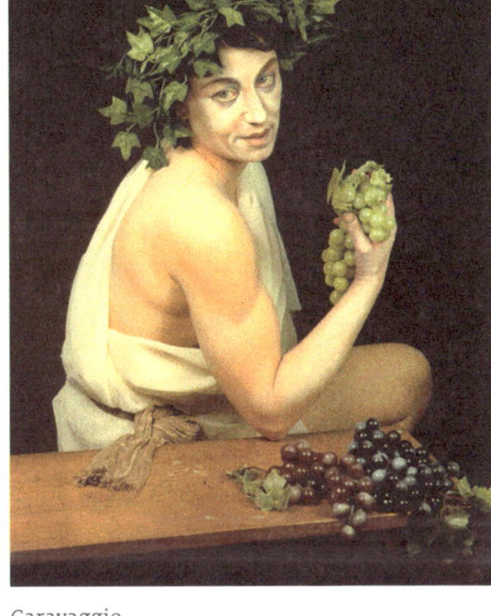

Caravaggio
Little Sick Bacchus, c. 1593
Oil on canvas
26 ½ x 21 in.
(67 x 53 cm)
Galleria Borghese, Rome

Untitled #224, 1990
Color photograph
48 x 38 in.
(121.9 x 96.5 cm)

25 On the rise of violence in American cinema, see the pioneering study by Carmen Shindy, *Harmed in Sync. Structure and Function of Violence in the Movies* (Widworth, Mass.: Crawford & Lauper, 1969).

26 Walker Evans's subway photographs were first published by Houghton Mifflin in 1966 under the title *Many Are Called*. The book was republished in 2004 by the Metropolitan Museum of Art in New York and Yale University Press, with the original introduction by James Agee and two essays by Luc Sante and Jeff L. Rosenheim.

naturally enough, when we consider that this pair of barely allegorized balls has no place in Sherman's version, given the sex of the artist gazing at us from beneath the thick makeup and garland of leaves. Caravaggio's *Bacchino Malato* is popularly held to be a self-portrait. *Untitled #224* is, then, a picture of a female artist impersonating a male artist impersonating a pagan divinity—a complex, multilayered representation that is also highly unusual, since it superimposes two relatively little used forms of self-portraiture. The first is that of the historiated self-portrait, in which the artist presents himself as a historical or mythological figure, like Caravaggio as the *Bacchino*, or Goliath in his *David and Goliath* (both in the Galleria Borghese in Rome). Other examples exist, of which Dürer's celebrated portrait of himself as Christ, painted in 1500, in the Alte Pinakotek in Munich, is perhaps the best known. The second type of self-portrait (a sub-group of the first type) is rarer still, namely the "portrait of the artist as another artist." Towards the end of his life, Rembrandt, who had already portrayed himself as the apostle Paul (in a painting now in the Rijksmuseum, Amsterdam), painted a *Self-Portrait as Zeuxis* inspired by a legend popularized in the 1604 *Book of Painting* by the Dutch writer Karel Van Mander. The legend tells how the ancient Greek painter Zeuxis, who had recorded the features of Helen of Troy, eventually died of laughter while painting the portrait of an ugly old woman.[27]

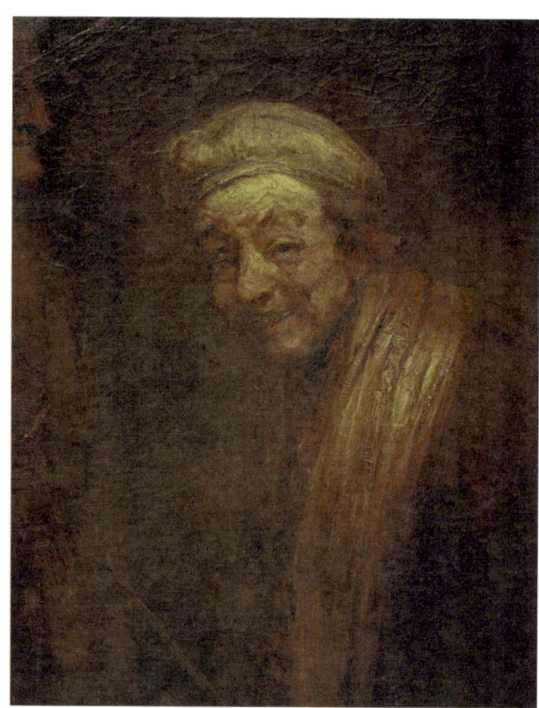

Rembrandt
Self Portrait as Zeuxis, c. 1662
Oil on canvas
32 ½ x 25 ½ in.
(82.5 x 65 cm)
Wallraf-Richartz-Museum, Cologne

To laugh, die, and be reborn. The classic cycle of Carnival. *Sia ammazzato!* ("To death!") was a cry still heard not so long ago at Roman carnival celebrations. In the best spirit of carnivalesque "misrule" the *History Portraits* are after the head (quite literally) of painting itself, the "high art" that Sherman has always sought to hijack and undermine. In its place, the series enthrones photography (the mechanical servant of painting, that Cinderella of the arts), which rises to the challenge with all the glee of a misshapen peasant girl jumping into a princess's bed. The usurper displays bodies compiled from an assortment of disparate parts, poorly

27
See Christopher White and Quentin Buvelot, eds., *Rembrandt by Himself* (London: National Gallery/The Hague: Mauritshuis, 1999): 216–19. This catalog refers to one other example of a *Self-portrait as Zeuxis*, iconographically more explicit than Rembrandt's version, and atributed to Rembrandt's pupil Arent de Gelder (1685, now in the Städelsches Kunstinstitut, Frankfurt).

28
See M. M. Bakhtin, *Rabelais and his World*, translated by Hélène Iswolsky (Cambridge, Mass.: MIT Press, 1968). Interestingly, Cindy Sherman featured in the 2004 exhibition "Disparities and Deformations: Our Grotesque," curated by Robert Storr at the Fifth International Santa Fe Biennial.

proportioned and shoddily assembled: the "grotesque body" described by the Russian art historian and literary theorist Mikhaïl Bakhtin, in his work on Rabelais, as perpetually unfinished and incomplete, always under construction, and itself engaged in the process of constructing another body altogether.[28] Renaissance grotesques, inspired by the rediscovery of murals in the Domus Aurea (the palace of the Roman emperor Nero, preserved in the foundations of the Baths of Trajan), took a similar morbid delight in hybrid and monstrous forms.[29] In exactly the same way, Sherman highlights the creation of a world where formal invention, fantasy, and satire reign supreme.

Complementing this fascination with the hybrid and grotesque, Sherman's images also share mannerism's love of masks. The first mask to be featured in Sherman's work is probably the diving mask in *Untitled Film Stills #45* and *#46* (1979), a plain glass "window" that conceals nothing, and which the wearer has pushed up onto her forehead (in #45), revealing a face which we are therefore tempted to consider (mistakenly, no doubt) as naked, guileless, and "unprepared." (Indeed, the exclusion of the classic "nude," and unfaked nudity of any sort, from Sherman's essential artistic vocabulary, constitutes one of the most important unifying elements in her work.) From 1985 onward, we see the appearance of a terrifying series of masks, complementing Sherman's exploration of more fantastical, macabre subject matter in her compositions. *Untitled #140* (1985), *Untitled #180* (1987), and *Untitled #191* (1989), among many others, revive ancestral fears, the terrors of infancy, and the nameless *larvae* engendered by the commingling of the animal and the human: "Like the Latin word *larva*, meaning both specter and an instrument of disguise, the [French] word *masque* and the Italian *maschera* (from which it derives) were used in the past to indicate a ghoul, a spectral creation of a demonic nature."[30] Cindy Sherman's play on the use of masks shows occasional similarities to the work of other photographers, such as Ralph Eugene Meatyard (d. 1972).[31] Meatyard often used rubber masks like those seen in Sherman's series *Untitled #314 A, B, C, D, E,* and *F* (1995), cut up and reassembled in absurd configurations which fill the picture space completely. The theme of masks invites infinite

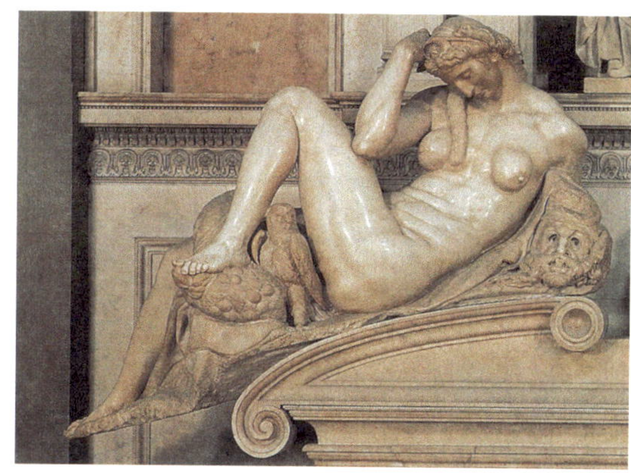

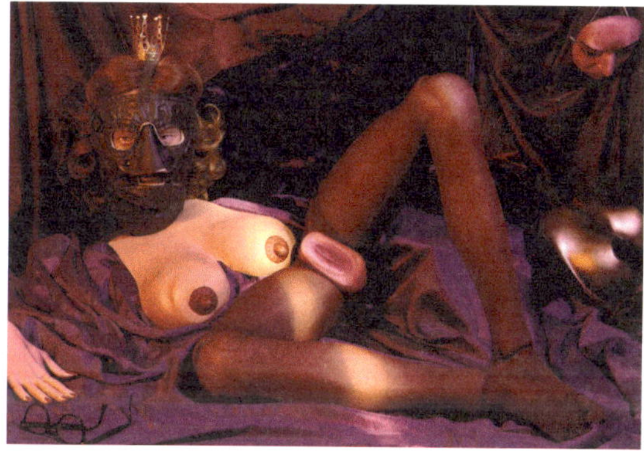

Michelangelo Night, 1526–31
Marble
76 ½ in (194 cm)
Tomb of Guiliano de' Medici, Medici Chapel, San Lorenzo, Florence

Untitled #264, 1992
Color photograph
50 x 75 in.
(127 x 190.5 cm)

29
See Philippe Morel's seminal study, *Les Grotesques. Les figures de l'imaginaire dans la peinture italienne de la fin de la Renaissance* (Paris: Flammarion, 1997).

30
André Chastel, *"Masque, mascarade, mascaron,"* in *Fables, formes, figures*, vol. 1 (Paris: Flammarion, 1978): 250. Translator's version.

31
This similarity is noted by Elizabeth A. T. Smith in her chapter "The Sleep of Reason Produces Monsters," in *Cindy Sherman: Retrospective* (London: Thames & Hudson, 1998): 19–33. The photographs by Meatyard date from the 1960s and early 1970s. See James Rhem's book *Ralph Eugene Meatyard: The Family Album of Lucybelle Crater and Other Figurative Photographs* (New York: D.A.P., 2002). The back cover of this book features the following statement by Sherman: "Ralph Meatyard was one of only a few photographers who had any sort of influence on my 'photographic roots' . . . I believed in his bizarre, fictional world."

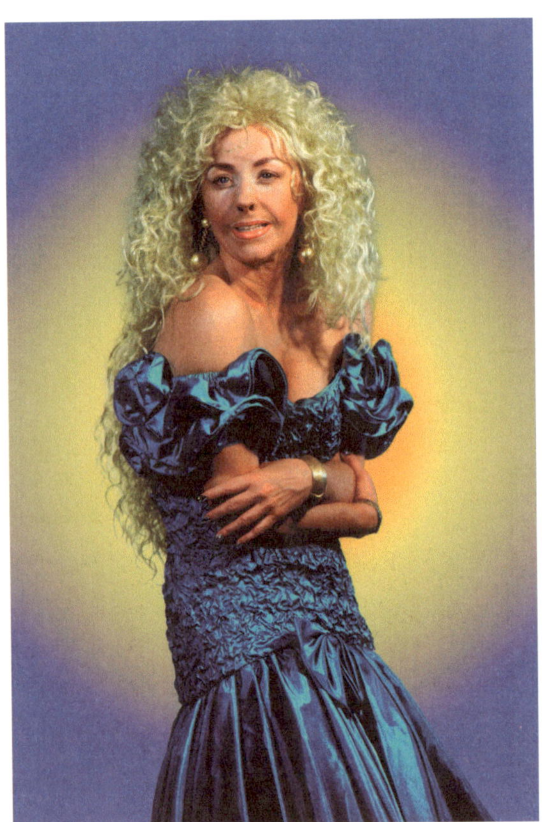

Untitled #408, 2002
Color photograph
54 x 36 in.
(137.2 x 91.4 cm)

comparisons; some viewers may see an echo of the carved mask beneath the figure of *Night* on Michelangelo's tomb for Giuliano de' Medici, in the New Sacristy at San Lorenzo in Florence. Similarly (and just as subjectively or arbitrarily) Sherman's photograph *Untitled #264* (1992)—which apes the fetishistic world of bondage and its particular representation in the photographs of Robert Mapplethorpe—is, for me, reminiscent of the reclining female nude wearing a gas mask in Edward Weston's photograph *Civilian Defense*, taken in 1942. On a purely personal level, my fascination for *Untitled #327* (1995) owes much to its connection with Marcel Schwob's novella *Le Roi au masque d'or*.

On another level, it goes without saying that makeup is a variation on the same theme. More than any other artist, Sherman has taken makeup to its utmost extreme, using it as a kind of weapon against the figures in her pictures. The *History Portraits* and numerous other, earlier works are animated by a kind of destructive frenzy (directed against art history in the case of the former); and there is also, it seems, an abhorrence of woman—a *horror mulieris*, like nature's *horror vacui*—in many of Sherman's images. Certainly, the pictures seem to express a horror of woman *as an image*. To take just two examples, *#359* (2000) and *#408* (2002) from the *Hollywood Portraits* series represent something of a tour de force (cathartic, perhaps) in the economy of their expression of the very "essence of the unbearable." The second woman—the optical equivalent of a gastric lavage—seems, like Herodias emerging from some murderous spree, to whisper lines from the French Symbolist poet Mallarmé's eponymous verse drama: "I love the horror of being virgin /and I wish to live in the terror my tresses make."[32]

32
Stéphane Mallarmé, *Herodias*, in *Selected Poems*, trans. C. F. MacIntyre, University of California Press, 1957.

*

Disguised and masked, the child experiences a moment of euphoria but then, in the transports of its own outrageous pantomime, commits some irreparable blunder, trips on its improvised costume, and, finally, turns its rage upon itself:

> Hot and angry, I rushed to the mirror and with difficulty watched the mask through the working of my hands. But for this the mirror had just been waiting. Its moment of retaliation had come. While I strove in boundlessly increasing anguish to squeeze somehow out of my disguise, it forced me, by what means I do not know, to lift my eyes and imposed on me an image, no, a reality, a strange, unbelievable and monstrous reality, with which, against my will, I became permeated: for now the mirror was the stronger, and I was the mirror. I stared at this great, terrifying unknown before me, and it seemed to me appalling to be alone with him. But at the very moment I thought this, the worst befell: I lost all sense, I simply ceased to exist. For one second I had an indescribable, painful, and futile longing for myself, then there was only he: there was nothing but he.[33]

Alone in front of the mirror, or behind the camera, Cindy Sherman, too, has gone beyond this nostalgic longing for the self, to create a body of work in which the endlessly reiterated exhibition of artifice transforms the making of her pictures image into their subject-matter. Here, all is mere fiction or "vision" (in the creative sense of a "dreamlike, chimerical image"). But there is, too, an effort to resist the temptations of idleness, expressed in an ironic, propitiatory manner in so many of the *Untitled* photographs (#179, for example, from 1987). That Sherman, in so doing, should disappear as a person, as an individual like everyone and no one else, is simply the necessary condition that allows her work to "emerge" most fully: "When concealment appears, concealment, having become appearance, makes 'everything disappear,' but of this 'everything has disappeared' it makes another appearance. It makes appearance from then on stem from 'everything has disappeared.' 'Everything has disappeared' appears."[34]

33
Rilke, *The Notebooks of Malte Laurids Brigge*, translated by M. D. Herter Norton (New York: W.W. Norton & Co. Inc., 1940): 94–95.

34
Maurice Blanchot, "The Essential Solitude and Solitude in the World," in *The Space of Literature*.

LAURA MULVEY

A PHANTASMAGORIA OF THE FEMALE BODY[1]

When I was in school I was getting disgusted with the attitude of art being so religious or sacred, so I wanted to make something which people could relate to without having read a book about it first. So that anybody off the street could appreciate it, even if they couldn't fully understand it; they could still get something out of it. That's the reason why I wanted to imitate something out of the culture, and also make fun of the culture as I was doing it.

Cindy Sherman [2]

Cindy Sherman's art is certainly postmodern. Her works are photographs; she is not a photographer but an artist who uses photography. Each image is built around a photographic depiction of a woman. And each of the women is Sherman herself, simultaneously artist and model, transformed, chameleon-like, into a glossary of pose, gesture and facial expression. As her work developed between 1977 and 1987 a strange process of metamorphosis took place. Apparently easy and accessible postmodern pastiche underwent a gradual transformation into difficult, but still accessible, images that raise serious and challenging questions for contemporary feminist aesthetics. And the metamorphosis provides a hindsight that then alters the significance of her early production. In order to work through the critical implications of this altered perspective, it is necessary to fly in the face of Sherman's own expressly non-, even anti-, theoretical stance. Paradoxically, it is because there is no explicit citation of theory in the work, no explanatory words, no linguistic signposts, that theory can come into its own. Sherman's work stays on the side of enigma, but as a critical

1
This essay was first published in the *New Left Review*, July–August 1991, coinciding with the display of a selection of Cindy Sherman's works at the Saatchi Gallery in London in a joint exhibition with Richard Artschwager and Richard Wilson that ran from 11 January to 28 July 1991. It was updated by the author for this publication.

2
Sandy Nairne, *The State of the Art. Ideas and Images in the 1980s*, Chatto & Windus, London 1987, p. 132.

challenge not as insoluble mystery. Figuring out the enigma, deciphering its pictographic clues, applying the theoretical tools associated with feminist aesthetics, is—to use one of her favourite words—fun, and draws attention to the way theory, decipherment and the entertainment of riddle- or puzzlesolving may be connected.

A New Politics of the Body

During the seventies, feminist aesthetics and women artists contributed greatly to the questioning of two great cultural boundary divisions. Throughout the twentieth century, inexorably but discontinuously, pressure had been building up against the separation of art theory from art practice on the one hand, and the separation between high culture and low culture on the other. The collapse of these divisions, crucial to the many and varied components of postmodernism, was also vital to feminist art. Women artists made use of both theory and popular culture through reference and quotation. Cindy Sherman, first showing work in the late seventies, used popular culture as her source material without using theory as commentary and distanciation device. When her photographs were first shown, their insistent reiteration of representations of the feminine, and her use of herself as model, in infinite varieties of masquerade, won immediate attention from critics who welcomed her as a counterpoint to feminist theoretical and conceptual art. The success of her early work, its acceptance by the centre (the art market and institutions) at a time when many artists were arguing for a politics of the margins, helped to obscure both the work's interest for feminist aesthetics and the fact that the ideas it raised could not have been formulated without a prehistory of feminism and its theorization of the body and representation. Sherman's arrival on the art scene certainly marks the beginning of the end of that era in which the female body had become, if not quite unrepresentable, only representable if refracted through theory. But rather than sidestepping, Sherman reacts and shifts the agenda. She brings a different perspective to the 'images of women question' and recuperates a politics of the body that had, perhaps, been lost or neglected in the twists and turns of seventies feminism.

In the early seventies, the women's movement claimed the female body as a site for political struggle, mobilizing around abortion rights, above all, but with other ancillary issues spiralling out into agitation over medical marginalization and sexuality itself as a source of women's oppression. A politics of the body led logically to a politics of representation of the body. It was only a small step to include the question of images of women in the accompanying debates and campaigns, but it was a step that also moved feminism out of familiar terrains of political action onto that of political aesthetics. And this small step called for a new conceptual vocabulary and opened feminist theory up to the influence of semiotics and psychoanalysis. The initial idea that images contributed to women's alienation from their bodies and from their sexuality, with an attendant hope of liberation and recuperation, gave way to theories of representation as symptom and signifier of the way problems posed by sexual difference under patriarchy could be displaced onto the feminine.

Not surprisingly, this kind of theoretical/political aesthetics also affected artists working in the climate of seventies feminism, and the representability of the female body underwent a crisis. At one extreme, the film-maker Peter Gidal said in 1978 'I have had a vehement refusal over the last decade, with one or two minor aberrations, to allow images of women into my films at all, since I do not see how those images can be separated from the dominant meanings.'[3]

Women artists and film-makers, while rejecting this wholesale banishment, were extremely wary about the investment of 'dominant meanings' in images of women; and while feminist critics turned to popular culture to analyse these meanings, artists turned to theory, juxtaposing images and ideas, to negate dominant meanings and, slowly and polemically, to invent different ones. Although in this climate Cindy Sherman's concentration on the female body seemed almost shocking, her representations of femininity were not a return, but a re-representation, a making strange.

A visitor to a Cindy Sherman retrospective, who moves through the work in its chronological order, must be almost as struck by the dramatic nature of its development, as by the individual, very striking, works themselves. It is not a question of

3
Teresa de Lauretis and Stephen Heath, eds., *The Cinematic Apparatus*. For an overview of the discussion that followed Peter Gidal's statement see 'Technology and Ideology in/through/and Avant Garde Film: An Instance', New York 1980, p. 169.

observing an increasing maturity, a changed style, or new directions, but of following a certain narrative of the feminine from an initial premiss to its very end. And this development takes place over ten years, between 1977 and 1987. The journey through time, through the work's chronological development, is also a journey into space. Sherman dissects the phantasmagoric space conjured up by the female body, from its exteriority to its interiority. The visitor who reaches the final images and then returns, reversing the order, finds that with the hindsight of what was to come, the early images are transformed. The first process of discovery, amusement and amazement is completed by a new curiosity, reverie and decipherment. And then, once the process of bodily disintegration is established in the later work, the early, innocent, images acquire a retrospective uncanniness.

Parodying Voyeurism

The first series of photographs, which also established Sherman's reputation, are called *Untitled Film Stills*. In each photograph Sherman poses for the camera, as though in a scene from a movie. Each photograph has its own *mise en scène*, evoking a style of film-making that is highly connotative but elusive. The black-and-white photographs seem to refer to the fifties, to the New Wave, to Neo-realism, to Hitchcock, or to Hollywood B pictures: This use of an amorphous connotation places them in a nostalgia genre, comparable to the American movies of the eighties that Fredric Jameson describes as typifying the postmodern characteristic of evoking the past while denying the reference of history.[4] They have the Barthesian quality of 'fifties-ness': that American collective fantasy of the fifties as the time of everyone's youth in a white and mainly middle America setting, in the last moment of calm before the storms of Vietnam, civil rights, and finally feminism. But Sherman twists nostalgia to suggest its dependence on constructing images and representations that conceal more than they record. She also draws attention to the historical importance of this period for establishing a particular culture of

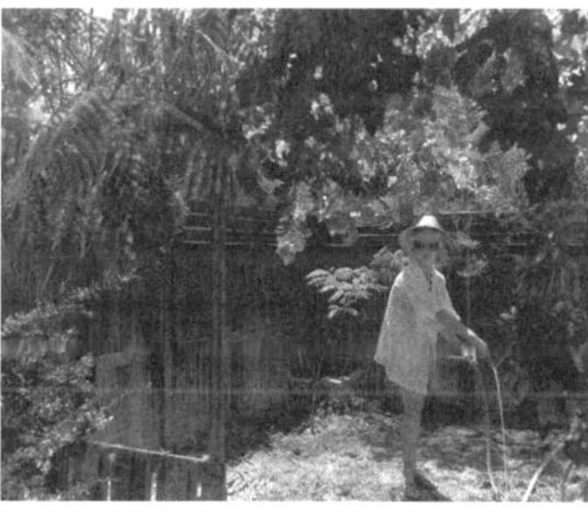

Untitled Film Still #47, 1979
Black-and-white photograph
8 x 10 in.
(20.3 x 25.4 cm)

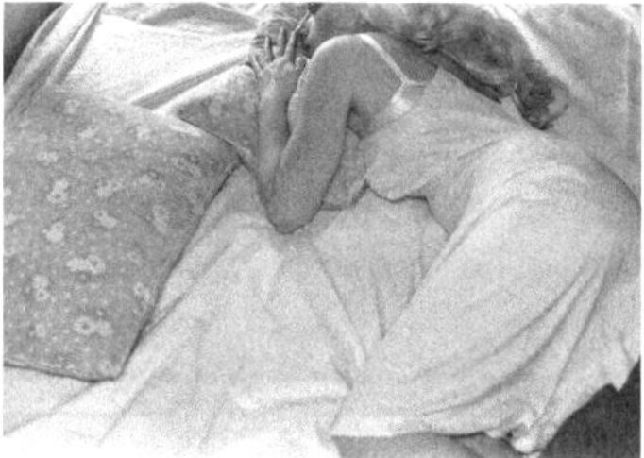

Untitled Film Still #52, 1979
Black-and-white photograph
8 x 10 in.
(20.3 x 25.4 cm)

4
F. Jameson, *Postmodernism, or, The Cultural Logic of Late Capitalism*, Duke University Press, Durham, 1991, p. 19.

appearances—specifically, the feminine appearance. The accoutrements of the feminine struggle to conform to a facade of desirability haunt Sherman's iconography. Make-up, high heels, hair, clothes are all carefully 'put on' and 'done'. Sherman-the-model dresses up into character, while Sherman-the artist reveals her character's masquerade. The juxtaposition begins to refer to a 'surface-ness', so that nostalgia begins to dissolve into unease. An overinsistence on surface starts to suggest that it might be masking something or other that should be hidden from sight, and a hint of another space starts to lurk inside a too plausible facade. Sherman accentuates the uneasiness by inscribing vulnerability into both the *mise en scène* of the photographs and the women's poses and expressions.

These *Film Still* scenes are set mainly in exteriors. Their fascination is derived from their quality as *trompe l'oeil*. The viewer is subjected to a series of double takes, estrangements and recognitions. The camera looks; it 'captures' the female character in a parody of different voyeurisms. It intrudes into moments in which she is unguarded, sometimes undressed, absorbed into her own world in the privacy of her own environment. Or it witnesses a moment in which her guard drops as she is suddenly startled by a presence, unseen and off screen, watching her. Or it observes her, simultaneously demure and alluring, composed for the outside world and its intrusive gaze. The viewer is immediately caught by the voyeurisms on offer. But the obvious fact that each character is Sherman herself, disguised, introduces a sense of wonder at the illusion and its credibility. And, as is well known in the cinema, any moment of marvelling at an illusion immediately destroys its credibility. The lure of voyeurism turns around like a trap, and the viewer ends up aware that Sherman-the-artist has set up a machine for making the gaze materialize uncomfortably, in alliance with Sherman-the-model. Then the viewer's curiosity may be attracted to the surrounding narrative. But any speculation about a story, about actual events and the character depicted, quickly reaches a dead end. The visitor at a Cindy Sherman show must be well aware that the *Film Still* is constructed for this one image only, and that nothing exists either before or after the moment shown. Each pregnant moment is a cutout, a tableau suggesting and denying the presence of a story.

As they pretend to be something more, the *Film Stills* parody the stillness of the photograph and ironically enact the poignancy of a 'frozen moment'. The women in the photographs are almost always in stasis, halted by something more than photography, like surprise, reverie, decorum, anxiety, or just waiting.

The viewer's voyeurism is uncomfortable. There is no complementary exhibitionism on the part of the female figures, and the sense of looking on, unobserved, provokes a mixture of curiosity and anxiety. The images are, however, erotic. Sexuality pervades the figures and their implied narratives. Sherman performs femininity as an appearance, in which the insistent sexualization of woman is integrated into style and respectability. Because Sherman uses cosmetics literally as a mask she makes visible the feminine as masquerade. And it is this homogeneous culture of fifties-like appearance that Sherman uses to adopt such a variety of same, but different, figurations. Identity, she seems to say, lies in looks. But just as she is artist and model, voyeur and looked-at, active and passive, subject and object, the photographs set up a comparable variety of positions and responses for the viewer. There is no stable subject position in her work, no resting point that does not quickly shift into something else. So the *Film Stills*' initial sense of homogeneity and credibility break up into the kind of heterogeneity of subject position that feminist aesthetics espoused in advance of postmodernism proper.

Soft-Core Pastiche

In 1980 Sherman made her first series of colour photographs, using back-projections of exteriors rather than actual locations, moving into a closer concentration on the face, and flattening the space of the photograph. Then, in 1981, she produced a series of colour photographs that start to suggest an interior space, and initiate her exploration inside the masquerade of femininity's interior/exterior binary opposition. The photographs all have the same format, horizontal like a cinemascope screen, so most of the figures lie on sofas or beds, or on the floor. As the series originated with a centrefold for *Artforum*, they give a strong sense of soft-core pastiche. These photographs concentrate on the sphere of feminine emotion, longing and reverie, and are set in private spaces that reduplicate the privacy of emotion. But, once again, an exact sensation is impossible to pin down. The young women that Sherman impersonates may be daydreaming about a future romance, or they may be mourning a lost one. They may be waiting, in enforced passivity, for a letter or telephone call. Their eyes gaze into the distance. They are not aware of their clothes, which are sometimes carelessly rumpled, so that, safe alone with their thoughts, their bodies are, slightly, revealed to the viewer. They exude vulnerability and sexual availability like lovesick heroine/victims in a romantic melodrama. There are some precedents in the *Untitled Film Stills* for this series, but the use of colour, the horizontal format and the repeated pose create a double theme of inside space and of reverie. The intimate space of a bedroom provides an appropriate setting for daydream or reverie, and combines with Sherman's erotic, suggestive, poses to accumulate connotations of sexuality. These photographs reiterate the 'to-be-looked-at-ness' of femininity. While the *Untitled Film Stills* fake a surrounding narrative, so the camera does not draw undue attention to its presence; the 1981 *Untitleds*, on the other hand, announce themselves as photographs and, as in a pin-up, the model's eroticism, and her pose, are directed towards the camera, and ultimately towards the spectator. However, the spectator who looks back at the gaze that sometimes comes out from the image, or is drawn into voyeuristic involvement with the figure displayed, must then remember that the artist both poses herself in a mirror and photographs the scene herself by means of a remote control.

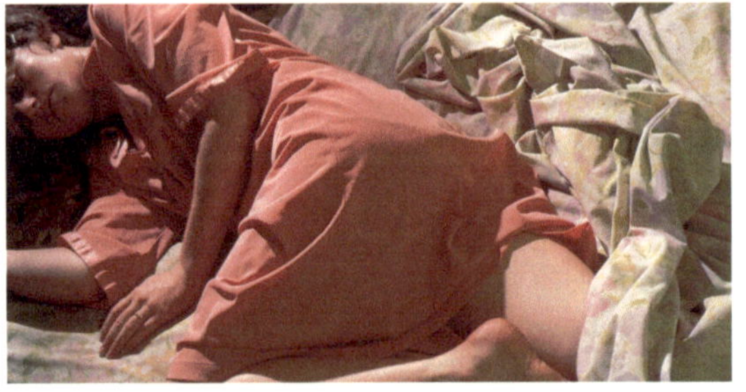

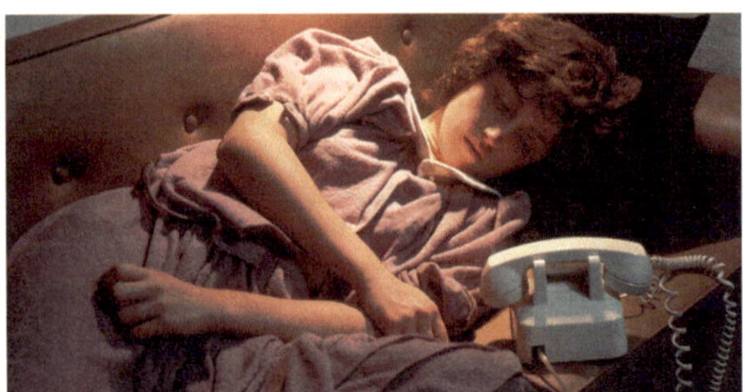

Untitled #89, 1981
Color photograph
24 x 48 in.
(61 x 121.9 cm)

Untitled #90, 1981
Color photograph
24 x 48 in.
(61 x 121.9 cm)

In most of the *Untitled Film Stills* the female figure stands out in sharp contrast to her surroundings, exaggerating her vulnerability in an exterior world. In some, however, a visible grain merges the figure with the texture and material of the photograph. In the 1981 series, Sherman's use of colour and of light and shade merges the female figure and her surroundings into a continuum, without hard edges. Pools of light illuminate patches of skin or bathe the picture in soft glow. Above all, the photographs have a glossy, high-quality finish in keeping with the codes and conventions of commercial photography. While the poses are soft and limp—polar opposites of a popular idea of fetishized femininity (high-heeled and corseted, erect, flamboyant and exhibitionist)—fetishism returns in the formal qualities of the photography. The sense of surface now resides, not in the female figure's attempt to save her face in a masquerade of femininity, but in the model's subordination to, and imbrication with, the texture of the photographic medium itself.

Metamorphoses

Sherman's next important phase, the *Untitleds* of 1983, first manifests the darkness that will, from then on, increasingly overwhelm her work. This turn was, in the first place, a reaction against the fashion industry that first invited her to design photographs for them and then tried to modify and tone down the results. 'From the beginning there was something that didn't work with me, like there was friction. I picked out some clothes I wanted to use. I was sent completely different clothes that I found boring to use. I really started to make fun, not of the clothes, but much more of the fashion. I was starting to put scar tissue on my face to become really ugly.'[5]

These photographs use bright, harsh light and high-contrast colour. The characters are theatrical and ham up their roles. A new Sherman body is beginning to emerge. She grotesquely parodies the kind of feminine image that is geared to erotic consumption, and she inverts conventional codes of female allure and elegance. Whereas the language of fashion photography gives great emphasis to lightness, so that its models seem to defy gravity, Sherman's figures are heavy in body and groundedness. Their unselfconsciousness verges on the exhibitionist, and they strike professional poses to display costumes that exaggerate their awkward physiques, which are then exaggerated again by camera angle and lighting. There is absolutely nothing to do with nature or the natural in this response to the cosmetic svelteness of fashion. Rather, they suggest that the binary opposition to the perfect body of the fashion model is the grotesque, and that the smooth glossy body, polished by photography, is a

5 Nairne, p. 136.

defence against an anxiety-provoking, uneasy and uncanny body. From this perspective the surface of the body, so carefully conveyed in the early photographs, seems to be dissolving to reveal a monstrous otherness behind the cosmetic facade. The 'something' that had seemed to be lurking in the phantasmatic topography of femininity, begins, as it were, to congeal.

After the *Untitleds* of 1983, the anti-fashion series, the metamorphoses become more acute and disturbing. The series *Untitled 1984* is like a reversal of Dorian Gray; as though the pain, anger and stupidity of human nature left their traces clearly on human features, as though the surface was failing in its task of masking. In the next series, inspired by the monsters of fairy stories, the figures become supernatural; and, rather like animistic personifications, they tower above or return to the elements. By this time the figures seem to be the emanations of irrational fears, verging on terror, relics of childhood nightmares. If the 'Centerfold' series conveyed, through pose and facial expression, the interiority of secret thoughts, now Sherman seems to personify the stuff of the unconscious itself. While the earlier interiority suggested soft, erotic reverie, these are materializations of anxiety and dread. Sherman seems to have shifted from conveying or suggesting the presence of a hidden otherness to representing its inhabitants. This is a shift that differentiates between reverie and the stuff of the repressed, the unconscious. Increasingly grotesque and deforming make up blurs gender identity, and some figures are horned or snouted, like horrific mythological hybrids. If the earlier iconography suggested a passive aspiration to please, deformation and distortion seem to erupt in some kind of ratio to repression. These figures are active and threatening.

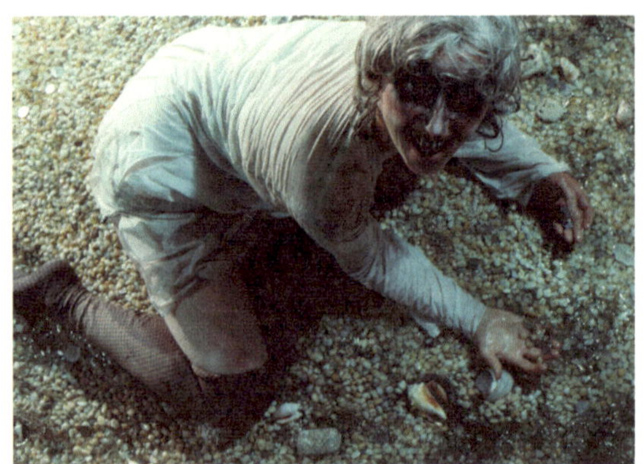

Untitled #156, 1985
Color photograph
49 ½ x 72 ½ in.
(126 x 184 cm)

Finally, in the last phase, the figure disappears completely. Sometimes body bits are replaced by prosthetics, such as false breasts or buttocks, but, in the last resort, nothing is left but disgust—the disgust of sexual detritus, decaying food, vomit, slime, menstrual blood, hair. These traces represent the end of the road, the secret stuff of bodily fluids that the cosmetic is designed to conceal. The topography of exterior/interior is exhausted. Previously, all Sherman's work had been centred and structured around a portrait, so that a single figure had provided a focus for the viewer's gaze. Surrounding *mises en scène* gradually vanished as though Sherman was denying the viewer any mitigation or distraction from the figures themselves as they gradually became more and more grotesque. Around 1985, settings make a comeback in the photographs, but diffused into textures. Natural elements—pebbles, sand or soil, for instance—develop expressive and threatening connotations. Colour, lighting, and the texture of the figures themselves merge them visually into their settings. The camera angle now looks down onto the ground where the figures lie lifeless, or, perhaps, trapped in their own materiality.

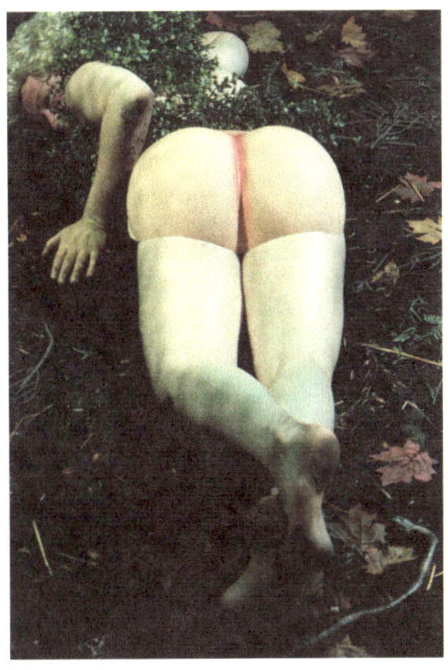

Untitled #155, 1985
Color photograph
72 ½ x 49 ¼ in.
(184.2 x 125.1 cm)

The shift in perspective, to downward camera angle, heralds Sherman's final transformation. When the body, in any homogeneous or cohesive form, disappears from the scene, its traces and detritus are spread out on the ground, on pebbles or sand, or submerged in water. With the disintegration of the body, the photographs also lose any homogeneous and cohesive formal organization and the sense of physical fragmentation is echoed in the fragmentation of the images. Now the edge of the image may be as significant as any other section of its space. At the same time, the photographs have become monstrously enlarged. One of the first series, *Untitled Film Stills*, were all in a similar format (between 20.3 x 25.4 cm and 25.4 x 20.3 cm). The photographs from the 1990s have grown to dimensions such as seventy-two by forty-nine inches. The viewer could take in the early work with a glance and sense of command over the image; the later photographs overwhelm the viewer and force the eye to scan the surface, searching for a specific shape or pattern that might offer some formal reassurance against the disturbing content.

De-fetishizing the Female Body

From the perspective of feminist aesthetics, this narrative of disintegration, horror and finally disgust, raises, first and foremost, the question of the source, or origin, of this phantasmagoria of the female body, and, secondly, how it might be analysed. Sherman depicts a phantasmatic space, projected onto and then into the female body. A variety of issues are raised by the question of spatial metaphor. First of all, there is certainly a sense in which Sherman's ironic 'unveiling' also 'unveils' the use of the female body as a metaphor for division between surface allure and concealed decay, as though the stuff that has been projected for so long into a mythic space 'behind' the mask of femininity had suddenly broken through the delicately painted veil. This veil is exemplified by the myth of enchantress-turned-hag, out of which the dualistic mythology of the female body came to represent the opposition between truth and artifice. Barbara Spackman, in her discussion of the appropriation of the female body as metaphor by symbolist aesthetics, comments on this figuration: 'As a figure for hermeneutics itself, it may be read as enacting the discovery of essence that lies beneath appearance, truth beneath falsehood, reality beneath fiction, plain speech beneath cosmetic rhetoric. Indeed . . . Nietzsche uses this very topos in order to overturn it, in order to critique the hermeneutic model that would find an essence beneath appearance. These are, of course, valid interpretations. Yet they discard the literal in order to concentrate on the figural and do not ask why woman is favoured as the vehicle of the metaphor.'[6]

As Spackman argues, woman becomes 'the favoured vehicle of the metaphor' once she is seen as the site of castration, so the origin of this phantasmagoria of the female body may be found in the structure of the unconscious, and may be deciphered with the aid of psychoanalytic theory. A cosmetic, artificial appearance then conceals the wound or void left in the male psyche when it perceives sexual difference. In this sense, the topography of the feminine masquerade echoes the topography of the fetish itself. It could certainly be argued that the metamorphosis of the feminine in Sherman's work traces this mythic figuration, and, in parodying the metaphor, returns in the last resort to the 'literal', to the bodily fluids and wastes that become

6 Barbara Spackman, *Decadent Genealogies. The Rhetoric of Sickness from Baudelaire to D'Annunzio*, Ithaca 1989, p. 165.

condensed with wounded body in the iconography of misogyny. But she also, dramatically, draws attention to the regime of representational and mythological contradiction lived by women under patriarchy. Although the origin of the image may be in the unconscious, and although the image may be a phantasm, these collective fantasies also have an impact in reality and produce symptoms that mediate between the two. The late photographs are a reminder that the female psyche may well identify with misogynistic revulsion against the female body and attempt to erase signs that mark her physically as feminine. The images of decaying food and vomit raise the spectre of the anorexic girl, who tragically acts out the fashion fetish of the female as an eviscerated, cosmetic and artificial construction designed to ward off the 'otherness' hidden in the 'interior'.

It is hard to trace the collapse of the female body as successful fetish without re-representing the anxieties and dreads that give rise to the fetish in the first place, and Sherman might be open to the accusation that she reproduces the narrative without a sufficiently critical context. It is here that the *Untitled Film Stills* may be re-read with the hindsight of the future development of Sherman's work in mind. To return to the early photographs in this way is to see how the female body can become a conduit for different ideas superimposed, as it were, and condensed into a single image. For instance, the uncanniness of the women characters, behind their cosmetic facades, starts to merge with the instability of the photograph as object of belief. The structure of fetishism indicates a homology between these different ideas, and the theory of fetishism helps to unravel the process of condensation.

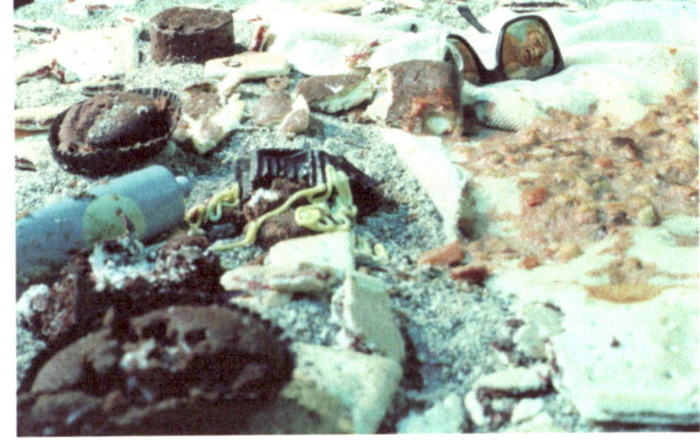

Untitled #175, 1987
Color photograph
47½ x 71½ in.
(120.7 x 181.6 cm)

Between Knowledge and Belief

For Freud, fetishism is particularly significant (apart, that is, from his view that it 'confirmed the castration complex') as a demonstration that the psyche can sustain incompatible ideas, at one and the same time, through a process of disavowal. Fetishistic disavowal acknowledges the possibility of castration (represented by the female, penis-less, genital) and simultaneously denies it. Freud saw the coexistence of these two contradictory ideas, maintained in a single psyche, as a model for the ego's relation to reality: the 'splitting of the ego', which allowed two parallel, but opposed, attitudes to be maintained in uneasy balance. Switching back and forth between visual duping, followed by perception of the duping mechanism, a willing suspension of disbelief followed by a wave of disillusion—'I know . . . but all the same . . .'—the viewer of Sherman's *Film Stills* can almost physically feel, and indeed relish, the splitting open of the gap between knowledge and belief.

This 'oscillation effect' is important to postmodernism. The viewer looks, recognizes a style, doubts, does a double take, then recognizes that the style is a citation, and meanings shift and change their reference like shifting perceptions of perspective from an optical illusion. This effect is, perhaps, particularly exciting because it dices with credibility in a manner similar to the fetish. In this sense, Cindy Sherman pushes postmodern play to its limits. When the viewer reaches the final photographs of disintegration and only reluctantly recognizes the content for what it is, the art aspect of Sherman's work returns. It is not so much that the colours of the detritus images are more 'painterly' and their reference is more to the shape of the frame than the figure, but that their place on the gallery wall affirms their status as art, just as the viewer is about to turn away in revolted disbelief. In this sense, they, too, create an 'oscillation effect', this time between reverence and revulsion. This kind of theme is present in Sherman's works from 1990 to 1991, which are outside the 1978–87 'narrative' and return to the figuration of the human body, now refracted through art itself. She reproduces old masters, taking the role of the central figure, or impersonating a portrait. Again, she distorts the body with false additions, such as the breast in a Virgin and Child. Although these images lack the inexorability and complexity of her previous phase, she still plays on the structures of disavowal and draws attention to the art-historical fetishization of great works and their value.

For Freud, the structure of fetishism was not the same as the structure of repression. While providing a substitute and a replacement and literally a screen against a traumatic memory,

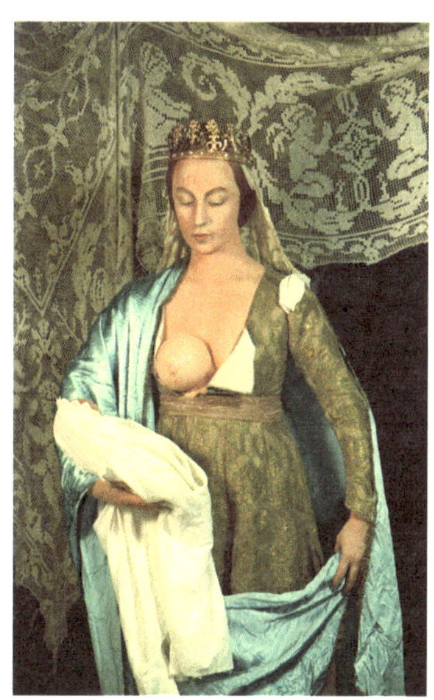

Untitled #216, 1989
Color photograph
87 x 56 in.
(221 x 142.2 cm)

the fetish is also a memento of loss and substitution. And in these circumstances, how the female body, the original provoker of castration anxiety, is represented, may be symptomatic and revealing. When Sherman depicts femininity as a masquerade in her succession of 'dressings-up', the female body asserts itself as a site of anxiety that it must, at all costs, conceal. And it acquires a self-conscious vulnerability that seems to exude tension between an exterior appearance and its interiority. In this way, Sherman plays with a 'topography' of the female body. But the early photographs illustrate the extent to which this 'topography' has been integrated into a culture of the feminine. In order to create a 'cosmetic' body a cosmetics industry has come into being, so that the psychic investment the patriarchy makes in feminine appearance is echoed by an investment on the part of capitalism. And cosmetics are also, of course, the tools of Sherman's trade.

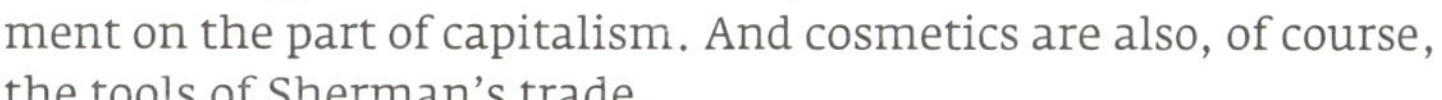

Fetishism depends on a phantasmatic topography, setting up a screen and shield, closely linked to the ego's defence mechanism, as Freud pointed out. At the same time, fetishism is the most semiotic of perversions, screening and shielding by means of an object that is, unavoidably, also a sign of loss and substitution. But its semiotic enterprise is invested in the deceit of artifice. The fetish is, as Nietzsche said of woman, 'so artistic'. As feminist theorists have noted, the female body not only reduplicates this structure—of a surface as screen and anxiety-provoking interior, the enchantress/hag dichotomy—but it can incarnate the fetish object itself. This syndrome came into its own with the Hollywood star system, the mass production of pin-ups, and the equation, in contemporary consumer culture, between the feminine and glamour.

Cindy Sherman traces the abyss or morass that overwhelms the defetishized body, deprived of the fetish's semiotic, reduced to being 'unspeakable' and devoid of significance. Her late work comes close to depicting the Kristevan concept of the abject: that

7
Julia Kristeva, *The Powers of Horror. An Essay on Abjection*, New York 1982.

8
See Barbara Creed, '*Alien* and the Monstrous-Feminine', in Annette Kuhn, ed., *Alien Zone. Cultural Theory and Contemporary Science Fiction Cinema*, London 1990.

is, the disgust aroused in the human psyche by lifeless, inanimate bodily matter, bodily wastes and the dead body itself.[7] For Kristeva, abjection is closely associated with separation from the mother's body. The small child, of both sexes, in the process of establishing autonomous subjectivity, has to establish an autonomous 'clean and proper body'. While previously the child found pleasure in its bodily wastes and the satisfying undifferentiation between its body and that of its mother, when it needs to define boundaries and separations, feelings of disgust come into play. Barbara Creed's argument that abjection is central to the recurring image of the 'monstrous feminine' in horror movies is also applicable to the monstrous in Sherman.[8] Although her figures materialize the stuff of irrational terror, they also have pathos and could easily be understood in terms of 'the monster as victim'. Her photographs of atrophied figures (for instance, the corpse that lies like a soiled waxwork, eyes staring and blending with colour tones into the grass) could be collected into a lexicon of horror and the uncanny, just as the *Untitled Film Stills* are like a lexicon of poses and gestures typical of respectable, but still uncanny, femininity. The 1987 series suggests that, although both sexes are subject to abjection, it is women who can explore and analyse the phenomenon with greater equanimity, as it is the female body that has come, not exclusively but predominantly, to represent the shudder aroused by liquidity and decay.

FIFTIES AMERICA: THE DEMOCRACY OF GLAMOUR

By referring to the fifties in her early work, Sherman joins many others in identifying Eisenhower's America as the mythic birthplace of postmodern culture. Reference to the fifties invokes the aftermath of the Korean War and the success of the Marshall Plan, American mass consumption and the 'society of the spectacle'; a time when, in the context of the Cold War, advertising, movies and the actual packaging and seductiveness of commodities all marketed glamour. Glamour proclaimed the desirability of American capitalism to the outside world and, inside, secured American-ness as an aspiration for the newly suburbanized, white, population as it buried incompatible memories of immigrant origins. In Sherman's early photographs, connotations of vulnerability and instability flow over on to the construction and credibility of the wider, social masquerade. The image of fifties-ness as a particular emblem of American-ness, also masks the fact that it was a decade of social and political repression while profound change gathered on the horizon—the transition, that is, from Joe McCarthy to James Dean. Rather than simply referring to 'fifties-ness' in nostalgia mode, Sherman hints at a world ingesting the seeds of its own decay. She is closer, therefore, to *Blue Velvet* than to *American Graffiti*.

It is interesting, in the light of the American postmodern citation of the fifties, to consider the pivotal place occupied by Marilyn Monroe, as an icon in her own right, and as source of all the subsequent Marilyn iconography, kept alive by gay subculture, surfacing with Debbie Harry in the late seventies and perpetuated by Madonna in the eighties (particularly, of course, her 'Material Girl'). In 1982 Cindy Sherman appeared on the cover of the Anglo-American avant-garde magazine ZG. She is immediately recognizable as Marilyn Monroe, in cover-girl pose. She is not the Marilyn of bright lights and diamonds, but the other, equally familiar, Marilyn in slacks and a shirt, still epitomizing the glamour of the period, hand held to thrown-back head, eyes half closed, lips open. But refracted through Sherman's masquerade, Marilyn's masquerade fails to mask her interior anxiety, and unhappiness seems to seep through the cracks. America's favourite fetish never fully succeeded in papering over her interiority, and the veil of sexual allure now seems, in retrospect, to be haunted by death.

Cindy Sherman's impersonations predate, and in some ways prefigure, those of Madonna. Madonna's performances make full use of the potential of cosmetics. As well as fast changing her own chameleonlike appearance on a day-to-day basis, she performs homages to the artificial perfection of the movie stars and also integrates the 'oscillation effect' into the rhythm of her videos, synchronizing editing, personality change and sexual role reversals. Although Madonna, obviously, does not follow the Cindy Sherman narrative of disintegration, her awareness of this, other, side of the topography of feminine masquerade is evidenced in her well-documented admiration for Frida Kahlo. Frida depicted her face, in an infinite number of self-portraits, as a mask, and veiled her body in elaborate Tehuana dresses. Sometimes the veil falls, and her wounded body comes to the surface, condensing her real, physical, wounds with both the imaginary wound of castration and the literal interior space of the female body, the womb, bleeding, in her autobiographical painting, from miscarriage. Frida Kahlo's mask was always her own. Marilyn's was like a trademark. While Cindy Sherman and Madonna shift appearance into a fascinating debunking of stable identity, Marilyn's masquerade had to be always absolutely identical. Her features were able to accept cosmetic modelling into an instantly recognizable sign of 'Marilyn-ness'. But here, too, the mask is taut, threatened by the gap between public stardom and private pressures (as was the case for everyone caught in the Hollywood Babylon of the studio system's double standards) and also by the logic of the topography itself.

In becoming the democracy of glamour, fifties America completed a process, through the movies and through mass-produced clothes and cosmetics, that had been launched in the thirties and interrupted by the Second World War. It was also a paradigmatic moment for commodity fetishism. Baudrillard has noted the origin of the word 'fetish' in the Portuguese *feitiço*, derived from the Latin *factitius*: 'From the same root (*facio, factitius*) as *feitiço* comes the Spanish *afeitar*: "to paint, to adorn, to embellish" and *afeite* "preparation, ornamentation, cosmetics".'[9] He suggests that this etymology from the artificial and the cosmetic implies a homology between the fetishized figure of bodily beauty and the fetishism of the commodity. The commodity, too, is haunted by the gap between knowledge and belief. By exploiting the gap between knowledge and belief, inherent in the complexity of value, the commodity can erase its origin in the labour of the working class, at the production line, and turn a phantasmatic, cosmetic, face to the world. And, as feminists have so often noted, the seal and guarantee of its success in the market place is so often the veneer of sexualized glamour generated by juxtaposition to the sexualized glamour of femininity in advertising. Although Cindy Sherman's work is not about the commodity, the citation of the fifties brings to mind this complex network of homologies. The failure of the fetish, which she traces through images of the feminine, is similar to the polarization of gloss in

9
Jean Baudrillard, *For a Critique of the Political Economy of the Sign*, St. Louis 1981, p. 91.

the shop window, and disavowals of the factory that flourish when society cannot find a way of narrating the contradictions in its history.

In refusing the word/image juxtaposition, so prevalent in the art of the seventies and eighties, Sherman may draw the accusation that she is, herself, stuck in the topographic double bind of the fetish and its collapse. Although she may be thus unable to inscribe the means of decipherment into the work itself, her use of *Untitled* to describe her works turns inability into refusal. Her work does, however, vividly illustrate the way that the human psyche thrives on the division between surface and secret, and that, standing for repression of all kinds, this recurring spatial metaphor cannot be swept away. The wordlessness and despair in her work represents the wordlessness and despair that ensues when a fetishistic structure, the means of erasing history and memory, collapses, leaving a void in its wake. The fetish necessarily wants history to be overlooked. That is its function. The fetish is also a symptom, and as such has a history which may be deciphered, but only by refusing its phantasmatic topography. Freud described the structure of the psyche through spatial metaphor to convey the burying action of repression, but he analysed the language of the unconscious, its formal expression in condensation and displacement, in terms of signification and decipherment. In the last resort, decipherment is dependent on language. The complete lack of verbal clues and signifiers in Cindy Sherman's work draws attention to the semiotic that precedes a successful translation of the symptom into language, the semiotic of displacements and fetishism, desperately attempting to disguise unconscious ideas from the conscious mind. She uses iconography, connotation, or the sliding of the signifier, in a trajectory that ends by stripping away all accrued meaning to the limit of bodily matter. However, even this bedrock—the vomit and the blood for instance—returns to cultural significance: that is, to the difficulty of the body, and above all the female body, while it is subjected to the icons and narratives of fetishism.

*

I wrote the article 'A Phantasmagoria of the Female Body' for *New Left Review* after seeing a Cindy Sherman retrospective held at the Saatchi Gallery in London in 1992. (It was later republished in my book *Fetishism and Curiosity* as 'Cosmetics and Abjection: Cindy Sherman 1977–87'). I had been deeply involved with the feminist psychoanalytic theory that had been applied to images of women since the 1970s and to see Cindy Sherman's work as it unfolded between 1977 and 1987 was to see these ideas both materialised and displaced. Her 'narrative' of femininity, as representation, mythology and symptom began with the *Untitled Film Stills*. These images of women had been constructed, seemingly, as a response to a desiring male gaze but then mutated, with the *Untitled* series, seemingly in response to male anxiety, so that gradually an abject body emerged, ultimately collapsing into its own detritus. But the inscribed consciousness of both of recognisable cultural connotations and of feminist theoretical concepts creates an extra level of irony, even of parody in the work. For instance, while the *Untitleds* refer to a culture of cosmetics and to feminist analyses of 'masquerade', Sherman's own masquerade, as she produces her own multiple performances, displaces both the constructed images of women and the psychoanalytic theory that deciphered them. I said: 'The viewer is subjected to a series of double takes, estrangements and recognitions.' This generates a viewing experience in which cliché images create clues so that the enigma of femininity and the displacement of its signs lead to the pleasure of decipherment.

Later, at an exhibition at the Serpentine Gallery in London in 2003, I was struck by the importance of pose in Sherman's work [during the 1990s...] which took me back to the *Untitled Film Stills* of the 1970s from a different perspective. In my earlier article I had been interested in the *Stills* as images extracted from phantasmatic, non-existent narratives, redolent with suggestions of genres. At the Serpentine, I was more interested in the way that the images referred to moments of stillness as the site of uncertainty in cinema, bringing to the fore its paradoxical existence within the film strip and the illusion of movement. Losing the resonances of masquerade and narrativity, these images now seemed more grounded in the discourse of photography, a unique presence caught at a specific moment of time. The persistence of pose in Sherman's work took on a more temporal significance. But while her women's performance related as much to the camera as to cultural connotation, the two folded back on each other so that iconicity and index* appeared in an uneasy, uncertain balance.

This consciousness of the temporal in Sherman's work seemed to be, in itself, an effect of the passing of time. The question of age became more prevalent in her work, as certain figures seem to be poised between past and present. But also the aesthetic of the photograph itself begins to fade with changing technologies. The Serpentine show ended with the series *Clowns*. These images no longer struggle for identity and their digitally generated backgrounds suggest that Cindy Sherman's 'narrative' is moving across an aesthetic threshold in which the relation between the human body and time moves away from the visual discourse of cinema and photography.

*
Editor's note: These terms refer to the philosophy of signification of C. S. Pierce (1839–1914), and particularly to his tripartition of the sign into symbol, icon, and index.

CINDY SHERMAN was born in 1954 in Glen Ridge, New Jersey, and was raised in Huntington, in the suburbs of Long Island. She received a Bachelor of Arts degree in 1976 from the State University of New York at Buffalo. She founded there *Hallwalls*, with Robert Longo and Charles Clough, an independent gallery of art. She moved to New York City in 1977 where she currently lives and works.

SELECTED SOLO EXHIBITIONS

An asterisk denotes the publication of an accompanying catalog.

1979
- Hallwalls, Buffalo, New York

1980
- *Contemporary Arts Museum, Houston, Texas
- Metro Pictures, New York
- The Kitchen, New York

1981
- Metro Pictures, New York
- Saman Gallery, Genoa
- Young/Hoffman Gallery, Chicago

1982
- Galerie Chantal Crousel, Paris
- Larry Gagosian Gallery, Los Angeles
- Metro Pictures, New York
- Contemporary Arts Museum, Houston
- Texas Gallery, Houston
- **Cindy Sherman*, The Stedelijk Museum, Amsterdam; (1982–84) Gewad, Ghent, Belgium; Watershed Gallery, Bristol, England; John Hansard Gallery, University of Southampton, England; Palais Stutterheim, Erlangen, West Germany; Haus am Waldsee, West Berlin; Centre d'Art Contemporain, Geneva; Sonja Henie-Niels Onstadt Foundation, Copenhagen; Louisiana Museum, Humlebæk, Denmark

1983
- *Fine Arts Center Gallery, State University of New York at Stony Brook; Zilka Gallery, Wesleyan University, Connecticut
- Galerie Schellmann & Kluser, Munich
- Metro Pictures, New York
- *Musée d'Art et d'Industrie de Saint Etienne, France
- Rhona Hoffman Gallery, Chicago
- *The St. Louis Art Museum

1984
- *Cindy Sherman*, Akron Art Museum, Ohio; (1984–86) Institute of Contemporary Art, Philadelphia; Museum of Art, Carnegie Institute, Pittsburgh, Pennsylvania; Des Moines Art Center, Iowa; The Baltimore Museum of Art, Maryland
- Galerie Grita Insam, Vienna
- Monika Sprüth Galerie, Cologne
- *Laforet Museum, Tokyo
- *Seibu Gallery of Contemporary Art, Tokyo

1985
- Metro Pictures, New York
- *Westfalischer Kunstverein, Munster, West Germany

1986
- Galerie Crousel-Hussenot, Paris
- *Portland Art Museum, Oregon
- The New Aldrich Museum, Ridgefield, Connecticut
- Wadsworth Atheneum, Hartford

1987
- HoffmanBorman Gallery, Los Angeles
- Metro Pictures, New York
- Provinciaal Museum, Hasselt, Belgium
- *The Whitney Museum of American Art, New York; The Institute of Contemporary Art, Boston; The Dallas Museum of Art, Texas

1988
- Galeria Comicos, Lisbon
- Monika Sprüth Galerie, Cologne
- La Maquina Española, Madrid
- Galeria Lia Rumma, Naples

1989
- Galerie Crousel-Robelin, Paris
- Galerie Der Wiener Secession, Vienna
- Galerie Pierre Hubert, Geneva
- Metro Pictures, New York
- *National Art Gallery, Wellington, New Zealand; Waikato Museum of Art and History, New Zealand

1990
- Monika Sprüth Galerie, Cologne
- Kunst-Station, St. Peter, Cologne
- Linda Cathcart Gallery, Santa Monica, California
- Metro Pictures, New York
- Padiglione d'arte Contemporanea, Milan
- University Art Museum, University of California, Berkeley

1991
- **Cindy Sherman*, Basel Kunsthalle, Switzerland; Staatsgalerie Moderner Kunst, Munich; The Whitechapel Gallery, London
- *Milwaukee Art Museum; Center for the Fine Arts, Miami; The Walker Art Center, Minneapolis, Minnesota
- Saatchi Collection, London
- Studio Guenzani and Le Case d'Arte, Milan

1992
- Monika Sprüth Galerie, Cologne
- Galerie Six Friedrich, Munich
- Linda Cathcart Gallery, Santa Monica, California
- Metro Pictures, New York
- Museo de Monterrey, Mexico

1993
- Galerie Ascan Crone, Hamburg
- Galerie Ghislaine Hussenot, Paris
- Galleri Susanne Ottesen, Copenhagen
- Tel Aviv Museum of Art, Tel Aviv
- Texas Gallery, Houston
- Wall Gallery, Fukuoka, Japan

1994
- *Cindy Sherman: Untitled 1987–1991*, Galerie Borgmann Capitain, Cologne *Cindy Sherman Display*, Comme des Garçons, New York
- **Cindy Sherman - New York Photographien*, ACC Galerie Weimar, Germany
- *Cindy Sherman - Possession*, Manchester City Art Gallery, Manchester, England
- Offshore Gallery, East Hampton, New York
- **From Beyond the Pale—Cindy Sherman Photographs 1977–1993*, The Irish Museum of Modern Art, Ireland

1995
- Metro Pictures, New York
- Norton Gallery and School of Art, West Palm Beach, Florida
- *Directions: Cindy Sherman—Film Stills*, Hirshhorn Museum and Sculpture Garden, Washington, D.C.
- **Cindy Sherman Photographien 1975–1995*, Deichtorhallen Hamburg, Germany; Malmo Konsthall, Sweden; Kunstmuseum Luzerne, Switzerland
- **Cindy Sherman: The Self Which Is Not One*, Museu de Arte Moderna de Sao Paulo, Brazil

1996
- *New Works*, PaceWildenstein, Los Angeles
- **Cindy Sherman*, Museum Boymans-van Beuningen, Rotterdam; Museo Nacional Centro de Arte Reina Sofia, Madrid; Sala de Exposiciones REKALDE, Bilbao; Staatliche Kunsthalle, Baden-Baden, The Netherlands
- **Cindy Sherman*, Museum of Modern Art, Shiga, Japan; Marugame Genichiro-Inokuma Museum of Contemporary Art, Japan; Museum of Contemporary Art, Tokyo
- *Metamorphosis: Cindy Sherman Photographs*, The Cleveland Museum of Art, Cleveland, Ohio
- Metro Pictures, New York

1997
- Studio Guenzani, Milan
- *Cindy Sherman: Works 1975–1995*, Deichtorhallen, Hamburg
- **Cindy Sherman. A Selection From the Eli Broad Foundation's Collection*, Museo de Bellas Artes, Caracas, Venezuela
- *Cindy Sherman: The Complete Untitled Film Stills*, Museum of Modern Art, New York; Centre for Contemporary Art, Ujazdowski Castle, Warsaw, Poland; Ludwig Museum Budapest, Royal Palace, Budapest, Hungary; Austin Museum of Art, Austin, Texas
- **Cindy Sherman: Retrospective*, Museum of Contemporary Art, Los Angeles; Museum of Contemporary Art, Chicago; Galerie Rudolfinum, Prague; Centro Cultural de Belém Exhibition Centre, Lisbon; capc Musée, Bordeaux, Museum of Contemporary Art, Sydney, Art Gallery of Ontario, Toronto
- **Cindy Sherman*, Museum Ludwig, Cologne

1998
- Metro Pictures, New York
- *Cindy Sherman Multiples*, Kurtz Contemporary, London

1999
- Metro Pictures, New York
- Galerie Edition Kunsthandel, Essen
- Art + Public, Geneva
- Monika Spruth Gallerie, Cologne

2000
- Metro Pictures, New York
- *Hasselblad Center, Goteborg, Sweden
- Gagosian Gallery, Beverly Hills
- *Fairy Tales*, Skarstedt Fine Art, New York
- Gallerie Ghislaine Hussenot, Paris
- Monika Sprüth Gallerie, Cologne
- Philomene Magers, Munich
- **Early Work of Cindy Sherman*, Glenn Horowitz Bookseller, New York
- Galería Juana de Aizpuru, Madrid
- Greengrassi, London

2001
- *Cindy Sherman: Early Works*, Studio Guenzani, Milan
- *Cindy Sherman*, Nikolaj Copenhagen Contemporary Art Center, Copenhagen, Denmark

2003
- *Cindy Sherman, Centerfolds, 1981*, Skarstedt Fine Art, New York
- **Cindy Sherman*, Serpentine Gallery, London; Scottish National Gallery of Modern Art, Edinburgh

2004
- **The Unseen Cindy Sherman—Early Transformations 1975/1976*, Montclair Art Museum, Montclair, New Jersey
- **Her Bodies*, Arario Gallery, Chung Nam, Korea
- **Clowns*, Kestnergesellschaft, Hanover, Germany

2005
- *Clowns*, Monika Sprüth & Philomene Magers, Munich, Germany
- Guild Hall, East Hampton, New York
- **Cindy Sherman: Working Girl*, Contemporary Art Museum, St. Louis, Missouri
- *Office Killer*, MoMA, New York

2006
- **Cindy Sherman*, Jeu de Paume, Paris; Kunsthaus Bregenz, Austria

2007
- **Cindy Sherman*, Louisiana Museum for Modern Art, Denmark; Martin Gropius Bau, Berlin

SELECTED GROUP EXHIBITIONS

An asterisk denotes the publication of an accompanying catalog.

1976
- Albright-Knox Art Gallery, Buffalo, New York
- *Hallwalls*, Artists Space, New York

1977
- Albright-Knox Art Gallery, Buffalo, New York

1978
- *Four Artists*, Artists Space, New York

1979
- *Re-figuration*, Max Protetch Gallery, New York

1980
- **Ils se Disent Peintres, Ils se Disent Photographes*, Musée d'Art Moderne, Paris
- **Likely Stories*, Castelli Graphics, New York
- Metro Pictures, New York

1981
- **Autoportraits*, Centre Pompidou, Musée d'Art Moderne, Paris
- **Body Language: Figurative Aspects of Recent Art*, Hayden Gallery, Massachusetts Institute of Technology, Cambridge, Massachusetts; Fort Worth Art Museum, Texas; University of South Florida, Tampa; Contemporary Arts Center, Cincinnati, Ohio
- *Erweiterte Fotografie*, 5. Wiener Internationale Biennale, Vienna Secession
- *Il Gergo Inquieto*, Museo Sant'Agostino, Genoa
- *Photo*, Metro Pictures, New York
- **Young Americans*, Allen Memorial Art Museum, Oberlin, Ohio

1982
- *Art and the Media*, The Renaissance Society, University of Chicago
- *Body Language*, Massachusetts Institute of Technology, Cambridge, Massachusetts
- **Documenta 7*, Kassel, West Germany
- **Eight Artists: The Anxious Edge*, Walker Art Center, Minneapolis
- **La Biennale di Venezia*, Venice
- *Lichtbildnisse: The Portrait in Photography*, Rheinisches Landesmuseum, Bonn
- **New Figuration in America*, Milwaukee Art Museum, Wisconsin
- **Recent Color*, San Francisco Museum of Modern Art
- **Faces Photographed*, Grey Art Gallery, New York University
- **The Image Scavengers: Photography*, Institute of Contemporary Art, Philadelphia
- *20th Century Photographs from the Museum of Modern Art*, Seibu Museum of Art, Tokyo; University of *Hawaii Art Gallery, Honolulu
- *Urban Kisses*, Institute of Contemporary Art, London
- *Subject: Women*, University Art Galleries/ University of Southern California

1983
- **Back to the U.S.A.*, Kunstmuseum Lucerne; (1983–84) Rheinisches Landesmuseum, Bonn; Wurttembergischer Kunstverein, Stuttgart
- **Faces Since the 50s*, Bucknell University, Pennsylvania
- **Big Pictures by Contemporary Photographers*, The Museum of Modern Art, New York
- **Directions 1983*, Hirshhorn Museum, Washington, D.C.
- *Drawings Photographs*, Leo Castelli Gallery, New York
- **Presentation: Recent Portrait Photography*, Taft Museum
- *Facets of the Collection: Recent Acquisitions*, San Francisco Museum of Contemporary Art
- **1983 Biennial Exhibition*, Whitney Museum of American Art, New York
- *The New Art*, The Tate Gallery, London

1984
- **Alibis*, Centre Pompidou, Musée d'Art Moderne, Paris
- *Color Photographs: Recent Acquisitions*, The Museum of Modern Art, New York
- **Content: A Contemporary Focus, 1974–1984*, Hirshhorn Museum, Washington, D.C.
- *La Narrativa Internacional de Hoy*, Museo Rufino Tamayo, Mexico City; P.S. 1, New York
- **The Heroic Figure*, Contemporary Arts Museum, Houston, Texas; Brooks Memorial Art Gallery, Memphis, Tennessee; Alexandria Museum, Alexandria, Louisiana; The Santa Barbara Museum of Art, Santa Barbara, California
- **The Fifth Biennale of Sydney, Private Symbol: Social Metaphor*, Art Gallery of New South Wales, Sydney, Australia
- **Sex-Specific: Photographic Investigations of Contemporary Sexuality*, The School of the Art Institute of Chicago
- *Umgang mit der Aura*, Stadtische Galerie Regensburg, West Germany

1985
- **Anniottanta*, Galleria Comunale d'Arte Moderna Bologna, Italy
- **Autoportrait a l'Epoque de la Photographie*, Musée Cantonal des Beaux-Arts, Lausanne; Wurttembergischer Kunstverein, Stuttgart
- *The Making of Modern Museum*, San Francisco Museum of Modern Art
- *1985 Carnegie International*, Museum of Art, Carnegie Institute, Pittsburgh
- **American Images: Photography 1945–1980*, The Barbican Art Gallery, London
- *Eau de Cologne*, Monika Sprüth Galerie, Cologne
- *Figuring It Out: Exploring the Figure in Contemporary Art*, Laguna Gloria Art Museum, Austin, Texas
- **1985 Biennial Exhibition*, Whitney Museum of American Art, New York
- **New York 85*, ARCA Centre d'Art Contemporain, Marseilles
- *Self-Portrait*, The Museum of Modern Art, New York

1986
- *Jenny Holzer/Cindy Sherman*, The Contemporary Arts Center, Cincinnati
- **Altered Egos: Samaras, Sherman, Wegman*, Phoenix Art Museum, Arizona
- **Art and Its Double: A New York Perspective*, Fundacio Caixa de Pensions, Barcelona and La Caixa de Pensions, Madrid
- *Eve and the Future*, Hamburger Kunsthalle, Hamburg
- **Individuals: A Selected History of Contemporary Art, 1945–1986*, Museum of Contemporary Art, Los Angeles
- **La Magie de l'Image*, Musée d'Art contemporain de Montreal
- *Prospect 86, Frankfurter Kunstverein, Frankfurt
- **Staging the Self: Self-Portrait Photography 1840s–1980s*, National Portrait Gallery, London; Plymouth Arts Centre; John Hansard Gallery, Southhampton; Ikon Gallery, Birmingham
- **Stills: Cinema and Video Transformed*, Seattle Art Museum
- **The American Exhibition*, The Art Institute of Chicago

1987
- *Art Against AIDS*, Metro Pictures, New York
- **Avant-Garde in the Eighties*, Los Angeles County Museum of Art
- **Implosion: A Postmodern Perspective*, Moderna Museet, Stockholm
- **L'Epoque, la mode, la morale, La Passion: Aspects de l'art d'aujourd'hui, 1977–1987*, Musée National d'Art Moderne, Centre Georges Pompidou, Paris
- **New York; Des Moines Art Center, Iowa*
- **Photography and Art: Interaction Since 1946*, Los Angeles County Museum of Art; Museum of Art, Fort Lauderdale, Florida; Queens Museum, New York; Des Moines Art Center, Iowa
- **Aspects of Conceptualism in American Work, Part II*, Ave. B Gallery, New York
- **This Is Not a Photograph: Twenty Years of Large-Scale Photography 1966–1986*, The John and Mable Ringling Museum of Art, Sarasota, Florida; The Akron Art Museum, Ohio; The Chrysler Museum, Norfolk, Virginia

1988
- **Matris*, Malmo Konsthall, Sweden
- **1988: The World of Art Today*, Milwaukee Art Museum, Wisconsin
- **Just Like a Woman*, Greenville County Museum of Art
- **Presi Per Incantamento*, Padiglione d'Arte Contemporanea di Milano, Milan
- Studio Guenzani, Milan (two-person exhibition with Louise Lawler)
- *The Pop Project*, The Clocktower, New York
- **Visions/Revisions: Contemporary Representation*, Marlborough Gallery, New York

1989
- **A Forest of Signs: Art in the Crisis of Representation*, The Museum of Contemporary Art, Los Angeles
- *Bilderstreit*, Mense Rhineside Halls, Cologne
- *Encore II: Celebrating Fifty Years*, The Contemporary Arts Center, Cincinnati, Ohio
- **Image World: Art and Media Culture*, Whitney Museum of American Art, New York
- **Re-Presenting the 80s*, Simon Watson Gallery, New York
- *Invention and Continuity in Contemporary Photography*, The Metropolitan Museum of Art, New York
- **Making Their Mark: Women Artists Move into the Mainstream, 1970–85*, Cincinnati Art Museum; New Orleans Museum of Art, Loiusiana; Denver Art Museum, Colorado; Pennsylvania Academy of the Fine Arts, Philadelphia
- *Moscow - Vienna - New York*, The Vienna Festival, Vienna
- *Peinture Cinema Peinture*, Centre de la Vielle Charite, Musée de Marseille
- **Photography Now*, The Victoria and Albert Museum, London
- **Surrogate Selves*, The Corcoran Gallery of Art, Washington, D.C.
- **The Art of Photography: 1839–1989*, The Museum of Fine Arts, Houston; Ministry of Culture of the Soviet Union; Royal Academy of Arts, London
- *Tenir l'image a distance*, Musée d'Art Contemporain de Montreal
- **Three Decades: The Oliver Hoffman Collection*, Museum of Contemporary Art, Chicago
- *The Photographer's Eye: A Selection by Chris Kellep*, Victoria and Albert Museum, London
- **The Photography of Invention: American Pictures of the 1980s*, National Museum of American Art, Smithsonian Institution, Washington D.C.
- **Konzeptuelle Fotografie*, Wiener Secession, Vienna, Austria

1991
- *Art That Happens to be Photography*, The Texas Gallery, Houston
- **1991 Biennial Exhibition*, Whitney Museum of American Art, New York
- *Art of the 1980s: Selections from the Collection of the Eli Broad Family Foundation*, Duke University Museum of Art, Raleigh, North Carolina
- *Metropolis*, Martin-Gropius-Bau, Berlin
- *Self-Portraits of Women in the Eighties*, Tokyo Metropolitan Museum of Photography
- *Places with a Past: New Site-Specific Art in Charleston*, Spoleto Festival, Charleston, South Carolina
- **1st Internale Foto-Triennale Esslingen*, Villa Merkel; Bahnwartehaus; Schwarhaus, Altes Rathaus; Galerie im Heppacher; Esslingen am Neckar
- *Devil on the Stairs: Looking Back on the Eighties*, Institute of Contemporary Art, Philadelphia; Newport Harbor Art Museum, Newport Beach, California
- *A Visage Decouvert*, Fondation Cartier, Jouy-en-Josas, France
- *Displacements*, Atlantic Center for Contemporary Art, Las Palmas, Canary Islands
- *Carroll Dunham, Mike Kelley, Cindy Sherman*, Metro Pictures
- *Art & Art*, Castello di Rivoli, Turin, Italy
- *Altrove: Fra immagine e identità fra identità e tradizione*, Centro per l'Arte Contemporanea Luigi Pecui, Italy
- *Just What is it that Makes Today's Home So Different, So Appealing*, The Hyde Collection, Glens Falls, New York
- *Adam and Eve*, The Museum of Modern Art, Saitama, Japan
- *"No Laughing Matter"*, Independent Curators Incorporated (traveling exhibition)

1990
- *Affinities and Intuitions: The Gerald S. Elliot Collection of Contemporary Art*, The Art Institute of Chicago
- **Culture and Commentary*, The Hirshhorn Museum, Washington, D.C.
- **Energies*, The Stedelijk Museum, Amsterdam
- *Figuring the Body*, Museum of Fine Arts, Boston
- *Fotografie*, Galerie Max Hetzler, Cologne
- *Louise Lawler, Cindy Sherman, Laurie Simmons*, Metro Pictures, New York
- **Je EST un Autre*, Galeria COMICOS/LUIS SERPA, Lisbon; Fundacao de Serralves
- **Photography Until Now*, The Museum of Modern Art, New York
- **The Art of Photography: 1839–1989*, Sezon Museum of Art, Tokyo
- *The Decade Show*, The Museum of Contemporary Hispanic Art, The New Museum and the Studio Museum of Harlem, New York
- **The Readymade Boomerang*, Eighth Biennial of Sydney, Australia
- **To Be and Not to Be*, Centre D'Art Santa Monica, Barcelona

1992
- *Quotations: The Second History of Art*, The Aldrich Museum of Contemporary Art, Ridgefield, Connecticut
- *Pleasures and Terrors of Domestic Comfort*, The Museum of Modern Art, New York
- *More Than Photography*, The Museum of Modern Art, New York
- Galerie Max Hetzler, Cologne

Ars Pro Domo, Museum Ludwig, Cologne
- **Post Human*, Musée d'Art Contemporain, Pully/Lausanne, Switzerland; Castello di Rivoli, Turin; Deste Foundation, Athens; Deichtorhallen, Hamburg; Israel Museum, Jerusalem
- *Dirty Data. Schürmann Sammlung*, Ludwig Forum für Internationale Kunst, Aachen
- **Dirt and Domesticity*, Whitney Museum of American Art, Equitable Center, New York
- *Art in Embassies Program*, American Embassy in Prague
- **Imagenes de Guerra*, Centro Cultural Arte Contemporanea, Mexico City
- *Erotiques*, A.B. Galerie, Paris
- **Perils et Coleres*, capc Musée d'Art Contemporain, Bordeaux
- **Hollywood, Hollywood: Identity Under the Guise of Celebrity*, Art Center College of Design, California
- *Not For Sale*, Tel Aviv Museum of Art
- **American Art of the 80s*, Museo d'Arte Moderna e Contemporanea di Trento, Italy
- *Selected Works from the Early Eighties*, K-Raum Daxer, Munich
- *Spiellholle. Asthetik und Gewalt*, Akademie der Kunste und Wissenschaften, Frankfurt; Grazer Kunstverein, Graz, Austria; Galerie Sylvana Lorenz, Paris

1993
- **Louise Lawler, Cindy Sherman, Laurie Simmons*, Kunsternes Hus, Oslo; Museum of Contemporary Art, Helsinki
- **1993 Biennial Exhibition*, Whitney Museum of American Art, New York
- *Body Doubles*, Ansel Adams Center, San Francisco
- *American Art of This Century*, Martin-Gropius-Bau, Berlin; Royal Academy of Arts, London
- **The Uncanny*, Sonsbeek '93, Geementemuseum, Arnhem, Holland
- *Commodity Image*, International Center for Photography, New York; ICA. Boston
- *Vivid: Intense Images of American photographers*, Raab Galerie, Berlin Galerie Ursula Schurr, Stuttgart
- *Cindy Sherman, Laurie Simmons*, Fay Gold Gallery, Atlanta, Georgia
- *The Legacy of Hans Bellmer*, Jan Turner Gallery, Los Angeles
- *1920. The Subtlety of Subversion, the Continuity of Intervention*, Exit Art, New York
- Metro Pictures, New York
- Studio Guenzani, Milan
- *Daydream Nation*, Luhring Augustine Gallery, New York
- *Konstruktion Zitat*, Sprengel Museum, Hannover, Germany
- *Strange Hotel*, Aarhus Kunstmuseum, Denmark
- *l'envers des choses*, Centre Pompidou, Paris
- **Das Bild des Körpers*, Frankfurter Kunstverein, Frankfurt
- *8 American Artists*, Galerie Bernd Klüser, Munich
- *Up in Smoke*, Knoedler & Company, New York
- *Network*, Kunsternes Hus, Oslo
- Centre Pompidou, Paris
- **Diskurse der Bilder: Photokunstlerishe Reprisen kunsthistorisher Werke*, Kunsthistorisches Museum, Vienna, Austria
- **Real Sex*, Salzburg Kunstverein, Austria,

1994
- *Pictures of the Real World (In Real Time)*, Paula Cooper Gallery, New York, Galleria Massimo De Carlo, Italy
- **World Morality*, Kunsthalle, Basel
- *Suture-Phantasmen der Vollkommenheit*, Salzberger Kunstverein
- Galerie Samia Saouma, Paris
- **Against All Odds: The Healing Powers of Art*, The Ueno Royal Museum and The Hakone Open-Air Museum, Japan
- *Body and Soul*, The Baltimore Museum of Art, Maryland
- **Dialogue with the Other*, Kunsthallen Brandts Klaedefabrik, Denmark
- *Ike + de Ander - Dignity for All: Reflections on Humanity*, Beurs van Berlage, Amsterdam
- *Art in the Present Tense: The Aldrich's Curatorial History 1964–1994*, The Aldrich Museum of Contemporary Art, Ridgefield, Connecticut
- *Opera Prima*, Kulturna Manifestacija, Ex Opificio Gaslini, Pescara, Trevi Flash Art Museum of Contemporary Art, Cankarjev Dom, Slovenija, Italy
- *New York 'Unplugged'*, Gallery Cotthem, Zeedijk
- *The Century of the Multiple: From Duchamp to the Present*, Deichtorhallen, Hamburg
- **Jurgen Klauke - Cindy Sherman*, Sammlung Goetz, Munich
- *Genres in Painting*, Centro Atlantico de Arte Moderno, Canary Islands
- *Transformers: The Art of Multiphrenia*, Marieluise Hessel & Richard Black Center for Curatorial Studies & Art in Contemporary Culture, Bard College, Annanale on Hudson, New York; Decker Galleries, Maryland Institute, College of Art, Baltimore, Maryland; Herbert F. Johnson Museum of Art, Cornell University, Ithaca, NY; Nexus Contemporary Art Center, Atlanta, Georgia; Art Center of Windsor, Ontario, Canada; Illingworth Kerr Art Gallery of the Alberta College of Art 7 Design, Alberta
- *Facts and Figures*, Lannan Foundation, Los Angeles
- **Quotation: Re-Presenting History*, Winnipeg Art Gallery
- *Virtual Reality: Contemporary Art*, National Gallery of Australia
- *Fotografinnen der Gegenwart*, Museum Folkwang Essen, Germany
- **After Art: Rethinking 150 Years of Photography*, Henry Art Gallery, University of Washington, Seattle, WA
- *It's How You Play the Game*, Exit Art/The First World, New York
- **The Making of a Modern Museum*, San Francisco Museum of Modern Art

1995
- *Call it Sleep*, Witte de With, Rotterdam, The Netherlands
- *Projections*, Ydessa Hendeles Art Foundation, Toronto
- **1995 Biennial Exhibition*, Whitney Museum of American Art, New York
- **Photography Today*, Sonje Museum of Contemporary Art, Kyungsangbuk-Do, Korea
- **Zeichen & Wunder*, Kunsthaus Zurich, Switzerland
- *Alternatives: 20 Years of Hallwalls Contemporary Art Center 1975–1995*, Burchfield-Penny Art Center, Buffalo, New York
- *Komix*, Brooke Alexander Editions, New York
- *Art and Film Since 1945*, The Museum of Contemporary Art, Los Angeles
- **XLVI Esposizione Internazionale d'Arte 1995*, La Biennale di Venezia
- *Regards croisés*, ELAC, Centre d'Echanges de Perrache, Lyon
- *Large Body*, Pace MacGill, New York
- **Die Muse?: Transforming the Image of Women in Contemporary Art*, in conjunction with Salzburger Festival, Galerie Thaddaeus Ropac, Paris
- *Histoire de l'infamie*, Biennale de Venise, Cercle de l'Arsenal
- **Autres Victoires*, Montiucon, chateau de la Louviere, Paris
- S.L. Simpson Gallery, Toronto
- *Cenas Domesticas*, Modula
- **The Monster Show*, Museum of Contemporary Art, Miami, Florida
- *Mode et Art: 1960–1990*, Palais des Beaux-Arts, Brussels
- **FeminiMasculin: Le Sexe de l'Art?*, Musée National d'Art Moderne, Centre Georges Pompidou, Musée d'Art Moderne Paris
- **L'Effet Cinéma*, Musée d'art Contemporain de Montréal
- **Laughter Ten Years After*, Center for the Arts, Wesleyan University, Connecticut
- **1995 Carnegie International*, The Carnegie Museum of Art, Pittsburgh, Pennsylvania
- *Imaginary Beings*, Exit Art, New York
- **Playtime: Artists and Toys*, Whitney Museum of American Art at Champion, Stamford, Connecticut
- *Passions Privee*, Musée d'Art Moderne de la Ville de Paris

1996
- *Everything that's Interesting is New: The Dakis Joannou Collection*, Athens School of Fine Arts "the factory", Greece
- *Empty Dress*, The Rubelle & Norman Schafler Gallery, Pratt Institute, Brooklyn
- *Controfigura*, Studio Guenzani, Milan
- *TECHNIK: FOTOGRAFIE. Teil 2*, Busche Galerie, Berlin
- *Altered and Irrational: Selections From the Permanent Collection*, Whitney Museum of American Art, New York
- **Sex & Crime: On Human Relationships*, Sprengel Museum, Hannover
- *Deformations: Aspects of the Modern Grotesque*, The Museum of Modern Art, New York
- **Prospect 96: Photographie in der Gegenwartskunst*, Frankfurter Kunstvereins im Steinernen Haus und der Schirn Ksnthalle, Frankfurt
- **L'Informe: le Modernisme a Rebours*, Centre Georges Pompidou, Musée National d'Art Moderne, Paris
- **Sexual Politics: Judy Chicago's Dinner Party and Feminists in Art History*, UCLA Armand Hammer Gallery, Los Angeles, California
- *Nudo & Crudo: Sensitive Body, Visible Body*, Claudia Gian Ferrari Arte Contemporanea, Milan
- *Multiple Pleasure*, Tanya Bonakdar Gallery, New York
- **Hall of Mirrors: Art and Film Since 1945*, The Museum of Contemporary Art, Los Angeles; The Wexner Center for the Arts, Columbus, Ohio; Palazzo delle Esposizioni, Rome; The Museum of Contemporary Art, Chicago
- *Laughter Ten Years After*, Houghton House Gallery, Hobart and William Smith Colleges, Geneva, New York; Beaver College Art Gallery, Glenside, Pennsylvania
- Galeria 56, Budapest
- *New York 'Unplugged II'*, Gallery Cotthem, Knokke-Zoute, Belgium
- **Radical Images*, 2nd Austrian Triennial on Photography 1996, Neue Galerie am Landesmuseum Joanneum, Graz
- *Doll House*, Illinois State University
- *Lobby*, Arizona State University Art Museum, Tempe, AZ
- **Fragments*, Museu d'Art Contemporani, Barcelona
- **New Persona/New Universe*, Biennale di Firenze, Florence, Italy
- **Picasso: A Contemporary Dialogue*, Galerie Thaddeus Ropac, Salzburg/Paris,
- *Jocaste en Arcadie a Madame de Sevigne - une evocation contemporaine du XVIIe Siecle*, Chateau des Adhemar, Montelimar; Chateau de Grignan; FRAC Basilico Fine Arts, New York
- Rhone-Alpes, Lyon, France
- **Face Value: American Portraits*, The Parrish Art Museum, Southampton, New York; Wexner Center for the Arts, Columbus, Ohio; Tampa Art Museum, Tampa, Florida
- **A/drift*, Center for Curatorial Studies, Bard College, New York

1997
- **Making it Real*, The Aldrich Museum of Contemporary Art, Ridgefield, Connecticut, The Reykjavik Municipal Art Musuem, Reykjavik, Iceland, Portland Museum of Art, Portland, Maine, Bayly Art Museum, University of Virginia, Charlottesville, Virginia,
- **Gender Performance in Photography*, Solomon R. Guggenheim Museum, New York
- *Portraits: 19th & 20th Century Photography*, Malborough, New York
- *Metamorphosis*, Claudia Gian Ferrati Arte Contemporanea, Milan, Italy
- **Making Pictures: Women and Photography, 1975–Now*, Benard Toale Gallery, Boston, Massachusetts
- *Gothic*, The Institute of Contemporary Art, Boston, Massachusetts
- **Mascara i Mirall*, Museu D'Art Contemporani, Barcelona, Spain
- *The Age of Modernisn, Art in the 20th Century*, Zietgeist-Gesellschaft, Berlin (ex. CD-ROM)
- **Finders Keepers*, Contemporary Arts Museum, Houston, Texas,
- *Altered Egos*, Hallwalls Contemporary Art Center, Buffalo, New York
- *Artisti Per Sarajevo*, Fondazione Bevilacqua La Masa San Marco, Venice, Italy
- Metro Pictures, New York
- **:Angel: Angel*, Kunsthalle Wien, Galerie Rudolfinum Prag, Astria
- *Landscape: The Pastoral to the Urban*, Center for Curatorial Studies: Bard College, New York
- *Tuning Up #4*, Kunst Museum, Wolfsburg, Germany
- *Autoportraits*, Galerie Municipale du Chateau D'Eau, Toulouse, France
- **160 Years of Photography: Masterworks of the San Francisco Museum of Modern Art*, Ho-Am Art Museum, Seoul, Korea
- **On the Edge: Contemporary Art from the Werner and Elaine Dannheisser Collection*, The Museum of Modern Art, New York
- **Scene of the Crime*, The Armand Hammer Museum of Art and Cultural Center, Los Angeles, California
- *Defining Eye: Women Photographers of the 20th Century*, the Saint Louis Art Museum; the Museum of Fine Arts, Santa Fe; the Mead Museum of Art, Amherst; the Witchita Art Museum
- **Deslocacoes From Here to There*, Centro de Arte Moderna José de Azeredo Perdigao, Lisbon; Centro Portugues de Fotografia, Porto
- *Laughter Ten Years After*, Exquisite Corpse, Burlington, Vermont
- **Body*, the Art Gallery of New South Wales, Sydney, Australia
- **Elvis + Marilyn: 2 x Immortal*, Hokkaido Obihiro Museum of Art, Obihiro, Japan; Daimaru Museum, Umeda, Osaka, Japan; Takamatsu City Museum of Art, Takamatsu, Japan; Sogo Museum of Art, Sogo, Japan; Mitsukoskohi Museum of Art, Fukouka, Japan; Kumamoto Prefectural Museum of Art, Kumamoto, Japan
- **Stills: Art and Cinema in the Marieluise Hessel Collection*, Centro Cultural Light, Rio de Janeiro
- *Signs of Age: Representing the Older Body*, the Contemporary Arts Forum, Santa Barbara, California

1998
- *I Love Art*, In Kahn, New York
- *Real Stories*, Friedrich Petzel & Marianne Boesky, New York
- *Mysterious Voyages*, Contemporary Museum, Maryland, Baltimore
- *Exterminating Angel*, Galerie Ghislaine Hussenot, Paris
- **Pop Surrealism*, Aldrich Museum of Contemporary Art, Ridgefield, Connecticut
- *Culturgest*, Galerias do Edifício Sede da Caixa Geral de Depósitos, Lisbon, Portugal
- *Avatar*, De Oude Kerk, Amsterdam, The Netherlands
- **Mirror Images: Women, Surrealism, and Self-Representation*, MIT List Center, Cambridge, Massachusetts; Miami Art Museum, Miami, Florida; San Francisco Museum of Modern Art, CA
- **Stills: A Selection from the Marieluise Hessel Collection*, Center For Curatorial Studies, Annandale-on-Hudson, New York
- **Read my Lips*, National Gallery of Australia, Canberra, Australia
- *Is This Art?*, Toyota Municipal Museum of Art, Toyota Aichi; Kawamura Memorial Museum of Art; Contemporary Art Center, Art Tower Mito, Mito-shi, Ibaraki, Japan
- **Corps à vif, Art et anatomie*, Musée d'Art et d'Histoire, Geneva, Switzerland
- **Beyond Belief: Modern Art and the Religious Imagination*, National Gallery of Victoria, Australia
- **Double Trouble: The Patchett Collection*, Museum of Contemporary Art, San Diego; Museo de las Artes and Instituto Cultural Cabanas, Gaudalahara, Mexico; Museo de Monterrey, Mexico; Museo Universitario Contemporáneo de Art, Mexico City; Auditorio de Galicia and Inglesia San Domingos de Bonaval, Santiago de Compostela, Spain; Sala Amós Salvador, Logroño, Spain
- **Connections and Contradictions: Modern and Contemporary Art from Atlanta Collections*, Michael C. Carlos Museum, Emory University, Atlanta, Georgia
- **From Warhol to Mapplethorpe: Three Decades of Art at ICA*, Institute of Contemporary Art, Pennsylvania
- **American Playhouse: The Theatre of Self-Representation*, The Power Plant, Toronto, Canada

- *Scratches on the Surface of Things*, Museum Boijmans Van Beuningen, Rotterdam
- *Shoot Me*, Goldstrom Gallery, New York
- **Art and the American Experience*, Kalamazoo Institute of Arts, MI
- **A Portrait of Our Times: An Introduction to the Logan Collection*, San Francisco Museum of Modern Art
- **Escences de L'Imaginari: Festival internacional de Teatre visuali de Titelles de Barcelona. XXV aniversari*, Institut del Teatre, Barcelona, Spain
- **Everything of Value*, Slot Loevestein, Gorcums Museum, The Netherlands

1999

- *...on the sublime...*, Rooseum, Malmö, Sweden
- *Six Americans*, Skarstedt Fine Arts, New York
- **Looking at Ourselves: Works by Women Artists from the Logan Collection*, San Francisco Museum of Modern Art,
- **Rosso vivo*, Padiglione d'Arte Contempoanea, Milan
- **Art at Work: Forty Years of the Chase Manhattan Collection*, Museum of Fine Arts, the Contemporary Arts Museum, Houston, Texas
- *Das Versprechen der Fotografie*, Kestner Gesellschaft, Hannover
- **Skin Deep*, The Israel Museum, Jerusalem
- *Gesammelte Werke 1: Zeitgenössische Kunst seit 1968*, Kunstmuseum, Wolfsburg
- *Notorious*, Museum of Modern Art, Oxford
- *Ceramic Millennium*, Museum Het Kruithuis, 's-Hertogenbosch
- *The Hand*, The Power Plant, Toronto
- **The Time of Our Lives*, New Museum, New York
- **American Century*, Whitney Museum of American Art, New York
- **Der Anagrammatische Körper*, Jahresmuseum, Mürzzuschlag, Austria; ZKM Medientheater, Karlsruhe
- *Who's That Girl*, Sandra Gering Gallery, New York
- *Inverted Odysseys*, Grey Art Gallery, New York
- *Rattling the Frame: The Photographic Space 1974–1999*, San Francisco Camerawork, San Francisco
- *The Century of the Body: Photoworks 1900–2000*, Musée de l'Elysée, Lisbon
- *Triennale Exhibition: Sentiment of the Year 2000*, Triennale di Milano, Milano
- *Macht und Fürsorge*, Trinitatiskirche, Cologne
- **Regarding Beauty*, Hirshhorn Museum, Washington, D.C.
- *Framed and Shot*, The Allen Memorial Art Museum
- **Notorious: Alfred Hitchcock and Contemporary Art*, Museum of Modern Art, Oxford, England; Museum of Contemporary Art, Sydney, Australia; Art Gallery of Hamilton, Ontario, Canada; Kunsthallen Brandts Klaedefabrik, Denmark; Tokyo Opera City Art Gallery, Japan; Hiroshima City Museum of Contemporary Art; Centre Cultural de la Fundacio 'la Caixa' de Lleida, Lleida, Spain; Centre Cultural de la Fundacio 'la Caixa' de Tarragona, Tarragona, Spain

2000

- **Let's Entertain*, Walker Art Center, Minneapolis; Centre Georges Pompidou, Paris; Portland Art Musuem, Oregon; Museo Rufino Tamayo, Mexico City, Mexico; Kunstmuseum Wolfsburg, Wolfsburg, Germany (2001); Miami Art Museum, Miami (2001)
- *Ich ist etwas Anderes*, Kunstsammlung, Dusseldorf
- *What's New: Recent Acquisitions in Photography*, Whitney Museum of American Art, New York
- *End Papers*, Neuberger Museum of Art, Purchase, New York
- *Looking Back*, Bard College Center for Curatorial Studies, Annandale-on-Hudson, New York
- *Representing: A Show of Identities*, The Parrish Art Museum and Southampton High School, Southampton, New York
- *Inverted Odysseys: Claude Calhoun, Maya Deren, Cindy Sherman*, Grey Art Gallery, New York University, New York
- *Ghost in the Shell*, LA County Museum of Art, New York
- *Staged: Constructions of Reality in Contemporary Photography*, Bonakdar Jancou Gallery, New York
- MoMA 2000/Walker Evans and Company, Museum of Modern Art, New York
- Art in America 2000, US Department of State Art in Embassies Program, Washington D.C.
- *Limited and Unlimited Editions*, Artists Space (benefit exhibition), New York
- *Studio Visit*, (benefit auction) Art Gallery Ontario, Toronto
- *Bizarre*, John Gibson Gallery, New York
- **Présumés innocents- L'art contemporain et l'enfance*, capc, Musée d'Art Contemporain, Bordeaux
- **Around 1984- A Look at Art in the 80's*, P.S. 1, New York
- **The Century of the Body*, Musée de l'Elysée, Lausanne, Switzerland,
- *Open Ends*, Museum of Modern Art, New York
- **Hitchcock and Art: Fatal Coincidences*, The Montreal Museum of Fine Arts, Quebec; Centre Georges Pompidou, Paris (2001)
- **Surface and Depth: Trends in Contemporary Portrait Photography*, Hood Museum of Art, Dartmouth College, Hanover, New Hampshire
- *The Bigger Picture*, Art Gallery of Ontario, Toronto
- **Is Seeing Believing?*, North Carolina Museum of Art, Raleigh, North Carolina (2001); The Cummer Museum of Art and Gardens, Jacksonville, Florida (2001)
- *Hyper Mental*, Kunsthaus Zürich (2001); Hamburger Kunsthalle (2001)
- *Oehlen, Zhen, Sherman*, Art & Public, Geneva

2001

- *Postmodern Americans*, The Menil Collection, Houston
- *Angles of Incidence*, Center for Curatorial Studies, Bard College, Annandale-on-Hudson, New York
- **Double Vision: Photographs from the Strauss Collection*, University Art Museum, California State University, Long Beach, California
- **Settings & Players*, White Cube, London
- **Kindly Lent Their Owner*, Bellagio Gallery of Fine Art, Las Vegas
- **Collaborations with Parkett: 1984 to Now*, Museum of Modern Art, New York
- *Bodily Acts*, Center for Curatorial Studies, Bard College, Annandale-on-Hudson, New York
- **Moving Pictures*, Galerien der Stadt Esslingen, Esslingen, Germany
- *Without Hesitation [Ohne Zögern]- The Olbricht Collection Part 2*, Neues Museum Weserburg Bremen, Bremen, Germany
- *Extra Art*, Logan Galleries, California College of Arts and Crafts, San Fransisco
- *Bogus: Conterfeit Images and Contemporary Art*, Castle Gallery, The College of New Rochelle, New Rochelle, New York
- **Jasper Johns to Jeff Koons: Four Decades of Art from the Broad Collections*, Los Angeles County Museum of Art; Museum of Fine Arts, Boston (2002)
- **Double Life*, Generali Foundation, Vienna, Austria
- **Naked Since 1950*, C&M Arts, New York
- Sommer Contemporary Art, Tel-Aviv, Israel
- *Issues of Identity in Recent American Art*, Roland Gibson Art Gallery, The State University of New York at Potsdam; University Galleries, Illinois State University, Normail, Illinois; The Ewing Gallery of Art and Architecture, University of Tennessee, Knoxville, Tennessee; Ben Shahn Galleries, William Patterson University, Wayne, New Jersey (2002); Samek Art Gallery, Bucknell University, Lewisburg, Pennsylvania (2002)
- **ABBILD: Recent Portraiture and Depiction*, Landesmuseum Joanneum, Graz, Austria
- **Lateral Thinking: Art of the 1990s*, Museum of Contemporary Art, San Diego, California; Colorado Sprigs Fine Art Center, Colorado Springs, Colorado (2002); Hood Museum, Dartmouth University, Hanover, New Hampshire (2004); Dayton Art Institute, Dayton, Ohio (2004)

2002

- **Chic Clicks: Creativity and Commerce in Contemporary Fashion Photography*, Institute of Contemporary Art, Boston, Massachusetts; Fotomuseum Winterthur, Winterthur, Switzerland
- *Popcorn and Politics—Artists on Art*, Museum of Contemporary Art, Helsinki, Finland
- Metro Pictures, New York
- *In the Blink of an Eye- Photo/ Art*, Sammlung Essl, Vienna
- *Super Heroes*, Galerie Edward Mitterand, Geneva
- **Tableaux Vivants*, Kunsthalle Wien, Vienna
- **Hautnah- The Goetz Collection*, Museum Villa Stuck, Munich
- **Espelho Cego [Blind Mirror]*, Museu de Arte Moderna de São Paulo, Brazil
- *Something/ Anything*, Matthew Marks Gallery, New York
- **AMERICAN STANDARD: (Para)Normality and Everyday Life*, Barbara Gladstone Gallery, New York
- *Moving Pictures*, Solomon R. Guggenhein Museum, New York
- **Ahead of the 21st Century—The Pisces Collection*, Fürstenberg Sammlungen, Donaueschingen, Germany
- **Visions from America: Photographs from the Whitney Museum of American Art*, Whitney Museum of American Art, New York
- *Gloria*, White Columns, New York
- **Fabric of Vision*, National Gallery, London
- *Die Wohltat Der Kunst*, Staatliche Kunsthalle Baden-Baden, Baden-Baden, Germany
- *Extension*, Magasin 3 Stockholm Konsthall, Stockholm, Sweden
- **The Arch of Desire*, Center for Curatorial Studies, Bard College, Annandale-on-Hudson, New York
- *Rapture*, Barbican Gallery, London
- **Some Assembly Required: Collage Culture in Post-War America*, Everson Museum of Art, Syracuse, New York
- **Die Wohltat der Kunst*, Staatlichen Kunsthalle Baden-Baden, Baden-Baden, Germany
- **Contemporary American Photography 1970–2000*, Ho-Am Art Gallery, Seoul, Korea
- **Life, Death, Love, Hate, Pleasure, Pain*, Museum of Contemporary Art, Chicago

2003

- **Witness: Theories of Seduction*, Dorsky Gallery Curatorial Programs, Long Island City, New York
- *Constructed Realities: Contemporary Photography*, Orlando Museum of Art, Orlando, Florida
- **The Auroral Light: Photographs by Women from Grolier Club Member Collections*, The Grolier Club, New York
- *Bull's Eye: Works from the Astrup Fearnley Collection*, ARKEN Museum of Modern Art, Ishøj, Germany
- *Brightness*, Museum of Modern Art, Dubrovnik, Croatia
- **The Burbs*, DFN Gallery, New York
- **Just Love Me, Post / Feminist Positions of the 1990s from the Goetz Collection*, Fries Museum Leeuwarden, Leewarden, Germany; Bergen Art Museum, Bergen, Germany; Sammlung Goetz, Munich; Staatliche Kunsthalle Baden-Baden, Baden-Baden, Germany
- *Pletskud*, Arken Museum for Moderne Kunst, Skøvej, Germany
- **The Last Picture Show: Artists Using Photography 1960–1982*, Walker Art Center, Minneapolis, MN; UCLA Hammer Museum, Los Angeles
- *Artist's Choice: Mona Hatoum, Here Is Elsewhere*, Museum of Modern Art, Queens, New York
- Everyday Aesthetics, Astrup Fearnley Museum of Modern Art, Oslo
- *Reality/Fiction: (Re)Constructing Representation*, Jamaica Center for Arts&Learning, Jamaica, New York
- **Himmel & Helvete*, Kistefos Museum, Kistefoss, Norway
- **The Last Picture Show: Artists Using Photography 1960–1982*, Walker Art Center, Minneapolis;
- Miami Art Central, Florida
- **Through the Looking Glass—Women and Self-Representation in Contemporary Art*, Palmer
- Museum of Art, University Park, Pennsylvania
- *After Image*, The Fruitmarket Gallery, Edinburgh, Scotland, traveled to Victoria Miro, London (2004)
- *American Beauty—From Muybridge to Goldin*, Art Gallery of New South Wales, Sydney, Australia
- **Only Skin Deep: Changing Visions of the American Self*, International Center of Photography, New York

**A Clear Vision*, Internationales Haus der Photographie, Deichtorhallen Hamburg, Germany
Masquerade, John Michael Kohler Arts Center, Sheboygan, Wisconsin
Metacorpos, Paço das Artes, São Paulo, Brasil

2004

- *Explosive Photography*, Nassau County Museum of Art, Roslyn Harbor, New York
- *Treasure Island*, Kunstmuseum Wolfsburg, Wolfsburg, Germany
- *La Grande Parade – Portrait de L'artiste en Clown*, Galeries nationals du Grand Palais, Paris; National Gallery of Canada, Ottawa
- *Sugar & Snails*, The Park School Gallery, Baltimore, Maryland
- *Fashioning Fiction—In Photographing Since 1990*, Museum of Modern Art, New York
- *Art by MacArthur Fellows*, Carl Solway Gallery, Cincinnati, Ohio
- *Love/Hate—From Magritte to Cattelan, Masterpieces from MCA Chicago*, Villa Manin Center of Contemporary Art in Passariano, Italy
- *North Fork/South Fork*, Parrish Art Museum, Southampton, New York
- *I am the Walrus*, Cheim and Read, New York
- *NY Collects Buffalo State*, Buffalo State College, New York
- *Disguise*, Manchester Art Gallery, Manchester, England
- **Disparities & Deformations—Our Grotesque*, 5th International Site Santa Fe Bienniale, Site Santa Fe, New Mexico
- **The Amazing & The Immutable*, University of South Florida, Tampa
- **Perspectives at 25*, Contemporary Arts Museum, Houston, Texas
- **Der Hamburger Bahnof*, Museum für Gegenwart, Basel, Switzerland

2005

- **Print Me: An Exhibition*, curated by Philippe Segalot, Galerie Emmanuel Perrotin, Paris
- *Nudes in Vogue*, curated by Dodie Kazanjian for December Vogue, Mitchell-Innes & Nash, New York
- **In Limbo*, Victoria H. Myhren Gallery, University of Denver, Colorado
- **Contemporanea*, Fundación Juan March, Madrid
- **High Drama: Eugene Berman and the Legacy of the Melancholic Sublime*, McNay Art Museum, San Antonio, Texas
- *Inside Out Loud*, Mildred Lane Kemper Art Museum, Washington University, St. Louis, Missouri
- *Girls on Film*, Zwirner and Wirth, New York
- *Vertiges*, Printemps de septembre, Toulouse Festival of Contemporary Images, France
- *Empreinte Moi: Philippe Segalot's Exposition* Galerie Emmaneul Perrotin, Paris
- *The Art of 9/11*, Apexart, New York
- *Self Portraits*, Skarstedt Fine Art, New York
- *Flashback: Revisiting the Art of the Eighties*, Kunstmuseum Museum for Gegenwartskunst, Basel
- *Pandemic: Imaging AIDS*, Umbrage Editions, New York
- *25th Anniversary Exhibition*, Fay Gold Gallery, Atlanta
- *American Matrix: Contemporary Directions for the Harn Museum Collection*, Samuel P. Harn Museum of Art, University of Florida, Gainsville

2006
- Galerie Nicola von Senger, Zurich, Switzerland
- *Masquerade*, The Museum of Contemporary Art, Sydney, Australia
- Metro Pictures, New York
- *The Downtown Art Show: The New York Art Scene 1974–1984*, The Grey Art Gallery, Fales Library, New York University, New York

MUSEUM AND PUBLIC COLLECTIONS

- Akron Art Museum, Ohio
- Albright-Knox Art Gallery, Buffalo
- Allen Memorial Art Museum, Oberlin, Ohio
- Art Gallery of New South Wales, Sydney
- Art Gallery of Ontario, Toronto
- Art Institute of Chicago
- Astrup Fearnley Museet, Oslo
- Australian National Gallery, Canberra
- Baltimore Museum of Art, Maryland
- Birmingham Museum of Art
- Brooklyn Museum, New York
- Burchfield Art Center, Buffalo
- Carnegie Museum of Art, Pittsburgh,
- Centre Georges Pompidou, Paris
- Centro de Arte Reina Sofia, Madrid
- Chrysler Museum, Norfolk, Virginia
- Corcoran Gallery of Art, Washington, D.C.
- Dallas Museum of Fine Arts
- Des Moines Art Center
- Duke University Museum of Art, Durham, North Carolina
- Eli Broad Family Foundation, Los Angeles
- Emmanuel Hoffmann Foundation, Basel
- Everson Museum, Syracuse
- Fundacio "la Caixa", Barcelona
- Galleria d'Arte Moderna e Contemporanea Pallazzo Forti, Verona, Italy
- George Eastman House, Rochester
- Goetz Collection, Munich
- Henry Art Gallery, Washington
- Hamburger Bahnhof Museum fur Gegenwart, Berlin
- Hamburger Kunstalle, Hamburg
- Hara Museum of Contemporary Art, Tokyo
- Hayden Gallery, Massachusetts Institute of Technology, Cambridge
- High Museum, Atlanta
- Indianapolis Museum of Art
- International Center of Photography, New York
- Israeli Museum, Israel
- Kunsthalle Hambourg, Germany
- Kunsthaus, Zurich
- Kunstmuseum Wolfsburg, Germany
- Los Angeles County Museum of Art
- Louisiana Museum, Humlebaek, Denmark
- Madison Art Center, Wisconsin
- Malmo Konsthall, Sweden
- Metropolitan Museum of Art, New York
- Milwaukee Art Museum
- Moderna Museet, Stockholm
- Modern Art Museum of Fort Worth, Texas
- Mount Holyoke College Art Museum, South Hadley, Massachusetts
- Musée d'art Contemporain, Montréal
- Museo Nacional Centro de Arte Reina Sofia, Madrid
- Museum Boymans-van Beuningen, Rotterdam
- Museum Folkwang, Essen, Germany
- Museum des 20, Jahrunderts, Vienna
- Museum Ludwig, Koln
- Museum of Art, Carnegie Institute, Pittsburgh
- Museum of Contemporary Art, Chicago
- Museum of Contemporary Art, Helsinki
- Museum of Contemporary Art, Los Angeles
- Museum of Contemporary Art, Luxembourg
- Museum of Contemporary Art, Wright State University, Dayton
- Museum of Fine Arts, Boston
- Museum of Fine Arts, Houston
- Museum of Modern Art, New York
- Museum of Modern Art, Oslo
- New Britain Museum of American Art, New Britain, Conneticut
- Palmer Museum of Art, Pennsylvania State University, University Park, Pennsylvania
- Philadelphia Museum of Art
- Patchett Collection, San Diego
- Portland Art Museum, Oregon
- Power Gallery of Contemporary Art, University of Sydney, Australia
- Queensland Art Gallery, Brisbane, Australia
- Rijksmuseum Kroller-Muller, Otterlo, Holland
- Ringling Museum, Sarasota, Florida
- Rose Art Museum, Brandeis University, Walthan, Massachusetts
- Saatchi Collection, London
- San Francisco Museum of Modern Art
- Scottish National Gallery, Edinburgh
- Solomon R. Guggenheim Museum, New York
- Sprengel Museum, Hannover
- St. Louis Art Museum
- Staatsgalerie Stuttgart, Germany
- Stedelijk Museum, Amsterdam
- Tamayo Museum, Mexico City
- Tampa Museum of Art
- Tate Gallery, London
- Tokyo Metropolitan Museum of Photography
- University Art Gallery, SUNY, Binghamton
- University of Kentucky Art Museum, Lexington
- University of Virginia Art Museum
- Vasser College Art Gallery, Poughkeepsie, New York
- Victoria and Albert Museum, London
- Wadsworth Atheneum, Hartford
- Walker Art Center, Minneapolis
- Weatherspoon Art Gallery, Greensboro, North Carolina
- Whitney Museum of American Art, New York
- Williams College Museum of Art, Williamstown, Massachusetts
- Yale University Art Gallery, New Haven, Connecticut
- Ydessa Hendeles Art Foundation, Toronto
- Yokohama Museum of Art, Japan

FILM AND VIDEO DIRECTION

1997
- *Office Killer*, feature-film starring Molly Ringwald, Carol Kane, Jeanne Tripplehorn, Barbara Sukowa, Good Machine and Kardana/Swinsky Films

DOCUMENTARIES

1994
- *Nobody's Here But Me*, a 55 minute Cinecontact production for the BBC and the Arts Council of England, Director: Mark Stokes; Producer: Robert Mcnab

SELECTIVE BIBLIOGRAPHY

1978
- *Four Artists*, exh. cat., Artists Space, New York

1979
- "Cindy Sherman: Recent Pictures," *Sun & Moon*, autumn, p. 129–136
- Douglas Crimp, "Pictures," *October*, n°8, p. 75–88
- Valentine Tatransky, "Cindy Sherman, Artists Space," *Arts Magazine*, n°5, p. 19

1980
- Joseph Bishop, "Desperate Character," *Real Life Magazine*, n°4, p. 8–10
- Linda Cathcart, *Cindy Sherman: Photographs*, exh. cat., Contemporary Arts Museum, Houston
- Andy Grundberg, "Lies for the Eyes," *The Soho News*, 17 December
- Ben Lifson, "Masquerading," *The Village Voice*, 31 March
- *Likely Stories*, exh. cat., Castelli Graphics, New York
- Michel Nuridsany, *Ils se disent peintres, ils se disent photographes*, exh. cat., ARC/Musée d'Art Moderne de la Ville de Paris, Paris
- Craig Owens, "The Allegorical Impulse: Toward a Theory of Postmodernism, Part 2," *October*, n°13, p. 59–80
- Michael Shore, "Punk Rocks the Art World," *Artnews*, n°9, p. 78–85
- Abigail Solomon-Godeau, "Sexual Difference: Both Sides of the Camera," *CEPA Quarterly*, spring/summer, p. 17–24
- Valentine Tatransky, "Cindy Sherman," *Arts Magazine*, n°10, p. 27

1981
- *Autoportraits Photographiques*, exh. cat., Centre Georges Pompidou, Éditions du Centre Georges Pompidou/Éditions Herscher, Paris
- Germano Celant, *Inespressionismo Americano*, Bonini editore, Genoa
- Douglas Crimp, "Cindy Sherman: Making Pictures for the Camera," in *Young Americans*, exh. cat., Allen Memorial Art Museum, Oberlin
- Douglas Crimp, "The Photographic Activity of Postmodernism," *October*, n°15, p. 99–102
- Richard Flood, "Cindy Sherman, Metro Pictures," *Artforum*, n°7, p. 80
- Andy Grundberg, "Cindy Sherman: A Playful and Political Post Modernist," *The New York Times*, 22 November, p. 35
- Michael Klein, "Cindy Sherman," *Arts Magazine*, n°7, p. 5
- Roberta Smith, *Body Language: Figurative Aspects of Recent Art*, exh. cat., Hayden Gallery, Massachusetts Institute of Technology, Cambridge;; Fort Worth Art Museum, Fort Worth; University of South Florida, Tampa; Contemporary Arts Center, Cincinnati
- Roberta Smith, "Art," *The Village Voice*, 18 November
- Lynn Zelavansky, "Cindy Sherman, Metro Pictures," *Flash Art*, n°102, p. 43

1982
- Julia Ballerini, "Artificiality and Artifice: The Portraits of Diane Arbus and Cindy Sherman," *Center Quarterly*, autumn, Catskill Center for Photography Pub., Woodstock
- Els Barents, *Cindy Sherman*, exh. cat., The Stedelijk Museum, Amsterdam, Schirmer/Mosel Verlag, Munich
- Rosetta Brooks, "New York: Heroic City," *The Literary Review*, London
- *Cindy Sherman*, Déjà Vu Éditions, Dijon
- "Cindy Sherman Untitled Film Stills," portfolio, *Paris Review*, November, p. 133–139
- "Cindy Sherman," portfolio, *File Magazine*, n°3, p. 22–25
- *Documenta 7*, exh. cat., Kassel
- Hal Foster, "New York Art: Seven Types of Ambiguity," *Artforum*, n°6, p. 14–24
- Jamey Gambrell, "Cindy Sherman, Metro Pictures," *Artforum*, n°6, p. 85–86
- Grace Glueck, "Cindy Sherman," *The New York Times*, 22 October
- Roselee Goldberg, "Post-TV Art," *Portfolio*, July–August, p. 76–79
- Ellen Handy, "Cindy Sherman, Metro Pictures," *Arts Magazine*, n°4, p. 33
- Eleanor Heartney, "Anxiety show at the Walker," *The New Art Examiner*, n°9, p. 12
- John Howell and Shelley Rice, "Cindy Sherman's Seductive Surfaces," *Alive Magazine*, New York, September/October, p. 20–25
- Christopher Knight, "Photographer with an Eye on Herself," *The Los Angeles Herald Examiner*, 10 October, p. E–5
- Rosalind Krauss, "Reflecting on Post-Modernism," *Brand. New York, The Literary Review*, London, p. 54–57
- Kay Larsen, "Art," *The New York Magazine*, 8 November
- Ben Lifson, *Faces Photographed: Contemporary Camera Images*, exh. cat., The Grey Art Gallery, New York University, New York
- Kate Linker, "Melodramatic Tactics," *Artforum*, September, p. 30–32
- Lisa Lyons, *Eight Artists: the Anxious Edge*, exh. cat., The Walker Art Center, Minneapolis
- Paula Marincola, *Image Scavengers: Photography*, exh. cat., Institute of Contemporary Art, Philadelphia
- Dorothy Martinson, *Recent Color*, exh. cat., San Francisco Museum of Modern Art, San Francisco
- Paul Pouvreau and Jacques Ristorcelli, "Les Autoportraits de Cindy Sherman," *Les Cahiers du cinéma*, February, p. 13–14
- Richard Rhodes, "Cindy Sherman's 'Film Stills'," *Parachute*, September/October, p. 4–7
- Peter Schjeldahl, "Shermanettes," *Art in America*, March, p. 110–111
- Peter Schjeldahl and Russell Bowman, *New Figuration in America*, exh. cat., Milwaukee Art Museum, Milwaukee
- Christian Schlatter, "De l'Avant-garde, avant toute chose," *Vogue France*, October, p. 88
- Carol Squires, "The Difference Between Fibs and Fictions," *The Village Voice*, 2 November, p. 82
- John Szarkowski, *20th Century Photographs from the Museum of Modern Art*, exh. cat., The Museum of Modern Art, New York; Seibu Museum, Tokyo

1983
- *1983 Biennial Exhibition*, exh. cat., The Whitney Museum of American Art, New York
- Janet Borden, *Presentation: Recent Portrait Photography*, exh. cat., The Taft Museum, Cincinnati
- Christian Caujolle, *Cindy Sherman*, exh. cat., Musée d'Art et d'Industrie, Saint-Étienne
- Jack Cowart, *Currents 20. Cindy Sherman*, exh. cat., The Saint Louis Art Museum, Saint Louis
- Fausta Daldini, "Due Donne USA," *Reflex*, March, p. 74–79
- Matt Damsker, "Portrait of an Artist," *The Hartford Courant*, 16 January, p. 4–5
- Douglas David, "Big Pix," Newsweek, 2 May, p. 80
- "Ein Star der Ungedrehten Filme," *Der Spiegel*, 24 January, p. 162–163
- Vicki Goldberg, "Portrait of a Photographer as a Young Artist," *The New York Times*, 23 October, p. 29
- Susan Hapgood, "Cindy Sherman/Metro Pictures," *Flash Art*, January, p. 63
- Klaus Honnef, *Back to the U.S.A.*, exh. cat., Kunstmuseum, Lucerne; Rheinisches Landesmuseum, Bonn

- Klaus Honnef, "Cindy Sherman," *Kunstforum international*, April, p. 105–121
- Joseph Jacobs, *Faces Since the 50's*, exh. cat., Bucknell University, Lewisberg
- Ronald B. Kuspit, "Idolatry and Authority: Notes from NYC," *Vanguard*, March, p. 22–23
- Lee Lescaze, "Making Faces: A Photographer Dresses Up for Success," *The Wall Street Journal*, 15 November, p. 32
- Therese Lichtenstein, "Cindy Sherman," *Arts Magazine*, January, p. 3
- Kate Linker, "Cindy Sherman, Metro Pictures," *Artforum*, January, p. 79
- Gerald Marzorati, "Imitation of Life," *ARTnews*, September, p. 78–87
- Lisbet Nilson, "Q & A: Cindy Sherman," *American Photographer*, September, p. 70–77
- "Openings: Cindy Sherman," *Esquire*, July, p. 115
- Phyllis Rosenzweig, *Directions 1983*, exh. cat., The Hirshhorn Museum and Sculpture Garden, The Smithsonian Institution Press, Washington
- "Scene Stealers," *Life Magazine*, May, p. 10–16
- Peter Schjeldahl, "Falling in Style: The New Art and Our Discontents," *Vanity Fair*, March, p. 115–116, 252
- Roberta Smith, "Art," *The Village Voice*, 29 November, p. 119
- Michael Starenko, "What's an Artist to Do?: A Short History of Postmodernism and Photography," *Afterimage*, January, p. 4–5
- Thom Thompson, *Cindy Sherman*, exh. cat., Fine Arts Center, State University of New York, Stony Brook
- Judith Williamson, "Images of 'Woman': The Photographs of Cindy Sherman," *Screen*, November–December, p. 102–116
- Lynn Zelavansky, "Cindy Sherman, Metro Pictures," *Artnews*, January, p. 145–146

1984

- Bernard Blistène et al., *Alibis*, exh. cat., Musée national d'Art moderne, Centre Georges Pompidou
- Linda Cathcart and Craig Owens, *The Heroic Figure*, exh. cat., Museum of Contemporary Art and USIS, Houston
- *Cindy Sherman*, exh. cat., Laforet Museum, Tokyo
- *Cindy Sherman*, exh. cat., The Seibu Contemporary Art Gallery, Tokyo
- "Cindy Sherman,"," *Camera Austria*, n°15/16, p. 40–49
- Michelle Cone, "Cindy Sherman, Metro Pictures,"," *Flash Art*, March, p. 39
- Brigitte Cornand, "Cindy Sherman : la star-caméléon," *Public*, May/October, p. 49
- *El Arte Narrativo*, exh. cat., Museo Rufino Tamayo, Mexico
- Phillipe Evans-Clark, "Cindy Sherman, Metro Pictures," *Artpress*, January, p. 46
- Anthony Faucett and Jane Withers, "Expo: Photographer's Gallery," *The Face*, March, p. 44–50
- Joyce Fernandes, *Sex-Specific: Photographic Investigations of Contemporary Sexuality*, exh. cat., The School of The Art Institute of Chicago, Chicago
- Howard N. Fox et al., *Content: A Contemporary Focus 1974–1984*, exh. cat., The Hirshhorn Museum and Sculpture Garden, The Smithsonian Institution Press, Washington
- Jamey Gambrell, "Marginal Acts," *Art in America*, March, p. 114–119
- Hervé Guibert, "Quel est le vrai visage de Cindy Sherman ?," *Le Monde*, Paris
  Andy Grundberg, "Self-Portraits Minus Self," *The New York Times Book Review*, 22 July, p. 11–12
- Ellen Handy, "Cindy Sherman," *Arts Magazine*, January, p. 56
- Klaus Honnef, *Szene New York*, exh. cat. Art Cologne International Kunstmarkt, Cologne
- Andreas Kallfelz, "Cindy Sherman: Ich Mache Keine Selbsportraits," *Wolkenkratzer Art Journal*, September/October, p. 44–49
- Freddy Langer, "Cindy Sherman," *Frankfurter Allgemeine Magazine*, September, p. 10–18
- Lisa Liebman, "Cindy Sherman, Metro Pictures," *Artforum*, March, p. 95
- Lisa Liebman, "Books, Books, Books: Cindy Sherman," *Artforum*, December, p. 74
- Alain Lopez and Anne de Margerie, "Moi Cindy Sherman," *Libération*, 12 August, p. 25
- Diana Morris, "Cindy Sherman," *Women Artists News*, November, p. 18–19
- "Photography Now: Cindy Sherman," *Photo Japan*, Tokyo, June, p. 148–155
- Carter Ratcliff, *The Fifth Biennale of Sydney, Private Symbol: Social Metaphor*, exh. cat., The Art Gallery of New South Wales, Sydney
- John B. Ravenal, "Cindy Sherman," *Arts Magazine*, January, p. 21
- Rosemary Robotham, "One-Woman Show: Cindy Sherman Puts Her Best Face Forward," *Life Magazine*, June, p. 14–22
- Peter Schjeldahl and I. Michael Danoff, *Cindy Sherman*, Pantheon Books, New York
- John Sturman, "The Art of Becoming Someone Else," *Artnews*, November, p. 35
- "The Best of the New Generation: Men and Women Under Forty Who Are Changing America," *Esquire*, December, p. 142

1985

- *1985 Biennial Exhibition*, exh. cat., The Whitney Museum of American Art, New York
- *Anniottanta*, exh. cat., Nuove edizioni Gabriele Mazzotta, Milan
- Gerry Badger, *American Images: Photography 1945–1980*, exh. cat., The Barbican Art Gallery, London
- Douglas David, "Seeing Isn't Believing," *Newsweek*, 3 June, p. 69
- Andy Grundberg, "Cindy Sherman's Dark Fantasies Evoke a Primitive Past," *The New York Times*, 20 October
- Ellen Handy, "Cindy Sherman, Metro Pictures," *Arts Magazine*, December, p. 116
- Gary Indiana, "Enigmatic Makeup," *The Village Voice*, 22 October, p. 41
- Alan Jones, "Friday the 13th: Cindy Sherman," *N.Y. Talk*, October, p. 44–45
- *L'Autoportrait*, exh. cat., musée cantonal des Beaux-Arts, Lausanne
- Gerald Mazeroti, "Self-Possessed," *Vanity Fair*, October, p. 112–113
- *New York 85*, exh. cat., ARCA Centre d'Art Contemporain, Marseille
- Maralyn Lois Polak, "She Shoots Herself (sort of)," *The Philadelphia Inquirer Magazine*, 13 January, p. 7–8
- Mark Rosenthal, *Art of Our Time: The Saatchi Collection*, Lund Humphries, London and Rizzoli, New York
- Ingrid Sischy, "On Location: Cindy Sherman's Camera Kabuki," *Artforum*, December, p. 4–5
- Nicholas Serota et al., *1985 Carnegie International*, exh. cat., Carnegie Museum of Art, Pittsburgh
- Marianne Stockebrand, *Cindy Sherman*, exh. cat., Westfälischer Kunstverein, Münster
- John Sturman, "Cindy Sherman, Metro Pictures," *Artnews*, December, p. 117
- Betsy Sussler, "Cindy Sherman interview," *Bomb*, spring/summer, p. 30–33
- Paul Taylor, "Cindy Sherman," *Flash Art*, October/November, p. 78–79
- "Today's American Works: Cindy Sherman," *Photo Japan*, February, p. 60–61
- Leo Van Damme, "Cindy Sherman: I Don't Want to Be a Performer," *Arte Factum*, Anvers, June/August, p. 15–21

1986

- H. Arnason, *A History of Modern Art : Painting, Sculpture, Architecture, Photography*, troisième édition, Harry N. Abrams, New York and Prentice Hall, Englewood Cliffs
- Neal Benezra and A. James Speyer, *Seventy-Fifth American Exhibition*, exh. cat., The Art Institute of Chicago, Chicago
- Dan Cameron, *Art and Its Double: A New York Perspective*, exh. cat., Fundacio Caixa de Pensions, Barcelona
- Christian Caujolle, "Cindy Sherman : 'Tout va bien, merci!'," *Actuel*, October, p. 136–143
- "Cindy Sherman," *Kunstforum*, June/July/August, p. 88–89
- Ruth Cloudman, *Perspective 4: Cindy Sherman*, exh. cat., Portland Art Museum, Portland
- Alain D'Hooghe, "Cindy Sherman : qui est cette femme ?," *Clichés*, n°31, p. 40–51
- Deborah Drier, "Cindy Sherman at Metro Pictures," *Art in America*, January, p. 136–138
- *Individuals: A Selected History of Contemporary Art, 1945–1986*, exh. cat., The Museum of Contemporary Art, Los Angeles, Abbeville Press, New York
- Larry Frascella, "Cindy Sherman's Tales of Terror," *Aperture*, n°103, p. 48–53
- Paulette Gagnon, *La Magie de l'image*, exh. cat., musée d'Art contemporain de Montréal, Montréal
- Stephen W. Melville, "The Time of Exposure: Allegorical Self-Portraiture in Cindy Sherman," *Arts Magazine*, January, p. 17–21
- Andrea Miller-Keller, *Cindy Sherman*, exh. cat., The Wadsworth Athenaeum Museum of Art, Hartford
- Jed Perl, "Starring Cindy Sherman," *The New Criterion*, January, p. 14–25
- Mark Power, "Cindy Sherman's Multiple Exposures," *The Washington Post*, 14 July, p. C1, C4
- *Prospect 86*, exh. cat., Frankfurter Kunstverein and Schirn Kunsthalle, Frankfurt
- *Staging the Self: Self-Portrait Photography 1840's–1980's*, exh. cat., National Portrait Gallery, London
- Alice Steinbach, "Cindy Sherman's Photos Make Her Art and Artist," *The Baltimore Sun*, 3 June, p. 1C
- Elizabeth Stevens, "New Approach to Self-Portraits," *The Baltimore Sun*, 3 June, p. 1C, 2C

1987

- *Aspects of Conceptualism in American Work, Part II*, exh. cat., Ave. B Gallery, New York
- Gretchen Bender, "Interview with Cindy Sherman," *Bomb*, winter, p. 20–24
- David Bonetti, "Portraits of a Lady: Cindy Sherman's fleurs du mal," *The Boston Phoenix*, 4–10 December, p. 5, 15
- Michael Brenson, "Art: Whitney Shows Cindy Sherman Photos," *The New York Times*, 24 July, p. C31
- Dan Cameron, "Art and It's Double: A New York Pespective," *Flash Art*, May
- Germano Celant et al., *Implosion: A Postmodern Perspective*, exh. cat., Moderna Museet, Stockholm
- *Cindy Sherman*, exh. cat., Parco Co. Ltd, Tokyo
- Laura Cottingham, "Cindy Sherman," *Flash Art*, October, p. 97
- Arthur C. Danto, "Art: Cindy Sherman," *The Nation*, 15–22 August, p. 134–137
- Howard N. Fox, *Avant-Garde in the Eighties*, exh., The Los Angeles County Museum of Art, Los Angeles
- Frederick Garber, "Generating the Subject. The Images of Cindy Sherman," *Genre XX*, autumn/winter, p. 359–382
- Kathleen McCarthy Gauss and Andy Grundberg, *Photography and Art: Interactions Since 1946*, exh. cat., The Museum of Art, Fort Lauderdale; The Los Angeles County Museum of Art, Los Angeles
- Andy Grundberg, "The 80's Seen Through a Postmodern Lens," *The New York Times*, 5 July, p. 25, 29
- Mary Ellen Haus, "Cindy Sherman: Metro Pictures, Whitney Museum of American Art," *Artnews*, October, p. 167–168
- Eleanor Heartney, "Two or Three Things I Know About Her," *Afterimage*, October, p. 18
- Marvin Heifferman and Joseph Jacobs, *This Is Not a Photograph: Twenty Years of Large-Scale Photography 1966–1986*, exh. cat., The John and Mable Ringling Museum of Art, Sarasota
- Gary Indiana, "Untitled (Cindy Sherman Confidential)," *The Village Voice*, 2 June, p. 87
- Ken Johnson, "Cindy Sherman and the Anti-Self: An Interpretation of Her Imagery," *Arts Magazine*, November, p. 47–53
- Howard Kissel, "The Ego Has Landed," *The Daily News*, 10 July, p. 61
- Donald Kuspit, "Inside Cindy Sherman," *Artscribe*, September/October, p. 41–43
- Kay Larson, "Who's That Girl?," *The New York Magazine*, 3 August, p. 41–43, 52–53
- *L'Époque, la mode, la morale, la passion*, exh. cat., Musée national d'Art Moderne, Centre Georges Pompidou, Paris
- Kim Levin, "Cindy Sherman," *The Village Voice*, 19 May
- Gerald Marzorati, "Sherman's March," *Vanity Fair*, August, p. 135
- Margot Mifflin, "The Fine Art of Shooting Oneself: Cindy Sherman," *Elle USA*, July, p. 26
- Sandy Nairne, *State of the Art: Ideas & Images in the 1980's*, Chatto & Windus Ltd, London
- "Narziss und Alptraum: Die Fotokunst Der Cindy Sherman," *Wiener*, December, p. 74–77
- Peter Schjeldahl and Lisa Phillips, *Cindy Sherman*, exh. cat., The Whitney Museum of American Art, New York; The Institute of Contemporary Art, Boston; The Dallas Museum of Art, Dallas
- Michael Small, "Photographer Cindy Sherman Shoots Her Best Model-Herself," *People*, 30 November, p. 157–160
- Roberta Smith, "Art: Cindy Sherman at Metro Pictures," *The New York Times*, 8 May, p. C27
- Carol Squiers and Charles Stainback, *Portrayals*, exh. cat., The International Center of Photography, New York
- Sidney Tillim, "Cindy Sherman at Metro Pictures and Whitney Museum," *Art in America*, December, p. 162–163
- Adam Versanyi, "Camera Theatron: Sherman/Steichen," *Theater*, The Yale School of Drama, summer
- Amei Wallach, "Cindy Sherman," *Newsday*, 12 July, p. 4–5
- Kelly Wise, "An Artist Walking Past Formula," *The Boston Globe*, 20 November, p. 33, 38
- Peter Wollheim, "Photography and Politics: The Post-Modern Perspective," *Center Quarterly*, spring, p. 4–6

1988

- Russell Bowman, *The World of Art Today*, exh. cat., The Milwaukee Art Museum, Milwaukee
- L. Brea, "Cindy Sherman: Uno Es Siempre Otro," *Sur Expres*, December/January, p. 97–101
- "Cindy Sherman," *Bijutsu Techo*, October, p. 28–33
- *Contemporary Art from New York*, exh. cat., The National Museum of Contemporary Art, Séoul
- Fredrick Garber, *Repositionings: Readings of Contemporary Poetry, Photography, and Performance Art*, The University of Oklahoma Press, Norman
- Rita Gilbert and William McCarter, *Living with Art*, Alfred A. Knopf Pub., New York
- Charles Guiliano, "Cindy Sherman," *Art New England*, December/January, p. 8–9
- Anne H. Hoy, *Fabrications: Staged, Altered and Appropriated Photographs*, Abbeville Press, New York
- Sam Hunter, *Visions/Revisions: Contemporary Representation*, exh. cat., Marlborough Gallery, New York
- Sue Lile Inman et al., *Just Like a Woman*, exh. cat., The Greenville County Museum of Art, Greenville
- Margaret Iverson, "Fashioning the Feminine Identity," *Art International*, n°2, spring, p. 52–57
- Margo Jefferson, "The Image Culture: Michael Jackson, Cindy Sherman and the Art of Self-Manipulation"
- Paolo Marini, "Mass-Media Manipulation," *Contemporanea*, May/June, p. 117–121
- *Matris*, exh. cat., Malmö Kunsthall, Malmö
- *Modern Dreams*, exh. cat., The Institute for Contemporary Art, New York and The MIT Press, Cambridge
- Javier Olivares, "Les Cindy De Sherman," *La Luna de Madrid*, December/January, p. 32–37
- Pablo Perez-Minquez, "Las Obsesiones de mi Prima Cindy," *La Luna de Madrid*, December/January, p. 32–37
- *Presi Per Incantamento*, exh. cat., Padiglione d'Arte Contemporanea, Milan and Giancarlo Politi, Milan
- Jeanne Siegel, *Art Talk: the Early 80's*, DaCapo Press, New York, p. 269–282
- *Three Decades: The Oliver Hoffman Collection*, exh. cat., The Museum of Contemporary Art, Chicago

1989

- *A Forest of Signs: Art in the Crisis of Representation*, exh. cat., The Museum of Contemporary Art, Los Angeles and The MIT Press, Cambridge
- Alan G. Artner, "Sherman Photos Halfway into New Subject," *The Chicago Tribune*, 21 July, p. 51

- Edward Ball, "The Beautiful Language of My Century," *Arts Magazine*, January, p. 65–72
- Germano Celant, *Unexpressionism: Art Beyond the Contemporary*, Rizzoli, New York
- A. D. Coleman, "Postmodern but, Surprisingly, Both Beautiful and Unnerving," *The New York Observer*, 23 January, p. 14
- Laura Cottingham, "The Feminine De-Mystique," *Flash Art*, summer, p. 91–95
- Arthur C. Danto, "Women Artists, 1970–85," *The Nation*, 25 December, p. 794–798
- Elaine Equi, "Cindy Sherman," *Arts*, September, p. 72
- Wolfgang Max Faust, "Kunst mit Fotografie heute," *Wolkenkratzer Art Journal*, January/February, p. 24–45
- Merry A. Foresta and Joshua Smith, *The Photography of Invention*, exh. cat., The National Museum of American Art, The Smithsonian Institution Press, Washington and The MIT Press, Cambridge
- Fredrick Garber, "Generating the Subject: The Images of Cindy Sherman," *Postmodern Genres*, The University of Oklahoma Press, Norman
- Andy Grundberg, "The Galleries: Cindy Sherman," *The New York Times*, 31 March, p. C1, C26
- Katherine Harrison, "Cindy Sherman, Metro Pictures," *Flash Art*, summer, p. 146
- Elizabeth Hayt-Atkins, "Cindy Sherman, Metro Pictures," *Artnews*, September, p. 170–171
- Mark Hayworth-Booth, *Photography Now*, exh. cat., The Victoria and Albert Museum, London and Dirk Nishen Publishing, London
- Jack Hobbs and Robert Duncan, *Ideas and Civilisation*, Prentice Hall, Englewood Cliffs
- Robert Hughes, "Mucking with Media," *Time*, 25 December, p. 93
- Gary Indiana et al., *Re-Presenting the 80's*, exh. cat., Simon Watson, New York
- Richard Lacayo, "Drawn by Nature's Pencil," *Time*, 27 February, p. 64–67
- Robert Leonard and Priscilla Pitts, *Cindy Sherman*, exh. cat., The National Art Gallery, Wellington
- Lisa Liebman, "About Face: Cindy Sherman's Self-transformations...," *Mirabella*, October, p. 45
- Lisa Phillips *and* Marvin Heifferman, *Image World: Art and Media Culture*, exh. cat., The Whitney Museum of American Art, New York
- "Photography: Borrowed Images," *The New Yorker*, 10 April
- Peter Plagens, "Into the Fun House," *Newsweek*, 21 August, p. 52–57
- David Rimanelli, "New York, Cindy Sherman, Metro Pictures," *Artforum*, summer, p. 165
- Randy Rosen, *Making Their Mark: Women Artists Move into the Mainstream, 1970–85*, exh. cat., The Cincinnati Art Museum, Cincinnati; The New Orleans Museum of Art, La Nouvelle-Orléans; The Denver Art Museum, Denver; The Pennsylvania Academy of Fine Arts, Abbeville Press Publishers, New York and The Royal Academy of Arts Pub., London
- Peter Schjeldahl, "Little Show of Horrors," *7 Days*, 12 April, p. 64–65
- Mira Schor, "From Liberation to Lack," *Heresies 6*, p. 15–21
- Howard Smagula, *Currents, Contemporary Directions in the Visual Arts*, Prentice Hall, Englewood Cliffs, p. 209–213
- Terrie Sultan, *Surrogate Selves: David Levinthal, Cindy Sherman, Laurie Simmons*, exh. cat., The Corcoran Gallery of Art, Washington
- Alexander Tonay, *1st Internationale Foto Triennale Esslingen*, exh. cat., Esslingen am Neckar
- Michael Weaver and Daniel Wolf, *The Art of Photography 1839–1989*, exh. cat., The Museum of Fine Arts, Houston; Ministère de la Culture de l'Union soviétique, Moscou; The Royal Academy of Art, London; The Sezon Museum of Art, Tokyo and The Yale University Press, New Haven
- Susan Weiley, "The Darling of the Decade," *Artnews*, April, p. 143–150
- *What does she want? Current Feminist Art from the First Bank Collection*, exh. cat., First bank Systems, Northfield
- Rick Woodward, "Film Stills," *Film Comment*, April, p. 51–54.
- Richard B. Woodward, "Documenting an Outbreak of Self-Reresentation," *The New York Times*, 22 January, p. 31

1990

- Brooks Adams, "Cindy Sherman at Metro Pictures," *Art in America*, June, p. 172–173
- *Affinities and Intuitions: The Gerald S. Elliot Collection of Contemporary Art*, exh. cat., The Art Institute of Chicago, Chicago
- Hildegund Amanhauser, "Cindy Sherman," *Camera Austria*, n°35, p. 14–21
- Rene Bloch, *The Readymade Boomerang: The Eighth Biennial of Sydney*, exh. cat., The Art Gallery of New South Wales, Sydney
- Dan Cameron et al., *To Be and Not to Be*, exh. cat., Centre d'Art Santa Monica, Barcelona
- Whitney Chadwick, *Women, Art, and Society*, Thames and Hudson, London
- A. D. Coleman, "Sherman Effects Tour de Force in Mature and Funny Show," *The New York Observer*, 22 January, p. 17
- A. D. Coleman, "Appropriate Appropriations? Cindy Sherman and Richard Prince," *The Photo Review*, p. 4–5
- Glenn Collins, "A Portraitist's Romp through Art History," *The New York Times*, 2 February, p. C17, C20
- Thomas Connors, "Self-portrait with Silver Screen," *The International Herald Tribune*, 6–7 October
- Laura Cottingham, "Cindy Sherman," *Contemporanea*, May, p. 93
- Peggy Cyphers, "Cindy Sherman," *Arts Magazine*, April, p. 111
- Arthur C. Danto, *Cindy Sherman: Untitled Film Stills*, Rizzoli, New York and Schirmer/Mosel Verlag, Munich
- Arthur C. Danto, "The State of the Art World: The Nineties Begin," *The Nation*, 9 July, p. 64–68
- Cathy N. Davidson, "Photographs of the Dead: Sherman, Daguerre, Hawthorne," *The South Atlantic Quarterly*, autumn, p. 667–701
- *Energies*, exh. cat., The Stedelijk Museum, Amsterdam
- Andy Grundberg, "Photography: Images of the Past and Future," *The New York Times*, 12 January, p. C29
- Kathy Halbreich, *Culture and Commentary: An Eighties Perspective*, exh. cat., The Hirshhorn Museum and Sculpture Garden, The Smithsonian Institution Press, Washington
- Eleanor Heartney, "Cindy Sherman, Metro Pictures," *Artnews*, May, p. 207–208
- "Insert: Cindy Sherman," *Parkett*, n°24, p. 119–133
- Steven Jenkins, "The Metamorphosed Self," *Artweek*, 20 September, p. 11–12
- Susan Kandel, "Cindy Sherman at Linda Cathcart," *Art Issues*, September/October, p. 36
- Christopher Knight, "Cindy Sherman: A Painted Lady," *The Los Angeles Times*, 8 June, p. F1, F18
- Kay Larsen, "Art: Cindy Sherman's Latest Series...," *The New York Magazine*, 29 January, p. 59
- Chakè Matossian et al., *Je EST un Autre*, exh. cat., Galeria COMICOS/LUIS SERPA, Lisbon; Fondation Serralvès, Porto
- Patrick McGrath, "The Doll," *Aperture*, autumn, p. 15–19
- "Photography," *The New Yorker*, 22 January, p. 22
- Robert Rosenblum and Peter Schjeldahl, "The New Shermans: Robert Rosenblum and Peter Schjeldahl at Metro Pictures, January 30"
- Peter Schjeldahl, "Portrait: She is a Camera," *7 Days*, 28 March, p. 17–19
- Roberta Smith, "A Course in Portraiture by an Individualist with a Camera," *The New York Times*, 5 January, p. C19
- Constance Sullivan, *Women Photographers*, Harry N. Abrams, New York
- John Szarkowski, *Photography Until Now*, exh. cat., The Museum of Modern Art, New York
- Jerome Tarshis, "One Woman Plays Many Parts," *The Christian Science Monitor*, 8 November, p. 17
- Kees van der Ploeg, "Spotlight: Cindy Sherman," *Flash Art*, summer, p. 142

1991

- *1991 Biennial Exhibition*, exh. cat., The Whitney Museum of American Art, New York
- Dolene Ainardi-Argence, *La Revanche de l'image*, exh. cat., Galerie Pierre Huber, Genève
- Alexandra Anderson-Spivy, "Who is that Girl, Anyway?," *Esquire*, February, p. 86
- Amnon Barzel et al., *Altrove: Fra immagine e identita fra identita e tradizione*, exh. cat., Centro per l'Arte Contemporanea Luigi Pecui, Prato
- Norman Bryson, "The Ideal and the Abject: Cindy Sherman Historical Portraits," *Parkett*, n°29, p. 91–102
- John M. Carvalho, "Repetitions. Appropriation Representation in Contemporary Art," *Philosophy Today*, winter, p. 307–323
- *Cindy Sherman: Specimens*, Kyoto Shoin International, Kyoto
- *Contemporary American Women Artists*, Cedco Publishing, San Rafael
- Sasha Craddock, "Fluff with a Fairground Feel," *The Guardian*, London, 16 January
- Arthur C. Danto, *History Portraits*, Schirmer/Mosel, Munich and Rizzoli, New York
- Wilfried Dickhoff, "Untitled #179," *Parkett*, n°29, p. 103–111
- Charles Gandee, "Art à la Carte," *House and Garden*, November, p. 198–200
- Andrew Graham-Dixon, "The Self and Other Fictions," *The Independent Magazine*, London, 19 January, p. 42–43
- Andy Grundberg, *Crisis of the Real. Writings on Photography, 1974–1989*, Aperture, New York
- Nancy G. Heller, *Women Artists. An Illustrated History*, Abbeville Press, New York
- Ursula Pia Jauch, "I am Alway the Other," *Parkett*, n°29, p. 74–81
- Elfriede Jelinek, "Sidelines," *Parkett*, n°29, p. 82–90
- Thomas Kellein, *Cindy Sherman*, exh. cat., Basel Kunsthalle, Basel; Whitechapel Art Gallery, London; Staatsgalerie Moderner Kunst, Munich and Hatje Cantz Verlag, Ostfildern-Ruit
- Linda S. Klinger, "Where's the Artist? Feminist Practice and Poststructural Theories of Authorship," *The Art Journal*, summer, p. 39–47
- Laura Mulvey, "A Phantasmagoria of the Female Body: The Work of Cindy Sherman," *The New Left Review*, n°188, July/August, p. 136–151
- Barry Nemett, *Images, Objects and Ideas. Viewing the Visual Arts*, Harcourt Brace and Jovanovich, San Diego
- Jill Quasha, *The Quillan Collection of Nineteenth and Twentieth Century Photographs*, Quillan Company Limited, New York
- Ingrid Sischy, "Photography, Let's Pretend," *The New Yorker*, 6 May, p. 86–96
- Dean Sobel, *Currents 18: Cindy Sherman*, exh. cat., The Milwaukee Museum of Art, Milwaukee
- Abigail Solomon-Godeau, "Suitable for Framing: The Critical Recasting of Cindy Sherman," *Parkett*, n°29, p. 112–121
- Paul Taylor, "Cindy Sherman, Old Master," *Art & Text*, May, p. 38
- Hugo Williams, "Her Dazzling Career. The Saatchi Collection by Cindy Sherman," *The Times Literary Supplement*, 11 January, p. 10
- Philip Yewanine, *How to Look at Modern Art*, Harry N. Abrams, New York

1992

- Jan Avgikos, "Welcher Natur ist dieses Begehren?," *Texte zur Kunst*, June, p. 159–163
- Lita Barrie, "On the Scene: Los Angeles," *Artspace*, September/October, p. 66–67
- David Bonetti, "Canvassing N.Y. Galleries: Sherman and Schnabel, still the talk of the town," *The San Francisco Examiner*, 21 May
- Elizabeth Bronfen, *Over Her Dead Body*, Manchester University Press, Manchester
- Brian D'Amato, "Cindy Sherman: Limbless Hermaphrodites and Dismembered Devil Dolls," *Flash Art*, summer, p. 107
- Joshua Decter, "Cindy Sherman aus der Sicht des männlichen, sich selbst beobachtenden Betrachters," *Texte zur Kunst*, June, p. 157–159
- Jeffrey Deitch, *Post Human*, exh. cat., Musée d'Art Contemporain, Lausanne; Castello di Rivoli, Turin; Deste Foundation, Athènes; Deichtorhallen, Hambourg; Israel Museum, Jérusalem
- Rebecca J. DeRoo, "Cindy Sherman's Untitled Film Stills: Masquerade...," *The Wittenberg Review*, autumn, p. 21–41
- Fred Fehlau et al., *Hollywood, Hollywood: Identity Under the Guise of Celebrity*, Art Center College of Design, Pasadena
- Gloria K. Fiero, "The Global Village of the Twentieth Century," *The Humanistic Tradition*, n°6, Brown and Benchmark, Dubuque
- Catherine Francblin, "Cindy Sherman : personnage très ordinaire," entretien, *Artpress*, n°165, p. 12–19
- Ellen G. Landau, "Cindy Sherman déconstruite ? Une reconstruction," *Les Cahiers du Musée national d'Art moderne*, winter, p. 37–47
- Justin Hoffmann, "Cindy Sherman," *Artis*, September
- Rita Gilbert, *Living with Art*, McGraw-Hill, New York
- David S. Gomez, "Photographer Cindy Sherman Assaults the Flesh at Metro Pictures," *Splash*, spring, p. 24–25
- Charles Hagen, "Cindy Sherman at Metro Pictures," *The New York Times*, 24 April, p. C32
- Eleanor Heartney, "Cindy Sherman at Metro Pictures," *Art in America*, September, p. 127–128
- Elizabeth Hess, "Sherman's Inferno," *The Village Voice*, 5 May, p. 107–108
- Susan Kandel, "Cindy Sherman at Linda Cathcart," *Art Issues*, September/October, p. 43
- Susan Kandel, "Madonnarama," *Artspace*, December, p. 42–43
- Ivo Kranzfelder, "Cindy Sherman: Die Gleichschaltung der Bilder," *Kunstler: Kritisches Lexikon der Gegenwartskunst*, Weltkunst and Bruckmann Verlag, Munich
- Bruce D. Kurtz, *Contemporary Art 1965–1990*, Prentice Hall, Englewood Cliffs
- Donald Kuspit, *Périls et colères*, Capc Musée d'Art Contemporain de Bordeaux, Bordeaux
- Therese Lichtenstein, "Cindy Sherman," *The Journal of Contemporary Art*, autumn, p. 78–88
- Alfred MacAdam, "Cindy Sherman at Metro Pictures," *Artnews*, September, p. 112–113
- David Pagel, "Going for Effects," *The Los Angeles Times*, 28 May, p. F4
- Michael Petry, "Letter from New York II," *The Arts Review*, June, p. 249–250
- Robert Pinto, "Cindy Sherman, Le Case D'Arte Studio Guenzani," *Flash Art*, March/April, p. 127
- Roee Rosen, "Art, Money, Identity: Fragments from Contemporary American Art," in *Not For Sale*, exh. cat., The Tel Aviv Museum of Art, Tel Aviv
- Jerry Saltz, *American Art of the Eighties*, exh. cat., Museo d'Arte Moderna e Contemporanea di Trento, Trente
- Barry Schwabsky, "Shamelessness," *Sculpture*, July/August, p. 44–45
- Cindy Sherman, *Fitcher's Bird*, livre d'artiste, Rizzoli, New York
- Susan Slesin, "Oh, So Traditional, Oh, So Subversive," *The New York Times*, 5 November, p. C1–C5
- Amei Wallach, "Tough Images to Face," *The Los Angeles Times*, 7 June, p. 77
- Frazer Ward et al., *Dirt & Domesticity: Constructions of the Feminine*, exh. cat., The Whitney Museum of American Art, New York
- Christoph Wiedemann, "Sex and Crime poetisch verpackt," *Süddeutsche Zeitung*, 11 September
- Judith Williamson, "Images of 'Woman': The Photography of Cindy Sherman," in *Knowing Women: Feminism and Knowledge*, The Open University, Milton Keynes, p. 222–225

1993

- *1993 Biennial Exhibition*, exh. cat., The Whitney Museum of American Art, New York
- Kathy Acker, *Meine Mutter: Damonologie*, MAAS Verlag, Berlin
- Jan Avgikos, "Cindy Sherman: Burning Down the House," *Artforum*, January, p. 74–79
- Pamela Church Gibson and Roma Gibson, *Dirty Looks: Women, Pornography, Power*, BFI Pub., London

- David Goldsmith, "Cindy Sherman," *On Location with*, Aperture, p. 34–43
- Cathy Hainer, "For Cindy Sherman, art has many guises," *USA Today*, 18 November, p. 6D
- Ann Hindry, "Les Images et les mots," interview with Rosalind Krauss, *Artpress*, September, p. 42–47
- Robert Hirsch, *Exploring Color Photography*, Brown & Benchmark, Indianapolis
- Christopher Knight, "Crushed by Its Good Intentions," *The Los Angeles Times*, 10 March, p. F1, F8–F9
- Rosalind Krauss, *Cindy Sherman: 1975–1993*, Rizzoli, New York
- Rosalind Krauss, "Cindy Sherman's Gravity: A Critical Fable," *Artforum*, September, p. 163–164, 206
- Kay Larson, "What a Long, Strange Trip," *The New York Magazine*, 22 March, p. 71–72
- Jim Lewis, "The New Cindy Sherman Collection," *Harper's Bazaar*, May, p. 144–149
- *Louise Lawler, Cindy Sherman, Laurie Simmons*, exh. cat., Kunsternes Hus, Helsinki; Museum of Contemporary Art, Helsinki
- Stella Pandell Russell, *Art in the World*, Harcourt Brace Jovanovich College Publishers, Fort Worth
- Peter Plagens, "Fade from White," *Newsweek*, 15 March, p. 72–73
- Françoise-Claire Prudhon, "Cindy Sherman at Ghislaine Hussenot," *Flash Art*, November/December, p. 119
- *Real Sex*, exh. cat., Salzburg Kunstverein, Salzbourg
- Roberta Smith, "A Whitney Biennial with a Social Conscience," *The New York Times*, 5 March, p. C1, C27
- Deborah Solomon, "A Showcase for Political Correctness," *The Wall Street Journal*, 5 March, p. A7
- Marcia Tucker, Elaine King, Jan Riley, Robert J. Shiffler, *Mettlesome & Meddlesome*, The Contemporary Arts Center Publication, Ohio
- Amei Wallach, "Art with an Attitude," *New York Newsday*, 5 March, p. 52–53
- Amei Wallach, "Sherman Going Extreme," *New York Newsday*, 12 April, p. 47, 57

1994

- *After Art: Rethinking 150 Years of Photography*, exh. cat., The Henry Art Gallery, University of Washington, Seattle
- *Against All Odds: The Healing Powers of Art*, exh. cat., The Ueno Royal Museum, Tokyo; The Hakone Open-Air Museum, Kanagawa
- Jan Avgikos, "To Hell and Back Again," *Women's Art*, n° 59, p. 38–39
- Rachel Barnes, "Desperately Seeking an Identity," *The Guardian*, 24 October
- Hans Belting, *Das Ende der Kunstgeschichte*, Verlag C.H. Beck, Munich
- Phyllis Braff, "Photography as a Tool for the Artist," *The New York Times*, 23 October, p. 26
- Michel V. Cheff and al., *Quotation: Re-Presenting History*, exh. cat., The Winnipeg Art Gallery, Winnipeg
- *Cindy Sherman and Juliao Sarmento*, exh. cat., The Irish Museum of Modern Art, Dublin
- Wayne Craven, *American Art: History and Culture*, Brown & Benchmark and Harry N. Abrams, New York, p. 639–640
- Emmanuela De Cecco, "Opera Prima," *Flash Art*, December, p. 55
- *Dialogue with the Other*, exh. cat., Kunsthallen Brandts Klaedefabrik, Odense
- Andrea Dietrich and Cindy Sherman, *Cindy Sherman: New York Photographien*, exh. cat., ACC Galerie, Weimar
- *Diskurse der Bilder*, exh. cat., Kunsthistorisches Museum, Vienna
- Johanna Drucker, *Theorizing Modernism: Visual Art and the Critical Tradition*, Columbia University Press, New York
- Silvia Eiblmayer, *Die Frau als Bild*, Dietrich Reimer Verlag, Berlin, p. 190–196
- William Ewing, *The Body*, Thames and Hudson, London
- Stephen Robert Frankel, "Cindy Sherman Comes to Tea," *Art & Auction*
- *From Beyond the Pale-Cindy Sherman Photographs 1977–1993*, exh. cat., The Irish Museum of Modern Art, Dublin
- Betty Freudenheim, "Dinnerware, Noted Names and Chuckles," *The New York Times*, 3 December, p. 21
- *Genres in Painting: a Contemporary Vision*, exh. cat., Centro Atlantico de Arte Moderno, Iles Canaries
- Emily B. Greenberg, "Cindy Sherman and the Female Grotesque," *Art Criticism*, vol. 9, n°2, p. 49–55
- *Jurgen Klauke-Cindy Sherman*, exh. cat., Sammlung Goetz, Munich and Hatje Cantz Verlag, Ostfildern-Ruit
- John R. Lane and Kara Kirk, *The Making of a Modern Museum*, The San Francisco Museum of Art, San Francisco
- Susanne Lingemann, "7 starke Frauen in New York," *Art*, December, n°12, p. 22–25
- Robert Long, "The Art of the Offbeat," *The Southampton Press*, 6 October
- Edward Lucie-Smith, *Race, Sex, and Gender in Contemporary Art*, Art Books International, London
- Andrew Menard, "Cindy Sherman: The Cyborg Disrobes," *Art Criticism*, vol. 9, n°2, p. 38–48
- Jeremy Mitchell and Richard Maidment, *Culture: The United States in the Twentieth Century*, The Open University, Milton Keynes
- Linda Nochlin, *The Body in Pieces: The Fragment as Metaphor of Modernity*, Thames and Hudson, London
- James Carey Parkes, "The Art of Playing a Part," *The Pink Paper-London*, 16 September
- Naomi Rosemblum, *A History of Women Photographers*, Abbeville Press, New York
- Antonella Russo, "Picture This," *Art Monthly*, November, p. 8–11
- Allan Schwartzman, "Art and Saucers," *Interview*, December
- Rose C. S. Slivka, "From the Studio," *The East Hampton Star*, 3 November
- Amy Spindler, "The Lure of the Ugly," *The New York Times*, 14 June, p. B10
- Jackie Stacen, *Star Gazing: Hollywood Cinema and Female Spectatorship*, Routledge, New York
- Urszula Szulakowska, "Rose Farrell and George Parkin: Art History and 'Primitivism' in Contemporary Australian Performance Photography," *Continuum*, vol. 8, n°1, p. 396–401
- Susan Tallman, "Feet of Clay," *Arts Magazine*, p. 15–17
- Frazer Ward, "Abject Lessons," *Art + Text*, May, p. 50
- Marion Wolberg Weiss, "Art Commentary," *Dan's Papers*, 6 October
- "Why is Cindy Sherman Such a Key Figure for Women Photographers?," *Women's Art*, n°59, p. 40
- *World Morality*, exh. cat., Kunsthalle Basel, Basel

1995

- *XLVI Esposizione Internazionale d'Arte*, exh. cat., La Biennale di Venezia, Venice
- Danilo Angrimani, "MAM exibe a polemica Cindy Sherman," *Diario do Grande ABC*, São Paulo, 21 June, p. 2
- Karen W. Arenson, "Relief Expert Missing in Chechnya Is Among MacArthur Grant Recipients," *The New York Times*, 13 June, p. A22
- Michel Arnaud, "The Show of Shows," *Harper's Bazaar*, March, p. 331–333
- *Autres Victoires*, exh. cat., Château de la Louivière, Montluçon
- Carlos Basualdo, *Cindy Sherman: The Self Which Is Not One*, exh. cat., Museu de Arte Moderna de São Paulo, São Paulo
- Eva Gesine Baur, "Ich befurchte, irgenduo bin ich romantische," *Suddeutsche Zeitung Magazin*, 26 May, p. 22–27
- Eva Gesine Baur, *Meisterwerke der erotischen Kunst*, DuMont Buchverlag Koln, Cologne, p. 47–48
- Dike Blair, "Cindy Sherman-Metro Pictures," *Flash Art*, March/April, n°181, p. 103
- Mario Cesar Carvalho, "Arte brasileira para a globaliza cao," *Terca Feira*, 28 March, p. 1
- Bonnie Clearwater, *The Monster Show*, exh. cat., The Museum of Contemporary Art, North Miami
- *Cindy Sherman*, Kunst Heute, n°14, Kiepenheuer & Witsch, Cologne
- "Cindy Sherman esta no MAM," *Shopping News*, São Paulo, 2 July, p. C4
- "Cindy Sherman: repulsa e satira," *Vogue Brazil*, n°214, p. 202–205
- "Cindy Sherman," *Bijutsu Techo*, June, p. 56–57
- "Cindy Sherman fotografa resti umani non identicati," *Lapis*, Milan, June
- Gabi Czoppan, "Künstler des jahres," *Focus*, October, p. 146–150
- Keith Davis, *An American Century of Photography: The Hallmark Photographic Collection*, Harry N. Abrams, New York
- Donna De Salvo et al., *Face Value: American Portraits*, exh. cat., The Parrish Art Museum, South Hampton
- *Die Muse?: Transforming the Image of Women in Contemporary Art*, exh. cat., Galerie Thaddaeus Ropac, Paris, in association with the Salzburger Festival
- "Early Cindy Sherman Memories," *The Georgetowner*, April, p. 12
- "Extremistiennen," *Deutsch Vogue*, March, p. 260–263
- Zdenek Felix, Martin Schwander, Elisabeth Bronfen and Ulf Erdmann Ziegler, *Cindy Sherman: Photoarbeiten 1975–1995*, exh. cat., Deichtorhallen, Hambourg; Malmö Konsthall, Malmö; Kunstmuseum, Lucerne and Schirmer/Mosel, Munich
- *Féminin/Masculin: le sexe de l'art?*, exh. cat., Musée national d'Art moderne, Centre Georges Pompidou, Paris
- Jean-Christian Fleury, "Cindy Sherman : portrait d'une inconnue," *Camera International*, n°40, summer, p. 62–69
- Charles Hagen, "Cindy Sherman," *The New York Times*, 3 February, p. C27
- "Here's the Money. Now Go Make Some Art," *The New York Times*, 25 June
- George Howell, "Anatomy of an Artist," *Art Papers*, July/August, p. 2–7
- Ken Johnson, "Cindy Sherman at Metro Pictures," *Art in America*, May, p. 112–113
- Joyce Jones, "Sherman: Making Movies," *The Washington Post*, 24 March, p. 55
- Klaus Kertess et al., *1995 Biennial Exhibition*, exh. cat., The Whitney Museum of American Art, New York
- Michael Kimmelman, "Portraitist in the Halls of Her Artistic Ancestors," *The New York Times*, 19 May, p. C1, C7
- Janet Kutner, "Multiple artists, singular viewpoints," *The Dallas Morning News*, 16 April, p. 1C, 8C
- *Laughter Ten Years After*, exh. cat., Center for the Arts, Wesleyan University; Beaver College Art Gallery, Glenside; Hobart & William Smith Colleges, Geneva
- *L'Effet Cinéma*, exh. cat., Musée d'art Contemporain de Montréal, Montréal
- Jo Ann Lewis, "How She Ought to Be in Pictures," *The Washington Post*, 2 April, p. G4
- Lucy Lippard, *The Pink Glass Swan: Selected Feminist Essays On Art*, The New Press, New York
- Georgia Lobacheff, "A arte abjeta de Cindy Sherman," *Jornal Da Tarde*, 24 June, p. 1
- Georgia Lobacheff, "Todas as Mulheres de Cindy Sherman," *Jornal da Tarde/SP*, 2 January, p. 12A
- Anja Losel, "Die Frau, die mit der Gansehaut spielt," *Stern Magazine*, May, p. 200–201
- Edward Lucie-Smith, *Artoday*, Phaidon Press, London
- Martha McWilliams, "Women's Work," *The Washington City Papers*, 19 May, p. 44–45
- Donald Miller, "Out With the Old," *Pittsburgh Post-Gazette*, 3 November, p. 14
- Suzanne Muchnic, "Interactive? It's virtually a Reality," *The Los Angeles Times*, 26 November, p. 58, 61
- Diane Neumaier, *Reframings: New American Feminist Photographies*, Temple University Press, Philadelphia, p. 214–217
- Joyce Carol Oates, *Die unsicht baren Narben Roman*, Deutscher Taschenbuch Verlag, Munich
- Kim Paice, "Cindy Sherman," *Frieze*, n°22, May, p. 60
- Victoria Pedersen, "Gallery Go 'Round," *Paper*, February, p. 111
- Daniel Piza, "Sherman faz rir do que e aterrorizante," *Folha De São Paulo*, 26 June, p. 4
- John Pultz, *The Body and the Lens: Photography 1839 to the Present*, Harry N. Abrams, New York
- "Quest for Lost Image 15," *Seven Seas*, March, n°79, p. 172–175
- Paulo Reis, "O ano da fotografia," *Jornal Do Brasil*, 20 March
- Paul Richard, "Cindy Sherman's Moving Pictures," *The Washington Post*, 2 April, p. G4
- "Schaurige Welt der Puppen," *Der Spiegel*, p. 214–216
- Peter Schjeldahl, "Master Class," *The Village Voice*, 7 February, p. 77
- Christa Schneider, *Cindy Sherman: History Portraits*, Schirmer/Mosel, Munich
- Ben Sederowsky, "Cindy Sherman: Forklaudnadens Mastrinna," *Manadens Femina Magasin*, 9 September, p. 106–110
- Carol Squiers, "Lingerie: A Brief History," *American Photo*, September/October, p. 46–49
- Mary Anne Staniszewski, *Believing Is Seeing: Creating the Culture of Art*, Penguin Books, New York
- Alexandra Stoddard, "Around Town in May," *WETA Magazine*, May, p. 2
- Paul Taylor, *After Andy: SoHo in the Eighties*, Schwartz City, Victoria
- Stephen Todd, "Photo Finished," *NOT ONLY Black + White*, October, p. 86–94
- Eugenie Tsai et al., *Playtime: Artists and Toys*, exh. cat., The Whitney Museum of American Art, Champion, Stamford
- Janet Tyson, "Focus on Photography," *The Fort Worth Star Telegram*, 16 April, p. F1, F4
- Neville Wakefield, "Cindy Sherman," *Artforum*, April, p. 89
- Amei Wallach, "Cindy Sherman's Demonology of Dolls," *New York Newsday*, 20 January, p. B6
- Marina Warner, "The Unbearable Likeness of Being," *Tate*, n°7, winter, p. 41–47

1996

- *100 Photographs from the Collection of the Stedelijk Museum Amsterdam*, THOTH Publishers Bussum, Stedelijk Museum, Amsterdam
- Allison Adato, "Camera At Work," *Life Magazine*, May, p. 120–124
- Hilton Als, "She Came From SoHO," *The New Yorker*, 22 April, p. 38–39
- Amelia Arenas et al., *Cindy Sherman*, The Museum of Modern Art, Shiga; The Marugame Genichiro-Inokuma Museum of Contemporary Art, Marugame; The Museum of Contemporary Art, Tokyo
- Dike Blair, "A Chat With Cindy Sherman," *Flash Art*, March/April, p. 82
- Ina Blom, "Mike Kelley," *Material*, n°28, p. 11–12
- Yves-Alain Bois and Rosalind Krauss, *L'Informe : le modernisme à rebours*, exh. cat., Musée national d'Art moderne, Centre Georges Pompidou, Paris
- Francesco Bonami and Roberto Pinto, "MoMA Buys Cindy Sherman's Film Stills," *Flash Art*, March/April, p. 39
- Kerry Brougher et al., *Art and Film Since 1945: Hall of Mirrors*, exh. cat., The Museum of Contemporary Art, Los Angeles; The Wexner Center for the Arts, Columbus; Palazzo delle Esposizioni, Rome; The Museum of Contemporary Art, Chicago; Biennale di Firenze, Florence
- David Carrier, "Carnegie International", *Artforum 34*, January, p. 39
- "Cindy Sherman," *BT Monthly Art Magazine*, October, p. 16–72
- *Collective Vision: Creating a Contemporary Art Museum*, The Museum of Contemporay Art Press, Chicago
- Jeff Cornelis, "Call It Sleep," *Witte de With Cahier*, March, p. 29–55
- Holland Cotter, "Cindy Sherman," *The New York Times*, 15 November, p. C21
- Gabi Czoppan and Tine Nehler, "Kunstler des Jahres," *Focus*, 21 October, p. 148–149
- Arthur C. Danto, *Playing With the Edge: The Photographic Achievement of Robert Mapplethorpe*, The University of California Press, Berkeley and Los Angeles, p. 55–57
- David D'Arcy, "Screen Romance," Art and Auction, October, p. 124–131
- Deborah Drier, "Art Couture: Comme des Garcons," *Guggenheim Magazine*, p. 14–19
- Régis Durand, "Cindy Sherman : le caméléonisme mélancolique des *Film Stills*," *Artpress*, February, p. 50–55
- Ronald Ehmke and Elizabeth Licata, *Consider the Alternatives: 20 Years of Contemporary Art at Hallwalls*, Hallwalls Inc., Buffalo

- *Face Value: American Portraits*, exh. cat., The Parrish Art Museum, South Hampton; Wexner Center for the Arts, Columbus; Tampa Art Museum, Tampa
- "Film Stills by Cindy Sherman," *Sotheby's*, September/October, p. 7
- *Fragments*, exh. cat., Museu d'Art Contemporani, Barcelona
- Peter Galassi, *Commentary: Cindy Sherman's Untitled Film Stills*, The Museum of Modern Art 1995–96 Annual Report, New York
- Peter Galassi, "Placeres y Terrores del Confort Doméstico," *Papel Alpha*, n°2, p. 3–33
- Timothy Greenfield-Sanders, *Timothy Greenfield-Sanders: Selected Portraits*, exh. cat., Kunst-Station Sankt Peter, Cologne
- Fritz Haarmann and Ulrich Krempel, *Sex & Crime: On Human Relationships*, exh. cat., Sprengel Museum, Hanover
- Charles Hagen, "An Undiminished Wave of Interest and Excitement," *Artnews*, February, p. 116–119
- Ann Hindry, "Operating With the 'Informe'," interview with Rosalind Krauss, *Artpress*, n°213, p. 34–41
- Amelia Jones et al., *Sexual Politics: Judy Chicago's Dinner Party in Feminists Art History*, exh. cat., The UCLA Armand Hammer Gallery, Los Angeles
- Michael Kimmelman, "Rediscovering Upstate Collections," *The New York Times*, 12 July, p. C24
- Danielle Knafo, "Dressing-Up and Other Games of Make-Believe: The Function of Play in the Art of Cindy Sherman," *American Imago: Studies in Psychoanalysis and Culture*, vol. 53, n°2, p. 139–164
- Irene Lacher, "Putting Yet Another Face on Her Career," *Los Angeles Times*, 10 February, p. F1, F13
- Ann Landi, "Art Talk: Art Stalk," *Artnews*, April, p. 34
- Bonita Y. Lei, "Cindy Sherman," *Hsiung Shih Art Monthly*, April, p. 93–96
- Maria Lind, "Retracing the Steps of Cindy Sherman," *Material*, n°28, p. 5
- Peter Lunenfeld, "Technofornia," *Flash Art*, March/April, p. 69–71
- Belinda Luscombe, "People: Seen & Heard," *Time*, 26 February, p. 71
- Michael Mack, *Surface: Contemporary Photographic Practice*, Booth Clibborn, London
- Robert Mapplethorpe, "Everything THt Lives, Eats," *Aperture*, spring, p. 19
- Jackie McAllister, "Cindy Sherman: "Untitled"," portfolio, *Grand Street*, n°58, p. 168–175
- Marsha Meskimmon, *The Art of Reflection*, Scarlet Press, London
- Laura Mulvey, *Fetishism and Curiosity*, Indiana University Press/British Film Institute, p. 65–76
- David Pagel, "Art," *The Los Angeles Times*, 15 February, p. F10
- *Picasso: A Contemporary Dialogue*, exh. cat., Galerie Thaddeus Ropac, Salzbourg/Paris
- *Prospect 96: Photographie in der Gegenwartskunst*, exh. cat., Frankfurter Kunstvereins im Steinernen Haus und der Schirn Kusnthalle, Frankfurt
- *Radical Images*, exh. cat., 2nd Austrian Triennial on Photography, Neue Galerie am Landesmuseum Joanneum, Graz
- Juliane Rebentisch, "Abject, Informe und die Frage nach der Angemessenheit von Interpretationen," *Texte zur Kunst*, n°24, p. 83–93
- Kaja Silverman, *The Threshold of the Visible World*, Routledge, p. 195–227
- Whitnet Scott, "Creep Show," *Manhattan File*, October, p. 69
- Liz Smith, ""Killer" Role for Tripplehorn," *Los Angeles Times*, 22 March, p. F2
- Paul Smith, "Rei Kawakubo: The First Lady of Fashion," *Dazed & Confused*, n°16, p. 45–49
- Roberta Smith, "A Neo-Surrealist Show With a Revisionist Agenda," *The New York Times*, 12 January, p. C23
- Roberta Smith, "Modern Museum Buys Sherman Photo Series," *The New York Times*, 23 January, p. C16
- Roberta Smith, "Finding Art in the Masses," The New York Times, 1er December, p. 43–44, 46
- Betty van Garrel, Verena Lueken, Hal Foster, Margrit Brehm, Peter Schjeldahl, *Cindy Sherman*, exh. cat., Museum Boijmans Van Beuningen, Rotterdam; Museo Nacional Centro de Arte Reina Sofia, Madrid; Sala de Exposiciones REKALDE, Bilbao; Staatliche Kunsthalle, Baden-Baden
- Amei Wallach, "Genre Busters," *The Village Voice*, 26 November, p. 45–46
- William Zimmer, "No Simple Innocence, Childhood Now Invoked Has More in Tow," *The New York Times*, 21 January, p. CN 16

1997

- Daniel Ammann, *Kunst und Gentechnologie*, Schwabe & Co. AG Verlag, Basel
- John Anderson, "*Office Killer*, Takes Aim at Horror Genre," *Los Angeles Times*, 5 December, p. F4
- *Angel, angel*, exh. cat., Kunsthalle Wien, Vienna; Galerie Rudolfinum, Prague
- Michael Archer, *Art Since 1960*, Thames & Hudson, p. 178–179, 180, 186
- David D'Arcy, "The Bigger Picture," *Avenue*, February, p. 64–69
- Paul Ardenne, *Art : l'âge contemporain*, Éditions du Regard, Paris, p. 89
- Gunnar Árnason, "The Remains of the Past: Cindy Sherman is Putting Humanity on the Map Again," *Siski*, Helsinki, summer, p. 15
- *Autoportraits*, exh. cat., Galerie Municipale du Château d'eau, Toulouse
- Kenneth Baker, "Image Conscious in Los Angeles," *The San Francisco Chronicle*, 5 November, p. E1, E3
- William Bartman, *The portraits speak: Chuck Close in conversation with 27 of his subjects*, ART. Press, New York
- Julie L. Belcove, "The Sherman Act," *W Magazine*, June, p. 187–193
- Jennifer Blessing et al., *Rrose Is a Rrose Is a Rrose: Gender Performance in Photography*, Solomon R. Guggenheim Publications, New York
- Anthony Bond, *The Body*, exh. cat., The Art Gallery of New South Wales, Sydney
- David Bonetti, "Subversive Photography," *San Francisco Examiner*, 31 December, p. C1, C7
- David Bonetti, "Laugh & Scream with Cindy Sherman," *The San Francisco Examiner*, 12 December
- Leslie Camhi, "Crossover Artists," *The Village Voice*, 16 December, p. 76
- Clare Carolin, "Cindy Sherman: History Portraits," *Contemporary Visual Arts*, n°17, p. 75
- Lance Carlson, "Scene of the Crime," *Artweek*, September, p. 23–24
- Graham Clarke, *The Photograph*, The Oxford University Press, New York
- José Miguel G. Cortés, *Irudi Lausotua Trabestismoa : eta identitatea artean : el rostro velado travestismo e identidad en el arte*, Diputación Foral de Guipuzkoa, p. 236–245
- Joan Crowder, "Exhibit Focuses on the Older Body," *The Santa Barbara News-Press*, 16 November
- Amanda Cruz, Amelia Jones, Elizabeth A. T. Smith, *Cindy Sherman: Retrospective*, exh. cat., The Museum of Contemporary Art, Los Angeles; The Museum of Contemporary Art, Chicago; Galerie Rudolfinum, Prague; The Barbican Art Gallery, London; Capc Musée d'Art contemporain de Bordeaux, Bordeaux; The Museum of Contemporary Art, Sydney; The Art Gallery of Ontario, Toronto, Thames & Hudson, New York
- Jean-Pierre Cuzin and Dimitri Salmon, *Georges de la Tour : histoire d'une redécouverte*, Éditions Gallimard, Paris
- "Dark Art at the ICA," *The Boston Phoenix*, 18 April
- Joshua Decter, *A/Drift*, exh. cat., The Center for Curatorial Studies Museum, Bard College, Annandale-on-Hudson
- Marlena Donohue, "Invented Identities," *The Los Angeles Daily Breeze*, 28 November, p. K30–31
- Gary Duehr, "'Gothic' is Spooky: ICA Exhibit Touches on Terror and Taboo," *The TAB*, 6–12 May
- *Engel, Engel*, exh. cat., Kunsthalle, Vienna; Galerie Rudolfinum, Prague
- Lena Eriksson, Paula Hoffman, "Nagra nedslag i konsthistorien," *Kollision*, p. 4–7
- "Faces to Watch," *The Los Angeles Times*, 5 January, p. 8–10
- Anne Field, "Maybe You Ought to be in Pictures," *Business Week*, 6 October, p. 174
- *Finders/Keepers*, exh. cat., The Contemporary Arts Museum, Houston
- "Focusing On Women As Photographers," *The Plain Dealer*, 12 September, p. 24
- Hal Foster, "The Real Thing," *Inter Communication*, n° 19, p. 48–53
- Noriko Fuku, "A Woman of Parts," *Art in America*, June, p. 74–81, 125
- Vicki Goldberg, "Photo's That Lie & Tell the Truth," *The New York Times*, 30 March, p. 33–34
- Christoph Grunenberg et al., *Gothic-Transmutations of Horror in Late-Twentieth-Century Art*, The Institute of Contemporary Art, Boston and The MIT Press, Cambridge
- Howard Halle, "Everyone Knows it's Cindy," *Time Out New York*, 24–31 July, p. 42
- Marvin Heiferman, "In Front of the Camera, Behind the Scene: Cindy Sherman's *Untitled Film Stills*," *Museum of Modern Art Magazine*, summer, p. 16–19
- Glen Helfand, "Role Model," *San Francisco Bay Guardian*, 1er December, p. 47–48
- Robert Hirsch, *Exploring Color Photography*, State University of New York, Buffalo, p. 170, 244
- Phoebe Hoban, "Sherman's March," *Vogue*, February, p. 240–243, 278
- A.M. Homes, "Cindy Sherman is Ready for her Close-up," *Mirabella*, November/December, p. 42–44, 46
- Marie Hullenkremer, "Bilder Bruchteil einer Sekunde," *Kolner Stadt Anzeiger*, 7 November, p. 29
- Christos Joachimides, "L'Art moderne au téléscope," *Artpress*, May, p. 30–37
- Fred Johnson, "Face to Face with Cindy Sherman," *Daily News*, 10 November, p. 10–11
- Andrew Johnston, "Office Killer," *Time Out*, 4–11 December, p. 83
- Julie Joyce, "Scene of the Crime," *Art Issues*, November/December, p. 36–37
- Christopher Knight, "Look Out World, Here They Come," *Los Angeles Times*, 3 March, p. 63, 64
- Christopher Knight, "Camera Ready," *Los Angeles Times*, 2 November, p. 5, 92
- Vasif Kortun and Ivo Mesquita, *Stills: Art and Cinema in the Marieluise Hessel Collection*, exh. cat., Centro Cultural Light, Rio de Janeiro
- Olivia Lahs-Gonzales & Lucy R. Lippard, *Defining Eye: Women Photographers of the 20th Century*, exh. cat., The Saint Louis Art Museum, Saint Louis
- Stephen Lemons, "The Many Faces of Cindy," *The Los Angeles Downtown News*, 17 November
- Barbara Lippert, "Vanity Farrah," *The New York Times*, 14 July, p. 18–19
- D. Dominick Lombardi, "All the World is Staged," *The Record-Review*, 11 April, p. 23
- Verena Leken, "Oh, gruase dich, es ist so schon," *Feuilleton*, 26 June
- Verena Lueken, "Blonde Frauen in Gefahr," *Frankfurter Allgemeine*, 23 July
- Barbara A. Macadam, "Madonna & Cindy Playing Themselves," *Artnews*, September, p. 27
- *Making it Real*, exh. cat., The Aldrich Museum of Contemporary Art, Ridgefield; The Reykjavik Municipal Art, Reykjavik Musuem, Reykjavik; Portland Museum of Art, Portland; Bayly Art Museum, University of Virginia, Charlottesville
- *Mascara i Mirall*, exh. cat., Museu d'Art Contemporaini de Barcelona, Barcelona
- Nanette Maxim, "Photo Synthesis," *Ms.*, July/August, p. 76–77
- Christopher Miles, "Fantastic Voyage: Sherman's Troubling familiarity," *The Bay Area Reporter*, 20 November
- Christopher Millis, "Gothic Lite: Few Chills or Thrills in the ICA's 'Transmutations of Horror'," *The Boston Phoenix*, 2 May, p. 10–11
- Helen Molesworth, "The Comfort of Objects: Helen Molesworth on Cindy Sherman's 'Untitled Film Stills' 20 Years on," *Frieze*, September/October, p. 45–47
- Tami Mnoian, "Reality Bites," *Daily Nexus: University of California*, 13 November, p. 7A
- Herbert Muschamp, "Knowing Looks: Cindy Sherman's Sixty-Nine "70"," *Artforum*, summer, p. 106–111
- Douglas R. Nickel and Misook Song, *160 Years of Photography: Masterworks of the San Francisco Museum of Modern Art*, exh. cat., Ho-Am Art Museum, Séoul
- Frederica Palomero and Joanne Heyler, *Cindy Sherman. A Selection From the Eli Broad Foundation's Collection*, exh. cat., Museo de Bellas Artes, Caracas
- Robert L. Pincus, "From Film Brilliance, Show Fades to Bleak," *Diego Union Tribune*, 23 November, p. E1, E10
- Abby Remer, *Pioneering Spirits: The Lives and Times of Remarkable Women Artists in Western History*, Davis Publications, Worcester, p. 143–144
- David Rimanelli, "A/Drift," *Artforum*, February, p. 83
- Stefan Römer, "Wem gehort die Apropriation art?," *Texte zur Kunst*, n°26, p. 128–137
- Ralph Rugoff, "Master of the Grotesque," *LA Weekly*, October/November, p. 30–34
- Ralph Rugoff, "Voices," *UCLA Today*, 29 August
- Peter Sager, "Der ganz normale Horror," *Die Zeit Magazin*, November, p. 30–39
- Elissa Schappell, "The Killer Inside Her," *Details*, December, p. 96, 99
- Katharina Schmidt and Marc Scheps, *Cindy Sherman*, exh. cat., Museum Ludwig, Cologne
- David Schonauer, "Buy! Sell! Hold!," *American Photo*, March/April, p. 40–66
- Ken Schulman, "A Touch of Class," *ARTnews*, May, p. 87
- Bernhard Schulz, "Das verraterische Rollenspiel," *Der Tagespiegel*, 29 December, p. 30
- Whitney Scott, "Madonna-Art Impresario," *The New York Post*, 26 June, p. 46
- *Sensation: Young British Artists From the Saatchi Collection*, exh. cat., Royal Academy of Arts, London
- Paul Sherman, "ICA's Gothic Film Series is a Frightfuly Good Time," *The Boston Herald*, 5 May
- Mary Sherman, "ICA Show Slakes First for Horror," *The Boston Herald*, 25 April
- Lesley Smith and Jane HM Taylor, *Women & the Book: Assessing the Visual Evidence*, University of Toronto Press, Toronto
- Roberta Smith, "A Horror Movie, Complete with Zombies," *The New York Times*, 30 November, p. 41
- Roberta Smith, "Starlet Cliches, Real and Artificial at the Same Time," *The New York Times*, 27 June, p. B1, B25
- Michael P. Spelvin, "Three Exhibitions Open at Aldrich Next Sunday," *The Ridgefield Press*, 16 January
- Carol Squires, "Market Report," *American Photo*, March/April, p. 71–72, 87
- Susan Fisher Sterling, "Persistent Presence," *Women In the Arts*, winter, p. 6–10
- Robert Storr and Kirk Varnedoe, *On the Edge: Contemporary Art from the Werner and Elaine Dannheisser Collection*, exh. cat., The Museum of Modern Art, New York
- Michael Tarantino, *Deslocacoes/From Here to There*, exh. cat., Centro de Arte Moderna José de Azeredo Perdigao, Lisbon; Centro Portugues de Fotografia, Porto
- Christine Temin, "At ICA, Art that Goes Bump in the Night," *The Boston Globe*, 25 April
- *The Quick and the Dead*, Royal College of Art, London; Mead Gallery, Warwick Arts Centre, Coventry; Leeds City Art Gallery, Leeds
- "This Month," *Art and Auction*, summer, p. 115
- Scott Timberg, "Postmodernism & its Discontents," *The New Time Los Angeles*, 27 November
- "Vanities: Untitled Film Stills New From Cindy Sherman," *Vanity Fair*, November, p. 214
- Anthony Vidler and Peter Wallen, *Scene of the Crime*, exh. cat., The Armand Hammer Museum of Art and Cultural Center, Los Angeles
- Carol Vogel, "Inside Art," *The New York Times*, 21 March, p. C26
- "Voice Choices-Photo," *The Village Voice*, 1er July, p. 4
- Barbara Welter, "Auf Hrer See," *Fraz Frauenzeitung*, September/October, p. 30–31
- William Wison, "Intimate Multiples in 'Silent & Violent'," *Los Angeles Times*, 4 April
- "Women Behind the Lens," *The Blade*, 24 September, p. 32–33

- "Women Behind the Lens," *Ventura County*, 24 July, p. 38
- Dana Wood, "Camera Ready," *W Magazine*, September, p. 210
- Joanna Woodall, *Portraiture: Facing the Subject*, The Manchester University Press, Manchester, p. 8, 19, 65–67, 243–245
- Josef Woodard, "The Art of Aging," *Los Angeles Times*, 18 December, p. 56
- Larry Worth, "Mixed-Up 'Office Killer' Falls Down on Job," *The New York Post*, 3 December, p. 49
- "Wrinkles in Time," *The Independent*, 13 November, p. 43
- Linda Yablonsky, "Killing Time," *Paper Magazine*, December, p. 58–59
- Paul Young, "Portraits of the Artist as…," *The Los Angeles Magazine*, November, p. 99–101
- William Zimmer, "Life with a Twist; Fiction-Based Photography, Realism in Paint," *The New York Times*, 30 March, p. 12

1998
- "200 Women Legends, Leaders, and Trailblazers," *Vanity Fair*, November, p. 250
- Elizabeth Armstrong et al., *Double Trouble: The Patchett Collection*, exh. cat., Museum of Contemporary Art, San Diego; Museo de las Artes and Instituto Cultural Cabanas, Guadalajara; Museo de Monterrey, Monterrey; Museo Universitario Contemporáneo de Art, Mexico; Auditorio de Galicia and Inglesia San Domingo de Bonaval, Saint-Jacques-de-Compostelle; Sala Amós Salvador, Logroño
- Genevieve Arnold, *Connections and Contradictions: Modern and Contemporary Art from Atlanta Collections*, exh. cat., Michael C. Carlos Museum, Emory University, Atlanta
- *Avatar: of Postmodern Times and Multiple Identities*, exh. cat., De Oude Kerk, Amsterdam
- Joan Baixas and Victor Molina, *Escences de L'Imaginari: Festival internacional de Teatre visuali de Titelles de Barcelona. XXV aniversari*, Institut del Teatre, Barcelona
- Wim Beeren et al., *Everything of Value*, exh. cat., Slot Loevestein Gorcums Museum, Gorinchem
- Hans Belting, *Das Unsichtbare Meisterwerk*, C.H. Beck'sche Verlagsbuchhandlung, Munich, p. 451
- Frauke Berndt, "Aristote: Towards a Poetics of Memory," *The Poetics of Memory*, p. 23–42
- Frances Borzello, *Seeing Ourselves: Women's Self-Portraits*, Harry N. Abrams, London, p. 6, 170
- Mark Brakeman, "The Third Thursday a Success," *The Weekly Press*, Philadelphia, 24 September, p. 8
- William F. Buckley JR., "The Irresistible Memory," *Forbes ASAP*, November, p. 128
- Claire Carolin, "Cindy Sherman: History Portraits," *Contemporary Visual Arts*, n°17, p. 75
- *Century*, Benedikt Taschen, New York, p. 667, 672, 677, 679
- Richard Cork, "Private Gift for the Public Eye," *The Times*, 24 February, p. 37
- Rosemary Crumlin, *Beyond Belief: Modern Art and the Religious Imagination*, exh. cat., National Gallery of Victoria, Victoria
- Maia Damianovic, "Cindy Sherman," *Tema Celeste*, Milan, September, p. 72
- Arthur C. Danto, "American Realities," *Artforum*, January, p. 92–93
- Dame Darcy, "Dame Darcy Reads the Palm of Cindy Sherman," *Index*, January/February, p. 86–89
- John Alan Farmer, "Devotion," *Art Journal*, New York, p. 64, 75
- Birgit Flos et al., "Brennpunkt Kinno ein Roundtable," *Noëma*, Vienna, n°49, p. 66–73
- Eva Forgács, "Cindy Sherman," *Art Issues*, January/February, p. 45
- R. Forgáes, "Cindy Sherman," *Art Issues*, January/February, p. 48
- Gary Garrels, *A Portrait of Our Times: An Introduction to the Logan Collection*, exh. cat., San Francisco Museum of Modern Art, San Francisco
- Irene Genhart, "Mauerblümchens Rache," *Tagblatt der Stadt Zürich*, 15 January
- Alice Rose George and Lee Marks, *Hope Photographs*, Thames & Hudson, p. 131
- Grace Glueck, "Cindy Sherman," *The New York Times*, 8 May, p. E 33
- M. A. Greenstein, "The Icky Side of Beauty," *Exposure*, Florida, n°31, p. 39–43
- Melissa Harris, *Master Breasts*, Aperture, New York
- Phoebe Hoban, "Cindy Sherman: Moving Pictures," *The New York Magazine*, 6 April, p. 178
- Klaus Honnef et al., *Art of the 20th*, Benedikt Taschen, New York, p. 667, 672, 677, 679
- Peter Hossli, "Ich Lache Dauernd in Horrorfilmen," *Facts*, n°33, p. 110–112
- Michael Kimmelman, "How the Tame Can Suddenly See Wild," *The New York Times*
- Michael Kimmelman, "In Connecticut Where Caravaggio First Landed," *The New York Times*, 17 July
- Richard Klein, Dominique Nahas, Ingrid Schaffner, *Pop Surrealism*, exh. cat., The Aldrich Museum of Contemporary Art, Ridgefield
- Dominick Lombardi, "An Art Lover's Candy Store at the Aldrich Museum," *The Record-Review*, 26 June
- Kathrin Luz, "Das Melodram in der Zeitenössischen Kunst," *Noëma*, Vienna, n°49, p. 38–45
- Carlo McCormick, "Surrealism Goes Pop," *Juxtapoz*, winter
- David McNeill, "Body," *Art/Text*, February/April, p. 81–82
- Steven Madoff, "Pop Surrealism," *Artforum*, October, p. 120
- Joanna Manning, "Learning to Love Patriarchy," *Conscience*, Washington, vol. XIX, n°1, p. 2–5
- Jan van der Marck, *Art and the American Experience*, exh. cat., The Kalamazoo Institute of Arts, Kalamazoo
- Maia Da Claudia Mesch, "Cindy Sherman's *Office Killer*," *Dialogue*, Columbus, July/August, p. 13
- Ivo Mesquita, *Stills: A Selection from the Marieluise Hessel Collection*, exh. cat., The Center For Curatorial Studies, Annandale-on-Hudson
- *Mirror Images: Women, Surrealism, and Self-Representation*, exh. cat., The San Francisco Museum of Modern Art, San Fransisco and The MIT Press, Cambridge
- Dominic Molon, Lisa Corrin, Carol S. Eliel, *Mariko Mori*, exh. cat., The Serpentine Gallery, London; The Museum of Contemporary Art, Chicago, p. 4
- Philip Monk, *American Playhouse: The Theatre of Self-Presentation*, exh. cat., The Contemporary Art Gallery, Power Plant, Toronto
- Suzanne Muchnic, "Cindy Sherman," *Artnews*, February, p. 123
- Lynda Nead, "The Naked and the Damned," *The Times Higher Education Supplement*, April, p. 15
- Lillian Pacce, "Quase Obsessaõ," *Elle*, April, p. 86–89
- Deanna Petherbridge, Claude Ritschard, Andrea Carlino, *Corps à vif, art et anatomie*, exh. cat., Musée d'Art et d'Histoire, Geneva
- William Pirl, "On the Couch with Cindy Sherman," *Artnews*, December, p. 168
- Carrie Rickey, "The Show of Shows," *Inquirer Magazine*, 18 October, p. 13–14
- John Roberts, *The Art of Interruption*, The Manchester University Press, Manchester, p. 16–27
- Jan Rosiek, *Patos*, Aarhus Universitetforlag, Aarhus
- Miranda Sawyer, "The Invisible Woman," *The Observer*, U.K., p. 14–19
- Karel Schampers, *Scratches on the Surface of Things*, exh. cat., Museum Boijmans Van Beuningen, Rotterdam
- Ursula Sinnreich, "Lust und Last des Totens," *Neue Zurcher Zeitung*, 16 January
- "Spotlight: Making it Real," *The Gallery Guide*, January, p. 13
- Carol Squires, "Defining Women: A Portfolio of Modern Masters," *American Photo*, March/April, p. 69–81
- Carol Squires, "Original, Savvy, Fearless and Female," *American Photo*, March/April, p. 50–65, 91
- Jan-Ove Steihaug, *Abject/Informe/Trauma: Discourses in American Art of the Nineties*, For Art, Oslo, p. 4–7, 16, 35, 40–41, 43–49
- Margaret Steele & Cindy Estes, *The Art of the Body*, MOCA, p. 9–10
- Amy Talkington, "Cindy Sherman," *Ray Gun*, California, n°50
- Mark C. Taylor, *Hiding*, The University of Chicago Press, Chicago, p. 302, 316, 317
- "The 100 Most Important People in Photography," *American Photo*, April/May, p. 48
- Jan van Toorn, *Design Beyond Design*, Jan van Eyck Editions, Amsterdam, p. 56–57
- Caroline Torem-Craig, "Cultural Storage," *Paper*, December, p. 142
- Grady T. Turner, "Cindy Sherman," *Flash Art*, October, p. 123
- Brigitte Ulmer, "Genüsslich durchwühlte Magen," *Extra*, January
- Betty Van Garrel, "Cindy Sherman," *Snoeks*, Belgique, p. 334–348
- Steven Vincent, "What's the Hurry?," *Art & Auction*, 16–29 November, p. 44–49
- Catherine Weir, *Read my Lips*, exh. cat., The National Gallery of Australia, Canberra
- Wolfgang Welsch, *Ästhetisches Denken*, Philipp Reclam Jun. Verlag, Ditzingen, p. 225
- William Zimmer, "Recipe for a Good Time: Surrealism and Pop Culture," *The New York Times*, 2 August

1999
- Vince Aletti, "Doll Parts," *The Village Voice*, 1er June, p. 131
- "Art and Theory on Voyeurism," *Bijutsu Techo*, March, p. 71, 80
- Lyle Ashton Harris, "The Sublime, the Grotesque, the Epic," *aRUDE*, n° 15, p. 6–7, 50–54
- Terry Barrett, *Criticizing Photographs*, Mayfield Publishing Company, Mountain View, p. 23
- Julie L. Belcove, "W2000: Image: Photography," *W*, March, p. 313–322
- Carla Benedetti, *L'ombra lunga dell'autore*, Feltrinelli, Milan
- Neil Benezra and Olga Viso, *Regarding Beauty*, exh. cat., The Hirshhorn Museum and Sculpture Garden, Washington, p. 74–77
- *Bilder Erleben und Verstehen*, Kirschenmann/Schulz, Leipzig, p. 49
- Johannes Bilstein, *Macht und Füsorge*, Oktagon, Cologne, p. 45–46
- Michael Boodro, "People are Talking About Art," *Vogue*, November, p. 292
- Hugo Bousset, *Bevlogen Lichtheid*, Meulenhoff, Amsterdam, p. 141
- Hamish Bowles, "Venice Rave," *Vogue*, September, p. 230
- Ariella Budick, "Guides to the Complex Nature of Femininity," *Newsday*, 19 November, 1999
- Dan Cameron, "(The Century's Most Influential Artists) Camera Cameleon," *Artnews*, May, p. 143, 148
- Judy Chicago and Edward Lucie-Smith, *Women and Art: Contested Territory*, Weidenfeld & Nicholson, London
- "Cindy's self-portraits get French star treatment," *The Art Newspaper*, April, p. 16
- Bonnie Clearwater, "Slight of Hand: Photography in th 1990s," *Art Papers*, September/October, p. 22–27
- *Collection*, Astrup Fearnley Museum of Modern Art, Oslo, p. 146–151
- *Das 20.Jahrhundert*, DuMont, Cologne, p. 168–169
- Keith F. Davis and Donald J. Hall, *An American Century of Photography*, Harry N. Abrams, New York, p. 428
- Cecelia Dean, *Woman*, Visionaire Publishing, New York
- Thomas Deecke, *Originale echt Falsch*, exh. cat., Neues Museum Weserburg, Bremen, p. 120–123
- Gillo Dorfles, *Ultime Tendenze Nell'Arte D'Oggi*, Feltrinelli, Milan, p. 157
- Maura Egan, "Art and Commerce," *The New York Magazine*, 24 May, p. 16
- Trevor Fairbrother and Bagley Wright, *The Virginia & Bagley Wright Collection*, exh. cat., The Seattle Art Museum, Seattle, p. 162
- David Frankel, "Cindy Sherman: Metro Pictures," *Artforum*, November, p. 136
- "From Eminence to Emptiness: The Lure of Celebrity," *The New York Times*, 9 July, p. E31–E34
- Jay Gates, *Dallas Museum of Art: A Guide to the Collection*, The Dallas Museum of Art, Dallas, p. 288
- Benjamin Genocchio, "Images of a soul in torment," *The Australian*, 11 June
- Grace Glueck, "Playing Dress Up In Personas," *The New York Times*, 3 December, p. E40
- Roselee Goldberg, *Performance: Live Art Since 1960*, Harry N. Abrams, New York, p. 201
- Vicki Goldberg and Robert Silberman, *American Photography: A Century of Images*, Chronicle Books, San Francisco, p. 191
- Will Gompertz, *Zoo*, The Friary Press, London, October, p. 192–193
- Andy Grundberg, *Crisis of the Real*, Aperture, New York
- Michel Guerrin, "Cindy Sherman, entre attraction et répulsion," *Le Monde*, 7–8 February, p. 24
- Howard Halle, "Welcome to the Dollhouse," *Time Out*, 27 May–3 June, p. 71–72
- Peter Hay Halpert, "Collecting: Cindy Sherman For All," *American Photo*, March/April, p. 50
- Dave Hickey, "Best of the '90s," *Artforum*, December, p. 112–113
- Jeffrey Hogrefe, "Cindy Sherman's Résumé: Receptionist, Lingerie Buyer…," *The New York Observer*, 31 May, p. 24
- Jed Jackson, *Art: A Comparative Study*, Kendall/Hunt Publishing, Iowa, p. 264–265
- Jonathan R. Jones, "Cindy Sherman," *Contemporary Visual Arts*, n°25, p. 67
- Michiko Kashara, *Information Design: Photography*, Kadokawa Shoten Publishing, Japon, p. 85
- Jeffrey Kastner, "American Angst," *Art Monthly*, July/August, p. 19–23
- Taka Kawachi, "Cindy Sherman," *Esquire Japan*, October, p. 25
- Wolfgang Kemp, *Von Beuys bis Cindy Sherman-Sammlung Lothar Schirmer*, Schirmer/Mosel, Munich, p. 259–279
- Jutta Koether, "Feiste Fetische," *Spex*, July, p. 56
- Jutta Koether, "Old Witnesses," *Camera Austria*, n°67, p. 18–29
- Janet Kraynak, "Cindy Sherman at Metro Pictures," *Documents*, autumn, p. 54–58
- Suzanne Landau, Danielle Knafo, Yvonne Fleitman, *Skin-Deep: Surface and Appearance in Contemporary Art*,
- exh. cat., The Israel Museum, Jerusalem, p. 32
- Martha Langford, "Mutant, Dearest," *Border Crossings*, n° 72, p. 66–67
- Jim Lewis, "Twelve Inches of Plastic Fun," *Manhattan File*, May, p. 66–67
- Anthony Macris, "Confessions of a Serial Thriller," *The Bulletin*, 15 June, p. 108–110
- Nick Madigan, "Thousand Word's Worth," *The Daily Variety*, 24 May, p. 43
- Sandrine Malinaud, "Cindy Sherman: The Woman With a Hundred Faces," *Cimaise*, March/April, p. 33–40
- Bernard Marcadé, "Cindy Sherman : féminin pluriel," *Beaux-Arts*, February, p. 40–47
- Brook S. Mason, "Sherman's March," *Artnews*, September, p. 72
- Charles Melcher and Steven Diamond, *Voyeur*, Harpercollins, New York
- Francesco Alfano Miglietti et al., *Rosso vivo. Mutazioni, Trasfigurazione e sangue nell'Arte Contemporanea*, exh. cat., Padiglione d'Arte Contemporanea, Milan
- Catherine Morris, *The Essential Cindy Sherman*, Harry N. Abrams, New York
- Mohammad Mottahedan, Tony Godfrey, *Once Upon A Time In America: The Mottahedan* Collection, Christie's Books, London, p. 82
- Pia Müller-Tam, *Puppen Körper Automaten*, Oktagon, Cologne
- Alfred Nemeczek, *Das Bild der Kunst, 20 Jahre ART-Das Kunstmagazin*, Verlag Gruner + Jahr, Hamburg, p. 184, 212
- Victoria Pedersen, "Gallery Go 'Round: The Allure of the Alter Ego," *Paper*, June, p. 148
- Victoria Pedersen, "Gallery Go 'Round," *Paper*, November, p. 152
- Lisa Phillips, *The American Century: 1950–2000*, The Whitney Museum of American Art, New York, p. 279, 361
- Susan Platt, "Politically Indirect: Outing the Activist Artist," *Art Papers*, September/October, p. 32–37

- Barbara Pollack, "The 10 Best Living Artists: Self-Denial," *Artnews*, December, p. 146
- Jean-Louis Pradel, "Cindy Sherman madone underground," *L'Évenement*, 4–10 February, p. 60–63
- Duane Preble, *Artforms*, Longman, New York, p. 486–487
- Maura Reilly, "Cindy Sherman: Metro Pictures," *Zingmagazine*, September, p. 250–251
- Shelley Rice, *Inverted Odysseys, Claude Cahun, Maya Deren, Cindy Sherman*, exh. cat., The Grey Art Gallery, New York University, New York; The Museum of Contemporary Art, Miami and The MIT Press, Cambridge and London
- Laurence A. Rickels, "American Psychos," *Art/Text*, November, p. 58–63
- Burkhard Riemschneider and Uta Grosenick, *Art at the Turn of the Millennium*, Taschen, p. 466–469
- Robert Rosenblum, *Art at Work: Forty Years of The Chase Manhattan Collection*, exh. cat., The Museum of Fine Arts, Contemporary Arts Museum, Houston; The Chase Manhattan Corporation, New York, p. 266–267
- David A. Ross and Douglas R. Nickel, *Picturing Modernity: Highlights from the Photography Collection of the San Francisco Museum of Modern Art*, exh. cat., The San Francisco Museum of Modern Art, San Francisco
- Daniela Salvioni, *Looking at Ourselves: Works by Women Artists from the Logan Collection*, exh. cat., The San Francisco Museum of Modern Art, San Francisco
- Peter Scheldahl, "Beauty Contest," *The New Yorker*, 1er November, p. 108–110
- Peter Schjeldahl, "Valley of the Dolls," *The New Yorker*, 7 June, p. 94–95
- Laurie Schneider Adams, *Art Across Time*, The City University Press, New York, p. 939–940
- Mady Schutzman, *The Real Thing: Performance, Hysteria & Advertising*, The Wesleyan University Press, Middletown, p. 169–170
- Sebastian Smee, "Barbie suffers a meltdown," *The Sydney Morning Herald*, 2 June, p. 13
- Roberta Smith, "Cindy Sherman: Review," *The New York Times*, 4 June, p. E33
- Robert A. Sobieszek, *Ghost in the Shell*, The Los Angeles County Museum of Art, Los Angeles and The MIT Press, Cambridge, p. 174–283
- *Spaced Out: Late 1990s Works From the Vicki and Kent Logan Collection*, exh. cat., California College of Arts and Crafts, San Fransisco, p. 17, 39
- Peter Stepan, *Icons of Photography: The 20th Century*, Prestel, Munich, p. 173–174
- Mark Stevens, "Spice Girls," *The New York Magazine*, 21 June, p. 64–65
- *The Time of Our Lives*, exh. cat., The New Museum, New York, p. 95
- Nazif Topçuoglu, "Cindy Sherman/Metro Pictures," *Genis Aci*, August, p. 72–75
- "Traces: Making Faces," *International Herald Tribune*, 3 December, p. 5
- Dean Trackman, *Art Since 1950*, The National Gallery of Art, Washington, p. 76
- Louise Upton, "Shock Treatment," *Bazaar*, June/July, p. 68, 70
- Luisa Valeriani, *Dentro la Trasfigurazione*, Costa & Nolan, Milan, p. 96
- Mark Van Proyen, "Cindy Sherman," *The New Art Observer*, October, p. 46
- Simona Vendrame, "Manichini," *Tema Celeste*, October/December, p. 91–93
- Alexander Walker, "Hitchcock," *Quarterly*, summer, p. 48–49
- Isabelle de Wavrin, "Spéculation : le retour ?" *Beaux-Arts*, July, p. 97
- Lilly Wei, "Cindy Sherman: Metro Pictures," *Artnews*, September, p. 147

2000

- Vince Aletti, "The Lady Vanishes," *The Village Voice*, 21 November, p. 85
- Vince Aletti, "Best of 2000," *Artforum*, December, p. 130
- Pascale Antolin-Pirès, "Les « Clignotements de l'entrevision »: fragments et questionnements dans l'œuvre photographique de Cindy Sherman," *Fragmentaire et Fragmentation*, MSHA, Paris, p. 187–200
- *Art at Work-Forty Years of The Chase Manhattan Collection*, The Chase Manhattan Corporation, New York, p. 266–267
- Julie L. Belcove, "Lens Crafters," *W Magazine*, May, p. 186–189
- Dike Blair et al., *Let's Entertain: Life's Guilty Pleasures*, D.A.P., New York, p. 25–26, 29, 200–203, 292, 319
- Lisa Boone, "Galleries: Cindy Sherman at Gagosian Gallery," *The Los Angeles Times*, 30 March, p. 44
- Phyllis Braff, "Three Shows Investigate Provocative Images: 'Representing'," *The New York Times*, 19 March, p. 22
- David Bussel, "Tonight Matthew, I'm Going to Be," *i-D*, January, p. 168
- Stéphanie Busuttil-César, *Red*, Éditions Assouline, Paris and New York
- Graham Coulter-Smith, *The Visual-Narrative Matrix: Interdisciplinary Collisions and Collusions*, The Fine Art Research Centre, Southampton, p. 67, 70
- Arthur C. Danto, "Senssualita, Banalita, Identita," *Tema Celeste*, January/February, p. 70–71
- James Danziger, *American Photographs*, Éditions Assouline, New York and Paris, p. 182
- "Dead Funny," HQ, n°70, May, p. 15
- Tessa De Carlo, "Laying Bare the Uncertain Underside of the Truth," *The New York Times*, p. AR39–40
- *Der Anagrammatische Körper*, exh. cat., ZKM-Medientheater, Karlsruhe, p. 30
- Wilfried Dickoff, *After Nihilism*, The Cambridge University Press, Cambridge
- Chris Dunn, *People Looking at Art*, Hodder & Stoughton, London, p. 20–21
- Owen Edwards, "Graven Images," *American Photo*, May/June, p. 68–73
- William A. Ewing, *The Century of the Body*, Thames & Hudson, London, p. 166–167
- Felicity Fenner, "Film Noir, Fairytales and Hard-core Porn," *Art & Australia*, spring, p. 363–365
- Jonathon Fineberg, *Art Since 1940: Strategies of Being*, Calmann & King, London, p. 470
- Éva Forgács, "Cindy Sherman at Gagosian Gallery," *Art issues*, September/October, p. 46
- Laura French, "American Artists, a Journey Through Time," *Geico Direct*, summer, p. 32–33
- Charles Gandee, "Women on the Verge," *Talk*, May, p. 46
- Robin Gibson, *Painting the Century*, The National Portrait Gallery, London
- Christine Giles, Elizabeth Hayt, Katherine Plake Hough, *Duane Hanson: Virtual Reality*, exh. cat., The Palm Springs Desert Museum, Palm Springs, p. 58
- Jessica Glasscock, "Bridging the Art/Commerce Divide, Cindy Sherman and Rei Kawakubo of Comme des Garçons," *The Grey Gazette*, n° 1, p. 9
- Vicki Goldberg, "When Asserting A Self-Image Is Self-Defense," *The New York Times*, 4 April, p. 39–40
- Vicki Goldberg, "In New Galleries, a Collection of the Unexpected," *The New York Times*, 3 November, p. E31, E34
- Mark Gollom, "Gallery Patrons Get Chance to Enter Artists' World," *The National Post*, Ontario
- Daniela Gregori, "Ich ist Etwas Anders," *Frame Magazine*, July/August, p. 138
- Lynn Gumpert and Shelley Rice, "Inverted Odysseys," *The Grey Gazette*, n°1, p. 2–5
- Peter Halley, "Il Millenio é Finito nel 1968," *Tema Celeste*, January/February, p. 64–67
- Patricia Hills, *Modern Art in the USA: Issues and Controversies of the 20th Century*, Prentice Hall, Englewood Cliffs, p. 367
- Robert Hirsch, *Seizing the Light: History of Photography*, McGraw Hill, Boston, p. 448
- David Hopkins, *After Modern Art*, The Oxford University Press, Oxford, p. 201
- Sam Hunter, John Jacobus, Daniel Wheeler, *Modern Art*, Harry N. Abrahms, New York, p. 409
- *HyperMental*, exh. cat., Kunsthaus, Zürich; Hamburger Kunsthalle, Hambourg and Hatje Cantz Verlag, Ostfildern-Ruit, p. 101
- Glenis Israel, *Senior Artwise*, John Wiley & Sons, Hoboken, p. 203–214
- *Is Seeing Believing?*, exh. cat., The North Carolina Museum of Art, Raleigh, p. 48–51
- Amelia Jones, "Posing the Subject: Performing the other as Self," in *Making a Scene*, ARTicle Press, Birmingham, p. 33–56
- Michael Kimmelman, "Handing Out Modern Art By the Bushel," *The New York Times*, 18 January, p. E1–E9
- Michael Kimmelman, "Cindy Sherman," *The New York Times*, 24 November, p. E36
- Wayne Koestenbaum, "Fall Gals," *Artforum*, September, p. 148–151
- Gunilla Knape, *Cindy Sherman*, exh. cat., Hasselblad Center, Göteborg
- "Le Temps, Je. . .," *Vite Magazine*, Éditions du Centre Georges Pompidou, April, p. 20
- Corinna Lotz, "Beauty Now. Beauty in Art at the End of the 20th Century," *Contemporary Visual Arts*, summer, p. 43
- Diane Miliotes, *Surface and Depth*, exh. cat., Hood Museum of Art, New Hampshire
- Richard Morphet, *Encounters-New Art From Old*, exh. cat., National Gallery, London, p. 14, 16
- Linda Nochlin, "The Naked and the Dread," *Tate*, n° 21, p. 66–71
- Brigitte Ollier, Elisabeth Nora, Vanessa van Zuylen, "Autoportrait," *L'Insensé*, n°1, p. 15–17
- David Pagel, "Sherman is the Very Picture of How Others Fall Short," *The Los Angeles Times*, 14 April, p. F22
- Dominique Païni, Guy Cogeval, *Hitchcock et l'art : coïncidences fatales*, exh. cat., The Montreal Museum of Fine Arts, Québec, p. 279, 329; Musée national d'Art moderne, Centre Georges Pompidou, Paris, p. 279
- Daniela Palazzoli, *Sentimento del 2000*, Electra, Milan, p. 84–87
- Henrietta Palmer, "Ett erotiskt ogonblick," *MaMa: Magasin For Modern Arkitektur*, n° 26, p. 36–38
- *Présumés innocents-L'art contemporain et l'enfance*, exh. cat., Capc Musée d'art contemporain de Bordeaux, Bordeaux
- Jeremy Scott, "Best of 2000," *Artforum*, December, p. 31
- "Spring Fireworks for the Old Art Hub, Madison Avenue," *The New York Times*, 5 May, p. E35, E38
- Calvin Tompkins, "Her Secret Identities," *The New Yorker*, May, p. 74–83
- Calvin Tomkins, "Cindy Sherman und ihre Leichen im Keller," *Emma*, July/August, p. 100–109
- Kirk Varnedoe, Paola Antonelli, Joshua Siegel, *Modern Contemporary: Art at MoMA Since 1980*, The Museum of Modern Art, New York, p. 2, 3, 4, 5, 6, 41, 230, 347
- Jörg-Uwe Von Albig, "Kunst und Fotografie," *Geo Extra*, n°2, p. 134, 139, 149–50
- Edsel Williams, *Early Work of Cindy Sherman*, Glenn Horowitz Bookseller, New York
- Andrew Wilson, "Cindy Sherman: Greengrassi, London," *Art Monthly*, December/January, p. 33–34
- Linda Yablonsky, "Vanity Fare," *Time Out New York*, November/December, p. 91
- Dave Yorath, *Photography–A Crash Course*, Watson-Guptill, New York, p. 127
- *Zona F*, exh. cat., Espai d'Art Contemporani de Castelló, Castelló, p. 16

2001

- *American Visionaries*, exh. cat., The Whitney Museum of American Art, New York, p. 278
- Pernille Anker Kristensen, "Shermans rædselskabinet," *Morgenavisen Jyllands-Posten*, 3 June
- Pernille Anker Kristensen, "Shocking Sherman," *Morgenavisen Jyllands-Posten*, 3 June
- Marianne Bieger-Thielemann et al., *20th Century Photography*, Taschen, Cologne, p. 166–167
- Christian Bouqueret, *Histoire de la photographie en images*, Marval, Paris, p. 173
- John Peter Brakewood, "Cindy Sherman–California Dream," *Art Actuel*, January/February, p. 82–83
- Sabine Breitwieser, *Double Life: Identity and Transformation in Contemporary Arts*, Generali Foundation, Vienna and Verlag der Buchhandlung Walther König, Cologne
- Annette Brodersen, "Cindy Sherman's Shock Treatment," *Politiken*, 5 June
- *Catálogo de la Colección de Arte Contemporáneo Fundación "la Caixa,"* Fundación "la Caixa," Barcelona, p. 138
- Pierrette Crouzet et al., *La Confusion des genres en photographie*, Bibliothèque Nationale de France, p. 162–163
- *Die Nationalgalerie*, DuMont Literatur, Allemagne, p. 302
- Arne Ehmann, "ArtFacts-Cindy Sherman," *Art Investor*, Munich, n°2, p. 18–19
- *Fragments*, exh. cat., El Museu de la Universitat d'Alacant, Alicante
- Massimiliano Gioni, "New York Cut Up," *Flash Art*, January/February, p. 67–69
- David Gleeson, "Reviews-Cindy Sherman," *Time Out London*, 3–10 January, p. 52
- Constance W. Glenn, *Double Vision: Photographs from the Strauss Collection*, exh. cat., The University Art Museum, California State University, Long Beach, p. 36
- Uta Grosenick, *Women Artists*, Taschen, Cologne, p. 488–493
- Eleanor Heartney, *Postmodernism*, Tate Publishing, London, p. 58–59
- Ingeborg Hoesterey, *Pastiche*, The Indiana University Press, Bloomington, p. 28
- *I am a Camera*, exh. cat., The Saatchi Gallery, London and Booth-Clibborn Editions, London, p. 131–160
- Bill Ivey, *A Creative Legacy—A History of the National Endowment fo the Arts Visual Artists' Fellowship Program*, Harry N. Abrams, New York, p. 108
- *Jasper Johns to Jeff Koons: Four Decades of Art from the Broad Collections*, exh. cat., The Los Angeles County Museum of Art, Los Angeles
- Cheryl Kaplan, "Cindy Sherman, Metro Pictures, New York," *Tema Celeste*, January/February, p. 91
- Donald Kuspit, "Regressive Irony: Duchamp's Legacy," *Tema Celeste*, March/April, p. 42–47
- *Lateral Thinking: Art of the 1990's*, exh. cat., The Museum of Contemporary Art, San Diego, p. 104–105
- Edward Leffingwell, "Cindy Sherman at Metro Pictures," *Art in America*, June, p. 126
- Nicoletta Leonardi et al., *L'Altra Metà Dello Sguardo*, Agorà Editrice, p. 43
- Steve Martin, *Kindly Lent Their Owner*, exh. cat., The Bellagio Gallery of Fine Art, Las Vegas, p. 80–81
- Roy T. Matthews and F. DeWitt Platt, *The Western Humanities*, Mayfield Publishing Company, Mountain View, p. 611
- *Notorious: Alfred Hitchcock and Contemporary Art*, exh. cat., Tokyo Opera City Art Japan, Tokyo, p. 74–76
- Peter Pakesh, *ABBILD: Recent Portraiture and Depiction*, Landesmuseum Joanneum, Graz
- *Parkett: Collaborations and Editions Since 1984*, Parkett Publishers, New York, p. 29
- Francesco Poli, "Let's Entertain," *Tema Celeste*, March/April, p. 54–59
- Eva Pohl, "Det fan'me uhyggeligt du," *Berlingske Tidende*, 2 June
- Günther Regel et al., *Moderne Kunst*, Ernst Klett Schulbuchverlag Leipzig, p. 227
- Burkhard Riemschneider and Uta Grosenick, *Art Now*, Taschen, Cologne, p. 150–151
- Trine Ross, "Sandheden om Sherman," *Politiken*, 1er June
- Mette Sandbye, "Cindy rædsel," *Weekendavisen*, 2–3 June
- Uwe M. Schneede, *Die Geschichte Der Kunst Im 20. Jahrhundert*, Verlag C.H. Beck, Munich
- Laurie Schneider Adams, *A History of Western Art*, McGraw Hill, New York, p. 549
- *Settings & Players*, exh. cat., White Cube, London
- Nancy Spector, *Guggenheim Museum Collection A to Z*, Guggenheim Museum, New York, p. 314–315
- Wendy Steiner, *The Trouble With Beauty*, William Heinemann, London
- L. P. Streitfeld, "The Female Body is the Passage," *NY Arts*, July/August, p. 15
- Marita Sturken and Lisa Cartwright, *Practices of Looking*, The Oxford University Press, New York, p. 255
- Astrid Wege, "Arbeit Am Rollenklischee," *Frame*, March/April, p. 100–101
- Renate Wiehager, *Moving Pictures*, exh. cat., Galerien der Stadt Esslingen, Esslingen, p. 130–133
- Claire Wilcox, *Radical Fashion*, V&A Publications, London
- *Without Hesitation [Ohne Zögern]-The Olbricht Collection Part 2*, exh. cat., Neues Museum Weserburg Bremen, Brême

- "Women, Place, Memory, and Desire," *Women in the Arts*, summer, p. 12–17

2002

- *Ahead of the 21st Century—The Pisces Collection*, exh. cat., Fürstenberg Sammlungen, Donaueschingen and Hatje Cantz Verlag, Ostfildern-Ruit, p. 158–165
- *AMERICAN STANDARD: (Para)Normality and Everyday Life*, exh. cat., Barbara Gladstone Gallery, New York
- Dominique Baqué, *Mauvais genre*, Éditions du Regard, Paris, p. 155
- *Chic Clicks: Creativity and Commerce in Contemporary Fashion Photography*, exh. cat., The Institute of Contemporary Art, Boston, p. 98–99, 100–101, 108–111
- *Die Wohltat der Kunst*, exh. cat., Staatlichen Kunsthalle Baden-Baden, Baden-Baden, p. 147–157
- Erika Doss, *Twentieth-Century American Art*, The Oxford University Press, Oxford, p. 217
- *Dreaming In Print-A Decade of Visionaire*, Edition 7L, New York, p. 120
- *DuMonts Begriffslexikon zur Zeitgenössischen Kunst*, DuMont, Cologne, p. 115, 132
- Douglas Eklund et al., *Thomas Struth*, exh. cat., The Dallas Museum of Art, Dallas, p. 154, 160
- *Espelho Cego [Blind Mirror]*, exh. cat., Museu de Arte Moderna de São Paulo, São Paulo, p. 60
- *Extension*, exh. cat., Magasin 3 Stockholm Konsthall, Stockholm
- *Fabric of Vision*, exh. cat., National Gallery, London, p. 75
- Maria Luisa Frisa et al., *Total Living*, Charta, Milan, p. 58–59
- Claude Frontisi, *Histoire visuelle de l'art*, Larousse, Paris, p. 492
- Blake Gopnik, "The Broad Collections: Stars, Unevenly Arrayed," *The Washington Post*, March, p. G1
- Uta Grosenick and Burkhard Riemschneider, *Art Now*, Taschen, Cologne, p. 452–455
- Howard Halle, "Lite Show," *Time Out New York*, 5–12 September, p. 52
- *Hautnah-The Goetz Collection*, exh. cat., Museum Villa Stuck, Munich, p. 82–85
- Amelia Jones, "The Eternal Return'," *Signs*, summer, p. 955, 958, 962
- Michael Kelly, "Danto and Krauss on Cindy Sherman," in *Art History, Aesthetics Visual Studies*, The Yale University Press, New Haven, p. 122–146
- Klaus Kertess, *Photography Transformed*, Harry N. Abrams, New York, p. 187, 252
- *Life, Death, Love, Hate, Pleasure, Pain*, exh. cat., The Museum of Contemporary Art, Chicago, p. 222–223
- Gerald Marzorati, "Defining Moments-Imitation of Life," *ARTnews*, November, p. 229
- Scot Peacock, *Authors & Artists for Young Adults*, Thomson Gale, Farmington Hills, p. 149–155
- *Photography Past Forward: Aperture at 50*, Aperture Foundation, New York, p. 33
- *Qu'est-ce que la photographie aujourd'hui ?*, Beaux-Arts, Paris, p. 32, 166–169
- *Rapture*, exh. cat., The Barbican Gallery, London, p. 52–53
- Karl Ruhrberg, *The Kaiserring: The 25th Anniversary of the Goslar Prize*, 200 Seite-Wienand Verlag, Cologne
- Jeremy Simon, *The Visual Art Critic*, Columbia University, New York
- Ingrid Sischy, "Great Pretenders," *The New York Times Magazine*, summer, p. 56–60
- *Some Assembly Required: Collage Culture in Post-War America*, exh. cat., The Everson Museum of Art, Syracuse, New York, p. 74
- William F. Stapp, *Portrait of the Art World: A Century of ARTnews Photographs*, The Yale University Press, p. 137
- John Sturman, "Defining Moments-Cindy Sherman," *ARTnews*, November, p. 255
- *Tableaux Vivants*, exh. cat., Kunsthalle Wien, Vienna, p. 158–163
- *The Arch of Desire (Center For Curatorial Studies Tenth Anniversary)*, exh. cat., Center for Curatorial Studies, Bard College, Annandale-on-Hudson, p. 10
- *Visions from America: Photographs from the Whitney Museum of American Art*, exh. cat., The Whitney Museum of American Art, New York, p. 130, 140, 221
- Christine Walter, *Bilder Erzählen!*, Verlag und Datenbank für Geisteswissenschaften, Weimar, p. 56, 128–133
- Mary Warner Marien, *Photography: A Cultural History*, Laurence King Publishing, London, p. 426

2003

- Vince Aletti, "Preview, Cindy Sherman, Serpentine Gallery," *Artforum*, May, p. 64
- Willfried Baatz, "50 Klassiker Photographen," in *Gerstenberg Visuell*, Gerstenburg Verlag, Hildesheim, p. 252–255
- Gerry Badger, *Collecting Photography*, Mitchell Beazley pub., London, p. 10, 11, 15, 21, 84, 130, 131
- Hans Belting, *Art History After Modernism*, The University of Chicago Press, Chicago, p. 124f, 125, 211
- Betsy Berne, "Studio Visit: Cindy Sherman," *TATE*, London, May/June, p. 36–42
- Catriona Black, "End in the Clowns?," *The Sunday Herald*, Edinburgh, 21 December
- James Bone, "Desperately seeking Cindy," *The Times Magazine*, London, 31 May, p. 26–28
- Martha Buskirk, *The Contingent Object of Contemporary Art*, The MIT Press, Cambridge, p. 111–117
- Rachel Campbell-Johnston, "Behind the Masks," *The Times*, London, 4 June, p. 13
- "Cindy Sherman," *Grafik*, London, August, p. 52–53
- *Cindy Sherman*, exh. cat., The Serpentine Gallery, London; The Scottish National Gallery of Modern Art, Edinburgh
- *Cindy Sherman, Centerfolds 1981*, Skarstedt Fine Arts, New York
- *Cindy Sherman: The Complete Untitled Film Stills*, The Museum of Modern Art, New York
- Ajay Close, "Secret Identities," *The Scotsman*, Edinburgh, 6 December
- Jo Craven, "What Lies Beneath," *British Vogue*, June, p. 182–187
- Laura Cumming, "Clowns to the left of me...," *The Observer*, London, 8 June
- Charles Darwent, "Better than painting? Maybe...," *The Independent on Sunday*, London, 8 June
- Vera Dika, *Recycled Culture in Contemporary Art and Film: The Uses of Nostalgia*, The Cambridge University Press, New York, p. 9, 41–46, 75, 150, 152
- Régis Durand, "Un monde réellement renversé ?," *DITS*, Hornu, n°3, p. 12–23
- Caroline Evans, *Fashion at the Edge—Spectacle, Modernity and Deathliness*, The Yale University Press, New Haven and London, p. 164–165
- Angela Everitt, "Platform for Art," *Tube*, summer, p. 9–11
- Annateresa Fabris, "Cindy Sherman ou de alguns estereótipos cinematográficos e televisivos," *Estudos Feministas*, CFH/CCE/UFSC, p. 61–70
- Simon Ford, "Head to Head: Cindy Sherman and Barbara Kruger in London," *Art Monthly*, July/August, n°268, p. 35–37
- David Frankel, "Cindy Sherman Talks to David Frankel," *Artforum*, March, p. 54–55, 259–260
- Lain Gale, "Sex and suffering: bizarre images from the world of the ultimate chameleon," *Scotland on Sunday*, Edinburgh, 21 December
- Uta Grosenick, *Icons—Women Artists in the 20th and 21st Century*, Taschen, Cologne, p. 170–173
- Chris Hammonds, "Profiles. Cindy Sherman," *Tema Celeste*, n°99, September/October, p. 80–81
- Aaron Hicklin, "Face to Face With Cindy Sherman, America's Greatest Living Artist," *The Sunday Herald Magazine*, Edinburgh, 30 November, p. 6–12
- Henry Hitchings, "What's Right in Front of You," *The London Times Literary Supplement*, 18 July, p. 18
- Tom James, "Cindy's clowning is seriously good," *Metro Travel*, London, 3 June, p. 32
- Waldemar Januszczak, "Cindy Sherman is shyly and wittily teaching us what self-portraiture is all about," *The Sunday Times*, London, 15 June, p. 10–11
- Sarah Kent, "Losing Face," *Time Out London*, London, August
- Michael Kimmelman, "For London, a Summer of Photograhic Memory," *The New York Times*, p. E1–E5
- Michael Kimmelman, "Unambiguously Cindy," *The New York Times Magazine*, 5 October, p. 32
- Ann Landi, "Who Are the Great Women Artists?," *Artnews*, March, p. 94–97
- Tom Lubbock, "The Make-up Girl," *The Independent Review*, London, p. 14–15
- Mick Moore, "Underground Overground?," *The Journal of Photography*, London, 11 June, p. 7
- Charlotte Mullins, "Living doll," *The Financial Times*, London, 7 June
- Molly Nesbit, "Bright Light, Big City: The 80s Without Walls," *Artforum*, April, p. 184–189, 245–248
- Miles Orvell, *Oxford History of Art: American Photography*, The Oxford University Press, New York, p. 171–175
- William Packer, "Photography that is more than snapping a moment," *The Financial Times*, London, August
- David Pollock, "Portrait of an artist who's hard to identify," *The Evening News Edinburgh*, 17 December
- Michael Prodger, "Cruel and Tender Cindy Sherman," *The Sunday Telegraph*, London, 8 June
- Andrew Renton, "Life through a lens," *The London Evening Standard*, London, 27 May, p. 39
- Andrew Renton, "Snap judgements," *The Scotsman*, London, 30 May
- Joyce Henri Robinson and Sarah K. Rich, *Through the Looking Glass*, The Pennsylvania State University Press, University Park, p. 18–19
- Daniel B. Schneider, "Moving Pictures," *Artforum*, April, p. 213
- Collier Schorr, "Feminism & Art: Nine Views," *Artforum*, October, p. 140–149
- Adrian Searle, "Dressing up in public," *The Guardian*, London, 6 June, p. 12–13
- Brian Sewell, "You Won't See Cindy," *The London Evening Standard*, 6 June, p. 32–33
- Alan Singer, *Aesthetic Reason-Artworks and the Deliberative Ethos*, The Pennsylvania State University Press, University Park, p. 238, 255–258, 260, 264–267
- Brian Sewell, "Cindy Sherman," Metrolife Magazine, in *The London Evening Standard*, November
- John Slyce, "Beyond Recognition: The Unidentifiable Cindy Sherman," *Portfolio*, December, p. 42–49
- Sebastian Smee, "Viewfinder: Cindy Sherman," *The Telegraph*, London, 31 May, p. 3
- Jürgen Tesch and Eckhard Hollmann, *Icons of Art—The 20th Century*, Prestel, New York, p. 192–193
- Sarah Valdez, *Curve—The Female Nude Now*, Universe Publishing, New York, p. 177
- Amei Wallach, "Finding Mapplethorpe's Inner Cindy Sherman," *The New York Times*, 14 September, p. AR34
- Gabby Wood, "I'm every woman," *The Observer*, London, 18 May

2004

- "A Whiff of Spring," *The New York Times*, 20 March, p. A13
- Susan Anker and Dorothy Nelkin, *The Molecular Gaze, Art in the Genetic Age*, The Coldspring Harbor Laboratory Press, New York, p. 66–67, 76, 189
- Jan Avgikos, "Reviews-Cindy Sherman, Metro Pictures," *Artforum*, September, p. 265
- Brooks Barnes, "Art Appreciation," *The Wall Street Journal*, 23 January, p. W1, W10
- Gina Bellafante, Holly Brubach, Rosalind Krauss, "Art That Wears $780 Shoes," *The New York Times*, 11 April, p. AR29
- Nicholas Blincoe, "The Muse and Her Wardrobe," *ArtReview*, September, p. 64–67
- Mark Coetzee, *Not Afraid: Rubell Family Collection*, Phaidon, New York, p. 64, 122, 126–127
- Jean-Pierre Criqui, "High Art," *Artforum*, January, p. 53–54
- Cayre English, "Cindy Sherman: Imaging Art, Imaging Fashion," *NY Arts Magazine*, July/August, p. 29
- Jori Finkel, "Art Fragments From the Big Apple-Cindy Sherman," *Flash Art*, July/September, p. 64
- Jori Finkel, "Cindy Sherman, Metro Pictures," *Flash Art*, July/September, p. 64
- Helen A. Harrison, "Unforeseen Irises and a Meteor Asking Big Questions—North Fork/South Fork," *The New York Times*, 30 May, p. 9
- Eileen Kinsella, "Sex Sells and Sometimes Quite Well," *ARTnews*, January, p. 110–111
- Christopher Knight, "Photo Synthesis," *The Los Angeles Times*, 7 March, p. E1, E41
- Isabelle de Maison Rouge, *Mythologies Personnelles*, Éditions Scala, Paris, p. 95–99
- Charles Dee Mitchell, "Report From Santa Fe—Everything in Excess," *Art in America*, November, p. 84–91
- Gill Perry and Paul Wood, *Themes in Contemporary Art*, The Yale University Press, New Haven, CT, p. 156–158
- Ellen Ross, "Conversation with Cindy Sherman and Lorna Simpson," *Yard*, autumn, p. 20–27
- Maik Schlütter, *Cindy Sherman Clowns*, exh. cat., Kestnergesellschaft, Hanovre, Schirmer/Mosel, Munich
- Ingrid Sischy, "Fear and Clothing," *The New York Times Magazine*, April, p. 76–86
- Roberta Smith, "The Ever-Shifting Selves of Cindy Sherman, Girlish Vamp to Clown," *The New York Times*, 28 May, p. E33
- Roberta Smith, "Images of Fashion Tiptoe Into the Modern," *The New York Times*, 16 April, p. E39
- Mark Stevens, "Kitsch in Sync," *New York*, 31 May, p. 54
- *Stripped Bare, The Body Revealed in Contemporary Art, Works from the Thomas Koerfer Collection*, Merrell, New York, p. 40, 86–89, 123, 138–143, 213
- *Subjective Realities—Works from the Refco Collection*, Refco Group Ltd., New York and Chicago, p. 218–219
- "The Multiple Worlds of Cindy Sherman's History Portraits," *ABV44*, The Annual Journal of the National Gallery of Victoria, Victoria, p. 26–33
- *The Unseen Cindy Sherman: Early Transformations 1975/1976*, Montclair Art University, Montclair; Smart Art Press, Santa Monica
- Éric Troncy, Stéphanie Moisdon and Fabrice Bousteau, "NuméroScope," *Beaux-Art Magazine*, January, p. 64–75
- Richard B. Woodward, "Fun to Look Different," *Art News*, May, p. 108

2005

- *Big Bang : création et destruction dans l'art du XXe siècle*, exh. cat., Musée national d'Art moderne, Centre Georges Pompidou, Paris, p. 154
- Ilka Becker, "Peeping Cindy," in *Women Artists in the 20th and 21st Century*, Taschen, Cologne, p. 300–305
- Margrit Brehm, *YES YES YES YES*, exh. cat., Museum Morsbroich, Leverkusen, p. 5, 159–167
  Flashback: Revisiting the Art of the 1980s, exh. cat., Kunstmuseum Basel and Museum fur Gegenwartskunst, Basel and Hatje Cantz Verlag, Ostfildern-Ruit
  "Forbidden Fantasies: A Special Issue on Pornography," *The Village Voice*, 26 October–1 November, p. 90
- Martin Friedman, *Close Reading: Chuck Close and the Artist Portrait*, Harry N. Abrams, New York, p. 285–299
- Isabelle Graw, "Without Makeup," interview with Cindy Sherman, in exh. cat. *Vertiges-Printemps de Septembre*, Les Presses du Réel, p. 26–35
- Paul Greenhalgh, *The Modern Ideal: The Rise and Collapse of Idealism in the Visual Arts (from enlightment to postmodernism)*, V&A Publications, London, p. 91
- Elizabeth Hamilton, *The Blake Byrne Collection*, The Museum of Contemporary Art, Los Angeles, p. 68
- Helen A. Harrison, "Turning Dress-Up Into Fine Art: In East Hampton the Many Faces of Cindy Sherman," *The New York Times*, 18 September, p. 2, 12–13
  Ken Johnson, "In Shows Large and Small, Long Island Celebrates Its Artistic Abundance," *The New York Times*, 12 August, p. E27, E30

- Jason Edward Kaufman, "Lens Life: Unmasking iconic photographer Cindy Sherman," *Art and Antiques*, September, p. 51–54
- Dodie Kazanjian, "Body Language," *Vogue*, December, p. 330–331
- Tod Lippy, *Esopus*, Esopus Foundation Ltd., New York, p. 116
- Robert Long, "Cool Curtains, Creepy Clowns: Robert Rauschenberg and Cindy Sherman at Guild Hall," *The East Hampton Star*, 25 August, p. C1, C4
  Glenn D. Lowry, *Masterworks of Modern from the Museum of Modern Art, New York*, Scala vision, New York, p. 264
  Barry J. Mauer, "The Epistemology of Cindy Sherman: A Research Method for Media and Cultural Studies,"
- *Mosiac*, The University of Manitoba, Winnipeg, March, p. 93–113
- Alyce Mahon, *Eroticism & Art*, The Oxford University Press, Oxford, p. 244
  Catherine Morris, Cindy Sherman: *Working Girl*, exh. cat., The Contemporary Art Museum, St. Louis
- *Private View 1980–2000 Collection Pierre Huber*, jrp-ringier, Zurich, p. 56–61
- di Renato Diez, "Rene Magritte," *Arte*, September, p. 86–92
- Gabriele Schor, "Precarious Transformations: Cindy Sherman's Unknown Early Work in St. Louis," *Neue Zurcher*
- *Zeitung*, Zurich, 9 December, p. 26
- Philippe Segalot, *Empreinte-moi*, exh. cat., Galerie Emmanuel Perrotin, Paris
- Lisa Skolnik, "5 Things You Need to Know about Collecting Photography," *The Chicago Tribune Magazine*, 13 November, p. 19–21
- Daniel Soutif, *L'Art au XXe siècle 1939–2002*, Citadelles & Mazenod, Paris, p. 483–484
  Camiel van Winkel, *The Regime of Visibility*, Nai Publishers, Rotterdam, p. 47–105

2006
- *Contemporary Voices: L'UBS Art Collection hôte de la Fondation Beyeler*, exh. cat., Fondation Beyeler, Basel; The Museum of Modern Art, New York, p. 200–201
- Alan Fletcher, *The Art Book for Children*, Phaidon, New York, p. 48–51
- Uta Grosenick, *Art Now, Vol. 2*, Taschen, Cologne, p. 488–491
- Stephen Melville, *The Lure of the Object*, The Yale University Press, New Haven

LIST OF WORKS

An asterisk denotes works in the exhibition.

The titles of the works and series in italics are the original ones given by the artist. To make it possible to identify the large series that make up Cindy Sherman's oeuvre, the titles used by critics and art historians are given in parentheses.

A Cindy Book, c.1964–1975
Album with 26 black-and-white photographs and handwritten notes, 8 pages
8 ¾ x 11 ¾ in. (22.5 x 29.8 cm)
Courtesy of the artist and Metro Pictures, New York
p.1–8, 233

—

***Untitled A–E**, 1975
5 black-and-white photographs
Artist's prints 1/2
Editions of 10
A, C, D, and E: 20 x 16 in. (50.8 x 40.6 cm); B: 7 ¾ x 6 ¼ in. (20 x 16 cm)
Private collection, Courtesy Metro Pictures, New York
p.11–15, 235

—

Doll Clothes, 1975
DVD from Super 8 film, black and white, no sound, 2'22''
Courtesy of the artist and Metro Pictures, New York
p.271

—

Bus Riders, 1976–2005
p.17–21, 237

**Untitled #363–#377*
1976–2000
15 black-and-white photographs
Editions of 20
7 ⅜ x 5 in. (18.9 x 12.7 cm)
Courtesy of the artist and Metro Pictures, New York

**Untitled #430, #431, #433, #434, #439*
1976–2005
5 black-and-white photographs
Editions of 20
7 ⅜ x 5 in. (18.9 x 12.7 cm)
Courtesy of the artist and Metro Pictures, New York

—

Murder Mystery, 1976–2000

**Untitled #378–#394*
1976–2000
17 black-and-white photographs
Editions of 20
10 x 8 in. (25.4 x 20.3 cm)
Courtesy of the artist and Metro Pictures, New York
p.23–31, 239

—

**Untitled Film Stills #1–#27, #27 B, #28–#65, #81–#84*
1977–1980
70 black-and-white photographs
Exhibition prints
Editions of 10
10 x 8 in. (25.4 x 20.3 cm) to 8 x 10 in. (20.3 x 25.4 cm)
Courtesy Metro Pictures, New York
p.33–62, 241–245, 276–277, 287

—

[Rear Screen Projections], 1980

**Untitled #66*
1980
Color photograph
Edition of 5
16 x 24 in. (40.6 x 61 cm)
Private collection
p.65, 247

**Untitled #67*
1980
Color photograph
Edition of 5
20 x 24 in. (50.8 x 61 cm)
Frac-Collection Aquitaine, Bordeaux
p.66, 247

**Untitled #69*
1980
Color photograph
Edition of 5
20 x 24 in. (50.8 x 61 cm)
Nina and Frank Moore Collection, New York
p.76, 247

**Untitled #70*
1980
Color photograph
Edition of 5
20 x 24 in. (50.8 x 61 cm)
The Broad Art Foundation, Santa Monica
p.74, 247

**Untitled #71*
1980
Color photograph
Artist's print 1/1
Edition of 5
20 x 24 in. (50.8 x 61 cm)
Private collection
Courtesy Metro Pictures, New York
p.69, 247

**Untitled #72*
1980
Color photograph
Edition of 5
20 x 24 in. (50.8 x 61 cm)
Barbara and Richard S. Lane Collection
p.70, 247

**Untitled #74*
1980
Color photograph
Edition of 5
20 x 24 in. (50.8 x 61 cm)
Victoria and Albert Museum, London
p.73, 247

**Untitled #75*
1980
Color photograph
Artist's print 1/1
Edition of 5
20 x 24 in. (50.8 x 61 cm)
Private collection
Courtesy Metro Pictures, New York
p.67, 247

**Untitled #76*
1980
Color photograph
Artist's print 1/1
Edition of 5
20 x 24 in. (50.8 x 61 cm)
Private collection
Courtesy Metro Pictures, New York
p.68, 247

**Untitled #77*
1980
Color photograph
Artist's print 1/1
Edition of 5
20 x 24 in. (50.8 x 61 cm)
Private collection,
Courtesy Metro Pictures, New York
p.72, 247

**Untitled #78*
1980
Color photograph
Edition of 5
20 x 24 in. (50.8 x 61 cm)
Neda Young Collection
p.71, 247

**Untitled #79*
1980
Color photograph
Edition of 5
20 x 24 in. (50.8 x 61 cm)
Private collection
p.75, 247

—

[Centerfolds/Horizontals], 1981

**Untitled #85*
1981
Color photograph
Edition of 10
24 x 48 in. (61 x 121.9 cm)
Musée d'Art Moderne de Saint-Étienne Métropole
p.92–93, 249

**Untitled #86*
1981
Color photograph
Edition of 10
24 x 48 in. (61 x 121.9 cm)
The Eli and Edythe L. Broad Collection, Los Angeles
p.80–81, 249

**Untitled #87*
1981
Color photograph
Edition of 10
24 x 48 in. (61 x 121.9 cm)
Private collection
p.84–85, 249

**Untitled #88*
1981
Color photograph
Edition of 10
24 x 48 in. (61 x 121.9 cm)
The Museum of Contemporary Art, Los Angeles
The Barry Lowen Collection
p.82–83, 249

**Untitled #89*
1981
Color photograph
Artist's print 1/2
Edition of 10
24 x 48 in. (61 x 121.9 cm)
Courtesy Metro Pictures, New York
p.86–87, 249, 290

**Untitled #90*
1981
Color photograph
Artist's print 2/2
Edition of 10
24 x 48 in. (61 x 121.9 cm)
Artist's collection
Courtesy Metro Pictures, New York
p.88–89, 249, 290

**Untitled #91*
1981
Color photograph
Edition of 10
24 x 48 in. (61 x 121.9 cm)
Collection Neda Young
p.90–91, 249

**Untitled #92*
1981
Color photograph
Edition of 10
24 x 48 in. (61 x 121.9 cm)
The Eli and Edythe L. Broad Collection, Los Angeles
p.78–79, 249

**Untitled #93*
1981
Color photograph
Edition of 10
24 x 48 in. (61 x 121.9 cm)
Goetz Collection, Munich
p.94–95, 249

*Untitled #94
1981
Color photograph
Artist's print 2/2
Edition of 10
24 x 48 in. (61 x 121.9 cm)
Artist's collection
Courtesy Metro Pictures, New York
p.96–97, 249

*Untitled #95
1981
Color photograph
Edition of 10
24 x 48 in. (61 x 121.9 cm)
Collection Neda Young
p.100–101, 249

*Untitled #96
1981
Color photograph
Artist's print
Edition of 10
24 x 48 in. (61 x 121.9 cm)
Olbricht Collection
p.98–99, 249

—

[Pink Robes], 1982

*Untitled #97
1982
Color photograph
Edition of 10
45 x 30 in. (114.3 x 76.2 cm)
Per Skarstedt Collection, New York
p.103, 251

*Untitled #98
1982
Color photograph
Edition of 10
45 x 30 in. (114.3 x 76.2 cm)
The Eli and Edythe L. Broad Collection, Los Angeles
p.104, 251

*Untitled #99
1982
Color photograph
Edition of 10
45 x 30 in. (114.3 x 76.2 cm)
The Eli and Edythe L. Broad Collection, Los Angeles
p.105, 251

—

*Untitled #103
1982
Color photograph
Edition of 10
30 x 19 ½ in. (76.2 x 50.2 cm)
Barbara Schwartz Collection
p.107, 251

*Untitled #113
1982
Color photograph
Edition of 10
48 x 24 in. (122 x 61 cm)
Fonds National d'Art Contemporain, Ministère de la Culture et de la Communication, Paris, no. inv. 1907 [1]
p.108, 251

*Untitled #114
1982
Color photograph
Edition of 10
49 x 30 in. (124.5 x 76.2 cm)
The Broad Art Foundation, Santa Monica
p.109, 251

*Untitled #116
1982
Color photograph
Edition of 10
45 ½ x 30 in. (114.9 x 76.2 cm)
The Broad Art Foundation, Santa Monica
p.110, 251

*Untitled
1983
Color photograph
20 x 16 in. (50.8 x 40.6 cm)
Courtesy of the artist and Metro Pictures, New York
p.274

—

[Fashion], 1983–84

*Untitled #122
1983
Color photograph
Edition of 18
35 ½ x 21 ¼ in. (89.5 x 54 cm)
The Broad Art Foundation, Santa Monica
p. 113, 252

*Untitled #126
1983
Color photograph
Edition of 18
34 ½ x 22 ¾ in. (87.6 x 57.6 cm)
The Eli and Edythe L. Broad Collection, Los Angeles
p.119, 252

*Untitled #127
1983
Color photograph
Edition of 18
34 x 23 in. (86.4 x 58.4 cm)
Poju and Anita Zabludowicz Collection, London
p. 116, 252

*Untitled #131
1983
Color photograph
Edition of 18
34 ¾ x 16 ½ in. (88.3 x 41.9 cm)
The Broad Art Foundation, Santa Monica
p. 115, 252

*Untitled #133
1984
Color photograph
Edition of 5
71 ¼ x 47 ½ in. (181 x 120.7 cm)
Grässlin Collection, St. Georgen, Germany
p. 117, 252

*Untitled #137
1984
Color photograph
Edition of 5
70 ½ x 47 ¾ in. (179.1 x 121.3 cm)
The Broad Art Foundation, Santa Monica
p. 114, 252, 278

*Untitled #138
1984
Color photograph
Edition of 5
71 x 48 ½ in. (180.3 x 123.2 cm)
The Broad Art Foundation, Santa Monica
p. 118, 252, 278

—

[Fairy Tales], 1985

*Untitled #145
1985
Color photograph
Edition of 6
70 x 47 ¼ in. (178 x 120 cm)
M. J. S. Collection, Paris
p. 121, 255

*Untitled #146
1985
Color photograph
Edition of 6
72 ½ x 49 ¼ in. (184.2 x 125.4 cm)
Palm Collection, Inc.
p. 123, 255

*Untitled #150
1985
Color photograph
Exhibition print
Edition of 6
49 ½ x 66 ¾ in. (125.7 x 169.5 cm)
Courtesy Metro Pictures, New York
p. 122, 255

*Untitled #155
1985
Color photograph
Edition of 6
72 ½ x 49 ¼ in. (184.2 x 125.1 cm)
Estlander Collection
p. 124, 255, 293

*Untitled #156
1985
Color photograph
Edition of 6
49 ⅝ x 72 ½ in. (126 x 184 cm)
Private collection, Switzerland
p. 125, 255, 292

—

[Disasters], 1986–89

*Untitled #168
1987
Color photograph
Edition of 6
85 x 60 in. (215.9 x 152.4 cm)
Private collection
Courtesy Metro Pictures, New York
p. 127, 255

*Untitled #173
1986
Color photograph
Edition of 6
60 x 90 in. (152.4 x 228.6 cm)
Estlander Collection
p. 128–129, 255

*Untitled #174
1986
Color photograph
Edition of 6
71 x 47 ½ in. (180.3 x 120.6 cm)
Servais Collection, Brussels
p. 135, 255

*Untitled #175
1987
Color photograph
Edition of 6
47 ½ x 71 ½ in. (120.7 x 181.6 cm)
Private collection
Courtesy Metro Pictures, New York
p. 130–131, 255, 295

*Untitled #186
1989
Color photograph
Edition of 6
44 ¾ x 29 ¼ in. (113.7 x 74.3 cm)
Courtesy of the artist and Metro Pictures, New York
p. 134, 255

*Untitled #188
1989
Color photograph
Edition of 6
43 ½ x 65 ½ in. (110.5 x 166.4 cm)
The Museum of Modern Art, New York
Gift of the Dannheisser Foundation
p. 133, 255

*Untitled #191
1989
Color photograph
Edition of 6
90 x 60 in. (228.6 x 152.4 cm)
Courtesy of the artist and Metro Pictures, New York
p. 132, 255

—

[History Portraits/Old Masters], 1988–90

*Untitled #183
1988
Color photograph
Edition of 6
42 ½ x 28 ½ in. (108 x 72.4 cm)
Private collection
Courtesy Metro Pictures, New York
p. 145, 257

*Untitled #193
1989
Color photograph
Edition of 6
48 ¾ x 42 in. (124.1 x 106.5 cm)
The Broad Art Foundation, Santa Monica
p. 137, 257

*Untitled #194
1989
Color photograph
Edition of 6
42 x 28 in. (106.7 x 71.2 cm)
Private collection
Courtesy Metro Pictures, New York
p. 141, 257

*Untitled #195
1989
Color photograph
Edition of 6
30 ½ x 20 ½ in. (77.2 x 52.1 cm)
Courtesy of the artist and Metro Pictures, New York
p. 145, 257

*Untitled #196
1989
Color photograph
Edition of 6
66 x 44 in. (167.6 x 111.8 cm)
The Broad Art Foundation, Santa Monica
p. 148, 257

*Untitled #197
1989
Color photograph
Edition of 6
31 ½ x 21 in. (80 x 53.3 cm)
Courtesy of the artist and Metro Pictures, New York
p. 142, 257

*Untitled #198
1989
Color photograph
Edition of 6
38.5 x 27 ½ in. (97.5 x 70.8 cm)
The Broad Art Foundation, Santa Monica
p. 138, 257

*Untitled #199
1989
Color photograph
Edition of 6
25 x 18 in. (63.5 x 45.7 cm)
The Broad Art Foundation, Santa Monica
p. 146, 257

*Untitled #200
1989
Color photograph
Edition of 6
31 x 20 ¾ in. (78.6 x 53 cm)
The Broad Art Foundation, Santa Monica
p. 141, 257

*Untitled #205
1989
Color photograph
Edition of 6
53 ½ x 40 ¼ in. (135.9 x 102.2 cm)
Per Skarstedt Collection, New York
p. 142, 257

*Untitled #206
1989
Color photograph
Edition of 6
67 ½ x 45 in. (171.4 x 114.3 cm)
Collection Palm, Inc.
p. 144, 257

*Untitled #209
1989
Color photograph
Edition of 6
57 x 41 in. (144.8 x 104.1 cm)
Emily and Jerry Spiegel Collection
p. 149, 257

*Untitled #210
1989
Color photograph
Edition of 6
67 x 45 in. (170.2 x 114.3 cm)
Emily and Jerry Spiegel Collection
p. 139, 257

*Untitled #211
1989
Color photograph
Edition of 6
37 x 31 in. (94 x 78.7 cm)
The Eli and Edythe L. Broad Collection, Los Angeles
p. 145, 257

*Untitled #212
1989
Color photograph
Edition of 6
33 x 24 in. (83.8 x 61 cm)
Courtesy of the artist and Metro Pictures, New York
p. 141, 257

*Untitled #213
1989
Color photograph
Edition of 6
29 ½ x 25 in. (74.9 x 63.5 cm)
Barbara Schwartz Collection
p. 146, 257

*Untitled #214
1989
Color photograph
Edition of 6
29 ½ x 24 in. (74.9 x 61 cm)
Barbara Schwartz Collection
p. 138, 257

Untitled #215
1989
Color photograph
Edition of 6
74 ½ x 51 in. (188.6 x 129.5 cm)
Courtesy of the artist and Metro Pictures, New York
p. 149, 257

Untitled #216
1989
Color photograph
Edition of 6
87 x 56 in. (221 x 142.2 cm)
Courtesy Metro Pictures, New York
p. 140, 257, 297

Untitled #220
1990
Color photograph
Edition of 6
64 x 40 in. (162.6 x 101.6 cm)
Courtesy of the artist and Metro Pictures, New York
p. 150, 257

Untitled #221
1990
Color photograph
Edition of 6
48 x 30 in. (121.9 x 76.2 cm)
Ringier Collection, Switzerland
p. 146, 258

Untitled #222
1990
Color photograph
Edition of 6
59 ½ x 43 ½ in. (151 x 110.3 cm)
Goetz Collection, Munich
p. 147, 258

Untitled #224
1990
Color photograph
Edition of 6
48 x 38 in. (121.9 x 96.5 cm)
Thurn und Taxis Collection
p. 138, 258, 279

Untitled #225
1990
Color photograph
Edition of 6
48 x 33 in. (121.9 x 83.8 cm)
The Broad Art Foundation, Santa Monica
p. 149, 258

Untitled #226
1990
Color photograph
Edition of 6
48 x 30 in. (121.9 x 76.2 cm)
Courtesy of the artist and Metro Pictures, New York
p. 142, 258

Untitled #228
1990
Color photograph
Edition of 6
82 x 48 in. (208.4 x 122 cm)
The Museum of Modern Art, New York
Gift of Eileen and Peter Norton
p. 143, 258

—

[Civil War], 1991

Untitled #240
1991
Color photograph
Edition of 6
49 x 72 in. (124.5 x 182.9 cm)
Private collection
p. 152–153, 261

Untitled #242
1991
Color photograph
Edition of 6
49 x 72 in. (124.5 x 182.9 cm)
Courtesy of the artist and Metro Pictures, New York
p. 154–155, 261

Untitled #243
1991
Color photograph
Edition of 6
49 x 72 in. (124.5 x 182.9 cm)
Courtesy of the artist and Metro Pictures, New York
p. 156–157, 261

—

[Sex Pictures], 1992

Untitled #251
1992
Color photograph
Edition of 6
68 x 45 in. (172.7 x 114.3 cm)
Courtesy of the artist and Metro Pictures, New York
p. 161, 258

Untitled #253
1992
Color photograph
Edition of 6
75 x 50 in. (190.5 x 127 cm)
Per Skarstedt Collection, New York
p. 159, 258

Untitled #255
1992
Color photograph
Edition of 6
46 ¼ x 69 ¼ in. (117.5 x 176 cm)
Kunstmuseum Wolfsburg, Wolfsburg
p. 164, 258

Untitled #256
1992
Color photograph
Edition of 6
68 x 45 in. (172.7 x 114.3 cm)
Goetz Collection, Munich
p. 163, 258

Untitled #257
1992
Color photograph
Edition of 6
69 ¼ x 46 ¼ in. (176 x 117.5 cm)
Private collection, Courtesy Metro Pictures, New York
p. 162, 258

Untitled #258
1992
Color photograph
Edition of 6
68 x 45 in. (172.7 x 114.3 cm)
Servais Collection, Brussels
p. 167, 258

Untitled #259
1992
Color photograph
Edition of 6
60 x 40 in. (152.4 x 101.6 cm)
Private collection
p. 165, 258

*Untitled #263
1992
Color photograph
Edition of 6
39 ½ x 45 ¼ in. (100 x 115 cm)
American Fund Collection
Courtesy Peter Norton 2000
On loan to the Tate Gallery, London
p. 166, 258

Untitled #264
1992
Color photograph
Edition of 6
50 x 75 in. (127 x 190.5 cm)
Private collection, Amsterdam
p. 160, 258, 281

—

[Fitcher's Bird], 1992

Untitled #267
1992
Color photograph
Edition of 6
26 ½ x 40 in. (67.3 x 101.6 cm)
Courtesy of the artist and Metro Pictures, New York
p. 270

—

[Fashion], 1993–94

Untitled #275
1993
Color photograph
Edition of 6
63 x 88 in. (160 x 223.5 cm)
Olbricht Collection
p. 170–171, 252

Untitled #276
1993
Color photograph
Edition of 6
78 ½ x 59 in. (199.4 x 149.9 cm)
Neda Young Collection
p. 179, 252

Untitled #278
1993
Color photograph
Artist's print 1/1
Edition of 6
73 x 49 in. (185.4 x 124.5 cm)
Jennnifer McSweeney Collection, New York
p. 169, 252

Untitled #279
1993
Color photograph
Edition of 6
65 x 49 in. (165.1 x 124.5 cm)
Courtesy of the artist and Metro Pictures, New York
p. 180, 252

Untitled #280
1993
Color photograph
Edition of 6
53 x 35 in. (134.6 x 88.9 cm
Neda Young Collection
p. 174, 252

Untitled #282
1993
Color photograph
Edition of 6
90 x 60 in. (228.6 x 152.4 cm)
Courtesy of the artist and Metro Pictures, New York
p. 173, 252

*Untitled #299
1994
Color photograph
Edition of 6
48 x 32 in. (122 x 81 cm)
Goetz Collection, Munich
p. 172, 252

Untitled #300
1994
Color photograph
Edition of 6
78 x 53 in. (198.1 x 134.6 cm)
Private collection, Los Angeles
p. 177, 252

Untitled #302
1994
Color photograph
Edition of 6
67 ¾ x 45 in. (172.1 x 114.3 cm)
Olbricht Collection
p. 176, 252

Untitled #303
1994
Color photograph
Edition of 6
67 ¾ x 43 in. (172.1 x 109.2 cm)
Courtesy of the artist and Metro Pictures, New York
p. 178, 252

Untitled #304
1994
Color photograph
Edition of 6
61 x 41 in. (155.1 x 103.9 cm)
Courtesy of the artist and Metro Pictures, New York
p. 175, 252

—

[Horror and Surrealist Pictures], 1994–96

Untitled #305
1994
Color photograph
Edition of 6
49 ¾ x 73 ½ in. (126.4 x 186.7 cm)
Mr. and Mrs. Howard L. Ganek Collection
p. 182–183, 261

Untitled #307
1994
Color photograph
Edition of 6
79 x 42 ½ in. (200.7 x 108 cm)
Courtesy of the artist and Metro Pictures, New York
p. 187, 261

Untitled #308
1994
Color photograph
Edition of 6
69 ½ x 47 in. (176.5 x 119.4 cm)
Goetz Collection, Munich
p. 184, 261

Untitled #310
1994
Color photograph
Edition of 6
44 x 63 ½ in. (111.7 x 161.3 cm)
Private collection,
Courtesy Metro Pictures, New York
p. 185, 261

Untitled #311
1994
Color photograph
Edition of 6
76 x 51 in. (193 x 129.5 cm)
Private collection,
Courtesy Metro Pictures, New York
p. 186, 261

Untitled #312
1994
Color photograph
Edition of 6
61 x 41 ½ in. (154.9 x 105.4 cm)
Private collection,
Courtesy Metro Pictures, New York
p. 188, 261

—

[Masks], 1994–96

Untitled #314 A–#314 F
1994
6 color photographs
Editions of 6
30 x 44 in. (76.2 x 111.8 cm) (A, F) / 44 x 30 in. (111.8 x 76.2 cm) (B, C, D, E)
Courtesy of the artist and Metro Pictures, New York
p. 190–191, 263

Untitled #315
1995
Color photograph
Edition of 6
60 x 40 in. (152.4 x 101.6 cm)
Olbricht Collection
p. 193, 263

Untitled #316
1995
Color photograph
Edition of 6
48 x 32 in. (121.9 x 81.3 cm)
M. J. S. Collection, Paris
p. 195, 263

Untitled #323
1995
Color photograph
Artist's print 1/1
Edition of 6
58 x 39 in. (147 x 99.1 cm)
Artist's collection
Courtesy Metro Pictures, New York
p. 194, 263

Untitled #324
1996
Color photograph
Edition of 6
58 x 39 in. (147 x 99.1 cm)
The Broad Art Foundation, Santa Monica
p. 192, 263

—

[Broken Dolls], 1999

Untitled #332
1999
Black-and-white photograph
Edition of 10
38 ½ x 25 ½ in. (97.8 x 64.8 cm)
Private collection
Courtesy Metro Pictures, New York
p. 198, 265

Untitled #334
1999
Black-and-white photograph
Edition of 10
47 ½ x 31 ½ in. (120.6 x 80 cm)
Private collection
Courtesy Metro Pictures, New York
p. 199, 265

Untitled #335
1999
Black-and-white photograph
Edition of 10
21 ½ x 32 ½ in. (54.6 x 82.6 cm)
Private collection
Courtesy Metro Pictures, New York
p. 197, 265

Untitled #337
1999
Black-and-white photograph
Edition of 10
35 ½ x 25 ½ in. (90.2 x 64.8 cm)
Private collection
Courtesy Metro Pictures, New York
p. 200, 265

Untitled #343
1999
Black-and-white photograph
Edition of 10
38 ½ x 25 ½ in. (97.8 x 64.8 cm)
Private collection
Courtesy Metro Pictures, New York
p. 198, 265

Untitled #345
1999
Black-and-white photograph
Edition of 10
25 ½ x 38 ½ in. (64.8 x 97.8 cm)
Private collection, Los Angeles
p. 201, 265

**Untitled #347*
1999
Black-and-white photograph
Edition of 10
22 x 22 in. (55.9 x 55.9 cm)
Private collection
Courtesy Metro Pictures, New York
p. 200, 265

**Untitled #348*
1999
Black-and-white photograph
Edition of 10
38 ½ x 26 in. (97.8 x 66 cm)
Private collection, Courtesy Metro Pictures, New York
p. 199, 265

—

[Hollywood/Hampton Types], 2000–02

Untitled #351
2000
Color photograph
Edition of 6
30 x 20 in. (76.2 x 50.8 cm)
Courtesy of the artist and Metro Pictures, New York
p. 207, 267

**Untitled #352*
2000
Color photograph
Edition of 6
27 x 18 in. (68.6 x 45.7 cm)
Collection Metro Pictures, New York
p. 203, 267

**Untitled #355*
2000
Color photograph
Edition of 6
36 x 24 in. (91.4 x 61 cm)
Collection Metro Pictures, New York
p. 207, 267

**Untitled #358*
2000
Color photograph
Edition of 6
30 x 20 in. (76.2 x 50.8 cm)
Olbricht Collection
p. 204, 267

**Untitled #359*
2000
Color photograph
Edition of 6
30 x 20 in. (76.2 x 50.8 cm)
Metro Pictures Collection, New York
p. 204, 267

**Untitled #360*
2000
Color photograph
Edition of 6
30 x 20 in. (76.2 x 50.8 cm)
Olbricht Collection
p. 207, 267

**Untitled #399*
2000
Color photograph
Edition of 6
39 x 26 in. (99.1 x 66 cm)
Per Skarstedt Collection, New York
p. 205, 267

**Untitled #400*
2000
Color photograph
Edition of 6
36 ¾ x 26 in. (93.3 x 66 cm)
Courtesy of the artist and Metro Pictures, New York
p. 206, 267

**Untitled #401*
2000
Color photograph
Edition of 6
36 x 24 in. (91.4 x 61 cm)
Private collection, New York
p. 207, 267

**Untitled #402*
2000
Color photograph
Edition of 6
36 x 26 in. (91.4 x 66 cm)
Courtesy of the artist and Metro Pictures, New York
p. 204, 267

**Untitled #403*
2000
Color photograph
Edition of 6
22 x 15 in. (55.9 x 38.1 cm)
The Broad Art Foundation, Santa Monica
p. 204, 267

**Untitled #408*
2002
Color photograph
Edition of 6
54 x 36 in. (137.2 x 91.4 cm)
Courtesy of the artist and Metro Pictures, New York
p. 209, 267, 282

**Untitled #409*
2002
Color photograph
Edition of 6
54 x 36 in. (137.2 x 91.4 cm)
The Broad Art Foundation, Santa Monica
p. 208, 267

—

[Clowns], 2003–04

**Untitled #412*
2003
Color photograph
Edition of 6
51 ¼ x 41 ¼ in. (130.2 x 104.8 cm)
Margaret and Daniel Loeb Collection
p. 211, 269

**Untitled #413*
2003
Color photograph
Edition of 6
46 x 31 in. (116.8 x 79.1 cm)
The Broad Art Foundation, Santa Monica
p. 220, 269, 273

Untitled #416
2004
Color photograph
Edition of 6
55 x 48 ½ in. (139.7 x 123.2 cm)
Courtesy of the artist and Metro Pictures, New York
p. 216, 269

**Untitled #417*
2004
Color photograph
Edition of 6
60 x 90 in. (152.4 x 228.6 cm)
Private collection, Los Angeles
p. 218–219, 269

**Untitled #419*
2004
Color photograph
Edition of 6
55 ½ x 48 ¼ in. (141 x 122.6 cm)
Private collection, Lausanne
p. 221, 269

**Untitled #421*
2004
Color photograph
Edition of 6
54 ⅞ x 78 ⅞ in. (139.4 x 200.3 cm)
The Broad Art Foundation, Santa Monica
p. 213, 269

**Untitled #422*
2004
Color photograph
Edition of 6
48 x 54 in. (121.9 x 137.2 cm)
Courtesy of the artist and Metro Pictures, New York
p. 212, 269

**Untitled #423*
2004
Color photograph
Edition of 6
71 ¾ x 48 ½ in. (182.2 x 123.2 cm)
Olbricht Collection
p. 217, 269

**Untitled #424*
2004
Color photograph
Edition of 6
53 ½ x 54 ½ in. (135.9 x 138.4 cm)
Noah Garson and Ronald Schwartz Collection
p. 214–215, 269

**Untitled #425*
2004
Color photograph
Edition of 6
70 ½ x 89 ½ in. (179.1 x 227.3 cm)
Private collection
p. 222–223, 269

**Untitled #426*
2004
Color photograph
Edition of 6
79 ½ x 54 in. (201.9 x 137.2 cm)
Michael and Sandra Benhamou Collection
p. 224, 269

This work is published to coincide with the exhibition ***Cindy Sherman***, organized by the Jeu de Paume, Paris, in cooperation with the Kunsthaus Bregenz, the Louisiana Museum of Modern Art, Humlebæk and the Martin-Gropius-Bau, Berlin.

Jeu de Paume, Paris:
May 16–September 3, 2006

Kunsthaus Bregenz, Bregenz:
November 25, 2006–January 14, 2007

Louisiana Museum of Modern Art, Humlebæk:
February 9–May 13, 2007

Martin-Gropius-Bau, Berlin:
June 15–September 10, 2007

Exhibition curators:
Régis Durand and Véronique Dabin, assisted by Edwige Baron

—

Directed by Régis Durand and Véronique Dabin, assisted by Edwige Baron

Edited by Julie Rouart, assisted by Clément Dirié

Translated from the French by Louise Rogers

Copyediting: Bernard Wooding

Design: deValence

Typesetting: Claude Olivier Four

Proofreading: Penelope Isaac

Production: Corinne Trovarelli

Color Separation: Dupont, Paris

Printed in Italy by Egedsa

Distributed in North America by Rizzoli International Publications, Inc.

Simultaneously published in French as *Cindy Sherman* © Flammarion SA/Éditions Jeu de Paume, Paris, 2006

English-language edition

Éditions Flammarion

87, quai Panhard et Levassor

75647 Paris Cedex 13

www.editions.flammarion.com

06 07 08 4 3 2 1

FC0510-06-VI

ISBN-10: 2-0803-0522-0

ISBN-13: 9782080305220

Dépôt légal: 06/2006

The exhibition was organized with the support of **Olympus France** and **Manufacture Jaeger-LeCoultre**, in partnership with **Le Figaro** and **FIP**

The Jeu de Paume is a member of the **tram** network

Neuflize Vie support the Jeu de Paume

—

We wish to express our thanks to the collectors and institutions who have contributed to this retrospective by generously entrusting their works to us for an extended period of time:

- American Fund for the Tate Gallery, London
- Michael and Sandra Benhamou
- Collection Estlander
- Fonds National d'Art Contemporain, Ministry of Culture and Communication, Paris
- Frac-Collection Aquitaine, Bordeaux
- Howard and Julie Ganek
- Noah Garson and Ronald Schwartz
- Goetz Collection, Munich
- Grässlin Collection, St. Georgen
- Kunstmuseum Wolfsburg, Wolfsburg
- Barbara and Richard S. Lane
- Margaret and Daniel Loeb
- M. J. S. Collection, Paris
- Jennifer McSweeney, New York
- Metro Pictures, New York
- Nina and Frank Moore, New York
- Musée d'Art Moderne de Saint-Étienne Métropole, Saint-Étienne
- Olbricht Collection, Essen
- Collection Palm, Inc.
- Ringier Collection, Suisse
- Barbara Schwartz
- Servais Collection, Bruxelles
- Per Skarstedt, New York
- Emily and Jerry Spiegel
- The Broad Art Foundation, Santa Monica
- The Eli and Edythe L. Broad Collection, Los Angeles
- The Museum of Contemporary Art, Los Angeles
- The Museum of Modern Art, New York
- Thurn und Taxis Collection
- Victoria and Albert Museum, London
- Neda Young
- Poju and Anita Zabludowicz, London

as well as those who preferred to remain anonymous.

The exhibition and this book would never have been possible without the involvement of Janelle Reiring, Helene Winer, and Tom Heman from Metro Pictures and the help of Per Skarstedt from Skarstedt Fine Art in New York. We thank them, and all the individuals who have generously supported this project, whole heartedly:

- Claude Allemand-Cosneau, director, Fonds National d'Art Contemporain, Ministry of Culture and Communication, Paris
- Hölger Broeker, curator, Kunstmuseum Wolfsburg, Wolfsburg
- Markus Brüderlin, director, Kunstmuseum Wolfsburg, Wolfsburg
- Allison Card, Metro Pictures, New York
- Marie-Anne Chambost, head of the collection, Frac-Collection Aquitaine, Bordeaux
- Eli et Edythe L. Broad, The Eli et Edythe L. Broad Collection, Los Angeles
- Bärbel Grässlin, Bärbel Grässlin gallery, Frankfurt
- Lórand Hegyi, director, Musée d'Art Moderne de Saint-Étienne Métropole, Saint-Étienne
- Joanne Heyler, curator, The Broad Art Foundation, Santa Monica
- Ghislaine Hussenot, Ghislaine Hussenot gallery, Paris
- Mark Jones, director, Victoria and Albert Museum, London
- Susan Kismaric, curator, The Museum of Modern Art, New York
- Margaret Lee
- Simon Lee, Sprüth Magers Lee, London
- Hervé Legros, director, Frac-Collection Aquitaine, Bordeaux
- Glenn Lowry, director, The Museum of Modern Art, New York
- Thomas Olbricht, Collection Olbricht, Essen
- Peter Schuette, Metro Pictures, New York
- Rainald Schumacher, director, Collection Goetz, Munich
- Nicholas Serota, director, Tate, London
- Jeremy Strick, director, The Museum of Contemporary Art, Los Angeles
- Franziska von Hasselbach, Monika Sprüth Philomene Magers Gallery, Cologne

And finally we offer our warmest thanks to Cindy Sherman for her support throughout the preparations for both the exhibition and this book.

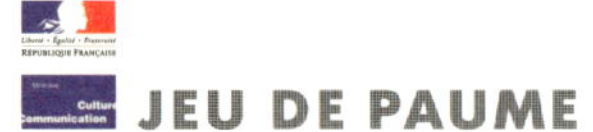

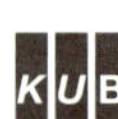

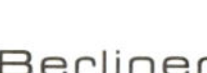

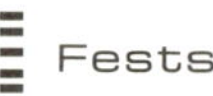

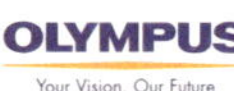

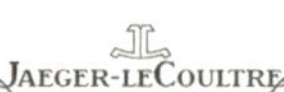

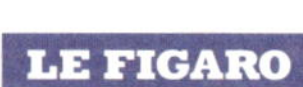